AMERICAN BIOGRAPHIES

American
Religious Leaders

TIMOTHY L. HALL

☑® Facts On File, Inc.

American Religious Leaders

Facts On File, Inc.
132 West 31st Street
New York NY 10001

Library of Congress Cataloging-in-Publication Data
Hall, Timothy L.
    American religious leaders / Timothy L. Hall.
        p. cm.—(American biographies)
Includes bibliographical references and index.
    ISBN 0-8160-4534-8
  1. Religious leaders—United States—Biography. I. Title. II. Series.

    BL72 .H33 2003
    200′.92′273—dc21   2002002454

Facts On File books are available at special discounts when purchased in bulk quantities for businesses, associations, institutions, or sales promotions. Please call our Special Sales Department in New York at (212) 967-8800 or (800) 322-8755.

You can find Facts On File on the World Wide Web at http://www.factsonfile.com

Text design by Joan M. Toro
Cover design by Cathy Rincon

Printed in the United States of America

VB Hermitage 10 9 8 7 6 5 4 3 2 1

This book is printed on acid-free paper.

For my mother and father

CONTENTS

Note on Photos   vi

List of Entries   vii

Acknowledgments   xi

Introduction   xiii

A to Z Entries   1

Glossary   398

Bibliography and Recommended Sources   404

Entries by Religious Affiliation   410

Entries by Year of Birth   413

Index   417

NOTE ON PHOTOS

Many of the illustrations and photographs used in this book are old, historical images. The quality of the prints is not always up to modern standards, as in some cases the originals are from glass negatives or are damaged. The content of the illustrations, however, made their inclusion important despite problems in reproduction.

LIST OF ENTRIES

Abbott, Lyman
Adler, Cyrus
Adler, Felix
Ainslie, Peter
Alexander, Archibald
Allen, Richard
Ames, Edward Scribner
Asbury, Francis
Avery, Martha Gallison Moore
Backus, Isaac
Ballou, Hosea
Bangs, Nathan
Bayley, James Roosevelt
Beecher, Henry Ward
Beecher, Lyman
Beissel, Johann Conard
Bellows, Henry Whitney
Black Elk
Blackwell, Antoinette Louisa
    Brown
Blake, Eugene Carson
Blavatsky, Helena Petrovna
Boehm, John Philip
Brainerd, David
Branham, William Marrion
Breck, James Lloyd
Bresee, Phineas Franklin
Briggs, Charles Augustus
Broadus, John Albert
Brooks, Phillips
Brownson, Orestes Augustus
Burke, John Joseph
Bushnell, Horace
Cabrini, Francesca Xavier

Cadman, S. Parkes
Campbell, Alexander
Candler, Warren Akin
Carroll, John
Cartwright, Peter
Cary, Lott
Cavert, Samuel McCrea
Cayce, Edgar
Channing, William Ellery
Chapman, John Wilbur
Chase, Philander
Chauncy, Charles
Cheney, Charles Edward
Cheverus, Jean Louis Lefebvre de
Clark, Francis Edward
Clarke, James Freeman
Clarke, John
Cody, John Patrick
Coffin, Henry Sloane
Coke, Thomas
Conner, Walter Thomas
Conwell, Russell Herman
Coppin, Fanny Jackson
Corrigan, Michael Augustine
Cotton, John
Coughlin, Charles Edward
Crosby, Fanny
Crummell, Alexander
Cushing, Richard James
Damien, Father
Davies, Samuel
Davis, Andrew Jackson
Day, Dorothy
De, Abhay Charan

De Smet, Pierre-Jean
Dickinson, Jonathan
Divine, Father
Dixon, Amzi Clarence
Drew, Timothy
Drexel, Katharine
DuBose, William Porcher
Duchesne, Rose Philippine
Dunster, Henry
Dwight, Timothy
Dyer, Mary
Eddy, Mary Baker
Edwards, Jonathan
Edwards, Jonathan, Jr.
Einhorn, David
Eliot, John
Emmons, Nathanael
England, John
Ewing, Finis
Falwell, Jerry
Farrakhan, Louis Abdul
Feehan, Patrick Augustine
Fillmore, Charles Sherlock
Finney, Charles Grandison
Flanagan, Edward Joseph
Ford, Arnold Josiah
Fosdick, Harry Emerson
Fox, Emmet
Frelinghuysen, Theodorus
    Jacobus
Frothingham, Octavius Brooks
Fuller, Charles Edward
Garnet, Henry Highland
Garrettson, Freeborn

Garrison, James Harvey
Gibbons, James
Ginzberg, Louis
Gladden, Solomon Washington
Grace, Sweet Daddy
Graham, Billy
Gratz, Rebecca
Hale, Edward Everett
Handsome Lake
Harris, Thomas Lake
Haven, Gilbert
Haygood, Atticus Greene
Heck, Barbara Ruckle
Hecker, Isaac Thomas
Hedge, Frederic Henry
Heschel, Abraham Joshua
Hicks, Elias
Hodge, Charles
Holmes, John Haynes
Hooker, Thomas
Hubbard, L. Ron
Hughes, John Joseph
Huntington, William Reed
Hutchinson, Anne Marbury
Ingersoll, Robert Green
Ireland, John
Jackson, Jesse
Johnson, Samuel
Jones, Bob
Jones, Jim
Jones, Rufus Matthew
Jones, Sam
Judson, Adoniram
Kaplan, Mordecai Menahem
Keith, George
Kimball, Spencer Woolley
King, Martin Luther, Jr.
King, Thomas Starr
Kino, Eusebio Francisco
Kirk, Edward Norris
Knudson, Albert Cornelius
Koresh, David
Krauth, Charles Porterfield
Kuhlman, Kathryn
Lamy, Jean Baptiste
LaVey, Anton
Lee, Ann
Lee, Jesse

Leeser, Isaac
Leland, John
Lewis, Edwin
Lipscomb, David
Machen, John Gresham
Macintosh, Douglas Clyde
Magnes, Judah Leon
Mahan, Asa
Makemie, Francis
Malcolm X
Mather, Cotton
Mather, Increase
Mather, Richard
Mathews, Shailer
Maurin, Aristide Peter
Mayhew, Jonathan
McCabe, Charles Cardwell
McCosh, James
McGarvey, John William
McGlynn, Edward
McKay, David Oman
McKendree, William
McPherson, Aimee Semple
Mendes, Henry Pereira
Merton, Thomas
Michel, Virgil George
Miller, William
Mitchell, Jonathan
Moody, Dwight Lyman
Moon, Lottie
Moon, Sun Myung
Morais, Sabato
Morse, Jedidiah
Mott, John Raleigh
Muhammad, Elijah
Muhlenberg, Henry Melchior
Mullins, Edgar Young
Murray, John Courtney
Nevin, John Williamson
Niebuhr, Helmut Richard
Niebuhr, Reinhold
Norris, J. Frank
Noyes, John Humphrey
Occom, Samson
Olcott, Henry Steel
Oxnam, Garfield Bromley
Palmer, Phoebe Worrall
Parker, Quanah

Parker, Theodore
Peale, Norman Vincent
Penn, William
Pennington, James William Charles
Pierson, Arthur Tappan
Pike, James Albert
Pilmore, Joseph
Powell, Adam Clayton, Sr.
Pratt, Parley Parker
Priestley, Joseph
Randolph, Paschal Beverly
Ransom, Reverdy Cassius
Rapp, George
Rauschenbusch, Walter
Rice, John Holt
Rigdon, Sidney
Roberts, Benjamin Titus
Robertson, Pat
Russell, Charles Taze
Rutherford, Joseph Franklin
Ryan, John Augustine
Sankey, Ira David
Schaff, Philip
Schmucker, Samuel Simon
Schneerson, Menachem Mendel
Scofield, Cyrus Ingerson
Scott, Orange
Scott, Walter
Seabury, Samuel
Sheen, Fulton John
Sheldon, Charles Monroe
Silver, Abba Hillel
Smith, Hannah Whitall
Smith, Joseph
Smith, Joseph, III
Smohalla
Spalding, Martin John
Spellman, Francis Joseph
Steinberg, Milton
Stetson, Augusta Emma Simmons
Stiles, Ezra
Stoddard, Solomon
Stone, Barton Warren
Strong, Augustus Hopkins
Strong, Josiah

Sunday, Billy
Suzuki, Daisetz Teitaro
Szold, Henrietta
Taylor, Nathaniel William
Tekakwitha, Kateri
Tennent, Gilbert
Tennent, William
Tenskwatawa
Tillich, Paul Johannes
Torrey, Reuben Archer
Turner, Henry McNeal
Tyler, Bennet

Verot, Jean Pierre Augustin
   Marcellin
Walther, Carl Ferdinand Wilhelm
Warfield, Benjamin Breckinridge
White, Alma Bridwell
Webb, Muhammad Alexander
   Russell
White, Alma Bridwell
White, Ellen Gould Harmon
Whitefield, George
Whitman, Marcus
Wilder, Robert Parmalee

Williams, Roger
Wise, Isaac Mayer
Wise, Stephen S.
Witherspoon, John
Woodruff, Wilford
Woodworth-Etter, Maria
Woolman, John
Wovoka
Young, Brigham
Zeisberger, David
Zinzendorf, Nikolaus Ludwig von

ACKNOWLEDGMENTS

I am indebted to Dean Samuel Davis and the Lamar Order of the University of Mississippi Law School for supporting my work on this project. Niler Franklin and Jennifer Ray Barnes at the University of Mississippi Law School helped to prepare the manuscript for publication. The staff of the University of Mississippi Law School Library, especially Lynn Murray, supported my research by assisting me in gathering more than two centuries' worth of biographical materials concerning American religious figures. I could not have finished this study if Lynn had not retrieved scores of books for me from other libraries. The students in my spring 2001 Law and Religion Seminar for first-year students at the University of Mississippi enthusiastically edited the essay on Anne Hutchinson as one of their writing assignments. If this one biographical entry stands out from the rest of the field, it is because of their careful attention.

I thank my friend at Salem Press, Kent Rasmussen, for suggesting that I contact Facts On File to write a young adult book about American religious leaders. Though I still have not written that book, I have now written two others: the present volume and *Supreme Court Justices: A Biographical Dictionary*. I have Nicole Bowen, my editor at Facts On File, to thank for both opportunities, and for overseeing both projects.

As always, I could not have written this book without the patience of my family—Lee, Ben, and Amy—who tolerated my working on this project on far more evenings than I should have. My wife, Lee, aided me in more tangible ways by helping to locate photographs and editing the manuscript. By the time these words find their way into print, she will have been my partner in marriage for 25 years. I have no closer friend, no surer ally, no more indispensable companion in all the world.

INTRODUCTION

This book traces the history of American religion through the lives of its leaders. Of course, other stories might be told concerning the nation's religious life, stories involving men and women mostly forgotten by history or never known at all, but whose impact on the course of American religion may have been, at least in its cumulative effect, greater than that made by those described here. The present volume does not attempt to tell these stories, not because they are less important, but only because they are less easily discovered. Of those whom William James referred to in his *Varieties of Religious Experience* as "great-souled" individuals, it may well be that most have escaped the notice of history. Nevertheless, for a biographical dictionary such as this one, history's discriminations are inevitably reproduced. This book therefore focuses on those who have occupied the spotlight of historical attention in one way or another: the founders, the pioneers, the heretics, the saints. It concentrates attention, in general, on those whose lives have summoned some measure of historical interest and left some historical record, either through journals and autobiographies of their own or through biographies written by others.

Even this limitation did not prevent the author from having to make hard choices about candidates for inclusion in this volume. Of the more than 18,000 individuals treated by the monumental 24-volume *American National Biography*, nearly 1,700 of these subjects are categorized as having some religious involvement or significance. In one respect at least, the field from which choices about which

figures to include have been made is even broader than that covered by the *American National Biography*, because, unlike that series, this volume includes figures still living. To create a one-volume biographical reference concerning American religious leaders, therefore, this study necessarily had to narrow the number of its subjects, since the scope of possible entries stretched from the earliest decades of the 17th century to the present moment. Readers are entitled to know something of the considerations that informed the decisions of whom to include and whom to neglect.

The author confesses to making these decisions with a large measure of attention to the anticipated readers of this book. Scholars will see soon enough that the present volume has not attempted to attend to their needs but to the needs of general readers and nonspecialists, those compelled either by their own curiosity or by the command of professors and teachers to learn something about the religious figures who richly populate American history. This work therefore provides information about individuals that these readers might be called upon to investigate and about whom they might simply be curious. Especially in the case of more recent figures, the author has not been overly troubled by judgments about whether this or that figure may be considered important a century from now, since scholars of history may presently lack a broad enough context to evaluate whether a particular individual has made an enduring contribution to the history of American religious life. The uncertainties that might plague such scholars are not relevant to the purposes of this book. Figures such as JIM JONES, who engineered the mass suicide of nearly a thousand followers at his People's Temple in Guyana, may eventually slip from historical memory in spite of the controversial circumstances of their lives. For the immediate future, however, such individuals command a popular attention that warrants their inclusion here.

In the main, however, the author has attempted to identify those generally recognized as having an important place in the history of American religion. Readers should be warned, however, that being classed as important for my purposes does not necessarily mean that each individual made some enduring contribution to the course of religion in America. ANNE MARBURY HUTCHINSON, for example, is more famous for having been driven out of the Massachusetts Bay Colony in the late 1630s than she is for having established a religious vision to compete with the Puritans' much vaunted "City Upon a Hill." Similarly, DAVID KORESH, in the 20th century, occupied a little populated fringe of fundamentalist Christian belief, famous—or infamous—not because it will have enduring significance but because his beliefs ultimately inspired his death and the death of many followers in a fiery conflagration inadvertently sparked by the Federal Bureau of Investigation (FBI). The importance of such individuals sometimes lies less in their individual contribution to the life of American religion than in their exemplification of some larger impulse or pattern. Hutchinson, for example, represents the enduring presence of dissent within American religious traditions. Koresh, depending upon the observer, speaks to the dangerous propensities of either cults or the governments that persecute them.

There are, of course, many religious leaders numbered here who did set in motion significant historical movements. Founders occupy a prominent place in this volume, even though America inherited many of its religious traditions from elsewhere in the world and thus can boast no particular founders of these. Even for these inherited traditions we commonly recognize the efforts of those who transplanted a religious tradition to American soil and tended its early years: FRANCIS ASBURY, the father of Methodism in the United States, appears here, as well as FRANCIS MAKEMIE, often referred to as the father of American Presbyterianism, for example, as do others who served as spiritual midwives for religious traditions conceived in other places. Americans are accustomed to thinking of themselves as the instigators of missionary activity, but during the 17th and 18th centuries, especially, the New World was frequently the *object of* missionary zeal by figures as varied as EUSEBIO FRANCISCO KINO, Catholic missionary to the Southwest, and COUNT NIKOLAUS LUDWIG VON ZINZENDORF, instrumental in planting the Moravian Church in North America. In addition, however, this country has witnessed the birth of more than a few indigenous religious movements, as well as significant tributaries of existing religious traditions. Founders of both sorts liberally populate the pages that follow.

Some leaders begot other leaders in this volume, whether this act of parenting was genetic or merely spiritual. JONATHAN EDWARDS, for instance, appears here in company with his grandfather, the Congregationalist preacher SOLOMON STODDARD, and his son, JONATHAN EDWARDS, JR. Founders of religious movements such as the Church of Jesus Christ of Latter-day Saints inspired leaders who followed them, as JOSEPH SMITH, JR., did BRIGHAM YOUNG, and the several other Mormon leaders. Smith, in fact, demonstrates that genetic and spiritual offspring may sometimes inhabit different tributaries of religious experience. Whereas Brigham Young became Smith's successor with respect to the main body of Mormons in the 19th century, JOSEPH SMITH III eventually became the patriarch for the smaller and lesser-known religious community, the Reorganized Church of Jesus Christ of Latter Day Saints, known, beginning in the 21st century, as the Community of Christ.

The leadership referred to in this volume took many forms. The charismatic preacher—such as AIMEE SEMPLE MCPHERSON or FULTON JOHN SHEEN—exercises one form of leadership, one often to be seen in the pages that follow, but certainly not the only form. There are institution builders here as well: administrators, organizers, university presidents, and the like. HENRIETTA

SZOLD, the 20th-century architect of Hadassah, shares pages here with REBECCA GRATZ, the founder of the first Jewish Sunday School. To these must be added spiritual exemplars of one form or another, whose influence often flows more after them than alongside them. KATERI TEKAKWITHA, for example, the 17th-century Native American convert to Christianity whose pious example led to her beatification by the Catholic Church in 1980, was such an exemplar, as was DAVID BRAINERD, whose autobiography made him a household word for generations of evangelical Protestants, even though he led a relatively obscure life before his early death. Here, even, are men and women who claimed to be God, as did FATHER DIVINE, or Christ, as did ANN LEE.

Saintliness is a common attribute of many of those religious figures represented here, though not an invariable one, and perhaps not even exhibited with such regularity as one might expect. The reader might consider William James's description of saints in *The Varieties of Religious Experience,* where he characterizes them as believing in the sacredness of every soul, and thus as practicing patterns of life appropriate in view of this belief. They are, he suggested, "the great torch-bearers of this belief, the tip of the wedge, the cleavers of the darkness. Like the single drops which sparkle in the sun as they are flung far ahead of the advancing edge of a wave-crest or of a flood, they show the way and are forerunners."

> The world is not yet with them, so they often seem in the midst of the world's affairs to be preposterous. Yet they are impregnators of the world, vivifiers and animaters of potentialities of goodness which but for them would lie forever dormant. It is not possible to be quite as mean as we naturally are, when they have passed before us. One fire kindles another; and without that over-trust in human worth which they show, the rest of us would lie in spiritual stagnancy.

James's understanding of saintliness does not parallel precisely the meaning of sainthood for each religious tradition described here. The Roman Catholic Church, for example, has its own, quite vigorous criteria and procedures for the establish-ment of sainthood. Nevertheless, the saintliness to which James draws our attention has decorated many of the lives dealt with in this volume.

Protestant Christians have a prominent place in the pages that follow, just as they have prominently featured in the nation's religious life. But the diversity that originally expressed itself on American soil chiefly through the various divisions among Protestantism that flourished here eventually embraced a spiritual pluralism that reached significantly beyond the channels forged by the Reformation, by Christianity generally, or even by the Judeo-Christian tradition, if such, in fact, exists. That diversity is mirrored, at least in part, in the biographies that follow. Native American prophets and spiritual leaders make their appearances, as do Theosophists, spiritualists, Black Muslims, Harmonialists, Scientologists, Transcendentalists, Swedenborgians, and Utopians. Even these categories do not exhaust the actual contours of American religious pluralism, which increasingly claims representatives of all the world's major religious traditions, as well as new religious movements such as unidentified flying object (UFO) and cargo cults, syncretistic religions such as Santería, and other manifestations of religious belief too numerous to be itemized here. If, as Mircea Eliade insisted, the religious vision divides the world between the sacred and the profane, it is nevertheless the case that apprehensions of the sacred in American history have yielded a vast assortment of religious perspectives. One volume could not possibly catalogue America's religious heterogeneity, and the present work has not attempted to do so. The limitations of this project relieved it of any aspirations toward comprehensiveness, and the author has labored rather to see that the figures included here were broadly representative of key forms of American religiosity.

One further explanation may help readers to understand the choices of inclusion and exclusion exercised in the preparation of this book. This biography was conceived by the publisher, Facts On File, as part of a series of books which includes volumes on American political, social, and religious leaders, as well as individuals in other fields of endeavor. These categories necessarily overlap, and particular individuals appear in more than one of these volumes, as in the case of African-American minister and civil rights leader Martin Luther King, Jr. But generally the authors have attempted to coordinate their biographical selections to prevent most duplications. Accordingly, readers disappointed by not finding a particular religious figure in this volume should consult *American Social Leaders* and *American Political Leaders* as well. These volumes include some individuals who made important contributions to American religious life in addition to those to its political or social life.

A weakness of the dictionary format is that it obscures broad patterns and themes in the history of American religion. There are, though, common themes that intersect the lives examined here. For example, the attempt by various religious traditions to address modernity features frequently in the biographical accounts that follow, especially of religious leaders in the closing years of the 19th and early years of the 20th century. More than one religious tradition grappled with Darwinism, higher biblical criticism, and the social needs spawned by industrialism. Protestantism, especially, found itself cleft in the first part of the 20th century between those believers prepared to embrace modernity, even if it caused them to modify important aspects of their faith, and those who steadfastly resisted modern developments, especially in the area of evolutionary theory and the application of critical methods to the study of Scripture. One after another denomination found itself divided over these issues, experiencing a kind of spiritual mitosis that

generated parallel denominational organizations, identical in many external respects, but following radically different theological trajectories. It would be a mistake, however, to view the battle between fundamentalism and liberalism in the 20th century as a new development in American religious history. "New divinities" have periodically surfaced, declaring their emancipation from older patterns of religious belief or practice. The Great Awakening, for example, produced no more illustrious theological craftsman than Jonathan Edwards, whose attempts to preserve both Calvinistic doctrine and revivalism produced the so-called New Divinity, which influenced New England theology for a century. The New Divinity had as its opponents those who distrusted the prominence of emotion in the revivals of the Great Awakening. Similar fractures exhibited themselves in the 19th century, again over revivalism especially.

To assist readers in recognizing at least some of the connections here between one religious leader and another, this work attempts to signal in the text occasions when an individual mentioned in passing in one essay is also the subject of a separate biographical entry. The names of such individuals will appear in all small capital letters on their first occurrence in an essay. Through this kind of cross-referencing, readers can gain a broader perspective on one leader by considering other related entries.

Abbott, Lyman
(1835–1922) *Congregationalist minister, author*

Lyman Abbott achieved national prominence toward the turn of the 20th century as a Congregationalist preacher and as the editor of an influential religious periodical, the *Outlook*. He exemplified the moderate progressivism common among mainstream Protestants during this period. Abbott was born on December 18, 1835, in Roxbury, Massachusetts, the son of Jacob Abbott and Harriet Vaughan Abbott. Jacob Abbott was a preacher and writer, who secured prominence through his authorship of the 28 volumes of the *Rollo* books, a series of stories for children. Lyman Abbott's mother died when he was seven, and he spent the remainder of his childhood and youth raised among relatives in Farmington, Maine, while his father worked in New York. Abbott earned his undergraduate degree from New York University in 1853. Thereafter, he worked in the law office of his brother while he studied law, and he passed the New York bar examination in 1856. The next year he married Abby Frances Hamlin, with whom he had six children.

Abbott and his wife settled initially in Brooklyn, New York, where he came under the preaching influence of HENRY WARD BEECHER, who was pastor of the Congregationalist Plymouth Church. In 1859, Beecher's preaching and a revival that had occurred the previous year prompted Lyman Abbott to abandon his infant legal career in favor of a preaching ministry of his own. After returning to Farmington for a brief period to pursue private theological study, Abbott received a pastoral call from a Congregational church in Terre Haute, Indiana, in 1860. When the Civil War ended, however, he returned to New York to undertake direction of the American Freedman's Union Commission. But by the end of the decade, he had settled into a career as a writer that would occupy him for the rest of his life.

In his early years as a full-time writer, Abbott edited the *Illustrated Christian Weekly*, but when his mentor, Henry Ward Beecher, invited him to become associate editor of the *Christian Union* in 1876, he leapt at this opportunity. Five years later, Beecher resigned as editor in chief and Abbott assumed control of the periodical. Toward the end of the 1880s, after Beecher died, the Plymouth Church in Brooklyn called Abbott to become its new pastor, thus allowing him to assume direction of Beecher's church as well as his newspaper.

In Abbott's position at the helm of an important Protestant journal, subsequently renamed the *Outlook,* and one of the nation's best-known churches, Lyman Abbott became increasingly prominent during the last decade of the 19th century and the first of the 20th. He used these venues to espouse an optimistic view of human prospects, clothed in the language of Charles Darwin's evolutionary theory. Abbott expressed his ideas about Christian faith in *What Christianity Means to Me: A Spiritual Autobiography:*

Congregationalist preacher Lyman Abbott achieved prominence as editor of the progressive religious periodical *Outlook*. *(Library of Congress, Prints and Photographs Division LC-USZ62-125670)*

Faith in ourselves and in our fellow men; in our infinite possibilities because in our infinite inheritance.

Faith in the great enterprise in which God's loyal children are engaged, that of making a new world out of this old world . . .

Faith in a Leader who both sets our task and shares it with us; the longer we follow him and work with him, the more worthy to be loved, trusted, and followed does he seem to us to be.

Faith in a companionable God whom we cannot understand, still less define, but with whom we can be acquainted, as a little child is acquainted with his mysterious mother.

Abbott's religious progressivism cast him naturally into alliances with moderate political progressives, none more significant than his friendship with Theodore Roosevelt. He supported Roosevelt's failed third-party candidacy for U.S. presi-

dent in 1912. Roosevelt's loss, combined with the blow to cultural optimism of all sorts dealt by World War I, marked the decline of Abbott's influence. He resigned as pastor of his church in 1899 but continued editing the *Outlook* through the first two decades of the 20th century. He died in New York City on October 22, 1922.

Lyman Abbott typified the progressive spirit of many mainstream Christians at the turn of the 20th century. Whereas more conservative believers saw in evolutionary science a threat to orthodox teachings, Abbott embraced evolution as a metaphor for the steady increase of Christian influence in the world. He spent a lifetime laboring on behalf of moral and social causes consistent with this view. By the time of his death, however, his brand of theological optimism had collided with the harsh face of world war and been humbled by it. Though Abbott was prominent in his own era, the continuing influence of his thought after his death suffered sharp decline.

Further Reading

Abbott, Lyman. "Can a Nation Have Religion?" *The Century* 41 (December 1890): 275–81; reprinted in *The Making of America*. Available online. URL: http://cdl. library.cornell.edu/moa/browse.author/a.13.html.

———. *Christianity and Social Problems.* Boston: Houghton, Mifflin, 1896.

———. *The Evolution of Christianity.* Boston: Houghton, Mifflin, 1892.

———. *Reminiscences.* Boston: Houghton, Mifflin, 1915.

———. *What Christianity Means to Me: A Spiritual Autobiography.* New York: Macmillan, 1921.

Brown, Ira V. *Lyman Abbott, Christian Evolutionist: A Study in Religious Liberalism.* Cambridge: Harvard University Press, 1953; Westport, Conn.: Greenwood Press, 1970.

Sweet, W. W. *Makers of Christianity: From John Cotton to Lyman Abbott.* New York: Macmillan, 1921.

Adler, Cyrus
(1863–1940) *Semitic scholar, educator, lay Jewish leader*

Born during the Civil War, Cyrus Adler lived to the brink of World War II and was an important voice for Jewish people in a rapidly changing era that eventually produced the darkness of the Holocaust. Adler lent his considerable scholarly and organizational skills to a wide range of projects on behalf of American and international Jews. He was born on September 13, 1863, in Van Buren, Arkansas, the son of Samuel Adler and Sarah Sulzberger Adler. While Adler was an infant, his family moved from Arkansas to Philadelphia and then to New York. In 1867, his father died and his family returned to Philadelphia, where Adler's uncle, David Sulzberger, became his guardian and a significant influence in his life.

After education in a Jewish parochial school and a public grammar school, supplemented by study with Jewish rabbis, including SABATO MORAIS, in Philadelphia, Cyrus Adler attended Center High School in Philadelphia and then enrolled in the University of Pennsylvania. There he received his B.A. in 1883 and then pursued graduate studies at Johns Hopkins University, where in 1887 he received the first American Ph.D. awarded in the subject of Semitics.

After teaching for several years at Johns Hopkins, Adler accepted a position as an assistant curator with the United States National Museum in 1888. Two years later, he was appointed a special commissioner of the Columbian Exposition in Chicago, Illinois, with responsibility for persuading Turkey, Egypt, Tunis, Algiers, and Morocco to participate in the exposition, which was held in 1893. Near the end of this period, Adler became the librarian for the Smithsonian Institute, a position he held until his appointment as assistant secretary of the Smithsonian in 1905. Significant among his accomplishments at the Smithsonian were his discovery and publication in 1904 of the "Jefferson Bible," the version of the New Testament extracted and arranged by Thomas Jefferson. The year after publishing this work, Adler married Racie Friedenwald, with whom he had one child.

Throughout the years of Adler's association with the Smithsonian Institute, he was also taking an increasingly active role in Jewish affairs. He helped establish the Jewish Publication Society of America in 1888, the American Jewish Historical Society in 1892, and the American Jewish Committee in 1906. He ultimately served as president of the Jewish Publication Society from 1898 to 1921 and of the American Jewish Committee from 1929 to 1940.

The first decade of the 20th century saw Adler return to academic environs when he became president in 1908 of Dropsie College for Hebrew and Cognate Learning in Philadelphia, an institution devoted to Judaic and Semitic studies. Soon after his acceptance of this position, Adler became the coeditor of the *Jewish Quarterly Review;* he held that position for three decades. In 1915, when the death of Solomon Schechter left the presidency of the Jewish Theological Seminary of America in New York City vacant, Adler agreed to add service as "temporary" president of this seminary to his responsibilities at Dropsie College. Nearly a decade later, the seminary abandoned the pretense of Adler's being there only temporarily and named him president. He remained in this position, as well as in his post at Dropsie College, until his death.

From World War I until his death at the outset of World War II, Cyrus Adler was active on behalf of the interests of international Jews. He helped establish Jewish relief agencies during World War I, and in the years that followed he sought to advance the interests of Palestinian Jews, though he opposed the creation of a Jewish state in Palestine. He died at the age of 76 on April 7, 1940, in Philadelphia, Pennsylvania.

Across a long lifetime, Cyrus Adler demonstrated that erudition could live harmoniously with action. Tethered firmly to the beliefs and practices of Conservative Judaism, Adler brought both great learning and indefatigable energy to the causes of both American and international Jews. Like Rabbi Sabato Morais, with whom he studied as a youth and with whom he had a long association in connection with the Jewish Theological Seminary, Cyrus Adler demonstrated that Conservative Judaism could respond to present needs even as it upheld the traditions of the past. Unlike Morais, Adler was not a rabbi, but the lack of a theological vocation did not prevent him from being one of the most respected Jewish leaders of his day.

Further Reading

Adler, Cyrus. *I Have Considered the Days.* Philadelphia: Jewish Publication Society of America, 1941; New York: Burning Bush Press, 1969.

Coolick, Gayle Meyer. "The Public Career of Cyrus Adler." Ph.D. dissertation, Georgia State University, 1981.

"Cyrus Adler: Biography," Center for Judaic Studies. Available online. URL: http://www.library.upenn.edu/cjs/FindingAids/Adler/Biography/Adlerbiomain.html. Updated on July 5, 2000.

Neuman, Abraham A. *Cyrus Adler: A Biographical Sketch.* Philadelphia: Jewish Publication Society of America, 1942.

Robinson, Ira. *Cyrus Adler: Selected Letters.* 2 vols. Philadelphia: Jewish Publication Society of America; New York: Jewish Theological Seminary of America, 1985.

Adler, Felix

(1851–1933) *founder of Ethical Culture*

Felix Adler, the son of a Jewish rabbi, migrated away from theism during postgraduate study in Europe. He eventually grew to believe that the universe was ordered by moral principles rather than a personal deity and established a kind of secular religion, the Ethical Culture Society. He was born on August 13, 1851, in Alzey, Germany, the son of Samuel Adler and Henrietta Frankfurter Adler. His family immigrated to New York City when Felix Adler was nearly six years old, and his father became the rabbi of Temple Emanuel. Adler briefly attended public school but then enrolled in Columbia Grammar School. In 1866, he entered Columbia College, from which he received his B.A. four years later. Intending initially to prepare himself to become a rabbi, Adler subsequently traveled to Europe to study at the University of Berlin and the nearby Academy for Jewish Learning (Hochschule für Wissenschaft des Judentums). In 1873, he transferred to the University of Heidelberg, where he was awarded his Ph.D.

By the time Adler returned to the United States, it was apparent that his views of the world no longer fit comfortably within the confines of Reform Judaism and that he would not assume the rabbinical post of his father in New York. Instead, he lectured for a time at Cornell University in the fields of Hebrew and Oriental literature. In the spring of 1876, Adler arranged to hold a meeting of those who might be interested in supporting a regular Sunday lecture series. At this inaugural meeting, he explained his general aim:

> The exercises of our meetings are to be simple and devoid of all ceremony and formalism. They are to consist of a *lecture* mainly, and, as a pleasing and grateful auxiliary, of music to elevate the heart and give rest to the feelings. The object of the lectures shall be twofold: First, to illustrate the history of human aspirations, its monitions and its examples; to trace the origin of many of those errors of the past whose poisonous tendrils still cling to the life of the present, but also to exhibit its pure and bright examples and so to enrich the little sphere of our earthly existence by showing the grander connections in which it everywhere stands with the large life of the race.

He launched his lecture series in October of that year and within a few months had taken steps to incorporate the Society for Ethical Culture in New York. The title of Adler's first book, *Creed and Deed* (1877), captured his break with traditional religion. The Ethical Culture Society, as Adler's group came to be known, emphasized the morality of deeds rather than the orthodoxy of creeds. Over the following decades, branches of the society sprang up in other cities, such as Chicago, Philadelphia, Saint Louis, and Boston.

In the years after the founding of the Ethical Culture Society, Felix Adler led its members to express their moral idealism through concrete programs. He helped establish a program that sent nurses into the poorer areas of the city and also established the first free kindergarten in the United States. At the beginning of the 1880s Adler added to these ventures marriage to Helen Goldmark, with whom he had five children.

Toward the beginning of the 20th century, Felix Adler returned to the academic environment he had left a quarter of a century before by accepting a position as professor of political and social ethics at Columbia University. He did not, however, abandon his leadership role in the Ethical Culture Society. For the remaining years of his life, Adler continued to lead the society in a demonstration of moral activism unhinged from traditional religious beliefs, even as he taught Columbia students in the area of ethics. He died on April 24, 1933, in New York City.

The late 19th century witnessed two major "free thought movements," which consciously attempted to break from traditional religious orthodoxies. One of these was the Free Religious Association, whose members splintered from mainstream Unitarianism because they thought it was too orthodox. The other principal free thought movement was the one founded by Felix Adler. Adler's nontheistic humanism, dressed in rituals reminiscent of the religious tradition he had abandoned, struck a chord of meaning for many Americans. He became a kind of Hebrew prophet, though he did not consider himself sent by God. Instead, he undertook to serve as the prophetic agent of moral impulses that were themselves a sign and seal of the divinity that was not personal, but that undergirded the universe.

Further Reading

Adler, Felix. "Founding Address," American Ethical Union. Available online. URL: http://www.aeu.org/adler1.html. Updated July 22, 1999.

———. *Life and Destiny; Or, Thoughts from the Ethical Lectures of Felix Adler.* New York: McClure, Phillips, 1903.

Cully, K. B. "Felix Adler: Founder of Ethical Culture." In *Distinguished American Jews.* Edited by Philip Henry Lotz. New York: Association Press, 1945.

Friess, Horace Leland. *Felix Adler and Ethical Culture: Memories and Studies.* Edited by Fannia Weingartner. New York: Columbia University Press, 1981.

Guttchen, Robert S. *Felix Adler.* New York: Twayne Publishers, 1974.

Kraut, Benny. *From Reform Judaism to Ethical Culture: The Religious Evolution of Felix Adler.* Cincinnati: Hebrew Union College Press, 1979.

Radest, Howard B. *Felix Adler: An Ethical Culture.* New York: P. Lang, 1998.

Ainslie, Peter

(1867–1934) *Disciples of Christ minister, ecumenical leader*

In the first decades of the 20th century, Peter Ainslie helped press the cause of the ecumenical movement, which sought to repair the fractures that denominationalism had visited on Christian churches. Though a Disciples of Christ minister, Ainslie made his most lasting contribution to the course of American religion through his dedication to the cause of ecumenical reform. He was born on June 3, 1867, near Dunnsville, Virginia, the son of Peter Ainslie II and Rebecca E. Ainslie. Both his father and his grandfather had been Disciples of Christ ministers, and by the time Peter Ainslie enrolled in Transylvania College in 1888, he had committed himself to the same vocation. Ill health, however, had prevented him from completing his studies when he left college, in 1891. Nevertheless, he was soon ordained a Disciples of Christ minister and undertook service as the minister of the Calhoun Christian Church in Baltimore, Maryland, a congregation of fewer than 50 members.

By the early years of the 20th century, Ainslie's church had flourished to the point that new facilities were needed to accommodate an ever expanding membership. He oversaw construction of what came to be called the Christian Temple, whose chapel was complete in 1905 and whose main building was opened two years later. Ainslie had already formed a fierce devotion to the principle of Christian unity, and this devotion found partial expression in his choice to inscribe a list of Christian leaders on the ceiling of his church's auditorium, a list that ranged from Old and New Testament figures across a wide spectrum of Catholic and Protestant religious leaders. This devotion found even more vivid expression when he was chosen to serve as president of the general convention of the Disciples of Christ and delivered his presidential address at the annual convention in 1910.

> We who wear the name of Christian only have climbed a hundred rugged steps and today, standing on God's balcony, we look down the past, and yonder is Jesus moving in that mightiest drama of all time. . . . Yonder is Luther nailing the ninety-five theses to the door of the castle church in Wittenberg, and Calvin, a refugee from persecution, writing his *Institutes.* Yonder are the Wesleys calling all believers in Jesus to the life of personal holiness and the Campbells pleading for a united church by the return to the New Testament

in name, in ordinances and in life. What a host of saints! Some were called "Nazarenes," others "Christians," still others "Roman Catholics," others "Reformers" and some "Disciples," but whatever be their names all these are our brethren.

In the wake of this address, Ainslie took the lead in establishing the Council on Christian Union of the Disciples of Christ, renamed in 1916 the Association for the Promotion of Christian Unity, and was promptly elected its president. The year of his address he also established a periodical to promote Christian fellowship, the *Christian Union Quarterly*, which he edited until his death a quarter of a century later. In the following years, Ainslie took an active part in the ecumenical movement. His emphasis on Christian unity, especially when it took the form of practicing open communion and open membership—that is, not requiring traditional evidencing of Disciples' orthodoxy for church membership or participation in communion—cast him at odds with other members of his denomination. But his fierce antipathy to denominationalism extended as well to denominational exclusivity when practiced by his own denomination. In addition to his work as editor of the *Christian Union Quarterly*, Ainslie wrote a number of books and lectured and preached widely outside his own church. On June 30, 1925, he married Mary Weisel, and the couple had two children. Ainslie died on February 23, 1934, in Baltimore, Maryland.

The 20th century witnessed the flourishing of the ecumenical movement, as Christians from many traditions sought to affirm their common bonds of faith and practice rather than to emphasize the differences that divided them. Peter Ainslie occupied a position on the leading edge of this movement. He died before it flowered in such organizations as the National Council of Churches and the World Council of Churches. But his efforts at fostering Christian union were important predecessors of these later ecumenical successes.

Further Reading

Ainslie, Peter. *God and Me.* Baltimore: Temple Seminary Press, 1908.
———. *The Scandal of Christianity.* Chicago: Willett, Clark & Colby, 1929.
———. *Towards Christian Unity.* Baltimore: Association for the Promotion of Christian Unity, 1918.
———. *Working with God; Or, the Story of a Twenty-five Year Pastorate in Baltimore.* St. Louis: Christian Board of Publication, 1917.
Garrett, Leroy. *The Stone-Campbell Movement: The Story of the American Restoration Movement.* Joplin, Mo.: College Press, 1995.
Idleman, Finis S. *Peter Ainslie: Ambassador of Good Will.* Chicago: Willett, Clark, 1941.
Moore, W. T., ed. *The New Living Pulpit of the Christian Church: A Series of Discourses, Doctrinal and Practical, by Representative Men among the Disciples of Christ.* St. Louis: Christian Board of Publications, 1918.

Alexander, Archibald
(1772–1851) *Presbyterian theologian*

Archibald Alexander was a prominent Presbyterian minister and theologian during the first half of the 19th century. He taught at Princeton Theological Seminary for more than 35 years, championing traditional Presbyterian orthodoxy against the excessive revivalism he saw in more recent theological currents. Alexander was born on April 17, 1772, in Rockbridge County, Virginia, the son of William Alexander and Ann Reid Alexander, who were prosperous farmers. Beginning in 1782, he studied with William Graham at Liberty Academy (later Washington and Lee University); the precise chronology of his life over the next decade is uncertain.

By the end of the 1780s, Alexander's father had obtained for him a position as a tutor in the home of General Thomas Posey in northwestern Virginia. While there, he had contact with a local Baptist revival and, after months of soul searching, experienced what he later believed was conversion. After a short period of additional study with William Graham, Alexander was licensed a Presbyterian preacher in 1791 and began an itinerant preaching ministry in Virginia and North Carolina. After three years he settled as a pastor of two churches in Charlotte County, Virginia.

In 1797 Alexander accepted the presidency of Hampden-Sydney College, a post that he held for the next nine years even as he continued to preach in churches and to achieve increased prominence among Virginia Presbyterians. He married Janetta Waddel in 1802; with her he had seven children. He took a sabbatical from his academic career in 1807 when he became the pastor of the Third Presbyterian Church in Philadelphia, Pennsylvania. That same year, he was elected moderator of Presbyterianism's highest denominational body, the General Assembly, and over the next few years, he involved himself in efforts to establish a seminary to train Presbyterian ministers. When the General Assembly voted to create Princeton Theological Seminary in 1812, Archibald Alexander became its first professor, holding the formal designation of professor of didactic and polemic theology.

In the 1820s, Presbyterians fractured into two theological camps: those who came to be known as Old School and those called New School. Old School Presbyterians championed traditional Presbyterian orthodoxy as enshrined in the Westminster Confession, the confession of faith that was adopted by English Presbyterians in the mid-1600s, and criticized the excesses of revivalism. Adherents of Old School Presbyterianism believed that traditional orthodoxy had been undermined in part by the alliance between Presbyterians and Congregationalists established in the first years of the 19th century, an alliance referred to as the Plan of Union. Under this plan, the two denominations had cooperated in establishing new churches west of the Hudson River. Alexander, in his days as president of Hampden-Sydney College, had supported this plan. But three decades later, Old School Presbyterians began to doubt the continued usefulness of this arrangement and, at the General Assembly of 1837, voted to dissolve the relationship with Congregationalists. Alexander, though having brushed against revivalism in his youth and having some sympathy for its role in the life of the church, nevertheless counted himself among the Old School Presbyterians.

At Princeton, Archibald Alexander influenced a generation of Presbyterian ministers, including two sons, James Waddel Alexander and Joseph Addison Alexander, who eventually joined him on the faculty of the seminary. An even more important protégé was CHARLES HODGE, who attended the seminary as a student and later joined the faculty in 1822 as professor of Oriental and biblical literature. Hodge carried on Alexander's Old School orthodoxy into the second half of the 19th century, and together the two men presided over a citadel of Reformed conservativism that stretched over most of the 19th century. Alexander died on October 22, 1851, in Princeton, New Jersey.

Archibald Alexander was no stranger to the revivalism that swept in a long current from the Great Awakening into the 19th century and ultimately became a permanent fixture of religious experience in the United States. Nevertheless, he helped perpetuate a conservative Christian faith that, although not utterly rejecting the element of personal experience, distanced itself from the more emotionally vigorous revivalism of preachers such as CHARLES GRANDISON FINNEY. Many Protestants of the 19th century responded to the skepticism and theological liberalism that inhabited their century with revivalistic exuberance. Archibald Alexander, however, devoted himself to the articulation of a reasonable faith consistent with Reformed orthodoxy.

Further Reading

Alexander, Archibald. *Evidences of the Authenticity, Inspiration, and Canonical Authority of the Holy Scriptures.* Philadelphia: Presbyterian Board of Publications, 1836; New York: Arno Press, 1972.

———. *Outlines of Moral Science.* New York: Scribner, 1852.

———. *Thoughts on Religious Experience.* Philadelphia: Presbyterian Board of Publication, 1841; London: Banner of Truth Trust, 1967.

Alexander, James W. *The Life of Archibald Alexander, D.D.: First Professor in the Theological Seminary, at Princeton, New Jersey.* New York: C. Scribner, 1854.

Hoffecker, W. Andrew. *Piety and the Princeton Theologians: Archibald Alexander, Charles Hodge, and Benjamin Warfield.* Grand Rapids, Mich.: Baker Book House, 1981.

Loetscher, Lefferts A. *Facing the Enlightenment and Pietism: Archibald Alexander and the Founding of Princeton Theological Seminary.* Westport, Conn.: Greenwood Press, 1983.

Noll, Mark A., ed. *The Princeton Theology, 1812–1921: Scripture, Science, and Theological Method from Archibald Alexander to Benjamin Breckinridge Warfield.* Grand Rapids, Mich.: Baker Book House, 1983.

Stewart, John William. "The Tethered Theology: Biblical Criticism, Common Sense Philosophy, and the Princeton Theologians, 1812–1860." Ph.D. dissertation, University of Michigan, 1990.

Allen, Richard

(1760–1831) *Methodist minister, founder and first bishop of the African Methodist Episcopal Church*

Richard Allen was born a slave but was able to purchase his freedom by the time he was 20 years old; earlier he had experienced a religious conversion and become a Methodist. In the years that followed he became a Methodist preacher and was instrumental in establishing the African Methodist Episcopal (A.M.E.) church and serving as its first bishop. He was born on February 14, 1760, in Philadelphia, Pennsylvania, into a slave family owned by a prominent Philadelphia lawyer, Benjamin Chew, who later served as chief justice of the Commonwealth of Pennsylvania. In 1777, Allen, his parents, and three of his siblings were sold to Stokely Sturgis, a slaveholder in Delaware. There he was influenced by Methodist preaching and experienced a religious conversion, which he later described in his autobiography, *The Life Experience and Gospel Labors of the Rt. Rev. Richard Allen*, in the following terms:

Richard Allen, the founder and first bishop of the African Methodist Episcopal Church, is pictured here with other A.M.E. bishops, along with scenes including Wilberforce University, Payne Institute, missionaries in Haiti, and the A.M.E. Church book depository in Philadelphia. *(Library of Congress, Prints and Photographs Division LC-USZ62-15059)*

I went with my head bowed for many days. My sins were a heavy burden. I was tempted to believe there was no mercy for me. I cried to the Lord both night and day. One night I thought hell would be my portion. I cried unto Him who delighted to hear the prayers of a sinner and all of a sudden my dungeon shook, my chains flew off, and "Glory to God" I cried. My soul was filled. I cried "Enough for me—the Savior died."

After Allen's conversion, his master was convinced by the preaching of the Methodist minister FREE-BORN GARRETTSON to offer Allen and his brother the opportunity to hire themselves out to purchase their freedom. They did so over the course of several years.

By 1780, Allen was a free man and licensed as a Methodist preacher. He traveled extensively as an itinerant preacher over the next seven years, preaching in Delaware, Maryland, New Jersey, and Pennsylvania. Eventually he associated himself with St. George's Church in Philadelphia, but the reluctance of white parishioners to welcome the increasing number of blacks who joined Allen caused Allen and others to begin meeting separately in 1787. Early that same year, Allen helped to establish the Free African Society, a benevolent association for African Americans. By 1794, Allen and other African Americans had been able to secure property and a building that had previously served as a blacksmith shop. These acquisitions resulted in the dedication by the Methodist bishop FRANCIS ASBURY of the Bethel African Episcopal Church of Philadelphia on June 29, 1794. Five years later, Asbury ordained Allen the first African-American deacon in the Methodist Episcopal Church.

Richard Allen served as de facto leader of the Bethel church from its inception, but he initially labored to maintain the church's connection to the Methodist Episcopal denomination. Attempts by St. Georgia's Church in Philadelphia to exert control over the Bethel church—and over its property—eventually led Allen and the members of Bethel to take steps toward independence. A decisive break occurred in 1816, when Allen invited a number of other African-American churches to send delegates to a meeting with the purpose of establishing a separate denominational structure.

The delegates assembled at Allen's invitation took the decisive step of forming the African Methodist Episcopal Church (A.M.E. Church) in April 1816. The delegates then ordained Richard Allen first an elder, and then on April 11, 1816, the first bishop of the A.M.E. church.

For the next 15 years, Bishop Allen helped to guide the affairs of the new denomination, which served not only as a spiritual center for the lives of many African Americans, but as the center of educational activities and a wide range of social services and programs. Allen also turned his attention to the general condition of African Americans, including slaves, in the United States. As early as 1797, he had joined with other black leaders in Philadelphia in seeking the repeal of the Fugitive Slave Law of 1793. Two decades later, after the formation of the American Colonization Society in 1817, Allen took a public stance against the viability of colonization. Finally, toward the end of his life he presided over the National Negro Convention convened at the Bethel church in the fall of 1830. Allen died in Philadelphia on March 26, 1831.

Rising from slavery to become a free man and a Methodist minister in the last decades of the 18th century, Richard Allen struggled for a time to remain within the Methodist Episcopal Church. Eventually, though, he and other African-American Methodists found themselves foreclosed from the possibility of an equal place in the life of then-existing American Methodist churches. Not willing to be treated as second-class spiritual citizens, they sought the spiritual fraternity of their own churches and, eventually, of their own denomination within the broader currents of Methodism. Allen played a leading role in the birth and early leadership of this denomination.

Further Reading

Allen, Richard. *The Life Experience and Gospel Labors of the Rt. Rev. Richard Allen.* Nashville: Abingdon Press, 1983.

Baxter, Daniel Minort. *Bishop Richard Allen and His Spirit.* Philadelphia: A.M.E. Book Concern, 1923.

George, Carol V. R. *Segregated Sabbaths: Richard Allen and the Emergence of Independent Black Churches 1760–1840.* New York: Oxford University Press, 1973.

Mathews, Marcia M. *Richard Allen.* Baltimore: Helicon, 1963.

Mwadilifu, Mwalimu I. *Richard Allen: The First Exemplar of African American Education.* New York: ECA Associates, 1985.

Raboteau, Albert J. "Richard Allen and the African Church Movement." In *A Fire in the Bones: Reflections on African-American Religious History.* Boston: Beacon Press, 1995.

Wesley, Charles H. *Richard Allen, Apostle of Freedom.* 2d ed. Washington, D.C.: Associated Publishers, 1969.

Ames, Edward Scribner

(1870–1958) *theologian, Disciples of Christ minister*

As a theologian, Edward Scribner Ames figured prominently in the Chicago school of theology. This version of theological liberalism sought to fashion a theology consistent with the insights of science and other aspects of modern thought. Ames was born on April 21, 1870, in Eau Claire, Wisconsin, to Lucius Bowles Ames and Adaline Scribner Ames. He received a B.A. and M.A. from Drake University in 1889 and 1891, respectively, then earned a B.D. from Yale University in 1892 and finally a Ph.D. from the University of Chicago in 1895.

After teaching at Butler College in Indianapolis, Indiana, for several years beginning in 1897, Ames moved in 1900 to Chicago, where he assumed the pastorate of the Hyde Park Church, a Disciples of Christ congregation, and became a professor of philosophy at the University of Chicago. Over the following decades, Ames pursued both ministerial and academic vocations. Influenced by the pragmatic philosophy of John Dewey and William James, Ames became an influential voice of the Chicago school, which sought to fashion a liberal theology consistent with the discoveries of modern science and thought.

In particular, Ames attempted to invigorate traditional religious understandings with the insights of social psychology. Impatient with a focus on Christian creeds, he preferred instead to train attention on the role of religious understandings in human interaction with the world. The task of re-ligion, he insisted in *Letters to God and the Devil*, "is not that of saving souls through some mysterious act of divine grace, but its task is the cultivation and nourishment of the better life through practical and effective methods." Formerly theologies had chained themselves to endless debates about the truth of various religious propositions; Ames, in contrast, measured the health of religious belief in terms of its social consequences.

Ames displayed a modernist's impatience with what he considered the "magical" elements of orthodox Christianity, such as the traditional doctrine of Jesus' resurrection from the dead. In his book *Religion*, he asserted that Jesus had survived death not in the form of a bodily resurrection but in the durableness of his ideas and example.

> No one can doubt the fact that he came to life in this world after he died upon the cross. No argument is needed to prove that he rose from a grave of obscurity to a life of renown; from a grave of ignominy to a place of love and honor. Already, in comparison with some thirty years of ordinary life, he has lived for nineteen hundred years beyond his death! And the secret of this conspicuous fact lies not in some miraculous magic but in the moral and spiritual character. It was the power of his living words and gracious spirit that carried him over the gulfs of death and gave him immortality.

To his work as a professor and a minister, Edward Ames added service as the editor of a Disciples of Christ theological journal *Scroll* for the quarter century from 1925 to 1951. He used this journal, as well as his pulpit at Hyde Park Church, to integrate his theological perspective into the life of his denomination. He also served as dean of the Disciples Divinity House at the University of Chicago from 1927 to 1945, an enterprise established to allow Disciples of Christ students at the University of Chicago Divinity School to live and study together. Ames retired first from his professorship at Chicago in 1935, then from his Hyde Park pulpit in 1940. Five years later he resigned from his position as dean of the Disciples Divinity House, though he pursued an active speaking and writing career until his death on June 29, 1958, in Chicago, Illinois.

What has been called the "liberal era" of American Protestantism flourished for about 60 years from the last quarter of the 19th century through around 1935. Edward Scribner Ames belonged to the second half of this era, a time when he and other liberal theologians had migrated substantially away from traditional Protestant orthodoxies. In place of inquiries into the truth of religious claims, Ames and others sought to define a theology by its helpfulness to men and women in the modern world, a theology partnered with science and psychology, even as it was severed from traditional sources of religious authority.

Further Reading

Ames, Edward Scribner. *Beyond Theology: The Autobiography of Edward Scribner Ames.* Edited by V. M. Ames. Chicago: University of Chicago Press, 1959.
———. *The Divinity of Christ.* Chicago: New Christian Century Company, 1911.
———. *The Higher Individualism.* Boston: Houghton Mifflin, 1915.
———. *Humanism.* Chicago: Chicago Literary Club, 1931.
———. *Letters to God and the Devil.* New York: Harper & Brothers, 1933.
———. *The New Orthodoxy.* Chicago: University of Chicago Press, 1918.
———. *The Psychology of Religious Experience.* Boston: Houghton Mifflin, 1910.
———. *Religion.* New York: H. Holt, 1929.
Anderson, Victor. *Pragmatic Theology: Negotiating the Intersections of an American Philosophy of Religion and Public Theology.* Albany: State University of New York Press, 1998.
Arnold, Charles Harvey. "A School That Walks the Earth: Edward Scribner Ames and the Chicago School of Theology." *Encounter* 30 (Fall 1969): 314–39.
Peden, Creighton. *The Chicago School: Voices in Liberal Religious Thought.* Bristol, Ind.: Wyndham Hall Press, 1987.

Asbury, Francis
(1745–1816) *Methodist bishop*

Though not the first Methodist minister in America, Francis Asbury became the most important

Francis Asbury is often referred to as the father of American Methodism. *(Library of Congress, Prints and Photographs Division LC-USZC4-6153)*

early leader of American Methodism. A keen sense of calling, a talent for toil, and powerful speaking and administrative gifts made Asbury the first American to become a Methodist bishop before he had turned 40 years of age. He was born August 20, 1745, in Staffordshire, England, to Joseph and Elizabeth Rogers Asbury. His formal education ended by the time he was 12 years old, and he was subsequently apprenticed to a craft, though its identity remains unknown. Before he had left his teenage years, however, Asbury had had contact with John Wesley's Methodism and had started preaching. In his early 20s, he was commissioned as an itinerant Methodist minister, and from 1767 to 1771, he traveled throughout Bedfordshire, Cochester, and Wiltshire. At a conference of Methodist ministers in 1771, John Wesley solicited volunteers to preach in America, and Ashley—who promptly stepped forward to undertake this calling—soon found himself in the New World. He wrote in his journal on the voyage over: "Whither am I going? To the New

World. What to do? To gain honour? No, if I know my own heart. To get money? No: I am going to live to God, and to bring others so to do." He arrived in Philadelphia, Pennsylvania, on October 27, 1771.

The following year, Asbury settled into preaching in New York and was designated by John Wesley as his assistant in America. Soon afterward, Wesley sent Thomas Rankin to America to take charge of Methodist affairs, and he and Asbury had difficulty working together. But Asbury's position as the leading Methodist minister in the New World was strengthened by the beginning of the Revolutionary War. Most of the other Methodist ministers who had originally arrived from England chose to return there once hostilities between the colonies and Great Britain were joined. Asbury, who alone remained to tend to the work in America, illustrated his reasoning on the issue in his journal:

> I can by no means agree to leave such a field for gathering souls to Christ, as we have in America. It would be an eternal dishonour to the Methodists, that we should all leave three thousand souls, who desire to commit themselves to our care; neither is it the part of a good shepherd to leave his flock in time of danger: therefore, I am determined, by the grace of God, not to leave them, let the consequence be what it may.

Asbury's decision to remain in the colonies was not without some measure of peril, because he and other Methodist ministers were viewed with distrust by American patriots. This distrust was compounded by John Wesley's writings in opposition to American independence. Asbury himself had to leave Maryland when he refused to take an oath forswearing any allegiance to the British Crown. For two years he centered his activities in Delaware, which did not require ministers to take such an oath.

After the Revolutionary War, American independence made a formal relationship between American and British Methodism untenable. In 1784, Wesley approved the ordination of Asbury as superintendent of Methodism in the United States, and Asbury, less than 15 years after arriving in America, became its first American bishop.

Wesley also made Thomas Cook a joint superintendent with Asbury, but Cook did not remain permanently in America. Though Cook made several visits to the United States subsequently, Asbury assumed the chief position among American Methodists by virtue of his continued presence.

Over the years that followed he tended a flock that grew exponentially. Before he died, 80 Methodist preachers had become more than 2,500; 15,000 members had swelled to 140,000. He rejected the role of a stationary executive, communicating long distance to an ever more far-flung ministry. Instead, he traveled mile upon mile each year, never establishing a permanent home, never marrying, never tarrying for long in any place. Toward the end, he could no longer travel by horse and had to move from place to place in a carriage. Sick more often than healthy, he nevertheless lived the life of an itinerant minister to the very end. He died on March 31, 1816, in Spotsylvania, Virginia.

John Wesley was the father of Methodism, but, in America at least, Francis Asbury was its midwife. On his arrival in North America, he found scattered congregations of Methodist piety and helped unite them into one of the country's fastest growing Protestant denominations. In 1968, the Methodist Episcopal Church, which he so diligently tended, merged with other branches of Methodism in the United States to become the United Methodist Church.

Further Reading

Asbury, Francis. *The Causes, Evils, and Cures of Heart and Church Divisions. Extracted from the Works of Burroughs and Baxter.* New York: Lane & Scott, 1849.

———. *The Journal of the Rev. Francis Asbury, Bishop of the Methodist Episcopal Church, from August 7, 1771, to December 7, 1815.* New York: N. Bangs & T. Mason, 1821.

Asbury, Herbert. *A Methodist Saint: The Life of Bishop Asbury.* New York: Knopf, 1927.

Baker, Frank. *From Wesley to Asbury: Studies in Early American Methodism.* Durham, N.C.: Duke University Press, 1976.

Carroll, H. K. *Francis Asbury in the Making of American Methodism.* New York: The Methodist Book Concern, 1923.

Du Bose, Horace Mellard. *Francis Asbury: A Biographical Study.* Nashville: Publishing House of the M.E. Church, 1909.

Duren, William Larkin. *Francis Asbury: Founder of American Methodism and Unofficial Minister of State.* New York: Macmillan, 1928.

Janes, Edwin. *The Character and Career of Francis Asbury, Bishop of the Methodist Episcopal Church.* New York: Carlton & Lanahan, 1872.

Lewis, James. *Francis Asbury, Bishop of the Methodist Episcopal Church.* London: The Epworth Press, 1927.

Ludwig, Charles. *Francis Asbury: God's Circuit Rider.* Milford, Mich.: Mott Media, 1984.

Mains, George Preston. *Francis Asbury.* New York: Eaton & Mains, 1909.

Nygaard, Norman E. *Bishop on Horseback: The Story of Francis Asbury.* Grand Rapids, Mich.: Zondervan, 1962.

Rudolph, L.C. *Francis Asbury.* Nashville: Abingdon, 1966.

Snethen, Nicholas. *A Discourse on the Death of the Rev. Francis Asbury: Late Bishop of the Methodist Episcopal Church in the United States.* Baltimore: John J. Harrod, 1816.

Tipple, Ezra Squier. *Francis Asbury: The Prophet of the Long Road.* New York: The Methodist Book Concern, 1916.

Wood, Timothy L. "'That They May Be Free Indeed': Liberty in the Early Methodist Thought of John Wesley and Francis Asbury." *Methodist History* 38 (2000): 231–41.

Avery, Martha Gallison Moore
(1851–1929) *Catholic lay preacher*

An influential Catholic lay preacher, Martha Gallison Moore Avery began her speaking career through her involvement in socialist causes. She eventually became disillusioned with socialism and converted to Catholicism, after which she employed her rhetorical skills to advocate her newfound faith. She was born on April 6, 1851, in Steuben, Maine, the daughter of Albion King Paris Moore and Katharine Leighton Moore. Her mother died when she was 13 years old, and because her father was frequently away from home, she was sent to live with her maternal grandfather,

Samuel Moore, from whom she acquired a keen interest in politics.

When she was 19 her grandfather helped to establish her in a hat-making business in Ellsworth, Maine. There, she joined a Unitarian church and became active in its affairs. She also met Millard Avery at the church, and the couple married in 1880. The following year Martha Avery had a daughter, the only child born of the union. Avery's husband became a traveling salesman sometime after the marriage, and Avery and her daughter eventually moved to Boston in 1888 to be closer to him. He died, however, in 1890.

In Boston, Martha Avery attended EDWARD EVERETT HALE's Unitarian church, but she was simultaneously drawn to socialist ideas. She became a member of the First Nationalist Club of Boston, which advocated the nationalization of all labor and capital. By 1891, Avery had joined the Social Labor Party, and from 1892 to 1895 she served on the party's State Central Committee. By the middle of that decade, she was making a living as a lecturer. In 1896 she established the Karl Marx Class, devoted to a discussion of Marx's works, and served as the class director and lecturer. The secretary of the class was David Goldstein, a young man almost 20 years her junior, with whom she would have a close association for the remainder of her life. Toward the end of the 1890s, Avery ran twice for elected office as a Socialist, first for the Boston school board in 1897 and the following year for state treasurer. She lost decisively each time.

In the fall of 1899, Avery sent her daughter to a Canadian school run by the Congregation of Notre Dame, an order of Catholic nuns. Within a few months, her daughter informed Avery that she had become Catholic. Avery herself became interested in Catholic teaching over the following months, and as she did so, she became more critical of socialism. By 1901, she had changed the name of her Karl Marx Class to the Boston School of Political Economy. She grew to believe that socialism was atheistic, anti-American at its core, and a threat to the family. She tried initially to reform socialism from within, but she left the party in 1903 and publicly criticized it in a 1903 article in *The Irish World* that characterized socialism as "this movement—this seducer of civic virtue—this deformer of God and man—this movement whose light is darkness and whose intellectual and moral darkness grows blacker, and by swift marches." Later that year, Avery and David Goldstein coauthored a more extended attack, *Socialism: The Nation of Fatherless Children* (1903). In May 1904, Avery joined the Catholic Church and modified her speaking career to embrace a Catholic perspective on social justice and a critique of socialism. A year later, her friend Goldstein converted to Catholicism as well. In 1912, the Common Cause Society, which advocated social justice reforms, was formed in Boston by lay Catholics, and Avery became an active participant in its affairs, serving from 1922 until 1929 as its president.

In her later years, Martha Avery focused less in her speaking career on social reform issues and more on straightforward proselytization for Catholicism as she became increasingly conservative in her views. She eventually opposed women's suffrage, feminism, and the idea of sexual equality, fearing that these causes would undermine the role of the family in American society. In 1917, Avery and Goldstein launched a street preaching project, the Catholic Truth Guild, in an attempt to make the Catholic Church "better known and loved." She

served as the project's president until her death on August 8, 1929, in Medford, Massachusetts.

Martha Gallison Moore Avery followed a spiritual path that took her from Unitarianism to Catholicism and a political one from socialism to markedly more conservative views. She was a protofeminist who ultimately opposed feminism. But she never retreated from a vigorous public life that eventually made her one of the foremost Catholic lay preachers of her generation.

Further Reading

Carrigan, D. Owen "A Forgotten Yankee Marxist." *New England Quarterly* 42 (March 1969): 23–43.

———. "Martha Moore Avery: The Character of a Crusader." Ph.D. dissertation, University of Maine, 1966.

———. "Martha Moore Avery: Crusader for Social Justice." *Catholic Historical Review* 54 (April 1968): 17–38.

Goldstein, David, and Martha Moore Avery. *Campaigning for Christ.* Boston: Pilot Publishing Co., 1924.

———. *Socialism: The Nation of the Fatherless Children.* Boston: T.J. Flynn, 1903.

Backus, Isaac
(1724–1806) *Baptist minister*

Isaac Backus was converted during the Great Awakening and became a leading figure among the religious groups that separated from the established churches at that time and afterward. He eventually became a Baptist minister and a tireless advocate for the cause of religious liberty. Backus was born on January 9, 1724, in Norwich, Connecticut, to Samuel and Elizabeth Tracy Backus. His father, a prosperous farmer, died when Isaac was 16 years old. Life in a farming family left little opportunity for education, and Isaac finished only seven years of school. In the early 1740s, the revival movement known as the Great Awakening swept through Backus's home in Norwich, and he experienced conversion. As he described it later in his diary:

> As I was mowing alone in the field, August 24th, 1741, all my past life was opened plainly before me, and I saw clearly that it had been filled up with sin. I went and sat down in the shade of a tree, where my prayers and tears, my hearing of the Word of God and striving for a better heart, with all my other doings, were set before me in such a light that I perceived I could never make myself better, should I live ever so long. Divine justice appeared clear in my condemnation, and I saw that God had a right to do with me as he would. My soul yielded all into his hands, fell at His feet, and was silent and calm before

Him. And while I sat there, I was enabled by divine light to see the perfect righteousness of Christ and the freeness and riches of His grace, with such clearness, that my soul was drawn forth to trust Him for salvation.

Backus became a member of the Norwich church (a Congregationalist one) in 1742, but within a few years he and his mother joined a group of believers who had separated from the church to form a congregation of their own. Backus soon felt that God had called him to preach. He spent two years as an itinerant minister before he settled in a newly formed church located near Middleborough and Bridgewater, Massachusetts, where he was ordained in 1748. In 1749 he married Susanna Mason, with whom he had nine children. Over the next few years, Backus began to reconsider the issue of infant baptism and ultimately became convinced that this practice was inconsistent with scriptural teaching. He thus became a Baptist himself and, in 1756, reorganized his church as the First Baptist Church of Middleborough.

For the next half century Backus advocated and defended Baptist principles, not the least of which was his firm conviction in religious liberty. He had personal reasons to favor such liberty, since 18th-century New England Baptists suffered more than a little religious persecution from the Congregational establishment, including the requirement that they pay taxes to support Congregational ministers. Out of frustration over lack of religious freedom, Backus eventually wrote *An Appeal to the Public for Religious Liberty* (1773), a tract that challenged New England's close association between church and state. His political activism on this front led him to other encounters with the great political issues of his day. For example, he supported the American Revolution and, later, the ratification of the U.S. Constitution.

Backus was instrumental in the growth of the Warren Baptist Association, an early group of Baptist churches. In 1788, this association sent Backus on a preaching tour of Virginia and North Carolina. His two years of itinerant preaching in these venues has been credited with assisting the spread of a new revival movement in the South—known as the Second Great Awakening. This important tour supplemented a steady career of evangelistic preaching missions, even while Backus cared for the needs of his church in Middleborough and penned a torrent of pages in tracts and books.

Backus served as a trustee of the College of Rhode Island (now known as Brown University) from 1765 to 1799. In 1800, Backus's wife died, and he himself died in Middleborough on November 20, 1806.

The most important Baptist of his day, Isaac Backus helped to form an enduring religious denomination out of the scattered spiritual congregations born of the Great Awakening. But his more enduring contribution to the history of American religion was his relentless advocacy of religious freedom and religious disestablishment. With the help of his efforts, both principles took root in the last decades of 18th-century America.

Further Reading

Backus, Isaac. *The Diary of Isaac Backus.* Edited by William G. McLoughlin. Providence, R.I.: Brown University Press, 1979.

———. *A History of New-England, with Particular Reference to the Denomination of Christians Called Baptists.* Boston: Edward Draper, 1777.

Diamond, Deborah. "The Role of Conscience in Defenses of Religious Liberty." Ph.D. dissertation University of Chicago, 1995.

Grenz, Stanley. *Isaac Backus—Puritan and Baptist: His Place in History, His Thought, and Their Implications for Modern Baptist Theology.* Macon, Ga.: Mercer University Press, 1983.

Hovey, Alva. *A Memoir of the Life and Times of the Rev. Isaac Backus.* Boston: Gould & Lincoln, 1859.

Maston, T. B. *Isaac Backus: Pioneer of Religious Liberty.* Rochester, N.Y.: American Baptist Historical Society, 1962.

McLoughlin, William G. *Isaac Backus and the American Pietistic Tradition.* Edited by Oscar Handlin. Boston: Little, Brown, 1967.

———, ed. *Isaac Backus on Church, State, and Calvinism.* Cambridge, Mass.: Belknap Press of Harvard University Press, 1968.

Ballou, Hosea
(1771–1852) *Universalist minister*

The most prominent preacher of Universalism's second generation, Hosea Ballou had a profound influence on the movement's doctrinal development. His work concerning the atonement of Christ especially reformulated this important Christian doctrine and redirected the course of Universalist thinking on this subject. Hosea Ballou was born on April 30, 1771, in Richmond, New Hampshire, the son of Maturin and Lydia Ballou. His mother died when he was two, and he was raised in relative poverty by his father, a farmer and Baptist minister. In his teens Ballou became a Universalist, and although he had had only a few years of formal education, he determined to become a Universalist preacher. He preached his first sermon in 1791, but, in the early years of his ministry, Ballou had to support himself by working as a schoolteacher while he pursued an itinerant preaching career in western Massachusetts and Vermont. He was ordained as a Universalist minister in 1794. The next year he married Ruth Washburn, with whom he had 13 children, only 9 of whom survived infancy.

In 1795, the year of his marriage, Ballou began to preach a Unitarian version of Universalism after he grew to believe that the doctrine of the Trinity lacked a scriptural basis. In the years that followed, he also revisited the orthodox doctrine of the atonement and eventually published in 1805 what would be perhaps his most important work, *A Treatise on Atonement*. Orthodox Christians commonly understood Christ's death to affect a vicarious or substitutionary atonement: human sin merited punishment to satisfy God's divine justice, and by his death Christ vicariously suffered the punishment warranted by human sin. Ballou rejected this account of Christ's death because it suggested that God needed Christ's death to reconcile him with humanity. On the contrary, Ballou insisted, an infinitely loving God did not need to be reconciled with humanity; humanity needed to be reconciled with God. Christ's death demonstrated God's love and thus signified to humanity the possibility of reconciliation.

> What an infinite difference there is between the All-gracious and Merciful, and his lost and bewildered creatures? He, all glorious, without a spot in the whole infinitude of his nature; all lovely, without exception, and loving, without partiality. Who can tell the thousandth part of his love to his offspring?

In 1809, Ballou finally ended his itinerant ministry to become the pastor of a Universalist congregation in Portsmouth, New Hampshire. In 1815, he moved on to the Universalist church in Salem. Then, at the end of 1817, Ballou accepted the call to become the minister of the Second Universalist Society in Boston, where he remained for the rest of his life. In Boston he began publication in 1819 of the *Universalist Magazine*, which was the chief denominational periodical of Universalists for the next nine years until it was absorbed into the *Trumpet and Universalist Magazine*. He also plunged into a debate over the prospect of future punishments, which inspired him to write *An Examination of the Doctrine of Future Retribution* (1834), in which he argued that such punishments, as sinful conduct merited, were administered by God in the present life rather than in the future one.

Toward the end of his long career as a champion of Universalism, Ballou wrote *A Short Essay on Universalism*, outlining the movement's doctrines. He also contributed a personal statement as its elder statesman:

> Owing to the age and infirmities of the writer of this article, he cannot expect to be able, much longer, to render any considerable service to the infinitely glorious cause to whose interest he has had the happy privilege of devoting his humble talents for nearly sixty years. But while holding himself ready to resign his armor, at the word of command, he cannot fully express his gratitude for what he sees of the wonderful spread of truth, and for the numerous army which he will leave in its future defense.

Ballou died in Boston, on June 7, 1852.

In spite of his lack of formal education, Hosea Ballou earned a position as the foremost apologist for Universalism in his day. He was a controversialist above all, and his immersion in particular religious debates has tended to limit the appeal of his works. Nevertheless, he articulated religious positions that would eventually find a settled place within theological liberalism.

Further Reading

Adams, John Coleman. *Hosea Ballou and the Gospel Renaissance of the Nineteenth Century.* Boston: Universalist Publishing House, 1903.

Ballou, Hosea. *The Ancient History of Universalism: From the Time of the Apostles, to Its Condemnation in the Fifth General Council, A.D. 553.* Boston: Marsh & Capen, 1829.

———. *An Examination of the Doctrine of Future Retribution.* Boston: Trumpet Office, 1834.

———. *A Treatise on Atonement.* Boston: Marsh, Capen and Lyon, 1832; Boston: Skinner House Books, 1986.

Ballou, Maturin Murray. *Biography of Rev. Hosea Ballou.* Boston: A. Tompkins, 1852.

Bressler, Ann Lee. "Popular Religious Liberalism in America, 1770–1880: An Interpretation of the Universalist Movement." Ph.D. dissertation, University of Virginia, 1992.

Cassara, Ernest. *Hosea Ballou and the Rise of American Religious Liberalism.* Boston: Universalist Historical Society, 1958.

———. *Hosea Ballou: The Challenge to Orthodoxy.* Boston: Universalist Historical Society, 1961; Washington, D.C.: University Press of America, 1982.

Safford, Oscar Fitzalan. *Hosea Ballou: A Marvellous Life-Story.* Boston: Universalist Publishing House, 1889.

Whittemore, Thomas. *Life of Rev. Hosea Ballou; with Accounts of His Writings, and Biographical Sketches of His Seniors and Contemporaries in the Universalist Ministry.* 4 vols. Boston: J. M. Usher, 1854–55.

Bangs, Nathan

(1778–1862) *Methodist minister*

One of the most important Methodist leaders of his generation, Nathan Bangs helped transform Methodism from a frontier sect into an established denomination in the 19th century. He served first as an itinerant minister in Canada and later occupied important leadership roles within the American Methodist Church. He was born on May 2, 1778, in Stratford, Connecticut, the son of Lemuel Bangs and Rebecca Keeler Bangs. In his teenage years, Bangs migrated with his family to Stamford, New York. Though lacking significant formal education, Bangs received an invitation in 1799 to teach school in Niagara, Canada. While there, he was converted to Methodism and licensed as an itinerant Methodist preacher in 1801. Prior to the War of 1812, Bangs preached widely, first in upper Canada from 1801 to 1804 and then in Quebec from 1804 to 1812. During the period of his Quebec ministry, in 1806, he married Mary Bolton, with whom he appears to have had at least two children.

After the outbreak of war between the United States and Great Britain in 1812 made life as an American citizen in Canada perilous, Bangs moved with his family to New York City, where he became a Methodist pastor and presiding elder. During these years he took up the pen to defend Methodist doctrine, publishing *Errors of Hopkinsianism* (1815) and *Examination of the Doctrine of Predestination* (1817). In these works, Bangs leveled a vigorous polemic against the Calvinistic doctrines of election and predestination. He also helped to found the Methodist Missionary Society in 1819, was chair of meetings that led to creation of the society, and helped to draft its constitution.

Bangs eventually took charge of the administration of the Missionary Society later in his life; earlier, he became manager of the Methodist Book Concern, in 1820. In this position and for the next 16 years, Bangs oversaw the principal publishing ventures of the Methodist Episcopal church. He added to this responsibility service as an editor, of *Methodist Magazine* from 1820 to 1828 and of *Christian Advocate and Journal* from 1828 to 1832. Beginning in 1836, Bangs assumed direction of the Missionary Society as its secretary. He found time during these years to publish perhaps his most important work, the four-volume *History of the Methodist Episcopal Church* (1838–40). He followed the post at the Missionary Society with a brief tenure of service as the president of Wesleyan University from 1841 to 1842. After returning to New York, where he ministered to several churches in the decade from 1842 to 1852, Bangs retired in 1852. He died ten years later on May 3, 1862, in New York City.

Nathan Bangs lived out his life during the years between the Revolutionary War and the Civil War. His lifetime witnessed the nation's birth and the early years of the great conflict that threatened its existence, the war between the North and the South. While his country grew up, Bangs played a significant role in the growing maturity of Methodism, second only in importance, some have suggested, to FRANCIS ASBURY, the father of Methodism in the United States. But however one gauges the rank of his influence, Nathan Bangs's contributions as a Methodist preacher, author, publisher, editor, and administrator made him a key figure in the first century of American Methodist history.

Further Reading

Bangs, Nathan. *An Authentic History of the Missions under the Care of the Missionary Society of the Methodist Episcopal Church.* New York: J. Emory & B. Waugh, 1832.

———. *A History of the Methodist Episcopal Church.* 4 vols. New York: T. Mason and G. Lane, 1838–1840.

———. *An Original Church of Christ.* New York: T. Mason & G. Lane, 1837.

———. *The Reformer Reformed.* New York: John C. Totten, 1818.

———. *A Vindication of Methodist Episcopacy.* N.p., 1820.

Herrman, Richard E. "Nathan Bangs: Apologist for American Methodism." Ph.D. dissertation, Emory University, 1973.

Lewis, Steven Wayne. "Nathan Bangs and the Impact of Theological Controversy on the Development of Early Nineteenth Century American Methodist Thought." Ph.D. dissertation, St. Louis University, 1998.

Rawlyk, George A. *The Canada Fire: Radical Evangelicalism in British North America, 1775–1812.* Kingston: McGill-Queen's University Press, 1994.

Stevens, Abel. *Life and Times of Nathan Bangs, D.D.* New York: Carlton & Porter, 1863.

Wigger, John H. *Taking Heaven by Storm: Methodism and the Rise of Popular Christianity in America.* New York: Oxford University Press, 1998.

Bayley, James Roosevelt

(1814–1877) *Catholic archbishop*

James Bayley converted from Episcopalianism to Catholicism when he was a young man, and he later became a priest. He was eventually consecrated the first bishop of Newark, New Jersey, and later the archbishop of Baltimore. Bayley was born on August 23, 1814, in New York City, the son of Guy Carleton Bayley and Grace Roosevelt Bayley. His father was a physician, whose half-sister, Elizabeth Ann Bayley Seton, was the founder of the American Sisters of Charity and the first native-born American to be canonized as a Roman Catholic saint. Bayley's uncle, Isaac Roosevelt, was the great-grandfather of Franklin D. Roosevelt. James Bayley studied at Amherst College from 1831 to 1833 and then transferred to Trinity College in Connecticut, where he received his B.A. in 1835.

Bayley had originally contemplated a career as a sailor and still later a vocation as a physician, but he decided after college to pursue a clerical calling. He was ordained an Episcopal priest in 1840 but almost immediately began to question his church's legitimacy. In 1841 he resigned as rector of his church in Harlem, New York, and traveled to Rome, where he was received into the Catholic Church at the Gesù the following year. Thereafter,

he studied theology in Paris and New York and was ordained a Catholic priest in 1844. Over the next several years, Bailey served as vice president of St. John's College (later Fordham University), as a parish priest in Staten Island, and then as secretary to Bishop (and later Archbishop) John J. Hughes in New York. During this period, he found time to write *A Brief Sketch of the History of the Catholic Church on the Island of New York* (1853).

When the Catholic Church created a new bishopric for Newark, New Jersey, in 1853, James Bayley became its first bishop. He proved an able spiritual overseer, helping to absorb into the Catholic Church the large numbers of immigrants who arrived in New Jersey over the next two decades. He understood their eagerness to create lives for themselves in a new country but tried to remind them, and all his spiritual charges, of the nearness of eternity.

> Everything that we hear, see, or read, is calculated to give us an extraordinary opinion of the importance of present things, and to shut out from our minds all thoughts of a future eternity—The present is all; everything that could remind us of God, and the necessity of preparing for a future life seems studiously kept out of sight. . . . We Catholics cannot live in this atmosphere without becoming in some degree affected by it.

While Bayley was bishop of Newark, the Catholic population in New Jersey doubled and he presided over the construction of 80 new churches to serve the needs of these new arrivals. He also founded Seton Hall College (later Seton Hall University), named for his famous aunt, Elizabeth Ann Bayley Seton, and the Immaculate Conception Seminary (later the School of Theology of Seton Hall University).

Toward the end of his life, Bayley reluctantly agreed to become archbishop of Baltimore in 1872. In this new office, he was less happy and less effective than during his tenure of service as bishop of Newark. Frequently plagued by illness after his consecration as archbishop, Bayley eventually asked for assistance, and in 1876 JAMES GIBBONS, the bishop of Richmond, was appointed coadjutor archbishop. Bayley died the next year in Newark on October 3, 1877.

James Roosevelt Bayley's most productive years were the nearly two decades he served as Newark's first bishop. He was a talented administrator, equal to the task of expanding the Catholic Church's ministries to respond to the rapid growth of the Catholic population in New Jersey in the second half of the 19th century. Less able at managing the ecclesiastical responsibilities of the archbishop of Baltimore, he had a brief tenure in the oldest see (jurisdiction of a bishop) within the American Catholic Church that climaxed a life characterized not by theological brilliance but by steady toil at his spiritual labor.

Further Reading

Bayley, James Roosevelt. *A Brief Sketch of the History of the Catholic Church on the Island of New York.* New York: E. Dunigan & Brother, 1853; New York: U.S. Catholic Historical Society, 1973.

Spalding, Thomas W. *The Premier See: A History of the Archdiocese of Baltimore, 1789–1989.* Baltimore: Johns Hopkins University Press, 1989.

Sullivan, Edwin Vose. "James Roosevelt Bayley." In *The Bishops of Newark, 1853–1978: The First 125 Years of the Archdiocese of Newark as Seen Through the Lives and Administrations of the Seven Men Who Have Been Its Leaders.* Edited by W. N. Field and F. Peters. South Orange, N.J.: Seton Hall University Press, 1978.

Yeager, Hildegarde. *The Life of James Roosevelt Bayley: First Bishop of Newark and Eighth Archbishop of Baltimore, 1814–1877.* Washington, D.C.: The Catholic University of America Press, 1947.

Beecher, Henry Ward
(1813–1887) *Congregationalist minister*

Henry Ward Beecher hailed from an influential family—his father was a prominent minister and his sister, Harriet Beecher Stowe, wrote *Uncle Tom's Cabin*—and he became one of the foremost preachers of his day. Beecher presided over the Congregationalist pulpit at Brooklyn's Plymouth Church and combined his ministerial duties with a writing and lecturing career that made him, in the words of American writer Sinclair Lewis, "the archbishop of American liberal Protestantism." He was born on June 24, 1813, in Litchfield, Connecticut, the son of LYMAN BEECHER and Roxana Foote Beecher. After preparatory education at the Boston Latin School and the Mount Pleasant Classical Institution at Amherst, Beecher received his college education from Amherst College, from which he graduated with his B.A. in 1834. Though he toyed with the idea of running away to sea for a time during his youth, he eventually followed the course of his father by preparing for a career as a minister. He studied theology at Lane Seminary in Cincinnati, Ohio, where his father had become president in 1832. Henry Ward Beecher graduated from the seminary in 1837 and the same year married Eunice Bullard White, with whom he had 10 children. He also assumed that year the pastorate of the Second Presbyterian Church in Indianapolis, Indiana.

A decade after entering the ministry, Beecher received a call to become the pastor of the Plymouth Church in Brooklyn, New York, where he labored until his death 40 years later. From his Brooklyn pulpit, Beecher quickly earned a reputation as an eloquent preacher, more in tune with the moral and political questions of his day perhaps than with traditional benchmarks of orthodoxy. His father, Lyman Beecher, had suffered the indignity of heresy proceedings that were ultimately dropped, and Henry Beecher eventually moved substantially further from the fold of Calvinism than his father had ever ventured. Toward the end of his life, he repudiated such tenets as a belief in hell and declared in his book *Evolution and Religion* his unabashed preference for an orthodoxy of love:

> To tell me that back of Christ is a God who for unnumbered centuries had gone on creating men and sweeping them like dead flies—nay, like living ones—into hell, is to ask me to worship a being as much worse than the conception of any medieval devil as can be imagined. But I will not worship the devil though he should come dressed in royal robes and sit on the throne of Jehovah, I will *not* worship cruelty, I *will* worship Love—that sacrifices itself for the good of those who err, and that is as

patient with them as a mother is with a sick child.

Beecher's theological liberalism veered toward a focus on social issues even as it turned away from the theological orthodoxies of his father. By the 1850s he had made a name for himself as an abolitionist. After the passage of the Kansas-Nebraska Bill in 1854 allowed new territories to decide whether to permit slavery, Beecher, who had opposed the bill, supported efforts to arm antislavery forces in Kansas. Guns sent to those opposed to slavery became known as "Beecher's Bibles." When the Civil War began, Beecher placed himself unabashedly on the side of the North.

By the 1870s, Henry Ward Beecher was one of America's most influential religious leaders. He served as editor of two prominent periodicals, the *Independent,* from 1861 to 1863, and the *Christian Union,* from 1870 to 1881. To a stream of journal articles, Beecher added a novel, *Norwood* (1868), and other books. But his position as the dean of Protestant liberalism suffered a sharp setback beginning in 1872, when rumors surfaced that he had had an adulterous affair with Elizabeth Tilton, the wife of a longtime friend. He was exonerated in a trial of the issue conducted by his church in 1874, but a civil suit tried the following year resulted in a hung jury, a verdict that he and his supporters claimed was a victory but that left his reputation indelibly stained. Beecher, though, continued to speak and write through most of the following decade, aligning himself with a variety of progressive social causes and naming himself an ally of the Darwinian theory of evolution then being grappled with by other American religious leaders. He died in Brooklyn on March 8, 1887.

Until scandal eclipsed his influence, Henry Ward Beecher commanded one of the most prominent reputations of any American preacher in the second half of the 19th century. He represented a strand of Protestantism eager to adapt to modernity by disentangling itself from traditional orthodoxies and committing itself to a progressive social vision. He championed a gospel of love and public morality rather than of

Henry Ward Beecher's career as a writer and a preacher made him a prominent voice for liberal Protestantism in 19th-century America. *(Library of Congress, Prints and Photographs Division LC-USZ62-102767)*

creed, but he suffered from accusations of sexual misconduct that tarnished the very message he delivered in the eyes of some observers. Others, though, especially members of his prominent church, continued to revere him as one of the century's great preachers.

Further Reading
Abbott, Lyman. *Henry Ward Beecher.* Cambridge: Riverside Press, 1904; New York: Chelsea House, 1980.
Beecher, Henry Ward. *American Rebellion: Report of the Speeches of Henry Ward Beecher.* Freeport, N.Y.: Books for Libraries Press, 1971.
———. *Autobiographical Reminiscences of Henry Ward Beecher.* Edited by T. J. Ellinwood. New York: Frederick A. Stokes, 1898.
———. *Freedom and War.* Freeport, N.Y.: Books for Libraries Press, 1971.
———. *The Life of Jesus the Christ.* 2 vols. New York: R. D. Dickinson, 1891.
———. *Norwood.* New York: C. Scribner, 1868.
———. *Yale Lectures on Preaching.* 3 vols. New York: J.B. Ford, 1872–1874.

Clark, Clifford Edward. *Henry Ward Beecher: Spokesman for a Middle-Class America.* Urbana: University of Illinois Press, 1978.

Elsmere, Jane Shaffer. *Henry Ward Beecher: The Indiana Years, 1837–1847.* Indianapolis: Indiana Historical Society, 1973.

Fox, Richard Wightman. *Trials of Intimacy: Love and Loss in the Beecher-Tilton Scandal.* Chicago: University of Chicago Press, 1999.

Hibben, Paxton. *Henry Ward Beecher: An American Portrait.* New York: G. H. Doran, 1927; New York: Beekman Publishers, 1974.

McLoughlin, William Gerald. *The Meaning of Henry Ward Beecher: An Essay on the Shifting Values of Mid-Victorian America, 1840–1870.* New York: Knopf, 1970.

Ryan, Halford Ross. *Henry Ward Beecher: Peripatetic Preacher.* New York: Greenwood Press, 1990.

Waller, Altina L. *Reverend Beecher and Mrs. Tilton: Sex and Class in Victorian America.* Amherst: University of Massachusetts Press, 1982.

Beecher, Lyman

(1775–1863) *Congregationalist and Presbyterian minister, seminary professor*

One of the foremost preachers of his day, Lyman Beecher attempted to meld Calvinistic Christianity with 19th-century revivalism and social reform movements. Though he considered himself essentially conservative in theological matters, he nevertheless had to fend off heresy charges from those who believed he had strayed beyond the bounds of orthodoxy. Lyman Beecher was born on October 12, 1775, in New Haven, Connecticut, the son of David Beecher and Esther Lyman Beecher. His mother died soon after his birth, and his father, a blacksmith, abandoned Lyman Beecher to the care of relatives, Lot and Catharine Benton, who lived on a farm in Connecticut.

After preparatory education, Beecher matriculated in 1793, at Yale College, where he was influenced by TIMOTHY DWIGHT, who assumed the presidency of Yale College in 1795, and under whose preaching at the college Beecher experienced conversion. After graduating in 1797, Beecher stayed on at Yale to study theology with President Dwight, and in the spring of 1798 he was baptized and became a member of the College Church. Under Dwight, Beecher was, as he would later describe it, "baptized in the revival spirit" and acquired a lifelong opposition to deism and other forms of infidelity to orthodox Christian faith. In October 1798, he was licensed to preach. The following year, he accepted the pastorate of a Presbyterian church in East Hampton, Long Island, and was ordained. That year he also married Roxana Foote, with whom he had nine children. In East Hampton, Beecher's preaching sparked a modest revival, and his concern for social problems in the community prompted him to help establish the Moral Society, designed to investigate and seek the redress of such problems. Beecher's confidence in the helpfulness of such voluntary societies became one of his major contributions to 19th-century American religion and society.

After a little more than a decade in East Hampton, Beecher accepted the call to become the pastor of the Congregational church in Litchfield, Connecticut, in 1810. Over the next 15 years, he continued to champion the value of voluntary organizations dedicated to the improvement of morals and the combat of vice. Law alone, he believed, would not rescue the nation from moral peril. "We may form free constitutions," he warned, "but our vices will destroy them; we may enact laws, but they will not protect us." The Kingdom of God was to be planted in the everyday world, and Beecher had no doubt that this planting was not only possible but necessary. Beecher's commitment to the necessity of social reform found many avenues of expression, perhaps the most prominent during this period his preaching against intemperance, published in 1825 as *Six Sermons on Temperance.*

The years in Litchfield saw Beecher's reputation as a preacher steadily advance, but they also included sorrow and changes in his personal circumstances. His wife Roxana died in 1816, and the following year he married Harriet Porter, with whom he had four children. Beecher's growing family would eventually enhance his own renown, since several of his children, including HENRY WARD BEECHER and Harriet Beecher Stowe (the author of *Uncle Tom's Cabin*), became famous through their own accomplishments. The prominence of Beecher's family inspired contemporaries to joke that America was "inhabited by saints, sinners, and Beechers."

In 1826, Beecher accepted the call to become the minister of the Hanover Street Church in Boston. There he had contact with two new spiritual antagonists: the Unitarians and the Catholics. He founded an evangelical magazine, *Spirit of the Pilgrims,* in 1828 to combat the spread of Unitarianism. He also supported various revival efforts to revitalize conservative faith, including the revival preaching of CHARLES GRANDISON FINNEY. Exposed to the growing Catholic population of Boston, Beecher—along with most other Protestants of his day—saw occasion for significant alarm. He increasingly viewed the American West as the object of popish cravings and sought to alert his Protestant contemporaries to what he saw as the vast acquisitiveness of the Roman Catholic hierarchy.

Lyman Beecher supplemented his career as a prominent Calvinistic preacher with service as president and professor at Lane Theological Seminary in Cincinnati, Ohio. *(Library of Congress, Prints and Photographs Division LC-USZ62-109964)*

In 1832 Beecher accepted a call to go west, where he became the first president and a professor of theology at Lane Theological Seminary in Cincinnati, Ohio. His career at Lane was a stormy one. Refusing to adopt a stance against slavery that might have jeopardized the future of the seminary, Beecher collided with an abolitionist student body who departed the seminary en masse in 1834 to join the newly founded school at Oberlin, Ohio. Following close on the heels of this setback, Beecher found himself accused of heresy by Old School Presbyterians the following year and was forced to defend himself in a trial before the Cincinnati presbytery. Beecher aligned himself with what was known as the New Haven theology, which generally affirmed traditional Calvinistic principles but departed from Old School Presbyterianism in emphasizing the capacity of individuals to respond to the gospel, in contrast with the Old School's insistence that sinful men and women lacked even this spiritual ability. Beecher prevailed in his defense of the heresy charges before the presbytery, and the charges were eventually dropped. Added to these tribulations was the death of his second wife in 1835.

In 1836, Beecher married Lydia Beals Jackson. Over the next 15 years he continued to preside over the affairs of Lane Seminary and to raise money for its support. Finally, he laid aside this responsibility in 1851, returning to Boston and busying himself with preparation of his collected *Works,* which was eventually published in 1852 and 1853. In 1856, he moved to Brooklyn, New York, to be close to his son, Henry Ward Beecher, who had become a prominent preacher. Beecher died there on January 10, 1863.

As America spilled west in the 19th century, Lyman Beecher became a symbol of its energy, optimism, and contradictions. He endeavored to defend the Calvinism he inherited from the previous century against new religious assaults, especially those of Unitarianism and Catholicism, but he also helped to transform this received faith. A confidence in the ability of men and women to choose salvation—and, more broadly, to live rightly—undermined the old school of Calvinism even as it undergirded an infectious optimism about the possibility of religious and social improvement.

Further Reading

Beecher, Lyman. *Autobiography*. Edited by Barbara M. Cross. Cambridge, Mass.: Belknap Press of Harvard University Press, 1961.

———. *Lyman Beecher and the Reform of Society: Four Sermons, 1804–1828*. New York: Arno Press, 1972.

———. *A Plea for the West*. Cincinnati: Truman & Smith, 1835; New York: Arno Press, 1977.

Fraser, James W. *Pedagogue for God's Kingdom: Lyman Beecher and the Second Great Awakening*. Lanham, Md.: University Press of America, 1985.

Harding, Vincent. *A Certain Magnificence: Lyman Beecher and the Transformation of American Protestantism*. Brooklyn, N.Y.: Carlson, 1991.

Hayward, Edward F. *Lyman Beecher*. Boston: The Pilgrim Press, 1904.

Henry, Stuart C. *Unvanquished Puritan: A Portrait of Lyman Beecher*. Grand Rapids, Mich.: W. B. Eerdmans, 1973.

Snyder, Stephen H. *Lyman Beecher and His Children: The Transformation of a Religious Tradition*. Brooklyn, N.Y.: Carlson, 1991.

Beissel, Johann Conrad

(1692–1768) *founder and leader of the Ephrata commune of Seventh Day Baptists*

The monastic life has flourished more often under the shadow of the Roman Catholic Church than that of its Protestant counterparts. Nevertheless, Johann Conrad Beissel, a Seventh Day Baptist who established the Ephrata commune, demonstrated that the monastic impulse may fasten itself to Protestant as well as Catholic piety. Beissel was born on March 1, 1692, in Eberbach, Germany, the son of Matthias Beissel and Anna Beissel. His father, an alcoholic baker, died shortly before his birth, and his mother died seven years later, leaving Beissel to be raised by older brothers and sisters. He was apprenticed to a baker while in his teens, and during this period he also became a pietist, the name given to Protestant believers in Germany who abandoned the state-sanctioned churches in their pursuit of personal holiness. Beissel's embrace of pietism eventually caused him to be banished from the region where he grew up and led to his migration to America in 1720.

Once in America, Beissel settled in Pennsylvania, where he may have intended to join a pietistic group called the Society of the Woman of the Wilderness. But the society had all but vanished by the time he arrived, and Beissel allied himself instead with a group of German Baptists—commonly referred to as Dunkards—led by Peter Becker. Soon dissatisfied with the Dunkards, however, Beissel sought a more solitary existence and settled in the Conastoga region of Pennsylvania, where he lived the life of a spiritual hermit for a time. An intrusion on this solitude subsequently presented itself, when a small group of German Baptists in the region persuaded Beissel to become their leader. Over the following decade, a community grew up around Beissel and, by the early 1730s, had moved from its home at a place called Falckner's Swamp to a location Beissel named Ephrata on the Cocalico Creek. Beissel and his followers at Ephrata were Seventh-Day Baptists—that is, Baptists who believed the appropriate day for Christian worship and rest was Saturday, the Old Testament sabbath. Beissel's first published work, titled *Mysterium Anomias* (1728), or "The Mystery of lawlessness," defended his sabbatarian views. The Ephrata community, at Beissel's insistence, also extolled the value of celibacy, even among its married members.

The Ephrata group practiced communal living and working arrangements that resembled those of a monastic order. By the 1750s, the community was home to more than 300 members. In addition to other forms of communal industry, Ephrata operated a printing press whose products included a Mennonite book, *Martyr-Spiegel* (1748), or "Martyr's mirror," whose pages exceeded 1,500, making it the longest book published in America prior to the 19th century, and a hymnbook, called *Die Turtle-Taube* (1747), or "The Turtledove," which consisted of hymns written primarily by Beissel for the Ephrata community.

Beissel governed the Ephrata community as a benevolent tyrant. Over the years, the community witnessed repeated internal disputes and external suspicion, especially centered on the rumors of sexual intrigue that accompanied the community's emphasis on celibacy, combined with Beissel's popularity among unmarried—and sometimes, married—women. Toward the later years of Beissel's leadership, the community's numbers declined, and at his death the Ephrata community all but vanished. Beissel died on July 6, 1768, at Ephrata, Pennsylvania.

Though the actual membership of the Ephrata community never exceeded several hundred, it was one of the best-known religious communities in colonial America. Johann Conrad Beissel, for his part, was a charismatic leader, but one whose spiritual vision was not married with the kind of pastoral or administrative gifts needed to produce a self-sustaining organization. When he died, Ephrata's center died, and its spiritual vision—shorn of an anchor—became a footnote to American religious history rather than a living tributary of it.

Further Reading

Alderfer, E. Gordon. *The Ephrata Commune: An Early American Counterculture.* Pittsburgh: University of Pittsburgh Press, 1985.

Erb, Peter, ed. *Johann Conrad Beissel and the Ephrata Community: Mystical and Historical Texts.* Lewiston, N.Y.: E. Mellen Press, 1985.

Gordon, Ronald J. "Conrad Beissel and the Ephrata Cloister," Church of the Brethren Network. Available online. URL: http://www.cob-net.org/cloister.htm. Downloaded on August 25, 2001.

Klein, Walter Conrad. *Johann Conrad Beissel: Mystic and Martinet, 1690–1768.* Philadelphia: University of Pennsylvania Press, 1942; Philadelphia: Porcupine Press, 1972.

Lamech, Brother. *Chronicon Ephratense: A History of the Community of Seventh Day Baptists at Ephrata, Lancaster County, Pennsylvania.* Translated by J. Max Hark. Lancaster, Pa.: S. H. Zahm, 1889.

Bellows, Henry Whitney
(1814–1882) *Unitarian minister*

A principal organizing force behind Unitarianism in the last half of the 19th century, Henry Whitney Bellows helped found the National Conference of Unitarian and Other Christian Churches in 1865. Less an original thinker than an administrator, Bellows aimed his considerable talents at crafting the-

ological statements and ecclesiastical forms around which Unitarians could find common cause. He was one of twin sons born on June 11, 1814, in Boston, Massachusetts, to John Bellows and Betsy Eames Bellows. His father was a successful merchant and bank president, and so Bellows grew up in affluent circumstances. After receiving a private preparatory education, Bellows attended Harvard College, from which he received a B.A. in 1832.

A decline in his father's financial circumstances, however, left Bellows unable to proceed directly on to Harvard Divinity School as he planned, so he found temporary employment as a teacher at a girls' school and then as a tutor to a wealthy family in Louisiana. He was finally able to enter Harvard's divinity school in 1834, and he graduated three years later. After a six-month trial of preaching in a church in Mobile, Alabama, Bellows was invited to become pastor of the First Unitarian Church in New York City and was ordained there in 1839. He remained in this ministerial office for the rest of his life. Later that first year in New York City, he married Eliza Nevins Townsend, with whom he had five children.

Secure in his New York church, over the following decades Bellows enjoyed growing prominence as a preacher and a writer. "The truth is," he would later declare,

> Divine Providence has led me by a way I knew not, and blessed me with a rigid discipline, a furnishing of rich opportunity, a fulcrum of influence in my pulpit, a position as your minister in this central seat of power, New York, that have elicited every faculty, aptitude, affection, sympathy I possessed, and enlisted every drop of blood in my veins, and every throb of my heart, in a most rewarding service.

In 1846, he founded and served as the initial editor of the *Christian Inquirer,* and 16 years later, he published a series of sermons, *Restatements of Christian Doctrine* (1860). In both sermons and writings, Bellows showed himself a centrist on theological questions, continuing to reject Trinitarianism but unwilling to cast off the whole of Christian orthodoxy. He was convinced that Unitarianism required continuing ceremonies and ritual forms.

When the Civil War erupted, Bellows added to his pastoral responsibilities a new field of endeavor by helping to guide early war relief efforts pioneered by New York women into a more enduring institutional structure, the U.S. Sanitary Commission. The War Department officially authorized the commission in June 1861, and Bellows became its first president. The commission acted as a clearinghouse by coordinating relief efforts, such as the provision of hospitals and nurses, both for the Union army and for Confederate prisoners.

The administrative experience Bellows gained as president of the U.S. Sanitary Commission inspired him to seek a greater measure of coordination among Unitarians. His dream lay in a "Liberal Christian Church of America," but he eventually aimed for the more manageable yet still daunting task of uniting Unitarians. Bellows was convinced that the growth of Unitarianism into a national denomination required articulation of a Unitarian creed, and he proved instrumental in the formation of both denomination and creed with the foundation of the National Conference of Unitarian and Other Christian Churches in 1865. He served as chairman of this organization's council from 1865 to 1875. Bellows's relative theological conservativism alienated some Unitarians, who subsequently formed the Free Religious Association as a counterpoint to the national conference, but Bellows had at least partially achieved his goal in forging a denominational identity for Unitarians. Bellows's first wife died in 1869; in 1874 he married Anna Huidekoper Peabody, with whom he had two children. He died on January 30, 1882, in New York City.

As early as the 1820s, Unitarians sought to establish cooperative associations to guide their common life, first the Berry Street Association in 1820 and, in 1825, the American Unitarian Association. But these associations only weakly linked the various Unitarian congregations in religious fraternity. It remained for Henry Whitney Bellows to craft a more comprehensive and durable form of unity in the National Conference of Unitarian and Other Christian Churches. Though little remembered today, he must be reckoned among the most influential Unitarian leaders in American religious history.

Further Reading

Bellows, Anna L. *Recollections of Henry Whitney Bellows.* New York: New York League of Unitarian Women, printed by the Branch Alliance of All Souls, 1897.

Bellows, Henry Whitney. "The Suspense of Faith: A Discourse on the State of the Church," Meadville Lombard Theological School. Available online. URL: http://www.meadville.edu/librarybellows.htm. Downloaded on September 5, 2001.

Kring, Walter Donald. *Henry Whitney Bellows.* Boston: Skinner House, 1979.

Wright, Conrad. *The Liberal Christians: Essays on American Unitarian History.* Boston: Beacon Press, 1970.

Black Elk
(Nicholas Black Elk)
(1863–1950) *Native American religious leader*

A holy man of the Oglala tribe of the Lakota Sioux, Black Elk experienced a vision when he was nine years old that eventually made him a spiritual leader of his people. When communicated to a broader public by the poet John G. Neihardt, Black Elk's vision played a central role in the rediscovery of Native American beliefs and values during the 1960s and 1970s. He was born in December 1863, on the Little Powder River, probably in what is now the state of Wyoming. His parents were Black Elk and Mary Leggins Down. The central event of his youth, growing up in the area west of the Black Hills, was the vision he experienced when he was nine. He disclosed it to elders of his tribe when he was 17 years old and thereafter embarked on a career as a medicine man.

In 1886 Black Elk decided to travel with Buffalo Bill's Wild West Show, visiting venues as remote as New York and Europe. He returned to South Dakota in 1889 in time to participate in the Ghost Dance movement. He saw its eclipse after the massacre at Wounded Knee on the Pine Ridge Indian Reservation in southwestern South Dakota on December 29, 1890, in which more than 200 Sioux men, women, and children were killed by U.S. soldiers. Two years after the Wounded Knee massacre, Black Elk married Katie War Bonnet, with whom he had three children. She died in

1904, and two years later Black Elk married Anna Brings White. The couple had three children.

Black Elk was exposed to Catholicism on the Pine Ridge Reservation and eventually converted to the Christian faith in 1904, at which point he assumed the name Nicholas Black Elk. Within two years he became a catechist for the Jesuit mission on the reservation and helped to spread Christianity among the Lakota. He also assisted in missionary ventures to other reservations.

Black Elk's migration from Native American holy man to Christian convert did not end his spiritual autobiography, however. In 1930 the poet John G. Neihardt visited Black Elk, initially seeking material to complete an epic poem, *Cycle of the West*. But in the course of this interview, Black Elk began what would become a lengthy process of revealing to Neihardt the vision he had experienced when he was nine and of conveying to Neihardt details of his life as a Lakota Sioux.

> My friend, I am going to tell you the story of my life, as you wish; and if it were only the story of my life I think I would not tell it; for what is one man that he should make much of his winters, even when they bend him like a heavy snow? So many other men have lived and shall live that story, to be grass upon the hills. It is the story of all life that is holy and is good to tell, and of us two-leggeds sharing in it with the four-leggeds and the wings of the air and all green things; for these are children of one mother and their father is one Spirit.

Neihardt published his interview with Black Elk in the 1932 book *Black Elk Speaks*. Although the book found only a limited audience at the time of its initial publication, when it was released again in paperback in 1961 it played a significant role in fostering renewed interest in Native American culture and religion. In the years after 1932, Black Elk repudiated neither his Catholicism nor the religious aspects of his childhood vision. He died on August 19, 1950, in Manderson, South Dakota.

The account of Black Elk's life presented to the world through John G. Neihardt ended at Wounded Knee and thus passed over his Catholic conversion. In truth, Black Elk's religious life possessed more complexity than *Black Elk Speaks* is able to convey. In the years after Wounded Knee, he converted to Christianity and was revered as a Native American holy man. Observers within both religious traditions have attempted to suppress one half or the other of Black Elk's religious identity. Nevertheless, Black Elk himself appears to have carried both the Christian and the traditional Native American aspects of his spiritual pilgrimage into his later years.

Further Reading

Black Elk DeSersa, Esther. *Black Elk Lives: Conversations with the Black Elk Family*. Edited by Hilda Neihardt and Lori Utecht. Lincoln: University of Nebraska Press, 2000.

The Black Elk Reader. Edited by Clyde Holler. Syracuse: Syracuse University Press, 2000.

Black Elk Speaks: Being the Life Story of a Holy Man of the Oglala Sioux, as Told Through John G. Neihardt (Flaming Rainbow). New York: William Morrow, 1932; Lincoln: University of Nebraska Press, 1961.

Holler, Clyde. *Black Elk's Religion: The Sun Dance and Lakota Catholicism*. Syracuse, N.Y.: Syracuse University Press, 1995.

Neihardt, John Gneisenau. *The Sixth Grandfather: Black Elk's Teachings Given to John G. Neihardt*. Edited by Raymond J. DeMallie. Lincoln: University of Nebraska Press, 1984.

———. *When the Tree Flowered: An Authentic Tale of the Old Sioux World*. New York: Macmillan, 1951.

Petri, Hilda Neihardt. *Black Elk and Flaming Rainbow: Personal Memories of the Lakota Holy Man and John Neihardt*. Lincoln: University of Nebraska Press, 1995.

Rice, Julian. *Black Elk's Story: Distinguishing Its Lakota Purpose*. Albuquerque: University of New Mexico Press, 1991.

Steltenkamp, Michael F. *Black Elk: Holy Man of the Oglala*. Norman: University of Oklahoma Press, 1993.

Blackwell, Antoinette Louisa Brown
(1825–1921) *Unitarian minister, social reformer*

The first woman ordained a minister by a mainline Protestant denomination, Antoinette Louisa Brown Blackwell had a public career that extended from before the Civil War into the 20th century. Although her religious affiliation migrated from Congregationalism to Unitarianism, she remained an influential advocate for women's rights for nearly 70 years. She was born on May 20, 1825, in Henrietta, New York, the daughter of Joseph Brown and Abigail Morse Brown. A precocious child, Antoinette Brown began attending school at an early age and joined her family's Congregationalist church when she was only nine years old. At the age of 16, she became a teacher, but a desire for further education prompted her in 1846 to enter Oberlin College, from which she graduated the following year. Although she remained at the college to study theology for another three years, Oberlin refused to grant her a degree because she was a woman. The college did not rectify this action until years later, when it awarded Brown an honorary A.M. in 1878 and, still later, a D.D. in 1908.

Undeterred by this setback to her educational aspirations, Brown lectured for a time on women's rights and other social issues, and she occupied such pulpits as invited her, until a Congregationalist church in South Butler, New York, proposed that she become its pastor in 1852. Her ordination to this ministry on September 15, 1853, made her the first woman ordained as a minister in a major U.S. denomination. Even after undertaking this new role, however, Brown continued her involvement in a variety of social issues, including the temperance movement. Elected a delegate to the World's Temperance Convention, which met in New York City in 1853, Brown had the distinction of being shouted off the podium by those who opposed being addressed by a woman. By 1854 Brown's agreement with basic tenets of Christian orthodoxy had eroded sufficiently to cause her to resign her ministerial position in South Butler. After leaving her Congregationalist post, Brown worked in New York City for a time with the prison reformer Abby Hopper Gibbons and wrote for Horace Greeley's *New York Tribune*. On January 24, 1856, she married Samuel Charles Blackwell of Cincinnati, Ohio. Her new husband shared her reformist spirit, and the marriage linked her by familial bonds with his sister, Elizabeth Blackwell, the first woman medical school graduate in the United States, and her longtime friend, Lucy Stone, who had married Samuel Blackwell's brother the previous year. Antoinette Blackwell had seven children with Samuel, and their marriage lasted until his death in 1901.

For the next half century, Blackwell wrote copiously. Her books included *Studies in General Science* (1869), *The Sexes throughout Nature* (1875), *The Physical Basis of Immortality* (1876), and *The Philosophy of Individuality* (1893). She published a novel as well in 1871, *The Island Neighbors*, and a volume of poetry in 1902, *Sea Drift; or Tribute to the Ocean*.

Blackwell also continued her participation in reformist causes, especially those involving women's rights, even though her views were sometimes at odds with those of other women leaders. In the 1860s, for example, she clashed with Elizabeth Cady Stanton and Susan B. Anthony over the issues of divorce and ratification of the Fifteenth Amendment to the U.S. Constitution: Blackwell opposed liberalizing the availability of divorce for women, in contrast with the position taken by Stanton and Anthony, and she supported ratification of the Fifteenth Amendment, which guaranteed the right to vote to males who had been newly freed from slavery. The National Woman Suffrage Association, however, led by Stanton and Anthony, opposed ratification, since the proposed amendment did nothing to secure women the right to vote.

Having left Congregationalism, Blackwell eventually aligned herself with Unitarianism, and she became a Unitarian minister in 1878. Later in life she helped establish the All Souls Unitarian Church in Elizabeth, New Jersey, and was elected pastor emeritus of the church in 1908. As the 20th century passed its second decade, only Blackwell remained of the leading women who had labored so insistently for equal rights in the late 19th century: Susan B. Anthony had died in 1906, Elizabeth Cady Stanton in 1902, and Blackwell's sister-in-law and friend, Lucy Stone, in 1893. But Blackwell lived to see the ratification of the Nineteenth Amendment in 1920 and to cast a vote in the presidential election of that year. She died on November 5, 1921, in Elizabeth, New Jersey.

Antoinette Louisa Brown Blackwell was born into a society that expected women to lead lives largely circumscribed by domestic duties. Though she bore herself the burden of such duties, she labored across seven decades to leap beyond the barriers that would have limited her to them. In the process, she became first a Congregationalist and later a Unitarian minister, even as she struggled to make her own accomplishments a possibility for other women.

Further Reading

Blackwell, Antoinette Louisa Brown. *The Making of the Universe: Evolution the Continuous Process Which Derives the Finite from the Infinite.* Boston: The Gorham Press, 1914.

———. *The Sexes Throughout Nature.* New York: G. P. Putnam, 1875; Westport, Conn.: Hyperion Press, 1976.

———. *The Social Side of Mind and Action.* New York: Neale, 1915.

Cazden, Elizabeth. *Antoinette Brown Blackwell: A Biography.* Old Westbury, N.Y.: Feminist Press, 1983.

Kerr, Laura Nowak. *Lady in the Pulpit.* New York: Woman's Press, 1951.

Lasser, Carol, and Marlene Merrill, eds. *Friends and Sisters: Letters Between Lucy Stone and Antoinette Brown Blackwell.* Urbana: University of Illinois Press, 1987.

———. *Soul Mates: The Oberlin Correspondence of Lucy Stone and Antoinette Brown, 1846–1850.* Oberlin, Ohio: Oberlin College, 1983.

Spies, Barbara Susan. "Antoinette Brown Blackwell and the Prophetic Voice of the Purity Movement: The Jeremiad in Purity Work." Ph.D. dissertation, Pennsylvania State University, 1994.

Blake, Eugene Carson

(1906–1985) *Presbyterian minister, ecumenical leader*

Eugene Carson Blake was a Presbyterian minister and a 20th-century champion of human rights, social justice, and church unity. He excelled at putting the organizational apparatus of mainline Christian churches at the service of humanitarian causes. Blake was born on November 7, 1906, in St. Louis, Missouri, the son of Orville Prescott Blake and Lulu Carson Blake. His parents were devout and theologically conservative Presbyterians who made religious devotion a central aspect of their children's lives. After completing his preparatory education at the Lawrenceville School in Lawrenceville, New Jersey, where his teachers included Thornton Wilder, later an esteemed American playwright and novelist, Blake entered Princeton University in 1924. While there, he experienced what he would later call conversion. "I decided that I was going to trust God and that religion was not going to be a problem for me anymore; that I was committed by faith to God in Christ." As a result of this experience, Blake determined to enter the Christian ministry.

When he graduated from Princeton in 1928, he worked briefly as a missionary in present-day Pakistan before marrying Valina Gillespie, with whom he had no children, and studying for a year at New College in Edinburgh, Scotland. Thereafter, he earned a Th.D. from Princeton Theological Seminary in 1932 and was licensed as an evangelist by the Presbyterian Church in the United States of America (PCUSA). For the next decade, Blake served in several pastoral positions that gave him increasing prominence, first as an assistant minister at the Collegiate Church of St. Nicholas in New York City; then, beginning in 1935, as senior pastor of the First Presbyterian Church in Albany, New York; and finally, beginning in 1940, as pastor of the Pasadena Presbyterian Church in California, one of the largest Presbyterian congregations in the nation.

Eugene Blake's prominence in American religious affairs was related less to his reputation as a preacher than to his work in denominational and ecumenical affairs from the late 1930s. He served on the board of trustees of the Protestant Radio and Television Commission and on the Board of Christian Education for his denomination. In 1951 he was elected stated clerk of the PCUSA. Later that decade he served as president of the National Council of Churches from 1954 to 1957, and he was general secretary of the World Council of Churches from 1966 to 1972.

Blake was adept at using the institutional organs of mainline Christianity to pursue the causes of social justice and church unity. He helped establish the Commission on Religion and Race within his denomination in 1963. This work supplemented his own commitment to racial justice, which led him to be arrested in Baltimore, Maryland, while trying to integrate an amusement park there, and prompted him to help plan and participate in the 1963 March on Washington. On the podium where MARTIN LUTHER KING, JR., delivered his "I Have a Dream" Speech, Blake also spoke in support of racial justice and reconciliation. Though his participation in the Civil Rights movement was controversial within some quarters, Blake insisted that "[m]inisters must risk being wrong rather than to be silent and safe." He also worked tirelessly for the cause of church unity, helping to establish and chairing the Consultation of Church Union, dedicated to proposing a plan for merging the mainline Protestant denominations.

In 1973, Blake's wife Valina died, and the next year he married Jean Ware Hoyt. He stayed involved in church and humanitarian causes throughout the 1970s, serving, for example, as president of Bread for the World. He died in Stamford, Connecticut, on July 31, 1985.

Though Eugene Carson Blake insisted that theological formulations of Christianity should be reformulated regularly, he nevertheless claimed that his social radicalism proceeded from an essentially conservative theological root.

> Only a theological "conservative," meaning one who takes seriously the good news of the transcendent God who entered into human history in Jesus Christ, His Son, can be a Christian radical on social questions. It is because the Christian is in the process of becoming a new man in Christ under the Cross, that he is able to be critical of the conservative assumptions of most men in most ordinary situations.

Whatever its theological foundations, Blake's Christian radicalism placed him at the forefront of important social issues of his day, not simply as an isolated prophetic voice, however, but as a spokesperson for institutional Protestantism.

Further Reading

Blake, Eugene Carson. *The Church in the Next Decade.* New York: Macmillan, 1966.

Brackenridge, R. Douglas. "'A Beginning Has Been Made': Eugene Carson Blake and the Soviet Union, 1956." *American Presbyterians* 68 (1990): 89–98.

———. *Eugene Carson Blake: Prophet with Portfolio.* New York: Seabury Press, 1978.

Crow, Paul A., Jr. "Eugene Carson Blake: Apostle of Christian Unity." *Ecumenical Review* 38 (April 1986): 228–36.

Niemöller, Martin. *The Challenge to the Church: The Niemoller-Blake Conversations, Lent, 1965.* Edited by Marlene Maertens. Philadelphia: Westminster Press, 1965.

Penfield, Janet Harbison. "Ecumenist of Our Time: Eugene Carson Blake, a Whole Man for the Whole World." *Mid-Stream: An Ecumenical Journal* 18 (July 1979): 311–24.

Blavatsky, Helena Petrovna
(Helena de Hahn, H. P. B.)
(1831–1891) *Theosophical Society founder*

A Russian aristocrat drawn early to spiritualism, Helena Petrovna Blavatsky (called H. P. B. by her close friends) became a cofounder of the Theosophical Society. This 19th-century religious movement combined elements of Eastern religious thought with strands of Western occultism. Blavatsky was born Helena de Hahn on July 31, 1831, in Ekaterinoslav (present-day Dnepropetrovsk), Ukraine. Her parents, Colonel Peter Hahn and Helena Pavlovna Fadeev, were Russian aristocrats. In 1848 or 1849, she married a middle-aged man, Nikifor Vasilievich Blavatsky, vice governor of the province, but she soon abandoned him and traveled widely in Asia, Europe, and the Middle East. For the next two decades, she flung herself enthusiastically into the investigation of occult matters. She began to view herself as in contact with various "masters," including various Eastern religious figures, who communicated mentally with her.

In 1871, Blavatsky traveled to the United States. A few years after arriving in America, she became acquainted with HENRY STEEL OLCOTT, a lawyer and journalist, whom she met in Vermont, where both had traveled to investigate a spiritualism phenomenon. The two would be closely associated for the next decade. The year after their initial meeting, Blavatsky and Olcott founded the Theosophical Society, with Olcott as its first president. Growing generally out of the spiritualism movement, Theosophy claimed to posit a middle way between the dogmatisms of science, on the one hand, and religion, on the other. In her first major work, *Isis Unveiled* (1877), Blavatsky emphasized that both matter and spirit derived from a single Consciousness, which she called the Universal Mind.

Though she became a United States citizen late in 1878, Blavatsky left the country, never to return, that same year when she and Olcott embarked to India. There, the two championed Theosophical ideas, while also showing respect for Hindu and Buddhist religious traditions as precursors of truths they had discovered. This respect has sometimes been credited with reinvigorating Buddhist and Hindu intellectual traditions among native Indians and indirectly sowing the seeds for the subsequent independence movement. Both Blavatsky and Olcott, while remaining dedicated to the Theosophy movement, became Buddhists during this period. In India, Blavatsky and Olcott founded the *Theosophist*, a magazine devoted to the exposition of Theosophical thought, in 1879. Three years later, they purchased an estate in Adyar, near Madras, where they established what became the world headquarters of the Theosophical Society. During the next few years, Blavatsky claimed to produce various supernormal phenomena, which her followers regarded as validation of her teaching. One of her associates, however, accused her of fraud, and England's Society for Psychical Research sent to India an investigator who published a report in 1885 that accused Blavatsky of chicanery.

In the wake of this scandal, Blavatsky left Olcott in Adyar and traveled to Germany and then to London. In London, she completed her second major work, *The Secret Doctrine*, which was published in 1888. Her new book suggested that the cosmos was rooted in "[a]n Omnipresent, Eternal, Boundless, and Immutable PRINCIPLE on which all speculation is impossible, since it transcends the power of human conception and could only be dwarfed by any human expression or similitude." The cosmos consisted of "a boundless plane; periodically the playground of numberless Universes incessantly manifesting and disappearing," thus illustrating the constant ebb and flow of all cosmic elements. Blavatsky finally insisted on the "fundamental identity of all Souls with the Universal OverSoul, the latter being itself an aspect of the Unknown Root."

In London, Blavatsky pursued an active writing career. She also founded the Blavatsky Lodge in 1887. She died in London on May 8, 1891.

Although Henry Steel Olcott took the lead in the organization and management of the early Theosophical Society, Helena Petrovna Blavatsky supplied the movement's religious ideas and vocabulary. Her merger of Western occultism with Eastern religious mysticism produced a synthesis often replicated among new religious groups of the 20th century. The influence of her ideas, which was substantial in the century after her death, was due partially to her ability to combine elements of Eastern religious thinking with the language of progress and evolution in which Western minds were fluent.

Further Reading

Bevir, Mark. "The West Turns Eastward: Madame Blavatsky and the Transformation of the Occult Tradition." *Journal of the American Academy of Religion* 62 (1994): 747–67.

Blavatsky, H. P. *Collected Writings.* Compiled by Boris De Zirkoff. 16 vols. Madras: Theosophical Publishing House, 1950.

———. *Personal Memoirs of H. P. Blavatsky.* Compiled by Mary K. Neff. London: Rider, 1937.

Cranston, S. L. *HPB: The Extraordinary Life and Influence of Helena Blavatsky, Founder of the Modern Theosophical Movement.* New York: G. P. Putnam's Sons, 1993.

Meade, Marion. *Madame Blavatsky: The Woman Behind the Myth.* New York: G. P. Putnam's, Sons, 1980.

Olcott, Henry Steel. *Old Diary Leaves: The True Story of the Theosophical Society.* New York: G. P. Putnam's Sons, 1895.

Boehm, John Philip
(1683–1749) *German Reformed minister*

John Philip Boehm played an instrumental role in planting the German Reformed Church in America. He also protected churches within this tradition from efforts by Count NIKOLAUS LUDWIG VON ZINZENDORF to merge them into an association of German evangelical churches. Boehm was born on November 25, 1683, in Hochstadt, Germany, the son of Philip Ludwig Boehm and Maria Boehm. The details of Boehm's childhood and education are unknown, other than that his father was a Reformed minister in Hochstadt.

In 1708 Boehm became the teacher for a school operated by the Reformed Church in Worms, Germany, and moved there with his wife, Anna Maria Stehler Boehm, with whom he had four children. After a stormy career in Worms, caused by opposition of influential members of the congregation to Boehm, he resigned in November 1715 and took a teaching position in Lambsheim, a nearby town. There, his first wife apparently died, and he married Anna Maria Scherer, a woman from Lambsheim, and this union produced four children.

Five years after taking the teaching position in Lambsheim, Boehm emigrated with his family to Pennsylvania. There he worked as a farmer, and German Reformed settlers persuaded him to serve as the reader in their church services. In 1725, several congregations pleaded with him to be their pastor, and though Boehm had not been ordained, he agreed to undertake this ministry. Two years later, another Reformed minister, George Michael Weiss, arrived in Pennsylvania and soon began to protest the irregularity of Boehm's service as a Reformed minister. Eventually, the matter was referred to the Classis of Amsterdam, which, in the summer of 1729, approved Boehm's work as a minister but instructed that he should seek ordination. The following November, Boehm was ordained by two Reformed ministers in New York.

For the next 20 years, Boehm ministered to his original congregations and engaged in an itinerant ministry of preaching and church building. He is credited with establishing 11 and perhaps 12 Reformed churches during his life. Over the years, Boehm defended these congregations both from the fragmenting impulse often characteristic of Protestantism and from the efforts of Count Nikolaus Ludwig von Zinzendorf to gather the various German-speaking churches of Pennsylvania into the "Congregation of God in the Spirit."

In the late 1720s, Zinzendorf had helped form the Church of the Brethren, also known as the Moravian Church, on his estate in Germany. In 1741, he began an 18-month visit to North America, in which he established the Moravian Church in America and attempted to persuade the German Protestants in Pennsylvania to form a unified association of churches. His "union movement," as it came to be called, would have drawn Protestant groups as varied as the Lutherans, the German Reformed Churches, the Sabbatarians, the Dunkers and Seventh-Day Dunkers, the Mennonites, and the Schwenkfelders into common synods. John Philip Boehm became a significant opponent of Zinzendorf's union movement, and in 1742 he published a book-length broadside against the movement, "True Letter of Warning addressed to the Reformed Congregations of Pennsylvania." This attack, combined with opposition from other German ministers in Pennsylvania, ultimately defeated Zinzendorf's plan of union.

Several years after the collapse of the union movement, Michael Schlatter, another German Reformed minister, arrived in Pennsylvania and set about organizing the various Reformed congregations, including those Boehm had established, into a coetus, an ecclesiastical body subordinate to the Classis of Amsterdam. Boehm assisted Schlatter in this work and served briefly as the president of the coetus during its second meeting, held in September 1748. He died the next year on April 29, 1749, in Hellertown, Pennsylvania.

An important branch of Protestant Christianity, the German Reformed Church helped to establish in North America a presbyterian form of church government and theological devotion to the Heidelberg Catechism, the influential summary of Reformed doctrine published in 1563. John Philip Boehm played a formative role in planting the German Reformed faith in Pennsylvania. The churches he established and the ecclesiastical structure he helped organize to govern them had a lasting impact on American religion.

Further Reading

Boehm, John Philip. *Life and Letters of the Rev. John Philip Boehm, Founder of the Reformed Church in Pennsylvania, 1683–1749.* Edited by William J. Hinke. Philadelphia: Publication and Sunday School Board of the Reformed Church in the United States, 1916; New York: Arno Press, 1972.

Dotterer, Henry S. *Rev. John Philip Boehm.* Philadelphia: n.p., 1890.

Moore, Wilson F. "A Sketch of the Life of John Philip Boehm." Available online. URL: http://www.kichline.com/carrie/boehm/jpb.htm. Downloaded on September 5, 2001.

Brainerd, David
(1718–1747) *Presbyterian missionary*

A Presbyterian missionary to Native Americans in New York, New Jersey, and Pennsylvania, David Brainerd might have occupied a more obscure place in American history had not a more famous man, the greater preacher and theologian JONATHAN EDWARDS, edited and published his diary. After Brainerd's death from tuberculosis, this diary became a model of the evangelical piety characteristic of the Great Awakening. Brainerd was born on April 20, 1718, in Haddam, Connecticut, the son of Hezekiah and Dorothy Hobart Mason Brainerd. Brainerd's father was an influential politician in Connecticut, who died when David was nine years old. His mother died six years later. Though David Brainerd grew up in a religious family, it was not until July 1739 that he experienced conversion. He later described the event in his diary:

> [A]s I was walking in a dark thick grove, unspeakable glory seemed to open to the view and apprehension of my soul. . . . [I]t was a new inward apprehension or view that I had of God, such as I never had before, nor anything

which had the least resemblance of it. . . . My soul was so captivated and delighted with the excellency, loveliness, greatness, and other perfections of God, that I was even swallowed up in Him. . . . Thus God, I trust, brought me to a hearty disposition to exalt Him and set Him on the throne, and principally and ultimately to aim at His honor and glory, as King of the universe. . . . If I could have been saved by my own duties, or any other way that I had formerly contrived, my whole soul would now have refused it. I wondered that all the world did not see and comply with this way of salvation, entirely by the righteousness of Christ.

The following fall, Brainerd entered Yale College to prepare for a ministerial career. While there, Brainerd and many other students were deeply influenced by the revivalistic fervor of the Great Awakening and soon began to find spiritual fault with those at Yale who were not similarly influenced. Those in charge of the college were not amused to find themselves the object of such criticism, and the trustees went so far as to order that "if any student of this College shall directly or indirectly say, that the Rector, either of the Trustees or Tutors are hypocrites, carnal or unconverted men, he shall for the first offense make a public confession in the Hall, and for the second offense be expelled." Brainerd violated this order when he was overheard telling his companions that one of Yale's tutors had "no more grace than this chair." When Brainard refused to apologize, Yale expelled him early in 1742.

A Yale education might well have been the preface to a ministerial career in one of New England's many churches. But Brainerd's expulsion directed his life to a different path. Although he already showed signs of having contracted tuberculosis, Brainerd felt himself called by God as a missionary to the Native Americans of New England, and he spent the remainder of his short life as an itinerant preacher to the Seneca and Delaware Indians of New York, New Jersey, and Pennsylvania. The Presbyterian Synod of New York eventually ordained Brainerd as a minister in the summer of 1744, but within three years his health was broken. He finally made his way to the home of Jonathan Edwards in Northampton, Massachusetts, in 1747. There he edited his diaries and composed an account of his early life and conversion. He died in Northampton on October 9, 1747. Jonathan Edwards published *An Account of the Life of the Late Reverend Mr. David Brainerd* in 1749, and this work became a classic of Christian devotional literature.

David Brainerd's success as a missionary to Native Americans of New England is difficult to estimate. His own missionary labors lasted scarcely five years before tuberculosis felled him. But he had a far deeper impact on American religion than might otherwise have flowed from this brief evangelistic career through Jonathan Edwards's published version of his early life and his diary. The account of his life became one of American religions' most celebrated autobiographies, and its spiritual influence continues to reach across the years even into the 21st century.

Further Reading

Edwards, Jonathan. *The Life of David Brainerd.* New Haven, Conn.: Yale University Press, 1985.

Page, Jesse. *David Brainerd: The Apostle to the North American Indians.* Des Moines, Iowa: LBS Archival Products, 1990.

Pettit, Norman. "Prelude to Mission: Brainerd's Expulsion from Yale." *The New England Quarterly* 59 (1986): 28–50.

Pointer, Richard, W. "'Poor Indians' and the 'Poor in Spirit': The Indian Impact on David Brainerd." *New England Quarterly* 67 (1994): 403–26.

Thornbury, John F. *David Brainerd: Pioneer Missionary to the American Indians.* Darlington, England: Evangelical Press, 1996.

Weddle, David L. "The Melancholy Saint: Jonathan Edward's Interpretation of David Brainerd as a Model of Evangelical Spirituality." *Harvard Theological Review* 81 (1988): 297–318.

Wynbeek, David. *David Brainerd: Beloved Yankee.* Grand Rapids, Mich.: Eerdmans, 1961.

Branham, William Marrion

(1909–1965) *charismatic minister, healer*

The father of the Christian healing movement in the second half of the 20th century, William Marrion Branham was a seminal figure in the rise of the charismatic movement during that period. He claimed to be a prophet sent from God to prepare the world for the end times, and, after his death, his followers began to believe that his words were inspired and infallible utterances. He was born near Burkesville, Kentucky, on April 6, 1909, to Charles and Ella Branham, an alcoholic father and a 15-year-old mother. Born in poverty and deprived of any substantial early education, Branham experienced conversion at the age of 19. Feeling that he was called by God to preach, he began an itinerant evangelistic ministry and, in his mid-20s, eventually settled as the pastor of a Baptist church in Jeffersonville, Indiana, where his congregation built the Branham Tabernacle.

In May 1946, Branham claimed that an angel had appeared to him and commissioned him an evangelist and a healer, and he soon began to con-

William Branham was a leading figure in the charismatic movement during the second half of the 20th century. *(Library of Congress, Prints and Photographs Division LC-USZ62-114787)*

duct revival and healing crusades that attracted thousands of people, many of whom declared that they had experienced miraculous healings in Branham's meetings. Branham reported that the angel who had originally visited him continued to accompany him onto the stage during his crusade services, often leaving him paralyzed and weakened by its presence. In the first part of the 1950s, Branham added crusades in South Africa, India, and Europe to an exhausting series of meetings in the United States. But even as his healing ministry was becoming nationally known, financial difficulties began to plague his ministry around 1955.

In the final decade of his life, Branham's healing ministry declined somewhat, and he devoted more attention to the development of particular doctrines that led to his followers' being referred to as Branhamists. Among these were a fierce antipathy to denominationalism and the doctrine of the "serpent's seed." Branham claimed to have had a revelation that Eve had sexual relations with Satan, in the form of a serpent, and that this unholy coupling produced a race of humans, through Cain, that was the "seed of the serpent" and doomed to damnation. Branham also taught his followers that they were living in the last times, and he implied that he was a prophet appointed by God during these times to prepare the church for Christ's second coming. Branham died on Christmas Eve 1965, in Amarillo, Texas, as a result of injuries received in an automobile accident.

In the last half of the 20th century, the charismatic movement, with its emphasis on continued supernatural gifts, such as the gift of healing and the gift of tongues, became one of the fastest growing religious groups in America. Although rooted initially in Pentecostal and Assemblies of God churches, it extended beyond these denominations and influenced the religious life of mainstream Protestant and even Catholic churches. Branham's career as a renowned healer, a career that reached its highest visibility from 1946 to 1955, contributed to the rise of the charismatic movement. Although Branham, and those who followed his message even after his death, ultimately traveled down theological pathways that were thought eccentric and even heretical by more mainstream Christians, he nevertheless had an enduring influ-ence on American Christianity through his formative role in the beginnings of the charismatic movement.

Further Reading

Branham, William. *Subject Encyclopedia of Sermons by Rev. William M. Branham*. Compiled by David Mamalis. Mesa, Ariz.: William Branham Library, 1978.

Chappell, Paul G. "William Branham." In *Twentieth-Century Shapers of American Popular Religion*. Edited by Charles H. Lippy. New York: Greenwood Press, 1989.

Lindsay, Gordon. *William Branham: A Man Sent from God*. Jeffersonville, Ind.: Spoken Word, 1950.

Stadsklev, Julius. *William Branham: A Prophet Visits South Africa*. Minneapolis: n.p., 1952.

Strohkorb, Mark. *Astonished at His Doctrine: A Historical Examination of the Doctrine of William Marrion Branham*. Tucson, Ariz.: MarksNet Publications, 1997.

Weaver, C. Douglas. *The Healer-Prophet: William Marrion Branham, A Study of the Prophetic in American Pentecostalism*. New ed. Macon, Ga.: Mercer University Press, 2000.

Breck, James Lloyd
(1818–1876) *Episcopal missionary*

James Lloyd Breck was an Episcopal missionary to the western frontier of the United States in the 19th century. Over the course of a ministry that spanned 35 years, he helped to establish six missions, from Wisconsin to California. He was born on June 27, 1818, in Philadelphia County, Pennsylvania, the son of George Breck and Catharine D. Israell Breck. A bequest from a wealthy uncle allowed Breck to attend the Flushing Institute in New York after early education in neighborhood schools. He was confirmed while studying there, and by the time he was 16 years old, he had determined to become an Episcopal priest. His stay at Flushing introduced Breck to the movement toward liturgical renewal then active within some quarters of Episcopalianism, represented especially by the Oxford movement in England during the 1830s and 1840s, which emphasized the importance of ritual and liturgy. Subsequently, Breck enrolled at the University of Pennsylvania and graduated in 1838. While at the General Theological Seminary in New York City, from which he received a B.D. in 1841, Breck was persuaded to become an Episcopal missionary to the West.

After his graduation, Breck and two classmates from seminary settled in Nashotah Lakes, Wisconsin, where they established an associate mission. In this enterprise several missionaries were to work together to form a kind of monastic order, which would be the center of various missionary endeavors such as the establishment of churches and schools. Breck and his colleagues adopted monastic-like rules, such as celibacy. At Nashotah they founded an academy (which eventually became Racine College), a school of theology (which became Nashotah House), and several churches. Breck's vision, though, generated conflict with other Episcopalians at Nashotah, who sniffed Roman Catholicism in his monastic zeal, and he eventually left in 1850 and helped to establish a mission in Saint Paul, Minnesota.

Beginning in 1852, Breck turned his attention to Native American missions. That year he founded Saint Columba's Mission for the Ojibwa at Gull Lake, Minnesota, and, in 1854, a mission at Leech Lake, Minnesota. Soon afterward, Breck abandoned his earlier commitment to celibacy and in 1855 married Jane Maria Mills, with whom he had two sons. Two years later he moved on to Faribault, Minnesota, where he established a new mission, with schools for boys and girls and a seminary (later to become Seabury Divinity School), and where he supervised the construction of a cathedral. His first wife died there, and in 1864 he married Sarah Styles. In 1867, missionary zeal impelled him to move once more, this time to Benicia, California, where he helped establish the Pacific Coast Mission. He died in Benicia, a little less than a decade later, on March 30, 1876.

The history of missionary activity has often turned on the heroic labors of isolated individuals who carried the word of faith into regions unfamiliar with it. But James Lloyd Breck gave Episcopal missions an alternative vision, that of the associate mission, which supplanted the lone evangelist with a community of souls who worked together to share the Christian message. In a sermon preached in Minnesota before he struck out to establish the mission in California, Breck described his vision of missions:

> There are instrumentalities, such as the organization of men and women for a variety of pious works, which alone will enable us to reach the people of our own or any country. . . . Impossible is it for isolated Pastors to do all the work required for the ministry of souls. There must be helps from every possible source, to meet the multiplied forms of wickedness that is in the world. Holy women must be organized. Men—clerical and lay—must be organized. The orphans of the land must be cared for. The sick and the aged poor must be looked after. Asylums, Hospitals, and Parish Schools must be largely cared for, by the self-denying and devoted lives of such as would live wholly for CHRIST. The world is to be won to CHRIST by these manifest and striking proofs of love for the souls of men. The wages of such will be paid them in the world to come.

The Episcopalianism of his day tended to cling to the prosperous and settled eastern coast of the United States. Breck carried his vision of missions to the western frontier and consequently assisted Episcopalianism in escaping the narrow regionalism into which it might otherwise have settled.

Further Reading

Breck, Charles. *The Life of the Reverend James Lloyd Breck, D.D.* New York: E. & J. B. Young, 1883.

Holcombe, Theodore Isaac. *An Apostle of the Wilderness: James Lloyd Breck and His Missions and His Schools.* New York: T. Whittaker, 1903.

Kiefer, James. "James Lloyd Breck: Priest, Educator, and Missionary (2 April 1876)," The Lectionary. Available online. URL: http://satucket.com/lectionary/JLBreck.htm.

Bresee, Phineas Franklin

(1838–1915) *Church of the Nazarene founder, minister*

Phineas Bresee devoted most of his life to the Methodist ministry, but he eventually migrated into the Holiness movement, which stressed Christians' potential to attain complete perfection in the present life. Finding Methodism increasingly inhospitable to this movement, Bresee eventually founded the Church of the Nazarene. He was born on December 31, 1838, in Franklin, New York, the son of Phineas Philips Bresee and Susan Brown Bresee, farmers and devout Methodists. Phineas Franklin Bresee worked on his family's farm and gained such formal education as was to be had, concluding with study at the Delaware Literary Institute for the school year of 1854–55.

In February 1856, Bresee was converted at a Methodist meeting and immediately "filled with great intensity for doing the work of the Lord." By the spring of the following year he had been licensed as an exhorter and soon afterward preached his first sermon. When his family moved to Iowa and settled on a new farm, Bresee accompanied them and was soon admitted on trial as an itinerant Methodist preacher by the Iowa Annual Conference. He received his first circuit appointment in 1858, was ordained a deacon in 1859, and became an elder in 1861. During these years, he also married Maria E. Hebberd, with whom he had seven children, in 1860.

Over the next three decades, Phineas Bresee cast himself into the work of the Methodist ministry, gradually assuming the responsibilities of a more senior clergyman. He was elected to attend the 1872 General Conference and served off and on as a presiding elder in Iowa. He eventually moved to Los Angeles, California, in 1883; there he became the pastor of the Fort Street Church. By 1891, he had been appointed presiding elder of the Los Angeles District.

Relatively early in his ministry, during the 1860s, Phineas Bresee had a formative religious experience as the pastor of the Methodist church in Chariton, which would eventually place him squarely within the Holiness movement. He later described the religious service over which he presided while enduring a personal period of depression.

> I turned toward the altar; in some way it seemed to me that this was my time, and I threw myself down across the altar and began

> to pray for myself. . . . [I]n my ignorance, the Lord helped me, drew me and impelled me, and, as I cried to Him that night, He seemed to open heaven on me, and gave me, as I believe, the baptism with the Holy Ghost . . .

Over the following years, Bresee understood this experience as one of "entire sanctification" or "the fullness of the blessing," an event in which a believer, subsequent to an initial conversion experience, becomes liberated from the effects of original sin. This understanding increasingly drew him to the Holiness movement.

In 1894, Bresee sought permission from Methodist authorities to work with the Peniel Mission in Los Angeles, a Holiness mission devoted to service to the poor. Denied this permission, he surrendered his position as a Methodist minister, which had generated increasing conflict with church authorities with no sympathy for the Holiness movement. The next year, however, the mission terminated its relationship with Bresee and his colleague, Joseph Pomeroy Widney, and the two men subsequently established the First Church of the Nazarene in Los Angeles in the fall of 1895. Widney soon returned to the Methodist Episcopal Church, leaving Bresee within a few years as the general superintendent of a new denomination as additional Nazarene churches sprang up and, beginning in 1902, as president of the Pacific Bible College, an institution established by the infant denomination.

Over the following years, Phineas Bresee labored at the task of uniting various Holiness groups in America in a single denomination, the Pentecostal Church of the Nazarene (renamed the Church of the Nazarene in 1919). In 1915, the General Assembly of the Pentecostal Church of the Nazarene elected him general superintendent of the newly united denomination. He died soon afterward, on November 13, 1915, in Los Angeles.

The Holiness movement had its American origins during the middle years of the 19th century, issuing partially out of the revivalism of CHARLES GRANDISON FINNEY and the perfectionist impulse long embedded in Methodism. It was not until the end of the decade, however, that the movement began to express itself in denominational form.

One of the most important and enduring of these was the Church of the Nazarene, which Phineas Bresee founded and superintended into the 20th century.

Further Reading

Bangs, Carl. *Phineas F. Bresee: His Life in Methodism, the Holiness Movement, and the Church of the Nazarene*. Kansas City, Mo.: Beacon Hill Press of Kansas City, 1995.

Bresee, Phineas F. *The Certainties of Faith: Ten Sermons by the Founder of the Church of the Nazarene*. Kansas City, Mo.: Nazarene Publishing House, 1958.

Brickley, Donald P. *Man of the Morning: The Life and Work of Phineas F. Bresee*. Kansas City, Mo.: Nazarene Publishing House, 1960.

Brown, Harrison D. *Personal Memories of the Early Ministry of Dr. Phineas F. Bresee*. Seattle: n.p., 1930.

Girvin, Ernest Alexander. *Phineas F. Bresee: A Prince in Israel, a Biography*. Kansas City, Mo.: Pentecostal Nazarene Publishing House, 1916.

Briggs, Charles Augustus

(1841–1913) *biblical scholar, seminary professor*

Charles Augustus Briggs, a professor at Union Theological Seminary in New York City, became a lightning rod in the theological war between conservatives and liberals in the waning years of the 19th century and the early decades of the 20th. His views on the authority of the Bible ultimately caused him to be tried and convicted of heresy by the Presbyterian Church. He was born on January 15, 1841, in New York City, the son of Alanson Briggs and Sarah Mead Berrian Briggs. His family owned and operated the largest barrel-making company in the United States. He attended the University of Virginia in the years immediately preceding the Civil War and experienced conversion in 1858 while a student there. With the outbreak of war, Briggs returned north and served briefly in the Union army before entering Union Theological Seminary to study for the ministry in 1861. He left the seminary two years later to manage the family business after his father's health declined, and he married Julia Valentine Dobbs in 1865;

with her he had one child. The following year he was ordained as a Presbyterian minister and traveled to the University of Berlin to complete his theological studies. There, he studied biblical criticism with Isaac August Dorner, a disciple of Julius Welhausen, often called the father of higher criticism of the Bible. This discipline sought to explore the composition of the biblical texts to identify their sources and historical contexts. Briggs returned to the United States in 1869 and became the pastor of the First Presbyterian Church of Roselle, New Jersey.

Briggs returned to the United States with the goal that biblical criticism would be accepted as one of the tools of orthodox theological inquiry, but his vantage as a pastor of a small congregation gave him little opportunity to see this aim fulfilled. In 1874, however, he accepted a position at Union Theological Seminary, where he had greater latitude to pursue his scholarly inquiries. As Union was at the time a Presbyterian seminary, Briggs soon found himself at odds with conservative members of the denomination when he published *Whither? A Theological Question for the Times* (1889), which advocated revisions to the Westminster Confession, the summary of doctrine adopted by English Presbyterians in the 17th century. The controversy over these proposed revisions was a prelude to an even more significant conflict with Presbyterian conservatives.

In 1891 the seminary installed Briggs in the Edward Robinson Chair of Biblical Theology. In his inaugural lecture for the occasion, delivered on January 20, 1891, Briggs seized the opportunity to focus the tools of higher criticism on orthodox Presbyterian views concerning the Scripture. He scandalized conservatives by declaring that the "great mass of the Old Testament was written by authors whose names or connection with their writings are lost in oblivion," and by solemnly proclaiming that "the theory that the Bible is inerrant is the ghost of modern evangelicalism to frighten children."

By May, heresy proceedings against him had commenced within the New York presbytery. Briggs successfully defended himself of heresy charges before the presbytery, but he found a less favorable reception when the matter went before the General Assembly of the Presbyterian Church in the United States of America. That body remanded the case to the New York presbytery; when the presbytery cleared him of all charges, the General Assembly once again took up the case and eventually suspended Briggs from the Presbyterian ministry, in May 1893. Union Theological Seminary, in the meantime, had in October 1892 severed its relation with the Presbyterian Church over the Briggs controversy. Briggs himself became an Episcopalian and was ordained a priest in 1899. He remained at Union Theological Seminary, where he became the professor of theological encyclopedia and symbolics in 1904. He died in New York City on June 8, 1913.

Charles Augustus Briggs spent almost half a century as a well-respected biblical scholar, publishing widely and teaching generations of students at Union Theological Seminary. But application of critical methods to the study of the Bible helped to pry open a wide fissure between Christian conservatives and liberals. Theological battles over the nature and authority of the Bible would spill over into the 20th century as views kindred to those of Briggs became ever more widely accepted.

Further Reading

Briggs, Charles Augustus. *The Bible, the Church, and the Reason.* New York: C. Scribner's Sons, 1892.

———. *The Higher Criticism of the Hexateuch.* New York: Charles Scribner's Sons, 1893.

———. *Theological Symbolics.* New York: C. Scribner's Sons, 1914.

Christensen, Richard L. *The Ecumenical Orthodoxy of Charles Augustus Briggs: 1841–1913.* Lewiston, N.Y.: Mellen University Press, 1995.

Hatch, Carl E. *The Charles A. Briggs Heresy Trial: Prologue to Twentieth-Century Liberal Protestantism.* New York: Exposition Press, 1969.

Massa, Mark Stephen. *Charles Augustus Briggs and the Crisis of Historical Criticism.* Minneapolis: Fortress Press, 1990.

Sawyer, M. James. *Charles Augustus Briggs and Tensions in Late Nineteenth-Century American Theology.* Lewiston, N.Y.: Mellen University Press, 1994.

Smith, H.P. "Chas. Augustus Briggs." *American Journal of Theology* 17 (October 1913): 497–508.

Broadus, John Albert

(1827–1895) *Baptist preacher, seminary professor*

A leading Baptist scholar and renowned preacher of the last half of the 19th century, John Albert Broadus joined the faculty of the Southern Baptist Theological Seminary, located first in Greenville, South Carolina, and later in Louisville, Kentucky. His preaching provided a model for a generation of Baptist ministers who studied at the seminary. Broadus was born on January 24, 1827, in Culpeper County, Virginia, the son of Edmund Broadus, a politician, and Nancy Sims Broadus. He studied at a school operated by one of his uncles for a few years and then taught school while he continued a program of self-study. He had a conversion experience when he was about 16 years old and, though intent at one time on studying medicine, became convinced that he should become a preacher. In pursuit of this vocation, Broadus enrolled in the University of Virginia in 1846 and graduated with an M.A. in 1850. That year he was ordained as a Baptist minister and married Maria Carter Harrison, with whom he had three daughters. His first wife died in 1857, and after two years Broadus married Charlotte Eleanor Sinclair, with whom he had five children.

After finishing his master's degree work at the University of Virginia, Broadus spent a year teaching at a small private school in Fluvanna, Virginia, and in 1851 he accepted a position as pastor of the First Baptist Church of Charlottesville in conjunction with a post as an instructor in his alma mater's department of ancient languages. After two years, he surrendered his teaching duties to concentrate all his energy on his work as pastor, which he continued for eight years, with an interlude from 1855 to 1857 when he also served as chaplain of the University of Virginia.

In 1859, Broadus accepted a position in the newly founded Southern Baptist Theological Seminary in Greenville, South Carolina, as professor of New Testament and preaching. The Civil War caused the seminary to suspend its activities after its firm beginning. "I am not a

John A. Broadus, a powerful Baptist preacher in his own right, also educated a generation of preachers as a professor at the Southern Baptist Theological Seminary in Louisville, Kentucky. *(Southern Baptist Historical Library and Archives)*

relocated to Louisville, Kentucky. During this time, Broadus published what would become his most enduring work, *Treatise on the Preparation and Delivery of Sermons* (1870), used by Baptist seminaries well into the 20th century. With the growth and success of the Louisville seminary, Broadus's reputation as a scholar, and especially as a teacher of homiletics, steadily increased. Harvard awarded him an honorary doctorate of divinity on its 250th anniversary in 1886, and Yale University invited him to deliver the Lyman Beecher Lectures on preaching in 1889. In later years, he became the president of the Southern Baptist Theological Seminary in Louisville. He served in this position until his death on March 16, 1895, in Louisville, Kentucky.

John Albert Broadus combined the gifts of a preacher and those of a scholar to become one of the most revered Baptists of his day. Many churches and educational institutions tried to tempt him away from the Southern Baptist Theological Seminary. Though he spoke widely and gained a reputation that extended beyond the limits of his denomination, Broadus nevertheless dedicated himself to the task of making the Louisville seminary a leading Baptist institution, whose denominational prestige extends to the present day.

secessionist . . . but I am a Virginian," Broadus recorded in his journal at the time. "Virginia in the Union, if men were wise enough, unselfish enough, virtuous enough to appreciate and preserve a union, is my favorite idea—but if Virginia cannot belong to the Union without servile degradation from Northern aggression and domination, then I am for Virginia and nothing else at present." He contented himself with part-time preaching in various churches and in army camps and, toward the end of the war, serving as aide-de-camp to Virginia's governor.

After the war, Broadus and the other faculty at the seminary commenced classes again, but the seminary struggled for more than a decade until it

Further Reading

Broadus, John Albert. *Favorite Sermons of John A. Broadus.* Edited by Vernon Latrelle Stanfield. New York: Harper, 1959.

———. *Jesus of Nazareth.* New York: A. C. Armstrong, 1890; Grand Rapids, Mich.: Baker Book House, 1962.

———. *A Treatise on the Preparation and Delivery of Sermons.* Philadelphia: Smith, English, 1870.

"John A. Broadus: Preacher Extraordinary," The Reformed Reader. Available online. URL: http://www.reformedreader.org/rbb/broadus/biography.htm. Downloaded on September 5, 2001.

McKibbens, Thomas R., Jr. *The Forgotten Heritage: A Lineage of Great Baptist Preaching.* Macon, Ga.: Mercer, 1986.

Robertson, Archibald Thomas. *Life and Letters of John Albert Broadus.* Philadelphia: American Baptist Publication Society, 1901.

Brooks, Phillips

(1835–1893) *Episcopal preacher, bishop*

An Episcopal minister and bishop, Phillips Brooks was one of the most revered preachers of his day. He brought high learning and aesthetic excellence to his calling as a minister, as well as a commitment to Christian orthodoxy coupled with a sympathetic spirit for those whose faith did not precisely parallel his own. These traits earned him respect beyond the bounds of his religious tradition while he was alive and an enduring place in the history of American religion in the century after his death. Phillips Brooks was born on December 13, 1835, in Boston, Massachusetts, the son of William Gray Brooks and Mary Ann Phillips Brooks. His mother was a descendant of the eminent Puritan preacher JOHN COTTON, and her forebears had founded Phillips Academy, Andover, Phillips Exeter Academy, and Andover Theological Seminary. Phillips Brooks was baptized in Boston's prestigious First Church, where John Cotton had preached in the 17th century, but after the church became Unitarian in 1835, his mother migrated with her family to Saint Paul's Episcopal Church.

After attending a public grammar school and then the Boston Latin School, Brooks matriculated at Harvard College in 1851 and received an A.B. four years later. He taught briefly at the Boston Latin School after graduating from Harvard but was dismissed for failure to keep order in his class. In the fall of 1856, he entered the Virginia Theological Seminary, where he received a B.D. in 1859.

The year he graduated from seminary, Phillips Brooks was ordained in the Episcopal Church and became the rector of the Church of the Advent in Philadelphia, Pennsylvania; in 1862, he was appointed as rector of Philadelphia's Holy Trinity Church and, in 1869, of Boston's Trinity Church. Since his days as a seminary student in Virginia, Brooks had grown to despise slavery, and during the Civil War he continued his criticism of this pernicious institution. After the war, he championed the right of African Americans to vote. He achieved a measure of national prominence when he preached a sermon about Lincoln after the president's assassination. Slavery, though techni-

cally abolished, had not been defeated absolutely, Brooks argued.

> Do not say that [slavery] is dead. It is not, while its essential spirit lives. While one man counts another man his born inferior for the color of his skin, while both in North and South prejudices and practices, which the law cannot touch, but which God hates, keep alive in our people's hearts the spirit of the old iniquity, it is not dead. . . . We must grow like our President, in his truth, his independence, his religion, and his wide humanity. Then the character by which he died shall be in us, and by it we shall live. Then peace shall come that knows no war, and law that knows no treason; and full of his spirit a grateful land shall gather round his grave, and in the daily psalm of prosperous and righteous living, thank God forever for his life and death.

The same year that Brooks preached the Lincoln sermon, he wrote the words to the Christian hymn "O Little Town of Bethlehem," for which he is best remembered. In his own time, though, Brooks enjoyed renown primarily for his preaching. Crowds overflowed Trinity Church, ultimately prompting the congregation to complete a new building in 1877 better to accommodate Brooks's following. His erudition prompted numerous invitations to undertake the leadership of colleges and universities, but he could not be tempted from his work as a minister. His response to an invitation to become provost of the University of Pennsylvania captured his sense of vocation: "I am a preacher to the end," he announced, "and also to the end and beyond." Not even an invitation to become a professor of ethics at Harvard College could dislodge Brooks from his pulpit at Trinity, though he did serve for a time on the Board of Overseers at his alma mater and preached there frequently. He also found time for personal ministry, including serving as a spiritual mentor for Helen Keller, who told him, "I knew all about God before you told me, only I didn't know His name."

Finally, toward the end of his life, Brooks stepped down from the pulpit at Trinity Church to accept election and consecration as the bishop of Massachusetts in 1891. But he held the position only 15 months. Death ended his episcopacy on January 23, 1893, in Boston.

Many of his contemporaries, and many subsequent historical observers, believed that Phillips Brooks was the finest preacher of his day. Born of Boston Brahmins, heir of the great Puritan preacher John Cotton, Brooks spent most of his life as a minister in the rarified intellectual regions of Boston and Harvard. Other preachers of his day, such as DWIGHT LYMAN MOODY, may have surpassed Brooks in bringing the Christian message to men and women in less august walks of life. Nevertheless, Brooks was, as he said, "a preacher to the end," and history has confirmed the enduring stature of his preaching.

Further Reading

Albright, Raymond Wolf. *Focus on Infinity: A Life of Phillips Brooks.* New York: Macmillan, 1961.

Allen, Alexander V. G. *Life and Letters of Phillips Brooks.* 2 vols. New York: Dutton, 1900.

Chesebrough, David B. *Phillips Brooks: Pulpit Eloquence.* Westport, Conn.: Greenwood Press, 2001.

Harp, Gillis J. "The Young Phillips Brooks: A Reassessment." *Journal of Ecclesiastical History* 49 (1998): 652–67.

———. "'We cannot spare you': Phillips Brooks's Break with the Evangelical Party, 1859–1873." *Church History: Studies in Christianity and Culture* 68 (1999): 930–53.

Howe, Mark Antony De Wolfe. *Phillips Brooks.* Boston: Small, Maynard, 1899.

Lawrence, William. *Life of Phillips Brooks.* New York: Harper & Brothers, 1930.

———. *Phillips Brooks: A Study.* Boston: Houghton Mifflin, 1903.

Woolverton, John Frederick. *The Education of Phillips Brooks.* Urbana: University of Illinois Press, 1995.

Brownson, Orestes Augustus
(1803–1876) *Catholic apologist*

Following a spiritual course that led him through Presbyterianism, Universalism, and Unitarianism before his conversion to Catholicism in midlife, Orestes Augustus Brownson became a prominent Catholic apologist of the 19th century. He never

quite surrendered, though, the fiercely independent spirit that had inspired these successive spiritual migrations. He was born on September 16, 1803, in Stockbridge, Vermont, the son of Sylvester Augustus Brownson and Relief Metcalf Brownson, who were farmers. The death of his father when he was two years old caused Brownson to be separated from his mother and twin sister and tendered to the care of a Congregationalist family. He was reunited with his family in Ballston Spa, New York, when he was 14 years old. He completed his teenage years with little in the way of formal education.

The spiritual journey that would move Brownson to Catholicism in his middle age had its first milestone in 1822, when Brownson joined the Presbyterian Church. This association lasted less than a year before he rejected the Calvinistic tenets of human depravity and divine election in favor of Universalism. After spending two years as a teacher in 1824 and 1825, Brownson became a Universalist minister. He married Sally Healy of Elbridge, New York, in 1827, and the couple had eight children. Toward the end of the decade, he abandoned the Universalist ministry in favor of a journalistic career advocating radical social causes, but his temporary absence from the pulpit ended within a few years. In 1831 Brownson returned to his ministerial career, first as a nondenominational preacher, and then, the following year, as a Unitarian minister. His first book, *New Views of Christianity, Society, and the Church* (1836), communicated his lasting commitment to an examination of social issues through the lens of religious faith, aligning himself with the Democratic Party and with working people. He published his influential "Essay on the Laboring Classes" in 1840.

In the early 1840s, Brownson began to reexamine his faith once again, and the fruit of this further reflection was his conversion to the Roman Catholic Church in 1844. That same year he began to publish *Brownson's Quarterly Review,* which, apart from a nine-year hiatus from 1864 to 1873, would be the chief vehicle for his journalistic talents for more than three decades. Brownson compared his conversion to Catholicism to arrival at a shore, after skipping across crumbling ice floes. He used *Brownson's Quarterly* to entice others to the same shore, though "enticement" is too delicate a characterization of the force and sometimes bluntness of Brownson's apologetic. Belligerent and terse, he was famous for his capacity to offend. The publisher of his periodical asked him humorously one day what reward he, a Protestant, might expect in the afterlife for publishing Brownson's Catholic magazine. Brownson replied: "Well, let me see. You will get a reward of course. It will be that once every million years you will be allowed to put your foot for the millionth part of a second on the coolest spot in hell."

The same spiritual temper that could aggravate those outside the Catholic Church could also irritate those within it. Though the American bishops endorsed Brownson's publication in 1849, they withdrew their endorsement five years later when some of their number concluded that certain of Brownson's positions, such as his insistence that only Catholics would be saved, amounted to spiritual error. He also angered Irish-American Catholics, who endured rising nativist hostility in

the 1840s and 1850s, by suggesting that they were insufficiently Americanized.

Ill health eventually caused Brownson to suspend publication of his *Review* in 1864, though he continued to express himself through lectures and other literary outlets. He resumed publication of the *Review* in 1873, but age and new illness again forced him to retire from this work two years later. He died in Detroit, Michigan, on April 17, 1876.

Orestes Brownson was a prominent convert to Catholicism during the 19th century and one of the most provocative apologists for his new faith during that century. Absorbed with the social and political problems of his age, he came to believe that only Catholic Christianity provided their solution. But he was a controversial spokesman for the church: one critic described him as too Catholic for Yankees and too Yankee for Catholics. Nevertheless, though not perhaps so effective as he might have wished at the time, Brownson's thought has continued to exert influence. Contemporary Catholics have frequently returned to his writings for insight on the relationship of the church to modern American society.

After O. A. Brownson was converted to Catholicism in his middle years, he became an influential apologist for the Catholic faith. *(Library of Congress, Prints and Photographs Division LC-USZ62-125936)*

Further Reading

Brownson, Henry Francis. *Orestes A. Brownson's Life.* 3 vols. Detroit: H. F. Brownson, 1898–1900.

Brownson, Orestes Augustus. *The American Republic: Its Constitution, Tendencies, and Destiny.* New York: P. O'Shea, 1866; Clifton, N.J.: A. M. Kelley, 1972.

———. *The Early Works of Orestes A. Brownson.* Edited by Patrick W. Carey. Milwaukee: Marquette University Press, 2000.

———. *Essays and Reviews Chiefly on Theology, Politics and Socialism.* New York: D. & J. Sadlier, 1852; New York: Arno Press, 1972.

———. *Selected Writings.* Edited by Patrick W. Carey. New York: Paulist Press, 1991.

———. *The Spirit-Rapper: An Autobiography.* Boston: Little, Brown, 1854.

Butler, Gregory S. *In Search of the American Spirit: The Political Thought of Orestes Brownson.* Carbondale and Edwardsville: Southern Illinois University Press, 1992.

Corrigan, Felicia. *Some Social Principles of Orestes A. Brownson.* Washington, D.C.: Catholic University of America Press, 1939.

Gilhooley, Leonard. *Contradiction and Dilemma: Orestes Brownson and the American Idea.* New York: Fordham University Press, 1972.

Lapati, Americo D. *Orestes A. Brownson.* New York: Twayne Publishers, 1965.

Marshall, Hugh. *Orestes Brownson and the American Republic: An Historical Perspective.* Washington, D.C.: Catholic University of America Press, 1971.

Maynard, Theodore. *Orestes Brownson: Yankee, Radical, Catholic.* New York: Macmillan, 1943; New York: Hafner, 1971.

McDonnell, James M. *Orestes A. Brownson and Nineteenth-Century Catholic Education.* New York: Garland, 1988.

Power, Edward J. *Religion and the Public Schools in 19th Century America: The Contribution of Orestes A. Brownson.* New York: Paulist Press, 1996.

Ryan, Thomas R. *Orestes A. Brownson: A Definitive Biography.* Huntington, Ind.: Our Sunday Visitor, 1976.

Schlesinger, Arthur M. *Orestes A. Brownson: A Pilgrim's Progress.* Boston: Little, Brown, 1939.

Whalen, Mary Rose Gertrude. *Granite for God's House: The Life of Orestes Augustus Brownson.* New York: Sheed & Ward, 1941.

Burke, John Joseph
(1875–1936) *Catholic priest*

John Joseph Burke was a Catholic priest who championed cooperative efforts by American Catholics on a variety of social, political, and ecclesiastical fronts. Beginning with his work in founding the National Catholic War Council during World War I and through his service as general secretary of the National Catholic Welfare Conference, Burke was a prominent force for national Catholic organization in the early decades of the 20th century. He was born on June 6, 1875, in New York City, the son of Patrick Burke and Mary Ragan Burke, Irish immigrants to the United States. He received a high school education at Saint Francis Xavier High School in New York City and remained in the city to attend the College of Saint Francis Xavier, from which he graduated in 1896. Subsequently, he entered the Missionary Society of Saint Paul the Apostle (the Paulists); studied at the Catholic University of

America in Washington, D.C.; and was ordained a priest on June 9, 1899. He remained at the university for two more years for advanced theological study.

After a few years as a parish priest, Burke became the assistant editor of the *Catholic World,* a Paulist publication. Within a year, he was placed in charge of all the Paulist publication outlets, including *Catholic World* and the Catholic Publication Society (later Paulist Press). From his vantage as a prominent Catholic editor, Burke became convinced of the necessity of coordinated Catholic efforts to address social issues. He helped found the National Catholic War Council during World War I to organize Catholic relief work and to represent Catholic views to the U.S. government. His administrative experience in this venture led to his appointment as general secretary of the National Catholic Welfare Conference from 1919 until 1936. This organization of the American Catholic hierarchy (later reorganized as the National Conference of Catholic Bishops after Vatican II) sought to continue the work of the War Council in post–World War I America by supporting Catholic activities, education, and social welfare work.

Beginning in the 1920s, Burke's gifts as an ecclesiastical statesman caused him to be summoned to assist negotiations between the Vatican and Mexico. These negotiations followed persecutions of the Catholic Church as early as 1925 by the government of Mexico under President Plutarco Elías Calles. After the church responded with an economic boycott and a general strike that suspended worship services and the Cristero Rebellion broke out at the beginning of 1927, Burke worked together with the U.S. State Department to find a resolution to the conflict. A provisional arrangement between Catholics and the Mexican government was finally reached in 1929, in significant part through the labors of John Joseph Burke. When persecution revived three years later, Burke again worked with the U.S. government to obtain relief for Mexican Catholics. Sudden death from an occluded coronary artery in Washington, D.C., ended this final diplomatic service on October 30, 1936.

Shortly before Burke's death, Pope Pius XI made him a domestic prelate or monsignor for his service as general secretary of the National Catholic Welfare Conference. This ecclesiastical honor recognized Burke's long devotion to the work of bringing the energy and theological perspective of the Roman Catholic Church to bear on contemporary issues. John Burke gave special attention to the church's role in achieving social justice and, in doing so, left an enduring mark on Catholic social engagement in the 20th century.

Further Reading

Burke, John Joseph. *Christ in Us: Meditations.* Philadelphia: Dolphin Press, 1934.

———. *Pray for Us: A Collection of Prayers for Various Occasions.* New York: P. J. Kenedy & Sons, 1936.

Piper, John F., Jr. "Father John J. Burke, C.S.P., and the Turning Point in American Catholic History." *Records of the American Catholic Historical Society of Philadelphia* 92 (March–December 1981): 101–13.

Sheerin, John B. *Never Look Back: The Career and Concerns of John J. Burke.* New York: Paulist Press, 1975.

Slawson, Douglas. *The Foundation and First Decade of the National Catholic Welfare Council.* Washington, D.C.: Catholic University of America Press, 1992.

Bushnell, Horace
(1802–1876) *Congregationalist minister*

Often referred to as the father of American religious liberalism, Horace Bushnell was an influential minister and theologian who attempted to reformulate important tenets of Protestant orthodoxy that were under attack during the 19th century. He distanced himself from, on one end of the theological spectrum, Protestant revivalism and, on the other end, Unitarianism. Horace Bushnell was born on April 14, 1802, in Bantam, Connecticut, near Litchfield, the son of Ensign Bushnell and Dotha Bishop Bushnell. He graduated from Yale College in 1827; briefly taught school in Norwich, Connecticut; and then worked for 10 months as an editor of the *Journal of Commerce* in New York City. Thereafter, he returned to Yale in 1829 and occupied the post of tutor while he studied law. That year he had a conversion experience, through which he was able to resolve doubts that had for some time plagued him, and in the course

of which, he said, "I was to think myself out of my over-thinking, and discover how far above reason is trust." After this experience, Bushnell turned away from the law to a ministerial calling, which he prepared for by entering Yale Divinity School, from which he graduated with a B.D. in 1833.

The year he left Yale, Bushnell accepted a ministerial call from Hartford's North Church, and he remained a Congregationalist for the next quarter of a century. The same year he married Mary Apthorp, and this union ultimately produced five children. Within a few years he had begun to suffer from tuberculosis, a disease that would stalk him for the rest of his life.

Though settled as the minister of North Church, Bushnell was inspired by his theological imagination to an active career as lecturer and writer. He soon took up a theological position at odds with Protestant revivalism. The revivalistic emphasis on a dramatic conversion experience seemed to Bushnell too individualistic and not sufficiently respectful of the role of Christian families and communities in communicating the Christian faith from one generation to the next. Thus, in *Discourses on Christian Nurture* (1847), Bushnell proposed that "the child is to grow up a Christian, and never know himself as being otherwise." Revivalism, he insisted, "is a religion that begins explosively, raises high frames, carries little or no expansion, and, after the campaign is over, subsides into a torpor."

In the year following his publication of *Christian Nurture*, Bushnell himself experienced what he would subsequently describe in his book *God in Christ* (1849) as a "personal discovery of Christ, and of God as represented in him."

> I seemed to pass a boundary. I had never been very legal in my Christian life, but now I passed from those partial seeings, glimpses, and doubts, into a clearer knowledge of God and into his inspirations, which I have never wholly lost. The change was into faith,—a sense of the freeness of God, and the ease of approach to Him.

This work attempted to restate the Christian doctrine of the Trinity. Bushnell refused to follow the radical monotheism of the Unitarians, which rejected the idea of a triune God. Nevertheless, he displayed impatience with classical Christian creeds that endeavored to capture as dogma the mystery of the Trinity. He accepted the Trinity not as a statement of what God was really like in some internal sense but simply as the means by which he revealed himself to humans.

Bushnell's exposition of the Trinity proved unpalatable to more orthodox Congregationalists. His church belonged to the Hartford North Consociation; an association of ministers within the consociation appointed a committee to investigate whether the views expressed by Bushnell in his most recent book amounted to heresy. This association ultimately voted against such a finding, but the possibility remained that the consociation might try Bushnell for heresy. To forestall this result, Bushnell's church withdrew from the consociation in 1852.

Bushnell eventually resigned from his pulpit at North Church in 1859, but he continued his career as a controversial theologian. Insisting that theological language was inherently metaphorical and poetic, he warred against dogma and creed, which he considered overly ambitious attempts to drain theology of its inherent mystery. On specific theological issues, he parted ways with orthodoxy; with respect to the doctrine of the atonement, for example, Bushnell rejected the substitutionary view of the atonement, by which Christ's death was understood as having paid a debt that men and women owed to God because of their sinfulness. He branded this account of the atonement a "gospel of dry wood and hay" and instead insisted that the atonement's effect was chiefly moral. It embodied "the Great Moral Power of God," in that as an act of love, Christ's death had the power to awaken in humankind the desire to be reconciled with God.

Bushnell's theological liberalism did not invariably ally itself with socially liberal views, however. He opposed suffrage for women, who he believed had been divinely ordained to occupy the domestic sphere. He also exhibited implacable hostility to Catholicism and to its spread in the United States through Catholic immigrants. He remained, though, best known for his theological views, expressed through lectures and a steady stream of books. After 1874, his health, regularly buffeted by his extended battle with tuberculosis, took a decided downward turn. He died on February 17, 1876, in Hartford, Connecticut, at the age of 74.

Horace Bushnell's impatience with attempts to strip theology of its mystery and his mystical appreciation for the language of metaphor and poetry placed him at odds with orthodox theological currents of his day. But his refusal to abandon key elements of Christian orthodoxy, such as Trinitarianism, also distanced him from the Unitarian and Universalist waves that flooded New England during the 19th century. Thus alienated from much of the thought of his own day, Bushnell's shadow stretched forward, as his unique theological station, expressed through lively prose, would have a significant impact on future American religious thought.

Further Reading

Adamson, William R. *Bushnell Rediscovered.* Philadelphia: United Church Press, 1966.

Archibald, Warren Seymour. *Horace Bushnell.* Hartford, Conn.: E. V. Mitchell, 1930.

Barnes, Howard A. *Horace Bushnell and the Virtuous Republic.* Philadelphia: American Theological Library Association; Metuchen, N.J.: Scarecrow Press, 1991.

Bushnell, Horace. *Christian Nurture.* New York: Charles Scribner, 1861.

———. *Forgiveness and Law Grounded in Principles, Interpreted by Human Analogies.* New York: Scribner, Armstrong, 1874.

Cheney, Mary Bushnell. *Life and Letters of Horace Bushnell.* New York: Arno Press, 1969.

Crosby, Donald A. *Horace Bushnell's Theory of Language: In the Context of Other Nineteenth Century Philosophies of Language.* The Hague: Mouton, 1975.

Cross, Barbara M. *Horace Bushnell: Minister to a Changing America.* Chicago: University of Chicago Press, 1958.

Duke, James O. *Horace Bushnell on the Vitality of Biblical Language.* Chico, Calif.: Scholars Press, 1984.

Edwards, Robert Lansing. *Of Singular Genius, of Singular Grace: A Biography of Horace Bushnell.* Cleveland: Pilgrim Press, 1992.

Haddorff, David W. *Dependence and Freedom: The Moral Thought of Horace Bushnell.* Lanham, Md.: University Press of America, 1994.

Hewitt, Glenn Alden. *Regeneration and Morality: A Study of Charles Finney, Charles Hodge, John W. Nevin, and Horace Bushnell.* Brooklyn, N.Y.: Carlson, 1991.

Munger, Theodore Thornton. *Horace Bushnell, Preacher and Theologian.* Boston: Houghton Mifflin, 1899.

Smith, David L. *Symbolism and Growth: The Religious Thought of Horace Bushnell.* Chico, Calif.: Scholars Press, 1981.

C

Cabrini, Francesca Xavier
(Maria Francesca Cabrini)
(1850–1917) *Catholic nun, missionary*

Francesca Xavier Cabrini devoted her life to Catholic missions, chiefly among Italian immigrants to the United States. She was the first American citizen to be canonized as a saint by the Roman Catholic Church. Cabrini was born Maria Francesca Cabrini on July 15, 1850, in Sant' Angelo Lodigiano, in the Lombardy region of Italy. Her parents, Agostino Cabrini and Stella Oldini Cabrini, were farmers who were sufficiently prosperous to provide Francesca with a solid education. She wished initially to become a nun but was rejected by two orders to which she had applied because of her frail health. Instead, Cabrini undertook service as a member of the Daughters of the Sacred Heart from 1863 to 1868; she first worked as a teacher; then on the staff of the House of Providence, an orphanage in Codogno; and later as the superior of the religious order in charge of the house. When the orphanage closed in 1880, Cabrini founded the Missionaries of the Sacred Heart with seven of her students from the orphanage, and took as her middle name Xavier, for the patron saint of missions, St. Francis Xavier.

Although Cabrini wished to become a missionary to the Orient, Pope Leo XIII dispatched her instead to the United States in 1889 to minister to the needs of Italian immigrants, "not to the East, but to the West." Once arrived in New York in the spring of 1889, she set about the task of es-

tablishing the orphanages, schools, and hospitals that would spring up in her wake all across the country. She began her missionary labors in New York's Lower East Side in St. Joachim's parish, where her early ministries included establishing an orphanage and providing education for children there, as well as for adults and children in the parish. Although her reception by Archbishop MICHAEL AUGUSTINE CORRIGAN of New York was chilly at first, Corrigan eventually became a dedicated supporter of Cabrini's missionary activities. Within a few years, she had founded Columbus Hospital (renamed Cabrini Medical Center in 1974). To these initial works, Cabrini added new institutions as she followed the steps of Italian immigrants south and west across the United States, to cities that included New Orleans, Chicago, Denver, Los Angeles, and Seattle. She became a U.S. citizen in 1909.

Francesca Cabrini devoted sustained energy to the work of educating orphans and other Italian immigrants. Her educational vision embraced both the practical—in the form of vocational training—and the spiritual. She believed in "education for the heart," which she understood to include the promotion of "feeling for God in an environment of affective relationships in which education becomes an act of love."

The United States remained the center of Cabrini's labors, though she returned frequently to Italy and also established institutions in Europe, Central America, and South America. In all, she founded nearly 70 schools, hospitals, and orphan-

Francesca Xavier Cabrini devoted her life to missions and became the first American citizen canonized as a saint by the Catholic Church. *(Library of Congress, Prints and Photographs Division LC-USZ62-103568)*

her principal missionary zeal, and she labored to give physical and spiritual relief to those who had been misplaced in the urban labyrinths. She ministered to those whose circumstances excluded them from the American dream—the poor, the orphaned, the sick—and by this focus helped to democratize that dream.

Further Reading

Cabrini, Francesca. *Meditations on the Blessed Virgin.* New ed. New York: Christian Press Association, 1911.

Green, Rose Basile, ed. and trans. *Mother Frances Xavier Cabrini.* Chicago: Missionary Sisters of the Sacred Heart, 1984.

Kuhn, Anna. *Watching at My Gates: Biographies of Rose Hawthorne, Francesca Xavier Cabrini and Theresa Martin.* Milwaukee: Bruce, 1948.

Maynard, Theodore. *Too Small a World: The Life of Francesca Cabrini.* Milwaukee: Bruce, 1945.

Sullivan, Mary Louise. *Mother Cabrini: Italian Immigrant of the Century.* New York: Center for Migration Studies, 1992.

ages in the United States, Europe, and Central and South America. Though from childhood afraid of water, she made 25 trips across the Atlantic. "If the Sacred Heart would give me the means," she once declared, "I would construct a boat called the Christopher (the Bearer of Christ), so as to carry the Name of Christ to all people—to those who as yet do not know Him, and also to those who have forgotten Him."

She died in Columbus Hospital in Chicago on December 22, 1917, at the age of 67. In the following years she was beatified by Pope Pius XI in 1938 and proclaimed a saint by Pope Pius XII on July 7, 1946. In 1950 she was declared to be the patron saint of immigrants.

Americans have often imagined themselves the agents of missionary efforts rather than the objects of it. But Francesca Xavier Cabrini made the great cities of the United States the objects of

Cadman, S. Parkes
(Samuel Parkes Cadman)
(1864–1936) *Methodist minister, radio personality*

A Methodist minister and pioneer of religious broadcasting, S. Parkes Cadman combined an infectious intellectual curiosity with a popular speaking style that made him one of the most respected preachers of his day. He was born Samuel Parkes Cadman on December 18, 1864, in Wellington, Shropshire, England, the son of Samuel Cadman and Betsy Parkes Cadman. His father operated a coal mine and served as a lay Methodist minister, and the elder Cadman's vocations charted the course for his son's first 20 years.

S. Parkes Cadman worked in the coal mines from the time he was 12 until he was 20, obtaining a sparse formal education during these years, supplemented by his own insatiable enthusiasm for reading. He experienced conversion during a Methodist revival service, or "mission," as it was called, when he was 16 years old. He later described the experience in the following words:

I knelt in humble confession and gave myself to Him. The choir sang of his changeless mercy and plenteous redemption. A holy man whom I loved and revered offered a prayer on my behalf. My heart melted in a deep and passionate resolve, uncolored by hectic emotion, but stamped with reality. I had glimpsed my Saviour, I felt I trusted Him for this world and the next. The assurance was mine that God for Christ's sake had taken away my sins—even mine—and that I was an adopted child of the All-Father.

Almost immediately, Cadman became convinced that God intended him to be a Methodist minister. He preached his first sermon when he was 17 and was licensed as a lay preacher when he was 20. In spite of his meager education, he subsequently won a scholarship to Richmond College of London University, and he left work in the mines, never to return. In 1888, while studying at Richmond, Cadman married Lillian Esther Wooding, with whom he had three children.

After graduating, Cadman set off for America and arrived in New York in the fall of 1890. An American bishop had promised him a church if he should ever immigrate to the United States, and Cadman had relatives on both sides of his family living there. On his arrival, he was assigned the pastorate of a small Methodist congregation in Milbrook, New York, and he soon added a ministry to a nearby congregation in Verbank. While serving these two churches, Cadman adopted the practice of beginning Sunday evening services with a question and answer period, during which he tried to apply Christian principles to questions posed about current issues of his congregations. He also began writing editorials for the *New York Ledger*. After Cadman's three years in Milbrook and Verbank, the young Englishman's growing reputation as a preacher attracted an offer for him to assume the pulpit of the Central Methodist Episcopal Church of Yonkers in 1893. Two years later he moved on to the Metropolitan Temple in Manhattan and, finally, in 1900, to the Central Congregational Church of Brooklyn, the ministerial position that he would hold for the next 36 years.

A voracious reader and a dynamic speaker, S. Parkes Cadman had a preaching style that attracted swelling audiences in New York, where he continued to find opportunities to use the question and answer sessions he had introduced earlier in his ministry. He employed this format with substantial success in conjunction with a weekly lecture he gave to men at a Young Men's Christian Association (YMCA) facility in Brooklyn. After World War I and the rapid growth of radio broadcasting in the early 1920s, Cadman's YMCA sessions were broadcast nationally, beginning in 1924. Two years later, he supplemented the reputation these broadcasts created when he began publishing a syndicated newspaper column with questions and answers. At the height of his popularity as a Christian speaker and writer, his radio broadcasts were estimated to reach between 5 and 7 million listeners and his newspaper column more than 10 million readers.

By the third and fourth decades of the 20th century, Cadman was recognized as one of the foremost preachers of his day. He was president of the Federal Council of the Churches of Christ in America from 1924 to 1928 and an internationally acclaimed speaker, second only to William Jennings Bryan as a popular lecturer. He died suddenly of peritonitis caused by acute appendicitis on July 12, 1936, in Plattsburg, New York.

S. Parkes Cadman was neither an original thinker nor a pioneer of religious doctrines. But he grappled with the pressing issues of his day as an essentially conservative evangelical Protestant minister, and he had the gift of conveying to broad audiences the insights that he gained. Though history tends to dote on founders and pioneers rather than on individuals such as Cadman, his was one of the foremost Christian voices of his time.

Further Reading

Cadman, S. Parkes. *Adventure for Happiness*. New York: Macmillan, 1935.

———. *Ambassadors of God*. New York: Macmillan, 1920.

———. *The Christ of God*. New York: Macmillan, 1929.

———. *Imagination and Religion*. New York: Macmillan, 1920.

Hamlin, Fred. *S. Parkes Cadman: Pioneer Radio Minister*. New York: Harper & Brothers, 1930.

Campbell, Alexander

(1788–1866) *Disciples of Christ founder, minister*

Alexander Campbell, together with his father, Thomas Campbell, founded the Christian Church, also known as the Disciples of Christ denomination. Ironically, Campbell waged a long campaign against the proliferation of Christian sects and denominations, believing that the churches he helped shepherd had simply returned to the authentic pattern of New Testament faith. He was born on September 12, 1788, in County Antrim, Ireland, the son of Thomas Campbell and Jane Corneigle Campbell. Campbell's father was a Presbyterian minister who migrated to the United States in 1807 and two years later established the Christian Association of Washington, Pennsylvania, after a dispute with other Presbyterians. When Alexander Campbell, who had completed a year of study at the University of Glasgow, and the rest of the Campbell family were able to reunite with Thomas Campbell in Pennsylvania in 1809, Alexander promptly joined his father's new religious association.

Alexander Campbell was licensed to preach in 1810. The following year, he and his father organized the Christian Association into the Brush Run Church, and, in 1812, Alexander was ordained as a minister of the church. Over the next two years, he substituted for his father as principal leader of the group of Christians sometimes referred to as Disciples of Christ or as Reformers. During the same period, in 1811, Campbell married Margaret Brown, with whom he had eight children before her death in 1827. Subsequently, he married Selina Bakewell, with whom he had six children.

Within a few years after the formation of the Brush Run Church, Campbell became convinced that baptism was appropriately reserved for believing Christians rather than for infants and that it should take the form of immersion. These tenets aligned him with the Baptists, who held the same beliefs, and in 1815, the Brush Run Church joined the Redstone Baptist Association. The following decade, disputes of Brush Run and other Reformer churches with more traditional Baptists led to the expulsion of the Reformer churches from the various Baptist associations with which they had affiliated. By the early 1830s, the Disciples of Christ formed a new spiritual alliance with the reform-minded Christians led by BARTON WARREN STONE, who called themselves the Christian Connection.

At the root of Campbell's spiritual impulse was the belief that divisions within Christendom, including the creeds these divisions proliferated, had obscured the authentic faith and practice of the New Testament and should be repudiated in favor of an exclusive focus on the Bible as the only source of guidance for Christians. He described the project in the preface to *The Christian System*, which he published in 1839:

> Tired of new creeds and new parties in religion, and of the numerous abortive efforts to reform the reformation; convinced from the Holy

Alexander Campbell's desire to recover the primitive purity of the early Christian church prompted him to found the Disciples of Christ with his father, Thomas Campbell. *(Library of Congress, Prints and Photographs Division LC-USZ62-104071)*

Scriptures, from observation and experience, that the union of the disciples of Christ is essential to the conversion of the world, and that the correction and improvement of no creed, or partisan establishment in Christendom, could ever become the basis of such a union, communion, and co-operation, as would restore peace to a church militant against itself, or triumph to the common salvation; a few individuals, about the commencement of the present century, began to reflect upon the ways and means to restore primitive Christianity.

By the 1830s, the "few individuals" had grown to a significant body of churches who shared Campbell's restorationist zeal. As early as 1823, Campbell had launched a monthly periodical, *Christian Baptist*, to make the case for Christian reform. By 1830, he had replaced this publishing venture with a new periodical, *Millennial Harbinger*. Similarly, Campbell had recognized the importance of creating educational institutions to further his biblical vision; he established the Buffalo Seminary in 1818 and Bethany College in 1840. By the end of the 1840s, the churches who named themselves Disciples of Christ organized themselves into a General Convention and named Campbell their president. Campbell himself lived long enough to see the number of churches in the convention climb to more than 2,000. By the time of his death, Disciples of Christ members numbered more than 200,000. Campbell died on March 4,1866, in Bethany, West Virginia.

The Protestant Reformation unleashed a splintering impulse within the Christian Church that produced, by the 19th century, a bewildering array of denominations and sects, with their attendant creeds. Finding these divisions perplexing, believers such as Alexander Campbell sought to recover the primitive principles of doctrine and religious practice that predated the creeds and to restore Christian unity around a common allegiance to these primitive principles. Campbell represents a kind of spiritual populism full of disdain for the theologies and creeds of the learned that has been common in the American religious experience. Yet, though he proved successful in guiding the Disciples of Christ Churches into a unified ecclesiastical association, he, in his own way, added yet another division to the ever expanding assortment of Protestant Christian sects and denominations.

Further Reading

Campbell, Alexander. *An Alexander Campbell Reader.* Edited by Lester G. McAllister. St. Louis: Mo.: CBP Press, 1988.
———. *The Christian System.* 2d ed. Pittsburg: Penn.: Forrester & Campbell, 1839.
Campbell, Selina Huntington. *Home Life and Reminiscences of Alexander Campbell.* St. Louis: J. Burns, 1882.
Garrett, Leroy. *The Stone-Campbell Movement: An Anecdotal History of Three Churches.* Joplin, Mo.: College Press, 1981.
Hughes, Richard T. *Reviving the Ancient Faith: The Story of Churches of Christ in America.* Grand Rapids, Mich.: W. B. Eerdmans, 1996.
Richardson, Robert. *Memoirs of Alexander Campbell, Embracing a View of the Origin, Progress and Principles of the Religious Reformation Which He Advocated.* 2 vols. Philadelphia: J. B. Lippincott, 1868–70.
Steed, Thomas Alan. "Alexander and Thomas Campbell's View of the Nature of Reality and Church: A Phenomenological, Rhetorical, and Metaphoric Analysis of the Restoration Movement." Ph.D. dissertation, Southern Illinois University at Carbondale, 2000.
West, Robert Frederick. *Alexander Campbell and Natural Religion.* New Haven, Conn.: Yale University Press, 1948.

Candler, Warren Akin
(1857–1941) *Methodist minister and bishop, educator*

An influential Methodist clergyman and educator, Warren Akin Candler was an idealistic southerner whose beliefs both supported traditional agrarian values of the 19th-century South and, on matters such as lynching, sometimes challenged them. His long and wide-ranging career was most closely associated with Emory University. He was born on August 23, 1857, in Villa Rica, Georgia, the son of Samuel Charles Candler and Martha Bernetta Beall Candler. He graduated from Emory College in 1876. During his college years he had originally prepared for a career as a lawyer but eventually determined that God had called him to be a minister. In his final year of college, he was admitted on trial to the North Georgia Conference of the Methodist Episcopal Church, South. His first assignments were to Convington and then to the Watkinsville circuit. In December 1877, he married Sarah Antoinette Curtright, with whom he had five children. That same month he was ordained a deacon and dispatched to a church and mission in Atlanta. By 1881 his enthusiasm and ability had earned him an appointment as presiding elder in the Dahlonega District. From there he moved to Sparta in 1882 and to Augusta in 1883.

While in Augusta, Candler and Bishop George Foster Pierce helped establish Paine College, a liberal arts college for African-American students, in conjunction with the Colored Methodist Episcopal Church. During these years, Candler gave evidence that his principles would not always mirror those of other southerners, particularly when he supported establishment of a racially integrated board to supervise the affairs of Paine College and when he publicly denounced the lynchings of African Americans. He did not, though, embrace a more vigorous notion of racial equality that would have integrated the Methodist hierarchy. For this reason, he opposed the union of Northern and Southern Methodists, in part because he opposed the idea of black Methodist bishops supervising white ministers.

In 1888, Candler became president of Emory College in Oxford, Georgia. He proved to be an energetic and generally progressive college administrator by substantially augmenting the college's financial support, expanding its course offerings, and making its degree requirements more stringent. But he unabashedly championed Christian education, which he defined as "a process of culture under Christian influences and from Christian motives resulting in Christian character." As a corollary of his focus on creating a culture of Christian influences, Candler opposed intercollegiate athletics, both for the gambling it sometimes encouraged and for the distraction from the educational process it generated.

Candler was elected as a bishop in the Methodist Episcopal Church, South, in 1898; he held that position for the next 36 years, until his mandatory retirement in 1934. This new role gave him supervisory responsibility for Methodist Episcopal churches in the Southeast. One of the duties it carried was ex officio membership on the Vanderbilt University Board of Trustees, a responsibility that thrust Candler into a controversy with the university's chancellor over Vanderbilt's Methodist affiliation. The chancellor, James Kirkland, was eager to sever Vanderbilt from its Methodist moorings and make it a free-standing secular institution. Candler, who had championed Christian education at Emory College, had no sympathy for the chancellor's ambition, and warred—unsuccessfully—against it. After Vanderbilt left the Methodist fold in 1914, the Methodist Episcopal Church, South, concentrated new resources on developing Southern Methodist University in Dallas, Texas, and Emory College, which migrated to Atlanta, Georgia, and became Emory University in 1914.

Candler became the newly elevated university's first chancellor in 1914. He displayed the same skill in strengthening the university's financial footing that he had when president of Emory's earlier incarnation as a college. In addition, he superintended the university's expansion to include professional schools for the study of theology, medicine, and law. By 1922, Chancellor Candler had become senior bishop for the Methodist Episcopal Church, South, an office he held until his retirement 12 years later. He died on September 25, 1941, in Atlanta, Georgia.

The history of higher education in the United States has been closely intertwined with the history of American religion, as religious leaders have frequently been educational leaders. Candler is a prominent Methodist example of the partnership between faith and education that produced institutions such as Harvard, Yale, Princeton, and, in Candler's case, Emory University. But his stormy relationship with Vanderbilt also illustrates a common feature of this partnership: the tendency of institutions to escape the control of their religious parents.

Further Reading

Bauman, Mark K. *Warren Akin Candler: The Conservative as Idealist.* Metuchen, N.J.: Scarecrow Press, 1981.

Candler, Warren Akin. *Current Comments on Timely Topics.* Nashville: Cokesbury Press, 1926.

———. *Great Revivals and the Great Republic.* Nashville: Publishing House Methodist Episcopal Church, South, 1904.

———. *Practical Studies in the Fourth Gospel.* 2 vols. Nashville: Publishing House Methodist Episcopal Church, South, 1914.

"History of Emory." Available online. URL: http://www.emory.edu/history. Updated on December 30, 1999.

Pierce, Alfred Mann. *Giant Against the Sky: The Life of Bishop Warren Akin Candler.* New York: Abingdon-Cokesbury Press, 1948.

Carroll, John
(1736–1815) *Catholic archbishop*

John Carroll was the first Catholic bishop in the United States. His leadership laid a secure foundation for the future of Catholicism in the early American republic, and his commitment to religious liberty and the separation of church and state made him an effective representative of his faith in the early days of the nation. He was born on January 8, 1736, in Upper Marlboro, Maryland, the son of Daniel Carroll and Eleanor Darnall Carroll. Carroll's father was a prosperous merchant, his mother, a member of a highly respected and socially influential family. Beginning in 1748, he attended school at St. Omer College, in French Flanders, a Jesuit institution, and he joined the Jesuits, also known as the Society of Jesus, in the fall of 1753. He studied philosophy and theology thereafter at Liège and was ordained a priest in 1769.

In 1773, Pope Clement XIV suppressed and dissolved the Society of Jesus, and Carroll, uprooted from his vocation, took the opportunity to travel to England before returning to his home in Maryland in the spring of 1774. There he lived with his mother, studied privately, and conducted mass for local Catholics at a chapel located on his mother's estate. In 1776, the Continental Congress solicited Carroll's assistance in connection with a mission to Canada. Together with Benjamin Franklin, Samuel Chase, and Charles Carroll, John Carroll traveled to Canada hoping to secure a pledge of Canadian neutrality in the Revolutionary War. The mission failed, however, and Carroll returned home to Maryland, though not without having created a favorable impression on Franklin, which would later influence the course of Carroll's life.

After the war with Britain, Carroll thought it no longer appropriate to accept direction from the vicar-general of the Vicar Apostolic of London. In 1783, Carroll was instrumental in organizing a number of other Catholic priests in Maryland under a plan to provide for their support and to safeguard their properties. The following year, partially at the suggestion of Benjamin Franklin, the pope appointed Carroll superior of Catholic missionary activity in the 13 American states. Carroll, as a Catholic in an overwhelmingly Protestant nation, had reason to value the principle of religious liberty. Soon after his appointment as superior, he had the opportunity to support this principle publicly when Charles Henry Wharton, a Jesuit who had converted to the Episcopal Church, accused the Catholic Church of opposing the idea of religious freedom. Carroll responded by publishing *Address to the Roman Catholics of the United States of America* (1784), the first book published in America by a Catholic. In it, he argued that "general and equal toleration, by giving a free circulation to fair argument, is the most effectual method to bring all denominations to a unity of faith."

Over the next few years, a variety of ecclesiastical disputes among Catholics in the United States convinced Carroll of the need for an American bishop, and in 1788, he petitioned the pope to appoint a bishop who would be elected by American priests and report directly to the pope. When the pope agreed to this plan, Carroll's American colleagues in the priesthood elected him to occupy the newly created office and he was named bishop of the diocese of Baltimore in November 1789. The affairs of American Catholics flourished under Carroll's leadership, and within a decade of his being named bishop, Carroll became an archbishop, with oversight of bishops in New York, Philadelphia, Boston, and Bardstown, Kentucky. He was instrumental in expanding Catholic higher education and was responsible, in particular, for the establishment of the educational institution that would become Georgetown University.

Archbishop Carroll was a respected American religious leader. Late in his life, he was invited to speak at the dedication of the Washington Monument, though he had to decline because of poor health. By the end of November 1815, his health was failing. "To all appearances," he spoke to a handful of acquaintances gathered around his bed in the last weeks of his life,

> I shall shortly appear before my God and my Judge. Entreat His infinite mercy to forgive me my sins, the abuse I have made of His graces and the bad example I may ever have given, the sacraments I have received without sufficient respect, the days of my life which I ought to have consecrated only to the promotion of His honor and glory. . . . I repose all my confidence in the goodness of God and the merits of our dear Lord Jesus Christ. I recommend myself to the powerful intercession of His Blessed Mother and of all the saints, in the hopes that they will obtain for me the pardon of my offences.

Archbishop John Carroll died soon after, on December 3, 1815, in Baltimore, Maryland.

John Carroll gave a distinctively American face to Catholicism and won for the Catholic Church a measure of respect it might not otherwise have enjoyed in the early American republic. If, as is sometimes said, religious disestablishment was a uniquely American invention, then Carroll embraced this invention as an American. By doing so, more than any other single individual, he created a solid foundation for the growth of Catholicism in the United States during the 19th century.

Further Reading

Agonito, Joseph. *The Building of an American Catholic Church: The Episcopacy of John Carroll.* New York: Garland, 1988.

Carroll, John. *The John Carroll Papers.* Edited by Thomas O'Brien Hanley. 3 vols. Notre Dame Ind.: University of Notre Dame Press, 1976.

Guilday, Peter Keenan. *The Life and Times of John Carroll, Archbishop of Baltimore, 1745–1815.* Westminster, Md.: Newman Press, 1954.

Kupke, Ramond J., ed. *American Catholic Preaching and Piety in the Time of John Carroll.* Lanham, Md.: University Press of America, 1991.

Melville, Annabelle M. *John Carroll of Baltimore: Founder of the American Catholic Hierarchy.* New York: Scribner, 1955.

Cartwright, Peter
(1785–1872) *Methodist minister*

A Methodist minister and sometime politician, Peter Cartwright became the archetypical backwoods preacher, or he at least delighted in conveying this impression as he grew older. He typified the sort of evangelical spirit that carried Methodism into the midwestern frontier. Peter Cartwright was born on September 1, 1785, in Amherst County, Virginia, the son of Peter and Christiana Garvin Wilcox Cartwright. When Cartwright was a child, his parents, who were poor farmers, moved the family to Logan County, Kentucky. There, in 1801, Cartwright had a conversion experience, which he described in his autobiography nearly 50 years later:

> Divine light flashed all around me. Unspeakable joy sprung up in my soul. I rose to my feet, opened my eyes, and it really seemed as though I was in heaven; the trees, the leaves on them, and everything seemed, and I really thought were, praising God. . . . [T]hough I have been since then in many instances unfaithful, yet I never have for one moment doubted that the Lord did then and there forgive me my sins and give me religion.

Cartwright promptly joined the Methodist Episcopal Church and was licensed as an exhorter (someone who assisted preachers in worship) a year later. By 1804, he had become a circuit-riding Methodist preacher. He supplemented his meager formal education after he became a preacher by studying theology with WILLIAM MCKENDREE, his presiding elder. FRANCIS ASBURY ordained Cartwright a deacon in 1806, and two years later, McKendree—now a bishop himself—ordained Cartwright an elder. That same year Cartwright married Frances Gaines, and the couple—who would have nine

Peter Cartwright, a frontier Methodist preacher, is pictured here with his wife. *(Library of Congress, Prints and Photographs Division LC-USZ62-95736)*

children together—settled on a farm in Christian County, Kentucky, while Cartwright continued his itinerant preaching ministry.

A stern opponent of slavery, Cartwright eventually found ministry in the South to be vexatious, and he obtained a transfer in 1824 to Illinois. He and his family settled in a small community north of Springfield that came to be called Pleasant Springs. Along with his responsibilities as presiding elder over various districts in the Illinois conference, Cartwright soon plunged into Illinois political affairs. He ran for the state legislature, winning two of the four times he stood for election. In 1932, he finished fourth in an at-large election that sent Cartwright and three other men to the state legislature. A young candidate from nearby New Salem, Illinois, Abraham Lincoln, finished eighth in the race. A little more than a decade later, Cartwright and Lincoln squared off politically again in a race for the U.S. House of Representatives in 1846. This time Lincoln prevailed over the Methodist preacher, in spite of Cartwright's attempt to make Lincoln's lack of church membership a campaign issue.

Cartwright played an increasingly prominent role in Methodist affairs his transfer to Illinois. In the early 1820s, he sided with those who advocated that bishops retain their episcopal authority to appoint presiding elders. This ecclesiastical struggle prompted the creation of the Methodist Protestant Church by those who opposed the allocation of such spiritual authority to the Methodist bishops. Cartwright also railed against the southern Methodists who formed the Methodist Episcopal Church, South, in 1846, after northern ministers, including him, attempted to curtail the spiritual authority of Bishop James O. Andrew because he owned slaves.

Cartwright gained further prominence when he began publication of the *Central Christian Advocate* in 1852; it was adopted as the official publication of the General Conference four years later. He also published his *Autobiography of Peter Cartwright, the Backwoods Preacher* in 1856, and this book further enhanced his reputation among Methodists. At the end of the following decade, Cartwright was honored by the Illinois conference for his 50 years of service as a presiding elder. He died on September 25, 1872, in Pleasant Plains, Illinois.

Peter Cartwright typified the frontier clergyman of the 19th century: at home in the saddle, relatively unschooled, but capable of supplying indomitable energy and native ability in the place of academic credentials. Even after the frontier gave way to settled communities, he relished labeling himself the "backwoods preacher." This designation may have correctly captured the character of his early ministry as a preacher, but it hardly did justice to a man comfortable both on the preaching circuit and in the legislative chamber, who took not only the Christian message but the foundations of a rich and stable society to the midwestern frontier.

Further Reading

Cartwright, Peter. *Autobiography of Peter Cartwright.* Nashville: Abingdon Press, 1986.

———. *Fifty Years as a Presiding Elder.* Ed. by W.S.Hooper. Cincinnati: Hitchcock and Walden, 1871.

Chamberlin, M. H. "Rev. Peter Cartwright, D.D." *Illinois State Historical Society Transactions* (1902): 27–56.

Dixon, Jonathan. "Order and Spontaneity in the Office of Presiding Elder: Peter Cartwright and the Growth of

Nineteenth Century American Methodism." Ph.D. dissertation, Saint Louis University, 2000.

Grant, Helen Hardie. *Peter Cartwright, Pioneer.* New York: Abingdon Press, 1931.

Hohlt, Brian Richard. "'Laws of the Lord': the Political World of Peter Cartwright, 1824–1848." Ph.D. dissertation, Saint Louis University, 1998.

Watters, Philip Melancthon. *Peter Cartwright.* New York: Eaton & Mains, 1910.

Cary, Lott

(ca. 1780–1828) *Baptist missionary*

Lott Cary was an African-American Baptist preacher who began his life as a slave and ended it as the governor of the American colony of Liberia in Africa. He was the first black American missionary to Africa. Lott was born around 1780 on a plantation in Charles City County, Virginia, the only son of slave parents whose names are not known. When he was about 20 years of age he married; with his wife, whose name is unknown, he had two children. In 1804, he was hired out as a day laborer in Richmond for the Shochoe Tobacco Warehouse.

While in Richmond he began attending the First Baptist Church, sitting with the other blacks in the gallery reserved for them, and there he eventually experienced conversion in 1807. On hearing a sermon about Jesus and Nicodemus taken from the third chapter of the Gospel of John, Cary was inspired to learn to read so that he could study the biblical passage himself. Once he could read, his warehouse supervisors made him a shipping clerk and allowed him the privilege of selling small bits of waste tobacco. With the earnings from these sales, Cary, who was widowed by this time, was able to save $850 and with it purchase freedom for himself and his two children in 1813. Two years later he remarried and with his new wife, whose name also is not known, had one other child.

By 1814, Lott Cary had felt a call to preach and around this time was licensed as a minister by the First Baptist Church. He began preaching to blacks around Richmond and soon turned his attention to the subject of foreign missions. Cary helped establish the Richmond African Baptist Missionary Society in 1815. Over the next few

years, Cary became convinced that he should undertake missionary work in Africa. By 1819, he had gained the endorsement of the Baptist Board of Foreign Missions and the American Colonization Society. In January 1821, he set sail with his family and other colonists for Africa. In a farewell address delivered to Richmond's First Baptist Church, he explained the reasons for his departure:

> I am about to leave you and expect to see your faces no more. I long to preach to the poor Africans the way of life and salvation. I don't know what may befall me, whether I may find a grave in the ocean, or among the savage men, or more savage wild beasts on the Coast of Africa; nor am I anxious what may become of me. I feel it my duty to go; and I very much fear that many of those who preach the Gospel in this country, will blush when the Saviour calls them to give an account of their labors in His cause and tells them, "I commanded you to go into all the world, and preach the Gospel to every creature" [(and with the most forcible emphasis he exclaimed)] the Saviour may ask where have you been? What have you been doing? Have you endeavored to the utmost of your ability to fulfill the commands I gave you, or have you sought your own gratification, and your own ease, regardles of My commands?

Cary and his fellow colonists arrived initially in Freetown, Sierra Leone, where his wife died soon afterward of tropical fever. In 1822, Cary and his children relocated to Mesurado (later named Cape Monrovia), a settlement that became part of the Republic of Liberia. Here he served as a health officer under the supervision of Jehudi Ashmun, colonial agent and representative of the American Colonization Society for the settlement. He also established a Baptist church and a day school in the settlement.

In 1825, the United States established Liberia as a colony and appointed Ashmun as its governor. Cary became vice agent of the colony in 1826. Two years later, illness forced Ashmun to leave the colony for the United States, and Cary assumed Ashmun's responsibilities; he was formally appointed governor of the colony after Ashmun's death in March 1828. That same year Cary died on November 10, 1828, of injuries that resulted from an explosion that occurred while he was making cartridges for the colonial militia.

Native ability, industry, and a willingness to bear hardship transported Lott Cary from slavery to service as the first black American missionary to Africa. After obtaining his freedom and a modest measure of financial independence, he could not contemplate the plight of Africans without committing himself to their service as a minister of the Christian gospel. The monument at his grave summarized his life's achievement: "Lott Cary's self-denying, self-sacrificing labors . . . have inscribed his name indelibly on the page of history, not only as one of Nature's Noblemen, but as an eminent Philanthropist and Missionary of Jesus Christ."

Further Reading

Cary, Lott. "'Circular Addressed to the Colored Brethren and Friends in America': An Unpublished Essay by Lott Cary, Sent from Liberia to Virginia, 1827." *Virginia Magazine of History and Biography* 104 (1996): 481–504.

Fisher, Miles Mark. "Lott Cary, the Colonizing Missionary." *Journal of Negro History* 7 (October 1922): 380–418.

Fitts, Leroy. *Lott Carey: First Black Missionary to Africa.* Valley Forge, Pa.: Judson Press, 1978.

———. *The Lott Carey Legacy of African American Missions.* Baltimore: Gateway Press, 1994.

Gurley, Ralph Randolph. *Life of Jehudi Ashmun, Late Colonial Agent in Liberia, with an Appendix Containing Extracts from His Journal and Other Writings, with a Brief Sketch of the Life of the Rev. Lott Cary.* Washington, D.C.: J. C. Dunn, 1835; Freeport, N.Y.: Books for Libraries Press, 1971.

Poe, William A. "Lott Cary: Man of Purchased Freedom." *Church History* 39 (March 1970):49–61.

Taylor, James B. *The Biography of Elder Lott Cary.* Baltimore: Armstrong & Berry, 1837.

Cavert, Samuel McCrea
(1888–1976) *ecumenical leader*

Samuel McCrea Cavert spent most of his life working within the organizational structures of ecumenical Christianity. He rose to prominence within these structures, serving as general secretary of the National Council of Churches and executive secretary of the World Council of Churches in the United States. He is a reminder that faith, also, has its bureaucracies, and that these have been important in the life of American religion. Cavert was born on September 9, 1888, in Charlton, New York, the son of Walter I. Cavert and Elizabeth Brann Cavert. He earned a bachelor of arts degree from Union College in Schenectady, New York, in 1910, and a bachelor of divinity from Union Theological Seminary in New York City five years later. He was ordained by the Presbyterian Church (U.S.A.) in 1915, and in 1918 he married Ruth Miller, with whom he had one child before her death two years later.

Apart from a brief period of service as an assistant to theologian William Adams Brown at Union Theological Seminary from 1915 to 1916, and as a military chaplain for a few months in the fall and winter of 1918, Cavert plunged almost immediately into a lifelong career of ecumenical administrative service. He served briefly on the staff of the General War-Time Commission of the Churches from the fall of 1917, then, from January 1919, as secretary of the Committee on the War and the Religious Outlook, organized under the auspices of the Federal Council of the Churches of Christ in America (FCC). In 1921, Cavert became one of the general secretaries of the FCC. Later in the decade, he married Ruth Twila Lytton. By 1933 he had become the FCC's senior general secretary, holding the organization's highest executive office.

Beginning in the 1930s, Samuel Cavert became an influential force behind the creation of an international organization of churches that would become the World Council of Churches (WCC), whose name Cavert himself suggested. His work as a midwife for this effort toward international ecumenism continued through that decade and into the next. World War II interrupted the efforts of Cavert and others to create the WCC, but after the war, momentum toward this worldwide expression of Christian unity resumed and culminated in the WCC's first assembly in Amsterdam in 1948, for which Cavert served as the chairman of the assembly's Committee on Arrangements. At this first assembly, Cavert made an address that emphasized the historic nature of the meeting:

> We enter now upon a new stage in the ecumenical movement: we inaugurate a continuous association of the Churches, under constitutional form, for whatever tasks they decide to undertake together. For the first time the official representatives of 150 Churches are creating a permanent instrument of fellowship and cooperation on a world-wide scale. This is an unprecedented hour. The path before us is so uncharted that we might well shrink from it if the Head of the Church had not promised the presence of the Holy Spirit.

When Cavert returned to the United States after this epochal assembly, he plunged into a new ecumenical project that would merge the Federal Council of Churches and other cooperative Christian ventures into the National Council of the Churches of Christ in the United States of America (NCC). Cavert served as the first general secretary of the NCC when it was formed in 1950. After four years in this position, Cavert resigned to become the executive secretary of the WCC in the United States, a position he held until 1958. Even after his retirement from this executive position in the organization he had helped bring into existence, Cavert remained active in ecumenical affairs for nearly 20 more years. He died on December 21, 1976, in Bronxville, New York.

A central religious event of the 20th century was the ecumenical movement, which sought to restore the unity lost to Christian churches through the splintering zeal inherited from the Reformation. Samuel McCrea Cavert spent most of his life immersed in this movement, bringing to bear upon it his considerable zeal and administrative skills. His career as an ecumenical administrator left him far from the center of public attention, of course, and less well known than many more popular religious figures during the 20th century. But it had a significant impact on the course of mainline Christianity.

Further Reading

Cavert, Samuel McCrea. *The Adventure of the Church: A Study of the Missionary Genius of Christianity.* New York: Missionary Education Movement and Council of Women for Home Missions, 1927.
———. *The American Churches in the Ecumenical Movement, 1900–1968.* New York: Association Press, 1968.
———. *Church Cooperation and Unity in America: A Historical Review: 1900–1970.* New York: Association Press, 1970.
———. *On the Road to Christian Unity: An Appraisal of the Ecumenical Movement.* New York: Harper, 1961; Westport, Conn.: Greenwood Press, 1979.
———. *Securing Christian Leaders for Tomorrow: A Study in Present Problems of Recruiting for Christian Life-Service.* New York: George H. Doran, 1926.
Schmidt, William J. *Architect of Unity: A Biography of Samuel McCrea Cavert.* New York: Friendship Press, 1978.
Warren, Heather Anne. "'That They All May Be One': Americans' Quest for Christian Unity, 1918–1948." Ph.D. dissertation, Johns Hopkins University, 1992.

Cayce, Edgar
(1877–1945) *psychic*

The 20th-century psychic Edgar Cayce was famous for his "Life Readings," in which he detailed the past lives of persons who consulted him. After his death, his readings continued to be studied by followers of spiritualism and other forms of New Age spirituality. Edgar Cayce was born on March 18, 1877, near Hopkinsville, Kentucky. His parents, Leslie B. Cayce, a tobacco farmer, and Carrie Elizabeth Major Cayce, belonged to the Disciples of Christ denomination. Cayce grew up in the church, read the Bible cover to cover, taught Sunday School, and even contemplated becoming a missionary. But his childhood was also punctuated by psychic episodes that would presage the course of his future life. As a teenager, he was reputed to be able to memorize the contents of books simply by sleeping on them. Though this talent might have made him an impressive student, his formal education ended when he left school as a teenager to work at a series of jobs.

By the first decade of the 20th century, Cayce claimed to have discovered the ability to enter a trancelike state and produce psychic diagnoses and cures of physical illnesses and other ailments. The *New York Times* carried an account of his psychic abilities on October 9, 1910, with the headline "Illiterate Man Becomes a Doctor When Hypnotized." This article, and the news of healings spread by grateful recipients of his psychic power, attracted a steady stream of inquires to his door and earned Cayce a reputation as "the sleeping prophet." Cayce received inquirers and, in self-induced trances, performed "readings" that diagnosed their physical ailments and offered suggested remedies for their cure. Cayce provided these readings not only to inquirers who visited him in person, but to those at a distance, whose names he was given.

In 1923, Edgar Cayce met Arthur Lammers, who acquainted Cayce with Theosophical teachings, including the concept of reincarnation. Lammers, who was quite wealthy, provided financial support for Cayce. Beginning that year, Cayce expanded his readings—previously focused on health issues—to include "Life Readings," which included revelations about past and future lives. Cayce is said to have predicted both world wars and the crash of 1929. Many of his readings touched on the history of the legendary civilization of Atlantis. In 1925, another wealthy benefactor financed the construction of the Cayce Hospital and Atlantic University in Virginia Beach. The onset of economic depression forced both these institutions to close in 1931, but that same year, friends and family cooperated to found the Association for Research and Enlightenment as a way of supporting Cayce and encouraging study of his work. He continued to conduct regular readings until his death on January 3, 1945, in Virginia Beach, Virginia.

After his death, the Association for Research and Enlightenment maintained files of more than 14,000 readings that Cayce conducted over his lifetime. Toward the end of his life, Cayce himself described the significance of these readings.

> For more than forty years now I have been giving readings to those who came seeking help. Thirty-five years ago the jeers, scorn and laughter were even louder than today. I have faced the laughter of ignorant crowds, the withering scorn of tabloid headlines, and the cold smirk of self-satisfied intellectuals. But I

have also known the wordless happiness of little children who have been helped, the gratitude of fathers and mothers and friends.

Cayce's readings continued to attract the attention and study of spiritualists and others interested in the occult in the decades since his death.

Further Reading

Bro, Harmon Hartzell. *A Seer out of Season: The Life of Edgar Cayce.* New York: NAL Books, 1989.

Carter, Mary Ellen. *Passage to the Millennium: Edgar Cayce and the Age of Aquarius.* New York: St. Martin's Paperbacks, 1998.

Cayce, Edgar. *The Lost Memories of Edgar Cayce: Life as a Seer.* Compiled and edited by A. Robert Smith. Virginia Beach, Va.: A.R.E. Press, 1997.

Church, W. H. *Many Happy Returns: The Lives of Edgar Cayce.* San Francisco: Harper & Row, 1984.

Johnson, K. Paul. *Edgar Cayce in Context: The Readings, Truth and Fiction.* Albany, N.Y.: State University of New York Press, 1998.

Kilpatrick, Sydney D. *Edgar Cayce: An American Prophet.* New York: Riverhead Books, 2000.

Stearn, Jess. *Edgar Cayce: The Sleeping Prophet.* Garden City, N.Y.: Doubleday, 1967.

Sugrue, Thomas. *There Is a River: The Story of Edgar Cayce.* New York: Holt, 1942.

Channing, William Ellery
(1780–1842) *Unitarian minister*

Often called the "apostle of American Unitarianism," William Ellery Channing was the leading theologian and spokesperson for Unitarianism during the first half of the 19th century. He remains a principal historical figure within this American religious tradition, renowned as a preacher, an essayist, and a social reformer. William Ellery Channing was born on April 7, 1780, in Newport, Rhode Island, to prominent parents. His father, William Channing, was a lawyer who held political posts including that of attorney general of Rhode Island. His mother, Lucy Ellery Channing, was the daughter of William Ellery, one of the signers of the Declaration of Independence. William entered Harvard College in the fall of 1794. He graduated four years later and gave the valedictory address for his class.

After graduation, Channing took a job in Richmond, Virginia, as a tutor for an important family, and this temporary occupation gave him time to study in preparation for an anticipated career as a minister. It also presented him a close view of slavery, which he grew to abhor and of which he would be a vigorous opponent in later years. After a year and a half in which he ruined his health with excessive study, Channing returned home to Newport. He was licensed to preach in 1802; in the following year, he accepted a call to become pastor of the Federal Street Church in Boston, a Congregationalist church, where he would serve for nearly 40 years.

Channing began his pastoral ministry at a time when adherents of the conservative and liberal poles of Congregationalism were openly at odds. Conservatives such as Jedidiah Morse, pastor of the First Congregational Church of Charlestown, Massachusetts, were anxious to halt the drift of Congregational liberals toward Unitarianism. Channing's church already occupied theological ground quite distant from Morse's Congregational orthodoxy, and Channing himself inclined to similar views. He rejected many tenets of traditional Calvinism, such as human depravity and the Trinity. He was Arian in his theology, believing that Jesus was less than God but nevertheless more than man.

In 1814, Channing married Ruth Gibbs, a childhood playmate and cousin, and the couple eventually had four children. His wife, a member of a wealthy family, brought assets to the marriage that allowed Channing and his family to live comfortably.

The second decade of the 19th century saw the theological skirmishes between the orthodox and liberal wings of New England Congregationalism reach a new pitch of intensity. The resulting war of sermons and pamphlets fractured the two theological camps and hastened the birth of Unitarianism not simply as a subspecies of Congregationalism but as a separate religious movement. A key moment in this severance occurred in the spring of 1819 when Channing was invited to preach the ordination sermon for a young liberal minister at the First Independent Church in Baltimore. His sermon, later published in pamphlet form as "Unitarian Christianity," attempted to articulate the essential elements of the new movement and became enormously influential in framing the theology of American Unitarianism.

Channing, though rejecting fundamental orthodoxies such as the Trinity and the divinity of Jesus, nevertheless considered himself firmly within the Christian household of faith. He believed that the Bible was the inspired word of God, but he insisted that orthodox Congregationalism had misread its revelation. Though Channing seems not to have consciously sought a formal break with orthodox Congregationalists, severance was forced on him in the following years, and in 1820 he helped establish the Berry Street Conference, a forerunner of the American Unitarian Association, which was founded five years later.

Over the following two decades, a steady stream of books flowed from Channing's pen on a copious variety of subjects, some expounding Unitarian theology, others addressing literary topics, and still others urging social reforms such as the abolition of slavery. Through these books and an active speaking career, Channing exerted an enormous influence on 19th-century liberal intellectuals, both in the United States and in Europe. He died on October 2, 1842, in Bennington, Vermont.

Toward the end of his life, Thomas Jefferson predicted that Unitarianism would soon become the dominant American religion. This prediction was spectacularly wrong. Evangelical Christianity proved to be more durable and more influential than Jefferson could have imagined. Though Unitarianism remained a powerful current within the American religious tradition, it never achieved the dominance he had expected. Consequently, William Ellery Channing, though a powerful religious figure during his day, tends to be overshadowed by the evangelical leaders of the 19th and 20th centuries.

Further Reading

Ake, Jeffrey James. *Channing: Paradigm Transition Figure.* Chicago: International Vision, 1995.

Brown, Arthur W. *Always Young for Liberty: A Biography of William Ellery Channing.* Syracuse, N.Y.: Syracuse University Press, 1956.

Brown, Arthur W. *William Ellery Channing.* New York: Twayne Publishers, 1961.

Channing, William Ellery. *Memoir of William Ellery Channing.* 3 vols. Boston: Wm. Crosby & H.P. Nichols, 1848.

———. *William Ellery Channing: Selected Writings.* Edited by David Robinson. New York: Paulist Press, 1985.

———. *Works of William Ellery Channing.* 6 vols. Boston: J. Munroe, 1841–43; New York: B. Franklin, 1970.

Delbanco, Andrew. *William Ellery Channing: An Essay on the Liberal Spirit in America.* Cambridge, Mass.: Harvard University Press, 1981.

Mendelsohn, Jack. *Channing, The Reluctant Radical: A Biography.* Boston: Little, Brown, 1971.

Patterson, Robert Leet. *The Philosophy of William Ellery Channing.* New York: Bookman Associates, 1952.

Rice, Madeleine Hooke. *Federal Street Pastor: The Life of William Ellery Channing.* New York: Bookman Associates, 1961.

Chapman, John Wilbur

(1859–1918) *Presbyterian revivalist*

John Wilbur Chapman was a prominent Presbyterian minister and evangelist who, for a brief period at the beginning of the 20th century, was one of America's best-known revival preachers. Assisted for a time by a young preacher named BILLY SUNDAY, Chapman would eventually find his career overshadowed by that of his protégé. Chapman was born on June 17, 1859, in Richmond, Indiana, the son of Alexander Hamilton Chapman and Lorinda McWhinney Chapman. He joined a Presbyterian church in 1876, and in spite of his father's warning that there were already more than enough poor ministers, Chapman was drawn toward a career as a preacher. He studied for a year at Oberlin College and then transferred to Lake Forest College, where he received a B.A. in 1879. While in college, Chapman attended a revival meeting conducted by DWIGHT LYMAN MOODY in Chicago, and in a brief encounter with Moody in an inquiry room after the meeting, he felt a renewed confidence that he was a Christian. At Lake Forest, Chapman also formed a friendship with B. Fay

Mills, with whom he would later have a close association. After graduating from college, Chapman enrolled in Lane Seminary in Cincinnati, Ohio, from which he received a B.D. in 1882. That year, he became the pastor of two Presbyterian churches, one in College Corner, Ohio, and the other in Liberty, Indiana, and he married Irene Steddom, a childhood friend with whom he had one child before her death in 1886.

In 1883, Chapman's college friend B. Fay Mills enticed him to accept the pastorate of a Dutch Reformed church in Schuylerville, New York, which placed the two young men in closer contact. In 1885, Chapman moved to the First Dutch Reformed Church of Albany. While in Albany, Chapman renewed his acquaintance with the great revival preacher Dwight L. Moody. With Moody's advice, Chapman restructured services at the church, introduced some of Moody's revival hymns, and preached evangelistic sermons that substantially increased the church's membership. He married Agnes Pruyn Strain in 1888, and the couple had four children. After five years at Albany, Chapman accepted the call to become the pastor of the Bethany Presbyterian Church in Philadelphia, Pennsylvania, in 1890. Again, the church flourished under Chapman's leadership, adding more than a thousand members in three years and expanding its institutional ministry to include a hospital, a bank, and Bethany College.

Chapman's ministry at Bethany received national attention and led to invitations to preach in revival services, not the least of which was Dwight L. Moody's solicitation of Chapman to be one of the evangelists Moody organized to preach at the 1892–93 Chicago World's Fair. The plentitude of revival engagements prompted Chapman to resign from his pulpit at Bethany in late 1892 in favor of full-time evangelistic work, assisted for a time by a young preacher named Billy Sunday, but he returned to the church in 1896. That same year he became vice president of the Moody Bible Institute. Chapman spent three more years at Bethany, expanding on the work he had launched in the early 1890s, but he left the church in 1899 to assume the pastorate of the prominent but struggling congregation of the Fourth Presbyterian Church of New York City. He labored there for a little less than four years before the Presbyterian General Assembly asked him in 1901 to undertake the responsibilities of corresponding secretary for its newly created Committee on Evangelism, with responsibility for supervising the activities of more than 50 evangelists.

Chapman's success at supervising Presbyterian evangelism campaigns again attracted invitations to conduct revival services. In 1903 he surrendered his administrative post with the Presbyterian General Assembly and embarked on a series of revival campaigns that took him across the country and around the world. He soon established the plan of "simultaneous meetings," an evangelistic arrangement in which several revivalists preached at different locations in a particular city while Chapman, joined after 1908 by the musician Charles Alexander, held services at some central location. He reached the height of his prominence as a revivalist from 1908 to 1910, but thereafter, his former assistant, Billy Sunday, began to eclipse him in reputation. Chapman continued to hold revival services around the world, though. Chapman's wife Agnes died in 1907, and in 1910 he married Mabel Cornelia Moulton. He died in New York City on Christmas Day 1918.

John Wilbur Chapman was a prominent revival preacher in his own day. He stands in a line of preachers who struggled to develop techniques for mass evangelism in urban America. In fact, his solid reputation as a Presbyterian pastor and denominational official helped to win acceptance for revivalism within mainstream Protestantism. Nevertheless, after Chapman's death, his historical reputation tended to be overshadowed by that of his mentor, Dwight L. Moody, and by the man who briefly served as his assistant, Billy Sunday.

Further Reading

Chapman, J. Wilbur. *The Personal Touch*. New York: Fleming H. Revell, 1911.

———. *Present-Day Evangelism*. New York: Baker & Taylor, 1903.

———. *Revivals and Missions*. New York: Lentilhon, 1900.

Harry, David Roy. "Two Kingdoms: Walter Rauschenbusch's Concept of the Kingdom of God Contrasted with the Theology of Revivalism in Early Twentieth Century." Ph.D. dissertation, Southwestern Baptist Theological Seminary, 1993.

Ottman, Ford C. *J. Wilbur Chapman: A Biography*. Garden City, N.Y.: Doubleday, Page, 1920.

Ramsay, John Cummins. *John Wilbur Chapman: The Man, His Methods and His Message*. Boston: Christopher Publishing House, 1962.

Chase, Philander
(1775–1852) *Episcopal bishop, educator*

A frontier bishop of the Midwest, Philander Chase served as bishop of Ohio and later Illinois during the first half of the 19th century. His independent and autocratic ways rankled many of his contemporaries, but they also sustained a rugged and persevering temper that helped to plant Episcopal faith and institutions in the Midwest. Chase was born on December 14, 1775, in Cornish, New Hampshire, the son of Dudley Chase and Allace Corbett Chase. He entered Dartmouth College in 1791, and while there he became acquainted with the Book of Common Prayer and converted from the Congregationalism of his youth to the Episcopal Church. After his graduation from Dartmouth in 1795, Chase studied theology with Thomas Ellison, an Episcopal minister in Albany, New York. In 1796, while studying in Albany, he married Mary Faye, with whom he had six children. Chase was ordained a deacon in 1798 and an Episcopal priest in the following year.

After several years spent tending churches in Poughkeepsie and Fishkill, New York, Chase moved with his wife to New Orleans. He hoped the geographic change would prove beneficial in curing her tuberculosis. In New Orleans in 1805 he organized Christ Church, the city's first Episcopal parish. After six years, though, Chase and his wife returned to New England and rejoined their children, whom they had left in the care of Vermont relatives. In 1811, Chase became the rector of Christ Church in Hartford, Connecticut.

Within several years of returning to New England, Chase began to look longingly toward the western frontier of the United States. In 1817, he migrated to Worthington, Ohio, where he accepted a position as principal of the Worthington

Academy. The following year his wife died of tuberculosis. In 1819, Chase married Sophia May Ingraham, with whom he had three children. The same year he was consecrated bishop of the newly formed diocese of Ohio. This appointment paid no salary, and Chase struggled to support his family by farming and by his work at the Worthington Academy. In 1821, he assumed the presidency of Cincinnati College, and during this period he began to contemplate the possibility of establishing an institution where Episcopal ministers might be trained. Eastern clergy opposed this idea, arguing that New York's General Theological Seminary, established in 1817, was more than adequate to train ministerial candidates from the Midwest. Chase, though, complained about the expense of sending candidates east to study and the likelihood that they would be tempted to remain there rather than

Philander Chase served as an Episcopal bishop of Ohio and Illinois during the early decades of the 19th century. *(Library of Congress, Prints and Photographs Division LC-USZ62-109898)*

return to the frontier. Consequently, he decided to travel to England to raise money for his planned institution. After a successful fund-raising trip in 1823–24, he returned home and established Kenyon College and Gambier Theological Seminary in 1824. He presided over these infant institutions with an autocratic hand that produced conflicts with trustees, faculty, and Ohio clergy. The Ohio Convention eventually insisted in 1831 that he surrender either his control of the institution or his post as bishop. Chase promptly resigned from both responsibilities.

Chase relocated his family to a small farm nearby and then to a farm in Gilead, Michigan. In 1835, however, he was summoned from his self-enforced retirement by his election as bishop of the newly formed diocese of Illinois. As he had in Ohio, Chase promptly turned his attention to securing the resources to establish a seminary. Again, he ventured to England to raise funds for the project. Though less successful in these efforts than he had been the previous decade, he raised enough money to establish Jubilee College in 1839.

Over the next decade, Chase tended to the affairs of the college and of his diocese. He became presiding bishop in 1843. Though the life of the Episcopal Church in Illinois prospered during this period, Jubilee College struggled to survive. Chase himself died at the age of 77, on September 20, 1852, in Jubilee, Illinois. Stripped of his support and indefatigability, Jubilee College was forced to close a decade later.

Philander Chase might have lived out a secure ecclesiastical ministry on the East Coast of the United States had he possessed a different temperament. But a rugged and independent spirit lured him west, where he found ample space to plant churches and educational institutions where none existed. He traded eastern comforts for the more arduous life of the frontier and superintendence of settled parishes for the life of a missionary. For more than 30 years he tended the affairs of infant parishes and educational institutions, twice hazarding trips to England to finance institutional visions not shared by Episcopal colleagues in America. His success as a frontier bishop earned him a lasting place in the history of the Episcopal Church.

Further Reading

Chase, Philander. *Bishop Chase's Reminiscences: An Autobiography.* Boston: J. B. Dow, 1847.

———. *A Plea for the West.* Philadelphia: William Stavely, 1826.

Clark, Jennifer. "'Church of Our Fathers': The Development of the Protestant Episcopal Church Within the Changing Post-Revolutionary Anglo-American Relationship." *Journal of Religious History* 18 (1994): 27–51.

Richmond, Andrew S. "The Papers of Philander Chase." Available online. URL: http://www2.kenyon.edu/khistory/chase/welcome2.htm. Updated on January 15, 2001.

Smith, Laura Chase. *The Life of Philander Chase: First Bishop of Ohio and Illinois, Founder of Kenyon and Jubilee Colleges.* New York: E. P. Dutton, 1903.

Chauncy, Charles

(1705–1787) *Congregationalist minister*

Often nicknamed the "Great Opposer of the Great Awakening," Charles Chauncy stood against what he believed to be the excesses of revivalism that visited New England during the 1740s. But history also remembers him for a theological liberalism that carried him away from the Puritanism he inherited from the 17th century. He was born on January 1, 1705, to Charles Chauncy and Sarah Walley Chauncy. After his father's death when he was six and his mother's subsequent remarriage, Chauncy studied at the Boston Latin School and then matriculated at Harvard when he was 12 years old. He received a B.A. in 1721 and an M.A. in 1724; by that time was he determined to become a Congregationalist minister.

In 1727, Chauncy was invited to become the assistant pastor for Boston's First Church (also known as Old Brick Church), where Thomas Foxcroft was senior minister. When he accepted this position and was ordained, he began what would ultimately be a 60-year career of service at Boston's oldest, most established, and most prominent church. Chauncy himself would become senior minister in 1769, when Foxcroft died. He married Elizabeth Hirst in 1727; with her he had three children before her death a decade later. In 1739 he married Elizabeth Phillips Townsend, who died in 1757. He married Mary Stoddard, whom he outlived by four years, in 1760.

Toward the beginning of the 1740s, the Great Awakening spread across New England. Its progress was marked by increasing emphasis on emotional conversion experiences. This emphasis, in turn, prompted divisions among church congregations, between those who supported the revival, the "New Lights," and those who distrusted and even opposed it, the "Old Lights." Whereas some prominent ministers, such as JONATHAN EDWARDS, pastor of the church at Northampton, Massachusetts, embraced the revival and sought to sustain its spiritual energy, others, none more prominent that Charles Chauncy, opposed it. He judged the revivalism of the Great Awakening by its fruits and found them unhealthy.

> Alas! what unchristian heats and animosities are there in many places, to the dividing and breaking in pieces of churches and towns? What a spirit of rash, censorious, uncharitable judging prevails too generally all over the land? What bitterness and wrath and clamour, what evil speaking, reviling and slandering, are become common; and among those too, who would be counted good christians? How alienated are many ministers from each other, and how instrumental of hurting rather than promoting one another's usefulness?

In the years following the Great Awakening, ministers such as Jonathan Edwards espoused a reinvigorated Calvinism, which emphasized the damnation of souls apart from Christ's saving grace. Chauncy considered this theological perspective, soon branded the New Divinity, repugnant. It was, in his estimation, "as bad, if not worse than paganism."

If Chauncy opposed the Great Awakening in part because it disrupted the settled peace of New England's Congregationalist churches, he nevertheless began to move toward a theological perspective in the years afterward that had ample potential for its own disruptive effects. Chauncy, convinced that a benevolent God would not consign even the most sinful men and women to eternal damnation, eventually began to believe in universal salvation. Orthodox Congregationalists believed that Christ had died only for the elect, whereas Chauncy became convinced that Christ had died for everyone and that his death would ultimately result in the atonement of all men and women. For many years, he kept this belief—quite alien to traditional Calvinism—a secret, discussed it only when among close friends, and even gave it a code name: the "pudding." Eventually, though, he began to make references to his universalist beliefs in his writings, culminating in the publication of his book *The Mystery Hid from Ages and Generations, Made Manifest by the Gospel-Revelation* (1784). In the century after Chauncy's death, this view would be championed by the Universalists and the Unitarians.

Chauncy was deeply involved in theological controversy during the middle years of his life. Toward the end, he also became involved in the political controversy that ultimately severed the colonies from Great Britain. He publicly supported colonial grievances against Britain and sided with the patriots when fiery rhetoric eventually gave way to armed resistance. He died in Boston on February 10, 1787, in time to witness the American Revolution and the drafting of the U.S. Constitution.

Charles Chauncy's career as a New England minister is remembered chiefly for his settled opposition to the Great Awakening and for a theological liberalism characterized by universalist views regarding salvation. The latter views were a precursor of the Universalist and Unitarian movements that would flourish in the next century. His distaste for revivalism would find additional allies after his death.

Further Reading

Chauncy, Charles. *The Mystery Hid from Ages and Generations, Made Manifest by the Gospel-Revelation.* London: Printed for C. Dilly, 1784; New York: Arno Press, 1969.

———. *Seasonable Thoughts on the State of Religion in New-England.* Boston: Rogers and Fowle for Samuel Eliot, 1743.

Corrigan, John. *The Hidden Balance: Religion and the Social Theories of Charles Chauncy and Jonathan Mayhew.* Cambridge: Cambridge University Press, 1987.

Griffin, Edward M. *Old Brick: Charles Chauncy of Boston, 1705–1787.* Minneapolis: University of Minnesota Press, 1980.

Lippy, Charles H. *Seasonable Revolutionary: The Mind of Charles Chauncy.* Chicago: Nelson-Hall, 1981.

Wells, Colin Peter. "Timothy Dwight, 'The Triumph of Infidelity', and the Universalist Controversy." Ph.D. dissertation, Rutgers University, 1995.

Cheney, Charles Edward

(1836–1916) *bishop of the Reformed Episcopal Church*

Evangelical sympathies led to Charles Edward Cheney's eviction from the Episcopal priesthood and his subsequent role of leadership with the Reformed Episcopal Church. But respect for traditional Episcopal practices such as the use of vestments by priests subsequently isolated him from this denomination as well. He was born on February 20, 1836, in Canandaigua, New York, the son of E. Warren Cheney and Alice Wheeler Chipman Cheney. After receiving an undergraduate degree from Hobart College in 1857, Cheney prepared for the Episcopal ministry by studying at the Virginia Theological Seminary in Alexandria, Virginia, from which he graduated in 1859. He was ordained an Episcopal priest the following year and almost immediately moved to Chicago, where he became the rector of Christ Church. Soon afterward, he married Clara Emma Griswold.

On undertaking his ministry at Christ Church, Cheney and his evangelical sympathies collided with the sentiments of "high church" Episcopalians. Cheney found himself at odds with those who denied the legitimacy of the ministers in nonepiscopal denominations whose ordinations were not rooted in apostolic succession. He also objected to conceptions of infant baptism that equated baptism with actual spiritual regeneration. By the late 1860s, Cheney had abandoned the Episcopal prayer book's description of baptism in these terms, thus setting the stage for a confrontation with the bishop of Illinois, Henry John Whitehouse.

When Cheney refused to follow the precise baptismal liturgy established in the prayer book,

Bishop Whitehouse commenced ecclesiastical proceedings against him; Whitehouse was judge and five Illinois priests were to sit in judgment. Cheney had for his representation a team of lawyers led by future U.S. Supreme Court justice Melville Weston Fuller. After Cheney's cause received initial setbacks at the beginning of the ecclesiastical trial in July 1869, his lawyers obtained an order from the Superior Court of Chicago temporarily barring further proceedings against Cheney. This order remained in effect until the first part of 1871, and when it was dissolved, Bishop Whitehouse promptly revived the proceedings against Cheney. This time, however, one of the original members of the court had been consecrated bishop of Arkansas, thus severing his connection with the Illinois diocese and with the court convened by Whitehouse. Whitehouse proceeded in spite of this vacancy, and the ecclesiastical court subsequently found Cheney guilty and ordered his suspension from the priesthood. After Cheney refused to obey the court's order, a second proceeding convened; it found him guilty of contumacious conduct and ordered him deposed from the priesthood.

With his congregation's support, Cheney remained as rector of Christ Church and fended off attempts by the Episcopal diocese of Illinois to take control of the church's property. Two years later, in the fall of 1873, Cheney found a new ally when George David Cummins, the assistant bishop of Kentucky, established a new denomination more consistent with Cheney's evangelical sympathies. Cheney was ordained a priest in December 1873 and was made bishop of Chicago within the new denomination in September 1875. In the years that followed Cheney served in prominent leadership positions with the Reformed Episcopal denomination.

Cheney, however, proved not so radically evangelical as some within the new denomination in terms of retention of certain Episcopal traditions. When the Fourteenth General Council of the Reformed Episcopal Church voted in 1897 to abolish the use of vestments by priests during worship, Cheney protested against this move and withdrew from most denominational affairs. He died on November 15, 1916, in Chicago.

Charles Edward Cheney found himself caught up in an ecclesiastical dispute that eventually produced a new Episcopal denomination. His own exodus from the denomination in which he had been ordained, however, occurred before the new Reformed Episcopal denomination was called into being by Bishop George David Cummins. In the interim, he had to content himself with the loyal support of his church, even though he was—for a time at least—a priest without a denomination. The independence exhibited by Cheney during this episode early in his Chicago ministry found its parallel nearly 30 years later, when the Reformed Episcopal Church took an ecclesiastical path Cheney was not prepared to follow. He retreated once more to his church, estranged from the wider denomination in which he served once again.

Further Reading

Cheney, Charles Edward. *The Barefoot Maid at the Fountain Inn.* Chicago: Chicago Literary Club, 1912.

———. *A Belated Plantagenet.* Chicago: Chicago Literary Club, 1912.

———. *The Second Norman Conquest of England.* Chicago: Chicago Literary Club, 1907.

Chorley, E. Clowes. *Men and Movements in the American Episcopal Church.* New York: Scribner, 1946; Hamden, Conn.: Archon Books, 1961.

Guelzo, Allen C. *For the Union of Evangelical Christendom: The Irony of the Reformed Episcopalians.* University Park: Pennsylvania State University Press, 1994.

Longmire, Rodney Howat. "Charles Edward Cheney, Bishop of the Reformed Episcopal Church." S.T.M. thesis, Lutheran Theological Seminary, 1965.

Cheverus, Jean Louis Lefebvre de
(1768–1836) *Catholic bishop*

An exile from revolutionary France, Jean Louis Lefebvre de Cheverus migrated to the United States at the end of the 18th century and eventually became the first bishop of Boston. After a quarter of a century in America, however, Cheverus returned to France, where he eventually became an archbishop and a cardinal. He was born on January 28, 1768, in Mayenne, France, the son of Jean-Vincent-Marie Lefebvre de Cheverus and Anne-Charlotte Lemarchand des Noyers. In 1781, Cheverus began study at the College of Louis-le-Grand in Paris; he continued his education at the Saint Magloire Seminary in Paris, from which he graduated in 1790.

In the December following his graduation, Cheverus was ordained a Catholic priest, but he found his circumstances in peril almost immediately when the French government attempted to seize control of the church and ordered priests to swear an oath supporting civil reorganization of the clergy. After Cheverus refused to do so, he served for a time as a priest in his hometown, but he was imprisoned briefly in the summer of 1792 and exiled from France later that year. He spent the following few years in England, teaching for a time at a boarding school in Berkshire and subsequently serving as a pastor in Tottenham, near London. In 1796, however, Francis Matignon, a Boston priest and French immigrant, suggested that Cheverus immigrate to America. Cheverus accepted this invitation and arrived in Boston in the fall of 1796. In a letter to Bishop JOHN CARROLL of Baltimore a few months later, he expressed the attitudes that would eventually make him one of the most respected Catholic prelates in America.

> I shall use my best endeavours to reconcile the people entrusted to my care, to all the measures of the humane and liberal government they live under. I shall on all occasions shew myself a hearty friend to the interest of the United states and to the Federal government. Everywhere I shall seek the peace of the Country which the Lord will have me dwell in.

Cheverus spent the following years partially as a missionary among Native Americans and as a pastor to French Canadian Catholics in Maine, but he labored primarily among Irish Catholic immigrants who settled in Boston.

True to his pledge to Bishop Carroll, Cheverus embraced the country in which he found himself and encouraged other Catholic immigrants to do the same. Over the following years, he earned warm praise even from Protestant leaders in Boston for his congenial temper and virtuous bearing. Three and a half decades after Cheverus arrived in Boston, the influential Unitarian minister WILLIAM ELLERY CHANNING lavished praise on the

Boston bishop in an article published in *The United States Catholic Miscellany:*

> Who, among our religious teachers, would solicit a comparison between himself and the devoted Cheverus? This good man . . . lived in the midst of us, devoting his days and nights, and his whole heart, to the service of a poor and uneducated congregation. We saw him declining . . . the society of the cultivated and refined, that he might be the friend of the ignorant and friendless . . . bearing with a father's sympathy, the burdens and sorrows of his large spiritual family.

Channing's praise of Bishop Cheverus used the past tense, for earlier in the 1820s the exiled Frenchman who had made his home in the United States received a summons from his king to return to France and accept a bishopric there. Louis XVIII's request tumbled Cheverus into a period of sustained anxiousness over whether he should abandon his post in America, but he ultimately determined that he must return to his homeland. There, in 1823, with the pope's blessing, he assumed the episcopacy of Montauban. Slightly less than three years later, he was named archbishop of Bordeaux. Finally, toward the beginning of 1836, he became a cardinal. He died that same year, in Bordeaux, on July 19, 1836.

Jean Louis Lefebvre de Cheverus devoted the major portion of his adult life to the service of the Catholic Church in the United States. Planted in Boston, the very citadel of Protestant America, he did much to forge a settled home for Catholic immigrants. He steadfastly insisted that Catholic immigrants should plunge themselves into the life of their new country and distinguish themselves less by adherence to the cultural practices of the lands they had left than by the virtuous lives they led in the land in which they now lived. Perhaps even more significantly, Cheverus followed his own advice, and, until his homeland finally reclaimed him, won both friends and converts by the graciousness of his character.

Further Reading
Hamon, André Jean Marie. *Life of the Cardinal De Cheverus, Archbishop of Bordeaux.* Translated by

Robert M. Walsh. Philadelphia: Hooker & Claxton, 1839.

Lord, Robert H. "Jean Lefebvre de Cheverus, First Catholic Bishop of Boston." *Proceedings of the Massachusetts Historical Society* 65 (1933): 64–78.

Lord, Robert Howard, John E. Sexton, and Edward T. Harrington. *History of the Archdiocese of Boston in the Various Stages of Its Development, 1604 to 1943.* New York: Sheed & Ward, 1944.

Melville, Annabelle M. *Jean Lefebvre de Cheverus, 1768–1836.* Milwaukee: Bruce, 1958.

O'Connor, Thomas H. *Boston Catholics: A History of the Church and Its People.* Boston: Northeastern University Press, 1998.

Clark, Francis Edward
(Francis Edward Symmes)
(1851–1927) *Congregational minister, founder of the Christian Endeavor Society*

In the late 19th century, Francis Edward Clark established an organization for youth called the Christian Endeavor Society. Its success in instilling evangelical faith in young people inspired a pattern for many similar organizations that sprang up in the 20th century. Clark was born Francis Edward Symmes on September 12, 1851, in Aylmer, Quebec, the son of Charles Carey Symmes and Lydia Clark Symmes. His father died of cholera in 1854, and a few years later, first his teenaged brother Charles and then his mother died in quick succession, leaving him at age seven an orphan without any immediate family. Subsequently, his uncle, Edward Warren Clark, adopted him, and Francis took the last name of his new parents. Clark's foster father was a Congregational minister, and the boy grew up in a religiously devout environment. He studied at the Kimball Union Academy in Meriden, New Hampshire, and then enrolled in Dartmouth College in 1869.

In college, Clark took an active role in religious affairs on campus, including the Theological and Missionary Society. He also served on the editorial board of the college newspaper, *The Dartmouth.* He graduated in 1873 and promptly enrolled in Andover Theological Seminary to pre-pare for a vocation as a Congregational minister. While at Andover, Clark devoted some of his extracurricular time to work at a local mission Sunday School. There he worked together with Harriet Abbott, whom he subsequently married in 1876 and with whom he had four children. After graduation from Andover, Clark moved with his wife to Portland, Maine, where he became the pastor of the Williston Memorial Congregational Church, a young congregation established as a mission some eight years before his arrival. Under Clark's energetic leadership, the church promptly swelled from 50 to 400 members.

To attract young people to his church, Clark established the Williston Young People's Society of Christian Endeavor, which held its first meeting on February 2, 1881. The society's original constitution specified that its object would be "to promote an earnest Christian life among its members, to increase their mutual acquaintance, and to make them more useful in the service of God." The constitution also set forth rather stringent requirements for attendance and participation at the society's meetings. In the late summer of the same year, Clark published an article in the *Congregationalist,* "How One Church Cares for Its Young People," and this article, which described the new society, became a blueprint for other churches, which soon began establishing societies mirroring Clark's. By June 1882, Clark had created an umbrella organization to superintend the rapidly growing number of Christian Endeavor Societies. By the time of this organization's second annual meeting in the summer of 1883, some 56 Christian Endeavor Societies had been formed, with a membership of nearly 3,000.

In October 1883, Clark undertook a new pastoral station at the Phillips Congregational Church in South Boston. There, he supervised the growing affairs of the Christian Endeavor Society, creating a national office for its oversight and beginning publication of a magazine for the organization, called at first the *Golden Rule* and later the *Christian Endeavor World.* By 1887, the Christian Endeavor Society had grown at such a pace that Clark resigned as pastor of his church to work full-time as president of the United Society of Christian Endeavor. He continued in this position for nearly four decades, until shortly before his death on May 26, 1927, in Newton, Massachusetts.

By the time of his death, the society that Francis E. Clark had established in 1881 stretched out across the globe. His vision of an organization that would inspire and harness to service the religious devotion of Christian youth found fertile ground in the waning decades of the 19th century and the early years of the 20th. In the years after his death, the Christian Endeavor movement continued to flourish. Perhaps even more significantly, it served as a model for many more interdenominational Christian youth organizations that came into being in the 20th century.

Further Reading

Chaplin, W. Knight. *Francis E. Clark, Founder of the Y.P.S.C.E.* N.p., 1902.

"Young People's Society of the Christian Endeavor," Christian Endeavor. Available online. URL:http://learn.union-psce.edu/timeline/Youth/christian_endeavor_history.htm.

Clark, Eugene Francis. *A Son's Portrait of Dr. Francis E. Clark.* Boston: Williston Press, 1930.

Clark, Francis Edward. *Christian Endeavor in All Lands.* Philadelphia: n.p., 1906.

Clarke, James Freeman
(1810–1888) *Unitarian minister*

A prominent Unitarian leader during the 19th century, James Freeman Clarke represented the strand of Unitarianism committed to continued expression through churches. His sympathies for transcendentalism and his friendship with more radical Unitarians made him a mediating figure in the conflicts among Unitarians that emerged in the 1860s. Clarke was born on April 4, 1810, in Hanover, New Hampshire, the son of Samuel C. Clarke and Rebecca Parker Hull. His parents named him for his stepgrandfather, James Freeman, an 18th-century Unitarian leader and pastor of King's Chapel in Boston. Clarke studied at Harvard College, from which he received an A.B. in 1829, and Harvard Divinity School, from which he graduated in 1833.

From 1833 to 1840, Clarke served as a Unitarian minister in Louisville, Kentucky. While there he founded a liberal religious magazine, *Western Messenger,* which he edited from 1833 to 1836. This periodical became an important voice for Transcendentalist thought. He married Anna Huidekoper, with whom he had four children, in 1839. But he felt isolated in Kentucky and remote from his New England roots. Consequently, he moved to Boston in 1840. By the following year he had founded the Unitarian Church of the Disciples, where, except for a period of convalescence the following decade, he would remain as minister for the rest of his life.

By the second half of the 19th century, some Unitarian congregations had begun to migrate away from their original Christian moorings, away, in fact, from any specific creedal formulations. Clarke, however, resisted this migration and remained committed to the identity of Unitarianism as one of the rooms within the larger household of Christian faith. He, thus, aligned himself with the relatively conservative Unitarian leaders, such as HENRY WHITNEY BELLOWS, who organized the National Conference of Unitarian Churches in 1865. Of course, Clarke's theology was a significant step removed from traditional Protestant orthodoxy. He formulated a well-known statement of Unitarian beliefs in *Vexed Questions in Theology* (1886) when he substituted for the classic five points of Calvinism his own credo: "the fatherhood of God . . . the brotherhood of man . . . the leadership of Jesus . . . salvation by character . . . and the progress of mankind onward and upward forever."

Although his own theological position allied him with the more conservative strand of Unitarianism, Clarke had a good deal of sympathy for the more radical currents that would turn away from the National Conference of Unitarian Churches to establish the Free Religious Association. In his earlier days as a Unitarian minister, he had himself been attracted to Ralph Waldo Emerson's Transcendentalism, and he never surrendered his affection for the ideas of more radical Unitarians such as THEODORE PARKER.

In the early 1850s illness forced Clarke to take a sabbatical from his ministerial position at the Church of the Disciples. He moved to the estate of his wife's family in Meadville, Pennsylvania, where he used the time to recuperate physically and to write. By 1853 he was able to return to Boston, where he resumed his post as minister of the Church of the Disciples and became increasingly prominent in Unitarian affairs. Beginning in 1867 he served as an adjunct professor at Harvard Divinity School, and, during the period from 1871 to 1873, he published his most important work, a two-volume study, *Ten Great Religions*. After a career that spanned nearly five decades, he died on June 8, 1888, in Boston.

The conciliatory spirit of James Freeman Clarke could not avoid the controversy that divided Unitarians in the 1860s. He found himself securely among the ranks of those who saw the value of the church as an institutional home for Unitarianism. "Churchly tastes," OCTAVIUS BROOKS FROTHINGHAM wrote in *Transcendentalism in New England: A History* (1876), "led him away from the company of thinkers where he intellectually belonged." Nevertheless, Clarke's fraternity with transcendentalists during the early years of his pastoral ministry imbued him with a greater tolerance for spiritual radicalism than was generally demonstrated among the more conservative Unitarians who helped establish the National Conference of Unitarian Churches in 1865. This tolerance, together with his interest in other religious traditions, including those of the Eastern religions, made him a kind of intellectual bridge between the dominant Unitarianism of the 19th century and the forms Unitarianism would increasingly take in the 20th.

Further Reading

Bolster, Arthur S. *James Freeman Clarke: Disciple to Advancing Truth*. Boston: Beacon Press, 1954.

Brasher, Alan. "James Freeman Clarke's Journal Accounts of Ralph Waldo Emerson's Lectures." *Studies in the American Renaissance* (1995): 83–100.

Clarke, James Freeman. *Autobiography, Diary, and Correspondence*. Edited by Edward Everett Hale. Boston: Houghton, Mifflin, 1891; New York: Negro Universities Press 1968.

———. *Ten Great Religions: An Essay in Comparative Theology*. 2 vols. Boston: Houghton, Mifflin, 1872–1883.

———. *Vexed Questions in Theology: A Series of Essays*. Boston: Geo. H. Ellis, 1886.

Neufeldt, Leonard. "James Freeman Clarke." In *The Transcendentalists: A Review of Research and Criticism*. Edited by Joel Myerson. New York: Modern Language Association of America, 1984.

Thomas, J.W. *James Freeman Clarke: Apostle of German Culture to America*. Boston: J. W. Luce, 1949.

Versluis, Arthur. *American Transcendentalism and Asian Religions*. New York: Oxford University Press, 1993.

Clarke, John
(1609–1676) *Baptist minister, colonial leader*

Famous as an advocate of religious freedom, John Clarke helped establish one of the first Baptist churches in North America and represented the interests of the Providence Colony (later Rhode Island) in England. He was born on October 8, 1609, in Westhorpe, Suffolk County, England, the son of Thomas and Rose Keridge Clarke. The measure and character of his later achievements indicate that he probably received some formal university education, including some study of medicine, but its details are not available. He married Elizabeth Harges, whose father was lord of the manor at Wreslingworth, Bedfordshire; the couple had no children.

In 1637, Clarke and his wife migrated to Boston, though his sympathies for the theological views of ANNE MARBURY HUTCHINSON—banished that same year by Massachusetts authorities—made the city unwelcoming to the Clarkes. They joined Hutchinson in relocating to the Providence Colony, where, in 1638, Clarke helped to purchase the island of Aquidneck from neighboring Indians and to found the town of Portsmouth there. The following year, he helped establish the town of Newport and soon became the pastor of its church. In the mid-1640s, Clarke came to oppose infant baptism and to believe that baptism was an ordinance reserved for adults who had been converted to the Christian faith and that it should be administered by immersion rather than by sprinkling. With these views, he led his church to become a Baptist congregation in 1648. Over the next few years he also undertook missionary activities that took him into the Massachusetts Bay Colony, which proved to be not at all tolerant of his Baptist beliefs. For holding an unsanctioned worship service in Lynn, he was jailed and fined. This experience prompted him to write what would become one of the 17th century's most famous polemics in favor of religious liberty: *Ill Newes from New-England: or a Narative of New-Englands Persecution. Wherein Is declared That While Old England Is Becoming New, New-England is Become Old,* published in London in 1652. Like ROGER WILLIAMS, who helped to found the Providence Colony after his own banishment from Massachusetts in 1635, Clarke protested the attempt by Massachusetts authorities to superintend the religious beliefs and practices of their citizens.

Together Clarke and Williams were instrumental in ensuring that the Providence Colony followed a course different from that of Massachusetts. In the early 1650s, Clarke was invited by the colony to serve as its agent in London, and he moved there with his wife. After the Restoration cast in doubt the colony's original charter—obtained by Roger Williams in the 1640s—the colony asked Clarke to work with Williams in obtaining a new charter. Though Williams eventually returned to Providence before the completion of this task, Clarke continued his efforts and ultimately secured the new charter in 1663. In keeping with the views of Clarke and Williams, the charter contained an expansive guarantee of religious liberty:

> No person within said colony, at any time hereafter, shall be any wise molested, punished, disquited, or called in question, for any differences in opinion in matters of religion, and do not actually disturb the civil peace of our said colony; but that every person and persons may . . . freely and fully have and enjoy his and their own judgements and consciences, in matters of religious concernments . . . they behaving themselves peaceably and quietly, and not using this liberty to licentiousness and profaneness, nor to the civil injury or outward disturbance of others.

After obtaining this charter, Clarke returned with his wife to Newport in 1664. He resumed preaching and continued involvement in the civil affairs of the colony, serving as deputy governor from 1669 to 1672. Personal and ecclesiastical troubles disturbed the peace of his final years, however. His first wife, Elizabeth, died around 1670, and in 1671 Clarke married Jane Fletcher. But his new wife died during childbirth a year later. Subsequently, in 1673, Clarke married the widow Sarah Davis and became the stepfather to her children. Affairs in Clarke's church followed a similarly troubled path, as doctrinal disagreements rent its peace during Clarke's final years. He died in Newport on April 20, 1676.

Providence Colony, eventually to become Rhode Island, was a despised stepsister in the New England of its day. Other colonies called it the "latrine" of New England, for the variety of spiritual dissenters it attracted. But the colony represented an early attempt to disentangle the affairs of church and state in the New World, and the future America would bear a closer likeness to Providence than to its more sophisticated neighboring colonies. To his credit, John Clarke played a significant role in the colony's early dedication to religious liberty.

Further Reading

Clarke, John. *Ill Newes from New-England: or a Narative of New-Englands Persecution. Wherein Is declared That While Old England Is Becoming New, New-England is Become Old.* London: H. Hills, 1652.

James, Sydney V. *John Clarke and His Legacies: Religion and Law in Colonial Rhode Island, 1638–1750.* Edited by Theodore Dwight Bozeman. University Park: Pennsylvania State University Press, 1999.

Nelson, Wilbur. *The Hero of Aquidneck: A Life of Dr. John Clarke.* New York: Fleming H. Revell, 1938.

Cody, John Patrick
(1907–1982) *Catholic cardinal*

Archbishop and later cardinal, John Patrick Cody presided over Catholic affairs in Chicago during the late 1960s and the 1970s. An imperious manner, combined with rapid changes occurring within Catholicism and American society, made Cody a controversial figure prior to his death in 1982. Cody was born on December 24, 1907, in Saint Louis, Missouri, to Thomas Joseph Cody and Mary Begley Cody, immigrants from Ireland. Beginning in 1927, Cody spent a decade in Rome, first as a seminarian at the North American College and then at the Pontifical Urbanian College of the Congregation de Propaganda Fide, where he received a Ph.D. in 1928 and an S.T.D. in 1932. Ordained a priest in 1931, Cody followed his seminary studies with service as assistant rector of the North American College from 1932 to 1938 and as a staff member of Cardinal Eugenio Pacelli's Secretariat of State. Work at the Secretariat gave Cody contact with two future popes: Pacelli, who later became Pope Pius XII, and the diplomat Giovanni Battista Montini, who became Pope Paul VI and who would eventually make Cody a cardinal.

In 1938, Cody returned to Saint Louis and became secretary to Bishop (and later Archbishop) John J. Glennon. Within 10 years, he had been named a bishop himself. The following years saw Cody serve several Catholic dioceses: Saint Joseph, Missouri, beginning in 1954; Kansas City Saint Joseph, beginning in 1956; and New Orleans, beginning in 1961. In 1964 he became archbishop of the New Orleans archdiocese and endured the controversy surrounding his efforts to continue the previous diocesan policy of integrating Catholic schools. He also earned a reputation as an authoritarian ecclesiastical administrator.

Cody's reputation as an autocrat blossomed in full flower once he had been named archbishop of Chicago in 1965 and elevated to the college of cardinals in 1967. On his arrival in Chicago in a stately railroad car, he consolidated control over an archdiocese that had previously enjoyed more broadly delegated power. Faced with a growing shortage of priests, Cody began closing parishes even as he worked to reorganize diocesan seminaries and create medical insurance and retirement programs for priests and a permanent diaconate program that soon became the largest in the nation. Almost immediately, though, his imperious style prompted Chicago priests to form a union, the Association of Chicago Priests (ACP), in 1966. Although Cody initially permitted the formation of this organization and tried to work with it, his relations with the ACP soon soured and cast him in a permanent state of antagonism with it. He further alienated Chicago priests by devoting considerable resources to establishing the ultimately unsuccessful Catholic Television Network of Chicago and lavishly renovating the Holy Name Cathedral, even as he closed several inner-city schools for lack of financial support.

By the beginning of the 1980s, Cody's ecclesiastical administration was plagued with allegations of financial and personal improprieties, including rumors that he had improperly funneled the insurance business of the archdiocese to the son of a stepcousin in Saint Louis and that he was supporting a mistress in a luxurious apartment. The prevalence of these rumors eventually stirred the U.S. Attorney's Office in Chicago to launch an investigation in 1981 and prompted withering criticism of Cody by the *Chicago Sun-Times*. Cody's health began to fail during this period, and he died in Chicago on April 25, 1982. The federal investigation ultimately closed without issuing any indictments, and no solid evidence of improprieties by Cody ever surfaced. Within a few months of Cody's death, Pope John Paul II appointed Joseph L. Bernardin to succeed him.

John Patrick Cody's superintendence of Catholic affairs in Chicago occurred during a period of momentous change in American society. In many ways, such as in his support for racial integration and for the ecclesiastical reformations initiated by the Second Vatican Counsel, Cody embraced these changes and helped to implement them within the Chicago archdiocese. But his autocratic manner frequently undermined his capacity for leadership in an age alive with new enthusiasm for democratic and social reform, making him one of the more controversial Catholic leaders of the 20th century.

Further Reading

Dahm, Charles W. *Power and Authority in the Catholic Church: Cardinal Cody in Chicago.* With Robert Ghelardi. Notre Dame, Ind.: University of Notre Dame Press, 1981.

Skerrett, Ellen, Edward B. Kantowicz, and Steven V. Avella. *Catholicism Chicago Style.* Chicago: Loyola University Press, 1993.

Coffin, Henry Sloane
(1877–1954) *Presbyterian minister, educator*

A leading voice among mainline Protestants during the first half of the 20th century, Henry Sloane Coffin resolutely defended theological liberalism from assaults by more conservative elements within his own denomination and among Protestants generally. Though a Presbyterian himself, he advocated a union among Christians that would preserve their differences even as it harnessed their collective strength. He was born on January 5, 1877, in New York City, the son of Edmund Coffin and Euphemia Sloane Coffin. Coffin studied at a private boy's school in New York City and then entered Yale College in 1893. His mother's devout Presbyterian faith had deeply influenced his childhood and youth, and this influence followed Coffin to college. At Yale, he was actively involved in the activities of the Yale Christian Association, serving as its president during his senior year, and, during summer vacations, he attended the student conferences organized by the revivalist DWIGHT LYMAN MOODY in Northfield, Massachusetts.

By the time Coffin graduated from Yale in 1897, he had determined to become a Presbyterian minister. He began graduate work in Europe, studying first at Edinburgh, Scotland, and then at Marburg, Germany. Subsequently, he returned to the United States for a final year of seminary study at Union Theological Seminary, from which he received a bachelor of divinity degree in 1900. That year he was ordained a Presbyterian minister and began work as pastor of the Bedford Park Presbyterian Church in the Bronx. He remained there for five years, before becoming the minister of the Madison Avenue Presbyterian Church in 1905.

During his last year at Bedford Park, Coffin added to his pastoral duties responsibilities as an associate professor at Union Theological Seminary. For the next 21 years, he labored as both a pastor and a seminary professor. In 1906 he married Dorothy Eells, with whom he had two children. During his years at Madison Avenue Presbyterian Church, his reputation as a leading voice of liberal Protestant theology grew steadily. In 1922, he became a member of the Yale Corporation, after being briefly considered to become its president. Two

years later, he placed himself at the forefront of the controversy between Presbyterian liberals and conservatives by playing an important part in the creation of what became known as the Auburn Affirmation. This statement was a manifesto of the theological liberals, which denied biblical inerrancy and insisted on liberty to reconsider the meaning of historic Presbyterian affirmations of faith.

In 1926, Coffin was named president of Union Theological Seminary, and for the next 19 years he guided the affairs of the institution. He persuaded two of the 20th century's most prominent American theologians, PAUL JOHANNES TILLICH and REINHOLD NIEBUHR, to join the faculty of the seminary. Though a Presbyterian at heart, Coffin used his growing influence to encourage efforts at church unity, both across the lines of Protestant denominations, such as the Presbyterians and the Episcopalians, and among Presbyterians themselves. In his influential article "Why I Am a Presbyterian" Coffin declared his interest in church unity.

> I am a Presbyterian only temporarily. The name carries many hallowed memories and associations, but it seems to me to belong to the past rather than to the present. . . . Once granted that no existing church is specially gifted with true doctrine or correct orders or the only valid mode of administering some sacrament, and that all have valuable historical heritages and large present contributions to make to the united Church of Christ, it ought not to be impossible to arrive at some form of organization which would combine liberty and unity, conserving the values in our differences and making possible the gains of united life and service.

The last significant ecclesiastical post Coffin occupied was that of moderator of the General Assembly of the Presbyterian Church (USA) in 1943. Two years later, he retired from his post at Union Theological Seminary in favor of a semiretirement of writing and lecturing. He died on November 25, 1954, in Lakeville, Connecticut.

Henry Sloane Coffin played a leading role in the affairs of mainline Protestantism during the first half of the 20th century. These were years when the mainline churches continued to exercise a predominant influence on American religious affairs. In the great theological controversy between liberals and conservatives of the period, Coffin unabashedly championed the cause of theological liberalism against the claims of conservatives who decried the drift of mainline denominations away from traditional orthodoxies. Coffin insisted that the verities of the faith were not fixed principles but rather living realities subject to reinterpretation by each age of the church.

Further Reading

Bains, David Ralph. "The Liturgical Impulse in Mid-Twentieth-Century American Mainline Protestantism." Ph.D. dissertation, Harvard University, 1999.

Coffin, Henry Sloane. *God Confronts Man in History.* New York: C. Scribner's Sons, 1947.

———. *A Half Century of Union Theological Seminary, 1896–1945: An Informal History.* New York: Scribner, 1954.

———. *In a Day of Social Rebuilding: Lectures on the Ministry of the Church.* New Haven, Conn.: Yale University Press, 1918.

———. *Some Christian Convictions: A Practical Restatement in Terms of Present-Day Thinking.* New Haven, Conn.: Yale University Press, 1915.

———. "Why I Am a Presbyterian." In *Twelve Modern Apostles and Their Creeds.* New York: Duffield, 1926.

Niebuhr, Reinhold. *This Ministry: The Contribution of Henry Sloane Coffin.* New York: Charles Scribner's Sons, 1945.

Noyes, Morgan Phelps. *Henry Sloane Coffin: The Man and His Ministry.* New York: Scribner, 1964.

Coke, Thomas
(1747–1814) *Methodist bishop*

Together with FRANCIS ASBURY, Thomas Coke served as one of the first bishops of the Methodist Episcopal Church in America. The personal representative of John Wesley in the United States, Coke acted as a bridge between English and American Methodism during the denomination's early years. He was born on September 28, 1747, in Brecon, South Wales, the son of Bartholomew Coke and Anne Phillips Coke. He studied at Oxford,

earning a B.A. in 1768, an M.A. in 1770, and a doctorate in civil law in 1775. White studying toward his doctorate, Coke was ordained a priest in the Church of England and ministered first as a deacon and then as a priest at the church in South Petherton, Somerset, from 1871 to 1877. His sympathies for Methodism, however, enhanced by a personal meeting with John Wesley in the late summer of 1876, ultimately derailed his career as an Anglican minister. In 1877 he was evicted from his parish, and from that point forward, he was a tireless advocate for Methodism.

On his departure from the Church of England, Coke became a trusted assistant to John Wesley, who eventually turned to him when circumstances required him to send a deputy to America in the years after the Revolutionary War. Given authority as Wesley's "superintendent" over American Methodist affairs, Coke made the Atlantic crossing in 1784 and attended the historic Christmas Conference held in Baltimore, Maryland, in December of that year, at which the Methodist Episcopal Church was formally organized. The delegates to this conference elected Asbury and Coke as the first two superintendents of the Methodist Episcopal Church, though Asbury later changed the designation of his spiritual office to bishop. Francis Asbury had tended Methodist affairs in America during the tumultuous years of the Revolutionary War, when other Methodist missionaries had retreated to England. As a consequence, he was able to take a dominant leadership role in the years after the birth of the Methodist Episcopal Church. He had also permanently attached himself to America soil, whereas Coke, nominally his cosuperintendent, had to travel back to England in 1787 to report to Wesley. But Coke returned again and again to the United States to assist in the spread of Methodist work there, nine times between 1784 and 1804.

Though American Methodists point to Thomas Coke as one of their first two bishops, English Methodists tend to refer to him as "the father of Methodist missions," for his zeal on behalf of evangelistic efforts. He led the effort to establish Methodist missionary outposts in the Caribbean, Nova Scotia, the Channel Islands, Scotland, Ireland, Wales, and the West Indies, traveling to the

West Indies in particular four times to supervise missionary activity there.

During his 20 years of itinerant travel back and forth across the Atlantic, Coke remained single. But he was married twice in the last decade of his life, first to Penelope Goulding Smith in 1805, and then, after her death in 1881, to Ann Loxdale soon afterward. Neither marriage produced any children. At the end of his life, Coke undertook a final missionary journey; he died at sea in route to Ceylon on May 3, 1814.

Thomas Coke helped to coordinate the spread of Methodism in the years after the Revolutionary War had disturbed relations between England and the United States. He learned, as did John Wesley, that American Methodists would inevitably chart a course separate from their English brethren, animated by a spirit of independence that spilled over from the political realm into the religious. Nevertheless, Coke labored diligently to maintain ties between those whose unity war had troubled, traveling regularly between the United States and Great Britain for two decades after his initial visit to America in 1784. Though Francis Asbury's influence among American Methodists during this period was greater than Coke's, Thomas Coke nevertheless must be reckoned one of the fathers of the American Methodist Church.

Further Reading

Candler, Warren A. *Life of Thomas Coke.* Nashville: Publishing House M.E. Church, 1923.

Coke, Thomas. *The Life of the Rev. John Wesley, A.M.: Including an Account of the Great Revival of Religion in Europe and America, of Which He Was the First and Chief Instrument.* Philadelphia: Parry Hall, 1793.

Collins, Vicki Tolar. "Perfecting a Woman's Life: Methodist Rhetoric and Politics in 'The Account of Hester Ann Rogers.'" Ph.D. dissertation, Auburn University, 1993.

Davey, Cyril James. *The Man Who Wanted the World: The Story of Thomas Coke.* London: Methodist Missionary Society, 1947.

Drew, Samuel. *The Life of the Rev. Thomas Coke, LL.D., Including in Details His Various Travels and Extraordinary Missionary Exertions, in England, Ireland, America, and the West-Indies.* London: T. Cordeux, 1817; New York: J. Soule & T. Mason, 1818.

Etheridge, John Wesley. *The Life of the Rev. Thomas Coke, D.C.L.* London: J. Mason, 1860.

Vickers, John A. "One-Man Band: Thomas Coke and the Origins of Methodist Missions." *Methodist History* 34 (1996): 135–47.

———. *Thomas Coke: Apostle of Methodism.* Nashville: Abingdon Press, 1969.

Conner, Walter Thomas
(1877–1952) *Baptist theologian, educator*

Sometimes dubbed "the people's theologian," Walter Thomas Conner translated a modest educational background into a position of respect and influence at the Southwestern Baptist Theological Seminary in Fort Worth, Texas. There, for nearly 40 years, Conner proclaimed a theology securely moored to the Southern Baptist roots from which he sprang but nevertheless conversant with some of the leading theological currents of his day. He was born on January 19, 1877, in Center, Arkansas (later Rowell, Arkansas), the son of Orlander Conner and Frances Jane Monk Conner. He grew up poor in Center, then Kingsland, Arkansas, and finally Tebo (later Tye), Texas, near Abilene. The public education he received as a child occupied only a few months of the year, leading Conner to observe wryly in later years that he "went to school enough each year to learn just about what [he] forgot the rest of the year."

Raised in a pious Southern Baptist family, Conner experienced a religious conversion when he was 17 years old while attending a revival meeting at a Methodist church. He was subsequently baptized in and became a member of a local Baptist church in November 1894. Soon afterward he began to consider seriously a vocation as a Christian minister, and he preached his first sermon in the fall of 1895. In 1898, Conner enrolled in Baylor University, though precarious financial circumstances prevented him from finishing at once. He had to leave the university after his freshman year and teach school for two years to support himself. At the same time, he was ordained a Baptist minister in the fall of 1899 and occupied the pulpits of Baptist churches in Tuscola and Caps, successively. Though he returned to Baylor in September 1901, he had to withdraw again two years later. He finally received a bachelor's degree in the spring of 1906. At the beginning of the summer that followed, he married Blanche Horne, with whom he had six children. Two years later he received a bachelor of theology degree from the newly established Southwestern Baptist Theological Seminary.

After his graduation, the seminary encouraged Conner to pursue a career in teaching. He subsequently added two years of graduate studies, first at Rochester Seminary in Rochester, New York, and then briefly at the University of Chicago. When he returned to Texas, he joined the faculty of the Southwestern Baptist Theological Seminary, recently relocated from Baylor to its new campus in Fort Worth, Texas. There he taught theology for nearly four decades, striving to establish a tradition of academic investigation and reflection in a denomination that had not always prized intellectual attainments. Although he never strayed far from traditional principles of Baptist orthodoxy, he chafed sometimes at the religious environment in which he found himself submerged. On one occasion, he mused in a private journal he kept and referred to as "Here and There":

> They tell us that orthodoxy means straight thinking. The orthodoxy that I have seen all my life was rather no thinking at all. It was an attitude of mind that accepted traditional doctrines, and then the mind, lest it should depart from what was accepted, committed suicide. Orthodoxy is an opiate to administer to young minds to guarantee that they will always be kept under control. Mind is a dangerous thing when it gets loose. It starts all kinds of uncomfortable things. It interferes with the established order and established interests.

Conner supplemented his work as a teacher of future Baptist ministers with an active writing career. He ultimately penned 15 books, characterized by an accessible writing style. He retired in 1949 and suffered a stroke that year from which he never completely recovered. He died on May 26, 1952.

Walter Thomas Conner labored mostly within the confines of a denomination in which the tra-

dition of an educated ministry was not yet securely fastened. He never strayed far from the verities of conservative Protestantism. Nevertheless, he approached theological discussions with an inquiring mind that separated him partially from the fundamentalist religious culture in which he lived his life.

Further Reading

Conner, W. T. *The Christ We Need.* Grand Rapids, Mich.: Zondervan Publishing House, 1938.

———. *The Cross in the New Testament.* Nashville: Broadman Press, 1954.

———. *Personal Christianity: Sermons.* Grand Rapids, Mich.: Zondervan Publishing House, 1937.

———. *A System of Christian Doctrine.* Nashville: Sunday School Board of the Southern Baptist Convention, 1924.

Givens, Jimmy McMath, Jr. "Christ as Hermeneutical Referent: an Analysis of the Extension of Christological Motifs Within the Theologies of A. H. Strong, E. Y. Mullins, and W. T. Conner." Ph.D. dissertation, Southwestern Baptist Theological Seminary, 2000.

Newman, Stewart A. *W. T. Conner: Theologian of the Southwest.* Nashville: Broadman Press, 1964.

Conwell, Russell Herman
(1843–1925) *Baptist minister, author*

Russell Herman Conwell, a lawyer turned preacher, was a prominent pastor and Christian speaker around the turn of the 20th century. He popularized a gospel of prosperity, which argued that God intended believers to be rich. He was born on February 15, 1843, in South Worthington, Massachusetts. His parents, Martin Conwell and Miranda Wickham Conwell, were Methodists and farmers. Conwell received his undergraduate education from Wilbraham Academy, a Methodist institution, and graduated in 1857. Thereafter he studied law at Yale College from 1861, but he left the following year to join the Union Army during the Civil War. Conwell was dismissed from the army in 1864. Charged with deserting his post at one point, he subsequently claimed to have been reinstated in time to fight and be wounded at the

Russell Herman Conwell's lecture "Acres of Diamonds" inspired many listeners to believe that God intended them to be prosperous. *(Library of Congress, Prints and Photographs Division LC-USZ62-110605)*

battle of Kennesau Mountain in the summer of that year. During this period, Conwell experienced a Christian conversion.

After the war, Conwell married Jennie Hayden in 1865, and this union produced two children before she died seven years later. Conwell also resumed his legal studies, though at Albany Law School in New York rather than Yale. After graduating in 1865, he established a law practice in Minneapolis, Minnesota, before he relocated in 1869 to Boston, where he practiced for the next 10 years. While he was working as a lawyer in Boston, Conwell had as a client MARY BAKER EDDY, the founder of Christian Science. After his first wife's death in 1872, he married Sarah Sanborn in 1874. During these years, Conwell supplemented his law practice with an active career as a speaker and a writer, as well as with participation in various lay religious activities, including teaching a popular

Sunday School class. He made a firm break from legal work in 1879, when, after he had temporarily filled the pulpit of a struggling church in Lexington, Massachusetts, the church asked him to remain permanently. The next year he was ordained and became the church's regular pastor.

Two years later, Grace Baptist Church in Philadelphia, Pennsylvania, persuaded Conwell to become its pastor, and with his guidance and powerful oratorical skills, the church soon became one of the largest Protestant churches in the country. When Conwell arrived, the church had around 90 members. A little more than a decade later, this membership had increased to 3,000, prompting the church to move into a new sanctuary, named the Temple, capable of seating 4,000. Conwell pioneered the idea of the "institutional church," which attempted to address not only the spiritual needs of the congregation but also the social needs of the community. Most significantly, Conwell oversaw the founding of Temple College in the mid-1880s to provide free evening classes to church members and Philadelphia workers generally, an institution that eventually became a full university and is said to have served more than 100,000 students by the time of Conwell's death. The church also ran two hospitals that provided free medical services to the poor.

Even as he presided over the explosive growth of the Baptist Temple, as his church came to be known, Conwell continued an active career as a lecturer and a writer. He became famous, especially, for the lecture "Acres of Diamonds," delivered thousands of times and eventually expanded into a best-selling inspirational book, published in 1915. In this and other lectures, Conwell developed a gospel of success, insisting that significant wealth was in the grasp of every man and woman.

> I say that you ought to get rich, and it is your duty to get rich. How many of my pious brethren say to me, "Do you, a Christian minister, spend your time going up and down the country advising young people to get rich, to get money?" "Yes, of course I do." They say, "Isn't that awful! Why don't you preach the gospel instead of preaching about man's making money?" "Because to make money hon-

estly is to preach the gospel." That is the reason. The men who get rich may be the most honest men you find in the community.

Conwell continued an active career as minister, lecturer, and writer into his 80s. He died in Philadelphia on December 6, 1925.

Russell Conwell advocated a gospel of wealth that has proved quite durable in American popular culture. World War I and the proliferation of urban social ills made this gospel less tenable by the second decade of the 20th century. Nevertheless, it experienced a revival in the last half of the 20th century through preachers such as NORMAN VINCENT PEALE, who resurrected and refitted Conwell's message for post–World War II society.

Further Reading

Bjork, Daniel W. *The Victorian Fight: Russell H. Conwell and the Crisis of American Individualism.* Washington, D.C.: University Press of America, 1979.

Burdette, Robert Jones. *The Modern Temple and Templars: A Sketch of the Life and Work of Russell H. Conwell.* New York: Silver, Burdett, 1894.

Burr, Agnes Rush. *Russell H. Conwell and His Work: One Man's Interpretation of Life.* Philadelphia: John C. Winston, 1917.

Conwell, Russell Herman. *Acres of Diamonds.* New York: Harper & Brothers, 1915.

Wimmer, John R. "Russell H. Conwell." In *Twentieth-Century Shapers of American Popular Religion.* Edited by Charles H. Lippy. New York: Greenwood Press, 1989.

———. "Symbols of Success: Russell H. Conwell and the Transformation of American Protestantism." Ph.D. dissertation, University of Chicago, 1992.

Coppin, Fanny Jackson
(1837–1913) *educator, religious leader*

One of the first African-American women in the United States to receive a college degree, Fanny Jackson Coppin became a leading educator of the late 19th century. Under her superintendence, the Institute for Colored Youth in Philadelphia, Pennsylvania, trained a generation of African-American teachers, artisans, and professionals. She was born a slave in 1837, in Washington, D.C., the daughter of Lucy Jackson. Her father's identify is unknown. When Fanny Jackson was 10 years old one of her aunts, Sarah Orr Clark, purchased the girl's freedom for $125 and sent her to live with another aunt, Elizabeth Orr, in New Bedford, Massachusetts.

In 1851, Jackson moved with the Orrs to Newport, Rhode Island. There, she found work as a domestic for the household of George Henry Calvert, the great grandson of Lord Baltimore, the founder of Maryland. With the earnings from her work, Jackson managed to hire a private tutor for one-hour lessons, three times a week. In addition, she took piano lessons and became the organist for the Colored Union Church in Newport. Toward the end of the six-year period when she worked for the Calverts, Jackson briefly attended the segregated public school system in Newport and then, around 1859, the Rhode Island State Normal School. By the following year, she had entered the ladies department of Oberlin College—an institution that accepted both women and blacks—and, within a year, was able to enroll in Oberlin's collegiate department.

At Oberlin, Jackson plunged into academic work, sustained by a vigorous determination to succeed, not merely for herself but for her race. She later recounted in her *Reminiscences of School Life and Hints on Teaching* the pressure that attended her work at the college: "I never rose to recite in my classes at Oberlin but I felt that I had the honor of the whole African race upon my shoulders." Jackson excelled as a student and began what would become a lifelong career as an educator by opening a night school for the freedmen who arrived in Oberlin at the beginning of the Civil War. She was also given teaching responsibilities in the preparatory division of the college. Jackson graduated in 1865 and was named class poet.

After her graduation, Fanny Jackson moved to Philadelphia, where she accepted a position as principal of the female division of the Institute for Colored Youth (ICY). She later narrated in her *Reminiscences* the cultural shock that this move occasioned, including a conversation she had with Oberlin's president, the famed revivalist CHARLES GRANDISON FINNEY, after she had taken the position in Philadelphia.

I had been so long in Oberlin that I had forgotten about my color, but I was sharply reminded of it when, in a storm of rain, a Philadelphia street car conductor forbid my entering a car that did not have on it "for colored people," so I had to wait in the storm until one came in which colored people could ride. This was my first unpleasant experience in Philadelphia. Visiting Oberlin not long after my work began in Philadelphia, President Finney asked me how I was growing in grace; I told him that I was growing as fast as the American people would let me.

On the departure of the ICY's principal in 1869 to become minister of Haiti, Fanny Jackson assumed leadership of the entire school, including both its male and its female divisions and their respective faculty. She presided over the ICY for more than 30 years, seeing it become one of the most prestigious centers of learning for African Americans in the country. Perhaps her greatest accomplishment was the addition of an industrial division to the school in 1889. Although Jackson had hoped to include professional-level training in disciplines such as engineering, the division ultimately had to content itself with more basic subjects such as carpentry, bricklaying, and dress making. Nevertheless, this vocational training attracted hundreds of new applicants to the school and helped its African-American graduates secure a place in the rising economic tides of Philadelphia.

In addition to her responsibilities as principal of ICY, Jackson played an active role in the affairs of the African Methodist Episcopal (A.M.E.) Church. She wrote regularly for the *Christian Recorder*, a publication of the church, and eventually, in 1881, married an A.M.E. minister, Levi Jenkins Coppin. Her husband seemed to have anticipated that Coppin would surrender her position at the ICY after their marriage, especially after he was transferred to the Bethel A.M.E. Church in Baltimore, Maryland. But Fanny Coppin insisted on remaining as principal of the school, and, within a few years, her husband was transferred to a small A.M.E. church in Philadelphia. Eventually, ill health caused her to retire in 1902, and she accompanied her husband to South Africa, where he served briefly as bishop of the 14th Episcopal Dis-

trict. By 1904, the Coppins had returned to the United States, where Levi Coppin became bishop of the Seventh Episcopal Church. Fanny Coppin's health, though, had declined precipitously, and she spent most of her remaining years confined in her home in Philadelphia. She died there on January 21, 1913.

Fanny Jackson Coppin escaped from poverty to become one of the 19th century's most famous educators. Uncommon determination melded with natural ability inspired her own studies as a young woman and then sustained her long career as a teacher and an administrator. The world that awaited the freed slaves in the years after the Civil War was frequently unwelcoming and hostile, but Fanny Coppin helped to equip a generation of African-American students with the skills necessary to forge a place in that world.

Further Reading

Coppin, Fanny Jackson. *Reminiscences of School Life and Hints on Teaching.* New York: G. K. Hall, 1995.

Coppin, Levi Jenkins. *Unwritten History.* Philadelphia, Pa.: A. M. E. Book Concern, 1919; New York: Negro Universities Press, 1968.

Perkins, Linda Marie. *Fanny Jackson Coppin and the Institute for Colored Youth, 1865–1902.* New York: Garland, 1987.

Corrigan, Michael Augustine
(1839–1902) *Catholic archbishop*

Archbishop of New York Michael Augustine Corrigan was an adept administrator of the largest Catholic archdiocese in the United Stated during the final years of the 19th century. He is best known as the champion of conservative Catholic values against attempts to infuse the Catholic Church with more liberal, Americanized values. Corrigan was born on August 13, 1839, in Newark, New Jersey, the son of Thomas Corrigan and Mary English Corrigan. His father was a wealthy businessman who was able to have Michael Corrigan educated in private schools. Corrigan studied at Saint Mary's College in Delaware from 1853 to 1855 and then at Mount Saint Mary's College in Maryland, where he received a B.A. in 1859. Afterward, he traveled to Rome and obtained a D.D. from the North American College in 1864.

On his return to the United States, Corrigan spent the next 12 years of his life as an academic, serving first as professor of dogmatic theology and sacred scripture at Seton Hall Seminary from 1864 to 1868, then as president of Seton Hall College from 1868 to 1876. While serving as president of Seton Hall, Corrigan was ordained bishop of Newark in 1873. He assumed the episcopacy at a time when the Catholic population in New Jersey was continuing to increase rapidly. Newark's new bishop soon consolidated control over the property of the diocese and instituted regular visitations of the priests in the diocese.

Corrigan's success in overseeing the affairs of the Newark diocese for seven years placed him in the position to be assigned to the more prestigious archdiocese of New York. He was initially appointed coadjutor of the archdiocese in 1880 with the right to succeed Cardinal John McCloskey of New York. During his five years as coadjutor, Corrigan introduced to the archdiocese of New York administrative reforms similar to those he had achieved in Newark. In addition, he helped to plan the Third Plenary Council of Baltimore in 1883–84. In 1885, Cardinal McCloskey died, and Corrigan assumed spiritual oversight of the New York archdiocese as its archbishop. During his years in New York, the archdiocese saw the creation of nearly 100 new parishes, 75 schools, and 24 new religious communities.

In the last decade of the 19th century, Catholics in the United States were increasingly divided between those eager to accommodate themselves to American values and social institutions and those conservatives who resisted these accommodations. Corrigan was a leader of the conservative majority, and he clashed prominently with the so-called Americanizing bishops over the matter of EDWARD McGLYNN, a priest in New York's largest parish, St. Stephen's. McGlynn advocated liberal social reforms and actively supported the mayoral campaign of Henry George in 1886. Corrigan deeply opposed McGlynn's progressive political activism. He eventually suspended McGlynn and appealed to Rome for a more decisive rebuke of the priest. When McGlynn refused to answer summons to

Rome and was excommunicated in the summer of 1887, controversy erupted in New York among supporters of McGlynn's progressivism.

Corrigan, for his part, viewed Edward McGlynn as representative of a deeper threat to traditional Catholic values in the form of what would later be called Americanism. He opposed relentlessly the efforts of Americanizers such as Archbishop JOHN IRELAND of Saint Paul, Minnesota, who advocated more rapid assimilation of Catholic immigrants into the institutions and cultural norms of American society. Ireland, for example, urged cooperative ventures between public school systems and Catholic parochial schools, which Corrigan

As archbishop of New York, Michael A. Corrigan championed conservative Catholic values. *(Library of Congress, Prints and Photographs Division LC-USZ62-106499)*

viewed as surrendering the peculiar values of traditional Catholic education. Corrigan criticized Ireland's Americanizing project relentlessly, and he opposed the foundation of the Catholic University of America in Washington, D.C., which he saw as a proposed citadel of Americanist heresy. In addition to his own efforts to oppose the religious and social program of individuals such as Ireland, Corrigan kept up a stream of communications with Rome, seeking support in his campaign against the Americanizers, and, in 1899, had significant vindication of his views when Pope Leo XIII issued the encyclical *Testem Benevolentiae*, which condemned Americanism as a heresy.

Michael Augustine Corrigan's role in the Americanist controversy has tended to obscure his successes as an ecclesiastical administrator. At a time when the ranks of the Catholic Church swelled with Catholic immigrants to the United States, Corrigan was adept at managing the institutional growth necessary to serve the growing number of Catholics in the New York area. But he is remembered primarily as a conservative and a traditionalist who opposed the acculturation of Catholics to what he viewed the overly secular values of American society. American Catholics would continue to wrestle with this issue long after Corrigan passed from the scene, but for a time, at least, he proved influential in resisting Catholic assimilation.

Further Reading

Andreassi, Anthony D. "'The Cunning Leader of a Dangerous Clique'? The Burtsell Affair and Archbishop Michael Augustine Corrigan." *Catholic Historical Review* 86 (October 2000): 620–39.

Curran, Robert Emmett. *Michael Augustine Corrigan and the Shaping of Conservative Catholicism in America, 1878–1902.* New York: Arno Press, 1978.

DiGiovanni, Stephen Michael. *Archbishop Corrigan and the Italian Immigrants.* Huntington, Ind.: Our Sunday Visitor, 1994.

Mahoney, Joseph F., and Peter J. Wosh. *The Diocesan Journal of Michael Augustine Corrigan, Bishop of Newark, 1872–1880.* Newark: New Jersey Historical Society, 1987.

Memorial of the Most Reverend Michael Augustine Corrigan, D.D., Third Archbishop of New York. New York: Cathedral Library Association, 1902.

Zwierlein, Frederick James. *Letters of Archbishop Corrigan to Bishop McQuaid, and Allied Documents.* Rochester, N.Y.: Art Print Shop, 1946.

Cotton, John
(1584–1652) *Puritan minister*

By the time he migrated to the Massachusetts Bay Colony in 1633, John Cotton had established a reputation as one of Puritanism's greatest preachers. Once transplanted to the New World, he added to this achievement a prolific writing career that made him a chief spokesperson for New England in the mid-17th century. He was born in Derby, England, on December 4, 1584, the son of Roland Cotton and Many Hurlbert Cotton. His father was a lawyer, and his family's financial circumstances were such as to allow him to attend Trinity College at Cambridge, where he matriculated at the youthful age of 13. He obtained a B.A. in 1603 and an M.A. in 1606 and then continued as a fellow in Emmanuel College, known for its hospitableness to Puritan sympathies. He was ordained in 1610 and became the vicar of Saint Botolph's Church in Boston, Lincolnshire, where he preached for the next two decades.

John Cotton proved more successful than most Puritan preachers of his day in adhering to nonconformist beliefs without drawing upon himself the hostility of Anglican authorities. Samuel Ward, one of his Puritan contemporaries, complained that Cotton did "nothing in the way of conformity, and yet hath his liberty, and I do everything that way, and cannot enjoy mine." Nevertheless, Cotton was suspended from his pulpit in 1615 and again in 1621, and as the third decade of the 17th century approached, he found himself increasingly at odds with the Anglican establishment. Cotton also suffered personal loss in 1631, when his wife of 18 years, Elizabeth Horrocks Cotton, died. The following year he married Sarah Hawkredd Story. His previous marriage had produced no children; his marriage to Sarah yielded six, including a daughter, Maria, who married IN-CREASE MATHER and became the mother of COTTON MATHER, two of New England's most famous Puritan preachers.

After the ascension of Charles I to the English throne in 1625, Puritan ministers in England, including John Cotton, found their positions increasingly more precarious. Consequently, many Puritans cast their attention to the New World. John Winthrop and his company departed for Massachusetts in 1630, and Cotton preached a sermon on the occasion of their leaving. He himself followed their course three years later and arrived in Boston in 1633, where he was soon installed as the teacher of the church of Boston.

Cotton's preaching emphasized the unconditional nature of God's gracious salvation of believers. He cautioned his audience against relying on the uprightness of their conduct as evidence that they were recipients of God's grace. He found an enthusiastic listener in ANNE MARBURY HUTCHINSON, who had migrated to Boston with her husband a year after Cotton had arrived and who had been influenced by Cotton's preaching while he was still in England. Hutchinson soon began to hold meetings in her home in which she discussed Cotton's sermons, adding to his voice her own in support of a steadfast focus on God's grace rather than on human works. For Hutchinson, the Holy Spirit dwelt in believers and the perception of this sacred presence was what allowed believers to know that they were the objects of God's grace. She soon began to contrast her focus on a "Covenant of Grace" with what she characterized as a "Covenant of Works." In particular, she insisted that those who measured their spiritual progress as believers by their adherence to various rules of moral conduct were hopelessly enslaved by a Covenant of Works.

Her opponents, in turn, branded Hutchinson and her followers Antinomians—opposers of moral and biblical law—and soon marshaled ministerial opinion against her. Hutchinson was eventually banished from the colony, and Cotton himself was scrutinized by his fellow ministers as a result of the Antinomian controversy. He ultimately distanced himself from the Hutchinson faction and tendered answers to questions submitted to him by his fellow New England ministers that convinced them of his orthodoxy.

The Antinomian controversy placed John Cotton temporarily at odds with Massachusetts orthodoxy, but on other issues, he was a leading defender

John Cotton's eloquent preaching made him perhaps the most well-known minister in the Massachusetts Bay Colony. *(Boston Public Library)*

of New England practices. Massachusetts's controversy with ROGER WILLIAMS, for example, found John Cotton solidly an ally of Puritan orthodoxy. The colony banished Williams, with the approval of Cotton, for his dissenting views, especially those regarding the appropriate relation of government and religion. Williams accused the Massachusetts Puritans of blurring the distinction between church and state, whereas Cotton rushed to the defense of the colony. In the years after Williams's banishment, the two men engaged in an extended written dispute over the issue, most famously represented by Williams's *The Bloudy Tenent of Persecution;* Cotton's *The Bloudy Tenent, Washed, and Made White in the Bloud of the Lambe;* and Williams's rebuttal, *The*

Bloudy Tenent Yet More Bloudy. Cotton also defended the Massachusetts Bay Colony from English critics of the congregational system of church government established in New England. In *The Way of the Churches of Christ in New-England,* published in 1645, Cotton supported this system.

By the time of his death in Boston on December 23, 1652, John Cotton had become one of the foremost representatives of New England Puritanism and had earned a place among its finest preachers. In the Massachusetts Bay Colony's tumultuous early years, as it sought to define its distinctive vision of government and religion, Cotton defended the colony's close alliance of church and state and its respect for the relative autonomy of individual churches. These were crucial pillars of the New England way, and John Cotton must be counted among their principal architects.

Further Reading

Cotton, John. *The Bloudy Tenent, Washed, and Made White in the Bloud of the Lambe.* London: Matthew Symmons, 1647; New York: Arno Press, 1972.

———. *The Way of the Congregational Churches Cleared* (1648), reprinted in *John Cotton on the Churches of New England,* edited by Larzer Ziff. Cambridge, Mass.: Harvard University Press, 1968.

Emerson, Everett. *John Cotton.* Rev. ed. Boston: Twayne Publishers, 1990.

Gallagher, Edward J. *Early Puritan Writers, A Reference Guide: William Bradford, John Cotton, Thomas Hooker, Edward Johnson, Richard Mather, Thomas Shepard.* Boston: G. K. Hall, 1976.

Polishook, Irwin H. *Roger Williams, John Cotton, and Religious Freedom: A Controversy in New and Old England.* Englewood Cliffs, N.J., Prentice-Hall, 1967.

Ziff, Larzer. *The Career of John Cotton: Puritanism and the American Experience.* Princeton, N.J.: Princeton University Press, 1962.

Coughlin, Charles Edward

(1891–1979) *Catholic priest, radio personality*

Father Charles Coughlin was the most prominent Catholic radio personality during the 1930s. He made a career out of railing, in Dickensian fashion, against "monied might," and he was for a time enormously influential in connecting with populist anxieties prompted by the Great Depression. Ultimately, though, his diatribes took on a decided anti-Semitic cast and Catholic authorities forced him to abandon his radio broadcasts. Coughlin was born on October 25, 1891, in Hamilton, Ontario, the son of Thomas Coughlin and Amelia Mahoney Coughlin. When he was 13 years old, Coughlin began preparations to become a priest by enrolling in Saint Michael's College in Toronto, a Catholic preparatory school and college from which he graduated with a B.A. in 1911. Thereafter he attended Saint Basil's Seminary in Toronto; he graduated in 1916 and was ordained as a priest that year.

Coughlin spent the first seven years of his life as a priest teaching at schools associated with the Basilian order. In 1923, however, he undertook work as a parish priest, serving as assistant pastor of Saint Leo's Church in Detroit, Michigan. From 1924 to 1926, he was pastor of the Catholic church in North Branch, Michigan. After these brief parish assignments, Coughlin was assigned to the parish in Royal Oak, Michigan, a suburb of Detroit, where he remained until his retirement in 1966. His church was named Shrine of the Little Flower, after Thérèse of Lisieux, who had recently been named a saint and was known as "The Little Flower of Jesus."

During his first year in Royal Oak, Coughlin was able to persuade a fellow Catholic to give him air time to broadcast his sermons over the radio. Coughlin's broadcasts were immediately successful. By 1930, CBS had picked up his program, *The Golden Hour of the Little Flower,* and through its network of stations gave Coughlin a weekly audience estimated at 40 million listeners at the peak of its popularity.

Although Coughlin's broadcast originally focused on religious and moral themes, with the advent of the Great Depression he turned his attention to economic subjects. Coughlin was quick to blame the depression and the general plight of American citizens caught in its grip on "predatory capitalists" who manipulated monetary markets to their own greedy ends. Father Coughlin saw government regulation of monetary policy as the only solution to the rapaciousness of these capitalists and originally viewed Franklin Delano Roosevelt as just the national leader who might muzzle the monetary tigers. The country, he believed, faced the stark option of "Roosevelt or ruin." Quite popular by the time of Roosevelt's election in 1932, Coughlin seems to have believed that he would be able to exert substantial influence within Roosevelt's administration. He founded the National Union for Social Justice in 1934 to advance issues of social justice, but he soon became disillusioned with Roosevelt when the president proved unwilling to grant Coughlin the influence he desired.

By 1936, Coughlin had turned decisively against Roosevelt, branding him the "great betrayer and liar . . . who promised to drive the money changers from the temple, [but] had succeeded [only] in driving the farmers from their homesteads and the citizens from their homes in the cities." The man who had welcomed Roosevelt as national savior four years before then asked Americans "to purge the man who claims to be a Democrat, from the Democratic party, and I mean Franklin Double-Crossing Roosevelt." Coughlin founded a newspaper, *Social Justice,* to advocate his own political vision, and—together with Gerald L. K. Smith, a Protestant minister who claimed to have inherited the political mantle of the recently assassinated Huey P. Long—helped to form the Union Party, with the little-known North Dakota congressman William Lemke as its presidential candidate. Coughlin promised that he would abandon his public career if Lemke did not receive at least 9 million votes, and when Roosevelt prevailed in the presidential election of 1936 and Lemke drew less than a tenth of the votes Coughlin had prognosticated, the radio priest disbanded both the Union Party and his own National Union for Social Justice and briefly retired from public life.

By 1938, however, Couglin's newspaper, *Social Justice,* and his radio broadcasts had begun to find new enemies against which to rail, and these enemies were overwhelmingly Jewish. In his new, anti-Semitic incarnation, the radio priest increasingly portrayed Adolf Hitler and nazism in a favorable light, while presenting Jewish communists (the two labels were virtually synonymous in his mind) as the real enemies of America. When he continued to publish and broadcast these positions after the United States had entered World War II, the Roosevelt administration suspended mailing privileges for Couglin's newspaper and warned the priest's ecclesiastical superior, Archbishop Edward Mooney, that Coughlin risked indictment for sedition if he did not curtail his public statements. In the spring of 1942, Coughlin announced that he was submitting to the wishes of church authorities and abandoning his public activities. He thereafter confined himself to his work as a parish priest until his retirement in 1966. He died on October 27, 1979, in Bloomfield Hills, Michigan.

In the years leading up to World War II, Father Charles Coughlin enjoyed immense popularity as a radio preacher, as a prophet not so much of religious truth as of economic justice. He learned, however, that popularity does not always equal political influence. President Franklin Roosevelt was able to keep Coughlin at arm's length from his own New Deal agenda, and Coughlin's radio popularity crashed against Roosevelt's even more formidable political popularity. This embarrassment alone might have discredited Coughlin, but his later anti-Semitism left a permanent stain on his historical reputation.

Further Reading

Athans, Mary Christine. *The Coughlin-Fahey Connection: Father Charles E. Coughlin, Father Denis Fahey, C.S.Sp., and Religious Anti-Semitism in the United States, 1936–1942.* New York: Peter Lang, 1991.

Brinkley, Alan. *Voices of Protest: Huey Long, Father Coughlin, and the Great Depression.* New York: Vintage Books, 1983.

Coughlin, Charles E. *Father Coughlin: Selected Discourses.* Philadelphia: Educational Guild, 1932.

———. *Father Coughlin's Radio Sermons.* Baltimore: Knox and O'Leary, 1931.

Marcus, Sheldon. *Father Coughlin: The Tumultuous Life of the Priest of the Little Flower.* Boston: Little, Brown, 1973.

Mugglebee, Ruth. *Father Coughlin: The Radio Priest, of the Shrine of the Little Flower.* Garden City, N.Y.: Garden City Publishing, 1933.

Tull, Charles J. *Father Coughlin and the New Deal.* Syracuse, N.Y.: Syracuse University Press, 1965.

Warren, Donald. *Charles Coughlin, the Father of Hate Radio.* New York: Free Press, 1996.

Crosby, Fanny
(Frances Jane Crosby)
(1820–1915) *hymn writer, poet*

One of the most prolific hymn writers of the 19th century, Fanny Crosby wrote the lyrics to approximately 9,000 hymns over the course of four decades. Many of them are still included in modern hymnbooks. She was born Frances Jane Crosby on March 24, 1820, in Putnam County, New York, the daughter of John Crosby and Mercy Crosby. In the second month of her life she contracted an eye infection. The local doctor was away at the time, and a man posing as a physician prescribed a mustard poultice for her eyes, which, when applied, permanently blinded Crosby. Her father died as well in her first year, and while her mother worked, Crosby's grandmother became her chief guardian. Intellectually precocious as a child, Crosby had memorized great portions of the Bible, including the Pentateuch and the gospels, by the time she was 10 years old. At the age of 15 Crosby entered the New York Institution for the Blind, where she remained first as a student and later as a teacher of grammar, rhetoric, and history for nearly a quarter of a century. In her student years she exhibited skill as a poet, and after she became a teacher, she published several volumes of poetry, beginning with *The Blind Girl and Other Poems* (1844). She also wrote the lyrics to a number of popular secular songs, including "Rosalie, the Prairie Flower"; "Glad to Get Home"; "Proud World, Good-bye"; and "There's Music in the Air."

Crosby experienced a religious conversion in the fall of 1850, while attending the Methodist Broadway Tabernacle in New York City. Later that decade, she finally left the New York Institute for the Blind on her marriage in 1858 to Alexander Van Alsteine, Jr., who was also a blind teacher at the New York Institute. This union produced one child, who died soon after birth, the only one Crosby would bear. The couple eventually separated and lived apart until the death of Van Alsteine—whose name Crosby declined to take—in 1902.

In the mid-1860s, Crosby met William Bradbury, a hymn writer who had formed his own company a few years earlier to publish the hymns he wrote. Bradbury encouraged Crosby to write hymns—primarily for Sunday School—and over the next four decades, thousands of lyrics spilled from her pen. Bradbury, who gave Crosby her start as a hymn writer, died several years afterward, but Crosby's reputation as a lyricist grew steadily. Though her earliest writing aimed to fill a need for hymns to be used in Sunday School, she soon became associated with revivalists such as DWIGHT LYMAN MOODY and his music leader, IRA DAVID SANKEY, who used Crosby's lyrics in their revival campaigns. She wrote prodigiously, sometimes as many as six or seven hymns a day. Nevertheless, her most enduring work was done early in her career as a hymn writer: within 10 years she had written most of the lyrics that would secure her prominent place in the history of American hymnody. She lived into the 20th century, continuing to write and proving popular as an evangelical speaker. Crosby died at the age of 94 on February 12, 1915, in Bridgeport, Connecticut. One of her most famous hymns, "All the Way My Savior Leads Me," written 35 years previously, is a fitting epitaph for her long career as a gospel hymn writer:

> And all the way my Savior leads me, oh the fullness
>   of His Love,
> Perfect rest in me is promised in my Father's house
>   above.
> When my spirit clothed immortal wings its flight to
>   realms of day,
> This my song through endless ages, Jesus led me all
>   the way.

Late 19th-century revivalism left a permanent mark on evangelical Christian faith in the century that followed, partially through its music. And of all the hymn writers whose lyrics and melodies gave musical content to the spirit of revivalism, none occupied a more commanding place of influence than Fanny Crosby, the blind poet of gospel hymns. Time has swallowed up much of her work, but many of her lyrics still populate hymnbooks and speak to Christian believers nearly a century after her death.

Further Reading

Albertson, Wayne Frederick. "Narcissism and Destiny: A Study of the Life and Work of Fanny J. Crosby." Ph.D. dissertation, Princeton Theological Seminary, 1992.

Crosby, Fanny. *Fanny Crosby's Life-Story.* New York: Every Where, 1903.

Harvey, Bonnie C. *Fanny Crosby.* Minneapolis: Bethany House Publishers, 1999.

Hearn, Chester. *Safe in the Arms of Jesus: The Story of Fanny Crosby.* Port Washington, Pa.: Christian Literature Crusade, 1998.

Loveland, John. *Blessed Assurance: The Life and Hymns of Fanny J. Crosby.* Nashville: Broadman Press, 1978.

Miller, Basil William. *Fanny Crosby: Singing I Go.* Grand Rapids, Mich.: Zondervan Publishing House, 1950.

Ruffin, Bernard. *Fanny Crosby.* Philadelphia: United Church Press, 1976; Ulrichsville, Ohio: Barbour, 1995.

Crummell, Alexander

(1819–1898) *Episcopal priest, missionary, educator*

A leading African-American intellectual of the 19th century, Alexander Crummell pursued an eclectic career across three continents. As a priest, a missionary, a college professor, and a popular writer and lecturer, Crummell became one of the foremost African-American leaders of his day. He was born on March 3, 1818, in New York City, the son of Boston Crummell, former slave, and Charity Hicks Crummell. A steady ambition to gain education characterized Crummell's youth. After receiving his early education from the African Free School in Manhattan and then from a high school Crummell's father had established, Crummell and several other companions briefly attended the Noyes Academy in Canaan, New Hampshire, in 1835. Soon after their arrival, however, nearby residents destroyed the racially integrated school by hitching teams of oxen to the school building and dragging it into a swamp. Crummell subsequently

attended the Oneida Institute in New York. During his studies there, he had a conversion experience and determined to prepare himself for the priesthood in the Episcopal Church. When he applied to the General Theological Seminary in New York, though, he was denied admission because of his race and had to content himself thereafter with private studies with ministers in Providence and Boston and with attendance at lectures at Yale College. While in New Haven, he helped form a new black parish, named Saint Luke's, in 1840. He was eventually ordained a deacon in 1842 and, two years later, an Episcopal priest.

Crummell's early years as a priest were spent ministering to congregations in Providence, Rhode Island, and Philadelphia, Pennsylvania, and, beginning in 1847, New York City. It appears that during this period (probably in 1841) he married Sarah Mabitt Elson, with whom he had at least five children. The facilities of Crummell's church in New York, the Church of the Messiah, were destroyed by fire in 1847, and he subsequently traveled to England to raise money for new facilities, and his family soon joined him. There, he lectured frequently to raise funds, but he also arranged to be admitted to Queen's College, Cambridge, where he received a bachelor's degree in 1853.

That same year Crummell decided to transplant his family to a new continent, this time to Liberia, West Africa, where he undertook service as a missionary of the Protestant Episcopal Church of America. He clashed repeatedly with his Episcopal superior, John Payne, a white man from Virginia. Crummell appears to have harbored ambitions of becoming the bishop of an independent black Episcopal church in Liberia and of playing an important role in Liberia, which he wanted to become an independent black Christian republic. Frustrated in these ambitions, Crummell resigned his post as a missionary and then taught school for a time in Cape Palmas before returning to the United States in 1861 to raise funds for the colonization of Liberia. After returning to Liberia in 1863, he served for a time as a professor at the newly established Liberia College, but when he departed abruptly in 1865 to retrieve his daughters, whom he had left in the States, the college dismissed him. On his return to Liberia, Crummell remained for a time, establishing a church in New Georgia in the spring of 1867 and engaging in local missionary activities. Finally, though, in late summer of 1871 he was forced to leave Liberia when the president, Edward James Roye, was assassinated.

In the United States once again, Crummell became the rector of Saint Mary's Church in Washington, D.C., in 1872 and subsequently organized and built facilities for a separate congregation known as St. Luke's Church. The new church held its first service in the fall of 1879, and Crummell served there as minister until 1894. His first wife died in 1878. She and Crummell were living apart at the time and had apparently been estranged for an extended period. He subsequently married Jennie Simpson in 1880. He retired from his ministerial position in 1895 but continued an active speaking and writing career. At one speaking event at Wilberforce University, W. E. B. Du Bois met Crummell, whom he subsequently memorialized in *The Souls of Black Folk* (1903):

> Instinctively I bowed before this man, as one bows before the prophets of the world. Some seer he seemed, that came not from the crimson Past or the gray To-come, but from the pulsing Now,—that mocking world which seemed to me at once so light and dark, so splendid and sordid.

The year after this meeting, Crummell organized the American Negro Academy to encourage African-American literary, artistic, and scholarly activities. He died on September 10, 1898, in Red Bank, New Jersey.

Possessed of copious ambition and significant ability, Alexander Crummell frequently found his aspirations frustrated, from the days when he labored to obtain an education in a society that deemed him unfit by reason of his race, to his attempts to secure a prominent place in the affairs of Liberia. But he possessed in equal measure a determination to find new avenues to substitute for those blocked before. The career of his life, accordingly, was characterized by sudden halts and abrupt turnings, but from them he emerged an important intellectual influence for the African-American community.

Further Reading

Crummell, Alexander. *Civilization and Black Progress: Selected Writings of Alexander Crummell on the South.* Edited by J. R. Oldfield. Charlottesville: Published for the Southern Texts Society by the University Press of Virginia, 1995.

———. *Destiny and Race: Selected Writings, 1840–1898: Alexander Crummell.* Edited by Wilson Jeremiah Moses. Amherst: University of Massachusetts Press, 1992.

———. *The Future of Africa.* New York: C. Scribner, 1862; New York: Negro Universities Press, 1969.

———. *The Greatness of Christ, and Other Sermons.* New York: T. Whittaker, 1882.

Ferris, William Henry. *Crummell: An Apostle of Negro Culture.* Washington, D.C.: The Academy, 1920; New York: Arno Press, 1969.

Moses, Wilson Jeremiah. *Alexander Crummell: A Study of Civilization and Discontent.* New York: Oxford University Press, 1989.

Oldfield, J. R. *Alexander Crummell (1819–1898) and the Creation of an African-American Church in Liberia.* Lewiston, N.Y.: E. Mellen Press, 1990.

Rigsby, Gregory U. *Alexander Crummell: Pioneer in Nineteenth-Century Pan-African Thought.* New York: Greenwood Press, 1987.

Cushing, Richard James
(1895–1970) *Catholic cardinal*

A popular Catholic archbishop and cardinal, Richard Cushing became known for his outgoing and approachable manner and his support of Catholic missions. His prominence as a Catholic leader was enhanced by his close relationship with the Kennedy family: he presided over the marriage and the funeral of John F. Kennedy, and he delivered the prayer at Kennedy's presidential inauguration. Richard James Cushing was born on August 23, 1895, in South Boston, Massachusetts, the son of Patrick Cushing and Mary Dahill Cushing. He attended Boston College from 1913 to 1915 and then transferred to St. John's Seminary in Brighton, Massachusetts, where he graduated with an M.A. in 1921. He was ordained a priest that same year.

Soon after his ordination, Cushing was appointed to the staff of the Society for the Propagation of the Faith, a Catholic mission organization. This appointment nurtured in Cushing a lifelong dedication to missionary efforts, which would, for example, prompt him to take an instrumental role in the formation in 1958 of the Society of Saint James the Apostle, a Latin American missionary endeavor. On the staff of the Society for the Propagation of the Faith, Cushing proved himself a gifted advocate of missionary efforts and an even more gifted mission fund-raiser; as a result, in 1928 he was named director of the diocesan office of this organization, where he remained until 1939. That year Cushing received an appointment as auxiliary bishop of Boston. Five years later he was named administrator of the archdiocese and, in November 1944, archbishop of Boston. Pope John XXIII elevated Cushing to the college of cardinals in 1958.

Richard Cushing assumed responsibility of the Boston archdiocese at a time when the Catholic population of the city had increased dramatically. He responded to this growth by increasing the number of parishes in the archdiocese by a third, as well as by overseeing the construction of new schools and hospitals. Yet his more enduring impact on Boston had perhaps less to do with these more tangible features of ecclesiastical life than with his own public character. In contrast with the austere personas of his predecessors, his approachable manner and his devotion to lay participation in Catholic affairs quickly made a name for him. He gave an avuncular face to Catholicism by broadcasting Catholic ceremonies via radio and later television. He also authored a variety of popular religious verse. Bostonians might see him officiating over a Catholic ceremony, but they might also catch a glimpse of him posing for cameras with a group of nuns he had assembled for an expedition to a baseball game.

At the same time, of course, Cushing cultivated relationships with prominent Massachusetts Catholics that one might expect of an archbishop. Perhaps most noteworthy of these was his relationship with Joseph P. Kennedy and Rose Kennedy, and later with their son John F. Kennedy. Cushing worked with Joseph and Rose Kennedy to support the cause of mentally handicapped children, and his friendship with John F. Kennedy made him a prominent presence in the Kennedys' life: Cushing officiated at John F. Kennedy's marriage to Jacqueline Bouvier in 1953 and supported Kennedy's presidential campaign in 1960. When Kennedy was elected the first Roman Catholic president, Cushing delivered a prayer at his inauguration. Still later, when an assassin's bullet struck Kennedy, Cushing presided over the slain president's funeral.

Throughout his long career as a Catholic leader, Cushing demonstrated himself a remarkable fund-raiser for Catholic concerns. He did not, however, always demonstrate an equal facility for

Cardinal Richard Cushing's personable manner gave a less authoritarian face to Catholic leadership during the middle years of the 20th century. *(Library of Congress, Prints and Photographs Division LC-USZ62-123871)*

managing money, and in his final years the Boston archdiocese struggled with debt. Cushing remained popular when he retired from the archdiocese in September 1970. He died two months later, on November 2, 1970, in Boston.

Richard Cushing championed a new style of Catholic leadership in the United States, less tinged with the austere severity of his predecessors and more accessible to lay Catholics. But he never exchanged his essential conservativism for more liberal vestments. He remained an outspoken opponent of communism and of birth control, as well as a friend of Senator Joseph McCarthy and the John Birch Society. In these political and moral commitments, he did not stray far from the common sensibilities of his generation. But he paired these commitments with equally vigorous dedication to the cause of the poor and the unchurched.

Further Reading

Cutler, John Henry. *Cardinal Cushing of Boston.* New York: Hawthorn Books, 1970.

Dever, Joseph. *Cushing of Boston, a Candid Portrait.* Boston: Bruce Humphries, 1965.

Devine, M. C. *The World's Cardinal.* Boston: St. Paul Editions, 1964.

Fenton, John H. *Salt of the Earth: An Informal Profile of Richard Cardinal Cushing.* New York: Coward-McCann, 1965.

Garneau, James Francis. "'Commandos for Christ': The Foundation of the Missionary Society of St. James the Apostle and the 'Americanism' of the 1960s." Ph.D. dissertation, Catholic University of America, 2000.

Damien, Father
(Joseph de Veuster, the Leper Priest of Molokai)
(1840–1889) *Catholic missionary*

Known as "the Leper Priest of Molokai," Father Damien became internationally prominent as a Catholic missionary to Hawaii who devoted himself to the physical and spiritual care of a leper colony on the island of Molokai. The disease whose ravages he attended eventually consumed him as well. Father Damien was born Joseph de Veuster on January 3, 1840, in Tremeloo, Belgium, the son of François de Veuster, a farmer, and Anne Catherine de Veuster.

In 1859, inspired by his brother, a Catholic priest, Joseph took the name *Damien* and began religious study that led to his taking vows as a brother of the Sacred Hearts of Jesus and Mary the following year. When his brother's plans to become a missionary to the Hawaiian Islands were aborted after he contracted typhus, Damien asked to be sent in his place. Damien arrived in Honolulu in the spring of 1864, was promptly ordained a priest, and ministered as a missionary for the next nine years.

As early as 1864, the island of Molokai had been made a leper colony, and by 1873, Hawaiian authorities had stepped up efforts to exile lepers to the island. That year, Damien heard his bishop express regret that the Molokai lepers had no priest and immediately asked to be sent there himself. On his arrival in Molokai, he discovered the pitiful condition of its inhabitants and undertook at once to relieve, insofar as possible, their physical suffer-

ings and to minister to them spiritually. Over the next 16 years, he labored to build medical facilities, schools, orphanages, and churches for the Molokai lepers, even as he besieged those with authority over the island for support to expand this work. So impressive were his sacrifices and his accomplishments on Molokai that when Princess Liliuokalani visited the island in 1881 she made Damien a knight of the Royal Order of Kalakaua.

Within a few years after his arrival on the island, Father Damien began to show signs that he had contracted leprosy. By the mid-1880s, his symptoms were severe. Nevertheless, the news that Damien had become a leper himself inspired renewed support for his mission to Molokai. Though he could frequently be disagreeable to those who assisted his labors on Molokai, his presence eventually drew additional missionaries to the island. Ira Barnes Dutton, referred to simply as Brother Joseph, was a lay brother who joined Father Damien in 1886 and eventually continued Damien's work well into the 20th century. Other nuns and priests assisted the Molokai mission. Father Damien succumbed to the disease of leprosy and died at Molokai on April 15, 1889. A short time before his death, he wrote to his brother Pamphile: "I am gently going to my grave. It is the will of God, and I thank Him very much for letting me die of the same disease and in the same way as my lepers. I am very satisfied and very happy."

After Damien's death, unseemly religious jealousies inspired by his renown produced rumors that his character had been less than saintly. One accusation, in particular, produced a memorable coda to Damien's life. Charles McEwen Hyde, a prominent Presbyterian minister in Honolulu, wrote a letter critical of Damien that found its way into the press. The letter, charging Damien with being "a coarse, dirty man, head-strong and bigoted," also included the scurrilous accusation that "[h]e was not a pure man in his relations with women, and the leprosy of which he died should be attributed to his vices and carelessness." This attack prompted a defense of Damien penned by Robert Louis Stevenson, who had visited Molokai shortly after Damien's death. Stevenson, himself nominally Presbyterian, accused Hyde of clothing himself in relative opulence in Honolulu, while Damien cast his lot with the miserable condition of the Molokai lepers:

> [W]hen we have failed, and another has succeeded; when we have stood by, and another has stepped in; when we sit and grow bulky in our charming mansions, and a plain, uncouth peasant steps into the battle, under the eyes of God, and succours the afflicted, and consoles the dying, and is himself afflicted in his turn, and dies upon the field of honour—the battle cannot be retrieved as your unhappy irritation has suggested. It is a lost battle, and lost for ever.

Stevenson imagined that a hundred years after Damien's death, he would be recognized as a

Father Damien, "the Leper Priest of Molokai," is pictured here with members of his mission on the island of Molokai in Hawaii. (*Library of Congress, Prints and Photographs Division LC-USZ62-103862*)

saint and Hyde would have been forgotten. In this, Stevenson was close to the truth. Subsequent investigations exonerated Damien of Hyde's charges and Hyde himself was only remembered for the nasty letter that inspired Stevenson's defense of the Leper Priest of Molokai. By the beginning of the 21st century, the process of naming Father Damien a saint had not been completed, but it was well under way. In 1995, Pope John Paul II beatified Damien, an important step in the recognition of him as a saint.

Further Reading

Beevers, John. *A Man for Now: The Life of Damien De Veuster, Friend of Lepers.* Garden City, N.Y.: Doubleday, 1973.

Bunson, Margaret. *Father Damien: The Man and His Era.* Rev. ed. Huntington, Ind.: Our Sunday Visitor Publishing Division, 1997.

Daws, Gavan. *Holy Man: Father Damien of Molokai.* New York: Harper & Row, 1973.

Dutton, Charles Judson. *The Samaritans of Molokai: The Lives of Father Damien and Brother Dutton Among the Lepers.* New York: Dodd, Mead, 1932.

Englebert, Omer. *The Hero of Molokai: Father Damien, Apostle of the Lepers.* Translated by Benjamin T. Crawford. Boston: St. Paul Editions, 1962.

Eynikel, Hilde. *Molokai: The Story of Father Damien.* Translated by Lesley Gilbert. New York: Alba House, 1999.

Farrow, John. *Damien, the Leper.* New York: Image Books, 1999.

Roos, Ann. *Man of Molokai: The Life of Father Damien.* Philadelphia: Lippincott, 1943.

Stewart, Richard. *Leper Priest of Moloka'i: The Father Damien Story.* Honolulu: University of Hawai'i Press, 2000.

Davies, Samuel
(1723–1761) *Presbyterian minister*

Samuel Davies was a Presbyterian minister who, in scarcely more than a decade of service, forged a place for Presbyterianism in Virginia. Before an early death, he also added to this career the titles of college president, poet, and hymn writer. He was born on November 3, 1723, in New Castle County, Delaware. His Parents, David Davies and Martha Thomas Davies, were farmers, who were able to secure for their son an education at an academy at Fagg's Manor, Pennsylvania, of which Samuel Blair was the master. By 1746, Samuel Davies had been licensed to preach by the New Castle Presbytery, an organization of "New Light" Presbyterians—that is, those who had been imbued with the spirit of revivalism embodied by the Great Awakening. In Davies's first year as a preacher, he married Sarah Kirkpatrick; Sarah's death during childbirth the following year severed this marital union. Davies noted the tragedy in his Bible: "Separated from her by Death & bereaved of an abortive Son Sep. 15."

Early in 1747, after a probationary period as an itinerant preacher, Davis was ordained by the New Castle Presbytery to engage in itinerant preaching in Virginia. Davies concentrated his work in Hanover Country and eventually settled permanently there in 1748. The same year he married again, this time Jane Holt, with whom he would have six children, one of whom—a daughter—died in infancy. Jane Holt Davies, or "Chara" as Samuel preferred to call her, became a topic in some of Davies's poetry. Of their courtship he wrote:

> *Chara,* beneath thy Influence I felt
> The charming Flame; my Soul was taught to melt
> In Ecstasies unknown, and soon began
> To put the Stoic off, and soften into Man.

The Anglican Church was established by law in Virginia and Davies had to obtain a license to preach from state officials. Though he was a minister of a dissenting faith, Davies exhibited erudition, eloquence, and a courteous demeanor that secured him a measure of acceptance by authorities who might otherwise have harried his preaching ministry with official disapproval. In fact, over the course of an energetic decade, Davies planted seven Presbyterian churches in Virginia and helped form a presbytery for the state.

During his years in Virginia, Samuel Davies combined the work of a pastoral and preaching ministry with a career as a poet and hymn writer. More than 90 of his poems have survived; the main portion was published in 1752 as *Miscellaneous Poems, Chiefly on Divine Topics*. At a time when many American churches sang only psalms, Davies contributed to a growing body of sacred hymns and encouraged their use in church services. One of the hymns written by Davies, "Great God of Wonders!" still finds a place in some Presbyterian and other Protestant hymn collections.

A little more than a decade after Davies began his ministerial career, the College of New Jersey (later Princeton University) asked him to become its president. Aaron Burr had been president until his death in 1757 and had been succeeded by the great Congregationalist preacher JONATHAN EDWARDS, who died within four months of assuming the presidency. When the trustees of the college first invited Davies to assume the vacant post in the summer of 1758, he refused, unwilling to surrender his pastoral ministry in Hanover. Over the next year, Davies continued to reject the college's overtures, until finally in the summer of 1759 he agreed to assume the presidency. Though he might have preferred to remain in Virginia, he became convinced that the call of God might lead him to remote places. "My life . . . I should look upon as secured to God and the Public: and the Service of God and Mankind is not a *local* Thing in my View: Wherever it appears to me I may perform it to the greatest Advantage, There, I hope, I should chuse to fix my Residence, whether in Hanover, Princeton, or even Lapland or Japan." The residence that Davies ultimately fixed in New Jersey proved only temporary, however. He died of pneumonia on February 4, 1761, at the age of 37.

Samuel Davies was one of the most influential Presbyterians of his day, though his public career lasted little more than a decade. He combined the erudition that Presbyterians wished to see in their ministers with the evangelistic fervor of a revivalist. To these qualities he added poetic eloquence and leadership ability. In all, he left an enduring legacy to southern Protestantism.

Further Reading

Bodeau, Carol Ann. "Faces on the Frontier: Indian Images from Colonial Virginia." Ph.D. dissertation, University of California, Davis, 1996.

Davies, Samuel. *Collected Poems*. Edited by Richard Beale Davis. Gainesville, Fla.: Scholars' Facsimiles & Reprints, 1968.

———. *The Reverend Samuel Davies Abroad: The Diary of a Journey to England and Scotland, 1753–55*. Edited by George William Pilcher. Urbana: University of Illinois Press, 1967.

———. *Sermons on Important Subjects*. New York: Dayton & Saxton, 1841.

Pilcher, George William. "Samuel Davies and the Instruction of Negroes in Virginia." *Virginia Magazine of Biography and History* 74 (1966): 293–300.

———. *Samuel Davies: Apostle of Dissent in Colonial Virginia*. Knoxville: University of Tennessee Press, 1971.

Davis, Andrew Jackson
(1826–1910) *spiritualist*

The most prominent spiritualist of 19th-century America, Andrew Jackson Davis produced works that became an important resource for the spread of spiritualism. The "Seer of Poughkeepsie," as he was called, was also a philosopher, whose attempts to explain the underlying nature of reality provided a theoretical underpinning for the spiritualism movement. Davis was born on August 11, 1826, in Blooming Grove, New York, the son of Samuel Davis and his wife, whose name is unknown. Davis's father earned a living partially as a shoemaker, and Davis himself was apprenticed for a time to this trade.

In his teenage years, Davis was introduced to mesmerism techniques and discovered that he had clairvoyant powers while in a trance. He claimed the ability to offer medical diagnoses of subjects he observed in a trance state, stating he could see their internal organs as though their bodies were partially transparent to his gaze. Soon, he declared that in visionary states he was able to travel to spiritual planes of existence and to converse with famous historical figures such as the Greek physician Galen and the 18th-century Swedish mystic, philosopher, and theologian Emanuel Swedenborg. Davis later incorporated aspects of Swedenborg's thought into his own reflections about the nature of the cosmos, such as its emphasis on love and wisdom as the organizing principles of the universe.

In 1847, Davis produced a compilation of lectures he delivered while in hypnotic trances, *The Principles of Nature, Her Divine Revelations, and a Voice to Mankind*. The 21-year-old became a sensation among spiritualists on the basis of this first book. Though he claimed not to have read the work of Swedenborg, *The Principles of Nature* appeared to be significantly influenced by the Swedish mystic's thought. Whatever its intellectual debts, Davis's book prophesied a coming commerce of spirits:

> It is a truth that spirits commune with one another while one is in the body and the other in the higher spheres—and this, too, when the person in the body is unconscious of the influx, and hence cannot be convinced of the fact; and this truth will ere long present itself in the form of a living demonstration. And the world will hail with delight the ushering in of that era when the interiors of men will be opened, and the spiritual communion will be established.

The year after publication of *The Principles of Nature*, Davis married Catherine DeWolfe Dodge, a wealthy divorcée. She died five years later and Davis subsequently married Mary Fenn Robinson in 1855. This marriage lasted nearly 30 years, until Davis eventually concluded that his wife was not his true soul mate and that he was therefore obliged to divorce her. The year after his 1884 divorce, he married Della E. Markham.

In the years after the publication of his first book, Davis briefly published his own periodical, *Univercolum and Spiritual Philosopher*, from 1847 to 1849. He produced a more substantial work in the following decade, when his five-volume treatise, *The Great Harmonia*, appeared from 1850 to 1855. This work developed his "Harmonial Philosophy," which posited the existence of spheres of existence through which souls passed after death, climaxing in the abode of those made finally perfect, called Summerland. These spheres, together with the natural order, were emanations from the Great Celestial Center, or God, the source of what Davis identified in Swedenborgian fashion as the twin principles of love and wisdom.

Late in his life, the Poughkeepsie seer added to his career as a writer and a lecturer a vocation as a physician. He obtained a medical degree from New York City's United States Medical College in 1886, and he practiced medicine thereafter in Boston, where he also operated a bookstore. He died on January 13, 1910, in Boston.

Andrew Jackson Davis was 19th-century spiritualism's principal philosopher. He labored to draw spiritualism out of the narrow confines of the séance room into the broader world of religious and philosophic contemplation. He did not achieve notable success in this venture, though his works continue to supply part of the theoretical apparatus of at least some 21st-century spiritualists.

Further Reading

Braude, Ann. *Radical Spirits: Spiritualism and Women's Rights in Nineteenth-Century America.* 2d ed. Bloomington: Indiana University Press, 2001.

Davis, Andrew Jackson. *Beyond the Valley.* Boston: Colby & Rich, 1885.

———. *The Harmonial Philosophy: A Compendium and Digest of the Works of Andrew Jackson Davis.* London: W. Rider & Son, 1917.

———. *The Magic Staff: An Autobiography.* New York: J. S. Brown, 1857.

Delp, Robert W. "Andrew Jackson Davis and Spiritualism." In *Pseudo-Science and Society in Nineteenth-Century America.* Edited by A. Wrobel. Lexington: University Press of Kentucky, 1987.

Moore, James Lowell. *Introduction to the Writings of Andrew Jackson Davis.* Boston: Christopher Publishing House, 1930.

Morita, Sally Jean. "Modern Spiritualism and Reform in America." Ph.D. dissertation, University of Oregon, 1995.

Schneider, Herbert F. *Writings of Andrew Jackson Davis: A Resumé.* Indianapolis, Ind.: Summit Publications, 1980.

Day, Dorothy

(1897–1980) *cofounder of the Catholic Worker movement*

After becoming a Catholic in her early 30s, Dorothy Day became the most influential lay

Dorothy Day helped found the Catholic Worker movement. *(Library of Congress, Prints and Photographs Division LC-USZ62-111099)*

woman in America, lending her voice to the cause of social justice. With a fellow social activist, ARISTIDE PETER MAURIN, Day cofounded the Catholic Worker movement as well as the *Catholic Worker*, the magazine devoted to its ideals. She was born on November 8, 1897, in Brooklyn, New York, the daughter of John Day and Grace Satterlee Day. While she was growing up, her family moved first to California, then to Chicago, where she was awarded a scholarship to the University of Illinois in 1914. Concerned already with the plight of the poor and dismayed by disparities in wealth and opportunity, Day became a socialist at the University of Illinois and abandoned college after her sophomore year. She moved to New York City, where she wrote for socialist and radical periodicals.

In the early 1920s, Day was briefly married to Barkeley Tobey, but their relationship dissolved quickly. Beginning in 1925, she shared a common law marriage with Forster Batterham, an anarchist

with whom she had a child the following year. Although Day had previously been disdainful of religion, she had her daughter baptized in a Catholic church. Day herself became a Catholic and was baptized in December 1927. This religious conversion did not blunt her zeal for the cause of social justice but rather gave her a new vision that incorporated the concerns that continued to dominate her life. It alienated her from Batterham, however, who was irreligious and unwilling to marry Day officially.

In 1932, Day met Peter Maurin, a Catholic who championed the idea of agrarian communities and who persuaded Dorothy Day to begin publication of a periodical they named the *Catholic Worker*. This magazine, in turn, inspired the formation of the Catholic Worker movement, which gave expression in deeds to the ideas being expressed in print in the *Catholic Worker*. Together, Day and Maurin oversaw the creation of hospitality houses and communal farms. Maurin suffered a stroke in the mid-1940s and died at the end of that decade. Day remained active on a variety of fronts, committed to the spiritual values of voluntary poverty, manual toil, and sacrificial love. The communities in which she plunged herself were not always idyllic, but they were nevertheless transformative. She wrote in the *Catholic Worker* in its January 1948 issue:

> I don't expect any success in anything we are trying to do, either in getting out a paper, running houses of hospitality or farming groups, or retreat houses on the land. I expect that everything we do will be attended with human conflicts, and the suffering that goes with it, and that this suffering will water the seed to make it grow in the future. I expect that all our natural love for each other which is so warming and so encouraging and so much a reward of this kind of work and living, will be killed, put to death painfully by gossip, intrigue, suspicion, distrust, etc., and that this painful dying to self and the longing for the love of others will be rewarded by a tremendous increase of supernatural love amongst us all.

Dorothy Day lived through the radicalism of the 1960s, and the marriage between traditional faith and social activism that characterized her life often seemed anachronistic to young activists unmoored from organized religion. But Day had long abandoned the search for justice apart from its concrete manifestation in Christian community, and the later decades of the 20th century gave her no cause to revise her long-held convictions. She died on November 29, 1980, in New York City.

Social activism in the second half of the 20th century frequently assumed a purely secular posture, as though faith could not be trusted to provide remedies for the ills of modern society. Dorothy Day herself was an activist before she was a Catholic. But her conversion to Christianity as a young woman provided the center for a social vision that she pursued for half a century and that inspired like-minded Catholics to see that faith need not be divorced from the world. For Dorothy Day, and the many for whom she served as an example, the life of faith could be both mystical and dynamic, a life of prayer and of deeds.

Further Reading

Coles, Robert. *Dorothy Day: A Radical Devotion.* Reading, Mass.: Addison-Wesley, 1987.
Day, Dorothy. *From Union Square to Rome.* New York: Arno Press, 1978.
———. *Loaves and Fishes.* New York: Curtis Books, 1972.
———. *The Long Loneliness: The Autobiography of Dorothy Day.* New York: Harper, 1952.
Forest, James H. *Love Is the Measure: A Biography of Dorothy Day.* New York: Paulist Press, 1986.
Kent, Deborah. *Dorothy Day: Friend to the Forgotten.* Grand Rapids, Mich.: W. B. Eerdmans, 1996.
Klejment, Anne, and Nancy L. Roberts, eds. *American Catholic Pacifism: The Influence of Dorothy Day and the Catholic Worker Movement.* Westport, Conn.: Praeger, 1996.
Merriman, Brigid O'Shea. *Searching for Christ: The Spirituality of Dorothy Day.* Notre Dame, Ind.: University of Notre Dame, 1994.
Miller, William D. *Dorothy Day: A Biography.* San Francisco: Harper & Row, 1982.
Roberts, Nancy L. *Dorothy Day and the Catholic Worker.* Albany: State University of New York Press, 1984.

De, Abhay Charan
(A. C. Bhaktivedanta, Śrīla Prabhupāda)
(1896–1977) *founder of the International Society for Krishna Consciousness*

A. C. Bhaktivedanta Swami Prabhupāda arrived in the United States late in life and founded the International Society for Krishna Consciousness (ISKCON). Before his death in 1977, he saw ISKCON become the most well-known Hindu religious movement in America. He was born Abhay Charan De on September 1, 1896, in Calcutta, India, the son of Gour Mohan De and his wife, Rajani De. Abhay's family was devoted to the worship of Krishna, in Hindu thought an avatar, or incarnation, of the god Vishnu. Abhay studied at the Scottish Churches College in Calcutta and, while a student there, entered into an arranged marriage with a child bride, Radharani Datta, with whom he would later live and have three children. Although he satisfied the requirements for graduation from college, he refused to accept a degree out of opposition to British colonialism.

After leaving college, Abhay worked for a time for a pharmaceutical company. In 1932, he became a disciple of Bhaktisiddhanta Sarasvati Thakura, who was the leader of a religious group devoted to the worship of Krishna called the Gaudiza Math Vaishnava movement. Shortly before Bhaktisiddhanta Sarasvati died in 1936, he appointed Abhay to carry the worship of Krishna to the English-speaking world. As a first step in this missionary task, Abhay began to publish the magazine, *Back to Godhead.* In the 1950s, Abhay eventually left his family and his secular occupation and undertook sannyāsa, the spiritual renunciation of the world. At this time he assumed the name Abhay Caranaravinda Bhaktivedanta Swami.

In 1965, at the age of 70, Bhaktivedanta immigrated to the United States. Arriving in the fall of that year, he soon attracted a group of followers with whom he founded ISKCON in 1966. His followers often referred to him as Śrīla Prabhupāda. Central to the activities of the group was the chanting of the Krishana mantra: "Hare Krishna Hare Krishna Krishna Krishna Hare Hare Hare Rama Hare Rama Rama Rama Hare Hare." In the chant, Rama is another name for Krishna and Hare an invocation of Krishna's consort, Rādhā. In traditional Hinduism, Krishna is regarded as one of the avatars of the god Vishnu. In ISKCON, however, Krishna is the central divine figure, and devotion to Krishna is the heart of the religious movement. After its founding, ISKCON spread rapidly in the United States and India especially as Bhaktivedanta presided over its affairs. Illness eventually forced him to return to his homeland, and he died in Vrndāvana, India, on November 14, 1977.

America, long the source of Christian missionary zeal around the world, became the object of such zeal itself on the part of other world religions in the 20th century. A. C. Bhaktivedanta Swami represented an influential Hindu version of this missionary phenomenon. At a time when most men his age had retired from their occupations, Bhaktivedanta cast himself across the Atlantic and transplanted the worship of Krishna to American soil. The group he founded, the International Society for Krishna Consciousness (commonly known as the Hare Krishnas), was not the only such eastern export of religion in the 20th century, but it was one of the most prominent such exports.

Further Reading

The Bhagavad Gita As It Is. Translated and edited by A. C. Bhaktivedanta Swami. New York: Macmillan, 1968.

Daner, Francine Jeanne. *The American Children of Krsna: A Study of the Hare Krsna Movement.* New York: Holt, Rinehart and Winston, 1976.

Gelberg, Steven J., ed. *Hare Krishna, Hare Krishna: Five Distinguished Scholars on the Krishna Movement in the West.* New York: Grove Press, 1983.

Gosvāmī, Satsvarūpa Dāa. *Srīla Prabhupāda-līlāmrta: A Biography of His Divine Grace A.C. Bhaktivedanta Swami Prabhupāda.* 6 vols. Los Angeles, Calif.: Bhaktivedanta Book Trust, 1980–83.

International Society for Krishna Consciousness. Edited by Elise Bjorkan. New York: Garland, 1990.

Knott, Kim. *My Sweet Lord: The Hare Krishna Movement.* San Bernardino, Calif.: R. Reginald, 1988.

Muster, Nori J. *Betrayal of the Spirit: My Life Behind the Headlines of the Hare Krishna Movement.* Urbana: University of Illinois Press, 1997.

Prabhupāda, A. C. Bhaktivedanta Swami. *The Path of Perfection: Yoga for the Modern Age.* Los Angeles: Bhaktivedanta Book Trust, 1979.

De Smet, Pierre-Jean
(Black Robe)
(1801–1873) *Catholic missionary*

Pierre-Jean De Smet, a Jesuit priest, was a leading promoter of Catholic missionary activity among Native Americans in the 19th century. He traveled more than 180,000 miles during his lifetime to solicit missionaries and money to introduce Christianity to the Native Americans in the American Northwest. He was born on January 30, 1801, in Termonde, Belgium, to Josse-Arnaud De Smet and Joanna Maria Buydens. Pierre-Jean attended a seminary at Malines for six years, beginning when he was 14 years old. In 1821, he joined a missionary expedition to the United States; he entered the Jesuit novitiate at Whitemarsh, Maryland, that year and later a novitiate near Saint Louis, Missouri, that would eventually become Saint Louis University. In 1827, De Smet was ordained a priest and remained at the novitiate as a teacher until ill health forced him to take a leave of absence and return to Europe in 1833. There, he recruited students and funds for the novitiate.

Soon after De Smet's return to Missouri in 1837, he was assigned the task of founding Saint Joseph's Mission among the Potawatoni at Council Bluffs, Iowa. A few years later, he was posted to Montana, where he helped to found St. Mary's Mission among the Salish tribe. For the next several years, De Smet lived the life of an explorer, missions promoter, and general administrator of Native American mission affairs in the Pacific Northwest. Among the Native Americans with whom he had constant commerce during these years, he became known simply as "Black Robe." His published accounts of these missionary activities became famous both in the United States and in Europe.

In the 1850s, federal officials began to lean on De Smet as a mediator between the federal government and Native Americans and as a general counselor concerning Indian affairs. In 1851, he served as "pacificator" at a general congress of tribes assembled in the Creek Valley near Fort Laramie. In 1858, De Smet accompanied General William S. Harney as chaplain on a military expedition against the Mormons in Utah. After the Mormons capitulated to federal authorities, he was posted to Oregon with the military. Subsequently De Smet was permitted to resign from this brief tenure of service for the U.S. military, and he spent the next decade traveling widely in support of missions and accompanying various government expeditions into Native American territories. In the most famous of these, in 1868, he traveled alone into the camp of Sitting Bull—the great Sioux chief and warrior, who had threatened to kill any white man who appeared—and was instrumental in securing the Treaty of 1868 between the U.S. government and the Sioux. De Smet died on May 23, 1873, in Saint Louis, Missouri.

Pierre-Jean De Smet was a chief emissary between whites and Native Americans during the 19th century. Though he frequently objected to federal treatment of Native American tribes, he nevertheless counseled the tribes to accept the peace offered to them through treaties. He held genuine affection for the Native Americans, for whom he was both an apostle of Christianity and a representative of the government of the United States; in turn, they appeared to have a similar affection for him.

Further Reading
Carriker, Robert C. *Father Peter John De Smet: Jesuit in the West.* Norman: University of Oklahoma Press, 1995.
De Smet, Pierre-Jean. *Life, Letters, and Travels of Father De Smet.* Edited by Hiram Martin Chittenden and Alfred Talbot Richardson. 4 vols. New York: Arno Press, 1969.
Killoren, John J. *"Come, Blackrobe": De Smet and the Indian Tragedy.* Norman: University of Oklahoma Press, 1994.
Laveille, Eugene. *The Life of Father De Smet, S.J. (1801–1873).* New York: P. J. Kenedy & Sons, 1915.
Pfaller, Louis. *Father De Smet in Dakota.* Richardton, N.D.: Assumption Abbey Press, 1962.
Terrell, John Upton. *Black Robe: The Life of Pierre-Jean De Smet, Missionary, Explorer & Pioneer.* Garden City, N.Y.: Doubleday, 1964.

Dickinson, Jonathan
(1688–1747) *Presbyterian minister*

Jonathan Dickinson was a prominent Presbyterian leader during the first half of the 18th century. He participated in key theological disputes among Presbyterians during this period and generally adhered to a middle course between more radical positions. He was born on April 22, 1688, in Hatfield, Massachusetts, the son of Hezekiah Dickinson and Abigail Blackman Dickinson. Most of the details of his early life remain unknown, except that he attended Yale College (known prior to 1718 as the Collegiate School or the School of the Church) and graduated in 1706. By 1709, presumably after private ministerial studies, he was ordained the minister of a church in Elizabeth Town (later Elizabeth), New Jersey, with responsibility for families scattered across nearby towns, including Rahway, Westfield, Connecticut Farms, Springfield, and Chatham. The same year he married Joanna Melyen, with whom he had eight children.

Dickinson arrived at his ministerial vocation at a time when Congregationalists and Presbyterians were beginning to take on separate denominational identities. The first presbytery organized in North America was that in 1707 in Philadelphia. A decade later, Dickinson persuaded his Elizabeth Town congregation to align themselves with this presbytery. Though he was the youngest minister in the presbytery in 1717, his skills as a preacher and a writer soon gave him prominence among Presbyterians of the Middle Colonies.

In the 1720s, Dickinson participated in one of the first significant theological disputes of the infant Presbyterian denomination. One element within the denomination pressed to have all ministerial candidates subscribe to the Westminster Confession, the statement of faith adopted by English Presbyterians in 1648, as a condition for ordination. Dickinson, a champion of spiritual liberty, opposed this proposal. In a sermon preached at a meeting of the synod of Philadelphia in September 1722, he argued that such attempts to control the orthodoxy of individual ministers amounted to a "bold invasion of Christ's royal power." Rather than excluding ministers who dissented from elements of the Westminster Confession, Dickinson argued that Presbyterians should "open the doors of the Church as wide as Christ opens the gates of Heaven; and receive one another, as Christ also receives us, to the glory of God." Although Dickinson and his allies were able to prevent passage of the subscription proposal in 1722, seven years later the issue arose again; this time the Philadelphia synod adopted the Westminster Confession as its official statement of faith. The synod also required that ministerial candidates henceforth signify their assent to the key elements of the confession as a condition of ordination.

In the years that followed what came to be known as the subscription controversy, Dickinson participated actively in another of the great controversies of early American Presbyterianism, one that arose from the revivalism associated with the Great Awakening. Presbyterians divided along the lines of those who opposed this revivalism, known as the Old Side, and those who supported the Great Awakening, known as the New Side. Dickinson was nominally aligned with the New Side in his general support for revivalism and, in fact, welcomed the great revivalist GEORGE WHITEFIELD into his Elizabeth Town pulpit. Nevertheless, he opposed those who seized on the Great Awakening to advance antinomianism—that is, freedom from traditional rules of religious conduct. He adopted a moderating position between the Old Side and New Side, seeking to prevent a decisive rupture within the Philadelphia synod. When he proved unsuccessful at this mediation, he ultimately joined other New Side Presbyterians in organizing the New York synod in 1745 as an alternative to the Philadelphia synod, which was controlled by more conservative Old Siders.

In the last significant activity of his ministerial career, Dickinson joined other New Side Presbyterians to establish a college hospitable to their spiritual vision. In 1746, the governor of New Jersey signed the charter to create the College of New Jersey. Originally located at Elizabeth Town, the college later relocated to Princeton, New Jersey, and eventually became Princeton University. Dickinson was appointed the college's first president, but he did not occupy this post for long. He died of pleurisy in Elizabeth Town on October 7, 1747, five months after the College of New Jersey held its first classes.

Although he could not avoid choosing sides in the controversies that defined early American Presbyterianism, Jonathan Dickinson earned a reputation among both his contemporaries and subse-

quent historians as a moderate on the key issues of his day. Uncomfortable with radicalism in any form, he steadfastly searched for a middle course in both the subscription controversy and the debates over the Great Awakening. His peaceable and reasonable temper made him one of the most respected Presbyterian ministers of his generation.

Further Reading

Cameron, Henry Clay. *Jonathan Dickinson and the College of New Jersey.* Princeton, N.J.: C. S. Robinson, 1880.

Harlan, David C. "The Travail of Religious Moderation: Jonathan Dickinson and the Great Awakening." *Journal of Presbyterian History* 61 (1983): 411–26.

———. "A World of Double Visions and Second Thoughts: Jonathan Dickinson's *Display of God's Special Grace.*" *Early American Literature* 21 (Fall 1986): 118–30.

Le Beau, Bryan F. *Jonathan Dickinson and the Formative Years of American Presbyterianism.* Lexington: University Press of Kentucky, 1997.

Schmidt, Leigh Eric. "Jonathan Dickinson and the Making of the Moderate Awakening." *American Presbyterians* 63 (1985): 341–53.

Sloat, Leslie W. "Jonathan Dickinson and the Problem of Synodical Authority." *Westminster Theological Journal* 8 (June 1946): 149–65.

Divine, Father
(George Baker, Jr., Major J. Divine, Reverend Major Jealous Divine)
(ca. 1879–1965) *Peace Mission movement founder*

Father Divine founded the Peace Mission movement and professed himself to be God. The precise date of his birth and the circumstances of his early life are largely unknown, partially because in later years he seems to have deliberately sought to keep these matters obscure. He was probably born in 1879 in Rockville, Maryland, the son of George and Nancy Baker and named George Baker, Jr. By 1899, he had left Rockville and migrated to Baltimore, where he worked as a gardener. There he was influenced by the teachings of CHARLES SHERLOCK FILLMORE, cofounder of the Unity school of

Christianity, who maintained that divinity was attainable by ordinary men and women who correctly channeled the spirit of God that was within them. In 1906, Baker visited California and had a spiritual experience, which included speaking in tongues, as a result of his participation in the Azusa Street Revival, conducted by an African-American minister, William Seymour. When Baker returned to Baltimore, he joined a Baptist church and became a popular teacher there.

While attending the church in Baltimore, Baker had contact with Samuel Morris, who claimed to be "the Father Eternal" or "Father Jehovia." By 1907, under Morris's influence, Baker claimed to be the son of God, or "the Messenger, God in the sonship degree." Together, the two men began conducting religious services in a house in Baltimore, but before 1912, Baker began to insist that he alone was the true expression of God. That same year, he left Baltimore in favor of an itinerant preaching ministry, teaching and preaching in a variety of settings and hosting sumptuous banquets patterned after the last supper of Jesus, which became characteristic of his evangelistic ministry. By 1914, he settled for a time in Valdosta, Georgia, where he announced that "God's second appearance on earth was in a form of Jew and that now he comes in the form of a negro." Authorities in Valdosta commenced involuntary commitment proceedings against Baker for his alleged insanity. He avoided being institutionalized, but he was nevertheless immediately charged with vagrancy after this victory and chose to leave the state.

Tiring of travel by 1915, Baker settled in Brooklyn, New York, where he soon established a religious community whose members pooled their resources and earnings, while practicing abstinence from sex, smoking, profanity, alcohol, and drugs. During his years in Brooklyn, Baker met and married an African-American woman named Pinninnah, though Baker claimed that the marriage was spiritual and not physically consummated. He also assumed the name of "Reverend Major Jealous Divine," though his followers referred to him more simply as "Father Divine" and to his wife Pinninnah as "Mother Divine." After four years in Brooklyn, Father Divine and Mother Divine were able to purchase a house in the village of Sayville in Suffolk County, Long Island, where they became the community's first black homeowners in 1919.

The new community Father Divine established in Sayville was conspicuous for its hardworking thrift and at first seemed to establish peaceful relations with its white neighbors. Eventually, though, the growing number of people who visited or joined the community precipitated local conflict. Father Divine continued to host sumptuous Holy Communion banquets, which, by 1931, turned into rotating meals that served as many as a thousand people over the course of each weekend. The steady tracks of pilgrims to Father Divine's door inevitably strained community relations and led to the arrest, in 1931, of Divine and many of his followers for disturbing the peace. Divine was eventually convicted before a hostile judge and sentenced to a year in jail and a $500 fine. An appellate court reversed the conviction because of the trial judge's prejudicial conduct, and the trial judge himself died three days after the trial. A commonly repeated anecdote suggests that Father Divine responded to the news of the judge's death with the quip "I hated to do it."

The collapse of community relations in Sayville forced Father Divine and his community to relocate to the home of one of his followers in Harlem, where Father Divine's movement earned its lasting name as the Peace Mission movement. In New York City, the movement began to establish low-cost restaurants, which soon were joined by a variety of other businesses that emphasized providing services for nominal costs. In 1943, Father Divine's wife died, and he created some measure of controversy among his followers when three years later he married Edna Rose Ritchings, a young white woman from Canada. The Peace Mission movement continued to spread to other cities, however, where it emphasized its founder's teachings concerning moral uprightness, economic self-reliance, and racial equality. Father Divine made one further relocation in the 1950s, when he settled at Woodmont, a 72-acre estate in a suburb of Philadelphia, Pennsylvania. He died there on September 10, 1965.

The success of the Peace Mission movement has puzzled many 20th-century commentators on Father Divine, who have devoted substantial attention to discrediting his divine pretensions. But efforts to discredit his claim of being God have sometimes obscured his movement's appeal. In a century in which racism still existed, his message of racial equality attracted both black and white followers. Moreover, the communal self-sufficiency of the movement and its ethic of social service proved especially desirable to many who had been economically scarred and dislocated by the financial hardships of the nation during the years of the Great Depression.

Further Reading

Burnham, Kenneth E. *God Comes to America: Father Divine.* Boston: Lambeth Press, 1979.

Divine, M. J. *The Peace Mission Movement: Founded by M. J. Divine, Better Known as Father Divine.* Philadelphia: Imperial Press, 1982.

Harris, Sara with Harriet Crittenden. *Father Divine.* Rev. ed. New York: Collier Books, 1971.

Hoshor, John. *God in a Rolls Royce: The Rise of Father Divine, Madman, Menace, or Messiah.* New York: Hilman-Curl, 1936; Freeport, N.Y.: Books for Libraries Press, 1971.

Parker, Robert Allerton. *The Incredible Messiah: The Deification of Father Divine.* Boston: Little, Brown, 1937.

Watts, Jill. *God, Harlem U.S.A.: The Father Divine Story.* Berkeley: University of California Press, 1992.

Weisbrot, Robert. *Father Divine and the Struggle for Racial Equality.* Urbana: University of Illinois Press, 1983.

Dixon, Amzi Clarence

(1854–1925) *Baptist minister*

Amzi Clarence Dixon's career as a Baptist minister and evangelist included service in some of the most famous churches of his day, including DWIGHT LYMAN MOODY's church in Chicago and the Metropolitan Tabernacle in London, which was founded by Charles Haddon Spurgeon, England's great Baptist preacher. But Dixon earned a more enduring place in American religious history through his role as an editor of the early volumes of *The Fundamentals,* an influential series of books that gave birth to 20th-century fundamentalism. Dixon was born on July 6, 1854, in Shelby, North Carolina, the son of Thomas Dixon and Amanda

Elvira McAfee Dixon. Amzi Dixon's father was a Baptist minister through whose preaching Amzi was converted, and the son followed the vocational footsteps of his father. He received his undergraduate degree from Wake Forest College in 1873 and then spent the next several years as pastor of churches in North Carolina. He was ordained a minister in 1875, after which he was able to study for a brief period with the famous Baptist theologian and educator JOHN ALBERT BROADUS, professor at the Southern Baptist Theological Seminary in Greenville, South Carolina.

In the following years Dixon occupied a series of pulpits in Baptist churches, beginning with one in Chapel Hill, North Carolina, in 1876 and, a few years later, the First Baptist Church in Asheville, North Carolina. He married Susan Mary Faison in 1880, and the couple had five children together. Though invited to assume the presidency of Wake Forest College in the early 1880s, Dixon decided to leave North Carolina instead, and in 1882 he became the pastor of Immanuel Baptist Church in Baltimore, Maryland. He spent the remainder of the decade in Baltimore, making contacts during those years that would eventually broaden his sphere of influence. These included forming a friendship with the 19th century's preeminent revivalist, Dwight L. Moody, and, in 1889, traveling to London, where he met the great English Baptist preacher Charles H. Spurgeon and preached at Spurgeon's church, the Metropolitan Tabernacle.

During the 1890s Dixon was pastor of the Hanson Place Baptist Church in Brooklyn, New York. Like many other conservative evangelicals of the time, Dixon held premillennialist views, which created a note of urgency in his evangelistic preaching. Premillennialists believed that Christ would return to the earth before inaugurating a thousand-year reign, unlike amillennialists, who saw biblical references to this millennial kingdom of Christ as metaphors to describe his presence in the world through the church, or postmillennialists, who thought a millennial kingdom of peace and righteousness would actually precede the coming of Christ. Dixon and other premillennialists viewed the return of Christ as imminent, necessitating vigorous efforts to convert souls before his second advent.

Dixon's association with the leading evangelical movements of his day flourished when he was a pastor in Brooklyn. He participated in Dwight L. Moody's campaign to target the Chicago World's Fair in 1893 for revival preaching. He also associated with England's Keswick movement, which embodied the "higher life" teaching that emphasized the possibility of a special experience of holiness for Christian believers.

In 1901, Dixon became the minister of the Ruggles Street Baptist Church in Roxbury, Massachusetts. Five years later, then prominent not only among Baptists but within the broader current of evangelical Protestantism, he was invited to assume the pulpit of the nondenominational Chicago Avenue Church in Chicago, Illinois. He preached there until becoming in 1911 the minister of the Metropolitan Tabernacle, the church founded in London by Charles H. Spurgeon.

Having thus occupied two of the most prominent pulpits of his day, Dixon might nevertheless have suffered the historical anonymity customarily reserved for all but the first rank of Christian preachers. But late in the first decade of the 20th century, his increasing reputation as a determined foe of theological liberalism won him an important role in the early history of the fundamentalist movement. Two wealthy California businessmen, Milton and Lyman Stewart, persuaded him to serve as editor of *The Fundamentals*. This influential collection of essays by conservative Protestant thinkers was published in 12 volumes between 1910 and 1915 and distributed free of charge to millions of Christian preachers and teachers. Dixon edited the first five volumes of the series, which attempted to restate and defend classic tenets of conservative Protestant orthodoxy, such as the virgin birth and divinity of Jesus.

After returning from England in 1919, Dixon lectured widely before assuming the pastorate of the University Baptist Church in Baltimore, Maryland, where he preached for the remainder of his life. After the death of his first wife in 1922, he married Helen Cadbury Alexander in 1924. Dixon died on June 14, 1925, in Baltimore.

By the beginning of the 21st century, Amzi Clarence Dixon was little known outside the ranks of church historians. But in his own day, he was a leading figure among conservative evangelical Protestants. He shared the theological emphases common among this group, its premillennialist views, its close association with the higher life movement, and—after the beginning of the 20th century—its escalating polemics against theological liberalism. His role as editor of the early volumes of *The Fundamentals*, especially, secured him an important place in the history of the fundamentalist movement, which itself played a significant role in the religious history of the 20th century.

Further Reading

Dixon, A. C. *Evangelism Old and New: God's Search for Man in All Ages.* New York: American Tract Society, 1905; New York: Garland, 1988.
———. *Lights and Shadows of American Life.* New York: Fleming H. Revell, 1898.
Dixon, Helen C. A. A. C. *Dixon: A Romance of Preaching.* New York: Garland, 1988.
The Fundamentals: The Famous Source Book of Foundational Biblical Truths. Edited by R. A. Torrey, Amzi Dixon, and others. Grand Rapids, Mich.: Kregel Publications, 1990.
Marsden, George M. *Fundamentalism and American Culture: The Shaping of Twentieth Century Evangelicalism, 1870–1925.* New York: Oxford University Press, 1980.
Martin, Donald Lewis, Jr. "The Thought of Amzi Clarence Dixon." Ph.D. dissertation, Baylor University, 1989.

Drew, Timothy
(Noble Drew Ali)
(1886–1929) *founder of the Moorish Temple*

Timothy Drew, who referred to himself as Noble Drew Ali in later years, demonstrated the affinity between black separatist ideas and Islamic faith that would flower after his death in the Nation of Islam. He was born of uncertain location in North Carolina on January 8, 1886; the names of his parents are not known. Virtually no information exits concerning Drew's life before he achieved a measure of prominence as an Islamic street preacher in approximately 1912. Drew claimed to have visited the Middle East, where he had received the name by which he thereafter called himself, Noble Drew Ali.

Ali founded the Moorish Holy Temple of Science in Newark, New Jersey, in 1913. There he taught blacks that they had originally been followers of Islam before being enslaved by whites and forced to adopt Christianity. He insisted that blacks in America traced their lineage not to Africa but to the Middle East and that they should refer to themselves as Asiatics or Moors. Noble Drew Ali's followers received an identification card, which proclaimed that they honored "all divine prophets, Jesus, Mohammed, Buddha and Confucius," and invoked the blessings of "the God of our Father Allah."

Noble Drew Ali's teaching was attractive to many urban blacks in the first decades of the 20th century, and additional Moorish Temples sprang up first in the Northeast, and later in the Midwest. By the mid-1920s, Ali had transferred the seat of his growing organization to Chicago, Illinois, and, in 1926, he formally incorporated the Moorish Temple of Science in Illinois. The following year, he published a collection of his teachings, *Holy Koran of the Moorish Holy Temple of Science*. In Chicago, though, Ali's followers attracted the unfavorable attention of authorities when male members of the Moorish Temple inaugurated the practice of "bumping," by which temple members in groups, often wearing red fezzes—conical hats with a flat top worn in some Islamic countries—would "bump" white pedestrians off of sidewalks. Ali attempted to discourage this practice but discovered that the movement he had started no longer responded readily to his dictates. He wrestled for control of the Moorish Temples with the organization's business manager, Claude Green. After Green was found murdered in the spring of 1929, Ali was arrested for the crime, even though he had been out of town at the time of Green's murder. Ali was released on bond, however, but mysteriously died of an apparent beating on July 20, 1929, in Chicago. The circumstances of his death remain obscure. Some of his followers insisted that he had died of a beating administered by the police, either while he was in jail or after his release. Other accounts suggested that opponents within the Moorish Temple had engineered his death.

After Noble Drew Ali's death, the Moorish Temple suffered a decline, though the movement still exists in a limited form at the beginning of the 21st century. Ali's more enduring legacy, however, was as a predecessor of the more successful Black Muslim movement, founded by Wallace Fard the year following Ali's death. By some accounts, Fard claimed to be the reincarnation of Noble Drew Ali, but in any event, the "Lost-Found Nation of Islam," which Fard established in 1930, offered its adherents a synthesis of Islamic teaching and racial pride whose pattern had been initially established by Noble Drew Ali.

Further Reading
Ali, Noble Drew. *The Holy Koran of the Moorish Science Temple of America.* Available online. URL: http://www.geocities.com/Athens/Delphi/2705/koran-index.html. Downloaded on April 30, 2002.
Fauset, Arthur. *Black Gods of the Metropolis.* Philadelphia: University of Pennsylvania Press, 1945; New York: Octagon Books, 1970.
Lincoln, C. Eric. *The Black Muslims in America.* 3d ed. Grand Rapids, Mich.: W.B. Eerdsmans, 1993.
Simpson, Frank T. "The Moorish Science Temple and Its Koran." *Moslem World* 37 (Jan. 1947): 56–61.

Drexel, Katharine
(1858–1955) *Catholic missionary*

In the fall of 2000, Katharine Drexel became the second American-born Catholic to be declared a saint. She was the heiress of a substantial estate who devoted both her life and a substantial portion of her wealth to the cause of Catholic missions to Native and African Americans. Katharine Drexel was born on November 26, 1858, in Philadelphia, Pennsylvania, the daughter of Francis Anthony Drexel and Hannah Jane Langstroth Drexel. Her father was a wealthy banker, who died in 1885, leaving Katharine and her sisters a trust fund of more than $14 million.

Shortly before her father's death, Katharine Drexel had been impressed with an appeal from Bishop Martin Marty for support of Native American missions. On a visit to Rome in 1887, she had an audience with Pope Leo XIII, who responded to her professed interest in supporting Native American and African-American missions by suggesting that she should become a missionary herself. Over the next two years, she visited various Native American missions in North and South Dakota and in Minnesota, and she became convinced of the need for an order of nuns to support these missionary projects. In 1889 she became a novitiate of the Sisters of Mercy in Pittsburgh, Pennsylvania; after she completed her novitiate in 1891, she established the Sisters of the Blessed Sacrament for Indians and Colored People and became the order's first sister. The purposes of the order were to include the personal sanctification of its members as well as "the service of Our Lord in the Blessed Sacrament by endeavoring to lead the Indian & Colored Races to the knowledge & love of God, & so make of them living temples of Our Lord's Divinity." In 1892 Drexel saw to the construction of a motherhouse for her new order in Cornwells Heights, Pennsylvania.

Beginning in 1894 with the opening of St. Catherine's School in Santa Fe, New Mexico, a school for Native American children, Katharine Drexel devoted her considerable financial resources and energy over the following years to establishing scores of religious institutions dedicated to ministering to Native Americans and African Americans. The most significant of these was Xavier College (later Xavier University) in New Orleans, a Catholic university for African-American students established in 1925, but the measure of her philanthropy far exceeded this one institution. By the time of her death, she had supported the establishment of more than 50 convents, 49 elementary schools, and 12 high schools. She also disbursed substantial portions of her wealth to the Bureau of Catholic Indian Missions, the Interracial Council in New York, and the National Association for the Advancement of Colored People (NAACP). In all, Drexel devoted more than $12 million of her inheritance to missionary activities and related social organizations for Native Americans and African Americans.

After a heart attack interrupted her work in 1935, Katharine Drexel retired from leadership of her order in 1937. She spent the remaining years of her life in meditation and prayer. She died on March 3, 1955, in Cornwells Heights. She was beatified in 1988 and canonized by Pope John Paul II on Sunday, October 1, 2000, the second American-born Catholic saint.

As a young adult, Katharine Drexel seemed poised to continue the philanthropic activities in which her wealthy family had become practiced. And, in fact, she did lavish a substantial portion of her wealth on charitable causes, chiefly those designed to benefit Native Americans and African Americans. Nevertheless, her life was distinguished not only by the measure of her generosity with the wealth she inherited but by her willingness to dedicate her life itself to these missionary causes.

Further Reading

Burton, Katherine. *The Golden Door: The Life of Katharine Drexel.* New York: Kennedy, 1957.

Duffy, Consuela Marie. *Katharine Drexel: A Biography.* Philadelphia: P. Reilly, 1966.

Tarry, Ellen. *Saint Katharine Drexel: Friend of the Oppressed.* Rev. ed. Boston: Pauline Books & Media, 2000.

DuBose, William Porcher
(1836–1918) *Episcopal priest, theologian, educator*

Today recognized as the foremost American theologian of the Episcopal Church, William Porcher DuBose spent the greater part of his adult life as a university professor, relatively unknown beyond his own campus. His progressive and liberal theology was out of step with the more conservative religious currents of the South, where he made his home, delaying his recognition as an important Episcopal thinker until well into the 20th century. DuBose was born on April 11, 1836, on a plantation near Winnsboro, South Carolina, the son of Theodore Marion DuBose and Jane Porcher DuBose, wealthy southern planters descended from 17th-century Huguenot settlers. He received his undergraduate education at the Citadel, a military school in South Carolina, from which he graduated in 1855. Four years later he completed an M.A. at the University of Virginia.

DuBose attended the Episcopal seminary in Camden, South Carolina, beginning in 1859; but the Civil War interrupted his plans to become an Episcopal priest. He left the seminary to join the Confederate army in 1861. During his military service he was wounded in battle and confined in a Union prisoner-of-war camp for two months. In the spring of 1863 he married Anna Barnwell Peronneau, with whom he had three children. By the end of that year, he was ordained to the Episcopal diaconate and served for the remainder of the Civil War as a military chaplain.

After the war, DuBose was ordained a priest in 1865 or 1866, and he spent his first years as a minister serving at St. John's Church, in Winnsboro, and St. Stephen's Chapel, in Ridgeway. Thereafter he became the rector of Trinity Church in Abbeville, South Carolina. Lifelong service as a parish priest was not to be his ultimate calling, however. In 1871, he moved to the University of the South in Sewanee, Tennessee, where he remained until his retirement in 1908. In his early years there he served as university chaplain. Later, beginning in 1872, he became professor of ethics and New Testament after the university established a theology department. The following year, his first wife died, and in 1878 he married Louisa Yerger. During his years at Sewanee, he wrote numerous articles as well as six major books. In 1894, he became the second dean of the university's school of theology. He died in Sewanee on August 18, 1918.

The heart of William Porcher DuBose's theology was his conviction that God was immanent in the world, not only in the incarnation of Christ but in the sufferings he had seen firsthand during the Civil War, in the human imperfections that war had made visible but not cured, and in the human condition generally. In an article written shortly before his death, he explained his ideas in an oft-quoted passage:

> God has placed forever before our eyes, not the image but the very Person of the Spiritual Man. We have not to ascend into Heaven to bring Him down, nor to descend into the abyss to bring Him up, for He is with us, and near us, and in us. We have only to confess with our mouths that He is Lord, and believe in our hearts that God has raised Him from the dead—and raised us in Him—and we shall live.

Comfortable with higher criticism of the Bible and with evolutionary theory, DuBose was a theological modernist who influenced a generation of students in the conservative cultural and theological milieu of the South.

Further Reading
Bratton, Theodore DuBose. *An Apostle of Reality: The Life and Thought of the Reverend William Porcher DuBose, S.T.D., D.C.L.* London: Longmans, Green, 1936.

Dubose, William Porcher. *A Dubose Reader: Selections from the Writings of William Porcher DuBose.* Compiled by Donald S. Armentrout. Sewanee, Tenn.: University of the South, 1984.

———. *William Porcher DuBose: Selected Writings.* Edited by Jon Alexander. New York: Paulist Press, 1988.

———. *Turning Points in My Life.* New York: Longmans, Green, 1912.

Luker, Ralph. *A Southern Tradition in Theology and Social Criticism, 1830–1930: The Religious Liberalism and Social Conservatism of James Warley Miles, William Porcher DuBose, and Edgar Gardner Murphy.* New York: E. Mellen Press, 1984.

Marshall, John Sedberry. *The Word Was Made Flesh: The Theology of William Porscher DuBose.* Sewanee, Tenn.: University Press, 1949.

Slocum, Robert Boak. *The Theology of William Porcher Dubose: Life, Movement, and Being.* Columbia: University of South Carolina Press, 2000.

Duchesne, Rose Philippine
(Quah-kah-ka-num-ad)
(1769–1852) *Catholic missionary*

Rose Philippine Duchesne was a 19th-century Catholic missionary to America. She helped to establish convents, schools, and orphanages in the area around Saint Louis, Missouri, and served briefly as a missionary to Native Americans late in her life. Duchesne was born on August 29, 1769, in Grenoble, France, the daughter of Pierre-François Duchesne and Rose-Euphrosine Perier, devout Catholics. She was educated at Sainte

Marie-d'en-Haut, a convent school of the Visitation order in Grenoble, and was then tutored privately in her home by a priest. She joined the Visitation order in 1788 but had to return home four years later when antireligious zeal spawned by the French Revolution caused the convent in Grenoble to be closed.

By 1801, Duchesne was able to rent the monastery of Sainte Marie d'en Haut, which the Visitation order had previously occupied. There she attempted to reestablish the order, but dissension among its members caused it to disband two years later. With a handful of nuns who remained at Sainte Marie d'en Haut, Duchesne renamed the community the Daughters of the Propagation of the Faith in the spring of 1803. The following year, Duchesne and the other members of the community attached themselves to the Society of the Sacred Heart, a religious order recently established by Madeleine-Sophie Barat.

Duchesne was sent to Paris in 1815; there she established a Sacred Heart convent, but her desire for some time had been to serve as a missionary in America. A decade earlier, she had sought permission from Mother Barat to undertake a mission to the United States but was refused. Finally, though, Bishop Louis DuBourg of Louisiana visited France in 1817 and solicited new missionaries for America. His appeal won from Barat permission for Rose Duchesne to pursue her missionary ambition. She arrived in New Orleans with other companions of the Sacred Heart in the spring of 1818 after 10 weeks at sea.

Bishop DuBourg promptly dispatched Duchesne and her companions to the area around Saint Louis, Missouri. There, in Saint Charles, Missouri, they established the first Sacred Heart convent. A year later, they relocated their motherhouse to Florissant, Missouri. Over the next decade, Duchesne helped to establish five additional convents and associated schools and orphanages in the area in and around Saint Louis. She served as superior of the Society of the Sacred Heart in America until finally relieved of this responsibility in 1840, when she was 71 years old.

Though the aging Duchesne had devoted more than two decades to Catholic missions in America, she still longed to participate more particularly in a mission to the Native Americans. Once unburdened of her responsibilities as mother superior, Duchesne was able to fulfill this last ambition in the summer of 1941, when she was sent to the Potawatomi Indian mission at Sugar Creek, Kansas. She spent a year there, until it became apparent that her health was too fragile to sustain her presence. During her time with the Potawatomi, they named Duchesne Quah-kah-ka-num-ad, or "Woman who prays always." She returned to the convent in St. Charles in July 1842; there she devoted the remaining years of her life to prayer and meditation. She died there on November 18, 1852.

Rose Philippine Duchesne immigrated to America as a middle-aged woman and endured hardships of frontier life that had broken spirits younger than hers. She was almost 50 years old when she stepped ashore in New Orleans and began the missionary work that would occupy her for the next two decades and eventually earn her an important place in the history of Catholic missions in the United States. She was beatified on May 12, 1940, and, on July 3, 1988, Pope John Paul II declared her a saint.

Further Reading

Callan, Louise. *Philippine Duchesne: Frontier Missionary of the Sacred Heart, 1769–1852.* Westminster, Md.: Newman Press, 1957.
Erskine, Marjory. *Mother Philippine Duchesne.* New York: Longmans, Green, 1926.
Korner, Barbara O. "Philippine Duchesne: A Model of Action." *Missouri Historical Review* 86 (1992): 341–62.
Mooney, Catherine M. *Philippine Duchesne: A Woman with the Poor.* New York: Paulist Press, 1990.
Schmitt, Catherine Marie Donlan. "The Spirituality of Philippine Duchesne as Revealed in Her Letters to Madeleine Sophie Barat and Joseph Rosati." Ph.D. dissertation, Saint Louis University, 1998.

Dunster, Henry
(1609–1659) *educator, minister*

A Puritan educated at Cambridge University and transplanted to the Massachusetts Bay Colony,

Henry Dunster became Harvard's first, and one of its most illustrious, presidents. Dunster was born in November 1609, in Lancashire, England, the son of Henry Dunster of Baleholt and a mother whose name is unknown. The younger Henry Dunster studied at Magdalene College at Cambridge University, where he received a bachelor's degree in 1630 and a master's in 1634. Though he was ordained as a minister in the Church of England, Dunster's Puritan beliefs made it difficult for him to remain in England. Consequently, he joined the great Puritan migration to the New World and landed in Boston in 1640.

A few weeks after his arrival in Massachusetts, Dunster was invited to assume the presidency of newly founded Harvard College, which would become the oldest institution of higher learning in the United States. For the next 14 years, Dunster carved a reputation as a gifted scholar and administrator of what became one of the nation's premier universities. Dunster proved to be an energetic administrator who enmeshed himself in the superintendence of the various aspects of college life, from the development of curriculum to the management of student expense accounts. Under his direction, the college held its first commencement in September 1642. Thomas Shepard, the pastor of the Cambridge church, described Dunster as "pious, painful, and fit to teach, and very fit to lay the foundations of the domesticall affairs of the College; whom God hath much honored and blessed." Henry Dunster married Elizabeth Harris Glover in 1641. A year after her death in 1643, Dunster remarried; with his new wife, Elizabeth, he had five children.

Henry Dunster's highly regarded career as president of Harvard ended with his resignation in 1654 when his religious beliefs fell out of step with the Congregational orthodoxy of the Massachusetts Puritans. In particular, Dunster opposed the practice of infant baptism, speaking out against it at the church in Cambridge and refusing baptism of his children. This opposition placed him among the number of the early colonial Baptists, who insisted that the ordinance of baptism should be administered only to believing adults and whom the Massachusetts Puritans harassed with banishments and other civil punishments. Massachusetts leaders attempted to rescue Dunster from the grip of what they viewed as erroneous and dangerous spiritual opinions but proved unable, as COTTON MATHER—a later Puritan preacher and historian described the matter—"to expedite the entangled out of the briars."

After Dunster resigned as president of Harvard College, he relocated his family from Cambridge to Scituate in the Plymouth Colony. Baptists in Ireland had written to urge him to relocate there, but Dunster chose to remain in the New World, where he pursued a vocation as a preacher. Five years after he surrendered the presidency of Harvard, he died in Scituate on February 27, 1659. In accordance with his wishes, the Massachusetts Puritans allowed Henry Dunster to be buried in a cemetery near the college that he had so successfully tended during its infancy.

Henry Dunster followed the course of many Puritans in migrating to the New World. Once there, he acted as midwife for the birth of higher education in what would become the United States, transplanting to his adopted continent a keen devotion to learning and scholarship. But his career as a college administrator ultimately crashed against the flinty orthodoxy of the Massachusetts Puritans. Like other religious dissenters before him, such as ROGER WILLIAMS and ANNE MARBURY HUTCHISON, Dunster discovered that the Puritans' attempt to erect a holy commonwealth was prepared to tolerate little in the way of doctrinal deviance. In particular, Dunster's repudiation of infant baptism alarmed the Puritans and inspired them to forgo his useful talents as a college administrator rather than be infected by his spiritual errors.

Further Reading

Chaplin, Jeremiah. *The Life of Henry Dunster, First President of Harvard College:* Boston: J. R. Osgood, 1872.

Dunster, Samuel. *Henry Dunster and His Descendants.* Central Falls, R.I.: E. L. Freeman, 1876.

"Harvard's First President was a man for All seasons." Available online, URL:http://www.curriculumunits. com/galileo/litcin/manseasons/harvardpresident article.htm. Downloaded on April 20, 2002.

Morison, Samuel Eliot. *The Founding of Harvard College.* Cambridge, Mass.: Harvard University Press, 1935.

Dwight, Timothy
(1752–1817) *Congregationalist minister, educator*

A grandson of JONATHAN EDWARDS, Timothy Dwight became nationally famous in the second half of the 18th century as a preacher, theologian, poet, and university president. He was a man of astonishing intellectual breadth who championed an orthodox and evangelical Calvinism. Timothy Dwight was born on May 14, 1752, in Northampton, Massachusetts, to Timothy and Mary Edwards Dwight. Intellectually precocious, he knew enough Latin by the age of eight to pass Yale's entrance examination. He studied first at home, and then, when he was 11 years old, with the Reverend Enoch Huntingdon of Middletown. At the age of 13, he entered Yale College, where he earned a bachelor's degree in 1769 and a master's degree in 1771. Thereafter, Yale invited him to remain as a tutor. While a tutor at Yale, Dwight helped form the "Connecticut Wits," also known as the "Hartford Wits," a group of poets who, in religion, steered according to a traditional Calvinistic perspective and, in politics, were staunch Federalists. Driven to excel in scholarly and intellectual pursuits, Dwight soon ruined his eyes with excessive reading, and weak vision would plague him for the rest of his life. In 1774, Dwight joined the Yale College Church, at the time a congregation imbued with an evangelical tenor dating from the Great Awakening. The details of his conversion experience have not survived, but his membership in the College Church suggests that Dwight had such an experience. In 1776 and 1777, Dwight began preparations for a ministerial career by studying with his uncle, JONATHAN EDWARDS, JR., who was pastor of the White Haven Church in New Haven, Connecticut. In the summer of 1777, he was licensed to preach. Timothy Dwight married Mary Woolsey on March 7, 1777, and this marriage lasted 40 years, until Dwight's death in 1817.

When the Revolutionary War began, Dwight obtained a military commission as a chaplain. During this period, he finished his major poem, *The Conquest of Canaan.* Dwight served a little less than two years and returned home on learning that his father—who had refused to embrace the cause of the revolution—had died while trying to establish a new homestead near Natchez on the Mississippi. Home again in Northampton, Dwight plunged into work on his family's farms and soon added political service to this labor, when his neighbors elected him to the Massachusetts Assembly in 1781 and 1782. Not content with these undertakings, Dwight also managed to establish and manage a school in Northampton and to preach in a variety of nearby pulpits. His talents as an educator proved so substantial that some Yale undergraduates even transferred to Dwight's school in Northampton.

Timothy Dwight, the grandson of Jonathan Edwards, was a prominent 18th-century preacher, theologian, and educator. *(National Archive NWDNS-111-SC-92819)*

In 1783, Timothy Dwight accepted an invitation to become pastor of the church in Greenfield, Connecticut, and was ordained in November of that year. As a preacher, Dwight followed his grandfather Jonathan Edwards's evangelical Calvinism, at war against theological liberalism, especially in the form of Universalism and Unitarianism. But in his years at Greenfield, he also continued his poetic enterprises, not the least of which was his publication of *Greenfield Hill* in 1788. The poem included a hymn to American cultural, intellectual, and spiritual solidarity:

> One blood, one kindred, reach from sea to sea;
> One language spread, one tide of manners run;
> One scheme of science, and of morals one;
> And, God's own Word the structure, and the base,
> One faith extend, one worship, and one praise.

While in Greenfield, Dwight again established an academy that soon attracted the sons and daughters of prominent New England families and secured his reputation as an academic administrator. This reputation soon bore prestigious fruit. EZRA STILES, the president of Yale, died in May 1795, and the following month, the college elected Timothy Dwight its new president. Under Dwight's tutelage, the college advanced from a regional institution into one of national stature. Dwight combined the office of presidency with service as professor of divinity and with a public career as a champion of Federalism in politics. He died on January 11, 1817.

Preacher, poet, and college administrator, Timothy Dwight dazzled his generation by his energy and erudition. To the consternation of his political and religious opponents, who were many, he waged a lifelong war against progressive impulses in both domains. His poetry, though well regarded in its day, has been displaced by that of more talented American voices. The American historian Henry Adams said of Dwight that he was a "man of extraordinary qualities, but one on whom almost every mental gift had been conferred in fuller measure than poetical genius." Dwight's reputation as an educator and a general

man of letters, though, remains among the most illustrious of the 18th century.

Further Reading

Cuningham, Charles E. *Timothy Dwight, 1752–1817, A Biography.* New York: Macmillan, 1942.

Dwight, Timothy. *The Conquest of Canaan: A Poem in Eleven Books.* Hartford, Conn.: Elisha Babcock, 1785; Westport, Conn.: Greenwood Press, 1970.

———. *Greenfield Hill: A Poem in Seven Parts.* New York: Childs and Swaine, 1794; New York: AMS Press, 1970.

———. *Theology, Explained and Defended, in a Series of Sermons.* 5 vols. Middletown, Conn.: Charles Lyman, 1818–1819.

———. *Travels in New England and New York.* 4 vols. New Haven, Conn.: T. Dwight, 1821–1822; modern ed., Barbara Miller Solomon, ed., with the assistance of Patricia M. King. Cambridge, Mass.: Belknap Press of the Harvard University Press, 1969.

Fitzmier, John R. *New England's Moral Legislator: Timothy Dwight, 1752–1817.* Bloomington: Indiana University Press, 1998.

Howard, Leon. *The Connecticut Wits.* Chicago: University of Chicago Press, 1943.

Silliman, Benjamin. *A Sketch of the Life and Character of President Dwight.* New Haven, Conn.: Haltby and Goldsmith, 1817.

Silverman, Kenneth. *Timothy Dwight.* New York: Twayne Publishers, 1969.

Dyer, Mary
(Mary Barrett)
(unknown–1660) *Quaker martyr*

Mary Dyer, born of uncertain date Mary Barrett, was a Quaker martyr of mid-17th-century New England. She ended her life on a gallows on the Boston Common after defying a sentence of banishment ordered by Massachusetts authorities. History notices her first on the occasion of her marriage on October 27, 1633, in London, to William Dyer, with whom she had six children. William Dyer was a successful merchant, and together they migrated in 1635 to the Massachusetts Bay Colony, where they promptly were admitted as members of the church in Boston.

Mary Dyer and her husband soon found themselves immersed in the antinomian controversy, one of New England's first social upheavals. Sparked by home religious meetings held by ANNE MARBURY HUTCHINSON in Boston, the controversy pitted Hutchinson and like-minded individuals such as the Dyers against the colony's established spiritual leaders. Hutchinson complained of these leaders' adherence to a "Covenant of Works" rather than the "Covenant of Grace" celebrated in the preaching of JOHN COTTON, the teacher of the Boston church. Hutchinson charged that other New England ministers placed excessive emphasis on external rules of conduct rather than relying simply on the indwelling presence of the Holy Spirit. Labeled a heretic by New England authorities, Anne Hutchinson earned the sentence of banishment for her perceived errors. The Boston church also excommunicated her in 1637, and Mary Dyer is said to have accompanied Hutchinson hand in hand when the excommunicate left the church. Dyer and her husband thereafter followed Hutchinson and her family to the Providence colony.

In 1652, Dyer and her husband traveled to England, and she remained there for five years. During this period, she became a Quaker. This religious group's focus on the inward presence of God and the irrelevance of creeds and clergy echoed theological inclinations that seem to have dated from her earliest days in the Massachusetts Bay Colony. In 1657 she joined a missionary effort intended to infiltrate New England Puritanism with Quaker teachings. But she and other Quakers soon collided with laws designed to resist Quaker evangelism. The Puritans promptly banished Quakers found within the colony but soon discovered that those they had banished refused to remain away. Consequently, beginning the very year that Mary Dyer returned to North America, the Massachusetts Bay Colony passed a law that inflicted harsh punishments on Quaker men who refused to stay out of the colony. A first return after an initial banishment earned the penalty of having one ear cut off; a second return would result in the loss of another ear, and a third return was to be met with a capital sentence. Finding this law ineffective in deterring Quakers from missionary activities in the colony, Massachusetts authorities soon replaced this law with one that decreed death for Quakers who reentered the colony after banishment.

Mary Dyer first encountered these new anti-Quaker policies when, in 1657, she landed at Boston en route to Providence on her way home from England. She was arrested because she was Quaker and released only after her husband posted bond. In 1659, three Quaker men, accompanied by an 11-year-old girl, ventured into Massachusetts in defiance of the colony's law. For this, they earned imprisonment. Mary Dyer then traveled to Boston to visit them but was soon arrested and consigned to prison. Two months after her arrest, Dyer and the three men were banished along with the girl. Two of the men, William Robinson and Marmaduke Stevenson, chose to defy the law and remain in Massachusetts, and though Dyer originally left, she soon returned to visit another friend who had been imprisoned. The three adults were arrested and sentenced to death. The two men were hanged, but Mary Dyer, expecting to receive the same punishment, was released after briefly wearing the hangman's noose. In the spring of 1660, however, she returned to Massachusetts. Not inclined to endure her defiance any longer, Massachusetts authorities sentenced her to death and executed her by hanging on June 1, 1660, in Boston.

By her death in 1660, Mary Dyer became the first and only woman executed for her religious beliefs in New England. Under pressure from England, colonial authorities were soon forced to abandon use of capital punishment against Quakers, and the executions of the mid-17th century eventually became an embarrassment to the colony. Today, a statue of Mary Dyer adorns the statehouse grounds in Boston, Massachusetts.

Further Reading

Crawford, Deborah. *Four Women in a Violent Time: Anne Hutchinson (1591–1643), Mary Dyer (1591?–1660),*

Lady Deborah Moody (1600–1659), Penelope Stout (1622–1732). New York: Crown Publishers, 1970.

Dyer, William A. "William Dyer, a Rhode Island Dissenter." *Rhode Island Historical Society Collections* 30 (1937): 9–26.

Moriarty, G. Andrews. "The True Story of Mary Dyer." *New England Historical and Genealogical Register* 104 (January 1950): 40–42.

Plimpton, Ruth Talbot. *Mary Dyer: Biography of a Rebel Quaker*. Boston: Branden, 1994.

Rogers, Horatio. *Mary Dyer of Rhode Island: The Quaker Martyr That Was Hanged on Boston Common, June 1, 1660*. Providence R.I.: Preston & Rounds, 1896.

Eddy, Mary Baker
(Mary Morse Baker)
(1821–1910) *Christian Science founder*

Mary Baker Eddy founded the Church of Christ, Scientist, and authored *Science and Health: With Key to the Scriptures* (1875). Though she was perhaps the most controversial woman of her day, she achieved a singular place in the history of American religion by establishing an indigenous religious movement that has survived more than a century. She was born Mary Morse Baker on July 16, 1821, in Bow, New Hampshire, the daughter of Mark Baker and Abigail Ambrose Baker. She became a member of her parents' Congregational church when she was 17 years old, though she did not believe in the doctrine of predestination, as she later explained, "for I was unwilling to be saved, if my brothers and sisters were to be numbered among those who were doomed to perpetual banishment from God." Religious faith, then, became a formative aspect of Baker's life, but so also did sickness, for she suffered a variety of illnesses in her childhood, adolescent, and young adult years.

In 1843, Eddy married George Washington Glover, a building contractor. After their marriage, the couple moved first to Wilmington, North Carolina, and then to Charleston, South Carolina. Glover died within six months of the marriage and left his bride, alone and penniless, to bear their son, named George Washington Glover II. Mary Baker Glover spent the following years cast upon the hospitality of her family members. Her mother

died in 1849, and her father remarried the following year, leaving her to depart from her family home to live with a wealthy sister. The sister, however, had no desire to include George Glover II in this living arrangement, so his mother gave him up in 1851 to be raised by Mahala Cheney, a former servant of her family. Mahala moved with her husband to Minnesota in 1856, and Mary Baker Glover thereafter had little contact with her son while he was growing up.

In 1853, she married Daniel Patterson, a dentist, and this relationship lasted until the couple separated in 1866 and then divorced in 1873. Illness continued to plague Mary Baker Patterson during this period, and she became acquainted in 1862 with Phineas Parkhurst Quimby, a mesmeric healer, who believed that sicknesses were illusions of the mind. She began to study with Quimby and experienced relief from her illnesses through his mesmeric techniques. On February 1, 1866, she suffered a serious fall that left her injured. Two days later, while reading an account of one of Jesus' healings in the New Testament, she experienced healing herself. She interpreted the event as an illustration that sickness and disease proceeded from the failure of individuals to recognize that they are Spirit and connected to the Divine Mind. Matter, she grew to believe, is an illusion, and all suffering can be traced to the hypnotic effects of this illusion.

Over the next decade, Mary Baker Patterson undertook the work of a healer and a teacher and began to graft onto a modified Christian cosmology

Mary Baker Eddy founded Christian Science. *(Library of Congress, Prints and Photographs Division LC-USZ62-100584)*

tinued growth of the movement. A key aspect of the church's organizational structure was a format for meetings in which readings from Eddy's *Science and Health* occupied a central place, unadorned with commentary by ministers that might alter the essential message that she wished to perpetuate. Toward the middle of the 1890s, Eddy also supervised the construction of the Mother Church for the movement in Boston.

Controversy, however, continued to attend the steady expansion of Eddy's movement. Mark Twain, for example, made Mary Baker Eddy the target of his vicious wit. Though he agreed with many of the teachings of Christian Science, he displayed overwhelming disdain for Eddy herself, who by this time had become successful financially as well as in her institutional role as founder and leader of the Church of Christ, Scientist. She was, Twain acerbically announced,

> grasping, sordid, penurious, famishing for everything she sees—money, power, glory—vain, untruthful, jealous, despotic, arrogant, insolent, pitiless where thinkers and hypnotists are concerned, illiterate, shallow, incapable of reasoning outside of commercial lines, immeasurably selfish.

her understanding of healing. In 1875, she published the first edition of *Science and Health: With Key to the Scriptures,* the text that she would continuously revise over the remaining 35 years of her life and would become the textbook of Christian Science. In 1877 she married Asa Gilbert Eddy, and this union lasted until her husband's death five years later. In 1879, Mary Baker Eddy formed the Church of Christ, Scientist. Over the years that followed, this movement rapidly gained adherents.

Although Eddy demonstrated herself to be a gifted administrator of the burgeoning movement, she also proved equally gifted at provoking dissension. A steady series of schisms and internecine conflicts accompanied the growth of the Church of Christ, Scientist. Eddy, however, worked to craft an organizational structure for the church that would ultimately be embodied in the *Manual of the Mother Church,* which she published initially in 1895 and which guided the con-

Added to tangible criticisms such as these, Eddy suffered toward the end of her life from the belief that her enemies were plaguing her with Malicious Animal Magnetism—that is, powers of mind devoted to her destruction. Her organization, however, continued to flourish in spite of these attacks, even as Eddy herself suffered the increasing frailties of age. She died on December 3, 1910, near Brookline, Massachusetts.

As American religious movements have been, overwhelmingly, founded by men, Christian Science serves as the chief counterexample to this general pattern. Religion in the United States has known many women leaders, but they have tended to labor in fields marked out by men before them. Mary Baker Eddy, an exception to this trend, founded a new religion and managed to stand at its head for nearly 35 years. Perhaps even more significantly, she was able to lay the foundation of a movement that would survive her into the 21st century.

Further Reading

Beasley, Norman. *Mary Baker Eddy.* New York: Duell, Sloan & Pearce, 1963.

Dakin, Edwin Franden. *Eddy: The Biography of a Virginal Mind.* New York: Blue Ribbon Books, 1930; New York: Scribner, 1970.

Eddy, Mary Baker. *Science and Health: With Key to the Scriptures.* Boston: Writings of Mary Baker Eddy, 2000.

Gardner, Martin. *The Healing Revelations of Mary Baker Eddy: The Rise and Fall of Christian Science.* Buffalo, N.Y.: Prometheus Books, 1993.

Gill, Gillian. *Mary Baker Eddy.* Reading, Mass.: Perseus Books, 1998.

Knee, Stuart E. *Christian Science in the Age of Mary Baker Eddy.* Westport, Conn.: Greenwood Press, 1994.

Nenneman, Richard A. *Persistent Pilgrim: The Life of Mary Baker Eddy.* Etna, N.H.: Nebbadoon Press, 1997.

Peel, Robert. *Mary Baker Eddy: The Years of Authority.* New York: Holt, Rinehart & Winston, 1977.

———. *Mary Baker Eddy: The Years of Discovery.* New York: Holt, Rinehart & Winston, 1966.

———. *Mary Baker Eddy: The Years of Trial.* New York: Holt, Rinehart & Winston, 1971.

Silberger, Julius. *Mary Baker Eddy: An Interpretive Biography of the Founder of Christian Science.* Boston: Little, Brown, 1980.

Thomas, Robert David. *"With Bleeding Footsteps": Mary Baker Eddy's Path to Religious Leadership.* New York: Knopf, 1994.

Edwards, Jonathan

(1703–1758) *Congregationalist minister, theologian*

Jonathan Edwards was a Congregationalist minister and theologian whose influence casts a long shadow across the history of American religious thought. His theology stands astride doctrines inherited from the Puritans of the 17th century and the currents of revival that swept across North America during the Great Awakening. He was born on October 5, 1703, in East Windsor, Connecticut, the son of Timothy Edwards and Esther Stoddard Edwards. His father was a Congregationalist minister, and his maternal grandfather was SOLOMON STODDARD, an influential Puritan minister of the previous century. After receiving a preparatory education from his father, Edwards entered Yale College at the age of 12 and graduated in 1720, adding to his undergraduate degree an M.A. in 1723. During his graduate studies, Edwards had a conversion experience. Though lacking in the traditional evangelical progress from remorse over sin to joyous acknowledgment of God's gracious forgiveness in Christ, Edwards's conversion yielded for him "new Dispositions" and a "new Sense of Things." After a brief ministry as a pastor in Bolton, Connecticut, Edwards returned to Yale the following year as a tutor; he remained there from 1724 until 1726, when he accepted a position as an assistant pastor of the Congregationalist church in Northampton, where his grandfather was senior pastor. He married Sarah Pierpont in 1727, and their union produced several children.

In Northampton, Edwards proved to be a prolific writer and a spirited preacher. He wrote the first of many books in 1731, and he soon developed a preaching style that pricked the consciences of his congregation and resulted in a revival in 1734 and 1735. He preached what would become his most famous sermon in the years immediately after this revival, "Sinners in the Hands of an Angry God." In it, he set before his congregation the image of the sinner suspended over damnation by the thinnest thread. He piled metaphor upon metaphor to emphasize the precarious condition of the unregenerate. "Unconverted men walk over the pit of hell on a rotten covering, and there are innumerable places in this covering so weak that they will not bear their weight, and these places are not seen."

> So that, thus it is that natural men are held in the hand of God, over the pit of hell; they have deserved the fiery pit, and are already sentenced to it; and God is dreadfully provoked, his anger is as great toward them as to those that are actually suffering the executions of the fierceness of his wrath in hell, and they have done nothing in the least to appease or abate that anger, neither is God in the least bound by any promise to hold them up one moment; the devil is waiting for them, hell is

gaping for them, the flames gather and flash about them, and would fain lay hold on them, and swallow them up; the fire pent up in their own hearts is struggling to break out: and they have no interest in any Mediator, there are no means within reach that can be any security to them. In short, they have no refuge, nothing to take hold of; all that preserves them every moment is the mere arbitrary will, and uncovenanted, unobliged forbearance of an incensed God.

The revival in Northampton that Edwards's preaching had contributed to in the mid-1730s was soon followed by a more sustained revival on both sides of the Atlantic, sparked by the preaching of Anglican minister GEORGE WHITEFIELD. Edwards enthusiastically supported this spiritual awakening. He delivered an influential address at Yale in 1741 in which he generally defended the new revival movement, and the following year he published *Some Thoughts Concerning the Present Revival of Religion* (1742), which although not ratifying every phenomenon associated with the Great Awakening, nevertheless attempted to create a place for religious enthusiasm alongside doctrinal purity.

Jonathan Edwards's grandfather, Solomon Stoddard, had been famous for liberalizing the requirements for participation in the Lord's Supper. Early Puritans had reserved this sacrament for those who had given public evidence that they had experienced conversion. But Stoddard had opened the Lord's Supper to all those who affirmed the basic tenets of orthodoxy and who led morally pure lives. In the late 1740s, Jonathan Edwards rejected his grandfather's liberality and insisted that those who participated in the ordinance of communion give evidence of conversion. He also repudiated the influential Half-Way Covenant, by which individuals who had themselves been baptized as infants but who had never given proof of a conversion experience could nevertheless have their children baptized. Edwards insisted that only those who had experienced conversion were eligible. Both theological positions alienated Edwards from his Northampton community, and he was eventually forced to leave the church in 1751.

Edwards took a less prestigious spiritual post in Stockbridge, Massachusetts, where he served as a missionary to local Native Americans and pastor of a small church. Though his outward circumstances suffered decline during this period, Edwards was able to devote considerable time to writing and scholarly investigations. After seven years in Stockbridge, though, just as Edwards had grown accustomed to life there, the College of New Jersey (later Princeton University) found itself without a president and turned to him to fill the vacancy. He consented to assume the post and was installed as president on February 16, 1758. Because the area where the college was located had suffered an outbreak of smallpox during the months before his arrival, Edwards chose to be inoculated, but this led to the onset of a fever that ended his life little more than a month after his arrival. He died on March 22, 1758, in Princeton, New Jersey.

In Jonathan Edwards, a copious intellect, conversant with the greatest theological and philosophical minds of his day, married an evangelical temper, at home with the revivalism of the Great Awakening. The years that followed his death would find this combination ever more rare. That Edwards refused to embrace a religion that had no place for emotion—even as he refused to unfetter his faith from his mind—was his enduring contribution to American religion.

Further Reading

Edwards, Jonathan. *Jonathan Edwards: Basic Writings.* Edited by Ola Elizabeth Winslow. New York: New American Library, 1978.

———. *A Jonathan Edwards Reader.* Edited by John E. Smith, Harry S. Stout, and Kenneth P. Minkema. New Haven, Conn.: Yale University Press, 1995.

———. *The Life of David Brainerd.* New Haven, Conn.: Yale University Press, 1985.

Griffin, Edward M. *Jonathan Edwards.* Minneapolis: University of Minnesota Press, 1971.

Jenson, Robert W. *America's Theologian: A Recommendation of Jonathan Edwards.* New York: Oxford University Press, 1988.

McClymond, Michael James. *Encounters with God: An Approach to the Theology of Jonathan Edwards.* New York: Oxford University Press, 1998.

Miller, Perry. *Jonathan Edwards.* New York: W. Sloane Associates, 1949.

Murray, Iain Hamish. *Jonathan Edwards: A New Biography.* Edinburgh: Banner of Truth Trust, 1987.

Smith, John E. *Jonathan Edwards: Puritan, Preacher, Philosopher.* Notre Dame, Ind.: University of Notre Dame Press, 1992.

Winslow, Ola Elizabeth. *Jonathan Edwards, 1703–1758: A Biography.* New York: Macmillan, 1940.

Edwards, Jonathan, Jr.
(1745–1801) *Congregational minister, educator*

History remembers JONATHAN EDWARDS, the father, more than Jonathan Edwards, Jr., the son. Nevertheless the younger Edwards enjoyed a prominent reputation in his own day, even though his conservative theology tended to alienate him from many of his contemporaries. He was born on May 26, 1745, in Northampton, Massachusetts, the son of Jonathan Edwards and Sarah Pierpont Edwards. Soon after the younger Edwards's birth, his father, a Congregationalist minister, was dismissed from his church at Northampton and relocated his family to a mission settlement at Stockbridge, Massachusetts. The Edwards family remained there until Jonathan Edwards, Sr., accepted the position of president of the College of New Jersey (later Princeton University) in 1758. Almost immediately after his arrival in Princeton, however, he died of the effects of a smallpox inoculation. Six months later, Sarah Edwards died as well. Jonathan Edwards, Jr., remained in Princeton, and three years after the death of his parents he entered the College of New Jersey as a student. He experienced a religious conversion in 1763 and graduated two years later. After a year of private theological study under Joseph Bellamy and Samuel Hopkins, who had been closely associated with his father, Edwards was licensed to preach in 1766. He occupied the next few years serving as a tutor at the College of New Jersey and preaching in New England churches.

Edwards received his ordination as the minister of the White Haven Congregational Church in New Haven in 1769. The following year he married Mary Porter, with whom he had four children, one of whom died in infancy. Edwards's tenure as the minister at White Haven began and ended controversially. Before his arrival, the White Haven church adhered to the Half-Way Covenant, according to which the children of full church members who had been baptized in their infancy but given no evidence of a conversion experience were admitted as church members themselves but not allowed to participate in the sacrament of the Lord's Supper. Apparently at Edwards's insistence, the church abandoned this arrangement just prior to his arrival, thus requiring evidence of conversion for all those who sought church membership. Aggrieved at this change, some of the members withdrew in 1771 to form a new church, the Fair Haven church. Edwards remained at White Haven for more than 25 years, but the stern Calvinist views he inherited from his father, frequently referred to as the New Divinity, proved increasingly unpalatable to his congregation. He enjoyed a more receptive audience among the ministerial students who studied with him during these years, including men of future note such as JEDIDIAH MORSE, who helped found Andover Seminary, and TIMOTHY DWIGHT, Edwards's nephew and a future president of Yale College. After the death of his first wife in 1782, he married Mercy Sabin the following year.

Over the years, Edwards's congregation steadily dwindled in size until it could—or would—no longer meet its salary obligations to him. In the spring of 1795, the church finally voted to dissolve its relationship with him, and Edwards found himself cast adrift from his ministerial station at the age of 50. Like his father, who had been dismissed from the Northampton church and had to settle for a much smaller mission church, the younger Edwards discovered that most New England pulpits were not eager to have him. He finally accepted a position as minister of the small Congregational church in Colebrook, Connecticut, at the end of 1795. Also like his father, who had been named the president of the College of New Jersey at the end of his life, the younger Edwards was presented with an academic opportunity after he had spent several relatively secluded years at Colebrook. Union College in Schenectady, New York, elected him its second president in 1799.

Edwards's brief tenure in this office left little in the way of concrete improvements in the institution. In his position as president of Union College, though, Edwards became closely involved in the final stages of deliberations that resulted in the Plan of Union adopted by Congregationalists and Presbyterians in 1801, according to which the two denominations agreed to participate in western missionary activities. He died in Schenectady soon after this event, on August 1, 1801.

Jonathan Edwards, Jr., never ascended to the pinnacle of influence his father had enjoyed. His vigorous Calvinism had been more palatable to his father's generation than it was to his own. The revolutionary times in which he lived preferred a God who made greater room for the possibility of human goodness than the younger Edwards was prepared to admit. Thus, he found himself largely isolated in his own age, heir to a theology that did not speak to the spiritual sensibilities of his own generation, however it may have undergirded the religious impulses of a previous time.

Further Reading

Edwards, Jonathan. *The Works of Jonathan Edwards.* 2 vols. New York: Garland, 1987.

Ferm, Robert L. *Jonathan Edwards the Younger, 1745–1801: A Colonial Pastor.* Grand Rapids, Mich.: Eerdmans, 1976.

Minkema, Kenneth Pieter. "The Edwardses: A Ministerial Family in Eighteenth Century New England." Ph.D. dissertation, University of Connecticut, 1988.

Valeri, Mark R. *Law and Providence in Joseph Bellamy's New England: The Origins of the New Divinity in Revolutionary America.* New York: Oxford University Press, 1994.

Einhorn, David
(1809–1879) *Reform rabbi*

A leading intellectual architect of Reform Judaism in America, David Einhorn immigrated to the United States in 1855. Though frequently at odds with other American Jews because of his theological view, Einhorn espoused ideas that dominated Reform Judaism in the United States until well into the 20th century. Einhorn was born on November 10, 1809, in Dispeck, Bavaria, the son of Maier Einhorn and Karoline Einhorn. He studied at an Orthodox

yeshiva and received his rabbinical certificate in 1826, when he was only 17 years old. Subsequently he attended a series of secular universities—at Erlangen, Würzburg, and Munich—where his theological views strayed substantially from orthodoxy. His radicalism, in fact, was sufficient to prevent him from finding a rabbinical post until the early 1840s.

In 1842, however, Einhorn became the rabbi in Birkenfeld, Germany. While there he married Julia Ochs, with whom he had nine children. At the Frankfort Rabbinical Conference in 1845, he urged changes to Jewish worship that would have included the use of the vernacular and elimination of any aspirations for the restoration of sacrifices or of the Jewish state. After five years in Birkenfeld, he became the chief rabbi of the Jewish congregation of Mecklenburg-Schwerin, but his radical views forced him to leave this post after several years and, after a brief tenure as a rabbi in Budapest, to immigrate to the United States in 1855.

The year before he left Europe, David Einhorn published his most important theological work, *The Principles of Mosaic Religion* (1854). In this and subsequent writings, Einhorn charted a theological course that would eventually dominate Reform Judaism in America. Its key elements were a rejection of the aspiration for a Jewish state and an attempt to unhinge Judaism from devotion to outmoded ceremonies in favor of a concentration on the ethical components of Jewish law. The divine law, he insisted, had a "perishable body" and an "imperishable spirit." Einhorn located the perishable in ceremonial rites and regulations practiced by Orthodox Jews and the imperishable in the enduring moral principles of Jewish law.

Einhorn arrived in America and assumed the post of rabbi for the Har Sinai congregation in Baltimore, Maryland. He appeared in the United States in time to participate in the Cleveland Rabbinical Conference, held in 1855, at which he clashed immediately with ISAAC MAYER WISE, who was willing to moderate some elements of Reform Judaism to create a broader sphere of cooperation among Jewish rabbis. Once settled in Baltimore, Einhorn published a German periodical, *Sinai,* which he used to advance his reformist project, from 1856 to 1862. He also prepared a new prayer book, mostly in German, *Olat Tamid.* His strident abolitionism, however, eventually forced him to abandon Baltimore in the face of mob violence threatened against him and to settle in Philadelphia, Pennsylvania, where he served as rabbi of the Kenesseth Israel congregation from 1861 to 1866. From 1866 until his retirement in 1879, shortly before his death, Einhorn was rabbi of Adath Jeshurun in New York, later renamed Temple Beth-El.

Einhorn attended the first conference for Reform rabbis in America, which was held in Philadelphia in 1866. He played a leading role in the proceedings of this conference, which produced a statement of principles that subsequently guided the course of Reform Judaism in America. The first two principles of the Philadelphia Conference embraced Einhorn's view of the Jews as a priestly rather than a political people.

> The Messianic goal of Israel . . . [i]s the union of all men as children of God. . . . The fall of the second Jewish commonwealth [i]s not punishment . . . [but] divine purpose . . . [t]he dispersion of the Jews to all parts of the earth, for the realization of their high priestly mission, to lead the nations to the true knowledge and worship of God.

Einhorn died a decade after the Pittsburgh Conference, on November 2, 1879, in New York City.

Before his death, David Einhorn had become a dominant voice within American Reform Judaism. Afterward, his influence survived through the leadership of his son-in-law and theological disciple, Kaufmann Kohler. Kohler convened another conference of Reform rabbis in Philadelphia in 1885, at which the platform substantially incorporated the elements of the Pittsburgh platform, over which Einhorn had exerted such significant influence. After the beginning of the 20th century, Kohler also assumed the presidency of Reform Judaism's most important educational institution, the Hebrew Union College in Cincinnati, Ohio. Through these developments, David Einhorn's intellectual presence guided Reform Judaism well into the 20th century.

Further Reading

Cohen, Bernard N. "David Einhorn, Some Aspects of His Thinking." In *Essays in American Jewish History*. Cincinnati: n.p., 1958; New York: Ktav Publishing House, 1975.

Cohen, Philip Martin. "David Einhorn: Biblical Theology as Response and Reform." Ph.D. dissertation, Brandeis University, 1994.

Friedland, Eric L. "'Olath Tamid' by David Einhorn." *Hebrew Union College Annual* 45 (1974): 307–32.

Greenberg, Gershon. "Mendelssohn in America: David Einhorn's Radical Reform Judaism." *Leo Baeck Institute Yearbook* 27 (1982): 281–93.

Meyer, Michael A. *Response to Modernity: A History of the Reform Movement in Judaism*. Detroit: Wayne State University Press, 1995.

Rutman, Herbert S. *Rabbi David Einhorn*. Baltimore: Jewish Historical Society of Maryland, 1979.

el-Shabazz, Malik   See MALCOLM X.

Eliot, John
(1604–1690) *Puritan minister, missionary*

John Eliot served as a Puritan minister in New England and as overseer of Harvard College during its early years, but history remembers him mainly for his missionary efforts to Native Americans. He was born in England and baptized on August 5, 1604, in Widford, Herfordshire, the son of Bennett Eliot and Lettice Aggar Eliot. he studied at Jesus College, Cambridge, and received a B.A. in 1622. Though ordained as a minister in the Church of England, Eliot had Puritan leanings that made him unwelcome to the Anglican establishment, so he instead accepted a position as a teacher at a grammar school in Little Baddow, Essex.

Eliot eventually joined other Puritans who migrated to the New World, arriving there in November 1631. He briefly served as pastor of the Boston church until John Wilson, the church's minister, returned from a trip to England. Afterward, the church offered Eliot the position of teacher, the post that JOHN COTTON, one of New England's most famous early preachers, would subsequently occupy. Eliot preferred to move to Roxbury, however, where some of his friends had settled, and he promptly accepted a position as teacher at the church there, where

Thomas Weld was pastor. He married Anne Mumford (or Mountfort) in 1632, and together the couple had six children. After Weld departed for England in 1641, Eliot became the church's senior pastor and continued in that position until he retired two years before his death. In all, Eliot served nearly 60 years in Roxbury, outliving most of the preachers of his generation and joking late in life that the other New England founders "got safe to heaven . . . would suspect him to be gone the wrong way, because he had stayed so long behind them."

In the 1640s, Eliot turned his attention to a study of Native American language with the goal of preaching to Native Americans. He focused on Algonquian and by the end of the decade had begun to engage in missionary activities that would dominate the remainder of his life and earn for him the title of "Apostle to the Indians." He raised money from English supporters for these activities, which, beginning in 1651, included establishing separate towns for Native American converts, who were referred to at the time as "praying Indians." Eliot encouraged his Native American hearers not only to adopt the truths of Christianity, but to adopt social practices of the English colonists, including their dress and trades. He also turned to the work of translating the Bible into Algonquin. Eliot's version of the Algonquin New Testament appeared in 1661, followed two years later by his translation of the Old Testament. Together, the two constituted the first complete text of the Bible printed in North America.

Eliot's missionary efforts among the Native Americans suffered a catastrophic setback with the outbreak of King Philip's War. Indian raids on New England frontier settlements prompted reprisals by colonial militia against Native American villages. The bloodletting on all sides poisoned relations between colonists and Native Americans generally, though at least some of the "praying Indians" found themselves enlisted as scouts against the tribes. More commonly, however, the Native Americans in the Christianized villages established by Eliot were viewed with distrust. The inhabitants of Natick, the original village of "praying Indians," were consigned to an island in Boston Harbor, where many of them died.

After King Philip's War drew to a bloody close in 1676, Eliot continued his missionary efforts. But his Native American parishioners had been decimated by the war, and his continued efforts yielded only scant results as compared to those of the previous two decades. He died on May 21, 1690, in Roxbury.

By contemporary standards of cultural respect and sensitivity, John Eliot is sometimes judged harshly for the extent to which he coaxed Native Americans not only into the folds of Christian faith but into that of European cultural mores as well. Among his contemporaries, however, Eliot was a beacon of respect for Native Americans. Unlike Puritans, such as COTTON MATHER, who considered Eliot to have humanized "miserable animals," Eliot himself viewed his mission as one to men and women who needed no humanizing, only converting.

Further Reading

Bowden, Henry W., and James P. Ronda. *John Eliot's Indian Dialogues: A Study in Cultural Interaction.* Westport, Conn.: Greenwood Press, 1980.

Cogley, Richard W. *John Eliot's Mission to the Indians Before King Philip's War.* Cambridge, Mass.: Harvard University Press, 1999.

Francis, Convers. *Life of John Eliot: The Apostle to the Indians.* Boston: Hilliard, Gray, 1836.

Mather, Cotton. *The Triumphs of the Reformed Religion in America: The Life of the Renowned John Eliot.* Boston: Benjamin Harris & John Allen, 1691.

Moore, Martin. *Memoirs of the Life and Character of Rev. John Eliot, Apostle of the N.A. Indians.* Boston: T. Bedlington, 1822.

Naeher, Robert J. "Dialogue in the Wilderness: John Eliot and the Indian Exploration of Puritanism as a Source of Meaning, Comfort, and Ethnic Survival." *New England Quarterly* 62 (1989): 346–68.

Winslow, Ola Elizabeth. *John Eliot: Apostle to the Indians.* Boston: Houghton, Mifflin, 1968.

Emmons, Nathanael
(1745–1840) *Congregational minister, theologian*

Nathanael Emmons championed the New England theology often referred to as the New Divinity. This form of Calvinism, inherited from JONATHAN EDWARDS, stressed both the predestined will of God and the possibility of revivalistic conversion. Emmons was born on April 20, 1745, in East Haddam, Connecticut, the son of Samuel Emmons and Ruth Cone Emmons. He attended Yale College and graduated in 1769. That year, he both experienced a religious conversion and accepted the New Divinity school of theology. Thereafter he taught school briefly, before studying privately with Nathan Strong of Coventry, Connecticut, and John Smalley of New Britain, Connecticut, to become a minister.

Emmons's embrace of the New Divinity won him as many theological enemies as friends, but he was licensed to preach in due time by the South Association of Hartford County, Connecticut. In the fall of 1772, he finally received a ministerial call from the Second Church of Wrentham, Massachusetts, where he was ordained a Congregational minister the following spring. Second Church would prove to be Emmons's only pastorate. Several years after he arrived there, the town divided, and the portion where Second Church was located was named Franklin. Emmons remained at the renamed Franklin Congregational Church for the rest of his life. In the spring of 1775, he married Deliverance French, with whom he had two children. After the sudden death of his wife and both children in quick succession three years later, Emmons married Martha Williams, with whom he had six children, in 1779. Late in life, after the death of his second wife, he married Abigail Moore Mills.

At Franklin, Emmons devoted himself wholeheartedly to the work of preaching, carrying on the New Divinity tradition. In this regard he emphasized the sovereignty of God, but he also stressed human freedom and responsibility. Emmons insisted that humans made choices according to their pleasure and thus were both free and responsible for those choices, even if they lacked the moral ability to choose rightly. More controversially, however, he denied the Calvinistic doctrine of original sin—that is, of an inherently corrupt human nature as the root of sinful conduct. There is, he contended, no such thing as a sinful nature antecedent to sinful "exercises," which he considered free and voluntary. Men and women are sinful not as a result of their nature, but of their free choice.

Emmons never attempted to write a systematic theology. Instead, he poured his energies week by week into the work of crafting sermons, which he subsequently published in collections. He also extended his theological influence by devoting significant attention to the training of ministerial students privately, thus multiplying the kind of mentoring relationship by which he himself had been trained. He was famous for his concise advice about the secret of good preaching: "First have something to say: then say it." Although Emmons's theology alienated many and denied him a broad preaching ministry in other pulpits, he did serve a leadership role in the Massachusetts Missionary Society, of which he was president for 12 years, beginning with the society's creation in 1799.

As many preachers of his day, Nathanael Emmons was not averse to commenting on public affairs from the pulpit. A Federalist who later drifted into the ranks of the Whigs, Emmons had nothing but disdain for President Thomas Jefferson and his Democrat-Republicans. On a fast day in 1801, he preached a sermon on Jeroboam, an Old Testament king of whom the Bible has little good to say, and painted the distant potentate in terms that levied a thinly veiled diatribe against President Jefferson. He died on September 23, 1840, in Franklin, Massachusetts.

Nathanael Emmons represented an important but controversial stand of New England theology. The New Divinity stretched from Jonathan Edwards through his students, Samuel Hopkins and Joseph Bellamy, and ultimately to Emmons. It was a theology born in the Great Awakening, ever afterward fixed on the task of reinterpreting classical Calvinist beliefs in ways that supported revivalism. In Emmons's hands, however, this reinterpretation took—at least on some issues such as original sin—the form of complete rejection and thus made him a lightning rod for critics who believed that he had ventured far from the fold of orthodox Calvinism.

Further Reading

Emmons, Nathanael. *The Works of Nathanael Emmons, D.D. Later Pastor of the Church in Franklin, Mass., with a Memoir of His Life.* Edited by Jacob Ide. Boston: Crocker & Brewster, 1842.

Kuklick, Bruce. *Churchmen and Philosophers: From Jonathan Edwards to John Dewey.* New Haven, Conn.: Yale University Press, 1985.

Park, Edwards Amasa. *Memoir of Nathanael Emmons.* Boston: Congregational Board of Publication, 1861.

Smith, Henry Boynton. "The Theological System of Emmons." *In Faith and Philosophy: Discourses and Methods.* Edited by G. L. Prentiss. New York: Scribner, Armstrong, 1877; New York: Garland Publishing, 1987.

Valeri, Mark R. *Law and Providence in Joseph Bellamy's New England: The Origins of the New Divinity in Revolutionary America.* New York: Oxford University Press, 1994.

Williams, Thomas. *A Discourse on the Official Character of Nathanael Emmons.* Boston: C.C.P. Moody, 1851.

England, John
(1786–1842) *Catholic bishop*

John England, the first bishop of Charleston, South Carolina, spent the last two decades of his life in America, after serving as a priest in Ireland. He gave to his later labors a boundless enthusiasm for the harmony he saw between the Catholic faith and the democratic traditions of the United States. England was born on September 23, 1786, in Cork, Ireland, the son of Thomas England and Honora Lordan England. He planned initially to practice law but in 1802 began study for the Catholic ministry at St. Patrick's College in Carlow, Ireland. He was ordained a priest six years later and returned to Cork, where he served until 1817 in a variety of capacities associated with the cathedral, including chaplain to the North Presentation Convent, the Magdalen Asylum, and the city jail. He also taught at the College of Saint Mary in Cork and became the college's president in 1812. The years from 1817 to 1820 he spent as a pastor in Bandon, Ireland.

In 1820, John England was ordained the first bishop of South Carolina, where he spent the remainder of his life. His diocese covered North and South Carolina as well as Georgia. England enthusiastically embraced the democratic traditions of the United States and found them compatible with the life and teachings of the Catholic Church. Unlike some religious believers, who detected in the U.S. Constitution's establishment clause a latent hostility to faith, England saw the Constitution's prohibition against laws "respecting an establishment of religion" as a safeguard for the church as well as the state.

England's respect for democratic principles spilled over into his administration of his diocese. Like the framers of the Constitution, who struggled to form a single union out of separate states, England searched for ways of uniting Catholics into established congregations and creating in these separate congregations a sense of belonging to a larger community of faith. To this end, he established in 1822 the *United States Catholic Miscellany,* the first Catholic newspaper to be published regularly in America.

The South Carolina bishop also approached diocesan affairs with a democratic concern for the role of the laity and for establishing clearly stated rules for governing the affairs of the diocese. He drafted a *Constitution for the Diocese of Charleston,* which sought to harness both clergy and laity into joint involvement in diocesan governance. The *Constitution* called for the appointment of lay delegates from each parish to serve in an annual convention. This convention bore a close likeness to the bicameral legislature of the federal government, though instead of a House of Representatives and a Senate, the convention established by England consisted of a House of Clergy and a House of Lay Delegates. Through the *Constitution* and the annual conventions it inaugurated, England was able to effect a measure of ecclesiastical peace in Catholic affairs that had been troubled before his arrival.

Though John England devoted his copious energies primarily to the management of the affairs of his diocese, his reputation as a conciliator drew the attention of a wider audience. He became the first Catholic to address Congress in 1826, and he used the occasion to reiterate his views concerning the harmony that should exist between the democratic institutions of the United States and the ecclesiastical institutions of the Catholic Church. The Vatican called on England to serve as an apostolic delegate from 1833 to 1837 to help negotiate a concordat between the church and the Haitian government. Though no agreement was forthcoming during John England's lifetime, two decades after his death the church signed a concordat with Haiti that incorporated key elements of England's early negotiation. England died on April 11, 1842, in Charleston, South Carolina.

Products of John England's democratic enthusiasm such as his *Constitution* and the conventions it generated did not survive his death. The bishops who followed him proved not to be enamored of his vision and reverted to more traditional forms of diocesan governance. They abandoned his *Constitution* and neglected to continue his annual conventions. England's steadfast commitment to the value of cooperative efforts by Catholics would become a pattern, though, for the influential councils of Catholic leaders that began in Baltimore in the half century after his death. For his tireless dedication to these efforts, he has sometimes been called the Father of the Baltimore Councils. It would remain until the 20th century, though, for the Catholic Church in America to reappropriate something like England's zeal for lay participation in the affairs of the church.

Further Reading

Carey, Patrick W. *An Immigrant Bishop: John England's Adaptation of Irish Catholicism to American Republicanism.* Yonkers, N.Y.: U.S. Catholic Historical Society, 1982.

Clarke, Peter. *A Free Church in a Free Society: The Ecclesiology of John England, Bishop of Charleston, 1820–1840—A Nineteenth-Century Bishop in the Southern United States.* Hartsville, S.C.: Attic Press, 1982.

England, John. *The Works of the Right Rev. John England.* Edited by Ignatius Aloysius Reynolds. 5 vols. New York: Arno Press, 1978.

Grant, Dorothy Fremont. *John England: American Christopher.* Milwaukee: Bruce, 1949.

Guilday, Peter. *The Life and Times of John England.* 2 vols. New York: American Press, 1927; New York: Arno Press, 1969.

"History of the Diocese of Charleston." Available online. URL: http://www.catholic-doc.org/ns-hist.html. Downloaded on April 22, 2002.

Ewing, Finis
(1773–1841) *Presbyterian minister, cofounder of the Cumberland Presbytery*

Finis Ewing was a cofounder and an early leader of the Cumberland Presbytery, which grew out of theological differences in the Presbyterian Church at the turn of the 19th century. Though he became a Presbyterian minister under controversial circumstances, he labored across four decades to create a revival on the western frontier. Named, appropriately enough, Finis, as the last of 12 children, he was born on July 10, 1773, in Bedford County, Virginia, the son of Robert Ewing and Mary Baker Ewing. The details of his early life are unknown, except that he eventually lived in Tennessee after the death of his parents, and in January 1793, he married Margaret Davidson, with whom he had 13 children.

By 1800, Ewing and his family had relocated to Logan County, Kentucky, where they joined a local Presbyterian church of which James McGready was minister. That year, McGready's fiery preaching had sparked revival in the area, and the Ewings experienced a religious conversion. Though Presbyterians normally required ministers to possess a classical education, the spiritual awakening ignited that year accelerated the need for preachers. In 1801, the Transylvania Presbytery, which encompassed the area in which revivalism had flourished, licensed four men, including Finis Ewing, who did not meet the normal educational requirements, as exhorters. The following year, the presbytery licensed Ewing and two others to preach, though a minority of the members of the presbytery—generally opposed to the revivalism that had flourished in the area—complained to the Synod of Kentucky about what they viewed as the irregular action of the presbytery. Soon afterward the synod divided the Transylvania Presbytery in two, creating a new Cumberland Presbytery and a reformed Transylvania Presbytery. The Cumberland Presbytery, controlled by a majority of ministers who supported the recent revivals, ordained Ewing as a minister in 1803.

In 1805, the Kentucky Synod moved against the actions of the Cumberland Presbytery, directing that Ewing and other new ministers refrain from preaching. This action sprang from the antirevival spirit that dominated the synod, its reluctance to ordain uneducated ministers, and, perhaps most important, its alarm that Ewing, and others who had recently been ordained, did not subscribe to the doctrine of reprobation as enshrined in the Westminster Confession, the statement of doctrine adopted by English Presbyterians in the 17th century. The following year, the synod dissolved the Cumberland Presbytery. But four years later, on February 4, 1810, Ewing and two other men— Samuel King and Samuel McAdow—reconstituted the Cumberland Presbytery as an independent presbytery, thus giving birth to the Cumberland Presbyterians. By 1813, growth among the Cumberland churches prompted the creation of the Cumberland Synod.

Over the years that followed, Ewing played a prominent role among the Cumberland Presbyterians. He eventually carried his revival preaching west, along with the spread of the new denomination, to Cooper County, Missouri, in the spring of 1820. He organized churches and a theological school in the new territory. In 1836 he moved to Lexington, Missouri, where he accepted an appointment as the U.S. register of the Land Office there, combining this salaried position with the work of establishing a new congregation and generally advancing the cause of Cumberland Presbyterianism. He died on July 4, 1841, in Lexington.

Born of early 19th-century revivalism, the Cumberland Presbyterian Church still thrives at the beginning of the 21st century, though it remains one of the lesser tributaries of Presbyterianism in the United States. Finis Ewing represented the evangelistic enthusiasm of those whom the fire of revival had made impatient with an overly keen preoccupation with ministerial qualifications other than divine calling. Though relatively uneducated, he possessed the spiritual willingness and the energy necessary to carry the Christian message to the edge of the frontier.

Further Reading

Barrus, Ben M., Milton L. Baughn, and Thomas H. Campbell. *A People Called Cumberland Presbyterians*. Memphis, Tenn.: Frontier Press, 1972.

Blake, T.C. *The Old Log House: A History and Defense of the Cumberland Presbyterian Church*. Nashville: Cumberland Presbyterian Publishing House, 1878.

Cossitt, Franceway Ranna. *The Life and Times of Rev. Finis Ewing, One of the Fathers and Founders of the Cumberland Presbyterian Church*. Louisville, Ky.: L. R. Woods, 1853.

Foster, Douglas A. "The Springfield and Cumberland Presbyteries: Conflict and Secession in the Old Southwest." *Restoration Quarterly* 32 (1990). Available online. URL: http://www.rq.acu.edu/Volume_032/rq03203foster.htm.

Stephens, John Vant. *The Genesis of the Cumberland Presbyterian Church*. Cincinnati: The Lane Seminary Building, 1941.

Falwell, Jerry
(1933–) *Baptist minister, television personality*

A fundamentalist Baptist preacher and conservative political activist, Jerry Falwell sprang onto the national stage in the late 1970s and 1980s with the creation of the Moral Majority, a conservative political action group. Falwell's influence was at its peak during the years of Ronald Reagan's presidency, and he continues to be an active voice of religiously rooted conservativism in national public debates. Falwell was born on August 11, 1933, in Lynchburg, Virginia, the son of Carey H. Falwell and Helen Falwell. His father was a successful local businessman who died in 1948 of cirrhosis of the liver; his mother was a fundamentalist Christian, whose influence was partially responsible for Falwell's conversion in 1952. According to Falwell's later account, his mother, unable to coax her son to church as he grew older, would leave the radio tuned to a prominent evangelist's program when she left for church. Through listening to this program and eventually attending a service at the Park Avenue Baptist Church in Lynchburg, Falwell responded to an invitation on January 20, 1952, and professed his faith in Christ. At the time, he was a student at Lynchburg College majoring in mechanical engineering. After becoming a "born again" Christian, as he would describe himself, Falwell transferred to the Baptist Bible College in Springfield, Missouri, where he gradu-

ated in 1956 with a Th.D. degree. Falwell married Macel Pate on April 12, 1958, and this union produced three children.

Falwell returned after college to Lynchburg, where he founded an independent Baptist church in the summer of 1956 with an initial membership of 35 adults. He started a radio broadcast immediately and, within six months, added a television program, *The Old-Time Gospel Hour*. After the first year, membership in the church, later named the Thomas Road Baptist Church, had neared 1,000. It grew phenomenally after that, numbering around 22,000 members by the beginning of the new millennium. In 1967, Falwell founded the Liberty Christian Academy and, in 1971, Lynchburg Baptist College (later called Liberty Baptist College) to add to the church's growing list of satellite ministries.

In the early years of his ministry, while the turbulence of the Civil Rights movement and protests against the Vietnam War engaged the nation's attention, Falwell insisted that the church had no business seeking to reform society. Rather, he maintained, it was commissioned by God simply to spread the gospel of salvation through Jesus Christ. In a sermon preached in 1965, "Ministers and Marches," Falwell spurned political involvement by clergy: "Nowhere are we commissioned to reform the externals; we are not told to wage war against bootleggers, liquor stores, gamblers, murderers, prostitutes . . . or any other existing evil as such." By the end of the 1970s, however, Falwell had decisively repudiated this position. Appalled by abortion rights, gay rights, banishment of prayer from public schools, and other social trends contrary to the norms of fundamentalist Christianity, Falwell turned his attention to political action. He organized "I Love America" to celebrate the country's Bicentennial and, in the summer of 1979, founded the Moral Majority to advance conservative political causes. Credited with helping to elect President Ronald Reagan in 1980, the Moral Majority condemned abortion, homosexuality, pornography, and the Equal Rights Amendment, and it advocated a balanced budget and increased military spending. For most of the 1980s, Falwell's position at the helm of the Moral Majority, combined with the television presence of his *The Old-Time Gospel Hour*, made him the most visible preacher in America.

By 1986, the Moral Majority had folded, replaced by the less prominent Liberty Federation. The influence of the Christian Right, moreover, of which Falwell's organization had been the most prominent example, seemed itself on the wane. Financial difficulties relating to Liberty Baptist College consumed much of Falwell's attention during the 1990s. But by the end of the decade, he was still visible on the national political scene, sponsoring a voter registration drive in connection with the presidential election of 2000 and appearing regularly on television talk shows devoted to current issues. All the while, he continued to preside as senior pastor of the Thomas Road Baptist Church, chancellor of the Liberty Baptist College, and president of *The Old Time Gospel Hour*.

Although Jerry Falwell has been enormously successful as the pastor of one of the largest churches in the nation, his more enduring significance for American religious life will probably be the role he has played in the reengagement of conservative Christians in political debate. In this role, he has been a lightning rod of criticism both by those who oppose his conservative political agenda and by those who complain that his overtly religious presence in the political arena threatens the so-called wall of separation between church and state. It remains to be seen whether the Christian Right, for which he was a leading voice in the final two decades of the 20th century, will continue to

play an influential part in the nation's political life in the 21st century.

Further Reading

D'Souza, Dinesh. *Falwell, Before the Millennium: A Critical Biography.* Chicago: Regnery Gateway, 1984.

Falwell, Jerry. *Champions for God.* Wheaton, Ill.: Victor Books, 1985.

———. *Falwell: An Autobiography.* Lynchburg, Va.: Liberty House, 1997.

———. *Listen, America!* Garden City, N. Y.: Doubleday, 1980.

———. *Strength for the Journey: An Autobiography.* New York: Simon & Schuster, 1987.

Harding, Susan Friend. *The Book of Jerry Falwell: Fundamentalist Language and Politics.* Princeton, N.J.: Princeton University Press, 2000.

Ide, Arthur Frederick. *Evangelical Terrorism: Censorship, Falwell, Robertson, and the Seamy Side of Christian Fundamentalism.* Irving, Tex.: Scholars Books, 1986.

Lloyd, Mark. *Pioneers of Prime Time Religion: Jerry Falwell, Rex Humbard, Oral Roberts.* Dubuque, Iowa: Kendall/Hunt, 1988.

Smolla, Rodney A. *Jerry Falwell v. Larry Flynt: The First Amendment on Trial.* New York: St. Martin's Press, 1988.

Snowball, David. *Continuity and Change in the Rhetoric of the Moral Majority.* New York: Praeger, 1991.

Strober, Gerald S., and Ruth Tomczak. *Jerry Falwell: Aflame for God.* Nashville: T. Nelson, 1979.

Farrakhan, Louis Abdul
(Louis Eugene Walcott, Louis X)
(1933–) *Nation of Islam leader*

Louis Abdul Farrakhan, the controversial leader of the Nation of Islam, achieved national notoriety during the 1980s for his virulent anti-Semitic remarks. By the beginning of the 21st century, he remained a prominent figure on the national scene as the leader of the most significant black separatist religion in the United States. He was born Louis Eugene Walcott on May 11, 1933, in New York City, the son of parents who had immigrated to the United States from the Caribbean. He grew up in Boston, Massachusetts, where he attended Boston English High School. Farrakhan completed two years of study at the Winston Salem Teachers College in North Carolina before leaving college to pursue a career as a singer-musician, referred to variously as "Calypso Gene" and "The Charmer." The year he left college he also married Betsy Ross (later known as Khadijah), with whom he had nine children. Farrakhan joined the Nation of Islam in 1955, first changing his name to Louis X, thus discarding his "slave" name, and later to Louis Abdul Farrakhan. As a member of the Nation of Islam, also referred to as Black Muslims, Louis embraced the teaching of ELIJAH MUHAMMAD, who asserted that Nation of Islam founder Wallace Fard had been the incarnation of Allah and that Elijah Muhammad was Allah's messenger. Muhammad also taught that whites were devils whose 6,000-year domination of the world was shortly to end and that blacks must practice self-sufficiency and moral purity to prepare themselves to claim their rightful place.

Soon after joining the Black Muslims, Farrakhan became the assistant to MALCOLM X in Boston and then minister of the Boston temple of the Nation of Islam when Malcolm X took charge of Temple No. 7 in Harlem. In 1963, conflict between Elijah Muhammad and Malcolm X resulted in Malcolm X's leaving the Nation of Islam and forming a competing religious organization. He was assassinated by three members of the Nation of Islam in February 21, 1965, and Farrakhan later admitted that his own inflammatory comments concerning Malcolm X had contributed to the climate that had produced the assassination. After Malcolm X's departure from the Black Muslims, Farrakhan assumed his leadership role within the Nation of Islam, becoming minister of the Harlem Temple and Elijah Muhammad's national representative. On the death of Muhammad in 1975, however, Muhammad's son, W. Deen Muhammad, took charge of the Nation of Islam and, over the next decade, sheered the movement of its black separatist identity and sought to bring it into the mainstream of Islamic faith.

Farrakhan resisted this transformation and eventually resurrected the Nation of Islam in 1978 along lines in keeping with the teachings of Elijah Muhammad. This rejuvenation of the Black Muslims coincided with the announcement by JESSE JACKSON in 1983 of his attempt to secure the Democratic nomination for president. Farrakhan campaigned aggressively for Jackson and, in doing so, captured national attention with anti-Semitic remarks, not the least of which was his suggestion in 1984 that Hitler had been a "great," though "wickedly great" man. The following year, he made news again when he was quoted as referring to Judaism as a "gutter religion." At the end of the decade, he made headlines once more by insisting that the international acquired immuno deficiency syndrome (AIDS) epidemic had been engineered by the U.S. government in an attempt to destroy blacks in Africa.

At the beginning of the 21st century, Louis Abdul Farrakhan was probably the most controversial religious leader in America. He continued to speak widely in the 1990s, and his orchestration of the Million Man March in 1995, which attracted thousands of African-American men to the National Mall in Washington, D.C., demonstrated that he had considerable influence among the black community. The same year, Qubilah Shabbaz, the daughter of slain African-American leader Malcolm X, was indicted for allegedly plotting to kill Farrakhan. She ultimately escaped conviction by agreeing to accept psychiatric and alcohol abuse treatment. Ironically, by the end of the 20th century, Farrakhan, like Malcolm X before him, seemed to have tamed some of his racist rhetoric and to have positioned himself more in line with traditional Islamic belief.

Further Reading

Farrakhan, Louis. *Back Where We Belong: Selected Speeches.* Edited by Joseph D. Eure and Richard M. Jerome. Philadelphia: PC International Press, 1989.

———. *A Torchlight for America.* Chicago: FCN, 1993.

Gardell, Mattias. *In the Name of Elijah Muhammad: Louis Farrakhan and the Nation of Islam.* Durham, N.C.: Duke University Press, 1996.

Magida, Arthur J. *Prophet of Rage: A Life of Louis Farrakhan and His Nation.* New York: Basic Books, 1996.

McCloud, Aminah Beverly. *African American Islam.* New York: Routledge, 1995.

Singh, Robert. *The Farrakhan Phenomenon: Race, Reaction, and the Paranoid Style in American Politics.* Washington, D.C.: Georgetown University Press, 1997.

White, Vibert L., Jr. *Inside the Nation of Islam: A Historical and Personal Testimony by a Black Muslim.* Gainesville: University Press of Florida, 2001.

Feehan, Patrick Augustine
(1829–1902) *Catholic archbishop*

The first Catholic archbishop of Chicago, Patrick Augustine Feehan presided over the spiritual affairs of his archdiocese competently but with little fanfare. However, ethnic controversies among Catholics in Chicago eventually made his final years as an archbishop turbulent. Feehan was born on August 28, 1829, in County Tipperary, Ireland, the son of Patrick Feehan and Judith Cooney Feehan. The future archbishop studied at Castle Knock College in Dublin and subsequently at Maynooth College Seminary. When his family immigrated to the United States in 1850, Feehan accompanied them. He completed his seminary training in Saint Louis and was ordained a Catholic priest there in 1852.

Feehan's early years as a priest were spent teaching at Kenrick's Carondelet College, of which he served as president from 1854 to 1857. Beginning in the latter year, he served as a priest in a succession of parishes in Saint Louis, distinguishing himself chiefly by his efforts to care for wounded soldiers who flooded into Saint Louis during and after the Civil War. He became bishop of Nashville in the fall of 1865 and set about the task of rebuilding churches that had been destroyed during the war. Over the next 15 years, the number of Catholic churches and priests in Tennessee doubled under Feehan's supervision. And when epidemics of cholera and yellow fever swept across his diocese, Feehan demonstrated again a keen willingness to care for the victims of these diseases.

In 1880, Feehan became the first archbishop of Chicago, and he spent the last two decades of his life superintending the affairs of one of the largest Catholic communities in the country, whose numbers quadrupled during his spiritual administration. By this time Feehan was a nationally prominent Catholic leader and took part in a variety of affairs affecting the Catholic Church in the United States, including service as the head of the committee on schools for the Third Plenary Council of Baltimore in 1884. In the main, though, Feehan discharged the responsibilities of his office without significant public attention.

In the final years of his life, however, controversy overtook Chicago's archbishop, in the form of ethnic conflicts among the Catholics of the archdiocese. The first involved Polish Catholics in St. Hedwig's parish, many of whom wished to see a young priest, Anthony Kozlowski, made senior pastor of the parish in place of the existing pastor. Matters eventually reached such a point that Feehan felt compelled to dismiss Kozlowski, but this action did not settle the controversy. When Kozlowski, supported by many members of the parish, refused to leave, the archbishop excommunicated him in the fall of 1895, but Kozlowski responded by departing with as many as 1,000 families from the parish to start an independent Catholic church.

The second conflict involved controversy over the appointment of an auxiliary bishop in Chicago. Many Irish Catholics, led by Jeremiah Crowley, a Chicago priest, opposed Feehan's desire to appoint the American-born priest Peter Muldoon to the position. Crowley made scandalous charges against Muldoon and was eventually excommunicated, and Feehan's choice prevailed. But this final controversy, accompanied by recurrent pneumonia, left Feehan's health weakened. He died in Chicago on July 12, 1902.

Religious leadership in America has often proceeded noisily, to the loud echoes of sermons and spiritual tirades. But as often, leaders have gone about their business more quietly. Archbishop Patrick Feehan was for most of his life among those who tended the spiritual affairs entrusted to him without fanfare. But in the turbulent decades at the end of the 19th century, when Catholic immigrants flooded into America, not even the retiring archbishop could wholly escape the controversies that followed in the wake of a rapidly increasing Catholic population.

Further Reading

Kirkfleet, Cornelius James. *The Life of Patrick Augustine Feehan, Bishop of Nashville, First Archbishop of Chicago, 1829–1902.* Chicago: Matre, 1922.

Sanders, James W. *The Education of an Urban Minority: Catholics in Chicago, 1833–1965.* New York: Oxford University Press, 1977.

Shanabruch, Charles. *Chicago's Catholics: The Evolution of an American Identity.* Notre Dame, Ind.: University of Notre Dame Press, 1981.

Stritch, Thomas. *The Catholic Church in Tennessee.* Nashville: Catholic Center, 1987.

Fillmore, Charles Sherlock

(1854–1948) *cofounder of the Unity School of Christianity*

Charles Fillmore, with his wife, Myrtle Fillmore, was a cofounder of the Unity School of Christianity. Unity is a spiritual cousin of the Church of Christ, Scientist, both of which stress the possibility for correct thinking to overcome physical adversity. Charles Sherlock Fillmore was born on August 22, 1854, on a Chippewa reservation near Saint Cloud, Minnesota, the son of Henry Fillmore and Mary Georgiana Stone Fillmore. His father was a second cousin of Millard Fillmore, the 13th president of the United States. Charles Fillmore grew up on the frontier, received an informal education, and eventually worked at a number of occupations, including mule team driver and real estate salesman. An injury when he was 10 years old left him with a permanently withered leg. He met Mary Caroline Page (known as Myrtle) in Denison, Texas, in 1876. Five years later the couple married and moved first to Pueblo, Colorado, where they lived from 1881 to 1884, and then to Kansas City, Missouri, where Charles sold real estate. The marriage produced three children.

In 1886, the couple attended a New Thought lecture delivered by Eugene Weeks, and through techniques learned in the lecture, Myrtle was cured of tuberculosis. This experience altered the course of both Myrtle's and Charles's lives. By 1889, Charles had begun to publish *Modern Thought,* a religious magazine, which generally dates the beginning of the Unity School of Christianity. The following year Myrtle founded the Society of Silent Help, later named Silent Unity, which was dedicated to praying for those in need of physical healing. In 1891, husband and wife were ordained by Emma Curtis Hopkins, the founder of New Thought, but within a few years they had established a distinct religious movement within the broader contours of New Thought. They founded the Unity Society of Practical Christianity in 1903, were ordained as its first ministers in 1906, and formally incorporated the movement as the Unity School of Christianity in 1914.

Like its parent, New Thought, the Unity School of Christianity taught that sickness was the product of harmful thinking, which could be eradicated by the application of positive thought and an awareness of the inner presence of God. Unity also insisted that poverty was a similar manifestation of negative thinking. Charles Fillmore added to these familiar New Thought principles the idea that positive thinking was capable of actualizing the divine nature that exists within each person, in the same way that Jesus actualized the divine nature of God.

In terms of practical orientation, the Unity School of Christianity differed from many other healing movements of the time in not charging fees for the healing techniques employed by its members. Instead, the movement relied on voluntary contributions to meet its financial needs. Fillmore spread the movement's religious teachings by publishing several periodicals and, beginning in 1922, airing radio broadcasts. By the end of the 1920s, the movement acquired 1,200 acres outside Kansas City, Missouri, and relocated to what became known as Unity Farm and, still later, as Unity Village. Myrtle Fillmore died in 1931; two years later Charles married Cora Dedrick. Charles himself died on July 5, 1948, at Unity Farm.

The movement that Charles and Myrtle Fillmore founded was the largest of the New Thought denominations at the beginning of the 21st century. Its membership hovered around 2 million, with more than 600 churches. The Fillmores' religious vision continued to be attractive to followers in search of practical deliverance from sickness or economic hardship, who were comfortable with an essentially Christian identity but intrigued by concepts such as reincarnation, more characteristic of Eastern religions.

Further Reading

D'Andrade, Hugh. *Charles Fillmore: Herald of the New Age.* New York: Harper & Row, 1974.

Fillmore, Charles. *Metaphysical Bible Dictionary.* Unity Village, Mo.: Unity Books, 1995.

———. *Prosperity.* Unity Village, Mo.: Unity Books, 1998.

Freeman, James Dillet. *The Story of Unity.* 4th ed. Unity Village, Mo.: Unity Books, 2000.

Finney, Charles Grandison

(1792–1875) *revivalist*

Charles Finney turned from a career as a lawyer to become one of the 19th century's greatest revival preachers. Where GEORGE WHITEFIELD, the foremost evangelist of the 18th century, forged a career in the fields of England and North America, Finney gravitated to the urban centers of American life. He was born on August 29, 1792, in Warren, Connecticut. His parents, Sylvester Finney and Rebecca Rice Finney, were farmers who eventually settled in Henderson, New York. After attending public school in Henderson and teaching briefly there, Finney attended Warren Academy in Connecticut. For four years, from 1814, he taught school in New Jersey, before returning home to study law as an apprentice in the law office of Benjamin Wright in Adams, New York. Over the years of his youth and young adulthood, Finney sat under the preaching of ministers from a variety of religious persuasions. Finally, when he was 29 years old, he had a conversion experience that climaxed a period of spiritual searching. During the period leading to this experience, Finney promised God that he would "preach the gospel" if he were ever converted. True to his word, Finney abandoned his pursuit of a legal career and studied theology with his pastor, George W. Gale, before being licensed to preach by the St. Lawrence Presbytery in December 1823. He was ordained a Presbyterian minister the following year.

For the next decade, Finney established himself as an itinerant evangelist, conducting revival services in cities across the northeastern United States, the most famous of which occurred in Rochester, New York, from September 1830 to June of the following year. For Finney, there was nothing miraculous about revival. It required, of course, "the blessing of God," as he explained in his *Lectures on Revivals of Religion.* But it was "a purely philosophical result of the right use of constituted means," and Finney did not hesitate to explore new means to draw men and women to Christ. He made frequent use of "inquiry meetings," in which those seeking salvation might be counseled to that end. Later he followed his sermons with direct invitations for seekers to walk forward at the close of his revival meetings to receive prayer for salvation. Unlike earlier spiritual predecessors who had seen conversion as the final result of a lengthy period of self-examination, Finney called on his hearers to receive salvation immediately. Though nominally within the Reformed tradition, Finney rejected the traditional emphasis on the individual's inability to receive salvation apart from God's election. He urged, instead, the responsibility of the individual to turn to God at once. "If there is a sinner in this house," he declared,

> let me say to him, Abandon all your excuses. You have been told to-night that they are all in vain. To-night it will be told in hell, and told in heaven, and echoed from the ends of the universe, what you decide to do. This very hour may seal your eternal destiny. Will you submit to God to-night—NOW?

Finney's emphasis on the ability of his hearers to accept salvation placed him increasingly at odds with more traditional Presbyterians, and he became a Congregationalist in 1836.

Toward the beginning of Finney's preaching career, he married Lydia Root Andrews, with whom he had six children. After Lydia's death in 1847, he married Elizabeth Ford Atkinson in 1848. After Elizabeth's death 15 years later, Finney married Rebecca Allen Rayl.

In 1832 Finney settled in his own church at the Chathan Street Theater in New York City. After a few years, however, Oberlin Collegiate Institute in Ohio was able to coax him to join its faculty in 1835 as a professor of theology by accepting his condition that he be permitted to return to New York City each winter to preach at the Broadway Tabernacle, which had been constructed according to his specifications. Two years later, Finney resigned from his New York ministry and became pastor of the First Church in Oberlin.

The social fruit of Charles Finney's evangelical faith had two aspects. First he valued education. Together with other evangelicals, he made Oberlin Collegiate Institute (where he was president from 1851 through 1865) an important venue for educational reform. The college was coeducational, and its academic affairs were governed by faculty rather than trustees. Second, Finney energetically supported the causes of abolition and temperance. He preached against slaveholding in particular and refused to offer communion to slave owners.

Finney served as a pastor in Oberlin until the later years of his life. He resigned as president of Oberlin Collegiate Institute in 1865. He died in Oberlin on August 16, 1875.

Charles Grandison Finney did not create revivalism in the 19th century, though he sometimes created that impression in speeches and writings. He was in a line of evangelistic preaching that stretched back a century to the days of George Whitefield. But Finney, more than any previous preacher, introduced revival to the urban centers of American life. He laid the foundation for the ministry of DWIGHT LYMAN MOODY, which would reach its most prominent heights near the time of Finney's death, and that of BILLY GRAHAM, who became the 20th century's most famous urban revivalist.

Further Reading

Finney, Charles Grandison. *Lectures on Revivals of Religion.* Edited by William G. McLoughlin. Cambridge, Mass.: Belknap Press of Harvard University Press, 1960.

———. *Lectures to Professing Christians.* New York: Garland, 1985.

———. *Memoirs.* Edited by Garth M. Rosell and Richard A.G. Dupuis. Grand Rapids, Mich.: Academic Books, 1989.

Hambrick-Stowe, Charles E. *Charles G. Finney and the Spirit of American Evangelicalism.* Grand Rapids, Mich.: W. B. Eerdmans, 1996.

Hardman, Keith. *Charles Grandison Finney, 1792–1875: Revivalist and Reformer.* Syracuse, N.Y.: Syracuse University Press, 1987.

Hewitt, Glenn Alden. *Regeneration and Morality: Study of Charles Finney, Charles Hodge, John W. Nevin, and Horace Bushnell.* Brooklyn, N.Y.: Carlson, 1991.

Weddle, David L. *The Law as Gospel: Revival and Reform in the Theology of Charles G. Finney.* Metuchen, N.J.: Scarecrow Press, 1985.

Flanagan, Edward Joseph
(1886–1948) *Catholic priest, founder of Boys Town*

Edward Joseph Flanagan spent the majority of his adult life devoted to the care of homeless boys. Most notably, he founded Boys Town, which became an internationally acclaimed home for boys and, some 30 years after Flanagan's death, for girls. He was born on July 13, 1886, in Leabeg, County Roscommon, Ireland, the son of John Flanagan and Honora Larkin Flanagan. He graduated from Summerhill College in Sligo, Ireland, in 1904 and promptly set sail for the United States, where his parents had previously immigrated to New York and where Flanagan hoped to become a Catholic priest. He received an undergraduate degree in 1906 from Mt. St. Mary's College in Emmitsburg, Maryland, and then continued studies toward the priesthood at St. Joseph's Seminary in Dunwoodie, New York. While a student at the seminary, however, he suffered an illness that forced him to withdraw and plagued him subsequently with lifelong respiratory ailments.

After leaving the seminary, Flanagan moved with his parents to Nebraska, where his older brother was a Catholic priest in Omaha. Once arrived there, Flanagan gained the attention of Omaha's bishop, who sent him to study at the

Gregorian University of Rome in 1907. Recurring illness forced Flanagan to withdraw from the university the following year, however. He was more successful, though, when dispatched to study at the Royal and Imperial Leopold Francis University in Innsbruck, Austria, beginning in 1909. In the summer of 1912 he was ordained a priest at St. Ignatius Church in Innsbruck and, after serving briefly in St. Patrick's Church in O'Neill, Nebraska, he became assistant pastor of Omaha's St. Patrick's parish in 1913.

A severe drought in 1916 left many farm laborers in Nebraska unemployed and helped to shape the course of Flanagan's future life. He opened a Workingmen's Hotel to respond to the needs of displaced men, but he soon became convinced that his attention should be focused on children instead. "I knew that my work was not with these shells of men," he subsequently explained, "but with the embryo men—the homeless waifs who had nowhere to turn, no one to guide them." This new vision prompted the priest to open Father Flanagan's Boys' Home in Omaha on December 12, 1917. In 1919 Flanagan became a U.S. citizen, and four years later, Flanagan relocated the Boys' Home to a 160-acre tract west of Omaha, called Overlook Farm, where it became known as Boys Town. There he applied innovative methods to the nurture of the boys in his home, rejecting the use of corporal punishment and soon allowing the boys themselves to govern the village into which the original Boys Home grew. "There's no such thing as a bad boy," became Flanagan's most famous proverb.

In the following years Flanagan's work at Boys Town received increasing attention as he struggled to raise funds. The priest began a radio program in the 1920s that helped to increase interest in the home for boys. The 1938 movie *Boys Town*, starring Spencer Tracy and Mickey Rooney, did even more to focus national attention on Flanagan's work. By the following decade, Flanagan was recognized as a national expert on delinquent children. A sequel to the movie *Boys Town*, called *Men of Boys Town*, appeared in 1941. In 1946, U.S. Attorney General Tom C. Clark appointed Flanagan to serve on a national advisory panel on juvenile delinquency. The following year, Flanagan traveled to Japan and Korea to study child welfare issues at the request of General Douglas MacArthur. When Flanagan's report reached the attention of President Harry S. Truman, the president called on Flanagan to make a similar investigation in Germany and Austria, but Flanagan died in Berlin on May 15, 1948, before he could complete this work.

Father Edward J. Flanagan established one of the 20th century's most prominent ministries to homeless children. Though he died shortly after the end of World War II, his benevolent institution endured and prospered. In 1979, Boys Home expanded its reach by accepting girls. By the end of the century, more than 30,000 boys and girls found shelter within the newly renamed Girls and Boys Town.

Edward J. Flanagan established an internationally acclaimed ministry to homeless boys called "Boys Town." *(Library of Congress, Prints and Photographs Division LC-USZ62-103880)*

Further Reading

Flanagan, Edward Joseph. *Understanding Your Boy.* New York: Rinehart, 1950.

Graves, Charles Parlin. *Father Flanagan, Founder of Boys Town.* Champaign, Ill.: Garrard, 1972.

Jendryka, Brian. "Flanagan's Island." *Policy Review* (Summer 1994): 44–51.

Lonnborg, Barbara A., ed. *Boys Town: A Photographic History.* Boys Town, Nebr.: Donning, 1992.

Oursler, Fulton, and Will Oursler. *Father Flanagan of Boys Town.* Garden City, N.Y.: Doubleday, 1949.

Stevens, Clifford, J. *Father Flanagan: Builder of Boys.* New York: P. J. Kenedy, 1967.

Ford, Arnold Josiah
(1877–1935) African-American Jewish leader

Arnold Josiah Ford, associated closely for a time with Marcus Garvey's Black Nationalism movement, rejected Christianity as a religion of white domination. Instead, he embraced Judaism and became a prominent black Jewish leader in the last decade of his life. Ford was born on April 23, 1877, in Bridgetown, Barbados, the son of Edward Thomas Ford and Elizabeth Augusta Braithwaite Ford. Ford's father was a Methodist minister, but his parents gave him an early exposure to Judaism by seeing that he took lessons in Hebrew and the Talmud while he was a child in Barbados. By the time Ford reached his young adult years he was a talented musician, and, in 1899, he enlisted these talents in the British Royal Navy, in which he served as a musician for close to two years. Afterward, he was assigned to work as a clerk for the Court of Federal Assize in Bermuda.

Little is known about Ford's life during this period, but by approximately 1910 he was living in New York City, where he settled in Harlem and married Olive Nurse, with whom he had two children. He earned a living writing music, giving music lessons, and playing for local orchestras. In the following decade, Ford became acquainted with Marcus Garvey, the Black Nationalist leader, and became prominent in the Universal Negro Improvement Association, which Garvey had founded in 1914. Beginning in 1920, Ford served as music director at the association's headquarters

in Harlem, called Liberty Hall, and while there he developed an interest in Judaism as an alternative to Christianity, which he increasingly characterized as the religion of the slave masters. Ford hoped that Garvey would turn to Judaism and make it the centerpiece of his nationalist ambitions, but Garvey declined.

Subsequently, Ford abandoned active participation in the Universal Negro Improvement Association and joined a black Jewish group known as the Moorish Zionist Temple Inc. In 1924, after he had disagreements with Mordecai Herrmenz, who had founded the temple in 1921, Ford left to start his own synagogue, Beth B'nai Abraham. The congregation practiced rites drawn from both the Reform and the Orthodox Jewish traditions. Attracting mostly blacks, the synagogue also had some white members. The congregation published *The Universal Ethiopian Hymnal,* a collection of hymns used at the synagogue, composed in the main by Ford. Internal disagreements that rent the peace of the synagogue, which eventually included disputes over Ford's opposition to classes in Yiddish—a white European language, he insisted—caused some members to leave. Beth B'nai Abraham survived this exodus, but it later collapsed after a corporation Ford established to finance a school building for the synagogue became bankrupt.

In December 1930, Ford left the United States for Ethiopia, and, once established there, tried to persuade the members of his congregation to join him. Around 50 did, though lack of work eventually forced them to return to the United States. Ford, however, remained in Ethiopia, turning again to music instruction and other odd jobs to support himself. He and his first wife had divorced in 1924, and in 1933 he married Mignon Innis, with whom he had two children. Ford died of a heart attack in Addis Ababa on September 16, 1935.

Although his father was a Christian minister, Arnold Josiah Ford eventually turned away from Christianity, rejecting it as a faith hopelessly tainted by its association with slavery. Swept up into the Black Nationalism movement that Marcus Garvey inspired, Ford turned to Judaism as a religious tradition that might replace Christianity in the black community. He never succeeded in communicating his Jewish faith to the broader

Black Nationalism movement, but he did attract a number of followers in Harlem for a brief period in the 1920s.

Further Reading

Berger, Graenum. *Black Jews in America: A Documentary with Commentary.* New York: Commission on Synagogue Relations, Federation of Jewish Philanthropies of New York, 1978.

Brotz, Howard M. *The Black Jews of Harlem: Negro Nationalism and the Dilemmas of Negro Leadership.* 2d ed. New York: Schocken Books, 1970.

Chireau, Yvonne, and Nathaniel Deutsch. *Black Zion: African American Religious Encounters with Judaism.* New York: Oxford University Press, 2000.

Kobre, S. S. "Rabbi Ford." *The Reflex* 4 (1929): 25–29.

King, K. J. "Some Notes on Arnold J. Ford and New World Black Attitudes to Ethiopia." *Journal of Ethiopian Studies* 10 (1971): 81–87.

Scott, William R. "Rabbi Arnold Ford's Back-to-Ethiopia Movement: A Study of Black Emigration, 1930–1935." *Pan African Journal* 7 (1975): 191–202.

Fosdick, Harry Emerson
(1878–1969) *Baptist minister*

Described as the Moses of theological modernism, Harry Emerson Fosdick was the foremost evangelical liberal of his era. He sided with liberalism in its great war against fundamentalism early in the 20th century and lent his significant popular influence to the defense of a faith unmoored from classical creedal statements. Fosdick was born on May 24, 1878, in Buffalo, New York, to Frank Sheldon Fosdick and Amie Inez Weaver Fosdick. Raised as a Baptist, Fosdick experienced conversion at the age of seven. He was a gifted student who graduated first in his high school class before earning a B.A. from Colgate University in 1900. Intent on preparing for a ministerial career, Fosdick attended Hamilton Theological Seminary before transferring to Union Theological Seminary in New York City. A nervous breakdown caused by severe depression interrupted his studies, but after a stay in a sanitorium and a period of convalescence, Fosdick returned to the seminary, where he received a

B.D. summa cum laude, in 1904. That same year he married Florence Allen Whitney, with whom he had two daughters.

On graduation from seminary, Fosdick accepted a call to pastor the First Baptist Church in Montclair, New Jersey. While there, he earned an M.A. in political science from Columbia University in 1908, taught part time at Union Theological Seminary, and wrote the first of many books, *The Second Mile*, in 1908. After 14 years at Montclair, he accepted a full-time position on the faculty of Union Theological Seminary in 1915. Though at first an adamant supporter of U.S. involvement in World War I, Fosdick toured the scene of the European conflict in 1918 and became thereafter a devout pacifist.

When Fosdick returned to the United States in 1918, he accepted an invitation to become the preaching minister for the First Presbyterian Church of New York City, a position that allowed him to continue most of his teaching activity at Union Theological Seminary. Fresh from the battlefields of World War I, Fosdick soon found himself engaged in a different kind of warfare as the conflict between liberalism and fundamentalism broke on the American theological scene. Fosdick cast himself firmly into the ranks of the theological liberals with his influential 1922 sermon, "Shall the Fundamentalists Win?"—a sermon made all the more influential when Fosdick's wealthy friend, John D. Rockefeller, Jr., saw to it that copies were distributed to every ordained minister in America.

Fosdick's public stance against fundamentalism soon drew the ire of conservative Presbyterians, among them William Jennings Bryan, who tried to have him dismissed from his pulpit at First Presbyterian. Although this attempt failed, pressure at the Presbyterian General Assembly for Fosdick to subscribe to the Westminster Confession—the statement of Presbyterian doctrine adopted by English Presbyterians in the 1640s—ultimately forced him to return to the Baptist fold. He resigned from First Presbyterian and became the minister of the Park Avenue Baptist Church in 1925. This was but a temporary ministry, during which Fosdick bided his time while his friend Rockefeller saw to the construction of the magnificent Riverside Church where Fosdick would be pastor from 1931 and would preside over an interdenominational congregation until his retirement in 1946. While he waited to occupy the Riverside pulpit, he began in 1927 the radio program *National Vespers Hour,* which would help to make him one of the best-known preachers in America.

A friend of WALTER RAUSCHENBUSCH, Fosdick supported the aims of the social gospel and did not flinch at suggesting that the Christian life and message inevitably possessed a social dimension. He remained adamant in his pacifism as the threat of World War II loomed in the late 1930s. In a sermon delivered on Armistice Day in 1933, he explained that he had "renounce[d] war for its consequences, for the lies it lives on and propagates, for the undying hatred it arouses, for the dictatorships it puts in the place of democracy, for the starvation that stalks after it." During the 1940s and 1950s, he took a public stance against racial discrimination and segregation, opening his pulpit to African-American preachers and supporting the National Association for the Advancement of Colored People (NAACP). He retired as pastor of the Riverside Church in 1946 but kept up an active career as a speaker and a writer. He died on October 5, 1969, in Bronxville, New York.

Fosdick claimed that his ministry had been formed partially out of the furnace of his own "struggle for a reasonable Christian faith, both against the reactionary dogmatism of the orthodox and against the skepticism of the atheists." His enemies dubbed him the "Jesse James of the theological world." But he became, in spite of this criticism, one of the most beloved and respected preachers of his generation, offering a way between a fundamentalism many found wedded to a discredited past and a skepticism that provided no hope for the future.

Further Reading

Abbott, Zane Allen, Jr. "Radio Preaching in the World War Two Era: The Cases of Harry Emerson Fosdick and Charles Coughlin on War and Peace." Ph.D. dissertation, Southern Baptist Theological Seminary, 1994.

Crocker, Lionel George, ed. *Harry Emerson Fosdick's Art of Preaching: An Anthology.* Springfield, Ill.: Thomas, 1971.

Ehrhard, James J. "An Analysis of the Popular Apologetics of Harry Emerson Fosdick During the Height of the Fundamentalist-Modernist Controversy, 1922–1932." Ph.D. dissertation, Mid-America Baptist Theological Seminary, 1997.

Fosdick, Harry Emerson. *The Living of These Days: An Autobiography.* New York: Harper, 1956.

Linn, Edmund Holt. *Preaching as Counseling: The Unique Method of Harry Emerson Fosdick.* Valley Forge, Pa.: Judson Press, 1966.

Miller, Robert Moats. *Harry Emerson Fosdick: Preacher, Pastor, Prophet.* New York: Oxford University Press, 1985.

Ryan, Halford Ross. *Harry Emerson Fosdick: Persuasive Preacher.* New York: Greenwood Press, 1989.

Scruggs, Julius Richard. *Baptist Preachers with Social Consciousness: A Comparative Study of Martin Luther King, Jr., and Harry Emerson Fosdick.* Philadelphia: Dorrance, 1978.

Fox, Emmet
(1886–1951) *New Thought minister*

During the 1930s and 1940s, Emmet Fox presided over the largest New Thought congregation in the world, New York City's Church of the Healing Christ. Through his lectures and books, Fox enunciated a hopeful religion that promised its adherents health, harmony, and happiness. He was born on July 30, 1886, in Ireland, the son of Catholic parents. His father, who died when Fox was 10 years old, was a surgeon and a member of Parliament. As a teenager, Fox attended Stamford Hill Jesuit College in London, but his reading of New Thought writers eventually caused him to veer away from the Catholicism of his parents, and he became an electrical engineer even as he continued his metaphysical studies. *New Thought* is the name widely given to a cluster of spiritual and philosophic movements that emphasize the presence of God (or, in secular variants, the universal mind) in all individuals and the application of that presence to the resolution of practical problems. The movement had roots in the transcendentalism of Ralph Waldo Emerson, enjoyed spiritual kinship with MARY BAKER EDDY's Christian Science, and found its most popular expression in the writings of NORMAN VINCENT PEALE during the 20th century, especially his *Power of Positive Thinking* (1952).

In 1914, Fox began to associate with the newly formed New Thought Alliance International. Fourteen more years passed, however, before Fox delivered his first New Thought lecture, in London's Mortimer Hall in 1928. The success of this venture inspired him to leave his career as an electrical engineer and to undertake a lecture tour through England, Scotland, and Ireland from 1928 through 1931. At the conclusion of this tour, Fox decided to lecture in the United States. In the fall of 1931, Harry Wolhorn, the secretary of New York City's Church of the Healing Christ, heard Fox lecture and proposed that Fox become the church's minister. The church was associated with the Divine Science branch of New Thought. Under the leadership of its previous minister, James Murray, the church had grown to more than 1,000 members, but after his death a few years earlier, membership had sharply declined. When Fox became minister in 1931, though, he reversed this trend, and his popularity as a New Thought lecturer caused the church to migrate through a series of meeting facilities, first in the Aston Hotel, then in the Metrodome, and finally in Carnegie Hall, where Fox lectured to crowds of several thousands each week for many years.

Emmet Fox gave popular expression to New Thought ideas that could be traced through Ralph Waldo Emerson, Phineas Quimby, and Mary Baker Eddy and would be carried into the second half of the 20th century through the speaking and writing of Norman Vincent Peale. At the heart of Fox's religious system was the insistence that God and Christ dwell in each individual and that perception of this reality creates the possibility of living in harmony with the basic essence of the universe. "You are the presence of God at the point where you are," he wrote in *Alter Your Life* (1950). In typical New Thought fashion, Fox maintained that a proper appreciation of reality might yield practical benefits. In *Alter Your Life*, he worked to show the connection between an appreciation of God's presence and the solution of life's various problems.

> You should never "put up" with anything. You should never be willing to accept less than Health, Harmony, and Happiness. These things are your Divine Right as the sons and daughters of God, and it is only a bad habit, unconscious, as a rule, that causes you to be satisfied with less. In the depths of his being man always feels intuitively that there is a way out of his difficulties if only he can find it, and his natural instincts all point in the same direction.

Emmet Fox's career as minister of the Church of the Healing Christ spanned some 20 years. In 1951, suffering from ill health, he made a trip to Europe seeking to recuperate. He died in Paris, France, on August 13, 1951.

Emmet Fox captivated New York audiences with his New Thought lectures for 20 years and, through the five books he wrote, influenced multitudes more. As America struggled out of the Great Depression and then confronted the secular totalitarianisms of the 20th century—nazism and communism—Fox's optimistic theology found a perennial audience. More than 50 years after his death, his books remained in print, testifying to the continued appeal of his New Thought message in the 21st century.

Further Reading

Braden, Charles Samuel. *These Also Believe: A Study of Modern American Cults and Minority Religious Movements.* New York: Macmillan, 1949.

Fox, Emmet. *Alter Your Life.* New York: Harper, 1950; San Francisco: HarperSanFrancisco, 1994.

———. *Make Your Life Worth While.* New York: Harper & Row, 1946.

———. *Power Through Constructive Thinking.* New York: Harper & Brothers, 1940.

———. *The Sermon on the Mount.* New York: Harper & Brothers, 1935.

———. *State Your Claim.* New York: Harper, 1952.

Gaze, Harry. *Emmet Fox: The Man and His Work.* New York: Harper, 1952.

Sikorsky, Igor I. *AA's Godparents: Three Early Influences on Alcoholics Anonymous and Its Foundation, Carl*

Jung, Emmet Fox, Jack Alexander. Minneapolis, Minn.: CompCare Publishers, 1990.

Wolhorn, Herman. *Emmet Fox's Golden Keys to Successful Living and Reminiscences.* New York: Harper & Row, 1977.

Frelinghuysen, Theodorus Jacobus
(1691–ca. 1747) *Dutch Reformed minister*

With his theological emphasis on the necessity of personal holiness and piety, Theodorus Jacobus Frelinghuysen, a Dutch Reformed minister who settled in New Jersey, helped till the theological ground in which the Great Awakening germinated. He was well regarded by more important figures of the awakening, such as GEORGE WHITEFIELD and JONATHAN EDWARDS. Frelinghuysen was born in 1691 in Lingen, Germany, the son of Johan Henrich Frelinghuysen and Anna Margaretha Brüggemann Frelinghuysen. His father was a Reformed minister. In 1711, Theodorus began study at the University of Lingen in Germany, where he was nurtured with a theological diet of pietism, which emphasized personal holiness and good works, as opposed to mere theological orthodoxy. He was licensed to preach in 1715 and began his first pastoral ministry in 1717 at Loegumer Voorwerk in East Friesland, where he was ordained. In 1719, however, after a flood had devastated his parish the previous Christmas Eve, Frelinghuysen accepted a call to serve as minister in the New World to a cluster of Dutch Reformed congregations in central New Jersey's Raritan Valley. Shortly after taking up his station as a minister in this area, Frelinghuysen married Eva Terhune, with whom he had seven children.

Soon after Frelinghuysen arrived in the New World, he embarked on the controversial career that would characterize the remainder of his life. He offended more orthodox Dutch Reformed ministers in New York with what they scoffed at as "howling prayers" and belief that use of the Lord's Prayer during religious services was overly formalistic. Once established as a minister in New Jersey, Frelinghuysen continued to emphasize personal holiness and piety and to prevent church members who failed to give evidence of having been converted from participating in the Lord's Supper. Frelinghuysen's rigorous examinations of even prosperous congregants earned their displeasure, as did his suggestion that "it has been very true that the largest portion of the faithful have been poor and of little account in the world." "If you remain ignorant," he pronounced to his hearers, "resting in your sins, unconverted and unholy, in the Lord's name I tell you that you will die the death, God's anger will remain upon you and you shall see yourself thrust out." Criticism of Frelinghuysen's ministry became such a commonplace that he eventually adorned the back of his sleigh with a rejoinder:

> No one's tongue, or no one's pen,
> Makes me other than I am.
> Speak, sland'rous speakers, speak on end.
> With words you no one here can rend.

Frelinghuysen further enraged some of his critics by pronouncing the sentence of excommunication on them. In all, contention swirled about his ministry until 1739, on the eve of the Great Awakening, when Dutch Reformed authorities finally effected a reconciliation between Frelinghuysen and his opponents in the Raritan Valley.

During the years of greatest controversy in his ministry, Frelinghuysen found an ally in the young Presbyterian preacher, GILBERT TENNENT, who became a minister in New Brunswick in the mid-1720s. Together, the men emphasized the necessity of personal conversion and developed a revivalistic style of preaching that, supplemented by the ministry of more famous men such as George Whitefield and Jonathan Edwards, would spark the Great Awakening in the 1740s. Frelinghuysen's own ministry suffered occasionally under what appear to have been episodes of mental illness. He died in the fall or winter of 1747; the precise date and location of his death remain unknown.

The Great Awakening, occasioned chiefly by preaching of George Whitefield in the American colonies that began in 1739, did not spring unannounced on the spiritual life of North America. The revival harvest had been planted earlier by less prominent ministers such as Frelinghuysen. He railed incessantly against those who confused orthodoxy with spiritual rebirth and elevated convention over piety. Though his name survives primarily among religious historians, his emphasis on personal piety would contribute to an enduring current within the broader stream of American religious life.

Further Reading

DeJong, Gerald Francis. *The Dutch Reformed Church in the American Colonies.* Grand Rapids, Mich.: Eerdmans, 1978.

Frelinghuysen, Peter H. B., Jr. *Theodorus Jacobus Frelinghuysen.* Princeton, N.J.: Princeton University Press, 1938.

Frelinghuysen, Theodorus Jacobus. *Forerunner of the Great Awakening: Sermons by Theodorus Jacobus Frelinghuysen (1691–1747).* Grand Rapids, Mich.: Eerdmans, 2001.

Harmelink, Herman. "Another Look at Frelinghuysen and His Awakening." *Church History* 37 (December 1968): 423–38.

Prozesky, Martin H. "The Emergence of Dutch Pietism." *Journal of Ecclesiastical History* 28 (January 1977): 29–37.

Scrag, F. J. "Theodorus Jacobus Frelinghuysen: The Father of American Pietism." *Church History* 14 (September 1945): 201–16.

Tanis, James. *Dutch Calvinistic Pietism in the Middle Colonies: A Study of the Life and Theology of Theodorus Jacobus Frelinghuysen.* The Hague: Martinus Nijhoff, 1967.

Frothingham, Octavius Brooks

(1822–1895) *Unitarian minister, writer*

A fierce opponent of religious dogma, Octavius Brooks Frothingham began his career as a Unitarian minister and grew increasingly estranged from this religious movement's more conservative elements. He found spiritual kinship for a time with Transcendentalists and became their chief 19th-century historian, but he was most significant in the role he played in the founding of the Free Religious Association. He was born on November 26, 1822, in Boston, Massachusetts, the son of a Unitarian minister, Nathaniel Langdon Frothingham, and Ann Gorham Brooks Frothingham. His education followed the same path as that of many 19th-century religious luminaries of New England: Boston Latin School, Harvard College, from which he received a B.A. in 1843; then Harvard Divinity School, from which he graduated in 1846. After divinity school, he married Caroline E. Curtis, with whom he had two children.

Frothingham became pastor of Salem's North Church in 1847, and while there, he was influenced by THEODORE PARKER, the Transcendentalist minister and abolitionist. His own abolitionist views estranged him ever more radically from traditional Christianity, which he considered complicit in the slavery trade and hopelessly entangled in doctrinal quarrels, and from more conservative Unitarianism. Subsequently, in 1855, he migrated to Jersey City, New Jersey, where he became the minister for several years of the Unitarian Society and developed a reputation not only as a learned preacher but as a scholarly writer. In 1859, he moved to New York City, where he helped establish a new Unitarian Society, eventually named the Independent Liberal Church, in 1870. There he achieved prominence as the prophet of radical religion, which he defined in his sermon "The Spirit of the New Faith" as one that

> seeks a supreme will in the ordinary texture of the world, rises above clarity, toleration, embraces radicals of all religions and cultures: Mohamet, Zoroaster, Confucious, Pythagoras, "infidels of the Enlightenment," challenges skeptics to create, atheists to live divinely.

After more conservative Unitarians such as HENRY WHITNEY BELLOWS founded the National Association of Unitarian Churches in 1865 in an attempt to establish creedal uniformity in Unitarianism, Frothingham joined other more radical Unitarians in forming the Free Religious Association in 1869. In a notorious sermon delivered shortly before Frothingham left his pastorate at Salem, he had asked, "How many spires are pushed up into the skies through spite?" This long-held antipathy toward the divisiveness of creeds fueled his participation in the Free Religious Association. He served as the association's president from its inception until 1878. During this period,

Frothingham gradually ceased to think of himself or his church as Unitarian.

In addition to fulfilling his pastoral responsibilities at the Independent Liberal Church and guiding the course of the Free Religious Association, Frothingham wrote prodigiously, both for periodicals such as *The Nation* and the *Radical*, and in books of his own. A transcendentalist himself for a time, he produced an enduring history of the movement, *Transcendentalism in New England* (1876). Frothingham sought to place the movement within the broader currents of American and European philosophy and to trace the careers of its major and minor prophets. Though able to view the movement critically, he nevertheless found much in it to praise:

> The moral enthusiasm of the last generation, which broke out with such prodigious power in the holy war against slavery; which uttered such earnest protests against capital punishment, and the wrongs inflicted on women; which made such passionate pleading in behalf of the weak, the injured, the disfranchised of every race and condition; which exalted humanity above institutions, and proclaimed the inherent worth of man,—owed, in larger measure than is suspected, its glow and force to the Transcendentalists.

In 1879, poor health caused Frothingham to resign from his pulpit at the Independent Liberal Church. After traveling in Europe for two years, he returned at last to the United States and eventually settled in Boston. Though retired from his ministerial post, he continued an active writing career until death intruded on November 27, 1895, in Boston, Massachusetts.

Late in life, in writing a history of the Unitarianism of his father's generation, Octavius Brooks Frothingham characterized his own religious views as "visionary and far off, a mist in the air, an almost inaudible note in a symphony." His early confidence that organized forms of religion were on the brink of extinction proved notoriously mistaken. Nevertheless, the distaste for creeds and vigorous pursuit of religious impulses unhinged from traditional forms of faith that Frothingham had espoused in his life have proved to be enduring aspects of American religious history.

Further Reading

Caruthers, J. Wade. *Octavius Brooks Frothingham: Gentle Radical.* University: University of Alabama Press, 1977.

———. *The Religion of Humanity.* New York: D. G. Francis, 1873.

Frothingham, Octavius Brooks. *Recollections and Impressions, 1822–1891.* New York: G. P. Putnam's Sons, 1891.

———. "Thou Lord of Hosts." Available online. URL: http://www.cyberhymnal.org/htm/t/h/o/thouloho.htm. Downloaded on April 23, 2001.

———. *Transcendentalism in New England: A History.* New York: G. P. Putnam's Sons, 1876; New York: Harper, 1959.

Quincy, Josiah Phillips. *Memoir of Octavius Brooks Frothingham.* Cambridge, Mass.: J. Wilson & Son, 1896.

Stedman, Edmund Clarence. *Octavius Brooks Frothingham and the New Faith.* New York: G. P. Putnam's Sons, 1876.

Fuller, Charles Edward
(1887–1968) *radio preacher*

Charles Edward Fuller was one of the most prominent radio evangelists of the 20th century, and his program, the *Old Fashioned Revival Hour,* became a phenomenal success. It was a dominant force in religious broadcasting until the advent of television in the 1950s. Fuller was born on April 25, 1887, in Los Angeles, California, the son of Henry Fuller and Helen Maria Day Fuller. During his childhood, Fuller's family moved to Redlands, California, where they ran a successful orange grove and participated actively in Methodist affairs. After high school, Fuller enrolled in Pomona College and graduated with a B.S. in chemistry in 1910. After finishing college, he returned to Redlands, where he ran an orange grove of his own and, in 1911, married his high school sweetheart, Grace Leone Payton. A hard freeze in 1913 disrupted his farming career and prompted Fuller to relocate to Placentia, California, where he managed a cooperative packing plant for orange growers and became a member of the Presbyterian church in Placentia.

In 1916, Fuller experienced a religious conversion while attending a revival service conducted by

Paul Rader, the pastor of Chicago's Moody Church. Within three years of this experience, Fuller left his job to begin studying for the Christian ministry and enrolled at the Bible Institute of Los Angeles, a fundamentalist institution. After graduation from the Bible Institute in 1921, Charles Fuller worked for a time as the president of the Orange County Christian Endeavor, while also teaching an increasingly popular Sunday School class at the Placentia Presbyterian Church. When the church, alarmed by Fuller's fundamentalist teaching, disowned the class in 1924, Fuller organized its membership into an independent congregation named Calvary Church and became its first pastor.

For the next several years, Fuller supplemented his pastoral work at Calvary Church with revival preaching in other West Coast venues. But 1929 marked a turning point in his ministry. That year he preached a sermon over the radio during an Indianapolis revival service and received a positive response from listeners. This experience convinced him to begin broadcasting the services at Calvary Church the following year. By 1933, though, his congregation had grown impatient with the time that Fuller was devoting to his radio broadcasts, and he ultimately resigned and formed the Gospel Broadcasting Association. The next year he finally settled on the form that would make him nationally prominent as a radio broadcaster when he began airing the *Old Fashioned Revival Hour.*

Within 10 years of its initial airing, the *Old Fashioned Revival Hour* had become one of the most popular programs on the air, broadcast on more than 450 stations of the Mutual Broadcasting Network. In 1944, however, the network decided to drop paid religious programming from its schedule, and Fuller had to scramble to arrange independent stations to carry his *Old Fashioned Revival Hour.* He was successful at doing so and managed to maintain a worldwide audience estimated at 20 million. Fuller's success as a radio broadcaster was complemented by his success as a revivalist during the years when his program occupied the pinnacle of popular radio broadcasts. In 1949, the American Broadcasting Company (ABC) picked up the program on its network of stations and continued to broadcast it until 1963. By then, television had edged aside radio broadcasts in popularity, but

Fuller had not been able to adapt his programming style to the new medium.

Even while Charles Fuller was capturing attention as perhaps the most popular radio personality of his time, he made plans to perpetuate the evangelical thrust of his ministry by founding a seminary that would train future Christian leaders. In 1947, Fuller Theological Seminary in Pasadena, California, began offering classes. Although Fuller himself sat squarely within the mainstream of fundamentalist Christianity, it soon became apparent that the seminary he founded would not follow this course, and the institution's early years witnessed significant tension between Fuller and the seminary over this issue. Eventually, Fuller acquiesced in the seminary's transformation into a solidly evangelical, though not fundamentalist, school, in part because he turned the seminary's leadership over to his son, Dan Fuller, whose theological temperament was more progressive than his father's. Charles Fuller died on March 18, 1968, in Pasadena, California.

As religion passed onto the airways of America in the 1920s, Charles Fuller proved especially successful at adapting this new medium of expression to the message of fundamentalist Christianity. He was less able, however, to migrate into the field of television programming when it appeared in the 1950s. By that time, his more enduring legacy lay in his founding of Fuller Theological Seminary, which became one of the most prominent evangelical institutions of the 20th century.

Further Reading

Fuller, Charles Edward, and J. Elwin Wright. *Manna in the Morning.* Boston: Fellowship Press, 1943.

Fuller, Daniel P. *Give the Winds a Mighty Voice: The Story of Charles E. Fuller.* Waco, Tex.: Word Books, 1972.

Hangen, Tona J. "Redeeming the Dial: Evangelical Radio and Religious Culture, 1920–1960." Ph.D. dissertation, Brandeis University, 1999.

Smith, Wilbur Moorhead. *A Voice for God: The Life of Charles E. Fuller, Originator of the Old Fashioned Revival Hour.* Boston: W. A. Wilde, 1949.

Wright, James Elwin. *The Old Fashioned Revival Hour and the Broadcasters.* Boston: Fellowship Press, 1940; New York: Garland, 1988.

Garnet, Henry Highland
(1815–1882) *Presbyterian minister, abolitionist*

Henry Highland Garnet escaped from slavery with his family when he was a child and subsequently became a Presbyterian minister. In the years leading up to the Civil War, he rose to national prominence as an abolitionist, and after the war, he became the first African-American minister to preach before Congress. He was born on December 23, 1815, on a plantation at New Market, Maryland, the son of George and Henrietta, who were slaves. When he was nine years old, his father engineered the family's escape to Wilmington, Delaware, and then along the Underground Railroad to New York City. Once arrived there, Henry's father led the family in a ceremony recognizing their new-found freedom, declaring, "By the blessings of God we are now free, come let us worship him." He gave each family member a name to mark the occasion, christening his young son, "Henry Highland Garnet."

In 1826, Garnet began to attend the African Free School #2 in New York City. By 1829, though, Garnet had found work on a schooner that plied the route between New York and Washington, D.C., with occasional trips to Cuba. He suffered a leg injury in the course of this work, however, that eventually required the amputation of his leg in 1841. But when he returned to New York, he discovered that his sister had been captured and returned to slavery and his fa-

ther and mother forced to flee into hiding. Garnet remained in New York and enrolled in 1831 at the High School for Colored Youth. He also began attending the First Colored Presbyterian Church. In 1834, Garnet, with ALEXANDER CRUMMELL and another friend, traveled to Canaan, New Hampshire, to enroll in a racially integrated school there, Noyes Academy. At Noyes Academy, Garnet met Julia Williams, whom he subsequently married in 1841 and with whom he had three children. Garnet's education at the academy abruptly ended when angry white residents of Canaan destroyed the school in 1835. He relocated to Whitesboro, New York, where he studied at an abolitionist school from 1836 until his graduation in 1839. Two years later he was ordained a Presbyterian minister and became the pastor of the Liberty Street Presbyterian Church in Troy, New York.

Soon after he became a minister, Garnet created a stir by delivering the speech "Call to Rebellion" to the National Negro Convention in Buffalo, New York, in August 1843. In his address, he forthrightly called on southern slaves to revolt against their masters.

> Brethren, arise, arise! Strike for your lives and liberties. Now is the day and the hour. Let every slave throughout the land do this and the days of slavery are numbered. You cannot be more oppressed than you have been—you cannot suffer greater cruelties

Henry Highland Garnet, a prominent African-American preacher and abolitionist, is pictured above left of Frederick Douglass (center). *(Library of Congress, Prints and Photographs Division LC-USZ62-7825)*

than you have already. Rather die freemen than live to be slaves. . . . Awake, awake; millions of voices are calling you! Your dead fathers speak to you from their graves. Heaven, as with a voice of thunder, calls on you to arise from the dust.

Although opposed by prominent black leaders such as Frederick Douglass, Garnet's proposal earned him a reputation as one of the more militant abolitionists.

Garnet spent the early 1850s abroad, first lecturing in Great Britain and subsequently serving as a missionary for the United Presbyterian Church of Scotland in Jamaica. In 1855, he returned to New York City, where he became the pastor of Shiloh Presbyterian Church. During the Civil War, he helped recruit black soldiers for the Union army, and, in 1864, he moved to Washington, D.C., to become pastor of the Fifteenth Street Presbyterian Church. After the war, he received a singular distinction when he was invited to deliver an address to Congress in the spring of 1865 to commemorate Congress's approval of the Thirteenth Amendment. He was the first African-American minister so honored. The years after the war also saw Garnet's increasing support for colonization efforts that would establish a homeland for blacks in Africa. After brief service as the president of Pittsburgh's Avery College, beginning in 1868, and a return to New York's Shiloh Presbyterian Church in 1870, Garnet was appointed U.S. minister to Liberia in 1881. Shortly before this appointment, he had married Sarah Smith Tompkins after the death of his first wife. He died in Liberia on February 13, 1882, a month after his arrival.

During his life, in spite of its notable achievements, Henry Highland Garnet endured periods when he felt too little appreciated. After his death, though, his reputation suffered even greater neglect as historians focused more attention on his contemporaries such as Frederick Douglass. He was, however, one of the most influential black leaders of the 19th century, a former slave who never swerved from the cause of freedom for those who had not escaped the bonds of servitude as he had.

Further Reading
Bremer, William. "Henry Highland Garnet." In *Blacks in White America Before 1865*. Edited by Robert V. Haynes. New York: D. McCay, 1972.
———. "Henry Highland Garnet." *Journal of Negro History* 13 (January 1928): 36–52.
Hutchinson, Earl Ofari. *Let Your Motto Be Resistance: The Life and Thought of Henry Highland Garnet*. Boston: Beacon Press, 1972.
Pasternak, Martin B. *Rise Now and Fly to Arms: The Life of Henry Highland Garnet*. New York: Garland, 1995.
Schor, Joel. *Henry Highland Garnet: A Voice of Black Radicalism in the Nineteenth Century*. Westport, Conn.: Greenwood Press, 1977.
Swift, David Everett. *Black Prophets of Justice: Activist Clergy Before the Civil War*. Baton Rouge: Louisiana State University Press, 1989.
Thomas-Holder, Susan Alexis. "Henry Highland Garnet: His Life, Times and an Afrocentric Analysis of His Writings." Ph.D. dissertation, Temple University, 1994.

Garrettson, Freeborn
(1752–1827) *Methodist minister*

An early American convert to Methodism, Freeborn Garrettson labored more than half a century as an itinerant preacher. During the Revolutionary War, especially, when few leaders were available to tend the scattered Methodist congregations or establish new ones, Garrettson helped to plant Methodism securely in the religious soil of his native South. He was born on August 15, 1752, in Hartford County, Maryland, the son of John Garrettson and Sarah Hanson Garrettson. His mother died when he was 10 years old and his father when he was 21, leaving Garrettson a comfortable inheritance, including a farm and several slaves.

He might have settled into the life of a southern planter gentleman but for the cumulative influence of several Methodist ministers. Beginning when he was 19, Garrettson heard the preaching of men such as Robert Strawbridge, Joseph Pilmoor, and, most important, FRANCIS

ASBURY. By the summer of 1775, this spiritual influence had drawn Garrettson to the brink of a conversion experience, which he subsequently described in his journal:

> On my way home, being much distressed, I alighted from my horse in a lonely wood, and bowed my knee before the Lord. . . . I knew the very instant when I submitted to the Lord and was willing that Christ should reign over me. I likewise knew the two sins which I part with last, pride, and unbelief. I threw the reins of the bridle on my horse's neck, and putting my hands together, cried out, "Lord, I submit." I was less than nothing in my own sight, and was now for the first time reconciled to the justice of God. The enmity of my heart was slain, the plan of salvation was open to me, I saw the beauty in the perfection of the Deity, and I felt the power of faith and love that I had ever been a stranger to.

Almost immediately after his conversion, Garrettson, who had taken to assembling his household for prayers, looked on his slaves one day and concluded to himself, "It is not right for you to keep your fellow creatures in bondage; you must let the oppressed go free." He therefore announced to his slaves that they did not belong to him, and ever afterward he was a determined foe of slavery. After his conversion, Garrettson also soon aligned himself with the infant Methodist movement and ceased attending the local Anglican parish church.

By May 1776, Freeborn Garrettson had been ordained a Methodist minister, and he undertook the vocation of itinerant preaching that would consume the next half century of his life. During the first years of his ministry, he road circuit mainly in the South, tending existing Methodist congregations and establishing new ones. His influence on the spread of Methodism during the years of the Revolutionary War was substantial, since many of the Methodist missionaries originally dispatched by John Wesley from England retreated across the Atlantic during the hostilities between Great Britain and the colonies. After the war, he helped to sum-

mon southern Methodist leaders to the Christmas Conference of 1784, at which the Methodist Episcopal Church was organized and Francis Asbury and THOMAS COKE became the church's first bishops. Garrettson himself was ordained a missionary to Nova Scotia at this conference, and he spent the next several years establishing Methodist congregations there.

In 1787, Garrettson returned to the United States and made New York the center of his evangelistic activities. In 1793, he married Catherine Livingston, with whom he had one child. He eventually built a house along the Hudson River, nicknamed "Traveler's Rest" by Francis Asbury and famous for its hospitality to Methodist circuit-riding preachers, over whom Garrettson had substantial supervisory responsibility during the later years of his life. He died in New York City on September 26, 1827.

In the early days after Freeborn Garrettson's conversion, while he was torn over whether to remain in the Anglican Church, he found himself drawn to the Methodist movement, thinking—as he recorded in his journal—"These are the people." Having cast his lot with the Methodists, he became one of the movement's most prominent early leaders in America. Across more than 50 years and innumerable miles, he carried the Methodist message, planting spiritual congregations up and down the Atlantic seaboard, from North Carolina and Virginia to New York and Nova Scotia. Although American Methodists generally name Bishop Francis Asbury as the father of the Methodist Church in the United States, Freeborn Garrettson had a spiritual influence exceeded only by Asbury's.

Further Reading

Andrews, Patricia Hayes. "'Mark the Perfect . . . Behold the Upright': Freeborn Garrettson Speaks for Methodism." *Methodist History* 16 (1978): 115–27.

Bangs, Nathan. *The Life of the Rev. Freeborn Garrettson.* Rev. ed. New York: G. Lane & C.B. Tippett, 1845.

Garrettson, Freeborn. *The Experience and Travels of Mr. Freeborn Garrettson, Minister of the Methodist-Episco-*

pal Church in North-America. Philadelphia: Joseph Crukshank, 1791.

———. American Methodist Pioneer: The Life and Journals of the Rev. Freeborn Garrettson, 1752–1827. Edited by Robert Drew Simpson. Rutland, Vt.: Academy Books, 1984.

Hughes, J. Theodore. An Historical Sketch of the Life of Freeborn Garrettson, Pioneer Methodist Preacher, 2d ed. Rhinebeck, N.Y.: Rhinebeck United Methodist Parish, 1984.

Payne, Roger M. "Metaphors of the Self and the Sacred: The Spiritual Autobiography of the Reverend Freeborn Garrettson." Early American Literature 27 (1992): 31–48.

Garrison, James Harvey
(1842–1931) *Disciples of Christ journal editor*

James Harvey Garrison edited the most prominent magazine of the Disciples of Christ for more than half a century. In this position he exerted considerable influence on the development of his denomination during its middle years. Garrison was born on February 2, 1842, in a log cabin near Ozark, Missouri, the son of James Garrison and Diana Kyle Garrison. He joined a local Baptist church when he was 15 years old. Three years later, after the outbreak of the Civil War, he joined the Union army; except for time spent recuperating from an injury he received at the Battle of Pea Ridge, he served until 1865. After being mustered out of the army, Garrison entered Abingdon College in Abingdon, Illinois, a Disciples of Christ institution. He hurried through the four-year undergraduate program in three years, contemplating a political career. But by the time he graduated in 1868, he had joined the Disciples of Christ and determined to pursue a Christian vocation. Also, immediately after graduation he married Judith E. Garrett.

In the fall of 1868, he became the associate pastor of a Disciples church in Macomb, Illinois, where John C. Reynolds was senior pastor. Early the following year, he joined Reynolds as coeditor of *The Gospel Echo*. As it turned out, Garrison never became an ordained minister, but he la-

bored as an editor for the next 60 years. Beginning in 1872, he took over the subscription list of a paper called *The Christian* and published from Quincy, Illinois, the *Gospel Echo and Christian*, which was later renamed simply *The Christian*. At the start of 1874, he began publishing *The Christian* from Saint Louis. Eight years later, he accomplished another merger, this time with a paper called *The Evangelist*. He joined this publication with his existing paper to publish the first issue of *The Christian-Evangelist* in the fall of 1882; he presided over the paper, first as a coeditor and later as editor in chief, until his retirement in 1912.

Garrison used his position as editor of an increasingly prominent Disciples paper to hew a generally moderate course in the denominational issues of his day. He possessed an inquiring, progressive temper coupled with a range of conservative theological commitments. *The Christian-Evangelist*, he insisted in an editorial on the eve of the 20th century, had "championed the right of Christian scholars to discover every fact, historical, chronological or literary, that throws any light upon any book of the Bible and report the same." Nevertheless, he did not agree with every conclusion reached by higher critics of the Bible.

> Some of these conclusions seem to us hostile to the integrity, inspiration and authority of the Scriptures; others seem to us to be lacking in sufficient evidence; concerning many others, we have not taken the time from a busy and crowded life to investigate the evidence, pro and con, and arrive at any satisfactory conclusion.

More conservative members of his denomination were not enthused by Garrison's moderate spirit in this matter, but the influence of his pen and of his editorial oversight of *The Christian-Evangelist* helped to steer the Disciples away from the fundamentalism to which they might otherwise have been prone. He played an equally prominent role in encouraging the Disciples to join in the cooperative venture with other mainline denominations that produced the Federal Council of Churches in 1908.

On his 70th birthday, Garrison stepped down as editor in chief of *The Christian Evangelist* and assumed the title of editor emeritus, a role in which he continued to write "The Easy Chair," an editorial column, for the paper. In January 1915, he and his wife moved to Claremont, California, to be near one of their sons. In the summer of 1920, after the son moved to Chicago, they chose to remain in California but relocated to Los Angeles. He continued to write his column regularly until 1928, when he was almost 87 years old. Garrison suffered a stroke in the spring of 1929, and he died on January 14, 1931, in Los Angeles.

Among the Disciples of Christ, an aphorism was common: "Disciples do not have bishops; they have editors." James Harvey Garrison, though never ordained, exercised something of the influence of a bishop among the Disciples. His pen traced the most important issues of his denomination for six decades, leaving him, at the end of his life, one of its leading patriarchs.

Further Reading

Foster, Douglas Allen. "The Struggle for Unity During the Period of Division of the Restoration Movement: 1875–1900." Ph.D. dissertation, Vanderbilt University, 1987.

Garrison, J. H. *Helps to Faith: A Contribution to Theological Reconstruction.* St. Louis: Christian Publishing, 1903.

———. *Memories and Experiences: A Brief Story of a Long Life.* St. Louis: Christian Board of Publication, 1926.

———. *A Modern Plea for Ancient Truths.* St. Louis: Christian Publishing, 1902.

———. *The Story of a Century: A Brief Historical Sketch and Exposition of the Religious Movement Inaugurated by Thomas and Alexander Campbell, 1809–1909.* St. Louis: Christian Publishing Co., 1909.

Major, James Brooks. "The Role of Periodicals in the Development of the Disciples of Christ, 1850-1910." Ph.D. dissertation, Vanderbilt University, 1966.

McMillan, Jim. "Stone-Campbell Restoration Movement Resources." Available online. URL: http://www.bible.acu.edu/stone-campbell.

Pope, Jesse Curtis. "The Restoration Ideal in American Religious Thought." Ph.D. dissertation, Florida State University, 1990.

Tucker, William Edward. *J.H. Garrison and Disciples of Christ.* St. Louis: Bethany Press, 1964.

Gibbons, James
(1834–1921) *Catholic cardinal*

In 60 years of service to the Catholic Church, James Gibbons became one of its most powerful voices in America. He aligned himself with progressive elements of the American Catholic hierarchy and celebrated the possibilities of harmony between the church and American society. Gibbons was born on July 23, 1834, in Baltimore, Maryland, the son of Thomas Gibbons and Bridget Walsh Gibbons. A few years after Gibbons's birth, his parents returned to their native Ireland; after Thomas Gibbons died in 1847, his wife and children ventured to the United States again in 1853 and settled in New Orleans.

After working for a time as a grocery clerk, James Gibbons was drawn to become a priest and began studies at St. Charles College in Baltimore in 1855. Two years later he continued preparation for the priesthood at St. Mary's Seminary in Baltimore. He was ordained on June 30, 1861, and following brief service as an assistant at St. Patrick's parish in Baltimore, he became the pastor of St. Bridget's, also in Baltimore, where his responsibilities included service as chaplain for Fort McHenry during the Civil War.

Gibbons had been a parish priest only a few years, however, when he was appointed secretary to Archbishop MARTIN JOHN SPALDING in 1865. In this capacity he helped the archbishop prepare for the Second Plenary Council of Baltimore. Once the council was convened, it recommended creating a new bishopric for North Carolina and—at the suggestion of Archbishop Spalding—recommended Gibbons to occupy this post. James Gibbons thus became the youngest Catholic bishop on August 16, 1868.

Throughout his long career as a Catholic prelate, James Gibbons proved to be more a spokesman for the Catholic faith than an architect of Catholic institutions. Sensing a need for a Catholic apologetic in 1876, he penned *Faith of*

Our Fathers, which became a classic statement of Catholic beliefs. After this book, others followed regularly from Gibbons's pen throughout the remainder of his life.

In 1872, Gibbons was appointed bishop of Richmond. Five years later, he succeeded JAMES ROOSEVELT BAYLEY as archbishop of Baltimore, America's premier see. In 1884, Pope Leo XIII appointed Gibbons to preside over the Third Plenary Council of Baltimore and, two years later, elevated Gibbons to the college of cardinals, thus making him the second American cardinal. In the spring of 1887, Gibbons received his formal appointment in Rome and preached a sermon to mark the event that aptly conveyed the general spirit of his ecclesiastical views. Although acknowledging that the church could flourish under a variety of forms of government, Gibbons insisted that the church had often "been hampered in her divine mission and has had to struggle for a footing wherever despotism has cast its dark shadow like the plant excluded from the sunlight of heaven, but in the genial air of liberty, she blossoms like a rose!"

Having himself breathed the air of liberty in the United States, Gibbons was unabashed in his enthusiasm for the potential for the church's flourishing there. In fact, as the 19th century drew to a close, Gibbons aligned himself with progressive elements within the American Catholic hierarchy—including Archbishop JOHN IRELAND and Bishop John J. Keane, who welcomed intercourse between the church and American society. With these allies, Gibbons won praise from workers for urging the pope not to condemn the Knights of Columbus as an illegal secret society. He also helped win the pope's permission to establish the Catholic University in Washington, D.C., which became a stronghold for the views of those, such as Gibbons, who were characterized by more conservative Catholics, such as Archbishop MICHAEL AUGUSTINE CORRIGAN of New York, as "americanizers."

In January 1899, Pope Leo XIII condemned "americanism" as a heresy in his letter *Testem benevolentiae*, but Gibbons remained influential among American Catholics in spite of this implicit

rebuke of his views. He earned the friendship of several American presidents, including, in particular, Theodore Roosevelt, even as he continued to preside over the Baltimore archdiocese. He remained active until shortly before his death on March 24, 1921, in Baltimore.

In the closing decades of the 19th century, American Catholics struggled to define their spiritual relationship to the country in which they found themselves. Many conservative Catholics looked upon American values and institutions with suspicion, out of which arose a keen interest in establishing a variety of religious and social institutions that would perpetuate their own religious and cultural visions. Cardinal James Gibbons, however, represented a counterview within American Catholicism, one that believed American values and institutions provided fertile

Cardinal James Gibbons was an important spokesperson for the Catholic Church in America during the 19th and early 20th centuries. *(Library of Congress, Prints and Photographs Division LC-USZ62-105240)*

grounds for the spread of Catholic faith. This view would remain prominent among American Catholics, though it would never have a more influential advocate than Cardinal Gibbons.

Further Reading

Ellis, John Tracy. *The Life of James Cardinal Gibbons: Archbishop of Baltimore, 1834–1921.* 2 vols. Milwaukee: Bruce, 1952.

Gibbons, James. *The Ambassador of Christ.* Baltimore: J. Murphy 1896.

———. *The Faith of Our Fathers: Being a Plain Exposition and Vindication of the Church Founded by Our Lord Jesus Christ.* New York: Arno Press, 1978.

Newcomb, Covelle. *Larger than the Sky: A Story of James Cardinal Gibbons.* London: Longmans, Green, 1945.

Ryan, James Emmett. "Inventing Catholicism: Nineteenth-Century Literary History and the Contest for American Religion." Ph.D. dissertation University of North Carolina at Chapel Hill, 2000.

Smith, Albert Edward, and Vincent de P. Fitzpatrick. *Cardinal Gibbons, Churchman and Citizen.* Baltimore: O'Donovan Brothers, 1921.

Spalding, Thomas W. *The Premier See: A History of the Archdiocese of Baltimore, 1789–1989.* Baltimore: Johns Hopkins University Press, 1989.

Will, Allen S. *Life of Cardinal Gibbons, Archbishop of Baltimore.* 2 vols. New York: E. P. Dutton, 1922.

Ginzberg, Louis

(1873–1953) *Talmudic scholar, educator*

A Talmudic scholar of dazzling erudition, Louis Ginzberg devoted a long academic career to the collection and preservation of Jewish lore and commentary on Jewish law. Especially in his monumental work *Legends of the Jews* (1909–38) he popularized Jewish traditions through scholarly work accessible not only to academics but to the broader public as well. Ginzberg was born on November 28, 1873, in Kovno, Lithuania, the son of Isaac Elias Ginzberg and Zippe Jaffe Ginzberg. He was descended from a long line of rabbinic scholars, especially on his mother's side, including his great-granduncle, Rabbi Eliyahu ben Shlomo Zalman of Vilna, often referred to as the Vilna Gaon ("ge-nius"). After studying at yeshivas in Telshe and Slobodka, Ginzberg moved to Germany, where he received a secular education at the universities of Berlin, Strasburg, and finally, Heidelberg, from which he received a Ph.D. in 1898.

The year after completing his doctorate, Ginzberg immigrated to the United States. Although he went to America expecting to be appointed to the faculty of the Hebrew Union College in Cincinnati, Ohio, on his arrival he discovered that no position would be forthcoming there. In New York City, however, he soon found work writing articles for *The Jewish Encyclopedia,* whose first volume appeared in 1900. In all, Ginzberg contributed 406 articles to this project. His position on the staff of *The Jewish Encyclopedia* ended in 1902, when Solomon Schechter, president of the newly reorganized Jewish Theological Seminary of America, which was located in New York City, appointed Ginzberg professor of Talmudic studies at the seminary. Seven years later, Ginzberg married Adele Katzenstein, with whom he had two children.

Even before Ginzberg joined the faculty of the Jewish Theological Seminary, he had approached the Jewish Publication Society about writing a small book about Jewish legends. The society approved the project, anticipating that Ginzberg would produce the work by 1903. The project eventually took on greater scope, however, and *Legends of the Jews* became a landmark of Jewish learning, published in seven volumes from 1909 to 1938. Its first two volumes were translated from Ginzberg's original German into English by HENRIETTA SZOLD, who subsequently founded Hadassah, a Zionist women's organization. Ginzberg's monumental work collected the various legendary embellishments on the biblical stories that flourished among Jewish communities over the centuries and organized them in an engaging narrative.

Ginzberg taught at the Jewish Theological Seminary in New York for more than half a century. During that period, he established himself as the premier American Talmudic scholar. He was the first president of the American Academy of Jewish Research, which he helped to found in 1920. Ginzberg held this position until 1947. His scholarly endeavors had an international dimension as well. He played a significant role in the early affairs of the Hebrew University in Jerusalem, whose cornerstone he laid in 1919. He taught there as a visiting professor in the academic year of 1928–29. Shortly before his death, the Hebrew University honored his contributions to the institution by establishing a chair for the Louis Ginzberg Professor of Talmud.

One of Ginzberg's last significant scholarly labors was to produce A Commentary on the Palestinian Talmud. Although he was not able to complete this project, three volumes of commentary appeared in 1941. He died on November 11, 1953, in New York City, a fortnight before his 80th birthday.

After a distinguished European education, Louis Ginzberg transplanted his learning to the United States on the brink of the 20th century. Already a gifted Talmudic scholar when he arrived in America, he adorned his early reputation with path-breaking scholarly efforts over the years that followed. His Legends of the Jews, especially, became a classic of Jewish learning, holding such enduring significance that its seven volumes were reissued in paperback in the final years of the 20th century.

Further Reading

Ginzberg, Eli. Keeper of the Law: Louis Ginzberg. Philadelphia: Jewish Publication Society of America, 1966.

Ginzberg, Louis. The Legends of the Jews. Translated by Henrietta Szold and others. 7 vols. Philadelphia: The Jewish Publication Society of America, 1909–38; Baltimore: Johns Hopkins University Press, 1998.

Goldman, Solomon. "The Portrait of a Teacher." In Louis Ginzberg: Jubilee Volume on the Occasion of His Seventieth Birthday. New York: American Academy for Jewish Research, 1945.

Schorsch, Rebecca. "Reclaiming Culture for American Jews: Louis Ginzberg's The Legends of the Jews Is at the Heart of the American Jewish Cultural Renaissance," National Foundation for Jewish Culture. Available online. URL: http://www.jewishculture. org/scholarship/99schorsch.htm.

Gladden, Solomon Washington

(1836–1918) Congregationalist minister, leader of the social gospel movement

Sometimes referred to as the "father of the social gospel," Washington Gladden, as he was known, emphasized the necessity for Christians to address the social needs of society. Confident that the gospel of love possessed the power not only to rejuvenate the lives of individuals but to cure the injustices of society, he called on Christian believers to engage in the work of social reform. He was born on February 11, 1836, in Pottsgrove, Pennsylvania, the son of Solomon Gladden and Amanda Daniels. He received a B.A. from Williams College in Williamstown, Massachusetts, in 1859 and, after teaching school for a few months, determined to pursue a vocation as a minister. Though having no formal theological training, he was licensed to preach and briefly occupied the pulpit of a church in LeRaysville, Pennsylvania. In 1860 he was ordained minister of the First Congregational Methodist Church of Brooklyn, New York, later renamed State Street Congregational Church. That year he also married Jennie O. Cohoon, with whom he had four children.

Soon afterward, the pressures of Gladden's urban ministry caused him to suffer a nervous collapse and to resign from his pulpit in June 1861. Subsequently, he accepted a ministerial position in nearby Morrisania, New York, where he served from 1861 to 1866. There he had the opportunity to compensate for his lack of theological training by attending classes (though without obtaining a degree) from Union Theological Seminary in New York City. Apart from three years in the early 1870s working as a religious editor of the Independent, a New York periodical, Gladden spent the remainder of his life occupying a succession of Congregational pulpits: in North Adams, Massachusetts, from 1866 to 1871; Springfield, Massachusetts, from 1875 to 1882; and finally, Columbus, Ohio, from 1882 until his retirement in 1914.

Early in his career as a minister, Gladden was influenced by the thought of HORACE BUSHNELL, believing that truth could not be reduced to precise verbal formulations such as those embodied in traditional creeds. From Bushnell, he also derived the principle that one could not impute to God through doctrinal positions any ethical position that was inconsistent with enlightened human norms of ethical conduct. Both theological perspectives led Gladden to abandon such tenets of Protestant orthodoxy as belief in the substitutionary atonement or eternal punishment. Moreover, in the later decades of the 19th century, Gladden made room in his theological reflection for the results of higher critical study of the Bible, as well as the implications of evolutionary theory.

Gladden, however, never won acclaim as a theologian, in part because his energies were directed down more practical paths. During his years in Columbus, Gladden became deeply involved in some of the pressing social issues of his day. Especially through his exposure to labor disputes, he grew sensitized to the social injustices that had accompanied modern industrial development. Even more significantly, he determined that the Christian gospel spoke to these social issues and not only to the spiritual salvation of individuals. He thus became a central proponent of the social gospel, a view held by generally liberal Christian thinkers of the late 19th and early 20th centuries, that Christian principles had application to the social problems and injustices of the world. The kingdom of God needed to be advanced not only in the domain of individual lives but within the wider institutions of society. For example, although Gladden was not a socialist and vigorously denied that government ought to assume possession of all private property for the common good, he insisted that wide disparities in wealth were inconsistent with the kingdom of Christ. "The broad equities of Christ's rule," he argued in *Applied Christianity: Moral Aspects of Social Questions* (1886), demanded that the great increases in wealth produced by the industrial revolution "be made, somehow, to inure to the benefit, in a far larger degree, of the people by whose labor it is produced."

Gladden did not shrink from translating the principles of the social gospel into concrete proposals for reform. Thus, for example, in the early years of the 20th century, he championed the

cause of labor unions. He even served as an alderman on the Columbus city council from 1900 to 1902, through which service he was able to work toward the practical implementation of his theological principles. Gladden's devotion to the work of social reforms also made him an early ally of the ecumenical movement, since interreligious cooperation provided a more solid basis for successful social renewal along biblical lines. Gladden eventually retired from his Columbus pulpit in 1914. He died on July 2, 1918, in Columbus.

The social gospel movement, in which Washington Solomon Gladden played such a formative role, helped to ignite the social consciousness of mainstream Protestant churches. Gladden's insistence that the New Testament gospel had application to the lives of societies as well as to those of individuals became a prominent theme among progressive churches during the 20th century. Without sophisticated theological training, Washington Gladden helped to launch one of the enduring theological impulses of modern Christianity.

Further Reading

Dorn, Jacob Henry. *Washington Gladden: Prophet of the Social Gospel.* Columbus: Ohio State University Press, 1966.

Fry, C. George, and Jon Paul Fry. *Pioneering a Theology of Evolution: Washington Gladden and Pierre Teilhard De Chardin.* Lanham, Md.: University Press of America, 1988.

Gladden, Washington. *Christianity: Moral Aspects of Social Questions.* Boston: Houghton Mifflin, 1886; New York: Arno Press, 1976.

———. *The Church and Modern Life.* Boston: Houghton Mifflin, 1908.

———. *Recollections.* Boston: Houghton Mifflin, 1909.

———. *Social Salvation.* Boston: Houghton Mifflin, 1902.

Knudten, Richard D. *The Systematic Thought of Washington Gladden.* New York: Humanities Press, 1968.

Phillips, Paul T. *A Kingdom on Earth: Anglo-American Social Christianity, 1880–1940.* University Park: Pennsylvania State University Press, 1996.

Grace, Sweet Daddy
(Charles Manuel Grace, Marceline Manoel da Graça)
(1881–1960) *founder of the United House of Prayer for All People*

Charles Manuel Grace, known to his followers as "Daddy Grace" or "Sweet Daddy Grace," founded a Pentecostal-style denomination whose membership consisted chiefly of poor urban blacks. He provided his followers not only a charismatic religious experience but also the promise of physical healing and a wide range of social services supported by the copious donations he collected. Most of the circumstances of Grace's early life are obscure, but he appears to have been born Marceline Manoel da Graça on January 25, 1881, in Brava, Cape Verde Islands, the son of Manuel de Graça and Gertrude Lomba de Graça, of Portuguese and African descent, respectively. Around 1900 he immigrated to the United States, where he settled in Bedford, Massachusetts, and earned a living primarily as a railroad cook. At some point he changed his name to Charles Manuel Grace and began a career as a Holiness preacher.

Grace seems to have established the first House of Prayer in about the 1920s, either in West Wareham, Massachusetts, or in Charlotte, North Carolina. By 1927, he had incorporated the United House of Prayer for All People on the Rock of the Apostolic Faith in Washington, D.C. In subsequent years new congregations of the House of Prayer sprang up in eastern urban centers, from Tampa, Florida, to Buffalo, New York, attracting hundreds of thousands of members. These congregations shared traits of Holiness and Pentecostal churches: they emphasized ecstatic worship, including charismatic elements such as healing and speaking in tongues, and insisted that members abstain from vices such as drinking and smoking. Grace, who chose the title of *bishop* for himself, was believed to have healing powers, and his publication, *Grace Magazine,* was thought by followers to provide miraculous cures if held against afflicted portions of the body.

Dynamic and flamboyant, with long flowing hair and fingernails painted red, white, and blue, Sweet Daddy Grace did not claim divinity for himself, though he challenged anyone to prove that he was not God. In the main, however, he took great pleasure in making plays on his adopted name *Grace.* "If you sin against God," he warned his followers, "Grace can save you, but if you sin against Grace, God cannot save you." He billed himself as the mediator between his disciples and God. "Grace has given God a vacation, and since God is on His vacation, don't worry Him."

If God was a kind of absent landlord, then Daddy Grace made sure that his disciples understood their charismatic leader as God's resident agent. He funneled some of the donations he collected into apartment buildings, food kitchens, pensions, and retirement homes. A good deal of the money he received, however, went to Grace himself, and he used it to finance an extravagant life-style and to acquire millions of dollars worth of property. He supplemented donations from his churches with a steady stream of business enterprises, chiefly the marketing of soaps, hair pomades, and other personal hygiene products.

Grace's opulent financial affairs attracted the kind of attention common in such circumstances. At least two women claimed that he had married them in earlier years and was the father of their children. It does, in fact, appear that Grace had married one of these women, Jennie L. Lombard, in 1909 and had a child with her before their later divorce. He also gained the attention of the Internal Revenue Service (IRS), which eventually collected nearly $2 million from his estate. Grace died of a heart attack in Los Angeles, California, on January 12, 1960.

Charles Manuel Grace orchestrated for his followers a Pentecostal-style religious experience clothed in the garb of financial opulence. For the poor and dispossessed urban blacks who were drawn to him, Grace symbolized the possibilities of self-improvement and material success. But, unlike some other African-American religious leaders, Grace never used his position to advance the cause of social reforms that might have benefited his disciples. His organization addressed the needs of urban blacks through church-sponsored activities such as free cafeterias, but it never tackled the larger issues of social justice that would become prominent during the civil rights era. Significantly, however, although Daddy Grace ruled the United House of Prayer organization during his life as its sole spiritual tsar, the movement did not collapse on his death. Rather, after initial internal battles over who would assume Grace's leadership position, in 1962 Walter McCollugh emerged as the successor who would guide the continued growth of the organization over which Sweet Daddy Grace had so colorfully presided.

Further Reading

Davis, Lenwood G. *Daddy Grace: An Annotated Bibliography.* New York: Greenwood Press, 1992.

Duré, Kathleen. "'Sweet Daddy Grace' and the United House of Prayer for All People," The Religious Movements Homepage at the University of Virginia. Available online. URL:http://religiousmovements.lib.virginia.edu/nrms/daddy_grace.html#3.

Fauset, Arthur. *Black Gods of the Metropolis.* New York: University of Pennsylvania Press, 1970.

Hodges, John O. "Charles Manuel 'Sweet Daddy' Grace." In *Twentieth-Century Shapers of American Popular Religion.* Edited by Charles H. Lippy. New York: Greenwood Press, 1989.

Jones, Charles Edwin. *Black Holiness.* Metuchen, N.J.: Scarecrow Press, 1987.

Leary, Richard. "Bishop Charles M. 'Sweet Daddy' Grace," New Bedford, Massachusetts: The Whaling City. Available online. URL:http://www.newbedford.com/nbhistory/daddygrace.html.

Moses, Wilson J. *Black Messiahs and Uncle Toms: Social and Literary Manipulations of a Religious Myth.* University Park: Pennsylvania State University Press, 1993.

Robinson, John W. "A Song, a Shout, and a Prayer." In *The Black Experience in Religion.* Edited by C. Eric Lincoln. Garden City, N.Y.: Anchor Press, 1974.

Washington, Joseph R., Jr., *Black Sects and Cults.* Garden City, N.Y.: Doubleday, 1972.

Graham, Billy
(William Franklin Graham, Jr.)
(1918–) *Baptist revivalist*

By the beginning of the 21st century, Billy Graham had preached to more people than any man or woman in the history of the world: in excess of 200 million, scattered across 185 countries and territories. Though firmly situated within the family of conservative Protestantism, Graham preached a simple message uncluttered with denominational specifics, urging audiences to accept Christ and discover a personal relationship with God. It was a message accepted by the hundreds of thousands of men, women, and children who responded to it in the crusades that have been a fixture of his evangelistic ministry. He was born William Franklin Graham, Jr., on November 7, 1918, on a farm near Charlotte, North Carolina, the son of William Franklin Graham and Morrow Coffey Graham. When he was 16 years old, he experienced conversion at a revival held in Charlotte by the itinerant evangelist Mordecai Ham.

After graduating from high school in 1936 and selling Fuller brushes door to door during the summer, Graham enrolled in Bob Jones College, a fundamentalist school then located in Cleveland, Tennessee. He found the college oppressively strict and left after a semester to enter the Florida Bible Institute, near Tampa. While a student at the institute, Graham became convinced that God had called him to preach. He was baptized at the end of 1938 and ordained a Southern Baptist minister the following year. In 1940 he continued his education at Wheaton College in Illinois, where he met Ruth McCue Bell, whom he married in 1943 and with whom he had five children. He obtained a B.A. from Wheaton that same year and chose to become the pastor of the First Baptist Church in Western Springs, Illinois, rather than continue on to seminary. A fixed pulpit soon proved too narrow for Graham. In 1944, and through the years immediately after World War II, he preached in evangelistic rallies in the United States and Europe for the Youth for Christ organization. Three years later, he accepted a post as president of Northwestern Schools, a college and seminary operated by First Baptist Church in Minneapolis, and juggled his administrative responsibilities for the five years he served in this position with a vigorous schedule of evangelistic rallies.

Graham stepped onto the national stage in 1949, when the remarkable success of his revival campaign in Los Angeles, California, caused the campaign to be extended from three weeks to eight. A steady series of crusades, as he began to call them, followed. Aware of perennial criticisms of itinerant evangelists for financial irregularities and for disruption of the congregations of local churches, Graham took pains to maintain the financial integrity of his ministry and to encourage those who experienced conversion in his crusades to find permanent homes in local churches. Graham also followed the lead of other evangelists and expanded his ministry in 1950 to include an influential radio broadcast, *Hour of Decision,* which operated under the newly formed Billy Graham Evangelistic Association (BGEA). Two years later, he began a syndicated newspaper advice column, "My Answer." To these evangelistic avenues, Graham added a number of books, including *Peace with God,* published in 1953, and helped to found *Christianity Today,* a conservative evangelical magazine, in 1955. Graham also promulgated his evangelistic message in the medium of film, through World Wide Pictures, which released its first feature film, *Mr. Texas,* in 1951.

During the 1950s and 1960s, Billy Graham carried his evangelistic message to every continent but Antarctica. London witnessed a crusade nearly a month long in which almost 1 million people attended and more than 40,000 made decisions during the altar calls or invitations that climaxed each night's service. But America remained the center of Graham's ministry. There was scarcely any major American city that did not reverberate to the sound of his voice, including New York, where more than 2 million people attended his 16-week crusade at Madison Square Garden in 1957.

By the 1960s, Graham was the dean of American evangelists, and his influence extended to the White House itself. Beginning with Harry Truman, one president after another made him a guest. Eisenhower, Kennedy, and Johnson all had the world-renowned preacher to the White House repeatedly. The relationship between Graham and President Richard Nixon was especially close: so close, in fact, that Graham's reputation suffered somewhat once Nixon's administration collapsed under the Watergate scandal during his second term in office and the president was forced to resign. Thereafter, Graham distanced himself further from partisan politics. By

Billy Graham, the foremost evangelist of the 20th century, is pictured here with President Richard Nixon. *(National Archives NLNP-WHPO-MPF-C3587(04))*

the beginning of the 21st century, Billy Graham was still preaching actively, though his son, William Franklin Graham, III, seemed poised to assume the leadership of the BGEA.

Billy Graham stands in a line of revivalists that stretches back to 18th-century figures such as JONATHAN EDWARDS, through 19th-century revivalists such as CHARLES GRANDISON FINNEY and DWIGHT LYMAN MOODY, and that continued into the 20th century through preachers such as BILLY SUNDAY. Consistent with the tradition of American revivalism, Graham's evangelistic message downplays creedal differences in favor of a straightforward appeal to his audiences to accept a personal relationship with God through faith in Christ. By avoiding the more rigid conservativism of some prominent preachers in the second half of the 20th century, such as JERRY FALWELL, and the financial scandals that have besieged others, Graham has remained a widely respected evangelical preacher for more than 50 years.

Further Reading

Ashman, Charles R. *The Gospel According to Billy.* Secaucus, N.J.: Lyle Stuart, 1977.

Bishop, Mary. *Billy Graham: The Man and His Ministry.* New York: Grosset & Dunlap, 1978.

Busby, Russ. *Billy Graham, God's Ambassador: A Lifelong Mission of Giving Hope to the World.* Alexandria, Va.: Time-Life Books, 1999.

Frady, Marshall. *Billy Graham: A Parable of American Righteousness.* Boston: Little, Brown, 1979.

Graham, Billy. *Just as I Am: The Autobiography of Billy Graham.* San Francisco: HarperSanFrancisco, 1997.

Kilgore, James E. *Billy Graham: The Preacher.* New York: Exposition Press, 1968.

Lockard, David. *The Unheard Billy Graham.* Waco, Tex.: Word Books, 1971.

Martin, William C. *A Prophet with Honor: The Billy Graham Story.* New York: Quill, 1991.

McLoughlin, William Gerald. *Billy Graham: Revivalist in a Secular Age.* New York: Ronald Press, 1960.

Mitchell, Curtis. *Billy Graham, Saint or Sinner.* Old Tappan, N.J.: F.H. Revell, 1979.

Paul, Ronald C. *Billy Graham: Prophet of Hope.* New York: Ballantine Books, 1978.

Pollock, John Charles. *Billy Graham, Evangelist to the World: An Authorized Biography of the Decisive Years.* San Francisco: Harper & Row, 1979.

———. *To All the Nations: The Billy Graham Story.* San Francisco: Harper & Row, 1985.

Walker, Jay. *Billy Graham: A Life in Word and Deed.* New York: Avon Books, 1998.

Wirt, Sherwood Eliot. *Billy: A Personal Look at Billy Graham, the World's Best-loved Evangelist.* Wheaton, Ill.: Crossway Books, 1997.

Gratz, Rebecca

(1781–1869) *Jewish lay leader*

Rebecca Gratz was an observant Jew who lived in the predominantly Christian culture of 19th-century America. Gracious, literate, and a skilled organizer,

she became the most famous Jewish woman of the 19th century in the United States through her success at establishing Jewish benevolence and educational organizations. She was born in Lancaster, Pennsylvania, on March 4, 1781, the seventh of 12 children born to the wealthy family of Miriam Simon and Michael Gratz. Rebecca Gratz was well educated and grew up among Philadelphia's upper class, acquainted with literary figures such as Washington Irving and James Kirke Paulding who contributed to the *Portfolio,* a literary magazine published in Philadelphia. According to literary legend Rebecca Gratz was the model for the character of Rebecca of York in *Ivanhoe,* Sir Walter Scott's 1820 novel, which portrays a beautiful young Jewish woman who declines to marry outside her faith and is considered the first positive portrayal of a Jew in English literature.

Widely read and an energetic correspondent, Gratz did not pursue a literary career herself. In-

Rebecca Gratz established the first Jewish Sunday school and spearheaded Jewish educational and philanthropic activities in Philadelphia. *(Library of Congress, Prints and Photographs Division LC-USZ62-109117)*

stead, she participated in civic activities. In 1801 she helped found the Female Association for the Relief of Women and Children in Reduced Circumstances and became the organization's secretary. This early benevolent activity set the course of her life. She was instrumental in the creation of the Philadelphia Orphan Asylum in 1815 and, again, served as the organization's secretary for many years.

As the Jewish community in Philadelphia expanded, Gratz turned her attention to organizing benevolent activities with other Jewish women. She was associated with Mikveh Israel, Philadelphia's most prominent synagogue; as did other women in the congregation, Gratz believed that the Jewish poor were often targets of Christian evangelism. To protect impoverished Jews both from want and from Christian proselytizing, she therefore helped establish the Female Hebrew Benevolent Society (FHBS) in 1819 and served as the organization's secretary for its first 40 years. The FHBS was the first nonsynagogal Jewish charity in the United States. Gratz and the women who joined her in this charitable organization sought to be "useful to their indigent sisters of the house of Israel." They believed in *tzedakah*, charity perceived as an obligation of justice and righteousness.

In the early years of the FHBS, Gratz wished to see the organization make efforts to provide education for Jewish children. She viewed Christian evangelism as a threat to the preservation of Jewish religious traditions in America, especially to indigent Jews, since charitable enterprises were frequently used as a vehicle for evangelistic efforts by Christians. She was also familiar with the success of Christian Sunday schools; the American Sunday School Union, devoted to the spread and support of Sunday schools, had been organized in Philadelphia in 1824 as the successor of the Sunday and Adult School Union of Philadelphia, founded in 1817. With these models in mind, Gratz convinced the FHBS to open a school for

Jewish students along the lines of Christian Sunday schools in 1838. Gratz became the superintendent of the resulting Hebrew Sunday School and taught there for many years.

In the later years of her life, Gratz summoned the energy for another benevolent enterprise. The Hebrew Sunday School had been enormously successful in providing education to Jewish children and thus helping to inoculate them against Christian evangelism. But Gratz remained concerned that some poor Jewish orphans were being cared for in orphanages that underminded their Jewish faith. She became convinced, accordingly, of the need for a Jewish orphanage and was instrumental in seeing the first in the United States—the Jewish Foster Home—opened in Philadelphia in 1855. At the age of 74, Gratz once again assumed the role of secretary for another of the organizations that she helped to create. Into her 80s, she continued to be actively involved in the Philadelphia Orphan Society, the Female Hebrew Benevolent Society, the Hebrew Sunday School, and the Jewish Foster Home. She died on August 27, 1869, in Philadelphia.

The organizations that Rebecca Gratz helped establish in Philadelphia survived after her death in part as a result of her talent for communicating her social and religious vision to the generation of Jewish women who followed her. A contemporary biographer of Gratz has summarized her achievement in perpetuating this vision. "In their work, these organizations continued to provide Jewish women and children a way to be both fully Jewish and fully American."

Further Reading

Ashton, Dianne. *Rebecca Gratz: Women and Judaism in Antebellum America.* Detroit, Mich.: Wayne State University Press, 1997.

Gratz, Rebecca. *Letters of Rebecca Gratz.* Edited by David Philipson. Philadelphia: Jewish Publication Society, 1929; New York: Arno Press, 1975.

Osterweis, Rollin Gustav. *Rebecca Gratz: A Study in Charm.* New York: G. P. Putnam's Sons, 1935.

H

Hale, Edward Everett

(1822–1909) *Unitarian minister, author, social reformer*

Remembered best as the author of the patriotic short story "The Man without a Country," Edward Everett Hale was one of the leading intellectual figures of his day. A popular speaker and prolific writer, he represented views characteristic of theological liberals during the late 19th and early 20th centuries. He was born on April 3, 1822, the son of Nathan Hale and Sarah Preston Everett Hale and the grandnephew of Nathan Hale, the Revolutionary era patriot famous for observing, "I regret that I have but one life to give for my country." Edward Everett Hale received an education at Boston Latin School and then Harvard College, from which he graduated second in his class in 1839. In the years after graduation he taught Latin at the Boston Latin School for two years, then wrote for his father's Boston newspaper, the *Daily Advertiser*.

In 1842 he was licensed as a Unitarian preacher and, four years later, ordained the minister of the Church of Unity in Worcester, Massachusetts. Even as he undertook this pastoral ministry, however, Hale turned his hand as well to the writing of short stories, the most famous of which, "The Man without a Country," he published in *Atlantic Monthly* in 1863. This tale, generally intended by Hale to inspire support for the Union cause during the Civil War, described the pathetic plight of a man who, in a fit of anger in a court, declares his wish never to hear of the United States again and then is sentenced to a long life in which his request is fulfilled. The enduring success of "The Man without a Country" began more than 20 years after Hale published his first short story. Hale soon added the essay to his repertoire of literary forms, using his skill as a writer especially to wage rhetorical war against slavery. In 1852, he married Emily Baldwin Perkins, the niece of Harriet Beecher Stowe and HENRY WARD BEECHER and the granddaughter of LYMAN BEECHER. They had eight children together.

In 1856, Hale undertook service as the minister of the South Congregational Church in Boston, where he would remain until the end of the century. He also continued his prodigious literary efforts, which yielded national prominence toward the end of the 1850s. To these activities, Hale added a steady diet of lectures and writings devoted to social causes such as abolitionism and educational improvement. He trained a generally optimistic and vigorous temperament on the social ills of his day, convinced that successful reform required, above all, effort and engagement. He took as a kind of life motto the lines he proposed in his 1869 Lowell Institute lectures and later included in his book *Ten Times One Is Ten* (1870): "Look up and not down, look forward and not back, look out and not in, and lend a hand." It was a sentiment that won him the friendship and regard of President Theodore Roosevelt.

As his years advanced, Edward Everett Hale grew in stature as one of the nation's leading historical reputation hinges chiefly on one creative effort, "The Man without a Country," a short story whose patriotism made it an enduring American classic.

Further Reading

Adams, John R. *Edward Everett Hale*. Boston: Twayne Publishers, 1977.

Hale, Edward Everett. "The Man without a Country." Available online. URL:http://www.Bartleby.com/310/6/1.html. Downloaded on April 23, 2002.

———. *Memories of a Hundred Years*. Rev. ed. New York: Macmillan, 1904.

———. *A New England Boyhood*. Upper Saddle River, N.J.: Literature House, 1970.

Hale, Edward Everett, Jr. *The Life and Letters of Edward Everett Hale*. Boston: Little, Brown, 1917.

Holloway, Jean. *Edward Everett Hale: A Biography*. Austin: University of Texas Press, 1956.

Handsome Lake
(Skaniadariio)
(ca. 1735–1815) *Seneca prophet, founder of the Longhouse Religion*

Handsome Lake has been credited with prompting a revitalization of Iroquois religion and culture after the defeats suffered by the Iroquois Confederacy (Cayuga, Mohawk, Oneida, Onondaga, Seneca, Tuscarora) during the Revolutionary War. Hemmed in by white settlers who deprived the tribes of hunting grounds and plagued by the alcoholism that accompanied idleness, the Iroquois received from Handsome Lake a nativist religious tradition that allowed them to coexist with European civilization, even if it proved unable to restore their former conditions. Little is known of the Seneca Prophet before he received the first of his religious visions at the end of the 18th century. He was born around 1735 at Canawagas, a Seneca village on the Genesee River near present-day Avon, New York. He was the half-brother of the Seneca chief Cornplanter. His name appears for the first time in historical records as a signer of the treaty of Big Tree in 1797, which established reservations for the Iroquois in New York. By 1799, he was an alcoholic, but in that year he experienced

Unitarian minister Edward Everett Hale is primarily remembered as the author of the patriotic short story "The Man without a Country." *(Library of Congress, Prints and Photographs Division LC-USZ62-99518)*

men of letters. Bostonians requested that he announce the new century with a reading from Psalm 19 on a statehouse balcony on December 31, 1900. When Hale was in his early 80s, the U.S. Senate unanimously chose him to serve as its chaplain; he occupied that post from 1903 to 1909. The year after he became chaplain of the Senate, Hale's long and distinguished career as a writer won him membership in the newly created Academy of Arts and Sciences. He died on June 10, 1909, in Boston.

A captain of New England Unitarianism, Edward Everett Hale achieved extraordinary prominence not only as a religious leader but as a writer, a lecturer, and a social reformer. From his pen flowed biographies, histories, travelogs, reminiscences, essays, and fiction, some 100 stories, and 18 novels. Though these made him a widely recognized man of letters in his own day, few have generated continued literary interest. His the first of a series of religious visions that became a source of reformation both for his own life and for those of his troubled people. Handsome Lake announced himself the recipient and prophet of the *Gaiwiio*, or "Good Word."

The essence of Handsome Lake's religious message was that Native Americans who refused to confess and abandon the sins that were wrecking their individual and social lives would be excluded from the heaven he had seen in his visions. He generally followed the Quaker missionaries who had preached among the Iroquois in identifying the chief sins as alcoholism and witchcraft, although Handsome Lake also insisted that the failure to practice traditional sacred ceremonies also threatened the spiritual ruin of the Iroquois. He traced such social evils as alcoholism and gambling to European influence, which had itself been occasioned by the Evil One, according to a narrative whose original version is attributed to Handsome Lake. According to his account, the Evil One had tricked a young man into inspiring colonial efforts designed to infect Iroquois culture.

> Across the ocean there is a great country of which you have never heard. The people there are virtuous, they have no evil habits or appetites but are honest and single-minded. A great reward is yours if you enter into my plans and carry them out. Here are five things. Carry them over to the people across the ocean and never shall you want for wealth, position or power. Take these cards, this money, this fiddle, this whiskey and this blood corruption and give them all to the people across the water. The cards will make them gamble away their goods and idle away their time, the money will make them dishonest and covetous, the fiddle will make them dance with women and their lower natures will command them, the whiskey will excite their minds to evil doing and will turn their minds, and the blood corruption will eat their strength and rot their bones.

In addition to morally indicting these European contagions, Handsome Lake warned against further sales of Iroquois lands. By these counsels he created the framework for Iroquois self-sufficiency and coexistence with white settlers. This counsel, of course, proved quite attractive to American leaders such as President Thomas Jefferson, who praised Handsome Lake for the reforms he was able to inspire among the Iroquois.

Handsome Lake, however, proved less gifted as a political leader than as a spiritual one. Although he briefly held the position of chief sachem of the New York Iroquois, he levied a steady stream of witchcraft accusations against political rivals and others, which sparked divisions and conflict among his people. He eventually became estranged from his half-brother, Cornplanter, who came to oppose Handsome Lake's stream of witchcraft allegations. Handsome Lake left his brother in 1803 and established a settlement of his own at Cold Spring, New York, near the Pennsylvania border. He died 12 years later while visiting the Onondaga Reservation in New York on August 10, 1815.

Handsome Lake's role in the revitalization of Iroquois religion was an enduring one. About 1818, his teachings and story were collected into the *Code of Handsome Lake*, of which there are various versions. The most popular version was preached by his grandson Jimmy Johans. The religion based on the code became known as the Longhouse Religion. Groups of Native Americans still practice the Longhouse Religion today. Handsome Lake offered the Iroquois a religious system of principally nativist elements that served as an alternative to Christianity. Unlike other Native American revivals, such as the 19th-century Ghost Dance movement, Handsome Lake's spiritual vision fostered peaceful coexistence with whites rather than conflict with them. His more pacifist vision of Native American religion did not inspire the opposition that later Native American traditions would, with tragic costs. As a consequence, it was and continues to be a durable spiritual tradition.

Further Reading

Deardorff, Merle H. "The Religion of Handsome Lake: Its Origin and Development." In *Symposium on Local Diversity in Iroquois Culture*. Edited by William N. Fenton. Washington: U.S. Government Printing Office, 1951.

Dowd, Gregory Evans. *A Spirited Resistance: The North American Indian Struggle for Unity, 1745–1815*. Baltimore, Md.: Johns Hopkins University Press, 1992.

Jacobs, Lyn Richard. "Native American Prophetic Movements of the Eighteenth and Nineteenth Centuries. Ph.D. dissertation, Syracuse University, 1995.

Parker, Arthur C. *The Code of Handsome Lake, the Seneca Prophet.* Albany: State University of New York, 1913.

Tooker, Elizabeth. "On the Development of the Handsome Lake Religion." *Proceedings of the American Philosophical Society* 133 (1989): 35–50.

Wallace, A. F. C. *The Death and Rebirth of the Seneca.* New York: Knopf, 1970.

Walker, Paul Robert. "Handsome Lake." In *Spiritual Leaders.* New York: Facts On File, 1994.

Harris, Thomas Lake

(1823–1906) *utopian leader, poet*

The spiritual migration of Thomas Lake Harris proceeded from Calvinism through Universalism, spiritualism, and Swedenborgianism. In the course of this migration, Harris participated in and established a succession of well-known 19th-century utopian communities. He was born on May 15, 1823, in Fenny Stratford, Buckinghamshire, England, the son of Thomas Harris and Annie Lake Harris. He emigrated to the United States with his parents when he was five years old and grew up in New York. Harris left home at an early age—rejecting the severity of the Calvinism in which he was raised—and eventually became associated with Universalism. By the mid-1840s, he was a minister to a Universalist congregation in Mohawk Valley, New York. In 1845 he married Mary Van Arnum, with whom he had two children.

Shortly after his marriage, Harris began a decade-long association with spiritualism, influenced especially in the early part of this period by ANDREW JACKSON DAVIS, a prominent 19th-century medium. By the early 1850s Harris was a member—and briefly the leader—of the Mountain Cove Community in Fayette County, Virginia. This community disbanded in 1853, and Harris undertook a lecturing tour on spiritualism while he began to publish volumes of poetry, beginning with *An Epic of the Starry Heaven* (1854), the first of several poetry books he dictated in a trance state. Harris's first wife died in 1850, and in 1855, he married Emily Isabella Waters; the couple had no children because, according to Harris, they maintained a celibate relationship until his wife's death 30 years later. This celibate relationship reflected Harris's belief, influenced by Andrew Jackson Davis, that one must seek out one's spiritual soul mate, who generally was not one's spouse. In one form or another, a preoccupation with celestial sexuality would characterize much of Harris's thought.

By 1857, Harris had abandoned spiritualism in favor of Swedenborgianism, a religious movement named for the 18th-century Swedish philosopher and mystic Emmanuel Swedenborg. Swedenborg emphasized the "law of correspondences," which posited a correlation between the phenomenal and spiritual planes. He was also famous for reconstructing the traditional Christian idea of the Trinity to argue that the universe was organized into three key principles: love, wisdom, and Spirit. Harris became minister of a Swedenborgian church in New York in 1857; he then decided to make a preaching tour of England.

When Harris returned to the United States in 1861, he founded his own religious community, named the Brotherhood of the New Life, near Wassaic, New York. He relocated the community in 1863 to land near Amenia, New York, and then again in 1867 to Brocton, New York. Laurence Oliphant, an influential and wealthy British politician whom Harris had converted to Swedenborgianism while he was preaching in England, joined the community after its relocation to Brocton. At Brocton, Harris taught his followers the respiratory technique of open breathing, by which, in a series of seven stages, the "Divine Breath" might move through them directly. In 1875, Harris relocated the Brotherhood of the New Life to Santa Rosa, California, where he established the community of Fountain Grove; some of the former New York community remained at Brocton and later severed their relationship with Harris. Harris himself remained at Fountain Grove until 1892. After the death of his second wife in 1885, he married Jane Lee Waring, a longtime disciple, and moved with her to New York City. He died there on March 23, 1906.

Thomas Lake Harris represents a minor tributary of the utopian impulse in American religious history. His own spiritual migration from Calvinism to the Brotherhood of the New Life exhibited a restlessness not uncommon in the religious life of his era. His focus on the Divine Breath was the organizing principle of his religious inquiry, suggested repeatedly in both his prose and his poetry, as illustrated by the following stanza from the poem "Fledglings."

Why should we waste and weep?
The Summers weave
A nest of blossoms deep.
Sad hearts, why grieve?
We downy birdlings are
Unfledged for flight:
God's love-wind woos afar;
Its name, Delight.

Harris's fascination with celestial sexuality, however, and the inferences of lurid conduct that some observers were happy to draw from this fascination, alienated him from religious pilgrims—such as Swedenborgians—who otherwise shared many of Harris's preoccupations. The connection between utopianism and nontraditional patterns of sexuality has nevertheless occupied an enduring, if marginal, place in American religious life.

Further Reading

Carroll, Bret E. *Spiritualism in Antebellum America.* Bloomington: Indiana University Press, 1997.
Cuthbert, Arthur A. *The Life and World-Work of Thomas Lake Harris.* New York: AMS Press, 1975.
Harris, Thomas Lake. *Arcana of Christianity: An Unfolding of the Celestial Sense of the Divine Word, Through T.L. Harris.* 3 vols. New York: New Church Publishing Association, 1858–67.
———. *God's Breath in Man and in Humane Society.* Santa Rosa, Calif.: The Author, 1891.
Hine, Robert V. *California's Utopian Colonies.* New Haven, Conn.: Yale University Press, 1966.
McAllister, Catherine Amy. "The Poetic Vision of Thomas Lake Harris: 'An Epic of the Starry Heaven.'" Ph.D. dissertation, State University of New York at Buffalo, 1993.
Schneider, Herbert Wallace. *A Prophet and a Pilgrim: Being the Incredible History of Thomas Lake Harris and Laurence Oliphant, Their Sexual Mysticisms and Utopian Communities.* New York: Columbia University Press, 1942; New York: AMS Press, 1970.
Swainson, William P. *Thomas Lake Harris and His Occult Teaching.* London: William Rider & Son, 1922.

Haven, Gilbert
(1821–1880) *Methodist bishop, abolitionist*

Gilbert Haven did not hurry into a career as a Methodist minister and a staunch abolitionist, but once he settled on these vocations, he cast himself into them with vigor. He lived through the turbulent years preceding and following the Civil War, and he made a name for himself as Methodism's most implacable foe of racial discrimination, whether it wore the face of slavery or of segregation. He was born on September 19, 1821, in Malden, Massachusetts, the son of Gilbert Haven, Sr., nicknamed "Squire Haven," and Hannah Burrill Haven. After public schooling, Gilbert Haven attended Wesleyan Academy in Wilbraham, Massachusetts, for a year in 1839; there he experienced a religious conversion, which he described in a letter to his parents as accompanied by feeling "the blessed assurance of sins forgiven, that my sins, which were as scarlet, have become white as snow through the blood of the Lamb." After a year at Wilbraham, however, Haven temporarily abandoned further education to work as a clerk in a succession of Boston stores for two years. He subsequently returned to Wilbraham and then continued his studies at Wesleyan University in Middletown, Connecticut, from which he graduated in 1846.

By the time of his graduation from college, Haven was a confirmed opponent of slavery and was inclined toward a career as a minister, though he was not immediately prepared to begin it. Instead, he worked for a time—first as a teacher and then as a principal—at the Amenia Seminary in New York. He preached a sermon two months after Congress passed the Compromise of 1850 that set the pattern for his remaining life. Appalled by the compromise, which contained provisions for the return of fugitive slaves, Haven launched the first of what would become many salvos at the institution of slavery. He brushed aside claims that the Constitution itself granted a harbor to slavery.

Instead, he argued, "[w]e should ever remember that there is a Law above the Constitution, a Lawgiver more exalted than Congress, obedience to whose will alone can make a people virtuous, prosperous, and happy." The following year he married Mary Ingraham, with whom he had two children, and he became a Methodist minister, undertaking the first of a series of pastorates that would carry him, in two-year successions, to five churches, beginning in Northampton and ending in Cambridge, Massachusetts.

In this first decade of ministry, Haven named slavery an offense to Christianity from his various pulpits. His abolitionism was inextricably entwined with his Christian beliefs, a marriage that found additional expression when he joined the Church Antislavery Society after it was established in 1859. On the eve of the Civil War, his wife, Mary, died in childbirth. He subsequently served briefly as a chaplain for the Eighth Massachusetts Regiment and then, after an equally brief pastoral position in New Jersey, traveled to Europe, Egypt, and the Holy Land.

When Haven returned to America, he served for a time as minister in a Boston church, where he continued his outspoken criticism of slavery from the pulpit and in articles published in religious periodicals. He also publicly denounced segregation, but his views on this issue outpaced those of his denomination. He found a new venue for his socially progressive ideas in 1867, when he became editor of the Methodist periodical Zion's Herald. From his perch as editor, he also led the periodical to champion such ecclesiastical reforms as increased participation by the laity in general and by women in particular in Methodist affairs.

Though Haven could not persuade his fellow Methodists to accept his belief in racial integration in the years after the Civil War, he nevertheless was elected bishop in 1872 and given responsibility for church affairs centered around Atlanta, Georgia. Though urged by other Methodist leaders to confine himself to religious matters, Haven used his new authority to denounce the social injustices that he had opposed for all of his adult life. By 1876, he had been effectively ostracized, however, when the general conference of the Methodist Episcopal Church dispatched him to inspect the Liberian Mission Conference in Africa. He returned, stricken by malaria that would trouble him for the rest of his life, and was offered no appointment. He died in Malden, Massachusetts, on January 3, 1880.

By the 20th century, social commentators routinely announced that 11 o'clock on Sunday morning—the traditional time of worship for most Christian denominations—was the most segregated hour of the week. Gilbert Haven railed against this social reality for all of his career as a Methodist minister, though he mainly crashed against the flinty walls of racial segregation in vain. His election to the Methodist episcopacy in spite of the widespread rejection of his views testifies nevertheless to the grudging respect that he won from many of his contemporaries, even if he could not make them embrace his religious and social vision.

Further Reading

Daniels, W. H., ed. "Graduated with Honor." Memorials of Gilbert Haven, Bishop of the Methodist Episcopal Church. Boston: B. B. Russell, 1880.

Fletcher, Thomas Richard. "Gilbert Haven: Jeremiad Abolitionist Preacher." Ph.D. dissertation, University of Oregon, 1982.

Gravely, William. Gilbert Haven, Methodist Abolitionist: A Study in Race, Religion, and Reform, 1850–1880. Nashville: Abingdon Press, 1973.

Haven, Gilbert. Christus Consolator; Or, Comfortable Words for Burdened Hearts. New York: Hunt & Eaton, 1893.

———. "Remarks by Rev. Gilbert Haven," Available online. URL:http://afroamhistory.about.com/library/bltruth_gilbert_haven.htm. Downloaded on April 23, 2002.

———. Sermons, Speeches, and Letters on Slavery and Its War. New York: Arno Press, 1969.

Wentworth, Erastus. Gilbert Haven: A Monograph. New York: Phillips & Hunt, 1880.

Haygood, Atticus Greene
(1839–1896) *Methodist bishop, educator*

In the years following the Civil War, Atticus Greene Haygood, a Southern Methodist leader, spoke against nostalgia for the prewar South and advocated what came to be known as "the New South." He championed the erection of modern economic institutions to replace slavery, and he insisted that African Americans be equipped with education to play a part in this new southern order. Though hailed by many northern progressives, he found himself generally out of step with the South of his day. Haygood was born on November 19, 1839, in Watkinsville, Georgia, the son of Greene B. Haygood and Martha Ann Askew Haygood. As a child, he suffered from epileptic seizures, but he grew healthy in his teenage years. His mother and father were devout Methodists, and Haygood experienced conversion and was baptized in 1854, when he was 14 years old. Two years later he enrolled at Emory College, in Oxford, Georgia, from which he received a bachelor's degree in 1859. Prior to his graduation, he determined to become a minister in the Methodist Episcopal Church, South, as did many other Emory students, and was licensed to preach in 1858. The year of his graduation, Haygood married Mary Yarbrough, with whom he had eight children, and began the first of a series of pastorates in small Methodist churches.

During the Civil War, Haygood served off and on again as a military chaplain. Afterward, he was pastor of the Trinity Church in Atlanta, Georgia, and from 1867 to 1870, he labored as presiding elder of the North Georgia Conference of the Methodist Episcopal Church, South. From this post he was appointed secretary of his denomination's Sunday School board and worked in the denominational headquarters in Nashville until his wife's poor health required him to resign in 1875. That year, however, Emory College named him its president.

Atticus Haygood proved to be an able administrator: His efforts yielded a substantial increase in the college's endowment as well as a doubling of its enrollment. During his years at Emory, he also wrote editorials for the *Southern Christian Advocate* from 1856 to 1878 and served as editor of the *Wesleyan Christian Advocate* from 1878 until 1882. These periodicals, as well as his speaking opportunities as Emory's president, offered Haygood opportunities to reflect on the condition of the South after the Civil War. In a commencement speech he delivered at the beginning of the 1880s, President Haygood took pains to distance himself from those locked in laments for the old South.

We do the illustrious dead no dishonor to look forward. . . . I protest . . . against the pessimistic folly of the whole race of cowards and croakers, . . . forever harping over what they call the ruin of the South. . . . I wish to say, deliberately and emphatically, the South of today has excellencies of character that were impossible to her twenty years ago. . . .

Of all people, in the civilized world, we of the South have the least reason to lament the overthrow of slavery. I, for one, do not lament it. . . . [W]hat the South needs, is not so much money, or manufacturers, or commerce, or political power, but whole-hearted men and women. . . . *The War is over.* . . . It becomes our duty, no less than our interest, to take an intelligent and active part in the general government.

In addition to advocating what became known as the "new South," Haygood insisted that African Americans be seated at the American table, given an equal political voice, the opportunity to work, and an education that would fit them for both pursuits. The advocacy of this cause, particularly in his book *Our Brother in Black*, published in 1881, became the segue into his work as an agent for the John F. Slater Fund, which promoted education among southern African Americans. Although Haygood was elected a bishop of the Methodist Episcopal Church, South, in the spring of 1882, he declined the appointment in favor of continuing at Emory. In that year, he began working part-time for the Slater Fund. In this capacity he vigorously supported vocational education for African Americans, though he opposed equipping blacks with a classical education, convinced that it would not suit their circumstances. Eventually, in 1884, Haygood resigned as president of Emory to work full-time for the Slater Fund until he was elected bishop again in 1890. This time he accepted the appointment, which he held until 1893. Illness and debt plagued his later years, however, and he retired in 1893 and died three years later on January 19, 1896, in Oxford, Georgia.

Atticus Haygood stood at the forefront of southern religious leaders who attempted to guide the South toward a new identity after the Civil War. He invested significant skills as an orator, a writer, and an educator in this task. Nevertheless, though northern progressives recognized him as a kindred spirit, Haygood's influence on southern social and political realities was slight except insofar as he helped to encourage education both within and without the church. This was his more durable contribution.

Further Reading

Dempsey, Elam Franklin. *Atticus Green* [sic] *Haygood*. Nashville: Parthenon Press, Methodist Publishing House, 1940.

Haygood, Atticus G. *The Man of Galilee*. New York: Hunt & Eaton, 1889.

———. *Our Brother in Black: His Freedom and His Future*. New York: Phillips & Hunt, 1881; Freeport, N.Y.: Books for Libraries Press, 1970.

Mann, Harold W. *Atticus Greene Haygood: Methodist Bishop, Editor, and Educator*. Athens: University of Georgia Press, 1965.

Owen, Christopher H. *The Sacred Flame of Love: Methodism and Society in Nineteenth-Century Georgia*. Athens: University of Georgia Press, 1998.

Heck, Barbara Ruckle
(1734–1804) *Methodist lay leader*

Called sometimes "the mother of American Methodism," Barbara Ruckle Heck immigrated to America in the years preceding the Revolutionary War and took with her a fervent Methodist piety. She eventually played a crucial role in the construction of one of the earliest Methodist church buildings in America. She was born in 1734, in Ballingrane, Country Limerick, Ireland, the daughter of Sebastian Ruckle and his wife, whose name is not known. The Ruckle family had fled persecution in Germany early in the century and eventually settled in Ireland. Barbara experienced a religious conversion and became a Methodist when she was 18 years old, perhaps after hearing the preaching of John Wesley, who made numerous missionary ventures to Ireland. She married Paul Heck, with whom she had seven children, in 1760, and the two immigrated that year to New York City along with a number of other relatives, including her cousin Philip Embury, who was a licensed Methodist preacher in Ireland before his

immigration to America. Lacking a Methodist society to attend, Barbara Heck, her husband, and the children soon added to their union attended Trinity Lutheran Church, where they were joined by other Methodists.

Five years after the Hecks arrived in New York, Barbara Heck's brother, Paul Ruckle, and other immigrants from Ballingrane joined them. In the following year, as traditional Methodist accounts have it, Barbara Heck discovered her brother and other men playing cards. Appalled at this exhibition of spiritual laxity, Heck entreated her cousin Philip to begin preaching in their new country. He consented to do so and in the fall of 1766, a Methodist fellowship sprang up from the gatherings Heck had prompted. The society soon prospered under the charismatic preaching of Captain Thomas Webb, newly arrived from England.

A year and a half later, again at Heck's suggestion, Phillip Embury and several other Methodist men took steps to erect a Methodist church by purchasing a lot on St. John Street in New York. There, relying on a design provided by Barbara Heck, the men constructed a stone chapel, which was opened for use on October 30, 1768. This structure may have been the first Methodist church building in America; it is not altogether clear whether a log building constructed by Robert Strawbridge in Frederick County, Maryland, near the same time may have slightly predated the New York chapel.

Near the beginning of the following decade, Heck and her family moved to what was then Albany County, New York, where they joined a nearby Methodist society. With the outbreak of the Revolutionary War, because they were loyalists, they decided to leave New York and settle outside Montreal. Once arrived in Canada, Paul Heck briefly served in a volunteer Canadian regiment and also became a prisoner of war of the Americans for a short time.

In 1785, Barbara Heck and her family relocated once more, to Augusta, Grenville County, in what is now Ontario. There they helped found a new Methodist society. Heck's husband died a decade later. Barbara Heck herself died on her son Samuel's farm in Ontario on August 17, 1804.

Early Methodist societies often created space for lay leadership, including lay women, unlike more established religious traditions. George Eliot's novel *Adam Bede,* for example, which was set in Britain, gave fictional testimony to this reality in her descriptions of the itinerant Methodist preacher Dinah Morris. Barbara Heck was a real-life American and Canadian example of the prominence of women in early Methodism. She frequently had to convince men to take the steps necessary to make her pious visions a reality, but she was—in important ways—the architect of the structures, both physical and spiritual, that they created with her promptings.

Further Reading

Baker, Frank. *From Wesley to Asbury: Studies in Early American Methodism.* Durham, N.C.: Duke University Press, 1976.

Bibbins, Ruthella Bernard Mory. *How Methodism Came: The Beginnings of Methodism in England and America.* Edited by Richard Larkin Shipley and Gordon Pratt Baker. Baltimore: The American Methodist Historical Society of the Baltimore Annual Conference, 1945.

Caddell, G. Lincoln. *Barbara Heck: Pioneer Methodist.* Cleveland, Tenn.: Pathway Press, 1961.

Shepherd, Victor A. "Barbara Heck: 1734–1804." Available online. URL: http://www.victorshepherd.on.ca/Heritage/barbara.html. Downloaded on April 23, 2002.

Stevens, Abel. *The Women of Methodism: Its Three Foundresses, Susanna Wesley, the Countess of Huntingdon, and Barbara Heck.* New York: Carlton & Porter, 1866; New York: Garland, 1987.

Withrow, William Henry. *Barbara Heck: Tale of Early Methodism.* Cincinnati: Cranston & Curts, 1895.

Hecker, Isaac Thomas

(1819–1888) *Catholic priest, founder of the Paulists*

Isaac Hecker founded the Society of Missionary Priests of Saint Paul the Apostle (better known as the Paulists), the first male religious order with origins in the United States, and he labored energetically to spread the Catholic faith to unbeliev-

ers. After his death, the publication of his biography in Europe prompted a controversy over whether Hecker and other progressive Catholics in the United States, labeled "americanists," had veered away from traditional Catholic principles in their hurry to accommodate the church to American values and institutions. Isaac Thomas Hecker was born on December 18, 1819, in New York, the son of John Hecker and Caroline Freund Hecker. With little in the way of formal education, Hecker had to work at an assortment of odd jobs to help support his family. His brothers established a bakery when Hecker was in his teens, and he worked with them until a religious experience when he was in his early 20s redirected the course of his life. Influenced by the Catholic apologist ORESTES AUGUSTUS BROWNSON, Hecker ultimately became a Catholic in 1844. Soon afterward he traveled to Europe to study for the priesthood with the Redemptorist order, first in Belgium and then in Holland. He was ordained a priest in London in 1849.

Two years later, Hecker returned to the United States eager to engage in evangelism to unbelievers. Over the following years, Hecker and other Redemptorist priests traveled among Catholic parishes seeking to encourage spiritual renewal, and Hecker produced two works in defense of the Catholic faith: *Questions of the Soul* (1855) and *Aspirations of Nature* (1857). Hecker traveled to Rome in 1857 to seek permission to organize an American house within the Redemptorist order, but he was dismissed from the order itself for failure to gain permission for his European journey from his American superior. Nevertheless, Pope Pius IX subsequently granted Hecker and four other Redemptorist priests a release from the vows of their order and suggested that Hecker consider establishing a new evangelistic order in the United States. The following year, when Hecker and his companions returned to the United States, they drew up a rule for their new order, approved by Archbishop JOHN JOSEPH HUGHES of New York, called the Missionary Priests of St. Paul the Apostle, also commonly known as the Paulists. Hecker became the first superior of the order and continued in this position until his death 30 years later.

In the decade that followed the founding of the Paulists, the order turned to publishing ventures as a means of carrying the Catholic faith to unbelievers and exploring the intersection between faith and American culture. In 1845, the Paulists began publication of *Catholic Ward*, a monthly commentary on religion and culture, and established the Catholic Publication Society (later renamed Paulist Press) in 1866. These ventures reflected Hecker's conviction that Catholics needed to be less preoccupied with issues relating to spiritual authority and more willing to engage the minds of unbelievers in order to draw them into the church. In 1870, Hecker attended Vatican I, whose ultimate recognition of papal infallibility seemed to him an example of the focus on authority that was frustrating Catholic evangelism. When he returned to the United States, he became ill, however, and found that his own missionary efforts had to be delayed while he traveled abroad seeking a recovery. He arrived again in New York in 1875, but the final years of his life, though devoted to leadership of the Paulists, were characterized by recurring illnesses. He died on December 22, 1888, in New York.

After Isaac Hecker's death, one of the men in his order, Walter Elliott, wrote Hecker's biography. The publication of an abridged translation of this biography in France stirred up controversy over whether Hecker and others who shared his general spiritual temper had undermined traditional principles of Catholic orthodoxy. More conservative Catholics branded Hecker and other progressive churchmen in the United States "Americanizers" and accused them of embracing a variety of heterodox opinions including the belief that particular Catholic tenets might be abandoned in order to make the faith more amendable to American culture. Whether Hecker and his spiritual allies ever held those opinions was and remains a contested issue. Nevertheless, a decade after Hecker's death, Pope Leo XIII wrote an apostolic letter, *Testem benevolentiae*, condemning Americanism as heresy, to the American cardinal JAMES GIBBONS.

The order that Isaac Hecker founded survived his death, but his own influence suffered decline after the pope's condemnation of Americanism in 1898. In the latter half of the 20th century, however, many Catholics found Hecker's spiritual perspective increasingly attractive. His zeal to integrate Catholic faith with American culture has sparked significant scholarly interest in the years since Vatican II.

Further Reading

Elliott, Walter. *The Life of Father Hecker.* New York: Columbus Press, 1891; New York: Arno Press, 1972.

Farina, John. *An American Experience of God: The Spirituality of Isaac Hecker.* New York: Paulist Press, 1981.

———, ed. *Hecker Studies: Essays on the Thought of Isaac Hecker.* New York: Paulist Press, 1983.

Hecker, Isaac Thomas. *Isaac T. Hecker, the Diary: Romantic Religion in Ante-Bellum America.* Edited by John Farina. New York: Paulist Press, 1988.

———. *Questions of the Soul.* New York: D. Appleton, 1855; New York: Arno Press, 1978.

Holden, Vincent F. *The Early Years of Isaac Thomas Hecker (1819–1844).* Washington, D.C.: Catholic University of America Press, 1939; New York: AMS Press, 1974.

———. *The Yankee Paul: Isaac Thomas Hecker.* Milwaukee: Bruce, 1958.

Kirk, Martin J. *The Spirituality of Isaac Thomas Hecker: Reconciling the American Character and the Catholic Faith.* New York: Garland, 1988.

McSorley, Joseph. *Father Hecker and His Friends: Studies and Reminiscences.* St. Louis: B. Herder, 1952.

O'Brien, David J. *Isaac Hecker: An American Catholic.* New York: Paulist Press, 1992.

Portier, William L. *Isaac Hecker and the First Vatican Council.* Lewiston, N.Y.: E. Mellen Press, 1985.

Hedge, Frederic Henry
(1805–1890) *Unitarian minister, educator*

At the beginning of the 21st century, Frederic Henry Hedge's name could be found most regularly in the pages of Protestant hymnbooks, listed as the translator for Martin Luther's hymn "A Mighty Fortress Is Our God." In his own day, though, Hedge played a prominent role in the early affairs of the Transcendentalist movement. He was born on December 12, 1805, in Cambridge,

Massachusetts, the son of a Harvard professor, Levi Hedge, and Mary Kneeland Hedge. After private lessons with his father and a tutor, Hedge traveled to Europe when he was 13 years old to study at schools in Ilfeld and Schulpforta (later Hanover and Saxony, respectively). He returned to the United States and entered Harvard in 1823. After he graduated two years later, he enrolled in Harvard Divinity School, where he received a bachelor of divinity degree in 1829. That same year he was ordained a minister of the Congregational Church in West Cambridge (later Arlington), Massachusetts, and he married Lucy Pierce, with whom he had three children.

During his years at West Cambridge, Hedge formed associations with Ralph Waldo Emerson and Margaret Fuller, who would be prominent in the Transcendentalist movement, which expressed a philosophical perspective that emphasized the role of intuition rather than sensory perception in the discovery of truth. Hedge himself wrote "Coleridge's Literary Character," an article about the Transcendentalism of Samuel Taylor Coleridge, published in the *Christian Examiner* in 1833. His article drew the attention of progressive American thinkers, and Hedge was thereafter closely associated with the movement in the United States. In 1835 he became the pastor of the Independent Congregational Church of Bangor, Maine, but continued his association with the Transcendentalist movement. In 1836 he founded the Transcendental Club—so closely associated with him that it was sometimes referred to as the Hedge Club—and he inspired the club to begin publication of the *Dial*, the chief periodical of the Transcendentalist movement, in 1840.

In parallel with other Transcendentalists, Hedge sought to recover a place for the intuitive perception of religious truth. He believed that men and women possessed an element of the divine nature that made such perception possible. In the essay "Critique of Proofs of the Being of God," he argued that intuitive knowledge of God was the most persuasive proof of God's existence.

> God is his own witness; and his writings of himself in every unsophisticated mind and every sound heart is the surest and most satis-

factory proof we can ever have of this primary truth. If God exists, it is incredible that the Being so named should not give assurance of himself to intelligible thought, should not bear witness of himself in intelligent minds.

Hedge displayed impatience with those who anchored religious truth to any form of revelation other than the internal perception of God. In his essay "Authorities and Scribes," he insisted that revelation was not "a voice without but a voice within, not a prodigious communication out of the skies, a doctrine appended to the tail of some portent, but the intuition of a rapt soul that has met the Spirit of God in its meditation."

As Emerson and other more radical Transcendentalists migrated away from Unitarianism and even Christianity, Frederick Hedge refused to follow this course. He was happy to mine Transcendental thought for insights that would revive Unitarian faith and practice, but he was unwilling to sever himself from the Christian tradition. His career after the 1830s thus included additional ministerial posts, at the Westminster Congregational Society in Providence, Rhode Island, from 1849 to 1857, and then at the First Unitarian Church in Brookline, Massachusetts, from 1857 to 1872. In 1859, Hedge began four years as the president of the American Unitarian Association. During his later years at Brookline, Hedge became a professor of ecclesiastical history at Harvard Divinity School. When he resigned from his Brookline church in 1872, he became a professor of German at Harvard College. He taught there until his retirement in 1884. Hedge died in Cambridge, Massachusetts, on August 21, 1890.

Thomas Carlyle wrote to Ralph Waldo Emerson concerning Frederick Henry Hedge: "Whenever new thought is marching onto the field, there we find Mr. Hedge in the front rank." Hedge's leading role in the early Transcendentalism movement certainly warrants this appraisal. Nevertheless, Hedge's refusal to follow the path of Transcendentalism out of Unitarianism altogether ultimately alienated him from Emerson and has perplexed more than a few historians since. Hedge wrote in "Destinies of Ecclesiastical Religion" that he was "ecclesiastically conservative, though intellectually radical," and this self-appraisal does much to explain the history of one of Unitarianism's most influential 19th-century leaders.

Further Reading

Grady, Charles. "Frederic Henry Hedge." Available online. URL: http://www.uua.org/uuhs/duub/articles/frederichenryhedge.html. Downloaded on April 23, 2002.

Hedge, Frederic Henry. *Atheism in Philosophy, and Other Essays.* Boston: Roberts Brothers, 1884.

———. *Christianity and Modern Thought.* Boston: American Unitarian Association, 1872.

———. *The Primeval World of Hebrew Tradition.* Boston: Roberts Brothers, 1870.

———. *Reason in Religion.* Boston: Walker, Fuller, 1865.

LeBeau, Bryan F. *Frederic Henry Hedge, Nineteenth Century American Transcendentalist: Intellectually Radical, Ecclesiastically Conservative.* Allison Park, Pa.: Pickwick Publications, 1985.

Wells, Ronald Vale. *Three Christian Transcendentalists: James Marsh, Caleb Sprague Henry, Frederic Henry Hedge.* New York: Columbia University Press, 1943; New York: Octagon Books, rev. ed. 1972.

Williams, George Huntston. *Rethinking the Unitarian Relationship with Protestantism: An Examination of the Thought of Frederic Henry Hedge (1805–1890).* Boston: Beacon Press, 1949.

Heschel, Abraham Joshua
(1907–1972) *Jewish theologian*

As a theologian, a writer, and a social activist, Abraham Joshua Heschel communicated traditional Jewish thought to 20th-century America. His actions spoke as prominently as his words as he participated energetically in the Civil Rights movement and protests against the war in Vietnam. He was born on January 11, 1907, in Warsaw, Poland, the son of Moses Mordecai Heschel and Rivka Reizel Perlow Heschel. His father was a Hasidic priest in a family of Jewish rabbis, and Heschel earned recognition early in his life as a religious prodigy. He was ordained a rabbi around the age of 15. After his early religious education, Heschel studied at the Real-Gymnasium in Vilna, Lithuania, and subsequently at Frederich

Wilhelm University (later renamed Humboldt University) and the Hochschule für die Wissenschaft des Judentums in Berlin. To this education he added a Ph.D. from the University of Berlin in 1933.

After teaching for several years, first in Berlin and subsequently in Frankfurt, Heschel was forced to leave Germany in 1938 along with other Polish Jews. He taught briefly in Warsaw and then traveled to London in the late summer of 1939 to establish an institute for Jewish studies there, thus escaping from Poland weeks before its invasion by Nazi Germany. Less than a year later, he accepted an invitation to join the faculty of the Hebrew Union College in Cincinnati, Ohio, thus transplanting his

Abraham J. Heschel combined a career as a theologian with active involvement in progressive social causes such as the Civil Rights movement. *(Library of Congress, Prints and Photographs Division LC-USZ62-123692)*

future to the United States, where he would remain the rest of his life. In 1945, Heschel left Hebrew Union College, a Reform Jewish institution, to join the faculty of the more conservative Jewish Theological Seminary in New York City. The same year he became a U.S. citizen and, in 1946, he married Sylvia Straus, with whom he had one child.

Heschel possessed a gift for translating theological concepts into a vernacular accessible to 20th-century Americans who struggled with the possibility of belief in an increasingly secular world. Although the horrors visited on the Jewish people during World War II might have driven Heschel to despair, he still found room for a wonder that perceived the face of the divine behind the sometimes inexplicable present. "Awareness of the divine," in fact, he suggested in *God in Search of Man: A Philosophy of Judaism* (1955), "begins with wonder." The world that we know is not the only reality, he argued in *Man Is Not Alone: A Philosophy of Religion* (1951): "For just as man is endowed with the ability to know certain aspects of reality, he is endowed with the ability to know that there is more than what he knows."

Although Heschel earned a reputation as one of the 20th century's leading Jewish theologians, he possessed a temperament that was prophetic as well as scholarly, and it led him to an active engagement in key social issues of his day. He participated with MARTIN LUTHER KING, JR., in the civil rights protests conducted in Selma, Alabama, and was a cofounder of Clergy Concerned about Vietnam, an organization (later renamed Clergy and Laity Concerned) that opposed United States involvement in the war in Vietnam. Heschel also participated behind the scenes in negotiations with Catholic authorities in preparation for Vatican II to modify long-standing attitudes concerning Jews within the church. Partially as a result of Heschel's labors, which included a private audience with Pope Paul VI in September 1964, Vatican II's Declaration on Non-Christian Religions, *Nostra Aetate*, took important steps toward the elimination of anti-Semitic references in the church's liturgical and educational materials. Heschel died the following decade, on December 23, 1972, in New York City.

Having barely escaped the Holocaust, Abraham Joshua Heschel became a leading Jewish voice in 20th-century America. Erudite and energetic, he plunged into a vigorous scholarly and teaching career when he arrived in America in 1940. He might have remained relatively unknown outside the Jewish community except for the eloquence and broad appeal of his writings and for the zeal of his social activism. As a writer and a social reformer, he leaped past the boundaries of the Jewish community and become a prominent public citizen of the nation he had adopted. However, he never surrendered the religious vision that had made him a rabbi.

Further Reading

Fierman, Morton C. *Leap of Action: Ideas in the Theology of Abraham Joshua Heschel.* Lanham, Md.: University Press of America, 1990.

Friedman, Maurice S. *Abraham Joshua Heschel and Elie Wiesel: You Are My Witnesses.* New York: Farrar, Straus & Giroux, 1987.

Gross, Victor. *Educating for Reverence: The Legacy of Abraham Joshua Heschel.* Bristol, Ind.: Wyndham Hall Press, 1989.

Heschel, Abraham Joshua. *Between God and Man: An Interpretation of Judaism, from the Writings of Abraham J. Heschel.* Edited by Fritz A. Rothschild. New York: Harper, 1959.

———. *God in Search of Man: A Philosophy of Judaism.* New York: Meridian Books, 1961.

———. *I Asked for Wonder: A Spiritual Anthology.* Edited by Samuel H. Dresner. New York: Crossroad, 1983.

———. *A Passion for Truth.* New York: Farrar, Straus & Giroux, 1973.

Kaplan, Edward K. *Holiness in Words: Abraham Joshua Heschel's Poetics of Piety.* West Fulton: State University of New York Press, 1996.

Kasimow, Harold. *Divine-Human Encounter: A Study of Abraham Joshua Heschel.* Washington, D.C.: University Press of America, 1979.

Kasimow, Harold, and Byron L. Sherwin, eds. *No Religion Is an Island: Abraham Joshua Heschel and Interreligious Dialogue.* Maryknoll, N.Y.: Orbis, 1991.

Moore, Donald J. *The Human and the Holy: The Spirituality of Abraham Joshua Heschel.* New York: Fordham University Press, 1989.

Sherman, Franklin. *The Promise of Heschel.* Philadelphia: Lippincott, 1970.

Sherwin, Byron L. *Abraham Joshua Heschel.* Atlanta: John Knox Press, 1979.

Hicks, Elias
(1748–1830) *Quaker minister*

A Quaker minister renowned for his eloquence, Elias Hicks played a central role in the split between Orthodox and Liberal Quakers in the early decades of the 19th century. Rejecting the evangelical orthodoxy of many urban Quakers, Hicks championed the traditional Quaker emphasis on "Inner Light," rather than the doctrines of revealed religion. He was born on March 19, 1748, in Hempstead, New York, the son of John Hicks and Martha Smith Hicks, who were farmers. His father, but not his mother, was a Quaker. Elias Hicks received a rudimentary education in a local school and then was apprenticed by his father to a carpenter. To the trade of carpentry, he soon added that of surveying. In 1770, he married Jemima Seaman, with whom he had 11 children, and moved with her to her family's farm, which he inherited seven years later.

Hicks participated actively in Quaker meetings and by 1778 had been recognized as a "recorded minister." The following year he began the first of what would be many itinerant journeys as a Quaker preacher, an apologist for the Inner Light. "Darkness and unbelief," he maintained, proceeded "from a want of due attention to, and right belief in, the *inward manifestation of the divine light,* which reveals itself in the heart of man against sin and uncleanness; and at the same time shows what is right, and justifies for right doing."

> [W]hile men disregard this inward divine principle, of grace and truth, and do not believe in it, as *essential* and *sufficient* to salvation; they are in danger of becoming either Atheists, or Deists . . . [or] becoming so blinded as not to believe in . . . the very essential doctrine of perfection, as contained in the clear, rational, and positive injunction of our dear Lord: Be ye therefore perfect . . . *It is by obedience to this inward light only,* that we

Elias Hicks, a prominent Quaker minister, championed traditional Quaker beliefs against more evangelical Quaker thinking that began to flourish in the early 19th century. *(Library of Congress, Prints and Photographs Division LC-USZ62-98115)*

are prepared for an admittance into the heavenly kingdom.

For Quakers such as Elias Hicks, obedience to the Inner Light had a profound social dimension, and he followed other influential Quaker leaders such as JOHN WOOLMAN in pronouncing malediction on the institution of slavery, which he considered a criminal offense in the sight of God. Hicks eventually published an antislavery tract, *Observations on the Slavery of the Africans and Their Descendants,* which sought to prick the consciences of whites who saw nothing wrong with slaveholding. His arguments found a wide circulation both in North America and in England. Hicks joined other Quakers in believing that slavery's pernicious reach extended to the production of products such as sugar and rice—and that opponents of slavery could not with good conscience enjoy such goods.

For Hicks, reliance on the Inner Light was inconsistent with doctrinal fastidiousness. He did not hold many of the beliefs of mainline Protestants of the time, the inevitable consequence, Hicks believed, of Quakerism's spiritual distinctiveness. In this respect, Hicks had much in common with other rural Quakers. By the second decade of the 19th century, however, other Quakers—many of them from urban centers—had been deeply influenced by Protestant evangelicals who increasingly emphasized the importance of doctrinal orthodoxy. In the 1820s, disagreement between Orthodox Quakers (as they came to be called) and Liberal Quakers ignited into schism. Hicks so prominently featured among the ranks of the more liberal Quakers that they soon were branded Hicksites by the more evangelical Quakers. For Orthodox Quakers, the exclusive emphasis by Hicks on the Inner Light, without any attention to doctrinal orthodoxy, resembled the confidence in reason of Unitarians and Universalists, whose assault on traditional tenets of Christianity, such as belief in the Trinity, was spreading rapidly in the early 19th century. In the last years of Elias Hicks's life, the controversy between Orthodox and Liberal Quakers had spread to the majority of the annual meetings held by Quakers across North America and resulted in the fracture of those meetings into Orthodox and Liberal factions. Hicks died at his home in Jericho on February 27, 1830, at the age of 81.

Elias Hicks was a controversial character in his day, and for many years after his death. He summoned his substantial rhetorical gifts to defend what he saw as a traditional Quakerism against the currents of evangelical orthodoxy that issued out of the Great Awakening and swept into the beginnings of the 19th century. Many Quakers of his generation, especially those in the urban centers of America and Great Britain, were prepared to forge a new alliance with evangelical Protestantism. Hicks, however, saw this alliance purchased at the cost of a distinctive Quaker inner life and, therefore, repudiated it.

Further Reading

Forbush, Bliss. *Elias Hicks: Quaker Liberal.* New York: Columbia University Press, 1956.
Hicks, Elias "The Foundation Principle Jesus Laid." Available online. URL: www.qhpress.org/quakerpages/qhoa/hicksbates.htm. Downloaded on April 24, 2002.
———. *Journal of the Life and Religious Labours of Elias Hicks.* New York: Arno Press, 1969.
Ingle, H. Larry. *Quakers in Conflict: The Hicksite Reformation.* Knoxville: University of Tennessee Press, 1986.
Wilbur, Henry W. *The Life and Labors of Elias Hicks.* Philadelphia: Friends' General Conference Advancement Committee, 1910.

Hodge, Charles
(1797–1878) *Presbyterian theologian, educator*

As a scholar and a seminary professor, Charles Hodge labored across nearly six decades to defend the orthodoxies of traditional Calvinism. He fought a rearguard action against the innovations of urban revivalism, on the one hand, and theological liberalism, on the other, two currents of religious thought that would eventually displace classic Reformed doctrine in the majority of the country's churches. Hodge was born on December 27, 1797, in Philadelphia, Pennsylvania, the son of Hugh Hodge and Mary Blanchard Hodge. He received his undergraduate education at the College of New Jersey (later Princeton University) and graduated in 1815. Subsequently, he attended Princeton Theological Seminary, established just four years prior to his entrance, and graduated in 1819, not, however, before being profoundly influenced by the seminary's first professor, ARCHIBALD ALEXANDER.

After graduation from seminary, Hodge studied Hebrew privately in Philadelphia until joining the faculty of Princeton Theological Seminary in May 1820 as an instructor of biblical languages. A year later, he was appointed professor of Oriental and biblical literature at the seminary, an academic post he held for approximately 20 years, before becoming professor of exegetical and didactic theology in 1840 at the death of his mentor, Archibald Alexander. The summer after he joined the seminary permanently as a professor, he married Sarah Bache, a great-granddaughter of Benjamin Franklin, with whom he had eight children. Following her death in 1849, Hodge married Mary Hunter Stockton, in 1852. After teaching several years at Princeton, Hodge took a leave of absence beginning in the fall of 1826 to study abroad, chiefly in Paris, Halle, and Berlin, for nearly two years. When Hodge returned to Princeton in 1828, he resumed his teaching responsibilities and resumed, as well, editorial work on the journal he had established the year before he left for his European sabbatical. Known by an assortment of names over the years—including *Biblical Repertory*, but principally as the *Princeton Review*—this periodical would become the chief outlet for Hodge's prodigious scholarship over the next half century. In the pages of *Princeton Review*, Hodge championed the traditional orthodoxies of the Westminster Confession—the statement of Presbyterian doctrine adopted by English Presbyterians in the 17th century—against the encroachments of new theological currents, chiefly the innovations of New Haven Theology and of 19th-century revivalists such as CHARLES GRANDISON FINNEY. With his spiritual forebear JONATHAN EDWARDS, Hodge emphasized the powerlessness of individuals to receive salvation apart from God's predestining grace. This emphasis collided with the ideas of 19th-century revivalists, who stressed the capacity of men and women to choose salvation, and of their theological allies, such as Yale Divinity School's NATHANIEL WILLIAM TAYLOR, who insisted that individuals always had "power to the contrary" to receive salvation in spite of their sinfulness. When "New School" Presbyterians adopted views similar to those advocated by the New Haven Theology, Hodge added this party within his own denomination to the list of his theological adversaries.

Although Hodge crowded the pages of the *Princeton Review* with theological reflections concerning the issues of his day, he also penned a number of significant books. The most important of these, his three-volume *Systematic Theology* (1871–72), dominated Presbyterian thought until well into the 20th century and remains influential within conservative Presbyterian circles to the present. Hodge's theological vision reached out across the future not only through his own work, but through the influence of his students, including two sons who became seminary professors, and one student, BENJAMIN BRECKINRIDGE WARFIELD, who became the most prominent conservative Presbyterian theologian of the early 20th century. Hodge died on June 19, 1878, in Washington, D.C.

By the time death drew Charles Hodge from academic life, he had taught nearly 60 years at Princeton Theological Seminary. Some 3,000 seminary students passed through his classrooms over the years, imbibing Old School Presbyterianism from its most able 19th-century expositor. He liked to boast that nothing new had ever been taught at Princeton Seminary, believing that innovation was not a proper product of theological activity. Instead, he sought to preserve classic Reformed doctrine in the face of advancing modernity.

Further Reading

Hewitt, Glenn Alden. *Regeneration and Morality: A Study of Charles Finney, Charles Hodge, John W. Nevin, and Horace Bushnell.* Brooklyn, N.Y.: Carlson, 1991.

Hicks, Peter. *The Philosophy of Charles Hodge: A 19th Century Evangelical Approach to Reason, Knowledge, and Truth.* Lewiston, N.Y.: Edwin Mellen Press, 1997.

Hodge, Archibald Alexander. *The Life of Charles Hodge.* New York: C. Scribner's Sons, 1880: New York: Arno Press, 1969.

Hodge, Charles. *Charles Hodge: The Way of Life.* Edited by Mark A. Noll. New York: Paulist Press, 1987.

———. *Systematic Theology.* 3 vols. Grand Rapids, Mich.: Eerdmans, 1952.

———. *What Is Darwinism? And Other Writings on Science and Religion.* Edited by Mark A. Noll and David N. Livingstone. Grand Rapids, Mich.: Baker Book House, 1994.

Hoffecker, W. Andrew. *Piety and the Princeton Theologians: Archibald Alexander, Charles Hodge, and Benjamin Warfield.* Phillipsburg, N.J.: Presbyterian and Reformed, 1981.

Noll, Mark A., ed. *The Princeton Theology, 1812–1921: Scripture, Science, and Theological Method from Archibald Alexander to Benjamin Breckinridge Warfield.* Grand Rapids, Mich.: Baker Book House, 1983.

Wells, David. "Charles Hodge." In *Reformed Theology in America: A History of Its Modern Development.* Edited by David F. Wells. Grand Rapids, Mich.: W. B. Eerdmans, 1985.

Wells, Jonathan. *Charles Hodges' Critique of Darwinism: An Historical-Critical Analysis of Concepts Basic to the 19th Century Debate.* Lewiston, N.Y.: Edwin Mellen Press, 1988.

Holmes, John Haynes

(1879–1964) *Unitarian minister, independent minister, pacifist*

A leading liberal minister of the 20th century, John Haynes Holmes championed what he referred to as the "religion of mankind." He gave a religious voice to the progressive issues of his day, especially pacifism, socialism, civil liberties, and racial equality. Holmes was born on November

The liberal minister John Haynes Holmes attempted to articulate a "religion of mankind." *(Library of Congress, Prints and Photographs Division LC-USZ62-112447)*

29, 1879, in Philadelphia, Pennsylvania, the son of Marcus M. Holmes and Alice Haynes Holmes. He received an A.B. from Harvard College in 1902 and an S.T.B. from Harvard Divinity School in 1904. Thereafter he was ordained a Unitarian minister and served as pastor of a Unitarian church in Dorchester, Massachusetts, from 1904 to 1907. In 1904, he married Madeleine Baker, with whom he had two children.

In 1907, Holmes became the minister at the Church of the Messiah in New York City, a Unitarian congregation at the time of his arrival, where he served for more than half a century. From the pulpit, and through engagement in a variety of civic activities, Holmes championed the progressive social ideas of his day. His dedication to the cause of civil rights and civil liberties prompted him to become a founding member both of the National Association for the Advancement of Colored People (NAACP) in 1909 and of the American Civil Liberties Union (ACLU) in 1920. During the later part of his ministerial career, he served as chairman of the board of directors of the ACLU from 1939 to 1949. To these progressive endeavors Holmes added a vigorous pacifism, which he did not hesitate to announce on the eve of World War I, although his stand on this issue might have cost him his pulpit. On April 3, 1917, he preached the sermon "A Statement to My People on the Eve of War," in which he described to his congregation his position on military combat:

> When hostilities begin, it is universally assumed that there is but a single service which a loyal citizen can render to the state: that of bearing arms and killing the enemy. Will you understand me if I say, humbly and regretfully, that this I cannot, and will not, do. When, therefore, there comes a call for volunteers, I shall have to refuse to heed. When there is an enrollment of citizens for military purposes, I shall have to refuse to register. When, or if, the system of conscription is adopted, I shall have to decline to serve. If this means a fine, I will pay my fine. If this means imprisonment, I will serve my term. If this means persecution, I will carry my cross. No order of president or governor,

no law of nation or state, no loss of reputation, freedom or life, will persuade me or force me to this business of killing. On this issue, for me at least, there is no compromise. Mistaken, foolish, fanatical, I may be; I will not deny the charge. But false to my own soul I will not be.

In subsequent years, Holmes's pacifism would be reinforced by his high regard for the nonviolent philosophy of Mohandas Gandhi.

In 1919, Holmes's church was destroyed by fire. He seized this moment to effect a spiritual reconstruction of his congregation, paralleling the physical reconstruction necessitated by the fire. Holmes and his church renamed their congregation the Community Church and severed its denominational affiliation with the American Unitarian Association, a spiritual affiliation that Holmes viewed as constricting and inconsistent with his ideal of a religion of mankind. Holmes led the Community Church actively as minister until 1947, when he retired. He continued to preach regularly at the church, however, until 1959. In 1960, he resumed his long-suspended affiliation with the American Unitarian Association. He died four years later, on April 3, 1964, in New York.

John Haynes Holmes epitomized liberal religion in the first half of the 20th century. He rejected the Protestant evangelical focus on individual salvation in favor of a salvation that found its locus in the community. This idea of collective salvation impelled him to plunge into the main currents of progressive political activism, expressed most visibly in his participation in the founding of the century's most prominent organizations on behalf of civil rights and civil liberties, the NAACP and the ACLU. Although he labored most of his life as the minister of a prominent New York church, he insisted that the church itself was not an institution within the community but instead was the community functioning spiritually.

Further Reading

Harrington, Donald Szantho. "John Hayes [sic] Holmes: The Community Church of New York: 1879–1964," Notable American Unitarians. Available online. URL: http://www.harvardsquarelibrary. org/unitarians/holmes.html. Downloaded on November 11, 2001.

Holmes, John Haynes. The Affirmation of Immortality. New York: Macmillan, 1947.

———. I Speak for Myself: The Autobiography of John Haynes Holmes. New York: Harper, 1959.

———. Patriotism Is Not Enough. New York: Greenberg, 1925.

———. Religion for To-Day, Various Interpretations of the Thought and Practice of the New Religion of Our Time. New York: Dodd, Mead, 1917.

Voss, Carl Hermann. Rabbi and Minister: The Friendship of Stephen S. Wiser and John Haynes Holmes. Cleveland: World, 1964.

Hooker, Thomas
(1586–1647) Puritan minister

One of the most famous Puritan ministers of the first colonial generation, Thomas Hooker played a leading role in the early affairs of the Massachusetts Bay Colony and helped to define the contours of early Congregationalism. His life began across the Atlantic, where he was born early in July 1586 in the English village of Marfield, located in Leicestershire. He was the son of the senior Thomas Hooker, who managed property of the Digby family, and a mother whose name is unknown. Beginning in 1604, Hooker attended Cambridge, matriculating initially at Queens College, but soon transferring his academic career to Emmanuel College, which had become closely associated with Puritan thinking. He received a B.A. from Emmanuel College in 1608 and remained there as a fellow, beginning in 1609. He served as a fellow until 1618, delivering lectures, dispensing spiritual instruction, and pursuing studies that earned an M.A. in 1611. Within a few years of receiving this graduate degree, Hooker experienced a religious conversion that convinced him that God had granted him salvation and called him to preach.

On leaving the college in 1618, Hooker accepted a position as rector of the parish church of St. George's in the village of Esher. There he met Susanna Garbrand, whom he married on April 3, 1621, and with whom he had at least six children.

Four years later, Hooker moved to Chelmsford, Essex, where he lectured at the Church of St. Mary and developed a reputation as one of the leading Puritan preachers of his day. By 1629, however, he had also attracted the unfavorable attention of Anglican authorities, and he was soon forced to flee England rather than face imprisonment. He joined the ranks of Puritan exiles in the Netherlands but, finding no permanent place of ministry there, decided to follow a number of his former Chelmsford parishioners who had migrated to the New World. Hooker arrived in Boston on September 4, 1633, and soon accepted a position as senior minister of the church in Newton.

Hooker arrived in Massachusetts in time to play a central role in some of its earliest disputes. Most significantly, he participated in attempts by the colony's leaders to deal with the dissenting views of ROGER WILLIAMS and ANNE MARBURY HUTCHINSON. In the case of Williams, Hooker earned the task of debating Williams, whom the colony ultimately banished in 1635 for his heterodox opinions, including his criticism of the alliance between church and state in Massachusetts. Two years later, Thomas Hooker was elected one of the two ministers who presided over a synod assembled in August and September 1637 to address the antinomian teachings of Anne Hutchinson and John Wheelwright.

In 1636, Hooker chose to follow other Newport residents who decided to relocate to the Connecticut Valley, where they established the town of Hartford. Two years later, on March 31, 1638, he delivered an influential sermon when the Connecticut General Court set about the task of establishing a framework for the government that would preside over Hartford, Windsor, Wetherfield, and the other Connecticut settlements. Hooker has thus been credited with playing an important role in the creation of one of America's earliest written constitutions, the Fundamental Orders of 1639. He also contributed significantly to the development and defense of the form of church order practiced by the New England Puritans. When English Puritans tilted toward Presbyterianism in the 1640s, Hooker defended the congregational structure of New England churches in *A Survey of the Summe of Church-Discipline*. This work, in turn, greatly influenced the formal statement of congregational principles adopted by the New England churches in the Cambridge Platform of 1648.

Hooker earned a reputation as one of the 17th century's greatest preachers. He excelled in explaining the progress of the soul's preparation to recognize Christ's salvation and in gently beseeching those outside the faith to have a care for the state of their souls. He exhorted his church members to display a similar attitude toward unbelievers. "We ourselves were once haters and hated of God, and ran the broad way to Hell and everlasting destruction, therefore shew pitty and compassion to such poore soules." Hooker's New England ministry extended beyond his gifts as a preacher, though. His New England contemporaries looked to him for assistance in resolving some of the early colony's most thorny theological disputes. In this role, Thomas Hooker championed the Congregationalist orthodoxy of the New England Puritans against dissidents such as Roger Williams and Anne Hutchinson, as well as against alternative forms of church government such as Presbyterianism.

Further Reading

Ball, John H. III. *Chronicling the Soul's Windings: Thomas Hooker and His Morphology of Conversion.* Lanham, Md.: University Press of America, 1992.

Bush, Seargent, Jr. *The Writings of Thomas Hooker: Spiritual Adventurer in Two Worlds.* Madison: University of Wisconsin Press, 1980.

Hooker, Thomas. *A Survey of the Summe of Church-Discipline.* London, 1648; New York: Arno Press, 1972.

Shuffelton, Frank. *Thomas Hooker, 1586–1647.* Princeton, N.J.: Princeton University Press, 1977.

Williams, George H., Norman Pettit, Winfried Herget, and Sargent Bush, Jr., eds. *Thomas Hooker: Writings in England and Holland, 1626–1633.* Cambridge, Mass.: Harvard University Press, 1975.

Hubbard, L. Ron
(Lafayette Ronald Hubbard)
(1911–1986) *founder of Scientology*

A science fiction author turned religious leader, L. Ron Hubbard founded one of the 20th century's indigenous American religions: Scientology. Centered in the teachings expressed in his book *Dianetics: The Modern Science of Mental Health* (1950), Scientology promises its adherents a rehabilitation of their spiritual nature and a realization of their potential. Hubbard was born Lafayette Ronald Hubbard on May 13, 1911, in Tilden, Nebraska, the son of Harry Ross Hubbard and Ledora May Waterbury de Wolfe Hubbard. He graduated from high school in Washington, D.C., and beginning in 1930 attended but did not graduate from George Washington University. Both before and after college, Hubbard traveled widely around the world, gaining a familiarity with Eastern religious traditions. He married Margaret Louise ("Polly") Grubb in 1933; with her he had two children prior to their divorce in 1947.

By the mid-1930s, Hubbard had established a career as a writer of pulp fiction, mostly of adventure and science fiction. His early science fiction novels included *Slave of Sleep* (1939), *Fear* (1940), *Final Blackout* (1940), *Death's Deputy* (1940), and *Typewriter in the Sky* (1940). He served in World War II as a lieutenant in the navy and spent time in navy hospitals for ulcers and other physical ailments. By some accounts in 1946—the year before his divorce from his first wife—he bigamously married Sara Northrup, with whom he had a child before their divorce in 1951.

In 1950, Hubbard published *Dianetics: The Modern Science of Mental Health*, the work that would frame the basis for a new religion. In this book, which became a best-seller, Hubbard proposed a technique he called "auditing," designed to free practitioners of unconscious mental images, called "engrams," which accumulated in what he referred to as the "reactive" mind and caused unwanted fears, distress, and psychosomatic illnesses. The following year, he supplemented this program of mental health by adding the idea of the "thetan" (his word for the human soul), which was capable of escaping the constraints of the physical body. By 1952, Hubbard had established the Hubbard Association of Scientologists International. That year he also married Mary Sue Whipp, with whom he had three children. Two years later, the Church of Scientology was formed in Los Angeles, California. In 1955, Hubbard relocated to Washington, D.C., where he established the Founding Church of Sci-

entology and assumed the position of its executive director.

Hubbard moved to England in 1959, and there he established the Hubbard College of Saint Hill, where he trained Scientology "auditors." These auditors, the equivalent of ministers in other religious traditions, assisted individuals in discovering and disabling engrams with the assistance of a device he called the "e-meter," to relieve individuals from the effects of all engrams and thus achieve the state of being "clear." In 1967, Hubbard chose some of his closest associates to form the Sea Organization, and with them he embarked on a series of cruises devoted to exploring the idea of the "operating thetan," or "OT," the spiritual being who achieves complete spiritual freedom. In subsequent years, Scientologists explored and developed techniques by which individuals might achieve the state of being operating thetans. Hubbard finally returned to land in 1975, settling first in Dunedin, Florida, and later at a ranch called La Quinta in Southern California. Late in life he returned to science fiction, by publishing *Battlefield Earth: A Saga of the Year 3000* (1982) and the multivolume series *Mission Earth* (1985–87). He died on January 24, 1986, in Creston, California.

Like many other 20th-century cults, Scientology attracted controversy almost from the moment of its birth. The movement engaged in a long legal battle, won only in 1993, after Hubbard's death, to receive the favorable treatment accorded to religious groups under U.S. tax laws. But the expenses associated with those seeking auditing services from the church, as well as the aggressive tactics pursued by the church against opponents, made it one of the more controversial new religious groups of the 20th century. In spite of this controversy, by the end of its first half century, the movement established by L. Ron Hubbard claimed millions of adherents, making it also one of the most successful indigenous religious movements ever given birth on American soil.

Further Reading

Chamblin, Laura "The Church of Scientology." The Religious Movements Homepage at the University of Virginia. Available online. URL: http://religious

movements.lib.virginia.edu/nrms/scientology.html. Downloaded on November 26, 2001.

Corydon, Bent, and L. Ron Hubbard, Jr. *L. Ron Hubbard: Messiah or Madman?* Secaucus, N.J.: L. Stuart, 1987.

Hubbard, L. Ron. *Dianetics: The Modern Science of Mental Health, a Handbook of Dianetic Therapy.* New York: Hermitage House, 1950.

Miller, Russell. *Bare-faced Messiah: The True Story of L. Ron Hubbard.* London: M. Joseph, 1987.

Widder, William J. *The Fiction of L. Ron Hubbard: A Comprehensive Bibliography and Reference Guide to Published and Selected Unpublished Works.* Los Angeles, Calif.: Bridges Publications, 1994.

Hughes, John Joseph
(1797–1864) *Catholic archbishop*

The first archbishop of New York, John Joseph Hughes, used his considerable oratorical and management skills to defend the Catholic Church against Protestant criticisms and to consolidate control over Catholic affairs under his direction, first in Philadelphia and later in New York. He was born on April 24, 1797, in Annaloghan, County Tyrone, Ireland, the son of Patrick Hughes and Margaret McKenna Hughes. In 1817, when he was 20 years old, he immigrated to the United States, where he worked at a variety of construction and farming jobs in Pennsylvania and Maryland. While he was laboring in Emmitsburg, Maryland, at the seminary run by John Dubois, later bishop of New York, Hughes applied to study there. Although Dubois initially rejected his application, Elizabeth Seton, whose order was located at the site of the seminary, convinced Dubois to admit the young man. Hughes studied first at Mt. St. Mary's College and then at the affiliated seminary, from 1819 to 1826. He was ordained a priest in 1826.

After his ordination, Hughes served as rector of St. Joseph's Church in Philadelphia from 1827 to 1832 and then, also in Philadelphia, at St. John's Church from 1832 to 1838. In Philadelphia, Hughes founded the *Catholic Herald* newspaper. He also had to contend with the legacy of colonial laws that had prohibited

Archbishop John Hughes consolidated authority of Catholic affairs first in Philadelphia and later in New York during the 19th century. *(Library of Congress, Prints and Photographs Division LC-USZ62-96710)*

Catholic clergy from owning church property and thus vested significant power in the hands of Catholic lay trustees. Hughes proved effective at reasserting clerical primacy by convincing the ordinary laity to side with him in conflicts with the trustees. In addition, he demonstrated considerable skill as a debater in conflicts with critics of the Catholic Church, perhaps most notably in an exchange of newspaper articles culminating in a public debate with John Breckenridge of Princeton Theological Seminary.

In 1838, Hughes was consecrated coadjutor bishop of New York, where he served with Bishop John Dubois, the man who had reluctantly admitted him to Mt. St. Mary's College nearly two decades previously. Dubois suffered a crippling stroke immediately after Hughes arrived in New York, making Hughes the de facto bishop of New York until he formally assumed this role on Dubois's death in December 1842. Bishop Hughes aggressively expanded the institutional resources of the New York diocese. His accomplishments in this regard included founding St. John's College (today Fordham University) in 1841. He also led Catholics to become a potent political force within New York City. When anti-Catholic violence erupted in Philadelphia, and Catholic homes and churches were burned by mobs, Hughes responded to the threat of similar mob violence in New York by ensuring that Catholic property was defended by parishioners and that New York politicians understood the consequences of their failure to prevent mob action in New York. He famously warned New York's mayor that "[i]f a single Catholic Church is burned in New York, the city will become a second Moscow," a reference to the destruction of over half of Moscow by fire in 1812, initiated by Russians who wished to see it burned to the ground rather than occupied by Napoleon. Hughes also fought a vigorous battle against Protestant control of public schools, a battle that led the way to the eventual secularization of these schools and the development of the Catholic parochial school system.

In the summer of 1850, New York became an archdiocese and John Joseph Hughes its first archbishop. Over the next 14 years, Hughes continued to consolidate control of Catholic affairs in the archdiocese and to represent Catholics in political matters. In 1858, he oversaw the beginning of construction on St. Patrick's Cathedral, located on Fifth Avenue and 50th Street in a spot that seemed remote at the time. After the Civil War began, President Abraham Lincoln solicited his aid in visiting various European leaders to persuade them not to recognize the Confederacy. When Archbishop Hughes returned from this successful venture, he had to deal with antidraft protests by New York's immigrant Catholic population. Devoted to the Union cause, Hughes made his last public appearance from the balcony of his residence, where he tried to persuade Catholics to end their protest against the draft. He died on January 3, 1864, in New York City.

John Joseph Hughes created a vigorous and autocratic face for Catholic leadership that would set its tone for nearly a century after his death. His opponents nicknamed him "Dagger John," and the violence of this moniker captured something of the spirit of New York's first archbishop, especially as applied to his spirited defense of Catholicism against its nativist and Know-Nothing critics. Though he never earned a cardinal's hat, he was the most influential American Catholic leader of his day, and he helped to shepherd one of the nation's most important archdioceses through a perilous period.

Further Reading

Brann, Henry A. *Most Reverend John Hughes, First Archbishop of New York.* New York: Dodd, Mead, 1892.

Hassard, John R. G. *Life of John Hughes, First Archbishop of New York.* New York: Arno Press, 1969.

Morris, Charles R. *American Catholic: The Saints and Sinners Who Built America's Most Powerful Church.* New York: Times Books, 1997.

Shaw, Richard. *Dagger John: The Unquiet Life and Times of Archbishop John Hughes of New York.* New York: Paulist Press, 1977.

Huntington, William Reed
(1838–1909) *Episcopal priest*

A leading Episcopal advocate for church unity, William Reed Huntington endeavored across nearly four decades to articulate a basis for a national church in America. Though never ordained as a bishop, he exercised more influence in the Episcopal Church of the late 19th century than most bishops. He was born on September 20, 1838, in Lowell, Massachusetts, the son of Elisha Huntington and Hannah Hinckley Huntington. William Huntington's father was a physician, and the son initially prepared himself for a similar vocation by attending prep school at Norwich University in Vermont. Subsequently, he enrolled in Harvard College, where he graduated in 1859.

Although Huntington remained at Harvard for a year after his graduation, teaching chemistry, he had determined as a college senior to become an Episcopal priest. His clerical ambitions collided initially with Bishop Manton Eastburn of Massachusetts, who, in the first part of 1861, initially refused to approve Huntington for ordination, because of Huntington's views on particular church doctrines. Eventually, however, in the fall of 1861,

Bishop Eastburn reconsidered, and Huntington was ordained first a deacon and then, in December 1862, an Episcopal priest. He then assumed the rectorship of All Saints Church in Worcester, Massachusetts. The following year he married Theresa Reynolds, with whom he had four children prior to her death during childbirth nine years later.

Huntington spent the remainder of his ministerial career as a parish priest, first at All Saints Church from 1862 to 1883, and then at Grace Church in New York City from 1883. With the publication of his 1870 book *The Church-Idea: An Essay toward Unity,* Huntington stepped onto the national stage of Episcopal affairs, a stage on which he would prove to be a dominant force for nearly 40 years. In *The Church-Idea,* he set forth a four-pronged statement of belief that he contended should be the basis for efforts at unifying the Christian church. These he proposed to substitute for the more extensive, and theologically restrictive, Thirty-Nine Articles (1563–71) that defined Anglican orthodoxy to that time. His proposals became the basis for the Chicago-Lambeth Quadrilateral, a statement of faith proposed as a basis of church unity first by the House of Bishops of the Episcopal Church in America in 1886 and then by a worldwide conference of Anglican bishops that met at Lambeth in 1888. The elements of this statement, as adopted by the Lambeth conference, were as follows:

(a) The Holy Scriptures of the Old and New Testaments, as "containing all things necessary to salvation," and as being the rule and ultimate standard of faith.

(b) The Apostles' Creed, as the Baptismal Symbol; and the Nicene Creed, as the sufficient statement of the Christian Faith.

(c) The two Sacraments ordained by Christ Himself—Baptism and the Supper of the Lord—ministered with unfailing use of Christ's words of Institution, and of the elements ordained by Him.

(d) The Historic Episcopate, locally adapted in the methods of its administration to the varying needs of the nations and peoples called of God into the Unity of the Church.

Huntington also turned his attention to the issue of liturgical reform within the Episcopal Church, but on this issue, he proved less immediately influential. His attempt to revise the Book of Common Prayer was rejected in 1886, though a half century later, in 1928, many of his proposed revisions were accepted. In all, he attended 13 General Conventions of the Episcopal Church in America from 1870 until his death, and he played a dominant role in the proceedings of the House of Deputies during these conventions. He died on July 16, 1909, in Nahant, Massachusetts.

William Reed Huntington was never elevated to the rank of bishop. Nevertheless, he commanded influence in the late 19th-century Episcopal Church far in excess of that which might have been expected from his ecclesiastical rank. Sometimes labeled the first presbyter of the church during this period, Huntington translated his dedication to church unity into significant reforms. Even when his reformist zeal did not immediately bear fruit, as in the case of his proposed revisions to the Book of Common Prayer, he continued to affect the life of his denomination long after his death.

Further Reading

Huntington, William Reed. *The Church-Idea: An Essay Toward Unity.* New York: E. P. Dutton, 1870.

———. *A Short History of the Book of Common Prayer; Together with Certain Papers Illustrative of Liturgical Revision, 1878–1892.* New York: T. Whittaker, 1893.

Northup, Lesley A. "William Reed Huntington: First Presbyter of the Late 19th Century." *Anglican and Episcopal History* 62 (June 1993): 303–5.

Suter, John Wallace. *Life and Letters of William Reed Huntington: A Champion of Unity.* New York: Century, 1925.

Woolverton, John F. "Huntington's Quadrilateral: A Critical Study." *Church History* (June 1970): 198–211.

———. "W. R. Huntington: Liturgical Renewal and Church Unity in the 1880s." *Anglican Theological Review* (April 1966): 175–99.

Hutchinson, Anne Marbury
(ca. 1591–1643) *Puritan lay leader*

Anne Marbury Hutchinson challenged elements of Puritan orthodoxy in the early years of the Massachusetts Bay Colony. For this she earned the sentence of banishment and a reputation as one of the colony's most significant early dissenters. Hutchinson was born in Alford, Lincolnshire, the child of Francis Marbury and Bridget Dryden Marbury. The precise date of her birth is unknown, but church records indicate she was baptized on July 20, 1591, and this rite normally followed birth by a few days. Her father was a minister in the Church of England who had been suspended from his clerical position and imprisoned for his criticisms of the church. In 1612, Anne Marbury married William Hutchinson, a wealthy businessman, with whom she had 15 children. Hutchinson and her family were eventually influenced by the preaching of JOHN COTTON, the Puritan minister and vicar of St. Botolph's Church in Boston, Lincolnshire. By 1633, Anglican authorities had suspended Cotton from his pulpit, and he chose to migrate to Massachusetts, where he soon became teacher of the Boston church. Hutchinson and her family followed Cotton the next year and on their arrival took up a prominent place in Boston society.

Once settled in Boston, Hutchinson began to conduct religious meetings in her home devoted to discussion of the sermons delivered by the ministers of the Boston church: John Wilson, its pastor, and John Cotton, the church's teacher. Hutchinson made clear her preference for the preaching of John Cotton, who emphasized the centrality of God's unconditional grace in salvation. Cotton urged that listeners, anxious to understand how they might know whether they were objects of this grace and among God's elect, not rely on the uprightness of their conduct but rather on the internal witness of the Holy Spirit, which God had made indwell his elect. Hutchinson believed that most New England ministers preached a "covenant of works" rather than the proper "covenant of grace" articulated in Cotton's sermons: they relied overmuch on external acts of righteousness as evidence that one was among the elect. Hutchinson's home meetings attracted a good deal of support, including the attendance of Henry Vane, a young man who briefly served as the colony's governor. In the end, they contributed to a polarization of Boston society that the colony's civil and spiritual authorities were

not inclined to tolerate. Hutchinson's opponents seized on her repudiation of external signs of righteousness as evidence of salvation to brand her an antinomian, suggesting that she did not believe in or was opposed to biblical law.

The ministers of the colony convened in late August 1637 and denounced Hutchinson's views. John Wilson, pastor of the Boston church, branded her a "dangerous instrument of the Devil raised up by Satan amongst us." In November, the Massachusetts General Court—the colony's highest judicial and legislative body—tried Hutchinson for heresy. There, Hutchinson deftly parried the accusations against her, which included claims that she was disrespectful of the colony's ministers and that she had improperly undertaken to teach men. The court eventually concluded that her beliefs were blasphemous, none more pernicious than what the court found to be her claim to have received immediate revelation from God on particular matters. For these errors, the court sentenced her to banishment and her church subsequently excommunicated her. It levied a similar edict against Hutchinson's brother-in-law, John Wheelwright, a minister in the colony who held views similar to those of Hutchinson. Once cast out of the Massachusetts Bay Colony, Anne Hutchinson and her family settled in a colony on Narragansett Bay in what became Rhode Island. Four years later, in 1642, her husband died, and she relocated, along with her six children who remained at home, to a part of the Dutch colony of New Netherlands in Long Island. The next year, she and five of her children were killed in an Indian massacre.

For a time, at least, in the mid-17th century, the Massachusetts Bay Colony was able to wield sufficient political power to harry dissenters such as Hutchinson out of its boundaries. Historians vary in their estimate of why Hutchinson triggered such adamant opposition from the Massachusetts authorities. For some, Hutchinson's offense lay chiefly in the area of her religious beliefs, which—by elevating inner spiritual perception over external norms of conduct—threatened the religious and political foundations of the Puritans' attempt to create a holy commonwealth. For others, Hutchinson's crime lay in her refusal to subordinate her own opinions to those of the clergy, or of men generally. In this reading, she was America's first feminist.

Further Reading

Battis, Emery John. *Saints and Sectaries: Anne Hutchinson and the Antinomian Controversy in the Massachusetts Bay Colony.* Chapel Hill: University of North Carolina Press, 1962.

Bremer, Francis J., ed. *Anne Hutchinson: Troubler of the Puritan Zion.* Huntington, N.Y.: R. E. Krieger, 1981.

Curtis, Edith. *Anne Hutchinson: Biography.* Cambridge: Washburn & Thomas, 1930.

Dunlea, William. *Anne Hutchinson and the Puritans: An Early American Tragedy.* Pittsburgh: Dorrance, 1993.

Hall, David D., ed. *The Antinomian Controversy, 1636–1638: A Documentary History.* 2d ed. Durham, N.C.: Duke University Press, 1990.

Pagnattaro, Marissa Anne. *From Anne Hutchinson to Toni Morrison: Women and Justice in American Literature.* New York: Peter Lang, 2001.

Williams, Selma R. *Divine Rebel: The Life of Anne Marbury Hutchinson.* New York: Holt, Rinehart & Winston, 1981.

I

Ingersoll, Robert Green
(1833–1899) *lawyer, atheist*

The 19th century's most famous skeptic was also one of its most famous lecturers. Robert Green Ingersoll, a lawyer by profession, disturbed crowds as often as he cheered them and forged a reputation as an eloquent challenger of America's religious sensibilities. He was born on August 11, 1833, in Dresden, New York, the son of John Ingersoll and Mary Livingston Ingersoll. Although his father was a Congregationalist minister. Ingersoll absorbed more from books than from his father. Though lacking in significant formal education, Ingersoll nevertheless succeeded in gaining admittance to the bar in 1854, along with his brother, Ebon Clark Ingersoll, after the two studied law briefly with an attorney in Marion, Illinois. Toward the end of the decade the brothers relocated to Peoria, where they built a legal practice together. Ingersoll married Eva A. Parker in 1862; with her he had two children.

During the Civil War, Ingersoll served for a time as an officer in the Union army and was briefly a prisoner of war in December 1862. The following summer he returned to the practice of law in Peoria, where he actively participated in Republican politics, even though his attempts to obtain a political office proved unsuccessful. He was able, however, to turn his growing oratorical skills to the support of his brother, Ebon Clark, who won election to Congress in 1864.

In 1872, Ingersoll launched his career as a public skeptic of religion with the lecture "On the Gods," in which he suggested that an "honest God is the noblest work of man." Gods were the flawed creations of human imagination, he insisted. Men created gods to deliver them from the perils and uncertainties of life. But, Ingersoll declared, "Man should cease to expect aid from on high."

> By this time he should know that heaven has no ear to hear, and no hand to help. . . . If abuses are destroyed, man must destroy them. If slaves are freed, man must free them. If new truths are discovered, man must discover them. If the naked are clothed; if the hungry are fed; if justice is done; if labor is rewarded; if superstition is driven from the mind; if the defenseless are protected and if the right finally triumphs, all must be the work of man. The grand victories of the future must be won by man, and by man alone.

Ingersoll never managed to win an elected office, but he played an increasingly prominent role in national Republican politics in the 1870s. He made the nomination speech for James G. Blaine at the Republican National Convention in 1876, and he subsequently campaigned vigorously for Rutherford B. Hayes, who won the Republican nomination and went on to win the disputed presidential election of that year. At the same time, Ingersoll enjoyed an increasing reputation as one of the more prominent lawyers of his day. In 1877 he transferred his legal practice to Washington, D.C., to be closer to his brother. After Ebon Clark Ingersoll's death in 1879, Robert Ingersoll moved to New York City in 1885. There, he continued to supplement his legal practice with a lucrative career as a lecturer, famously antagonizing religious believers with his skeptical wit. He died at Dobbs Ferry, New York, on July 21, 1899.

Robert Ingersoll made a career as a critic of creeds, but he was not afraid to advance his own creed, though it affirmed none of the spiritual verities to which most of his contemporaries adhered. "Happiness is the only good," he affirmed in his 1882 address "Creed."

> The time to be happy is now. The place to be happy is here. The way to be happy is to make others so. This creed is somewhat short, but it is long enough for this life, strong enough for this world. If there is another world, when we get there we can make another creed. But this creed certainly will do for this life.

Although Ingersoll died on the brink of the 20th century, his humanistic gospel became an increasingly prominent force in the century he did not live to see. In his hands, and those of his intellectual successors, religious skepticism was the tool not of despair but of hope, hope that the human race, once unshackled from religious superstition, would find lasting happiness.

Further Reading

Anderson, David D. *Robert Ingersoll*. New York: Twayne Publishers, 1972.
Cramer, C. H. *Royal Bob: The Life of Robert G. Ingersoll*. Indianapolis: Bobbs-Merrill, 1952.
Ingersoll, Robert Green. *The Letters of Robert G. Ingersoll*. Edited by Eva Ingersoll Wakefield. Westport, Conn.: Greenwood Press, 1973.
———. *The Works of Robert G. Ingersoll*. 12 vols. New York: Dresden, 1902; New York: AMS Press, 1978.
Kittredge, Herman Eugene. *Ingersoll: A Biographical Appreciation*. New York: Dresden, 1911.
Smith, Edward Garstin. *The Life and Reminiscences of Robert G. Ingersoll*. New York: National Weekly, 1904.
Smith, Frank. *Robert G. Ingersoll: A Life*. Buffalo, N.Y.: Prometheus Books, 1990.

Ireland, John
(1838–1918) *Catholic archbishop*

The first archbishop of Saint Paul, Minnesota, John Ireland is remembered chiefly for his role in the Americanist controversy toward the end of the 19th century. Ireland championed the assimilation of American Catholics into the institutions and values of American society and, by doing so, clashed with more conservative Catholic leaders who opposed Ireland's assimilationist vision. John Ireland was born on September 11, 1838, in Burnchurch, County Kilkenny, Ireland, the son of Richard Ireland and Judith Naughton Ireland. In 1849 Ireland's family immigrated to America, where they settled successively in Burlington, Vermont; Chicago, Illinois; and finally, in 1852, Saint Paul, in Minnesota territory. Almost immediately, though, Ireland returned to Europe, where he attended a preparatory seminary at Meximieux, France, and then the seminary at Montbel, France, from which he graduated in 1861.

When John Ireland returned to America in the fall of 1861, he was ordained a priest and served briefly as a curate of the cathedral parish in St. Paul. For a little less than a year, from June 1862 to April 1863, Ireland served as chaplain of the Fifth Minnesota Infantry Volunteers, an experience that he afterward valued greatly and that accounted, perhaps, for some of his later zeal for a Catholic appreciation of American values. He also carried away from his brief career in the Union army a deep antipathy to slavery. Nearly three decades later he preached a sermon against racial segregation that traced its roots to the pernicious institution of chattel slavery. "Certain stages of civilization, it has been said, rendered slavery a social necessity. Certain stages of barbarism they should be called, and Americans should not have lowered themselves to barbarism."

Returned once again to Saint Paul, Ireland resumed his work as curate and later rector of the cathedral parish. In 1875 he was appointed coadjutor bishop of the Saint Paul diocese and became bishop in 1884 with the retirement of his successor, Bishop Thomas Grace. Four years later, Ireland became the first archbishop of Saint Paul.

Ireland's prominent place in the history of American Catholicism owes most to his role in what came to be called the Americanist controversy. In this struggle between conservative and liberal elements within the church, Ireland cast himself vigorously in support of the rapid assimilation of Catholic immigrants into the mainstream of American society. This position placed Ireland at odds with more conservative Catholic leaders such as Archbishop MICHAEL AUGUSTINE CORRIGAN of New York, who feared Catholic acculturation to American values such as materialism and secularism. It also drew the opposition of German Catholic immigrants who insisted on the preservation of their European language and traditions.

The controversy spilled across the last decade and a half of the 19th century. Ireland, for his part, helped to found the Catholic University of America in Washington, D.C., and used it as a base for championing his liberal vision. He also attempted specific programs designed to hasten the assimilation of Catholic immigrants into the institutions and values of American society. Perhaps the most significant of these was his arrangement to lease parochial school property in Faribault, Minnesota, to the public schools in exchange for the right to supervise the secular education that would be offered in these facilities. Ireland's assimilationist zeal also expressed itself through his support of a Wisconsin law that required English-language instruction in all public and private schools.

In the final years of the 19th century Ireland's enthusiasm for a close partnership between Catholics and American values suffered significant reverses. Archbishop Ireland found the principle of church-state separation an attractive political principle and one that Catholics should embrace. Pope Leo XIII disagreed that the American pattern of religious disestablishment was a fit model for European countries in his 1895 encyclical letter, *Longingqua Oceani.* Four years later, Pope Leo delivered a further setback to Ireland's vision when he named Americanism a heresy in his encyclical letter *Testem benevolentiae.* Ireland and his allies denied, of course, that the heresy existed, but opponents such as Archbishop Corrigan rallied to the pope's encyclical as a decisive repudiation of the liberal element within American Catholicism.

Saint Paul's first archbishop never became a cardinal, in spite of efforts by his friends to press for this honor. Nevertheless, in spite of setbacks occasioned by the Americanist controversy, Ireland made lasting contributions to American Catholicism. The Catholic University of America, which he helped to found, survived the controversy. Ireland also founded St. Paul Seminary and oversaw the construction of the Cathedral of Saint Paul and the Basilica of St. Mary in Minneapolis. He died in Saint Paul on September 25, 1918.

The waves of European Catholic immigrants who arrived in the United States in the last two decades of the 19th century occasioned significant stresses in the American social fabric. Archbishop John Ireland attempted to resolve these social tensions by hurrying the assimilation of Catholic immigrants into American society. He was not widely successful in winning support for his vision among the Catholic hierarchy, and the process of assimilation stretched out longer than he might have wished. But Ireland's confidence that being an American and being a Catholic were not fundamentally inconsistent would find a more secure place in the later years of the 20th century.

Further Reading

Ireland, John. *The Church and Modern Society: Lectures and Addresses.* 2 vols. Chicago: D. H. McBride, 1896.

Moynihan, James H. *The Life of Archbishop John Ireland.* New York: Harper, 1953; New York: Arno Press, 1976.

O'Connell, Marvin Richard. *John Ireland and the American Catholic Church.* St. Paul: Minnesota Historical Society Press, 1988.

Peters, Richard Clayton. "Archbishop John Ireland's Faribault Plan and Stillwater Experiment and Their Implications for Church/State Relations." Ph.D. dissertation, Marquette University, 2000.

J

Jackson, Fanny Cobin See COPPIN, FANNY JACKSON.

Jackson, Jesse
(Jesse Louis Burns)
(1941–) *Baptist minister, civil rights leader, politician*

The foremost African-American religious leader during the last decades of the 20th century and the beginning of the 21st, Jesse Jackson has forged a role as the public successor of the slain civil rights leader MARTIN LUTHER KING, JR. In two failed but significant campaigns for the Democratic nomination for president, Jackson put the cause of the dispossessed and downtrodden at the center of the political table. He was born Jesse Louis Burns on October 8, 1941, in Greenville, South Carolina, the son of Helen Burns and Noah Louis Robinson, a prominent black neighbor who was not his mother's husband. Jesse's mother married Charles Henry Jackson in 1943, and in 1957 he adopted Jesse, who assumed his adopted father's last name.

Jackson was a talented athlete at Greenville's Sterling High School, from which he graduated in 1959. Subsequently, he attended the University of Illinois for a year and then transferred to North Carolina Agricultural and Technical State College in Greensboro. During college he married Jacqueline Lavinia Brown, with whom he had five children. He also became involved in the Civil Rights movement, helping to organize sit-ins and other demonstrations against racial segregation in and around Greensboro. After his 1964 graduation from college, where he had been student body president and quarterback of the football team, he enrolled in Chicago Theological Seminary. The following year, however, he joined Dr. Martin Luther King's civil rights demonstrations in Selma, Alabama, and subsequently left the seminary to work for the Southern Christian Leadership Conference (SCLC). He was appointed in 1966 to head the Chicago branch of Operation Breadbasket. This program sought to secure jobs and other economic advantages for African Americans. In 1967, Jackson became its national chairman.

After the assassination of Dr. Martin Luther King in 1968, Jackson appears to have aspired to assume control of SCLC. However, this post went to Ralph Abernathy instead. Jackson eventually left SCLC at the end of 1971 to found Operation PUSH (People United to Serve Humanity) in Chicago, an organization, like Operation Breadbasket, that aimed to empower African Americans economically. He leaped onto the national stage in the following decade, announcing in 1983 his intention to seek the Democratic nomination for president of the United States. At the Democratic convention, although the nomination went to Walter Mondale, Jackson received more than 400 delegate votes. "My constituency," he announced in a speech before the convention, "is the desperate, the damned, the disinherited, the disrespected, and the despised." He responded to controversy that had erupted during

Jesse Jackson, a protégé of Martin Luther King, Jr., has become an influential African-American religious and political figure. *(National Archives, NWDNS-412-DA-13800)*

his campaign over his association with LOUIS ABDUL FARRAKHAN, the leader of the Nation of Islam, and over Jackson's own derogatory remarks concerning Jews.

> If, in my low moments, in word, deed or attitude, through some error of temper, taste or tone, I have caused anyone discomfort, created pain or revived someone's fears, that was not my truest self. . . . I am not a perfect servant. I am a public servant doing my best against the odds. As I develop and serve, be patient. God is not finished with me yet.

Four years later, Jackson mounted another bid for the Democratic nomination. Although he arrived at the Democratic convention with more than 1,200 delegates, he lost to Michael Dukakis; however, he again demonstrated a solid political base, especially among African-American voters.

In the years after the 1988 presidential election, Jesse Jackson moved with his family to Washington, D.C., where he worked for a time to win statehood for the District of Columbia. By 1996, he had returned to Chicago, where he undertook leadership of PUSH again. During the last decade of the 20th century, he carried out several international missions. In 1991, for example, he was successful in persuading Saddam Hussein to release hundreds of foreign nationals whom he had been holding captive. At the end of the decade, he negotiated the release of three U.S. servicemen taken prisoner by the Yugoslav president, Slobodan Milosevic, during the war in Kosovo.

By the beginning of the 21st century, the Reverend Jesse Jackson commanded a prominent place in national political affairs. Though he had never won an elected office, he had mobilized African-American voters and helped to press their interests before state and national political bodies.

In addition, Jackson had enjoyed a measure of success as a kind of roving ambassador, as in his 1991 negotiations with Saddam Hussein, and he seemed poised to continue similar missions in the future. Perhaps most significantly, he had learned how to use his prominence to exert pressure on business organizations to allow African Americans a greater sphere of participation in the economic life of the United States.

Further Reading

Barker, Lucius J., and Ronald W. Walters, eds. *Jesse Jackson's 1984 Presidential Campaign: Challenge and Change in American Politics.* Urbana: University of Illinois Press, 1989.

Colton, Elizabeth O. *The Jackson Phenomenon: The Man, the Power, the Message.* New York: Doubleday, 1989.

Frady, Marshall. *Jesse: The Life and Pilgrimage of Jesse Jackson.* New York: Random House, 1996.

Jackson, Jesse. *Straight from the Heart.* Edited by Roger D. Hatch and Frank E. Watkins. Philadelphia: Fortress Press, 1987.

Reynolds, Barbara A. *Jesse Jackson: The Man, the Movement, the Myth.* Chicago: Nelson-Hall, 1975.

Reynolds, David Blackwell. "Movement Politics: Grassroots Progressive Political Activism as Seen Through Jesse Jackson's 1988 Campaign." Ph.D. dissertation, Cornell University, 1993.

Johnson, Samuel
(1696–1772) *Episcopal bishop*

Ordained while a young man as a Congregational minister, Samuel Johnson soon afterward converted to Anglicanism and became a tireless missionary for his new faith in the American colonies. He also achieved a measure of renown as a philosopher and an educator, in particular through his service as president of King's College in New York (later Columbia University). He was born on October 14, 1696, in Guilford, Connecticut, the son of Samuel Johnson and Mary Sage Johnson. At the age of 14, Johnson entered the Collegiate School at Saybrook, Connecticut (later relocated to New Haven, where it became Yale University). After graduating in 1714, he taught school at Guilford, Connecticut. After the Collegiate School relocated to New Haven in 1716, Johnson became

its first tutor. While in New Haven, Johnson read widely in the institution's meager library, which included works by divines in the Anglican Church, and gradually, over the following years, Johnson found himself increasingly dissatisfied with Congregational theology. In 1719 he resigned as tutor from Yale College, as the Collegiate School had been renamed the year before.

In 1720 Johnson was ordained a Congregational minister and became the pastor of the church in West Haven. Nevertheless, he soon became convinced that proper ordination to the ministry could not be had in the congregational structure and that it had to be conferred through the episcopal authority of the Church of England. Accordingly, after two years as a Congregationalist minister, Johnson joined two other men and traveled to England, venturing "in the arms of Almighty Providence to cross the ocean for the sake of that excellent church, the Church of England, and God preserve me, and if I err, God forgive me." There, in 1723, Johnson was ordained a deacon and a priest of the Anglican Church and appointed a missionary to Stratford, Connecticut, under the auspices of the Society for the Propagation of the Gospel (SPG). He returned to Stratford, where he organized the first Anglican congregation in Connecticut. In September 1725, he married Charity Floyd, a widow who entered their union with three children, and with whom he had two children.

Samuel Johnson became an energetic missionary for Anglicanism, helping to coordinate activities of other Anglican ministers and to train students who subsequently joined the church's ministerial ranks. He published numerous works defending Anglicanism from its copious New England opponents. His writing career also included a philosophy text influenced by his friendship with and persuasion by the idealistic philosophy of George Berkeley, who lived for a time, beginning in 1729, in Rhode Island. Johnson's *An Introduction to Philosophy* (1731) was eventually expanded and published in 1752 by Benjamin Franklin as *Elementa Philosophica.*

In 1754, nearing the age of 60, Johnson accepted the presidency of the newly established King's College (later Columbia University) in New York City. For nearly a decade he labored to set the new institution on a proper course, but personal tragedy clouded the years. One of his sons died in

1756 of smallpox contracted in London, after traveling there to be ordained in the Church of England as his father had. Two years later Johnson's wife died and then, in rapid succession, so did two of his stepchildren. Johnson himself had to remain away from New York for two extended periods when epidemics of smallpox, which he had never contracted, swept through the city. His second wife, Sarah Beach, whom he married in 1761, died two years later of smallpox. The year of her death, Johnson resigned as president of King's College and returned to his former church in Stratford. He died there on January 6, 1772.

Samuel Johnson's missionary efforts on behalf of the Church of England helped to plant Anglicanism firmly into the soil of New England, theological ground made inhospitable by the domination of Congregationalism. He established the colony's first Anglican congregation and, by the time of his death, saw more than 40 additional churches established. Although his career as a college administrator was less successful, his presidency of King's College added to his reputation as one of the most renowned Anglican thinkers of the New World during the colonial period.

Further Reading

Abelove, Henry. "John Wesley's Plagiarism of Samuel Johnson and Its Contemporary Reception." *Huntington Library Quarterly* 59 (1997): 73–79.

Beardsley, Eben Edwards. *Life and Correspondence of Samuel Johnson, D. D., Missionary of the Church of England in Connecticut, and First President of King's College, New York.* New York: Hurd & Houghton, 1874.

Carroll, Peter N. *The Other Samuel Johnson: A Psychohistory of Early New England.* Rutherford, N.J.: Fairleigh Dickinson University Press, 1978.

Chandler, Thomas Bradbury. *The Life of Samuel Johnson, D. D., the First President of King's College, in New-York.* New York: T. & J. Swords, 1805.

Ellis, Joseph J. *The New England Mind in Transition: Samuel Johnson of Connecticut, 1696–1772.* New Haven, Conn.: Yale University Press, 1973.

Johnson, Samuel. *Elementa Philosophica: Containing Chiefly, Noetica, or Things Relating to the Mind or Understanding: and Ethica, or Things Relating to the Moral Behaviour.* Philadelphia: B. Franklin and D. Hall, 1752; New York: Kraus Reprint, 1969.

———. *Samuel Johnson, President of King's College: His Career and Writings.* Edited by Herbert and Carol Schneider. 4 vols. New York: Columbia University Press, 1929; New York: AMS Press, 1972.

Jones, Bob
(Robert Reynolds Davis Jones)
(1883–1968) *revivalist, educator*

During the years between the evangelistic ministries of DWIGHT LYMAN MOODY in the 19th century and BILLY GRAHAM in the 20th, the most prominent revivalists in America were BILLY SUNDAY and Bob Jones. Jones, because he founded a fundamentalist university that survived into the 21st century, had the more enduring impact on American religious life. Robert Reynolds Davis Jones was born on October 30, 1883, in Skipperville, Alabama, the 11th of 12 children born to William Alexander Jones and Georgia Creel Jones. His parents were peanut farmers who struggled to make a living to support their large family.

Bob Jones displayed precocious speaking abilities from an early age, delivering his first speech in favor of the Populist Party when he was 12 years old. He was converted that same year and turned his rhetorical talent immediately to religious uses, preaching his first sermon soon afterward and ministering to his own small congregation by the time he was 13. The Alabama Conference of the Methodist Episcopal Church, South, licensed him to preach when he was 15 years old and commissioned him as a circuit-riding minister the following year. When not preaching, Bob Jones attended school and was able to enroll in Southern University in Greensboro, Alabama, in 1900. But personal loss preempted his attempt to gain a college education. His mother died when he was 14, and his father when he was 17. Before graduating, Jones left college to become a full-time evangelist.

In 1905 he married Bernice Sheffield, who died within a year of tuberculosis. Three years later he married Mary Gaston Stollenwerck, who had been converted in one of his revival meetings. Their only son, Bob Jones, Jr., was born in 1911.

In the quarter century after Bob Jones left college, he preached in revivals across the United States and traveled internationally as well. By the

1920s, his prominence as a revivalist was second only to Billy Sunday's. He did not confine his ministry to the conversion of souls, however. He also cast himself unabashedly into the cause of fundamentalism in the controversy with theological liberalism that sharpened during the first decades of the 20th century. As did many religious leaders, Jones determined that he might more effectively create a durable spiritual legacy by founding an educational institution that would perpetuate his theological visions. Consequently, he founded Bob Jones College in St. Andrews, Florida, in 1926.

Financial hardships caused by the Great Depression soon forced the college to relocate in 1933, to Cleveland, Tennessee. There it grew rapidly during the years leading up to World War II and, by 1947, had to move again to more expansive facilities in Greenville, South Carolina. Permanently settled in Greenville, Bob Jones University, as it was now known, became a bastion of fundamentalist higher education, steadfastly rejecting modern currents of theology and culture. Jones was so adamant in his opposition to theological liberalism that he ultimately clashed with Billy Graham, the generally conservative 20th-century revivalist who gained national prominence in the years after World War II. Graham's revival campaigns enlisted the cooperation of nonfundamentalist religious leaders and made no effort to steer converts toward fundamentalist churches. Consequently, Bob Jones, in an article published in *Christianity Today* in 1966, accused Graham of "doing more harm to the cause of Jesus Christ than any living man."

Bob Jones eventually passed on the administration of Bob Jones University to his son, Bob Jones, Jr., who would in turn bequeath governance of the university to Bob Jones III. As the institution continued into the later part of the 20th century, it remained closely wed to fundamentalist theology. The university became known especially for its anti-Catholicism and for its belief that racial segregation was justified by the Bible. Bob Jones himself died in Greenville, South Carolina, on January 16, 1968.

By the beginning of the 21st century, the institution founded by Bob Jones had proved to be one of the most prominent and durable legacies of fundamentalist theology. The university's segregationist policies survived well after Jones had died,

though these ultimately led to the university's loss of tax-exempt status in the early 1980s and the eventual collapse of its segregationist practices in the years that followed. But other aspects of the fundamentalist legacy inherited from Bob Jones accompanied the university into the new century.

Further Reading

Dalhouse, Mark Taylor. *An Island in the Lake of Fire: Bob Jones University, Fundamentalism, and the Separatist Movement.* Athens: University of Georgia Press, 1996.

Johnson, R. K. *Builder of Bridges: The Biography of Dr. Bob Jones, Sr.* Murfreesboro, Tenn.: Sword of the Lord, 1969.

Jones, Bob. *Things I Have Learned: Chapel Talks at Bob Jones University.* Greenville, S.C.: Bob Jones University Press, 1986.

Wright, Melton. *Fortress of Faith: The Story of Bob Jones University.* Grand Rapids, Mich.: Eerdmans, 1960.

Jones, Jim
(James Warren Jones)
(1931–1978) *founder of the People's Temple*

Jim Jones authored the mass suicide of some 900 religious followers in the late 1970s. By doing so, he captured in death a measure of worldwide attention not generally focused on minor cult leaders. He was born James Warren Jones on May 13, 1931, in Crete, Indiana, the son of James Thurman Jones and Lynetta Putnam Jones. While he was working as a hospital orderly in Richmond, Indiana, during high school, he met Marceline Baldwin, whom he married in 1949 on his graduation from high school. The couple had one child.

After three years of study at Indiana University in Bloomington, Jones and his wife moved to Indianapolis. There Jones, who had previously been involved with a Pentecostal church during his teens, became a student pastor for the Somerset Methodist Church. His wife was a Methodist and Jones was drawn to the denomination because its socially progressive views at least partially matched his own. Jones, though, outstripped the members of his church in his zeal for a spiritual community not divided along lines of race. By 1954 he had struck out on his own, renting a building in a racially mixed area of Indianapolis and establishing a congregation he called Community Unity. Over the next few years this congregation relocated and metamorphosed into "Wings of Deliverance" and, still later, the People's Temple.

Jones led his followers in Pentecostal-style religious services, whose elements included speaking in tongues and the exercise by Jones of healing and clairvoyance gifts. The congregation also emphasized the provision of social services such as free meals for the poor and nursing homes for the elderly. This emphasis reflected both Jim Jones's own progressive social views and the influence of FA-THER DIVINE, the charismatic black leader, whom Jones visited during the 1950s and whose religious community participated in similar activities. Jim and Marceline Jones also tried to emulate the kind of "rainbow" family that they wished their spiritual congregation to be by adopting a black child and two Korean orphans.

Jim Jones relocated the People's Temple to Ukiah, California, in 1965. He carried with him many of the congregation's Indiana members but also soon attracted somewhat more affluent and educated followers, as the People's Temple became one of the new religious movements that flourished during the 1960s and 1970s. The People's Temple also became a spiritual refuge for many urban blacks who found its combination of Pentecostalism and social activism appealing. Curiously, in 1968 Jones formally affiliated himself with the Disciples of Christ, though his People's Temple retained its pre-existing spiritual emphases. The following years saw the People's Temple grow dramatically in size, from fewer than 100 members immediately after the relocation to California to some 3,000 by the time of its final emigration to Guyana. The movement soon included members in San Francisco and Los Angeles as well as Ukiah.

During the 1970s Jim Jones became increasingly preoccupied with what he perceived as hostility to the People's Temple by the forces of government, organized religion, and American society generally. In 1977, he led approximately 1,000 members of the People's Temple from California to a 300-acre tract of land his agents had secured in Guyana, which soon became known as Jonestown. There he attempted to establish a new utopian community in the South American jungle, but dissenters in Guyana and critics in the United States soon began to circulate charges that Jones was engaging in brainwashing and other forms of abuse to prevent defections from Jonestown. These charges eventually prompted Leo Ryan, a California Democrat in the U.S. House of Representatives, to schedule a visit to Jonestown with several media representatives in November 1978. On November 18, as Ryan's delegation was preparing to leave Guyana, some of Jones's followers attacked the delegation and murdered Ryan, three media representatives, and a member of the People's Temple attempting to leave Jonestown. At the same time Jim Jones persuaded 913 members of the People's Temple to commit suicide by drinking a grape-flavored concoction containing potassium cyanide. Jones himself was subsequently found dead of a gunshot wound to the head, apparently delivered on the same date by one the members of the People's Temple, who subsequently committed suicide as well.

The years following the Jonestown tragedy have not produced a single explanation for an event that galvanized world attention on a relatively obscure religious group. Perhaps most commonly, Jonestown has become a byword for the dangers posed by cults. The Guyana suicides prompted waves of "deprogramming" efforts, aimed at rescuing hapless souls from the clutches of religiously inspired brainwashing. Other explanations, though, have focused on the enduring attractiveness of utopian communities such as the People's Temple in American religious history. These, too, have tried to explain how religious devotion tipped over into paranoia and how one man could engineer the suicide of so many followers. By the beginning of the 21st century, though, two decades of investigation had not succeeded in unraveling the essential enigma of Jonestown.

Further Reading

Chidester, David. *Salvation and Suicide: An Interpretation of Jim Jones, the Peoples Temple, and Jonestown.* Bloomington: Indiana University Press, 1988.

Feinsod, Ethan. *Awake in a Nightmare: Jonestown, the Only Eyewitness Account.* New York: Norton, 1981.

Hall, John R. *Gone from the Promised Land: Jonestown in American Cultural History.* New Brunswick, N.J.: Transaction Publishers, 1987.

Klineman, George, Sherman Butler, and David Conn. *The Cult That Died: The Tragedy of Jim Jones and the Peoples Temple.* New York: Putnam, 1980.

Maaga, Mary McCormick. *Hearing the Voices of Jonestown.* Syracuse, N.Y.: Syracuse University Press, 1998.

Naipaul, Shiva. *Journey to Nowhere: A New World Tragedy.* New York: Simon & Schuster, 1981.

The Peoples Temple and Jim Jones: Broadening Our Perspective. Edited by J. Gordon Melton. New York: Garland, 1990.

Reiterman, Tim. *Raven: The Untold Story of the Rev. Jim Jones and His People.* New York: Dutton, 1982.

Rose, Stephen C. *Jesus and Jim Jones.* New York: Pilgrim Press, 1979.

Jones, Rufus Matthew
(1863–1948) *Quaker theologian*

A Quaker scholar and a mystic, Rufus Matthew Jones was a major intellectual leader of liberal Protestantism during the early decades of the 20th century. He spent most of his life as a teacher, but he wrote voluminously and lectured widely, so that his influence was substantial. He was born on January 25, 1863, during the Civil War, on a farm in South China, Maine. His parents, Edwin Jones and Mary Hoxie, were both Quakers. He attended Haverford College in Pennsylvania, where he studied philosophy and received a B.A. in June 1885. The following year, he earned a master's degree from Haverford on the basis of research in the area of mysticism, the study of which subject would occupy the remainder of his life. During 1885 and 1886, Jones taught at the Oakwood Seminary, a Quaker boarding school in Union Springs, New York. The next year, he studied abroad in Europe and during this period had a mystical experience, which he later described in his book *The Trail of Life in College* (1929).

I was on a solitary walk, absorbed with my thoughts about the meaning and purpose of my life, wondering whether I should ever get myself organized and brought under the control and direction of some constructive central purpose of life, when I felt the walls between the visible and the invisible suddenly grow thin, and I was conscious of a definite mission of life opening out before me. I saw stretch before me an unfolding of labor in the realm of mystical. . . . I remember kneeling down alone in a beautiful forest glade and dedicating myself then and there in the quiet and silence, but in the presence of an invading Life, to the work of interpreting the deeper nature of the soul and its relation with God.

On his return from Europe, Jones accepted a teaching position at a Quaker school in Providence, Rhode Island. In the summer of 1888 he married Sarah ("Sallie") Hawkeshurst Coutant and also wrote a biography of his uncle and aunt, Eli and Sybil Jones, which was the first of 57 books he authored. Beginning in 1889, Jones served four years as the principal of the Oak Grove Seminary in Maine, a coeducational Quaker boarding school. There, Sallie gave birth to a son, Lowell, in 1892. The following year, Jones and his family moved to Pennsylvania, where he accepted a teaching position at Haverford College and also the editorship of *The Friends Review,* a Quaker magazine that became *The American Friend* in 1894. He continued as a professor at Haverford until 1934, when he was a professor emeritus until his death.

In 1899, Jones's wife, Sallie, died of tuberculosis, and he spent the following year studying philosophy and psychology at Harvard, with George Herbert Palmer, George Santayana, Francis G. Peabody, and Josiah Royce. He married Elizabeth Cadbury in 1902, but he suffered the death of his son, Lowell, the following year. His marriage with Elizabeth produced a daughter, Mary Hoxie Jones, born in 1904.

During the final years of the 19th century and the first of the 20th century, Jones labored diligently to unite the various separate annual Quaker meetings. He used *The American Friend* as an organ of this unification effort and helped draft the *Uniform Discipline* as a basis for coordinated Quaker activity. His opposition to creedal statements, however, placed him at odds with some evangelical Quakers.

Rufus Jones's mysticism did not drive him from the world, but rather more deeply into it in various forms of social engagement. In 1917 he helped to found and served as the first president of the American Friends Service Committee, a group that administered humanitarian relief in Europe after World War I. Together with a sister organization in Great Britain, the American Friends Service Committee won the Nobel Peace Prize in 1947. Jones died the following year, on July 16, 1948, in Haverford, Pennsylvania.

Rufus Matthew Jones was one of the 20th century's most prominent Quakers. His teaching influenced a generation of students and his writing, an even wider audience. In his thought, a Christian mysticism anchored securely to the past was also informed by contemporary philosophical and psychological investigations. Perhaps most significantly, he melded a life of contemplation with one of deeds. "The great mystics who must be our types," he wrote, "have learned that every new truth, every new vision, involves a new duty and leads to activity." To this model of mysticism, Rufus Jones proved himself abundantly faithful.

Further Reading

Hinshaw, David. *Rufus Jones: Master Quaker.* New York: Putnam, 1951.
Jones, Rufus Matthew. *A Call to What Is Vital.* New York: Macmillan, 1948.
———. *The Church, the Gospel and War.* New York: Harper, 1948.
———. *Rufus Jones: Essential Writings.* Edited by Kerry Walters. Maryknoll, N.Y.: Orbis Books, 2001.
———. *The Eternal Gospel.* New York: Macmillan, 1938.
———. *Finding the Trail of Life.* New York: Macmillan, 1926.
———. *New Studies in Mystical Religion: The Ely Lectures Delivered at Union Theological Seminary, New York, 1927.* New York: Macmillan, 1927.
———. *A Small-Town Boy.* New York: Macmillan, 1941.
Moore, James Floyd. *Rufus Jones: Luminous Friend.* Greensboro, N.C.: Guilford College, 1959.
Vining, Elizabeth Gray. *Friend of Life: The Biography of Rufus M. Jones.* Philadelphia: Lippincott, 1958.

Jones, Sam
(Samuel Porter Jones)
(1847–1906) *Methodist revivalist*

Often called the "Moody of the South," in comparison with the great 19th-century urban evangelist, DWIGHT LYMAN MOODY, Sam Jones thrilled crowds, mostly southern, with his homespun version of the gospel. During the final decade of the 19th century, he became the South's premier evangelist. Samuel Porter Jones was born on October 16, 1847, in Chambers County, Alabama, the son of John J. Jones and Nancy Porter Jones. He sprang from a family in which his grandfather and four uncles were Methodists ministers; his father was a lawyer. While in high school, he suffered a breakdown diagnosed at the time as caused by nervous dyspepsia. Although he had received a solid education in public schools and private academies, this breakdown seemed to foreclose the possibility of his attending college. Instead, Jones studied law privately and was admitted to the Georgia bar in 1868. In the same year, he married Laura McElwain, with whom he had seven children. At about the same time, he became an alcoholic.

Four years later, Jones experienced a religious conversion that cured him of his alcoholism and set him on the path to become a Methodist preacher. His father, shortly before death, had himself been converted, and on his deathbed he told his children that he expected to see all of them in heaven but Sam. "My poor, wicked, wayward reckless boy," the father is said to have told his son, "you have broken the heart of your sweet wife, and brought me down in sorrow to my grave." Sam Jones, pierced with conviction, promised, "I'll quit! I'll quit!" This deathbed confrontation prompted Jones to experience a religious conversion himself and to give up alcohol. He also became a Methodist preacher and spent the years from 1872 to 1880 as a circuit-riding preacher, tending small rural congregations in the North Georgia Conference of the Methodist Episcopal Church, South. Jones supplemented these duties with an increasing schedule of revival engagements. His appointment as a fund-raising agent for a Methodist orphanage in 1881 gave him broader exposure as a preacher and eventually enabled him to become a full-time revival minister.

By the mid-1880s, Sam Jones had become one of the South's most prominent evangelists; his preaching ministry stretched north as well to cities such as Chicago, where he is estimated to have preached to more than a quarter of a million people. An 1885 revival he conducted in Nashville,

Tennessee, witnessed the conversion of Tom Ryman, a wealthy riverboat owner against whose drinking and gambling establishments Jones had railed. As a result of this conversion, Ryman promised to clean up his riverboats and built the Union Gospel Tabernacle in Nashville as a home for future revivals. The tabernacle eventually housed the Grand Ole Opry from 1941 to 1975.

Jones preached straightforward evangelistic sermons dominated by appeals to his audiences to turn their lives over to Jesus. Conversion, as he understood it, involved a change of a life's direction and a change of its conduct. "Just quit your meanness," he told audiences, "and follow along in the footsteps of Jesus Christ." In an article published in the *Atlanta Journal*, he offered a similar message: "I stand squarely on the two propositions, that the best thing a man can do is to do right and the worst thing a man can do is to do wrong." The vigorous years of revival preaching eventually took their toll on Jones, however. He died on a train on the way home from a revival in Oklahoma City on October 15, 1906, the day before he would have turned 59 years old.

Though having no formal theological training, Sam Jones enjoyed enormous success as a revivalist. In fact, he never tired of pricking the pretentiousness of theology. "Theology is a good thing," he liked to say. "It is a good thing to stuff with sawdust, like the skin of a fish, and put in a museum as a relic of antiquity." Religion, though, was a different matter. As he often declared to revival audiences, "I always did despise theology and botany, but I do love religion and flowers."

Further Reading

Holcomb, Walt. *Sam Jones: An Ambassador of the Almighty, Commemorating the Centennial Year of the Birth of Sam Jones.* Nashville: Methodist Publishing House, 1947.

Jones, Laura McElwain. *The Life and Sayings of Sam P. Jones, a Minister of the Gospel.* 2d rev. ed. Atlanta: Franklin-Turner Co., 1907.

Jones, Sam P. *Famous Stories of Sam P. Jones, Reproduced in the Language in Which Sam Jones Uttered Them.* Edited by George R. Stuart. New York: F. H. Revell, 1908.

———. *Popular Lectures of Sam P. Jones.* Edited by Walt Holcomb. New York: F. H. Revell, 1909.

McLoughlin, William Gerald. *Modern Revivalism: Charles Grandison Finney to Billy Graham.* New York: Ronald Press, 1959.

Minnix, Kathleen. *Laughter in the Amen Corner: The Life of Evangelist Sam Jones.* Athens: University of Georgia Press, 1993.

Parker, David B. "'Quit Your Meanness': Sam Jones's Theology for the New South." *Georgia Historical Quarterly* 78 (Winter 1993): 711–27.

Rensi, Raymond Charles. "Sam Jones, Southern Evangelist." Ph.D. dissertation, University of Georgia, 1972.

Judson, Adoniram
(1788–1850) *Baptist missionary*

Often referred to as the father of American Baptist foreign missions, Adoniram Judson spent more than 35 years as a Christian missionary to Burma. As a result of his perseverance in this work in the face of tremendous hardships, Judson became a leading spiritual example for evangelical Christians during the 19th century. He was born on August 9, 1788, in Malden, Massachusetts, the son of Adoniram Judson and Abigail Brown Judson. Although his father was a Congregationalist pastor, Judson abandoned the Christian faith while he was a student at Brown University. After his graduation in 1807, he taught school briefly and then decided to enroll in the newly founded Andover Seminary, where he experienced conversion. He graduated in Andover's first class in 1810.

The year he finished seminary, Judson joined several other seminary graduates in persuading Massachusetts Congregationalists to establish the American Board of Commissioners for Foreign Missions to support their plans to undertake missionary work in Burma. This was the first foreign missionary organization in America. En route to London to seek cooperation from English Christians, Judson was captured by a French pirate ship and subjected to his first prison confinement. Once in London, Judson failed to obtain English support and returned to America, where he was ordained a missionary by the American Board in February 1812, the day after he married Ann Hasseltine. Together with his wife, Judson sailed the same month with another missionary couple for Calcutta. While studying the Bible aboard ship, Judson rejected the practice of infant baptism and, on arriving in Calcutta, became a Baptist. His new theological views cast him adrift from the Congregationalist mission board, but American Baptists rallied to his support by establishing the Baptist Board of Foreign Missions in 1814.

The Judsons settled in Burma, where he devoted more than three decades to missionary work. The years piled his life high with personal loss. His first wife died in 1826. He married Sarah Hall Boardman in 1834 but saw her die 12 years later. He finally married Emily Chubbuck in 1846, and she would survive him. The three children born to Judson by his first wife died, as well as three of his stepchildren by marriage to Sarah Boardman. In addition, Judson himself suffered frequent illness and time in prison.

In spite of these hardships and ongoing opposition from political authorities, Judson applied himself to the task of giving the Christian message to the Burmese. His first important breakthrough in this mission occurred after he established a Buddhist-style *zayat*, or meditation room, in Rangoon, which led to the first Christian conversion some six years after Judson arrived in Burma. More important, Judson devoted himself to the work of translating the Bible into the Burmese language, producing a New Testament in 1823 that was finally published in 1832, and completing a translation of the whole Bible in 1834. He added to these translations a Burmese-English dictionary, which he finished shortly before his death. He returned to America only once in the course of his long missionary career, for nine months in 1845 and 1846. While taking a voyage to recover from one of the many illnesses that had marked his life, Judson died on April 12, 1850, and was buried at sea.

Prior to Adoniram Judson's missionary career, American Christians had directed their evangelistic impulses mainly to the task of winning Native American converts to Christianity. Judson, though, saw a broader field for the propagation of the Christian message. He believed God had committed the work of evangelism to Christians as a sacred trust, and he believed that Christians of his day had failed to honor this trust. Shortly after embarking on the path that would take him to Burma, he wrote about that failure in a magazine article:

> How do Christians discharge this trust committed to them? They let three-fourths of the world sleep the sleep of death, ignorant of the simple truth that a Savior died for them. Content if they can be useful in the little circle of their acquaintances, they quietly sit and see whole nations perish for lack of knowledge.

For evangelical Christians of the 19th century, Adoniram Judson's tireless efforts to give knowledge of Christianity to the world became almost legendary, an example that would fuel continued missionary efforts for the next century and beyond.

Adoniram Judson devoted more than 35 years of his life to Christian missionary activity in Burma and is often referred to as the father of Baptist missions. *(Southern Baptist Historical Library and Archives)*

Further Reading

"Adoniram Judson." Available online. URL: http://www.reformedreader.org/rbb/judson/bio.htm. Downloaded on April 24, 2002.

Anderson, Courtney. *To the Golden Shore: The Life of Adoniram Judson.* Valley Forge, Pa.: Judson Press, 1987.

Judson, Edward. *The Life of Adoniram Judson.* New York: A. D. F. Randolph, 1883.

McElrath, William N. *To Be the First: Adventures of Adoniram Judson, America's First Foreign Missionary.* Nashville: Broadman Press, 1976.

Wayland, Francis. *A Memoir of the Life and Labors of the Rev. Adoniram Judson. D.D.* Boston: Phillips, Sampson, 1853.

Kaplan, Mordecai Menahem
(1881–1983) *Jewish rabbi, founder of Reconstructionism*

The founder of a separate branch of American Judaism known as Reconstructionism, Mordecai Menahem Kaplan sought to fashion Judaism as a living community unshackled from the traditions and even the beliefs of the past. Though he made his place primarily among the institutions and people of Conservative Judaism for most of his life, in his old age he finally turned his attention to establishing Reconstructionism as a separate denomination within Judaism. He was born on June 11, 1881, in Sventzian, Lithuania, the son of Israel Kaplan and Haya Nehama Kovarsky Kaplan. His father was a rabbi who led the family to immigrate to the United States and settle in New York City when Mordecai was eight years old. Kaplan subsequently received a B.A. from City College of New York in 1900, together with an M.A. from Columbia University and a rabbinate from the Jewish Theological Seminary in 1902.

Kaplan initially served as a rabbi for the Kehilath Jeshurun congregation in New York City, an Orthodox synagogue, from 1903 to 1909, although his theological views had already begun a relentless migration away from Jewish orthodoxy. During this period he married Lena Rubin, with whom he had four children. Uncomfortable in his rabbinical post, Kaplan leaped at the offer to become the first principal of the Jewish Theological Seminary's Teachers' Institute in 1909, and he remained associated with

the Jewish Theological Seminary, except for a brief hiatus, until his retirement in 1963. During the early years of the 20th century, the seminary became a stronghold of Conservative Judaism, which sought to find a middle way between Orthodox and Reform Judaism. But Kaplan's theological views were always estranged from prevailing thought at the seminary. In 1929, he described his only uneasy relationship with his colleagues in a journal he kept:

> My colleagues are worshippers of dead letters just as our ancestors were worshippers of lifeless images. To be a prophet one must not only be an iconoclast but also be able to speak in the name of the living God. Since in spite of all my strenuous searching I have not yet found Israel's living God and cannot speak in his name, I must abide with the idolaters and imitate their ways.

Kaplan's differences with the Conservative thought of the Jewish Theological Seminary prompted him to resign from the seminary in 1927 in favor of a teaching post at the Jewish Institute of Religion. But students and alumni of the Jewish Theological Seminary persuaded him to return to the seminary within a few months. He could not avoid conflicts with more Orthodox Jews, however. Kaplan believed it necessary to reconstruct the Jewish community to dispense with whatever rites and beliefs did not actually serve to strengthen the community in its 20th-century form. His reconstructionist efforts, for example, led him in 1945 to publish *The Sabbath Prayer Book*, which omitted some and altered other traditional Jewish prayers. This liturgical innovation so angered traditional Jewish leaders that the Union of Orthodox Rabbis of the United States and Canada excommunicated him and publicly burned his prayer book.

During his years as a teacher, Kaplan also held rabbinical posts. Beginning in 1918 he served as rabbi of the Jewish Center in New York City, a newly founded Orthodox congregation on the Upper West Side of Manhattan, until he could no longer tolerate its Orthodox climate. He subsequently left the center and established the Society for the Advancement of Judaism in 1922, often referred to as the cradle of Reconstructionist Judaism. He served as this congregation's rabbi until 1945. Kaplan officially retired from the Jewish Theological Seminary in 1963, and he devoted his remaining years to work as a writer and a lecturer. He also finally abandoned the hope that Reconstructionism might embrace the entire Jewish community and devoted his energies to strengthening what had essentially become a separate denomination with Judaism. He died at the age of 102, on November 8, 1983, in New York City.

Mordecai M. Kaplan developed the theological vision early in his rabbinical career that would become the fountainhead for Reconstructionist Judaism. He also founded, in the 1920s, the first Reconstructionist congregation, the Society for the Advancement of Judaism. But he remained attached to Conservative Judaism's flagship institution, the Jewish Theological Seminary in New York, for another four decades, hoping all the while that his Reconstructionist program might be embraced by the American Jewish community as a whole. Eventually, however, he had to acknowledge that he had founded yet another denomination of Judaism, to be added to the Orthodox, Reform, and Conservative movements whose members never accepted his vision.

Further Reading

The American Judaism of Mordecai M. Kaplan. Edited by Emanuel S. Goldsmith, Mel Scult, and Robert M. Seltzer. New York: New York University Press, 1990.

Breslauer, S. Daniel. *Mordecai Kaplan's Thought in a Postmodern Age.* Atlanta: Scholars Press, 1994.

Cohen, Jack. *Guides for an Age of Confusion: Studies in the Thinking of Avraham Y. Kook and Mordecai M. Kaplan.* New York: Fordham University Press, 1999.

Einstein, Ira, and Eugene Kohn. *Mordecai Kaplan: An Evaluation.* New York: Jewish Reconstructionist Foundation, 1952.

Gurock, Jeffrey S., and Jacob J. Schacter. *A Modern Heretic and a Traditional Community: Mordecai M. Kaplan, Orthodoxy, and American Judaism.* New York: Columbia University Press, 1997.

Kaplan, Mordecai Menahem. *Communings of the Spirit: The Journals of Mordecai M. Kaplan.* Edited by Mel Scult. Detroit: Wayne State University Press and Reconstructionist Press, 2001.

———. *The Future of the American Jew.* New York: Macmillan, 1948.

———. *The Meaning of God in Modern Jewish Religion.* New York: Behrman's Jewish Book House, 1937; Detroit: Wayne State University Press, 1994.

Libowitz, Richard. *Mordecai M. Kaplan and the Development of Reconstructionism.* New York: Edwin Mellen Press, 1983.

Scult, Mel. *Judaism Faces the Twentieth Century: A Biography of Mordecai M. Kaplan.* Detroit: Wayne State University Press, 1993.

Keith, George
(ca. 1638–1716) *Quaker theologian, Anglican priest*

First a Presbyterian, then a Quaker theologian, and last an Anglican priest, George Keith followed a remarkable spiritual odyssey. The abrupt transitions of his spiritual pilgrimage denied him a place within the first rank of American religious leaders but contributed to a career that significantly influenced the course of religious thought in 17th-century America and England. George Keith was born around the year 1638 in Aberdeenshire, Scotland. Little is known of his parents except that they disowned him when he became a Quaker.

Though in later years he branded universities as "the stews of Anti-Christ," Keith studied at Marischall College in Aberdeen and received an M.A. in 1658. Over the course of the next few years, he abandoned the Presbyterianism of his youth and became a Quaker and joined a meeting in Aberdeen that included a future influential Quaker theologian, Robert Barclay. This spiritual migration was influenced partially by Keith's reading of René Descartes and Cambridge Platonists such as Henry More and John Smith, who emphasized the importance of love and moral purity rather than of doctrinal correctness.

Over the following years, Keith rapidly became an intellectual leader among Scottish Quakers and was repeatedly imprisoned for his beliefs. During a six-month term of imprisonment in 1662, he wrote an influential early statement of Quaker principles, *Immediate Revelation . . . Not Ceased, but Remaining a standing and perpetual Ordinance in the Church of Christ,* which was eventually published in 1668. This book presented an account of the Quaker concept of "inner light," or immediate revelation, as "A Substance beyond all Shadows, Pictures, Representations, Comprehension, or Thoughts."

In 1672, George Keith married Elizabeth Johnston, an Aberdeen Quaker who would share her husband's zeal for this faith, and would one day abandon it with him in favor of Anglicanism. Together they had three children. In 1677, the couple joined several other influential Quakers, including George Fox and WILLIAM PENN, in a mission to Holland and Germany. In the course of this mission, Keith's influence as a Quaker writer and preacher increased. Afterward, he continued an itinerant ministry for a time, before finding work as a schoolmaster. But his role as a Quaker apologist landed him before Scottish authorities, who convicted him of *præmunire,* the offense of refusing to swear a prescribed oath, which was punishable by life imprisonment and forfeiture of his estate. An influential English Quaker was ultimately able to secure Keith's release, however, and Keith, for his part, soon decided to strike out for America.

He moved to New Jersey in 1684, became surveyor-general of East Jersey, and acquired land in both New Jersey and Pennsylvania. Within five years, he had settled into a position as headmaster of a school in Philadelphia, Pennsylvania, and coupled his responsibilities in this position with an active career as a Quaker preacher and a writer. In 1691, the Quaker founder George Fox died, and Keith may have attempted to assert himself as Fox's successor. In any event, influential Philadelphia Quakers accused Keith of various spiritual errors, and Keith responded by lodging accusations of his own against his Quaker opponents. The controversy produced a split between Keith's followers, called "Christian Quakers," and the main body of

American Quakers. Keith published a number of works during this period vindicating his position and exposing the supposed errors of his opponents. He also published, in 1693, the first American antislavery tract, *An Exhortation to Friends Concerning Buying or Keeping of Negroes.*

That same year, Keith left America to plead his case before English Quakers. When this attempt proved unsuccessful, he proceeded to include the English Quakers in his denunciations and was eventually disowned by them in 1695. Not content with the fractures that these denunciations occasioned, Keith included the famous American Quaker William Penn among the objects of his unflagging criticism.

By 1700, Keith's alienation from other Quakers finally drove him to the Church of England. He was ordained an Anglican priest that year, and, in 1702, he returned to America on behalf of the English Society for the Propagation of the Gospel. He applied the same missionary zeal on behalf of the Anglican Church that he had exhibited as a Quaker apologist, but his contentious manner made his errand mostly unsuccessful. He returned in 1704 to England, where he continued his campaign against the Quakers. He became the rector of Edburton in 1707 and died there on March 27, 1716.

George Keith inherited from Presbyterianism a keen interest in doctrinal formulations concerning religious life. His talent for reproducing in words the wordless Quaker devotion to the inner light made him an important early Quaker apologist. But his hunger for systematic doctrine ultimately led him out of the Quaker fold and into the Church of England, which proved more hospitable to his theological inclinations.

Further Reading

Butler, Jon. "'Gospel Order Improved,' the Keithian Schism and the Exercise of Quaker Ministerial Authority in Pennsylvania." *William and Mary Quarterly,* 3d ser., 31 (July 1974): 431–52.

Frost, J. William, ed. *The Keithian Controversy in Early Pennsylvania.* Norwood, Pa.: Norwood Editions, 1980.

———. "Unlikely Controversialists: Caleb Pusey and George Keith." *Quaker History* 64 (Spring 1975): 16–36.

Kirby, Ethyn Williams. *George Keith (1638–1716)*. New York: D. Appleton-Century, 1942.

Trowell, Stephen. "George Keith: Post-Restoration Quaker Theology and the Experience of Defeat." *Bulletin of the John Rylands University Library of Manchester* 76 (1994): 119–37.

Kimball, Spencer Woolley

(1895–1985) *president of the Church of Jesus Christ of Latter-day Saints*

The 12th president of the Mormon Church, Spencer Woolley Kimball, arrived at his office late in life. Nevertheless, in less than a decade of active service, he did much to remake the face of the Church of Jesus Christ of Latter-day Saints. He was born on March 28, 1895, in Salt Lake City, Utah, the son of Andrew Kimball and Olive Woolley Kimball. Kimball's grandfather—Heber C. Kimball—had been a counselor to BRIGHAM YOUNG, the second president of the Mormon Church. His father, Andrew Kimball, eventually became president of the St. Joseph Stake (an ecclesiastical territory comparable to a Catholic diocese). After two years as a Mormon missionary from 1914 to 1916, Spencer Kimball attended a semester of college at the University of Arizona in 1917, and the same year he married Camilla Eyring, with whom he had four children.

Over the following years, Kimball worked as a bank teller and then, beginning in 1929, as coowner of an insurance and real estate agency in Safford, Arizona. At the same time, he served in a series of positions within the Mormon Church: as clerk for his father's stake from 1917 until 1924, as counselor to the new stake president after the death of his father in 1924, and then, beginning in 1938, as president of the Mount Graham Stake. In 1943, Kimball was ordained an apostle in the Mormon Church and joined the Quorum of the Twelve Apostles. He labored in this office for the next three decades, during which his most notable work involved missionary activity among Native Americans. In particular, he established the Indian Student Placement Services, a program that promoted the placement of Native American children from reservations into the homes of Mormon families during the school year. But Kimball also suffered from a variety of physical ailments during his tenure as a Mormon apostle. Throat cancer required the removal of most of his vocal cords in 1957. He also experienced a heart attack in 1940 and had open-heart surgery in 1972.

In 1973, the 78-year-old Kimball was ordained the president of the Mormon Church after the death of Harold B. Lee. In spite of his advanced age, Kimball plunged into the work of restructuring important elements of Mormon faith and practice. He inaugurated sweeping changes in the church's hierarchical structure, including abolition of the office of patriarch. These changes reorganized the church's leadership to cope with its rapid growth. During Kimball's presidency, the number of stakes more than doubled, as did the number of Mormon temples. The number of countries in which the Mormons had an organized presence climbed from 50 to 96, and worldwide membership skyrocketed from 3.3 million to nearly 6 million. Perhaps most significant of all, in 1978 Kimball announced a new revelation that ended the church's refusal to admit blacks to the priesthood and to temple ordinances. The change in this aspect of the church's practice resulted almost immediately in growth among its world missionary efforts. Kimball also led the church to take public stands on key political issues of the times, including the church's formal opposition to the MX missile program—especially to the proposal that missiles be sited in the Utah-Nevada desert—and to ratification of the Equal Rights Amendment to the U.S. Constitution, which would have given formal expression to gender equality in the Constitution.

In 1979, Kimball twice underwent surgery for subdural hematomas. After a third such operation in 1981, his health declined rapidly and he had to entrust active leadership of the church to his counselors among the First Presidency, the highest executive council of the Mormon Church. Kimball died on November 5, 1985, in Salt Lake City, Utah.

Although Spencer Woolley Kimball assumed the office of Mormon president at a time when most individuals would have long since retired, he brought sweeping changes in the Church of Jesus Christ of Latter-day Saints. Near the end of the preceding century, another church president, WILFORD

WOODRUFF, had redirected the course of the church by repudiating polygamy, and Kimball's revelation concerning the admittance of blacks to the Mormon priesthood drew Mormons into a more harmonious relationship with emerging concepts of human rights. Partially as a result of this change and partially as a consequence of Kimball's own missionary zeal, the church experienced significant growth during the tenure of his presidency.

Further Reading

Gibbons, Francis M. *Spencer W. Kimball: Resolute Disciple, Prophet of God.* Salt Lake City, Utah: Deseret, 1995.

Kimball, Edward L., and Andrew E. Kimball, Jr. *Spencer W. Kimball, Twelfth President of the Church of Jesus Christ of Latter-day Saints.* Salt Lake City, Utah: Bookcraft, 1977.

Kimball, Spencer W. *The Miracle of Forgiveness.* Salt Lake City, Utah: Bookcraft, 1969.

———. *One Silent Sleepless Night.* Salt Lake City, Utah: Bookcraft, 1975.

———. *President Kimball Speaks Out.* Salt Lake City, Utah: Deseret, 1981.

———. *The Teachings of Spencer W. Kimball, Twelfth President of the Church of Jesus Christ of Latter-day Saints.* Edited by Edward L. Kimball. Salt Lake City, Utah: Bookcraft, 1982.

King, Martin Luther, Jr.
(Michael King, Jr.)

(1929–1968) *Baptist minister, civil rights leader*

The 20th century's most important civil rights leader, Martin Luther King, Jr., died of an assassin's bullet before he had reached the age of 40. Nevertheless, his struggle on behalf of the rights of African Americans remade the face of American society. He was born Michael King, Jr., on January 15, 1929, in Atlanta, Georgia, the son of Michael King (who later changed his name and his son's to Martin Luther King) and Alberta Williams King. King's grandfather was pastor of the prominent Ebenezer Baptist Church in Atlanta until his death in 1931, and subsequently, his father occupied the same pulpit. Martin Luther King, Jr., received his undergraduate education from Morehouse College

Martin Luther King, Jr., became the 20th century's most influential civil rights leader prior to his assassination in Memphis, Tennessee, in 1968. *(Library of Congress, Prints and Photographs Division LC-USZ62-122990)*

in Atlanta. The year prior to his graduation in 1948 he determined to follow the vocational path of his father and grandfather, and he was ordained a minister. He attended seminary at Crozer Theological Seminary in Chester, Pennsylvania, from 1948 to 1951, and after obtaining a bachelor of divinity degree there, he undertook work toward a Ph.D. at Boston University and obtained the degree in 1955. At Crozer and later Boston University, King absorbed the influence of Protestant liberal thought and of neoorthodoxy, the 20th-century theological reaction to liberalism. While studying at Boston University, King married Coretta Scott, with whom he had four children.

While he worked on his dissertation, King assumed the pulpit of the Dexter Avenue Church in Montgomery, Alabama, in 1954. At the close of the following year, the arrest of Rosa Parks for refusing to surrender her seat on a bus to a white man had galvanized the African-American community in

Montgomery. After the formation of the Montgomery Improvement Association to coordinate protests of bus segregation, King was chosen its president. For the next year, he presided over the bus boycott, which ended only after the U.S. Supreme Court struck down Alabama's segregated bus law. The success of the Montgomery bus boycott inspired King to organize the Southern Christian Leadership Conference (SCLC) in 1957, and he became its first president. By 1960, his growing involvement in civil rights activities prompted King to resign from his ministerial position at the Dexter Avenue Church and to join his father as copastor of the Ebenezer church in Atlanta. King, though, continued to devote his energies primarily to the cause of civil rights.

King's influence within the Civil Rights movement reached its peak in 1963. That year, he helped to orchestrate the civil rights demonstrations in Birmingham, Alabama. Television coverage of these demonstrations, including the use by police of dogs and water hoses against the demonstrators, forever changed the public face of the civil rights struggle, and King's role in the Birmingham protests put him at the forefront of national attention. Arrested during the demonstrations, he wrote his *Letter from a Birmingham Jail,* which has become a classic defense of civil disobedience. In the summer of that year he participated in the March on Washington, which drew more than 200,000 protesters. On the steps of the Lincoln Memorial in Washington, D.C., on August 28, 1963, he delivered perhaps his most famous speech, declaring his vision for America:

> I have a dream that one day on the red hills of Georgia the sons of former slaves and the sons of former slaveowners will be able to sit down together at a table of brotherhood. I have a dream that one day even the state of Mississippi, a desert state, sweltering with the heat of injustice and oppression, will be transformed into an oasis of freedom and justice. I have a dream that my four children will one day live in a nation where they will not be judged by the color of their skin but by the content of their character. I have a dream today. I have a dream that one day the state of Alabama . . . will be transformed into a situation where little black boys and black girls will be able to join hands with little white boys and white girls and walk together as sisters and brothers.

As a testimony to his national prominence, King received the Nobel Peace Prize in December 1964.

In the years that followed the Birmingham demonstrations, King collided with ever greater frequency against more militant forces within the Civil Rights movement, especially as represented by the Student Nonviolent Coordinating Committee. This organization increasingly questioned King's resolute commitment to nonviolent demonstrations, as its membership grew to believe that equal rights for African Americans could not be achieved through the use of nonviolent strategies such as King had learned from the writings of Mohandas Gandhi. King, though, adhered to his nonviolent campaign against racial inequality, as demonstrated by a high-profile voting rights campaign centered in Selma, Alabama, in 1965. In the spring of 1968, he led a march in support of sanitation workers in Memphis, Tennessee, that attracted violence and looting. He returned to Memphis a month later and delivered a speech at Bishop Charles J. Mason Temple, on April 3. Encouraging his audience to persevere in the struggle for civil rights, King declared that he had "been to the mountaintop" and that he had "seen the promised land." Like Moses, forbidden to lead the children of Israel in the Old Testament into the Promised Land, King hinted that though he had glimpsed that land, he might not enter it himself. The next day, April 4, 1965, standing on the balcony of the Lorraine Motel in Memphis, he was assassinated by James Earl Ray.

Nearly two decades after the death of Martin Luther King, Jr., the United States gave public recognition of his influence by declaring his birthday a national holiday, celebrated for the first time in 1986. The achievements of the Civil Rights movement in which he played such a dominant part from 1955 until his death in 1968 remain a subject of debate, as cultural observers variously celebrate its accomplishments or lament its unfinished work. But King himself, notwithstanding the criticisms sometimes leveled at him, remains the Moses for the Civil Rights movement. Even if his work was uncompleted, it changed the face of America in ways that could have scarcely been imagined a generation before.

Further Reading

Ansbro, John J. *Martin Luther King, Jr.: The Making of a Mind.* Maryknoll, N.Y.: Orbis Books, 1982.

Bennett, Lerone. *What Manner of Man: A Biography of Martin Luther King, Jr.* 4th rev. ed. Chicago: Johnson, 1976.

Branch, Taylor. *Parting the Waters: America in the King Years, 1954–63.* New York: Simon & Schuster, 1988.

———. *Pillar of Fire: America in the King Years, 1963–65.* New York: Simon & Schuster, 1998.

Colaiaco, James A. *Martin Luther King, Jr.: Apostle of Militant Nonviolence.* New York: St. Martin's Press, 1988.

Deats, Richard L. *Martin Luther King, Jr., Spirit-Led Prophet: A Biography.* London: New City Press, 2000.

Garrow, David J. *Bearing the Cross: Martin Luther King, Jr., and the Southern Christian Leadership Conference.* New York: W. Morrow, 1986.

King, Martin Luther, Jr. *A Testament of Hope: The Essential Writings of Martin Luther King, Jr.* Edited by James Melvin Washington. San Francisco: Harper & Row, 1986.

———. *The Autobiography of Martin Luther King, Jr.* Edited by Clayborne Carson. New York: Intellectual Properties Management in association with Warner Books, 1998.

Lewis, David L. *King: A Biography.* 2d ed. Urbana: University of Illinois Press, 1978.

Lischer, Richard. *The Preacher King: Martin Luther King, Jr., and the Word That Moved America.* New York: Oxford University Press, 1995.

Oates, Stephen B. *Let the Trumpet Sound: The Life of Martin Luther King, Jr.* New York: Harper & Row, 1982.

King, Thomas Starr

(1824–1864) Universalist minister

Thomas Starr King began his career as a Universalist minister in Charleston, Massachusetts. But history knows him best for his planting of Unitarianism in the soil of California. He was born on December 17, 1824, in New York City, the son of Thomas Farrington King and Susan Starr King. His father, who was a Universalist minister, died when King was 15 years old, and he had to work at odd jobs thereafter to support his family, including work as a bookkeeper for Charleston Naval Yard. This work prevented him from obtaining any formal education after the age of 15, and he sometimes referred to himself in later years as "a graduate of Charleston Naval Yard." During the early 1840s, however, King was able to study theology with the Universalist minister HOSEA BALLOU, and in 1846 he was ordained the minister of the Universalist Church of Charleston, Massachusetts, where his father had served at the time of his death. Two years later, he relocated to Boston, where he accepted a position as minister of the Hollis Street Unitarian Church. That same year, he married Julia Wiggin, with whom he had two children.

Thomas Starr King, a Universalist minister, is sometimes credited with persuading California to remain in the Union during the Civil War. *(Library of Congress, Prints and Photographs Division LC-USZ62-109959)*

During the 12 years he spent in Boston, King earned prominence as one of the city's leading preachers and lecturers. In 1860, he decided to transplant his ministerial career to California, where he assumed the pulpit of a Unitarian church in San Francisco. Almost immediately, he found himself immersed in the controversy over whether California would remain in the Union. King unabashedly supported the cause of the Union and urged Californians to support it. In a Fourth of July speech sponsored by an Episcopal Mission Sunday School and delivered by King in 1860, he made the case for national unity.

> Whoever works for the disunion of our nation, and hopes to succeed, must get up, not a convention or a rebellion, but an earthquake that shall pitch half the Mississippi towards the north pole, snap the Alleghenies at the center, turn the Ohio out of bed, and choke with ruins every pass of the Rocky Mountains.

After the start of the Civil War in 1861, King lectured widely against those willing to sacrifice the Union as a means of purchasing peace. His labors for the Union cause won him recognition by some observers as the "man who saved California to the Union." He also raised more than $1.5 million for the Sanitary Commission, an agency that provided medical supplies to the Union army. He did not live to see the Union's ultimate victory, however. After contracting diphtheria, King died of pneumonia in his San Francisco home on March 4, 1864.

The National Statuary Hall Collection in the United States Capitol consists of statues representing notable figures from the history of each state in the nation. After the creation of the collection, the federal government invited states to provide two statues each, and by the beginning of the 21st century, the collection consisted of 97 items. In the spring of 1931, California unveiled its own bronze figures representing two illustrious citizens from its past, and one of these figures was that of the Unitarian minister Thomas Starr King. Although the young minister arrived in California only four years before his untimely death, he made himself conspicuous by his efforts to prevent his new-found neighbors from bidding farewell to the Union. Though his efforts were not the only ones

devoted to this end, King's oratorical brilliance in service of the Union won him lasting admiration within the state of California and within the Union he helped to preserve.

Further Reading

Crompton, Arnold. *Apostle of Liberty: Starr King in California.* Boston: Beacon Press, 1950.

Frothingham, Richard. *A Tribute to Thomas Starr King.* Boston: Ticknor and Fields, 1865.

Monzingo, Robert A. *Thomas Starr King: Eminent Californian, Civil War Statesman, Unitarian Minister.* Pacific Grove, Calif.: Boxwood Press, 1991.

Simonds, William Day. *Starr King in California.* San Francisco: P. Elder, 1917.

Wendte, Charles William. *Thomas Starr King, Patriot and Preacher.* Boston, Mass.: Beacon Press, 1921.

Kino, Eusebio Francisco
(Eusebio Francisco Chini)
(1645–1711) *Catholic missionary, explorer*

A Jesuit missionary, Eusebio Francisco Kino helped to plant Catholicism in what became the southwestern portion of the United States. Kino also explored and mapped the region and established cattle ranches that became important economic centers and the nuclei of later towns in the Southwest. He was born on August 10, 1645, in Segno, Italy, the son of Francisco Chini and Mararita Chini; he later changed the spelling of his surname to *Kino*. In his late teens he suffered a severe illness, during the course of which he promised his patron saint, Saint Francis Xavier, that he would become a missionary if he recovered. Two years later, in 1665, he took the first steps toward fulfilling this promise when he entered the Society of Jesus (the Jesuits), undertaking his novitiate at Landsberg, Bavaria, followed by three years of study at the University of Ingolstadt, Bavaria, three years of teaching at the Jesuit college of Hale in Innsbruck, Austria, and then further theological studies at Ingolstadt and Oettingen, Bavaria. In the course of these studies, Kino also pursued an avid interest in mathematics and cartography. He was ordained a Jesuit priest in 1676.

In 1678, Kino's superiors granted his long repeated requests to serve as a missionary. He had sought from the Jesuit father general an appointment to a mission in the Indies or China or "some other difficult one in nature, if indeed, to the Divine Grace anything is difficult." It was finally decided, however, that Kino would undertake missionary service in Mexico. He arrived in Veracruz in 1681; from there he made his way to Mexico City. There he was assigned to join an expedition led by Admiral Isidro de Atondo y Antillón, which had as its purpose the establishment of a Jesuit mission in California. On October 5, 1683, Kino founded the first mission in California at San Bruno, near present-day Loreto. When Admiral Atondo decided to withdraw from the area in the spring of 1685, however, Kino had to abandon the mission. This retreat did not blunt the edge of Kino's missionary and exploratory zeal, though. Over the following years he launched expeditions that resulted in establishment of missions at Nuestra Señora de los Dolores, Caburica, Tubutama, Caborca, Guevavi, Cocóspera, and San Xavier del Bac, chiefly among the Pima Indians. In addition to these missionary accomplishments, Kino's cartographic skills proved invaluable in charting significant portions of what would one day be the southwestern United States. In particular, by the late 1690s, he had established that Lower California was a peninsula rather than an island, as commonly believed. But Kino was more than a migrant evangelist who moved from place to place. He helped introduce wheat farming and cattle raising to the areas surrounding the missions he established, thus laying a foundation for the economic as well as the spiritual lives of the communities he established. Toward the end of his missionary career he was appointed superior of the missions in Pimeria Alta, a region consisting of present-day southern Arizona and northern Sonora, Mexico. He died in Santa Maria Magdalena, Mexico, on March 15, 1711.

When he was a young man, Eusebio Francisco Kino dreamed of carrying the message of Christianity to China. But another continent was destined to feel the tread of his feet, and other peoples to become converts to his faith. Across more than a quarter of a century he carried the Christian gospel to southern Arizona and northern Mexico and established spiritual and economic communities that lasted long after his career as a Jesuit missionary had ended. Today a statute of Kino stands in the Statuary Hall representing the state of Arizona in the United States Capitol.

Further Reading

Bolton, Herbert Eugene. *Rim of Christendom: A Biography of Eusebio Francisco Kino, Pacific Coast Pioneer.* New York: Russell & Russell, 1936; Tucson: University of Arizona Press, 1984.

Burrus, Ernest J. *Kino and Manje, Explorers of Sonora and Arizona: Their Vision of the Future.* St. Louis, Mo.: St. Louis University, 1971.

Clark, Ann Nolan. *Father Kino: Priest to the Pimas.* New York: Farrar, Straus, 1963.

Kino, Eusebio Francisco. *Kino Writes to the Duchess: Letters of Eusebio Francisco Kino, S.J., to the Duchess of Aveiro.* St. Louis, Mo.: St. Louis University, 1965.

———. *Kino's Historical Memoir of Pimería Alta: A Contemporary Account of the Beginnings of California, Sonora, and Arizona.* 2 vols. Cleveland: Arthur H. Clark, 1919; New York: AMS Press, 1976.

Polzer, Charles W. *Kino, A Legacy: His Life, His Works, His Missions, His Monuments.* Tucson: Jesuit Fathers of Southern Arizona, 1998.

Smith, Fay Jackson, John L. Kessell, and Francis J. Fox. *Father Kino in Arizona.* Phoenix: Ariz.: Historical Foundation, 1966.

Wyllys, Rufus Kay. *Pioneer Padre: The Life and Times of Eusebio Francisco Kino.* Dallas, Tex.: Southwest Press, 1935.

Kirk, Edward Norris
(1802–1874) *Congregationalist minister*

Edward Norris Kirk was an evangelical Calvinist who participated in the wave of revivals that stirred 19th-century Protestantism. In the course of a ministerial career that spanned almost half a century, Kirk migrated from Presbyterianism to Congregationalism. He was born on August 14, 1802, in New York City, to George and Mary Norris Kirk. His father, an immigrant from Scotland, ran a dry goods store and served as an elder in New York's Magazine Street Presbyterian Church. Kirk graduated from the College of New Jersey (today, Princeton University) in 1820 with a B.A. and, against the wishes of his parents, who hoped he would become a minister, chose to prepare himself for a legal career. In 1822, however, he had a conversion experience, which convinced him that God had saved him and called him to preach. Kirk promptly enrolled in Princeton Theological Seminary; he graduated in 1825. After an additional year's study at Princeton, he was licensed to preach by the New York presbytery in 1826.

Kirk began his preaching career as an agent for the American Board of Commissioners for Foreign Missions. He traveled through the mid-Atlantic states and the South from 1826 to 1828, seeking to raise support for foreign missions. In 1828 Second Presbyterian Church in Albany, New York, invited him to occupy its pulpit for a time. The church had a prominent membership, including the future U.S. president Martin Van Buren, but its more influential members decided in 1829 that Kirk's revivalistic preaching was not to their liking. They consequently asked him to leave. But many of the congregation had approved of Kirk's preaching and soon founded Albany's Fourth Presbyterian Church and invited Kirk to become its pastor beginning in April 1829. There, he continued his own spirited preaching and lent his pulpit to other revivalists. In particular, he invited CHARLES GRANDISON FINNEY to preach at his church when every other pulpit in Albany refused to hear him. During his years in Albany, Kirk also combined zeal for revival with zeal for social reforms, especially abolitionism and temperance.

By the spring of 1837, Kirk was prepared to leave his church in Albany. From its founding membership, the church had added more than 1,000 new members over the years of Kirk's pastoral care. But Kirk was eager to witness the course of revivalism in Europe, and he spent two years traveling and preaching there before returning to the United States in 1839. For the next few years, he traveled widely in the United States, conducting revival meetings of his own. By the early years of the next decade, Kirk's views about church government had migrated toward Congregationalism, with its emphasis on the autonomy of local churches. In 1842, he agreed to become pastor of Mount Vernon Congregational Church in Boston, formed for the very purpose of offering Kirk a pulpit from which to preach. Over the next

15 years, Kirk grew to national prominence as a preacher, filling his church Sunday by Sunday. Occasionally, during this period, he ventured to Europe, including a period of absence from Boston while he helped establish the American Church in Paris in 1857.

As controversy over slavery increasingly captured the nation's attention during the 1850s, Kirk refused to cloak his fierce antislavery views. From the pulpit and elsewhere, he denounced slavery and the racist assumptions that supported its traffic in human misery, a traffic that he had witnessed personally during a tour of the South made shortly before Abraham Lincoln's election as president. In the speech "The Clergy and the Slave Power," Kirk expressed his agreement with Europeans who thought that "a man is a man,— under any parallel of latitude, with a skin of any color, a nose of any shape, a heel of any length, a hair of any degree of curliness."

After war erupted, Kirk supported the cause of the Union so vociferously and campaigned so actively for Lincoln's reelection in 1864 that he became known as the patriot preacher. He was frequently likened to the preachers who had supported the cause of revolution a century before. Edward Kirk never married, and he died on March 27, 1874, in Boston, Massachusetts.

Edward Norris Kirk gave an urbane and educated face to 19th-century Protestant revivalism. Though associated with the specific traditions of Presbyterianism, and later Congregationalism, his evangelicalism produced in him an ecumenical temper that allied him with a variety of revival movements of his day. Unlike some revivalists, however, whose faith separates them from worldly concerns, Kirk was propelled into the thick of social and political controversy, especially the controversy concerning slavery, by his Christianity.

Further Reading

Kirk, Edward Norris. *Lectures on Revivals.* Edited by David O. Mears. Boston: Congregational Publishing Society, 1875. Available online. URL: http://www.books-on-line.com/Book Display.cfm? Book Num = 2494. Downloaded on April 25, 2002.

Mears, David. O. *Life of Edward Norris Kirk.* Boston: Lockwood, Brooks, 1878.

Knudson, Albert Cornelius
(1873–1953) *Methodist theologian, educator*

Albert Cornelius Knudson combined the temper of an evangelical Methodist with the intellectual commitments of a Protestant liberal. Through his elaboration of a theology of personalism, he was able to espouse an evangelical liberalism influential during the first half of the 20th century. He was born on January 23, 1873, in Grandmeadow, Minnesota, the son of Asle Knudson and Susan Fosse Knudson, Norwegian immigrants. While a senior at St. Paul High School, he experienced a religious conversion and joined a Methodist church. After finishing high school in 1889, he attended the University of Minnesota, from which he graduated second in his class with a B.A. in classics in 1893. During college he decided to adopt the vocation of his father, who was a Methodist minister.

After completing his undergraduate studies, Knudson enrolled in the Boston University School of Theology. While in Boston, he supplemented his theological education with practical ministerial experience by serving as pastor of a Congregational mission called the Lenox Street Chapel for three years. On receiving his bachelor's degree in sacred theology in 1896, he decided to remain at Boston University to pursue a Ph.D. in philosophy under the direction of personalist philosopher Borden Parker Bowne. Knudson was awarded a fellowship to study in Germany at the universities of Jena and Berlin from 1897 to 1898. Once he returned to the United States, he took a teaching position at Illiff School of Theology in Denver, Colorado, while he continued work toward his Ph.D. He also married Mathilde Johnson in 1899. The couple had no children. During this period in Denver, Knudson was ordained a Methodist minister, although it was becoming increasingly apparent that he possessed the gifts of an academic in greater abundance than those of a pastor. Once he had earned the Ph.D. in 1900, Knudson spent the following several years teaching first at Baker University in Bladwin, Kansas, from 1900 to 1902, and then at Allegheny College in Meadville, Pennsylvania, from 1902 to 1906.

In 1905, Hinckley G. Mitchell, one of Knudson's former professors at Boston University, had been forced out of his professorial position as a result of his enthusiasm for higher criticism of the Bible. Knudson was invited to assume the vacant post, and, in 1906, he began what would ultimately be a 37-year career on the faculty of Boston University. For his first 15 years, he served as professor of Hebrew and Old Testament exegesis. Beginning in 1921, he refocused his academic concentration on systematic theology. Five years later, he added to his academic responsibilities a tenure of service as dean of the School of Theology from 1926 to 1938.

Knudson's theological labors concentrated on exploring the implications of the philosophy of personalism he had imbibed from Borden Parker Bowne, the father of American personalism, at Boston University. He offered his most significant elaborations of this theological vision in works such as *The Philosophy of Personalism* (1927) and *The Validity of Religious Experience* (1937). According to the philosophy of personalism, personality and relationships are the fundamental organizing concepts of philosophic reflection. Knudson devoted particular attention to the relationship between God, the infinite person, and individuals, who constitute finite persons. Through this emphasis religious experience and ethics were at the center of Knudson's theology, thus allowing the theologian to remain at home with traditional Methodist rhetoric even though he had decisively repudiated some of its more orthodox commitments.

After Knudson resigned his post as dean of the Boston University School of Theology in 1938, he continued to teach at the university another five years. He retired from active academic life in 1943. Ten years later he died, on August 28, 1953, in Cambridge, Massachusetts.

Albert Cornelius Knudson helped steer 20th-century Methodism away from the theological conservativism that had dominated its life in the preceding century. This theological migration mirrored that which occurred in other mainline Protestant denominations during the same period. But Knudson's personalist theology, with its emphasis on religious experience and ethics, allowed him to speak a theological language both sensitive to the currents of modernity and not wholly divorced from the evangelical commitments of Methodism's past.

Further Reading

Brightman, Edgar Sheffield, ed. *Personalism in Theology: A Symposium in Honor of Albert Cornelius Knudson.* Boston: Boston University Press, 1943; New York: AMS Press, 1979.

Deats, Paul, and Carol Robb, eds. *The Boston Personalist Tradition in Philosophy, Social Ethics, and Theology.* Macon: Mercer University Press, 1986.

DeWolf, L. Harold. "Albert Cornelius Knudson as Philosopher." *The Personalist* 35 (October 1954): 364–68.

Knudson, Albert Cornelius. *The Doctrine of God.* New York: Abingdon-Cokesbury Press, 1930.

———. *The Doctrine of Redemption.* New York: Abingdon-Cokesbury Press, 1933.

———. *The Philosophy of Personalism: A Study in the Metaphysics of Religion.* New York: Abingdon Press, 1927.

Lavely, John. H. "What Is Personalism?" *Personalist Forum* 7 (1991): 1–33.

Leslie, Elmer A. "Albert Cornelius Knudson: An Intimate View." *The Personalist* 35 (October 1954): 357–63.

Koresh, David
(Vernon Wayne Howell)
(1959–1993) *Adventist leader*

David Koresh captured national attention in 1993 when he participated in a widely televised standoff with the Federal Bureau of Investigation (FBI) outside Waco, Texas. The confrontation ended with the fiery deaths of Koresh and more than 70 followers after the FBI attempted to invade the compound in which Koresh had fortified himself. He was born Vernon Wayne Howell on August 17, 1959, in Houston, Texas, the son of an unwed 14-year-old mother, Bonnie Clark, and Bobby Howell. Howell's mother and grandmother exposed him to the teachings of the Seventh-Day Adventists as he was growing up. This theologically conservative Christian denomination emphasizes the imminent return of Christ to the world and the necessity of leading a pure life in anticipation of this return. Howell attended public school until the 11th grade, when he dropped out to work as a carpenter.

In 1981, the 22-year-old Howell moved to the Mount Carmel compound outside Waco, Texas, where a splinter group of the Seventh-Day Adventists, called the Branch Davidians, practiced their faith. Lois Roden led the Davidians at the time of Howell's arrival, and her son, George Roden, viewed himself as his mother's rightful successor. Howell, though, had an affair with Lois Roden and won her favor, threatening George Roden's prospects for assuming control of the Davidians. In 1984, Howell married 14-year-old Rachel Jones, with whom he had two children. That same year, a power struggle between Howell and George Roden resulted in Howell's leaving Mount Carmel with a number of disciples and settling for a time in Palestine, Texas. A few years later, however, after Roden was sentenced to jail for an unrelated crime, Howell and his followers returned to claim Mount Carmel as their own.

By the end of the 1980s, Vernon Howell had changed his name to David Koresh; *Koresh* is the transliteration of the Hebrew word for Cyrus, the Persian king mentioned in the Old Testament who permitted the Jews held captive in Babylon to return to Israel. Koresh also assumed for himself the title of the "Lamb" referred to in Revelation 5, who opens the seven seals referred to there. By the mid-1980s, Koresh had begun to understand his apocalyptic role to include fathering numerous children. Over the years that followed he insisted on the celibacy of male Davidians, while he sired some 17 children by female followers, including married and underage women. Convinced that the apocalypse was imminent and that America would be its staging ground, Koresh assembled a sizable cache of weapons that eventually attracted the attention of the Federal Bureau of Alcohol, Tobacco, and Firearms (ATF).

Seeking to investigate whether Koresh and his followers had broken federal firearms laws, the ATF raided the Mount Carmel compound on February 28, 1993. The Davidians responded with gunfire, and in the hail of bullets that followed, 4 ATF agents were killed and 24 were wounded, and 6 Davidians were killed. The FBI promptly took control of what became a siege that stretched across 50 days. Although 37 individuals left the compound during this period, the FBI, under the direction of U.S. Attorney General Janet Reno, eventually chose to invade the compound. This decision was prompted partially by suggestions, later proved unsubstantiated, that Davidian children were being abused. In any event, on April 19, 1993, the FBI used tanks to punch holes in compound buildings and inserted tear gas into them. Almost at once, however, fires started in the compound, and it was soon consumed in flames. Nine Davidians escaped the inferno, but more than 70 men, women, and children perished, some, including David Koresh, with gunshot wounds apparently inflicted by themselves or other Davidians. Many details of the Mount Carmel tragedy remain in dispute, such as whether Davidians themselves started the fires that engulfed the compound or whether the FBI accidentally triggered the fires when it assaulted the compound with tear gas.

The tragedy at Waco has defied ready categorization. Accusations of government misconduct share space in the public consciousness with incredulity about the religious beliefs of the Branch Davidians. David Koresh's sexually tinged apocalypticism finds parallels in such famous American utopian experiments as the Oneida colony of late 19th-century New York. Nevertheless, clothed in the garb of semiautomatic weapons, Koresh's religious vision also bore a disturbing resemblance to the Jonestown massacre that had briefly galvanized American attention a decade and a half before Koresh made his defiant stand against the ATF and the FBI. Whether he should be understood as a reminder of government overreaching or of dangerous religious fanaticism remains a hotly debated question.

Further Reading

Bailey, Brad, and Bob Darden. *Mad Man in Waco.* Waco, Tex.: WRS, 1993.

King, Martin, and Marc Breault. *Preacher of Death: The Shocking Inside Story of David Koresh and the Waco Siege.* New York: Signet Books, 1993.

Koresh, David. *The Decoded Message of the Seven Seals of the Book of Revelation.* Green Forest, Ark.: Stewart Waterhouse, 1993.

Lewis, James R., ed. *From the Ashes: Making Sense of Waco.* Lanham, Md.: Rowman & Littlefield, 1994.

Linedecker, Clifford L. *Massacre at Waco, Texas: The Shocking Story of Cult Leader David Koresh and the Branch Davidians.* New York: St. Martin's Paperbacks, 1993.

Reavis, Dick J. *The Ashes of Waco: An Investigation.* New York: Simon & Schuster, 1995.

Tabor, James D., and Eugene V. Gallagher. *Why Waco? Cults and the Battle for Religious Freedom in America.* Berkeley: University of California Press, 1995.

Krauth, Charles Porterfield

(1823–1883) *Lutheran minister, theologian, educator*

A champion of confessional Lutheranism in mid-19th-century America, Charles Porterfield Krauth steadfastly opposed a movement within Lutheranism to deemphasize traditional Lutheran doctrines in favor of personal piety. He viewed the revivalism that flourished in the 19th century as a threat to doctrinal purity and was a chief voice in support of continued faithfulness to classic Lutheran statements of theology such as the Augsburg Confession. He was born on May 17, 1823, in Martinsburg, Virginia, the son of Charles Philip Krauth and Catherine Susan Heiskell Krauth. Krauth's father was a Lutheran minister. His mother died when he was an infant, and he spent much of his childhood in the care of relatives. By the time Krauth was 10 years old, his father had become president of Pennsylvania College in Gettysburg, Pennsylvania, a Lutheran institution, and Krauth attended a preparatory school associated with the college. He enrolled in Pennsylvania College itself in 1834 and, after graduation in 1839, entered Gettysburg Seminary at the age of 16; he graduated three years later. At Gettysburg Seminary, the most prominent faculty member was SAMUEL SIMON SCHMUCKER, who had helped to found the institution in 1926 and who represented a form of evangelical Lutheranism that Krauth would vigorously oppose in future years.

Krauth was licensed to preach in 1841 and began a pastoral ministry that would last 20 years by tending briefly to a Congregational church in Canton, Maryland. He was subsequently ordained a minister in the fall of 1842, and he became the pastor of the Second English Church in Baltimore, Maryland. Two years later he married Susan Reynolds. After her death in 1853, Krauth married Virginia Baker in 1855. In all, he had five children with his two wives.

During his early years as a minister, Krauth flirted for a time with the evangelical style of Lutheranism then prominent, but he gradually rejected the ecumenical and pietistic emphases of revivalism in favor of a renewed appreciation for historic Lutheran doctrine, especially as enshrined in the Augsburg Confession. He traveled through a series of ministerial posts in the following years. From 1847 to 1848, he jointly tended congregations in Martinsburg and Shepherdstown, Virginia (later West Virginia). Thereafter he was pastor of a church in Winchester, Virginia, from 1848 to 1855; the English Lutheran Church in Pittsburgh, Pennsylvania, from 1855 to 1859; and finally St. Mark's Church in Philadelphia, Pennsylvania, from 1859 to 1861.

In the course of this pastoral migration, Krauth became increasingly fastened to the principles of confessional Lutheranism. He finally took leave of ministerial work in 1861 to become the editor of the *Lutheran and Missionary* magazine, which he used as a pulpit to advance the cause of confessionalism from 1861 to 1867. While an editor for this magazine, Krauth also became professor of systematic theology at the Lutheran Theological Seminary when it was established in Philadelphia in 1864, a position he held until his death. Four years later, he also accepted an appointment as professor of philosophy at the University of Pennsylvania, an academic post he also filled until he died. During these years of academic labor, Krauth published his most important work, *The Conservative Reformation and Its Theology* (1871). His years as a scholar and a teacher did not divert him from Lutheran Church affairs, however. He served as theologian and principal architect in 1867 of the formation of the General Council, a body of confessional Lutheran churches at odds with the more evangelical congregations that controlled the General Synod. Moreover, he moderated the national meetings of this new ecclesiastical body for its first decade. He died in Philadelphia, Pennsylvania, on January 2, 1883.

The revivalism that flowed across 19th-century America frequently took on an ecumenical character, as evangelicals from different traditions minimized their differences to collaborate in common evangelistic and missionary projects. But some observers of this trend looked on it with alarm, seeing in it a subordination of doctrinal truth to pietistic feeling. Charles Porterfield Krauth was one such observer. Though he studied with Samuel S. Schmucker, one of evangelical Lutheranism's leading 19th-century representatives, he ultimately became one of Schmucker's most prominent theological opponents. For Krauth, religious experience should be rooted not in the inner life of pietism but in the historic confessions of the Lutheran Church. His success in articulating a competing vision to evangelical Lutheranism made him one of the century's most important Lutheran theologians.

Further Reading

Griffioen, Arie J. "Charles Porterfield Krauth and the Synod of Maryland." *Lutheran Quarterly* 7 (1993): 277–91.

Krauth, Charles P. *The Conservative Reformation and Its Theology*. N.p.: 1871; Minneapolis: Augsburg Publishing House, 1963.

Reckzin, Dale Markham. "Three Doctors of the American Lutheran Church: Charles Porterfield Krauth, Carl Ferdinand Wilhelm Walther, Gustav Adolph Theodor Felix Hoenecke," Western Lutheran Seminary. Available online. URL: http://www.wls.wels.net/library/Essays/Authors/R/ReckzinDoctors/ReckzinDoctors.html. Downloaded on December 5, 2001.

Spaeth, Adolph. *Charles Porterfield Krauth*. 2 vols. New York: Christian Literature Company, 1898–1909; New York: Arno Press, 1969.

Tappert, Theodore G., ed. *Lutheran Confessional Theology in America, 1840–80*. New York: Oxford University Press, 1972.

Kuhlman, Kathryn
(ca. 1910–1976) *charismatic preacher, healer*

Famous for her healing services, Kathryn Kuhlman was a leader of the charismatic revival in the United States during the third quarter of the 20th century. She resisted being referred to as a faith healer, insisting that only God heals sicknesses, through divine healing power. Kathryn Kuhlman was born around 1910 in Concordia, Missouri, to a Baptist father, Joe Kuhlman, and a Methodist mother, Emma Walkenhorst Kuhlman. Kathryn Kuhlman's formal education ended with the 10th grade. In 1923, she began a religious career that would span more than half a century when she joined a traveling tent revival that was led by her brother-in-law and her sister. In 1928, at the age of 21, Kuhlman began an itinerant ministry of her own, traveling with Helen Gulliford through the Northwest and referring to their team as "God's Girls."

Beginning in 1933, Kuhlman settled for a time in Denver, Colorado, where she opened the Kuhlman Revival Tabernacle in a paper warehouse in 1934 and the Denver Revival Tabernacle in the following year. In the fall of 1938, Kuhlman married Burroughs A. Waltrip, a Texas evangelist who had preached in the tabernacle for two months the previous year and who divorced his wife and abandoned his children to marry Kuhlman. The resulting scandal drove away her Denver congregation and hampered her evangelist campaigns for the next several years. Kuhlman was forced to return to itinerancy with her new husband, conducting evangelistic meetings from place to place. In 1944, she had the charismatic experience of being "baptized with the Holy Spirit" and almost immediately left her husband in favor of a solo evangelistic career. Within two years she had made Franklin, Pennsylvania, near Pittsburgh, the hub of her evangelistic activities. She also began to study biblical teaching concerning healing. In 1947, the first of what would become thousands of reported healings occurred during services she conducted. Within a year, she began to refer to her meetings as "miracle services." By 1950, she had transferred the center of her now growing healing ministry to Pittsburgh.

Throughout the next decade, Kuhlman's reputation, though attacked by more conservative evangelical leaders who challenged the idea of women being preachers, increased, and her ministry, then including radio programs, flourished. She did not adopt the aggressive fund-raising techniques that would become routine among later television and radio evangelists but nevertheless succeeded in supporting the growing financial requirements of her ministry. She published her first book, *I Believe in Miracles*, in 1962, and it was followed by a number of other books over the next 14 years. In 1967 Kuhlman added a television ministry to her work and eventually produced more than 500 half-hour programs, which combined with her other work to make her one of the charismatic movement's most prominent figures during the 1960s and 1970s.

As early as 1955, Kuhlman had been diagnosed as having an enlarged heart, and during the last years of her life, she suffered the physical effects of a combination of this condition and a rigorous speaking and traveling schedule. By the mid-1970s her health declined precipitously, and she was hospitalized at the end of 1975 for open heart surgery. She died of complications of the surgery on February 20, 1976, in Tulsa, Oklahoma.

Often compared with early 20th-century Pentecostal preacher and healer AIMEE SEMPLE MCPHERSON, Kathryn Kuhlman was a less flamboyant preacher. But she succeeded in planting the charismatic movement squarely within middle-class America. She deliberately downplayed her own role in the miracles claimed to accompany her ministry and avoided the sometimes tawdry financial appeals that sometimes have characterized charismatic ministries. As a consequence, she helped shepherd the charismatic movement out of its historically close association with Pentecostalism and made it appealing to a more mainstream religious audience.

Further Reading

Buckingham, Jamie. *Daughter of Destiny: Kathryn Kuhlman, Her Story.* Plainfield, N.J.: Logos International, 1976.

Hinn, Benny. *Kathryn Kuhlman: Her Spiritual Legacy and Its Impact on My Life.* Nashville: Tenn.: T. Nelson, 1999.

Hosier, Helen Kooiman. *Kathryn Kuhlman: The Life She Led, the Legacy She Left.* Boston: G. K. Hall, 1976.

Kuhlman, Kathryn, with Jamie Buckingham. *A Glimpse into Glory.* Plainfield, N.J.: Logos International, 1979.

———. *Healing Words.* Edited by Larry Keefauver. Orlando, Fla.: Creation House, 1997.

———. *I Believe in Miracles.* Englewood Cliffs, N.J.: Prentice-Hall, 1962.

———. *Never Too Late.* Minneapolis: Bethany Fellowship, 1975.

McCauley, Deborah Vansau. "Kathryn Kuhlman." In *Twentieth-Century Shapers of American Popular Religion.* Edited by Charles H. Lippy. New York: Greenwood Press, 1989.

Spraggett, Allen. *Kathryn Kuhlman: The Woman Who Believes in Miracles.* New York: World, 1970.

Warner, Wayne E. *Kathryn Kuhlman: The Woman Behind the Miracles.* Ann Arbor, Mich.: Servant Publications, 1993.

L

Lamy, Jean Baptiste
(1814–1888) *Catholic missionary*

Influential in the spread of Catholicism in the southwestern United States during the 19th century, Jean Baptiste Lamy combined missionary zeal and perseverance with administrative skill. He left an enduring legacy in New Mexico and Arizona through the churches, schools, and hospitals built under his supervision. Lamy was born on October 11, 1814, in Lempes, France, to Jean Lamy and Marie Dié Lamy. When he was nine years old, his parents enrolled him in a Jesuit school at Billom. Thereafter, determined to be a priest, he studied first at a preparatory seminary at Clermont and then at the diocesan seminary of Mont-Ferrand, where he was ordained in 1838. After serving briefly at the parish in Capre, France, Lamy and his friend Joseph Machebeuf, also a priest, joined a group of priests and nuns immigrating to the United States for mission work in the summer of 1839. Once in America, Lamy was assigned to minister in Danville, Ohio, where he served as pastor and built several churches in the area before Bishop John Purcell, his superior, transferred him to Covington, Kentucky, in 1847.

After Mexico ceded the territory of New Mexico to the United States in 1848, Lamy's postings in Ohio and Kentucky became the preface to the ministry that would occupy the rest of his life. The American bishops petitioned Pope Pius IX to create a new vicariate apostolic for the New Mexico Territory, and the pope, agreeing to this request, appointed Lamy bishop of this new region the same year. Lamy suffered setbacks at the outset of his new responsibilities. A shipwreck off the coast of Texas delayed his arrival in New Mexico, and, once there, he discovered that many of the Catholics in New Mexico doubted his spiritual authority, believing themselves still subject to the authority of Mexico's bishop. But Lamy proved to be an indefatigable missionary. He inherited responsibility for territory in which Catholic affairs were in substantial disarray. Though Jesuit and Franciscan missionaries had established Catholicism in the Southwest, years of neglect had left the church's presence in this region scattered and weakened. Over the next 35 years, however, Lamy presided over the steady advance of Catholic influence first in New Mexico, then in Arizona. Under his spiritual administration the number of Catholics in these territories increased by the thousands, and he was especially able at persuading other priests and nuns to join him in the work of his diocese. He worked with orders including the Sisters of Loretto from Kentucky in 1852, the Sisters of Charity from Cincinnati in 1865, and Jesuits from Naples in 1867. Lamy also left an enduring mark on the region by overseeing the construction or repair of scores of churches, as well as a hospital, an orphanage, two colleges, and many schools. When he retired, he left the diocese with 238 churches; there had been only 66 when he arrived in Santa Fe.

In 1875, Santa Fe became an archdiocese, and Lamy was made its archbishop. He served a decade in this position before retiring in 1885. He died of pneumonia two and a half years later on February 13, 1888, in Santa Fe.

American religious leadership has not always expressed itself through oratorical or theological brilliance; persevering labor and energy have also played important roles. Jean Baptiste Lamy was a priest for 50 years and a bishop for 38. During his long career of service, a capacity for energetic labor and a boundless passion for the church's increase made him a prominent spiritual force in the Southwest during the 19th century.

Further Reading

De Aragon, Ray John. *Padre Martínez and Bishop Lamy.* Las Vegas, N.Mex.: Pan-American, 1978.

Ellis, Bruce T. *Bishop Lamy's Santa Fe Cathedral: With Records of the Old Spanish Church (Parroquia) and Convent Formerly on the Site.* Albuquerque: University of New Mexico Press, 1985.

Hanks, Nancy. *Lamy's Legion: The Individual Histories of Secular Clergy Serving in the Archdiocese of Santa Fe from 1850 to 1912.* Santa Fe, N.Mex.: HRM Books, 2000.

Horgan, Paul. *Lamy of Santa Fe: His Life and Times.* New York: Farrar, Straus & Giroux, 1975.

Lamy, John Baptist. *Archbishop Lamy: In His Own Words.* Albuquerque, N.Mex.: LPD Press, 2000.

LaVey, Anton Szandor
(Howard Stanton Levey)
(1930–1997) *Satanist*

The flamboyant founder of the Church of Satan, Anton Szandor LaVey capitalized on media attention to champion his own variety of antireligion. Along the way, he penned six books, including *The Satanic Bible* (1969), and attracted a minor cult following. He was born Howard Stanton Levey on April 11, 1930, in Chicago, Illinois, the son of Michael Levey and Gertrude Levey. Anton LaVey, as he began to call himself, was not averse to the manufacture of fictitious details about his past, and therefore the circumstances of his early

life are difficult to determine. He married a woman named Carole in 1951, with whom he had one child, a daughter named Karla, before their divorce in 1960. Two years later he began living with Dianne Hagerty, with whom he had another daughter, Zeena. During the 1950s and early 1960s he appears to have made a living playing the organ for various San Francisco nightclubs. Attracted to the study of the occult and magic, he also supplemented his income by offering lectures on these subjects.

In 1966, LaVey attempted to capitalize on that decade's surge of interest in the occult and new religions by founding the Church of Satan. The following year, he captured media attention by staging a satanic wedding, and, the year after that, by baptizing his daughter Zeena into the Church of Satan. By the end of the decade, he had published the first of six books, *The Satanic Bible* (1969), which eventually sold more than half a million copies.

Though clothed in the garb of magic and the occult, LaVey's version of Satanism was chiefly a diatribe against religious belief, particularly Christianity, and traditional middle-class values. "Satan is a symbol, nothing more," LaVey insisted in an interview published in the *Washington Post Magazine* in February 1986. "Satan signifies our love of the worldly and our rejection of the pallid, ineffectual image of Christ on the cross." LaVey's *Satanic Bible* self-consciously posed as a kind of anti–Sermon on the Mount, with declarations such as "If a man smite thee on one cheek, *smash* him on the other!" The Church of Satan, which is essentially atheistic, does not worship Satan per se but uses him as an iconoclastic symbol, representing subversion of what LaVey viewed as corrupt religious authority. LaVey, though, was happy to clothe himself in the trappings of the occult and the unusual. With shaved head and black clothes, he made his home in a family mansion finally deeded to LaVey and his second wife in the 1971, with rooms painted black and ceilings painted red. The house was surrounded by a high chain link fence capped with barbed wire, apparently necessary to contain the lion that LaVey kept for a time as a pet.

By the 1970s internal divisions of the Church of Satan proliferated and LaVey generally withdrew from public view, though he still offered lifetime membership in the church to those willing to pay a $100 fee. In 1984, LaVey and his second wife, Dianne, divorced. Prior to their separation, Dianne LaVey had served as high priestess of the Church of Satan. After the divorce, LaVey's younger daughter, Zeena, assumed this position from 1985 to 1990. After she departed from the church, her older sister, Karla, became high priestess. Late in life, LaVey had a child with his mistress and biographer, Blanche Barton. He died on October 29, 1997, at St. Mary's Hospital in San Francisco.

Anton LaVey possessed the soul of a religious iconoclast and the talents of a carnival hustler, which made him a controversial figure in the second half of the 20th century. The church he founded never claimed more than a few hundred members, and even these splintered into smaller cells after his death. Nevertheless his success in attracting media attention made him, for a time, one of the more exotic characters produced by the new religious currents that began to proliferate in America in the 1960s.

Further Reading

Barton, Blanche. *The Secret Life of a Satanist: The Authorized Biography of Anton LaVey*. Los Angeles, Calif.: Feral House, 1992.

Ellis, Bill. *Raising the Devil: Satanism, New Religions, and the Media*. Lexington: University Press of Kentucky, 2000.

Harrington, Walt. "Anton LaVey: America's Satanic Master of Devils, Magic, Music and Madness." *The Washington Post Magazine* (February 23, 1986).

LaVey, Anton Szandor. *The Satanic Bible*. New York: Avon Books, 1969.

———. *The Satanic Witch*. Oreg.: Feral House, 1989.

———. *Satan Speaks!* Venice, Calif.: Feral House, 1998.

Medway, Gareth J. *Lure of the Sinister: The Unnatural History of Satanism*. New York: New York University Press, 2000.

Wright, Lawrence. *Saints and Sinners: Walker Railey, Jimmy Swaggert, Madelyn Murray O'Hair, Anton LaVey, Will Campbell, Matthew Fox*. New York: Knopf, 1993.

Lee, Ann
(Mother Ann Lee)
(1736–1784) *founder of the Shakers*

"Mother" Ann Lee, as her disciples called her, believed that she was the second Christ, sent to Earth to inaugurate a millennial kingdom. The spiritual communities that she founded, called the Shakers, or, more formally, the United Society of Believers in Christ's Second Coming, have all but vanished. But for a time in the 1800s, they offered a communitarian alternative to the revivalism that swept 19th-century America. The circumstances of her early life are uncertain. She was born on February 29, 1736, in Manchester, England, the daughter of John Lee and his wife, whose name is not known. According to traditional accounts Lee's father worked as a blacksmith and Lee herself never received a formal education and remained illiterate all her life. She is said to have worked in a cotton mill prior to her 1762 marriage to Abraham Standerin (sometimes referred to as Standley or Stanley). This union produced four children who died in infancy or early childhood.

A few years before her marriage, Ann Lee joined a group of believers led by James and Jane Wardley. Lee soon became the acknowledged leader of this group, whose members were called the "Shaking Quakers" for the physical manifestations exhibited during their ecstatic worship and for their supposed links to Quakerism. The group clashed repeatedly with authorities in England, and Lee spent time in jail on two occasions. In the late spring of 1774, she migrated with her husband and several other Shakers to America, where they landed in New York in August of that year. Within a few years, Lee's husband had left her, and she and her Shaker followers had settled in Niskeyuna, New York, later known as Watervliet.

The small sectarian group attracted increasing attention over the next few years, partially because Lee and the other Shakers refused to align themselves on the side of independence during the Revolutionary War. Ann Lee found herself jailed again for several months in 1780, before New York's governor, George Clinton, eventually ordered her released. In the spring of 1781, soon after her release, Ann Lee undertook a missionary tour through New England, making Shaker converts and reinforcing the faith of believers already committed to her spiritual vision. A magnet for conflict, however, Lee did not escape trouble on her missionary journey. In Petersham, Massachusetts, she was dragged from the house where she was staying and forcibly evicted from the community.

Ann Lee clashed with New England authorities and communities chiefly over the contours of her spiritual teachings. Among these was her belief—based on a vision she had experienced and perhaps on her own tragic childbearing history—that sexual intercourse of all kinds was sinful—the original sin, in fact, that had cast Adam and Eve out of paradise. Even more significant was Ann Lee's claim that she was the second Christ and that her presence in the world had inaugurated a millennial kingdom. She therefore urged her disciples to separate themselves from the world and its carnal desires.

After Lee's 28-month missionary expedition, she returned to Niskeyuna. But tragedy struck soon afterward when her brother, William—who had become a close Shaker associate—died in July 1784. Ann Lee herself died in Niskeyuna, New York, less than two months later, on September 8, 1784.

The scattered Shaker communities that Ann Lee had helped to plant in the soil of New England continued to grow after Lee's death. In 1785, the first Shaker community was formally "ordered" in New Lebanon, New York. In the decades that followed, Shaker communities continued to flourish until their peak in approximately the 1840s, when Shakers numbered some 6,000 in nearly 20 communities. Today, the Shakers are all but extinct, though they bequeathed to American culture important traditions in arts and crafts. The longing for a millennial kingdom of order and purity that undergirded the Shakers' spiritual vision remains an important strand of American religious life.

Further Reading
Blinn, Henry Clay. *The Life and Gospel Experience of Mother Ann Lee.* East Canterbury, N.H.: Published by the Shakers, 1901.

Campion, Nardi Reeder. *Ann the Word: The Life of Mother Ann Lee, Founder of the Shakers.* Boston: Little, Brown, 1976.

Evans, F. W. *Ann Lee (The Founder of the Shakers): A Biography.* London: J. Burns, 1869.

Horowitz, Leslie Ann. "Women and Universal Salvation: Promise, Practice and Everyday Life in the Shakers, Universalists, and Universal Society of Friends, 1770–1820." Ph.D. dissertation, Cornell University, 2001.

Joy, A. F. *The Queen of the Shakers.* Minneapolis: T. S. Denison, 1960.

Stein, Stephen J. *The Shaker Experience in America.* New Haven, Conn.: Yale University Press, 1992.

Wright, Lucy. *The Gospel Monitor: A Little Book of Mother Ann's Word to Those Who Are Placed as Instructors & Care-takers of Children.* Canterbury, N.H.: n.p., 1843.

Lee, Jesse
(1758–1816) *Methodist minister*

Early Methodism in the United States spread primarily through the work of itinerant ministers who occupied no settled pulpit and often found their congregations in houses or fields or in front of courthouse steps. Methodism arrived in North America through missionaries from Great Britain, but its rapid diffusion across American society depended on indigenous apostles, and Jesse Lee was one of the most prominent of these during the final years of the 18th century and the first of the 19th. He was born on March 12, 1758, in Prince George County, Virginia. His parents, Nathaniel and Elizabeth Lee, were farmers and initially Anglicans who experienced religious conversions in 1772 and became Methodists two years later. Jesse Lee himself experienced conversion in 1773 and with his parents migrated to Methodism.

In the latter part of 1777, Lee moved to North Carolina to care for the farm of a relative recently widowed. While there, he began to teach Methodist classes and to hold prayer meetings in the area. On November 17, 1779, Lee preached his first sermon.

In the late summer of 1780, during the Revolutionary War, Lee was drafted to serve in the North Carolina militia, but this call to military service occasioned a crisis of conscience, for Lee believed that "as a Christian, and as a preacher of the gospel," he could not fight. He appeared before the military authorities and, after being briefly held under guard for refusing to take up arms, agreed to serve in various noncombatant positions, supplementing this work with ministry to his fellow soldiers as an informal chaplain. Toward the end of October, Lee was discharged from the militia.

Over the next several years, Jesse Lee served as an itinerant minister, preaching in a circuit across North Carolina and, later, Virginia and Maryland. In 1785, Lee traveled for a time as an assistant to FRANCIS ASBURY in his tour of the southern states. Asbury had recently been ordained bishop of the Methodist Episcopal Church, which had just been organized separately from its sister church in England. Toward the end of the decade, Lee directed his attention north and undertook an itinerant ministry in New England. There he preached and labored to establish the Methodist work in regions where Congregationalism had dominated religious life for more than a century and a half. He was ordained a deacon and an elder in 1790, a testimony to more than a decade of strenuous labor on behalf of Methodism.

In the last few years of the century, Francis Asbury again prevailed on Lee to accompany him as an assistant. For three years, beginning in 1797, the two men traveled widely together, tending to Methodist affairs. In 1800, they arrived together at the General Conference of Methodist preachers in Baltimore. After the conference voted to ordain a new bishop to assist Asbury, Jesse Lee was one of two men nominated for the position and only narrowly lost the election to the other candidate.

Though Lee never became a Methodist bishop, his influence and labors found other acknowledgments. From 1809 to 1813, he served as chaplain of the U.S. House of Representatives, and in 1814 he was elected chaplain of the U.S. Senate. His long association with Methodism in the United States gave him the background to write *A Short History of the Methodists, in the United States of America*, which was the first his-tory of Methodism in America and was published in 1810. Lee died on September 12, 1816, after contracting a cold at a Methodist camp meeting in Hillsborough, Maryland, where he had preached a few days before.

Jesse Lee never married. With other early Methodist circuit-riding preachers, he believed that his calling as a traveling minister of the gospel was inconsistent with the obligations of a husband and a father. Instead, he became a father to Methodist congregations created both in the North and in the South, which he tended with indefatigable zeal for more than 35 years.

Further Reading

Bangs Nathan. *History of the Methodist Episcopal Church.* 4 vols. New York: T. Mason and G. Lane, 1838–1841. Available online. URL: http://www.ccel.org/b/bangs/index.html. Downloaded on April 26, 2002.

Lee, Jesse. *A Short History of the Methodists, in the United States of America.* Baltimore: Magill and Clime, 1810; Rutland, Vt.: Academy Books, 1974.

Lee, Leroy M. *The Life and Times of the Rev. Jesse Lee.* Charleston, S.C.: J. Early, for the Methodist Episcopal Church, South, 1848.

Meredith, William H. *Jesse Lee: A Methodist Apostle.* New York: Eaton & Mains, 1909.

Thrift, Minton. *Memoir of the Rev. Jesse Lee with Extracts from His Journals.* New York: N. Bangs and T. Mason, for the Methodist Episcopal Church, 1823; New York: Arno Press, 1969.

Leeser, Isaac

(1806–1868) *Jewish teacher, author*

Isaac Leeser's long career as a Jewish writer and teacher helped to establish traditional Jewish faith and practice in America. Though hostile to Reform Judaism, he embraced the United States as a place where Jews might take a central role in the regeneration of the human race. He was born on December 12, 1806, in Neuenkirchen, Westphalia, the son of Uri Lippman and Sarah Isaac Cohen Lippman. After the death of his mother in 1814, Lesser was raised by his paternal grandmother. Both she and his father died in 1820, and Leeser was thereafter sent to study in a school in Münster.

At the invitation of a maternal uncle who had immigrated to the United States, Leeser suspended his formal education when he was 18 years old and joined his uncle in Richmond, Virginia, where he worked in his uncle's general store. He supplemented this work with active involvement in Richmond's Beth Shalome congregation, where its *hazzan,* or religious leader, Isaac B. Seixas, taught Leeser the synagogue's Sephardic rituals. He also achieved a measure of prominence by defending Judaism in print from a series of anti-Semitic articles that appeared in a Richmond newspaper. This activity, especially, prompted congregation Mikveh Israel in Philadelphia, Pennsylvania, to invite Leeser to become its hazzan in 1829.

For the 21 years that Leeser served at Mikveh Israel, he assumed a prominent place both in the Jewish life of Philadelphia and in America generally. A teacher by nature, he struggled to make Jewish traditions accessible to American Jews through such innovative practices as delivering sermons in English. Even more important, though, he seized the written word to inform an audience far wider than his Philadelphia congregation. A stream of books flowed from his pen in the 1830s: *Instruction in the Mosaic Law* (1830), *The Jews and Mosaic Law* (1837), a multivolume series of prayer books published in 1837 and 1838, and the initial volumes of *Discourses on the Jewish Religion* published in 1838. The same decade he demonstrated his commitment to Jewish education by supporting REBECCA GRATZ's efforts to establish the first Jewish Sunday School program in America.

Leeser's literary efforts in the 1840s were equally prolific. Again, though opposed to the theological innovations beginning to take the form of Reform Judaism, Leeser was eager to provide resources of the Jewish faith for American Jews who could not read Hebrew. Thus, in 1845 he published an English translation of the Torah. The previous decade he had translated prayers and rituals of the Sephardic Jews into English. In 1848 he translated those of Ashkenazic Judaism as well. Of perhaps equal significance, he began publication in 1843 of a monthly newspaper, *The Occident and*

Isaac Leeser, though never ordained as a rabbi, was a prominent Jewish leader during the 19th century, who is sometimes referred to as the father of Conservative Judaism. *(Library of Congress, Prints and Photographs Division LC-USZ62-97922)*

American Jewish Advocate, for which he served as editor until his death 25 years later.

Leeser was never trained as a rabbi, and his undertaking of activities such as preaching normally reserved for rabbis disturbed some members of his Philadelphia congregation. In 1850, he ended his career at Mikveh Israel and devoted the next seven years to writing and lecturing. During this period he completed his translation of the Hebrew Bible into English. In 1857 supporters from his previous Philadelphia congregation organized a new synagogue, the congregation Beth El Emeth, and made Leeser its hazzan.

In the final years of his life Leeser undertook one more significant project. Convinced of the need for American-trained rabbis, Leeser took the lead in establishing the country's first rabbinical school in 1867—Philadelphia's Maimonides College. He died soon afterward, on February 1, 1868, in Philadelphia, and the college survived only a few years after the loss of his influence.

Though Conservative Judaism, as a mediating theological position between the Orthodox and Reform traditions of Judaism, did not take formal shape until the 20th century, Isaac Leeser has sometimes been called its father. Although he was moored to the essential theological tenets and traditions of Orthodox Judaism, Leeser was eager to help Jewish faith flourish in the United States. To this end, he was prepared to embrace innovations such as sermons in the vernacular and translations of Jewish religious texts to the extent that these might assist American Jews in maintaining allegiance to their spiritual legacy.

Further Reading

Englander, Henry. "Isaac Leeser." *Yearbook of the Central Conference of American Rabbis* 28 (1918): 213–52.

Lesser, Isaac. *Catechism for Younger Children.* Philadelphia: Adam Waldie, 1839.

———. *Discourses, Argumentative and Devotional, on the Subject of the Jewish Religion,* 3 vols. Philadelphia: n.p., 1837–41.

———. *The Jews and the Mosaic Law.* Philadelphia: n.p., 1834.

Seller, Maxine. "Isaac Leeser's Views on the Restoration of a Jewish Palestine." *American Jewish Historical Quarterly* 58 (September 1968): 118–35.

Sussman, Lance Jonathan. *Isaac Leeser and the Making of American Judaism.* Detroit, Mich.: Wayne State University Press, 1995.

Whiteman, Maxwell. "Isaac Leeser and the Jews of Philadelphia." *Publications of the American Jewish Historical Society* 48 (June 1959): 207–44.

Leland, John
(1754–1841) *Baptist minister*

A fiery Baptist evangelist of the Revolutionary War era, John Leland was the implacable foe of government entanglements with religion. He championed religious liberty and religious disestablishment through the Revolutionary generation. He was born on May 14, 1754, in Grafton, Massachusetts, the son of James Leland and Lucy Warren Leland. Raised in the Congregational Church, Leland experienced a religious conversion in 1772 and was subsequently rebaptized in a Baptist church in Bellingham, Massachusetts. Licensed to preach by the Bellingham church in 1775, he carried his evangelistic message between New England and Virginia over the next few years. In the fall of 1776, he married Sally Divine, with whom he had seven children.

By 1778 Leland had been ordained and had settled in Orange County, Virginia, where he ministered to a circuit of churches in the vicinity. In Virginia he faced the long-standing governmental support of the Anglican Church and the official harassments visited on dissenting Protestants, such as the Baptists. This experience made him an ardent champion of religious liberty and a vigorous opponent of religious establishments, especially those that took the form of official public support for preferred Christian denominations. Leland's positions on these issues eventually cast him into a political alliance with his fellow Virginians James Madison and Thomas Jefferson, who both worked vigorously during the 1780s to untangle church-state relations in Virginia. Leland's exact participation in this campaign is unclear, but it is known that Virginia Baptists, joined with Presbyterians in the state, backed efforts to dissolve the official support for the Anglican Church. They worked as well for the adoption as state law of the Bill for Establishing Religious Liberty drafted by Jefferson and championed in the Virginia legislature by James Madison. This bill, enacted by the legislature in 1786, abolished taxes for support of religious teachers and institutions.

According to tradition, Leland's path crossed that of James Madison again after the Constitutional Convention proposed the Constitution for ratification by the states. Virginia Baptists were initially cool toward the Constitution, since it contained no explicit guarantee of religious liberty. At least some evidence suggests that Leland and Madison may have met in Orange County after the convention and that Madison was able to win Leland's support for the Constitution. In any event, shortly afterward Madison, by a narrow margin, was elected a delegate to the Virginia convention, which debated and ultimately ratified the Constitution. Baptists almost certainly played a significant role in his victory.

In 1791, Leland moved from Virginia to Massachusetts, where he discovered a Congregational establishment in New England paralleling that of the Anglicans that had flourished in Virginia. He settled in Cheshire, Massachusetts, and he remained there for the rest of his life, conducting an itinerant preaching ministry to churches in the vicinity but also devoting copious energy to protests of the Congregational establishment. The year he arrived in Massachusetts, he wrote the tract *The Rights of Conscience Inalienable, and Therefore Religious Opinions Not Cognizable by Law: or, The High-Flying Churchman, Stript of His Legal Robe, Appears a Yahoo*, in which he defended the case of religious liberty:

> Every man must give account of himself to God, and therefore every man ought to be at liberty to serve God in a way that he can best reconcile to his conscience. If government can answer for individuals at the day of judgement, let men be controlled by it in religious matters; otherwise, let men be free.

Later, he discharged another written salvo against tax support for religion, *The Yankee Spy, Calculated for the Religious Meridian of Massachusetts* (1794). Leland, after a long career as a Baptist minister, died on January 14, 1841, in Cheshire, Massachusetts.

In an autobiographical sketch penned late in life, John Leland suggested that "[n]ext to the salvation of the soul the civil and religious rights of men have summoned my attention, more than the acquisition of wealth or seats of honor." History remembers Leland most for his implacable opposition to entanglement of government and religious institutions. As did many other Baptists of the period, he opposed tax support of religion and insisted that the state had no business attempting to prop up religious teachers and institutions with public funds. This insistence was his most important legacy to the history of American religious life.

Further Reading

Boland, Martha Jo Eleam. "Render unto Caesar: Sources of the Political Thought of John Leland." Ph.D. dissertation, New Orleans Baptist Theological Seminary, 1997.

Butterfield, L. H. "Elder John Leland, Jeffersonian Itinerant." *Proceedings of the American Antiquarian Society* (1952): 151–242.

Congdon, Dale R. *A Leland Journey: An Historic Account of the Elder John Leland and Lemuel Leland Families, with Excursions into the Lives of the Families Case, Goodwin, Nickerson, Noble, Powell, and Wilder.* New Hope, Minn.: Dale R. Congdon, 1998.

Fearheiley, Don M. *The John Leland Story.* Nashville: Broadman Press, 1964.

Greene, L. F., ed. *The Writings of the Late Elder John Leland.* Lanesboro, Mass.: G. W. Wood, 1845; New York: Arno Press, 1969.

Hostetler, Michael J. "Liberty in Baptist Thought: Three Primary Texts, 1614–1856." *American Baptist Quarterly* 15(1996): 242–56.

Lewis, Edwin
(1881–1959) *Methodist theologian, educator*

Edwin Lewis followed a spiritual migration from liberalism to neoorthodoxy, from, as he described it himself, "philosophy to revelation." In this migration he traveled ground familiar to many liberal Protestant thinkers whose estimation of human potential was disillusioned by events of World War I and the Great Depression. Lewis was born on April 18, 1881, in Newbury, England, the son of Joseph Lewis and Sarah Newman Lewis. In his late teens he served as a Methodist missionary to Labrador. Subsequently he studied at Sackville College and Middlebury College before receiving a bachelor of divinity degree from Drew Theological Seminary in 1908. While in college, in 1904 he married Louise Newhook Frost, with whom he had five children. In 1915, Lewis received a B.A. from New York State College for Teachers; three years later, he completed a Th.D. at Drew Theological Seminary. He became a naturalized U.S. citizen in 1916.

In 1920 Edwin Lewis joined the faculty of Drew Theological Seminary, and he remained there for more than 30 years, until his retirement in 1951. Although he began his career as a seminary professor securely in the ranks of theological liberalism, he soon veered sharply toward more orthodox views. This transformation chiefly resulted from his appointment as coeditor of the *Abington*

Bible Commentary. He later described this period in his article "From Philosophy to Revelation," published in *Christian Century* in 1939:

> During the three years during which the Commentary was in process, I was under necessity of living with the Bible daily. Whether I would or not, it was my meat and drink, and the experience revolutionized my thinking. . . . I found myself faced with the Word of God, given it is true, by slow processes through the words of men, but a last in Christ, "made flesh." The Creator appeared as the Redeemer. He who acted in the primal miracle of creation acted again in the miracle of redemption. I saw that this must be either true or not true. If it be not true, then have we nothing but the confusions of naturalism. But if it be true—as it must be true if we are to have enduring hope—it can be true only as something revealed, not as something discovered. Creation and the incarnation are alike acts of God, and each has its meaning, but we know the act and we know the meaning because, and only because, they have been *disclosed* to us.

Lewis's retreat from philosophical speculation about God to a focus on God's disclosure of himself to the world mirrored the rise of neoorthodox theology in Europe and America in the years after World War I. Liberalism's confidence in human possibilities was less convincing to many theologians chastened by the experience of world war. These theologians, led especially by German thinkers such as Karl Barth and Emil Brunner, abandoned liberalism in favor of neoorthodoxy. Lewis's own theological transformation could be seen in the difference between his first book, *Jesus Christ and the Human Quest* (1924), and *A Christian Manifesto* (1934), published a decade later. The first held up Jesus as a model for the universal human quest; the second declared that Christianity was concerned with God's quest for us rather than our quest for God.

Lewis retired from Drew Theological Seminary in 1951, and two years later his first wife died. He subsequently married Josephine Stults. After his retirement from Drew, he taught as a visiting professor at Temple University School of Theology in Philadelphia, Pennsylvania, for three years. He died on November 28, 1959, in Morristown, New Jersey.

Theological liberals of the late 19th and early 20th centuries largely drained religion of its supernatural elements. The notion that God might intrude himself into the evolutionary progress of human history seemed a quaint relic of a preenlightened past. In the somber wake of a world war and the economic depression that followed on its heels, however, the essentially optimistic temper of liberalism seemed itself discredited, at least to observers such as Edwin Lewis. To this general historical climate Lewis had added the specific career circumstance of editing a Bible commentary. This experience exposed him to a sustained encounter with the Bible itself, an encounter that weaned him from liberalism and left him with an abiding conviction that Christianity was at its core a supernatural religion.

Further Reading

Hardwick, Charley D. "Edwin Lewis: Introductory and Critical Remarks." *Drew Gateway* 33 (Winter 1963): 91–104.

Lewis, Edwin. *The Biblical Faith and Christian Freedom.* Philadelphia: Westminster Press, 1953.

———. *A Christian Manifesto.* New York: Abingdon, 1934.

———. "From Philosophy to Revelation." *Christian Century* 56 (June 1939): 762–64.

———. *A Philosophy of the Christian Revelation.* New York: Harper & Brothers, 1940.

Mallow, Vernon R. *The Demonic, a Selected Theological Study: An Examination into the Theology of Edwin Lewis, Karl Barth, and Paul Tillich.* Lanham, Md.: University Press of America, 1983.

Seamands, Stephen A. *Christology and Transition in the Theology of Edwin Lewis.* Lanham, Md.: University Press of America, 1987.

Lipscomb, David
(1831–1917) *Disciples of Christ editor, educator*

One of the most prominent leaders among the Disciples of Christ during the last decades of the

19th century, David Lipscomb influenced the Disciples chiefly through his editing of the *Gospel Advocate* for nearly half a century. He also advanced the cause of Christian education by founding the Nashville Bible School. Lipscomb was born on January 21, 1831, in Franklin County, Tennessee, the son of Granville Lipscomb and Nancy Lipscomb. When he was four years old, his family moved to Illinois, but on the death of Lipscomb's mother soon afterward, Lipscomb's father returned the family to Tennessee in 1836. David Lipscomb experienced an evangelical religious conversion when he was 14 years old, and he was baptized in a Disciples of Christ church. Subsequently, he attended Franklin College in Nashville, Tennessee, from which he graduated in 1849. After college, he worked for two years as the manager of a plantation in Georgia and then returned to Tennessee, where he took up the life of a farmer.

By the mid-1850s, however, Lipscomb had become a lay preacher for the Disciples of Christ. In the summer of 1862, he married Margaret Zelner, with whom he had one child, who died in infancy. In 1866, after the Civil War, Lipscomb became coeditor with Tolbert Fanning of the *Gospel Advocate,* a Disciples paper that Fanning had helped establish in the 1850s and that became a leading paper of the Disciples of Christ. Fanning soon left the paper and Lipscomb became its editor in chief.

Lipscomb used the pages of the *Gospel Advocate* to advance positions characteristic of more conservative Disciples, who rejected all ecclesiastical innovations not authorized by the New Testament. He opposed with special vehemence various religious associations, including missionary societies, and the use of instrumental music in Christian worship. On the latter point, he saw no evidence of instrumental music in the New Testament, and therefore he insisted that Christians should not insert this innovation into worship services. In an article in the *Gospel Advocate* dated September 11, 1873, he asked why churches stopped at the organ. If the organ could be used as a substitute for singing, why should not beads be used as a substitute for praying? Lipscomb also used his pulpit in the lines of the *Gospel Advocate* to insist on pacifism among

Christians. He argued in the *Gospel Advocate* in December 1866, for example, that the only scriptural duty of Christians with respect to governments was the obligation of submission. "There is not a word of information in the sacred Scriptures that suggest it is the duty of any Christian to support, maintain, or defend any institution or organization of man, further than a quiet, passive, but conscientious and faithful submission to its requirements."

During the 1880s, Lipscomb turned his attention to the subject of Christian education. He helped establish the Fanning Orphan Home in 1884 and served on its board of directors for the remainder of his life. At the beginning of the following decade, he launched another educational venture, establishing the Nashville Bible School, an institution later renamed David Lipscomb University, in the fall of 1891. Over the following years, Lipscomb divided his energies among teaching at the school, preaching to Disciples of Christ churches, and editing the *Gospel Advocate,* until his retirement in 1913. He died on November 11, 1917, in Nashville.

During David Lipscomb's long career as a leader among the Disciples of Christ, the movement that began in the 1830s gradually began to fracture. Lipscomb was the most prominent voice among the more conservative Disciples, characterized, for example, by their steadfast objections to instrumental music in the church. Partially through Lipscomb's prodding, the U.S. Census Bureau formally recognized the fracture among Disciples in 1906 by allowing census respondents to declare their affiliation with either the Disciples of Christ (also known as the Christian Church) or the more conservative Churches of Christ. Sometimes referred to as the "bishop of the Southern Disciples of Christ"—though the Disciples had no bishops—David Lipscomb never swerved from his commitment to seeing the Christian church purged of its accretions and restored to its primitive purity.

Further Reading

Hooper, Robert E. *Crying in the Wilderness: A Biography of David Lipscomb.* Nashville: David Lipscomb College, 1979.

Lipscomb, David. *Salvation from Sin.* Edited by J. W. Shepherd. Nashville: McQuiddy Printing Company, 1913.

Richardson, Robert Randolph. "Speaking Where the Bible Speaks: The Rhetoric of the American Restoration Movement." Ph.D. dissertation, Wayne State University, 1994.

West, Earl Irvin. *The Life and Times of David Lipscomb.* Henderson, Tenn.: Religious Book Service, 1954.

M

Machen, John Gresham
(1881–1937) *Presbyterian theologian*

A central figure in the clash between liberalism and fundamentalism in the early 20th century, J. Gresham Machen waged a vigorous campaign against theological modernism. As a result of this conflict, he was cast out of the mainstream Presbyterian denomination and driven to start a new, more conservative, denomination of Presbyterians. John Gresham Machen was born on July 28, 1881, in Baltimore, Maryland, the son of Arthur Webster Machen and Mary Gresham Machen. Raised in a climate of southern affluence, Machen received an undergraduate education from Johns Hopkins University, from which he graduated first in his class in 1901 with a major in the classics. After an additional year of graduate study at Johns Hopkins, Machen began a joint course of study of philosophy at Princeton University and of divinity at Princeton Theological Seminary. He received an M.A. and a B.D. in 1904 and 1905, respectively. Encouraged to pursue an academic career, Machen spent a year in Germany, studying at Marburg and Göttingen.

On his return to the United States, Machen accepted a position as an instructor of New Testament studies at Princeton Theological Seminary. By 1914 he had been ordained a minister in the Presbyterian Church (U.S.A), and had received a regular appointment on the faculty of the seminary. There, apart from work as secretary of the Young Men's Christian Association (YMCA) in France during World War I (from 1917 to 1919), Machen labored until 1929.

From his seat in mainline Presbyterianism's most illustrious seminary, Machen soon began a scholarly campaign against assaults on such tenets of Christian orthodoxy as the virgin birth of Christ. By the early 1920s, he had lain siege to the encroachments of theological liberalism, insisting that orthodox Christianity differed fundamentally from its modern counterfeits. Above all, he declared, Christianity had at its center not simply a way of life but a historical message. In *Christianity and Liberalism* (1923), he attempted to elaborate this distinction.

> It is perfectly clear, then, that the first Christian missionaries did not simply come forward with an exhortation; they did not say: "Jesus of Nazareth lived a wonderful life of filial piety, and we call upon you our hearers to yield yourselves, as we have done, to the spell of that life." Certainly that is what modern historians would have expected the first Christian missionaries to say, but it must be recognized that as a matter of fact they said nothing of the kind. . . . The great weapon with which the disciples of Jesus set out to conquer the world was not a mere comprehension of eternal principles; it was an historical message, an account of something that had recently happened, it was the message, "He is risen."

In spite of his efforts, Machen proved unsuccessful at directing the course of either his seminary or his denomination down more conservative paths. By 1929 he had left Princeton and helped to organize Westminster Theological Seminary. A few years later, disturbed at waning orthodoxy among Presbyterian missionaries, he helped established the Independent Board of Presbyterian Foreign Missions in 1933. This act, especially, put him in direct conflict with his denomination. In 1934, the General Assembly of the Presbyterian Church (U.S.A) ordered Machen to abandon his association with the independent missions board. When he declined to do so, he was charged with contempt for church authority and stripped of his ordination in March 1935. Those disgruntled with Machen's treatment at the hands of the Presbyterian Church (U.S.A.) soon joined him in forming a new Presbyterian denomination. In the summer of 1936 Machen and other like-minded Presbyterians established the Presbyterian Church in America, later renamed the Orthodox Presbyterian Church. Machen, though, lived only a little more than a year after the new denomination's creation. While on a trip to Bismanck, North Dakota, he died there of pneumonia on January 1, 1937.

J. Gresham Machen was a founder of what came to be known in the early 20th century as fundamentalism. Convinced of the Bible's inerrancy, and of the truth of historic Christian doctrines such as the resurrection of Jesus and his virgin birth, Machen and others waged a rearguard action against the encroachments of theological modernity. In contrast with "fundamentalist" stereotypes, Machen was educated and erudite. But his learning had little sympathy for the predominant currents of modern theological thought. Thus, while mainstream Protestants were preoccupied with ecumenical efforts, Machen and other theological conservatives found it necessary to chart a different spiritual course, one that added new fragments to the already fractured life of Protestant Christianity in America.

Further Reading

Bratt, James D. "Abraham Kuyper, J. Gresham Machen, and the Dynamics of Reformed Anti-Modernism." *Journal of Presbyterian History* 75 (1997): 247–58.
Coray, Henry W. *J. Gresham Machen: A Silhouette.* Grand Rapids, Mich.: Kregel Publications, 1981.
Hart, D. G. *Defending the Faith: J. Gresham Machen and the Crisis of Conservative Protestantism in Modern America.* Baltimore: Johns Hopkins University Press, 1994.
Machen, J. Gresham. *The Christian Faith in the Modern World.* New York: Macmillan, 1936.
———. *Christianity and Liberalism.* New York: Macmillan, 1923.
———. *Historic Christianity: Selections from the Writings of J. Gresham Machen.* Edited by Stanley A. Mansfield, Carey C. Olson, and John H. Skilton. Philadelphia: Skilton House Ministries, Sowers Publication, 1997.
———. *What Is Christianity? and Other Addresses.* Edited by Ned Bernard Stonehouse. Grand Rapids, Mich.: W. B. Eerdmans, 1951.
Stonehouse, Ned Bernard. *J. Gresham Machen: A Biographical Memoir.* Grand Rapids, Mich.: Eerdmans, 1954.

Macintosh, Douglas Clyde
(1877–1948) *Baptist theologian, educator*

Though Douglas Clyde Macintosh intended early in his life to become a Baptist minister, a study of philosophy and theology turned his vocational interests toward teaching instead. As a consequence, he became a prominent liberal theologian of the 20th century. Macintosh was born on February 18, 1877, in Breadalbane, Ontario, Canada, the son of Peter Macintosh and Elizabeth Charlotte Everett Macintosh. His parents were evangelical religious believers, and Macintosh experienced a religious conversion and joined a local Baptist church when he was 14 years old. He enrolled in McMaster University in Toronto, Ontario, in 1899 and graduated with a B.A. in 1903. Although Macintosh had entered this Baptist institution to prepare himself for a ministerial career, by the time of his graduation he had decided to become an academic instead. To pursue this new vocational ambition, Macintosh entered the University of Chicago in 1904 and received a Ph.D. from that institution in 1909. During his years at Chicago, he was ordained a Baptist minister.

While he was completing his Ph.D. dissertation, Macintosh held a position as professor of biblical and systematic theology at Brandon College in Manitoba, Canada, from 1907 to 1909. Beginning in 1909, however, he joined the faculty of Yale University. He remained there, apart from brief absences, until his retirement in 1942. One of the absences occurred during World War I, when Macintosh received leave from Yale to serve as a chaplain for the Canadian army and then for the Young Men's Christian Association (YMCA) in Europe. He also took a leave of absence to teach at the University of Chicago first in 1919 and then again in 1923. In 1921, Macintosh married Emily Powell, who died in childbirth less than two years later. In 1925, he married Hope Griswold Conklin. The couple did not have any children.

Though Macintosh spent most of his adult life in the United States, he never became a U.S. citizen. When he attempted to enter the United States to assume his position at Yale, he encountered the first of the difficulties that his Canadian citizenship would present. After he announced to an immigration officer that he had a job waiting for him in New Haven, Connecticut, the officer almost prevented him from crossing into the country. Eventually, though, the officer asked Macintosh what he would be doing in New Haven, and when the young Canadian man indicated he would be a professor at Yale University, the immigration official responded, "That is all right. I thought you said you were coming over to work." When Macintosh later applied for U.S. citizenship in 1925, he became the subject of a celebrated case before the Supreme Court. His citizenship application required him to indicate whether he would be willing to bear arms in defense of the United States. Macintosh responded, "Yes, but I would like to be free to judge of the necessity." This application did not satisfy naturalization officials, who denied Macintosh's citizenship application. When Macintosh challenged this denial in court, the U.S. Supreme Court eventually decided in *United States v. Macintosh* (1931) that Macin-

tosh's constitutional rights had not been violated by this action. Macintosh therefore remained a Canadian citizen for the rest of his life.

At Yale, Macintosh became known for his interest in empirical theology. He attempted to plot a middle course between those who disconnected religious truth completely from religious experience and those who found no room at all in the age of science for religious experience. He remained active as a university professor and a scholar until he suffered a stroke in 1942 that forced him to retire from Yale. He died in Hamden, Connecticut, on July 6, 1948.

Though securely settled into the mainstream of 20th-century Protestant liberalism, Douglas Clyde Macintosh attempted to articulate what he called an "untraditional orthodoxy." In particular, he believed that religion could be investigated empirically and that the results of this investigation would demonstrate the truth of Christianity. His development of this theological approach, along with the celebrated pacifism that prevented him from becoming a U.S. citizen, made him a prominent figure in American religious history during the first half of the 20th century.

Further Reading

Grubbs, Gayle Gudger. "Irony, Innocence, and Myth: Douglas C. Macintosh's Untraditional Orthodoxy." Ph.D. dissertation, Rice University, 1996.

Heim, S. Mark. "The Path of a Liberal Pilgrim: A Theological Biography of Douglas Clyde Macintosh." *American Baptist Quarterly* 2 (September, 1983): 236–56.

Macintosh, Douglas Clyde. *Personal Religion.* New York: C. Scribner's Sons, 1942.

———. *Religious Realism.* New York: Macmillan, 1931.

———. *Social Religion.* New York: C. Scribner's Sons, 1939.

———. "Toward a New Untraditional Orthodoxy." In *Contemporary American Theology: Theological Autobiographies,* vol. I. Edited by Vergilius Ferm. New York: Round Table Press, 1932.

Warren, Preston. *Out of the Wilderness: Douglas Clyde Macintosh's Journeys Through the Grounds and Claims of Modern Thought.* New York: Peter Lang, 1989.

Magnes, Judah Leon
(1877–1948) *rabbi, educator*

Judah Leon Magnes presided over the earliest years of the Hebrew University in Jerusalem as its first chancellor and later as its first president. His successful administration of this institution was partially overshadowed by his controversial opposition to the creation of an independent Jewish state in Palestine. He was born on July 5, 1877, in San Francisco, California, the son of David Magnes and Sophia Abrahamson Magnes. Judah Magnes's parents were members of a Reform Jewish congregation, and from 1894 he attended Reform Judaism's most prominent institution, the Hebrew Union College in Cincinnati, Ohio, and the University of Cincinnati. He received a B.A. in 1898 and two years later was ordained a rabbi. Thereafter, he pursued graduate studies in Germany; he received a Ph.D. from the University of Heidelberg in 1902.

From 1904 to 1910, Magnes served a series of Jewish congregations as rabbi: Temple Israel in Brooklyn, New York, from 1904 to 1906; Temple Emanuel in New York from 1907 to 1910; and B'nai Jeshurun in New York briefly thereafter. He married Beatrice Lowenstein in 1908; with her he had three children. Almost from the beginning of his rabbinical career, Magnes plunged into the broader currents of Jewish religious and cultural life. From 1905 to 1908, he served as secretary of the Federation of American Zionists. More significantly, in 1909 he conceived and guided the creation of the New York Kehillah (community), an attempt to unite the fragmented Jewish community in New York in the service of an ambitious range of educational and social projects such as crime prevention. Magnes directed this organization from its inception in 1909 until its dissolution in 1922.

For much of his life, Judah Magnes occupied prominent roles of leadership within important Jewish institutions even as he alienated members of the Jewish community by the positions he took on controversial issues. His outspoken pacifism during World War I was an early case in point, and he maintained this position even though it cost him support among New York Jews and probably hastened the collapse of the Kehillah, to whose

creation and leadership he had devoted considerable energy.

By the mid-1920s, however, Magnes had found a new object of his attention. Through this period, he maintained important relationship with key Jewish leaders in the United States, and he traded on these relationships to help realize the creation of the Hebrew University in Jerusalem. His American contacts also secured for him the position as the university's first chancellor, a post he held from 1925 to 1935, and subsequently as president—an honorary position—from 1935 until his death. For the decade he was chancellor, Magnes poured himself into the work of structuring the original academic program of the university and raising funds to support its programs.

Even while Judah Magnes successfully shepherded the Hebrew University through its earliest years, however, he quickly placed himself at odds with the Zionist movement, which sought to create an independent state for Jews in Palestine. Committed to peace between Arabs and Jews, Magnes took the immensely unpopular position of opposing the creation of a Jewish state. Instead, he insisted that Jews press for increased immigration to Palestine and for settlement rights. Together with Jewish philosopher and theologian Martin Buber, Magnes was convinced that lasting peace between Arabs and Jews could not be accomplished through the formation of a separate Jewish state in Palestine, and that this Zionist aspiration would simply ignite perpetual war. He died in New York City on October 27, 1948, while on an unofficial mission to obtain Jewish support for a United Nations proposal to secure peace between Jews and Arabs in Palestine.

Rabbi Judah Leon Magnes lived to see the creation of Israel in 1948 as an independent state in Palestine, in spite of his best efforts to forestall this historic event. His opposition to this most cherished ambition of the Zionist movement alienated him from a broad spectrum of the international Jewish community. Had he commanded more popular influence, then historians might have devoted attention to him as a minor spoiler of Jewish nationalism. But in spite of Magnes's significant contributions to the history of Palestine through his early superintendence of the Hebrew

University, his opposition to the creation of Israel has led most historians to neglect him.

Further Reading

Bentwich, Norman De Mattos. *For Zion's Sake: A Biography of Judah L. Magnes, First Chancellor and First President of the Hebrew University of Jerusalem.* Philadelphia: Jewish Publication Society of America, 1954.

Biale, David. *Judah L. Magnes, Pioneer and Prophet on Two Continents: A Pictorial Biography.* Berkeley, Calif.: Judah L. Magnes Memorial Museum, 1977.

Brinner, William M., and Moses Rischin, eds. *Like All the Nations? The Life and Legacy of Judah L. Magnes.* Albany: State University of New York Press, 1987.

Kotzin, Daniel Phillip. "An American Jewish Radical: Judah L. Magnes, American Jewish Identity, and Jewish Nationalism in America and Mandatory Palestine." Ph.D. dissertation, New York University, 1998.

———. "An Attempt to Americanize the *Yishuv:* Judah L. Magnes in Mandatory Palestine," Israel Studies. Available online. URL: http://iupjournals.org/israel/iss5-1.html. Downloaded on November 27, 2001.

Magnes, Judah Leon. *Dissenter in Zion: From the Writings of Judah L. Magnes.* Edited by Arthur A. Goren. Cambridge, Mass.: Harvard University Press, 1982.

———. *In the Perplexity of the Times.* Jerusalem: The Hebrew University, 1946.

Mahan, Asa

(1799–1889) *Congregationalist minister, educator*

As the first president of Oberlin College in Ohio, Asa Mahan presided over that institution's early achievements. Oberlin occupies a prominent position in the history of American education because it admitted both male and female students, and because it admitted African-American students alongside whites. Mahan was born on November 9, 1799, in Vernon, New York, the son of Samuel Mahan and Anna Dana Mahan. When he was 17, he experienced a religious conversion, which he described in his autobiography:

[W]hen alone with God, I bowed the knee before Him and confessed that I had no right to ask or expect any favour at His hands, and that my whole eternity hung upon His mere grace and mercy. One favour I would venture to ask, that I might be kept from ever returning to that state of alienation from Him in which my life had been spent, and that I might have grace to appreciate His love, excellence, and glory; to love and venerate Him, and have a sacred respect for His will. If He would grant me this, I would accept of anything in time and eternity that He might appoint me. . . . I had no sooner pronounced these words than I was consciously encircled in the "everlasting arms." I was so overshadowed with a sense of the manifested love of a forgiving God and Saviour that my whole mental being seemed to be dissolved and pervaded with an ineffable quietude and assurance. I arose from my knees without a doubt that I was an adopted member of the family of God. With "the peace of God, which passeth all understanding," pervading every department of my mental nature, I could look upward, and, without a cloud between my soul and the face of God, could and did exclaim, "My Father and my God!" Such was my entrance into the inner life.

Subsequently, Mahan attended Hamilton College in New York, from which he graduated in 1824. Intent on becoming a minister, he completed his theological training at Andover Theological Seminary in Massachusetts in 1827. The following year he married Mary Hartwell Dix, with whom he had seven children.

Ordained a Congregational minister in 1829, Mahan began his ministerial career as a pastor of a Congregational church in Pittsford, New York, from 1829 to 1831; he then led the Sixth Presbyterian Church (later Vine Street Congregational Church) in Cincinnati, Ohio, from 1831 to 1835. While in Cincinnati, he served on the board of trustees of Lane Seminary there. In 1835, when the board responded to student agitation against slavery by prohibiting further discussion of the issue, Mahan cast the lone dissenting vote against this policy. The majority of the student body withdrew from Lane and enrolled in the recently established Oberlin Collegiate Institute (later Oberlin College) and Mahan was named the institution's first president. Oberlin became nationally prominent for its coeducational admissions and its admission of African-American students along with whites. With CHARLES GRANDISON FINNEY, the famous revival preacher who joined the faculty at Oberlin in the same year that Mahan assumed its presidency, Mahan emphasized the possibility of spiritual perfection. To these men, this theological vision also emphasized the possibility of social reform. Conflicts with faculty, however, ultimately led to Mahan's resignation as president in 1850.

After leaving Oberlin, Mahan moved to Cleveland, Ohio, where he helped to found Cleveland University and served as its president until the institution closed in 1855. Subsequently he was pastor of churches in Jackson and Adrian, Michigan, before serving as the first president of Adrian College from 1860 to 1871. After the death of his first wife in 1863, Mahan married Mary E. Munsell in 1866. In 1874 Mahan moved to England, where he spent the last 15 years of his life. He had long been associated with the Holiness movement, and in England he became a regular speaker at the annual Keswick Conference. He edited the newspaper *The Divine Light* from 1877 to 1889. He died on April 4, 1889, in Eastbourne, England.

Oberlin College exemplified the association of revivalism with social reform common in the middle years of the 19th century, and Asa Mahan's tenure as the institution's first president placed him firmly within this progressive evangelical tradition. In the years after he left Oberlin, he remained prominent as a spokesman for perfectionist theology. Though less well known than Charles G. Finney, who taught at Oberlin while Mahan presided over its affairs and who later became president himself, Asa Mahan continues to be revered as an eloquent spokesman for the modern descendants of the 19th-century Holiness movement.

Further Reading

Madden, Edward H., and James E. Hamilton. *Freedom and Grace: The Life of Asa Mahan.* Metuchen, N.J.: Scarecrow Press, 1982.

Mahan, Asa. *Autobiography: Intellectual, Moral, and Spiritual.* New York: AMS Press, 1979.
———. *Doctrine of the Will.* New York: AMS Press, 1979.
———. *Out of Darkness into Light.* New York: Garland, 1985.
———. *A System of Intellectual Philosophy.* Rev. and enlarged from the 2d ed. New York: A. S. Barnes, 1854.

Makemie, Francis
(ca.1658–ca.1708) *Presbyterian minister*

The father of Presbyterianism in America, Francis Makemie helped organize the first presbytery in the colonies and served as its first moderator. He also gained some notoriety after he was arrested on the order of New York's unpopular governor, Lord Cornbury; tried for preaching without a license; and eventually acquitted by a sympathetic jury. Important dates in Makemie's life are uncertain. He was born in County Donegal, Ireland, in approximately 1658 to parents of Scottish ancestry, of whom nothing else is known. He entered the University of Glasgow in 1676, was licensed to preach in 1681 or 1682, and was ordained in 1682.

In 1683, Makemie migrated to North America, where he took up an itinerant preaching career in Maryland, Virginia, and North Carolina. By 1687, he had settled in Accomack County, Virginia. In the next decade he married Naomi Anderson, with whom he had two daughters. He traveled to London toward the close of the 1680s and solicited ministerial support there for the colonies. During the decade of the 1690s he appears to have spent most of his time tending trading interests and preaching in Barbados, a regular stop on the route of ships traveling between England and the colonies. At the end of that decade, his wife's father died, and the couple inherited sizable holdings in Virginia.

At the junction of the 17th and 18th centuries, the Presbyterian Makemie was happy to cooperate with other Protestants, including Anglicans, to present a united face against Catholicism. Over the next few years, though, Anglican authorities made a concerted effort to expand the influence of the Church of England in the colonies, especially through the Society for the Propagation of the Gospel, which was founded in 1701. Presbyterians such as Makemie soon began to feel the pinch of Anglican orthodoxy. To respond to new threats against their religious liberties, Makemie encouraged other Presbyterian ministers in Maryland, Virginia, Delaware, and Pennsylvania to form the first American presbytery in 1706, and his ministerial colleagues elected him moderator of the infant presbytery.

The following year, Makemie and John Hampton, another Presbyterian minister, made a trip to New York, where they requested from the colonial governor, Edward Hyde, Lord Cornbury, a license to preach in New York's Dutch and French Reformed churches. Cornbury refused, eager to see Anglicanism established as the colonial religion. When Makemie and his colleague defied Cornbury by preaching in a house—with the doors propped open—Cornbury had the two arrested for preaching without a license. Charges against Hampton were ultimately dropped, but after several months Makemie stood trial before a jury, which promptly acquitted him. Even then, Cornbury attempted to make Makemie pay for the expenses of his imprisonment and trial, but the New York assembly passed a law the following year prohibiting the charge of such expenses to innocent parties. Cornbury later complained that Makemie was a "Jack of all Trades he is a Preacher, a Doctor of Physick, a Merchant, an Attorney, or Counsellor at Law, and, which is worse of all, a Disturber of Governments." But Cornbury's treatment of Makemie was of a piece with his general reputation for corruption and overreaching, a reputation that would eventually cause him to be jailed briefly for debt and recalled as colonial governor.

Makemie, for his part, was vindicated by the jury and praised by at least some of his contemporaries. During the trial, he had insisted that his license to preach in Virginia was sufficient to allow him to preach in New York as well. Though he might have appealed to the 1689 Act of Toleration, which commanded Anglican authorities to refrain from persecuting dissenting groups, Makemie insisted that he had no need of the act since the authority of the Church of England did not extend to the colonies. COTTON MATHER, Boston's famous Puritan preacher, spoke warmly of Makemie in the wake of his trial: "That brave man, Mr. Makemie, has after a famous Trial at N. York, bravely triumphed over the Act of Uniformity, and the other Poenal Lawes for the Ch. of England. . . . The Non-Con [formist] Religion and Interest, is, thro' the Blessing of God on the Agency of that Excellent person, Likely to prevail mightily in the Southern Colonies." Makemie himself returned to Accomack and died there in 1708.

Presbyterianism had an able and energetic advocate in Francis Makemie. He ministered to its earliest congregations in the New World and helped to unite them into America's first presbytery. For these efforts, he earned the title of "the father of American Presbyterianism."

Further Reading

Makemie, Francis. *A Good Conversation.* Boston: B. Green, 1707.
———. *The Life and Writings of Francis Makemie.* Edited with an introduction by Boyd S. Schlenther. Philadelphia: Presbyterian Historical Society, 1971; Lewiston, N.Y.: Edwin Mellen Press, 2d ed. 1999.
———. *A Narrative of a New and Unusual American Imprisonment, of Two Presbyterian Ministers.* Reprint ed. New York: H. Gaine, 1755.
———. *A Plain and Friendly Perswasive to the Inhabitants of Virginia and Maryland, for Promoting Towns and Cohabitation.* London: J. Humfreys, 1705.
Miller, Char. "Francis Makemie: Social Development of the Colonial Chesapeake." *American Presbyterians: Journal of Presbyterian History* 63 (1985): 333–40.
Page, Isaac Marshall. *The Life Story of Rev. Francis Makemie.* Grand Rapids, Mich.: Wm. B. Eerdmans, 1938.

Malcolm X
(Malcolm Little el-Hajj Malik el-Shabazz)
(1925–1965) *Nation of Islam leader*

A leading civil rights activist, Malcolm X became an influential leader within the Nation of Islam during the 1950s. Later, after a pilgrimage to Mecca during the final years of his life, Malcolm X abandoned the racist doctrines of the Black Muslims and embraced a more orthodox form of Islam. He was born Malcolm Little on May 19, 1925, in Omaha, Nebraska, the son of Earl Little and Louise Norton Little. By the end of that decade, his family had settled in East Lansing, Michigan. His father, a Baptist preacher, and his mother were members of Marcus Garvey's Universal Negro Improvement Association. After his father was run over by a streetcar and killed in 1931, rumors circulated that his death had been orchestrated by a white supremacist group. Thereafter the mental health of Malcolm's mother deteriorated, and, by 1936, she had been committed to an asylum.

Malcolm X, a minister within the Nation of Islam until shortly before his assassination, was a militant advocate of civil rights during the middle years of the 20th century. *(Library of Congress, Prints and Photographs Division LC-USZ62-115058)*

In 1941, after spending time in a variety of foster homes, Malcolm moved to Boston to live with his half sister, and over the following years he lived there and in New York City, working mainly for railroads and restaurants at odd jobs and becoming involved in criminal activities such as drug dealing. He was arrested and imprisoned in 1946 for grand larceny and breaking and entering. While in prison he was converted to the religious teachings of ELIJAH MUHAMMAD, the leader of the Nation of Islam, a black nationalist sect of Islam that taught that whites were "devils." When he was released on parole in 1952, he changed his name to Malcolm X—choosing the X to replace what he viewed as his slave name—and became a minister for the Nation of Islam, gaining prominence over the next five years second only to that of Elijah Muhammad. In 1958 he married Betty X, a member of the Nation of Islam, with whom he had six daughters.

Though actively engaged in the Civil Rights movement during the late 1950s and early 1960s, Malcolm X had little but criticism for MARTIN LUTHER KING, JR., and his nonviolent attempts to secure racial justice.

> There is nothing in our book, the Koran, that teaches us to suffer peacefully. Our religion teaches us to be intelligent. Be peaceful, be courteous, obey the law, respect everyone; but if someone puts his hand on you, send him to the cemetery. That's a good religion.

When King appeared with other civil rights leaders at the March on Washington in August 1963, Malcolm X attended the event. Nevertheless, he distanced himself from the march by commenting that he did not understand why blacks would be so enthusiastic about participating in a demonstration "run by whites in front of a statue of a president who has been dead for a hundred years and who didn't like us when he was alive."

During the early 1960s, Malcolm X also grew increasingly alienated from Elijah Muhammad, partially because of rumors of Muhammad's sexual affairs with women in the Nation of Islam and because of suspicions of Muhammad and his followers that Malcolm X wished to take over the Nation.

Friction between the two men reached a peak after Malcolm X observed of President John F. Kennedy's assassination that Kennedy "never foresaw that the chickens would come home to roost so soon." Muhammad had instructed Nation of Islam ministers not to comment on Kennedy's assassination, and he responded to Malcolm X's statement by suspending him for three months, beginning in December 1963. In March of 1964, Malcolm X publicly broke from the Nation of Islam and established a competing organization, Muslim Mosque, Inc.

The following month, Malcolm X made a pilgrimage to Mecca, and his experiences on this trip caused a decisive revision of his religious views, especially regarding whites. After his trip to Mecca, he abandoned talk of whites' being devils. Instead, he insisted that Islam provided the solution to racism.

> American needs to understand Islam, because this is the one religion that erases from its society the race problem. Throughout my travels in the Muslim world, I have met, talked to, even eaten with people who in America would have been considered "white"—but the "white" attitude was removed from their minds by the religion of Islam. I have never before seen sincere and true brotherhood practiced by all colors together, irrespective of their color.

On his return to the United States at the end of May 1964, Malcolm X announced that he had adopted a new name, el-Hajj Malik el-Shabazz. He also formed the Organization of Afro-American Unity to do "whatever is necessary to bring the Negro struggle from the level of civil rights to the level of human rights." But his assassination on February 21, 1965, by members of the Nation of Islam, as he was making a speech in New York City, cut short this new mission.

Black leadership within the Civil Rights movement frequently allied itself with African-American religion. Malcolm X represents one strand of this alliance, a strand that produced a militant and angry assault against racial discrimination in American society. The other strand had as its chief exemplar Martin Luther King, Jr., who sought to use nonviolent protest to unsettle the foundations of racial segregation and discrimination. Both men drew on their respective religious traditions: Malcolm X—at least until the very end of his life—relied on Nation of Islam teaching that whites were a malevolent source of evil; Martin Luther King, Jr., turned to his roots as an African-American Baptist preacher to prophesy against the evil of racism.

Though King was the more prominent force within the Civil Rights movement, Malcolm X widened that movement to include voices less patient than King's, voices more angry and more willing to use such force as necessary to do battle against the forms of racial discrimination entrenched in American society.

Further Reading

Benson, Michael. *Malcolm X.* Minneapolis: Lerner Publications, 2002.

Breitman, George. *The Last Year of Malcolm X: The Evolution of a Revolutionary.* New York: Merit Publishers, 1967.

Carson, Clayborne. *Malcolm X: The FBI File.* Edited by David Gallen. New York: Carroll & Graf, 1991.

Clarke, John Henrik, ed. *Malcolm X: The Man and His Times.* New York: Macmillan, 1969.

Curtis, Richard. *The Life of Malcolm X.* Philadelphia: Macrae Smith, 1971.

DeCaro, Louis A. *On the Side of My People: A Religious Life of Malcolm X.* New York: New York University Press, 1996.

Dyson, Michael Eric. *Making Malcolm: The Myth and Meaning of Malcolm X.* New York: Oxford University Press, 1995.

Gallen, David. *Malcolm X: As They Knew Him.* New York: Carroll & Graf, 1992.

Goldman, Peter Louis. *The Death and Life of Malcolm X.* New York: Harper & Row, 1973.

Malcolm X, with Alex Haley. *The Autobiography of Malcolm X.* New York: Grove Press, 1965.

———. *Malcolm X: The Last Speeches.* Edited by Bruce Perry. New York: Pathfinder, 1989.

———. *A Malcolm X Reader.* Edited by David Gallen. New York: Carroll & Graf, 1994.

———. *The Speeches of Malcolm X at Harvard.* Edited by Archie Epps. New York: W. Morrow, 1968.

Perry, Bruce. *Malcolm: The Life of a Man Who Changed Black America.* Barrytown, N.Y.: Station Hill, 1991.

Rummel, Jack. *Malcolm X.* New York: Chelsea House, 1989.

Strickland, William. *Malcolm X, Make It Plain.* New York: Viking, 1994.

Wolfenstein, E. Victor. *The Victims of Democracy: Malcolm X and the Black Revolution.* Berkeley: University of California Press, 1981.

Mather, Cotton
(1663–1728) *Puritan minister*

The Mather family towers over the first 100 years of New England history, and Cotton Mather joined his father, INCREASE MATHER, and his grandfather, RICHARD MATHER, to form a near dynasty of Puritan ministers. His mother, Maria, lent additional weight to the gravity of his spiritual heritage, since she was herself the daughter of JOHN COTTON, the most famous preacher of New England's first generation. Cotton Mather, the heir of two great Puritan lineages, was born in Boston on February 12, 1663. Like his father, Increase, Cotton entered Harvard College at the age of 12. He graduated in 1678 when he was 16 years old, and in 1681 he earned an M.A. from Harvard. Even before this later academic accomplishment, Cotton Mather had, like his father and two illustrious grandfathers, preached his first sermons. Beginning in rapid succession in late summer of 1680, he preached at Dorchester, where his grandfather, Richard Mather, had served before his death some 20 years earlier; then at Second or Old North Church in Boston, where his father preached; and then at the Boston church where John Cotton had preached. These and other early sermons were well received, although the young preacher battled with stuttering and acquired in his warfare against this impediment a deliberateness of speech that would characterize his preaching for the rest of his life.

The congregation of Old North Church determined on hearing Cotton Mather's first sermon that he would be a fit colleague for his father, Increase. But Increase was cool to the idea. Although persuaded to accept his son on probationary terms as one of the church's preach-

ers, he steadfastly opposed Cotton's ordination until his congregation's persistence finally caused him to relent five years after Cotton had preached his maiden sermon. Cotton Mather was ordained in North Church on May 13, 1685, and he served alongside his father at the church until Increase died nearly 40 years later.

Cotton Mather's father had combined a pastoral ministry with political activity in the Massachusetts Bay Colony, especially after its original charter had been revoked in the mid-1680s. The English Crown appointed Sir Edmund Andros to serve as governor of New England, as well as New York and New Jersey, and on his arrival in 1686, he proved to be a highly unpopular agent of royal policy. Increase set out for England, where he remained until after the Glorious Revolution, which deposed James II and enthroned William and Mary, and he was able to obtain a new charter for Massachusetts. Cotton, for his part, stayed in Massachusetts, tending the affairs of Old North Church but also participating to some extent in New England's own miniature revolution, in which Governor Andros was arrested and evicted from the colony. Cotton Mather wrote a defense of those who unseated Andros, *Declaration of the Gentlemen, Merchants, and Inhabitants of Boston and the County Adjacent.* Cotton, however, was generally less engaged in political matters than his father.

Increase Mather returned from England in 1692 and rejoined his son in the pulpit of the Old North Church. When he arrived home, the Salem witch trials were in progress and soon commanded the attention of both men. Though he had no doubt that Satan was busy at work in Salem as elsewhere, Increase Mather expressed dissatisfaction with the Salem court's reliance on "spectral evidence," that is, testimony from witnesses who claimed to have seen apparitions of those accused of witchcraft engaged in various nefarious activities. Increase ultimately published a book criticizing the methods employed at Salem to uncover witchcraft. Cotton Mather, however, though opposed as his father was to the use of spectral evidence, believed that the Salem proceedings had, in fact, ferreted out the devil's doings there, and he wrote a book defending the

Salem trials, *Wonders of the Invisible World.* Both at the time and since, Mather's defense of the Salem trials earned him scorn.

Cotton Mather married Abigail Phillips in 1686, and the couple had nine children before she died in 1702. Thereafter, he remarried, this time the widow Elizabeth Hubbard, with whom he had six children. After Elizabeth's death in 1713, Mather married Lydia Lee George in 1715. She was the wealthy widow of a prominent businessman, and she insisted on retaining control of the financial assets with which she had entered the marriage to Mather. By the time of his marriage to Lydia, only six of his children by previous marriages had survived. At the time of his death, only two of his children remained alive. His marriage to Lydia soon proved to be unhappy. Lydia was prone to "prodigious Paroxysms" of rage against her husband, so much so that he feared that she was mad and that public discovery of this fact would ruin his ministry. The marriage survived, though, until his death 13 years later. Mather died in Boston on February 13, 1728, the day after his 65th birthday.

Though prominent as a preacher in his day, Cotton Mather has a place in history that owes more to his pen than to his tongue. He wrote more than 400 volumes in his life, which revealed a dazzling breadth of interest and intellect, on subjects as diverse as scriptural exegesis, hymnody, and natural history. His interest and writing on scientific topics, including his *Curiosa Americana,* ultimately gained him membership in the Royal Society of London. The most famous of his works, *Magnalia Christi Americana,* published in 1702, chronicled the history of Puritan New England. Cotton Mather was the last great Puritan preacher of an illustrious lineage and was himself Puritanism written large, with all its energies, enthusiasms, and errors.

Further Reading

Boas, Ralph Philip, and Louise Boas. *Cotton Mather: Keeper of the Puritan Conscience.* New York: Harpers, 1928.

Levin, David. *Cotton Mather: The Young Life of the Lord's Remembrancer, 1663–1703.* Cambridge, Mass.: Harvard University Press, 1978.

Cotton Mather was the last of a celebrated dynasty of Puritan ministers, which included his grandfather, Richard Mather, and his father, Increase Mather. *(Library of Congress, Prints and Photographs Division LC-USZ62-92308)*

Lovelace, Richard F. *The American Pietism of Cotton Mather: Origins of American Evangelicalism.* Grand Rapids, Mich.: Christian University Press, 1979.

Mather, Cotton. *Magnalia Christi Americana.* London, 1702; New York: Arno Press, 1972.

———. *Paterna: The Autobiography of Cotton Mather.* Edited by Ronald A. Bosco. Delmar, N.Y.: Scholars' Facsimiles & Reprints, 1976.

———. *Selected Letters of Cotton Mather.* Compiled with commentary by Kenneth Silverman. Baton Rouge: Louisiana State University Press, 1971.

Mather, Samuel. *The Life of the Very Reverend and Learned Cotton Mather, D.D. & F.R.S.: Late Pastor of the North Church in Boston Who Died Feb. 13, 1727,8.* Boston: printed for Samuel Gerrish, 1729.

Middlekauff, Robert. *The Mathers: Three Generations of Puritan Intellectuals, 1596–1728.* Rev. ed. Berkeley: University of California Press, 1999.

Post, Constance J. *Signs of the Times in Cotton Mather's Paterna: A Study of Puritan Autobiography.* New York: AMS Press, 2000.

Silverman, Kenneth. *The Life and Times of Cotton Mather.* New York: Harper & Row, 1984.

Wendell, Barrett. *Cotton Mather: The Puritan Priest.* New York: Dodd, Mead, 1891.

Mather, Increase
(1639–1723) *Puritan minister*

Increase Mather earned a reputation as the most famous minister of New England's second generation. Together with his father, RICHARD MATHER, and his son, COTTON MATHER, Increase Mather formed a triumvirate of influential Puritan preachers. He was born in Dorchester, Massachusetts, on June 21, 1639, the son of Richard Mather and Katherine Holt Mather. He entered Harvard College at the age of 12 but soon left to pursue a private course of study with John Norton in Boston. The precocious young scholar returned to Harvard as a senior and received a B.A. in 1656. The year before his graduation, he had a conversion experience by which he became convinced that he had received God's grace. This followed close on the heels of a spiritual crisis precipitated by his mother's death, during which, he later recounted, "the Lord broke in upon my conscience with very terrible convictions and awakenings." These convictions and awakenings climaxed in Mather's conversion in May 1655, which he later described as a surrender to Christ.

> At the close of the day, as I was praying, I gave my selfe up to Jesus Christ, declaring that I was now resolved to be his Servant, and his only and his forever, and humbly professed to him that if I did perish, I would perish at his feet. Upon this I had ease and inward peace in my perplexed soul immediately; and from that day I walked comfortably for a considerable time, and was carefull that all my words and wayes should be such as would not offend God.

After leaving Harvard, Increase Mather attended Trinity College in Dublin and received an M.A. in 1658; he lived in England for a time. Though offered a fellowship at Trinity, Mather declined this academic post in favor of pastoral ministries first in Devonshire, then as chaplain of the garrison on Guernsey, and briefly, at a church in Gloucester. The Restoration placed his Puritan beliefs at odds with the Anglican hierarchy that resumed control along with King Charles II. Consequently, Increase Mather returned to Massachusetts in 1661. Soon afterward he married Maria Cotton, whose father, JOHN COTTON, was one of New England's most prominent preachers. The couple had nine children, the first born of whom, Cotton Mather, would become an even more famous Puritan minister than his father.

Shortly after Increase's return to Massachusetts, the colony convened a synod in 1662 that ultimately produced the Half-Way Covenant. This resolution of a doctrinal controversy concerning infant baptism put Increase and his father, Richard, at odds. Increase favored maintaining the traditional rule of baptizing only the children of full communing members of the New England churches. His father, however, led the synod to adopt the Half-Way Covenant, which permitted the baptism as well of children whose parents had themselves been bap-

Increase Mather was a prominent Puritan preacher during the second generation of the Massachusetts Bay Colony. *(Library of Congress, Prints and Photographs Division LC-USZ62-75070)*

tized but had never given proof of the conversion experience that would have made them full church members. Only later would Increase adopt his father's views on the covenant.

In 1664, Increase accepted a position as teacher of Boston's Second Church, a post he filled for nearly 60 years. Toward the close of that decade his father died, and the event, coupled with his own severe illness, thrust Increase into a depression that gripped him for more than two years. He finally emerged from this troubled time to become one of New England's most influential ministers. He played a significant role in the Reforming Synod of 1679, which pitted him against the innovative practice of the Lord's Supper by SOLOMON STODDARD, whose church allowed individuals to participate in the sacrament even if they had not yet given a public testimony of their conversion. A decade later, he traveled to England on behalf of the colony to obtain a new charter after the first had been abolished in the mid-1680s. He remained there from 1688 to 1692; he returned to New England during the height of the Salem witchcraft trials and earned demerits from history for his tepid opposition to them. During the last 15 years of the 17th century, he added to these achievements service as president of Harvard College from 1685 until 1701.

As the leading spiritual voice of New England's second generation, Increase Mather repeatedly lamented the colony's departure from the holy example of its founders. Over the years, he complained, New England had substituted worldly interests for religious ones. As a consequence, God had chastened the colony with judgments such as King Philip's War, which bathed New England in ferocious conflict with Native American tribes during the mid-1670s. Though Mather viewed the ultimate colonial victory in this war as a sign that God had rewarded at least the beginnings of a spiritual reformation, he nevertheless badgered his fellow New Englanders with a steady stream of jeremiads exhorting them to continue to reform. During his later years, he shared a preaching ministry at Boston's Second Church with his son Cotton Mather. His wife, Maria, died in 1714, and at the age of 76 he married Ann Lake Cotton. Toward the end of his career as a New England minister, he defended the autonomy of Congregational churches against attempts to make them subject to synods along Presbyterian lines. Increase Mather died in Boston on August 23, 1723.

Puritan orthodoxy, as redefined by the Half-Way Covenant, had no more illustrious defender than Increase Mather during the waning decades of the 17th century and the early years of the 18th. He resisted attempts to democratize church membership and to strip the Congregational churches of New England of their long-treasured autonomy. As much as any man of his time, he assisted in the perpetuation of the original spiritual vision of his father's generation, a generation he never ceased to admire.

Further Reading

Hall, Michael G. *The Last American Puritan: Increase Mather, 1639–1723*. Middletown, Conn.: Wesleyan University Press, 1988.

Lowance, Mason I., Jr. *Increase Mather*. New York: Twayne Publishers, 1974.

Mather, Increase. *The Doctrine of Divine Providence Opened and Applyed: Also Sundry Sermons on Several Other Subjects*. Boston: printed by Richard Pierce for Joseph Brunning, 1684.

Middlekauff, Robert. *The Mathers: Three Generations of Puritan Intellectuals, 1596–1728*. Rev. ed. Berkeley: University of California Press, 1999.

Murdock, Kenneth Ballard. *Increase Mather: The Foremost American Puritan*. Cambridge: Harvard University Press, 1925.

Sawyer, Kenneth Steven. "'Secret Walkings Before the Lord': Theology and Experience in the Life of Increase Mather, 1639–1723." Ph.D. dissertation, University of Chicago, 1992.

Scheick, William J., ed. *Two Mather Biographies: Life and Death and Parentator*. Bethlehem, Pa.: Lehigh University Press, 1989.

Mather, Richard
(1596–1669) *Puritan minister*

Richard Mather migrated to New England during the 1630s and became one of the chief spokesmen for the principles of Congregationalism that flourished there. He was born in Lancashire, England, in the hamlet of Lowton, a short distance from Liverpool. His parents, Thomas Mather and Margaret Abrams, tried to secure an education for him by enrolling him in a grammar school in Winwick. They could not, however, afford to send him on immediately for a university education. Instead, Richard Mather became a schoolteacher in Toxeth Park when he was 15 years old. While teaching, he lived with the family of Edward Aspinwall, and, exposed to this family's nonconformist views, Mather had a conversion experience. Subsequently, he was able to continue his education at Brasenose College, Oxford, where he matriculated in 1618. Nevertheless, the inhabitants of Toxeth Park persuaded him to return to them before he had spent even a year at Oxford, this time as a minister rather than a schoolteacher.

Although Richard Mather returned to Toxeth Park with Puritan sensibilities, he managed in his early years there to avoid attracting the unfavorable attention of Anglican authorities. He was ordained in 1619, and five years later, he married Katharine Holt, with whom he had six children. One of these, INCREASE MATHER, became a famous New England preacher himself and the father of the even more famous preacher and Puritan historian, COTTON MATHER. After Charles I ascended to the throne of England in 1625, the Anglican hierarchy displayed increasing intolerance toward Puritans. Mather himself was suspended from his ministerial position in 1633, though influential friends managed to restore him to his post shortly thereafter. But the following year, a synod convened near Toxeth Park to examine reports of nonconformity in the area, and Mather was summoned before it. When questioned, Mather revealed that in his 15-year career as a minister he had never worn the surplice, the formal outer garment usually worn by Anglican clergy. Dismayed by this announcement, one of the members of the synod exclaimed: "What, preach fifteen years and never wear a Surpless? It had been better for him that he had gotten Seven Bastards!" As a result of the synod's inquiry, Mather was again suspended.

Denied a pulpit in England and anxious that remaining there in the face of persecution by Anglican authorities might be accepting a kind of "self-murder," Richard Mather joined the great mi-

gration of Puritans to New England. He arrived in Boston with his family in August 1635. Once there, however, he received less than the welcome he might have expected. The church at Boston initially refused to receive him as a member. Mather's views regarding his ordination in the Church of England did not appear to mesh with the church's understanding of its own role in recognizing ministers. Eventually, the church admitted Mather as a member, but a new rebuff lay ahead. Inhabitants of Dorchester appealed to Mather to organize a new church there after many of the town's citizens had relocated to Connecticut. But when Mather petitioned the General Court of Massachusetts to recognize the new church, it refused to do so on the ground that some of Mather's charter members could not give a satisfactory explanation of their salvation. Only after Mather spent additional time preparing these members to respond appropriately did the General Court finally recognize his church in the summer of 1636.

In spite of Richard Mather's rocky introduction to New England's scheme of church government, he eventually became one of its chief defenders. The congregational system of the New England churches recognized individual churches as possessing substantial autonomy in the conduct of their affairs. This independence conflicted with Presbyterian models of church government that gained ascendancy in England during the mid-17th century. Influential Presbyterians challenged New England's congregationalism, and Richard Mather rose to the defense of the New England way in works such as An Apologie for Church Covenant (1643) and Church Government and Church Covenant Discussed in Answer to Two and Thirty Questions (1643). Subsequently, New England churches convened a synod to prepare a formal statement of their principles of church governance and, in 1649, adopted A Platform of Church Discipline Gathered Out of the Word of God (known more commonly as the Cambridge Platform). Richard Mather was a chief architect of this statement, and he also played an important role in articulating the Half-Way Covenant adopted by the New England churches in 1662. This covenant resolved the vexing question of what to do with the children of parents who had been baptized as infants but had not had an adult conversion experience and thus had never become full church members. The Half-Way Covenant provided that these children could themselves be baptized though they, like their parents, would not be admitted to full church membership without evidencing later some indication of conversion. Finally, after more than three decades of service as minister in Dorchester, Mather died there on April 22, 1669.

Richard Mather was neither the most renowned New England preacher of his day nor its brightest intellect. Other men, such as THOMAS HOOKER and JOHN COTTON, commanded more respect for their oratorical skills and intellectual abilities. But Mather's labors helped to secure the foundations of New England Congregationalism during its first generation, and his role in crafting the *Cambridge Platform* and in negotiating the Half-Way Covenant secured his place in colonial history.

Further Reading

Burg, B. R. *Richard Mather of Dorchester.* Lexington: University Press of Kentucky, 1976.

Gallagher, Edward J. *Early Puritan Writers, a Reference Guide: William Bradford, John Cotton, Thomas Hooker, Edward Johnson, Richard Mather, Thomas Shepard.* Boston: G. K. Hall, 1976.

Mather, Horace E. *Lineage of Rev. Richard Mather.* Hartford, Conn.: Press of the Case, Lockwood & Brainard, 1890.

Mather, Increase. *Life and Death of Richard Mather* (1670). A facsimile reprint with an introduction by Benjamin Franklin V and William K. Bottorff. Athens, Ohio: 1966.

Middlekauff, Robert. *The Mathers: Three Generations of Puritan Intellectuals, 1596–1728.* Rev. ed. Berkeley: University of California Press, 1999.

Mathews, Shailer

(1863–1941) *theologian*

Shailer Mathews taught for nearly 40 years at the University of Chicago Divinity School and occupied the position of dean for a quarter of a century.

He was an important early representative of the brand of theological liberalism commonly referred to as the Chicago school. Mathews was born on May 26, 1863, in Portland, Maine, the son of Jonathan Bennett Mathews and Sophia Lucinda Shailer Mathews. He received an undergraduate education at Colby University (known today as Colby College) in 1884 and then studied at New Theological Seminary, from which he graduated with a bachelor of divinity degree in 1887. Though his grandfather had been a preacher, Mathews determined to pursue an academic career, which he began as a professor of rhetoric at his undergraduate alma mater.

After Mathews had taught seven years at Colby University, the University of Chicago Divinity School invited him to join its faculty in 1894. As a professor of New Testament history, he began what would ultimately prove to be an association of nearly four decades with the Divinity School. Later, he concentrated in the areas of historical and comparative theology. Fourteen years after his arrival on the faculty, Mathews was named dean of the Divinity School, a role he filled until his retirement in 1933.

From his position at the helm of one of America's preeminent divinity schools, Shailer Mathews became a leading figure in the early Chicago School, an influential variant of liberal Christianity. He became dean of the University of Chicago Divinity School two years before the publication of the first booklets in the series *The Fundamentals*, which marked the birth of fundamentalism as a discrete movement within American religious history, one that sought to maintain the historic teachings of Christianity. Shailer Mathews epitomized the polar opposite of fundamentalist theology. The Christian faith, he argued in *The Faith of Modernism*, was not so much a repository of received doctrines as an organic community constantly adapting to the needs and circumstances of the present.

> If we are to understand our religion we must . . . do more than study its formulae and institutions. We must look beneath and through the Creeds and Confessions to the attitudes and convictions, the needs, temptations and

trials, the prayer and rites, in a word, the actual religious life of the ongoing and developing Christian group.

In contrast with fundamentalists, who saw scientific theories such as evolution to be a threat to theological orthodoxy, Mathews found in science a fit partner for his theological imagination. Evolution, he insisted in *The Faith of Modernism,* was "the history of an ever more complete revelation of how the infinite Person produces finite personalities."

Mathews combined his teaching and administrative responsibilities at the University of Chicago Divinity School with an active career as a writer, publishing more than 20 books and serving as the editor of two periodicals: *World Today* from 1903 to 1911, and *Biblical World* from 1913 to 1920. His commitment to the role of faith in the pursuit of social justice also made him an early proponent of the social gospel movement, and it involved him in the Federal Council of Churches—mainline Protestantism's flagship organization devoted to social issues—of which he served as president from 1912 to 1916. Mathews retired from active academic life in 1933 but continued to write. He died in Chicago on October 23, 1941.

When the tension between theological liberalism and conservativism long latent in American Protestantism erupted in the early years of the 20th century, Shailer Mathews positioned himself clearly on the side of liberalism. He championed a view of religion unmoored from historic creeds and the doctrines they embodied, a faith self-consciously structured to respond to modernity. He joined other theological liberals in embracing evolutionary theory as a valuable tool for articulating religious truths and in emphasizing the necessary social consequences of authentic religious belief.

Further Reading

Arnold, Charles Harvey. *Near the Edge of Battle: A Short History of the Divinity School and the Chicago School of Theology, 1866–1966.* Chicago: Divinity School Association, University of Chicago, 1966.

Lindsey, William D. *Shailer Mathews' Lives of Jesus: The Search for a Theological Foundation for the Social Gospel.* New York: P. Lang, 1996.

Mathews, Shailer. *The Faith of Modernism.* New York: Macmillan, 1924; New York: AMS Press, 1969.

———. *New Faith for Old: An Autobiography by Shailer Mathews.* New York: Macmillan, 1936.

Peden, Creighton. *The Chicago School: Voices in Liberal Religious Thought.* Bristol, Ind.: Wyndham Hall Press, 1987.

Maurin, Aristide Peter
(1877–1949) *Catholic lay leader*

A Catholic layman, Peter Maurin cofounded the Catholic Worker movement with DOROTHY DAY. Dedicated to the improvement of modern society, Maurin championed the establishment of hospitality houses and agrarian communities. Aristide Peter Maurin, who was known by his middle name, was born on May 9, 1877, in Oultet, a village in southern France, the son of Jean Baptiste Maurin and Marie Pages Maurin. When he was a teenager he joined the Christian Brothers, an order that stressed simplicity of life and care for the poor. He was, however, not exempt from French military service and spent time in the infantry over the next 10 years. Beginning in 1902, Maurin left the Christian Brothers and joined Le Sillon, a lay activist group devoted to Christian social justice.

In 1909, Peter Maurin immigrated to Canada, where he homesteaded with a friend for two years in Saskatchewan. After his friend's death, Maurin drifted across the United States, working intermittently for the railroad and at other odd jobs and being arrested on two occasions for vagrancy. He eventually settled for a number of years in Chicago, where he began to teach French. Subsequently, he moved to New York, where he found work as a handyman at a Catholic boys' camp.

After leaving France, Maurin had drifted away from the Catholic Church, but on settling in New York he returned to the church. A turning point in his life occurred in 1932, when he met Dorothy Day, a journalist and a recent convert to Catholicism. Maurin advocated the establishment of houses of hospitality to care for the poor and agrarian communities, which he called "agronomic universities," through which he hoped to encourage both scholarship and manual toil. He convinced Dorothy Day to begin publishing a newspaper, which she named *The Catholic Worker*, that would provide a forum for the advancement of social reform. This newspaper was the genesis of the Catholic Worker movement. The movement sponsored hospitality houses, inspired by Maurin's vision of beggars as "ambassadors of gods."

Maurin's corollary ambition to establish agronomic universities was partially fulfilled by the creation of a communal farm on Staten Island in 1935. A stroke suffered by Maurin in 1944 forced him to live the remaining years of his life quietly at farms operated by the Catholic Worker movement, first in Pennsylvania and later in New York. He died at the farm in Newburgh, New York, on May 15, 1949, and was buried in a suit and a grave donated to clothe his remains. "God has taken him into Paradise, with Lazarus who once was poor," Dorothy Day wrote of his death.

Peter Maurin shuddered at the society of "go-getters" in which he found himself and sought to transform it into one of "go-givers." He saw the Catholic Church as the natural ally of social reform, though he recognized that often this alliance had been frustrated in practice and that his own proposals were quite radical. Nevertheless, he doggedly persisted at his efforts to create "a new society within the shell of the old," on the basis of a philosophy "which is not a new philosophy but a very old philosophy, a philosophy so old that it looks like new."

Further Reading

Ellis, Marc H. *Peter Maurin: Prophet in the Twentieth Century.* New York: Paulist Press, 1981.

Maurin, Peter. *Catholic Radicalism: Phrased Essays for the Green Revolution.* New York: Catholic Worker Books, 1949.

———. *Easy Essays.* Chicago: Franciscan Herald Press, 1977. Selections available online. URL:http://www.catholicworker.com/Maurin.htm. Downloaded on April 26, 2002.

Miller, William. *A Harsh and Dreadful Love.* New York: Liveright, 1973.

Sheehan, Arthur T. *Peter Maurin: Gay Believer.* Garden City, N.Y.: Hanover House, 1959.

Mayhew, Jonathan
(1720–1766) *Congregationalist minister*

A liberal Congregationalist minister of the mid-18th century, Jonathan Mayhew served as a bridge between the Puritanism that colonized New England and the Unitarianism that flourished there by the 19th century. He contributed to this theological migration from his pulpit of the West Congregational Church in Boston, where he preached from 1747 until his death. Jonathan Mayhew was born on October 8, 1720, at Chilmark on Martha's Vineyard in Massachusetts, the son of Experience Mayhew and Remember Bourne Mayhew. He was descended from a family of Puritan missionaries who had settled on Martha's Vineyard and devoted themselves to communicating the gospel to the Pokanauket Indians who inhabited the island. With his father's blessing, though, Jonathan pursued a different career. He graduated from Harvard College in 1744 and then received a small stipend from the college while he pursued studies that led to an M.A. in 1747. That same year Mayhew was called to preach at the West Congregational Church and was ordained a minister there.

Over the next two decades, before his untimely death in 1766, Jonathan Mayhew placed himself outside the fraternity of New England Congregational orthodoxy but solidly within the currents of theological liberalism that would become a midwife for Unitarianism. Though he originally supported and admired the revivalistic efforts of GEORGE WHITEFIELD, Mayhew rejected Whitefield's evangelistic fervor in favor of a more rational Christianity. In the year of his ordination he heard Whitefield's farewell sermon in America, which he branded "a very low, confused, puerile, conceited, ill-natur'd, enthusiastick, &c. Performance as ever I heard in my life." By this time Mayhew had abandoned the doctrines of original sin and predestination as inconsistent with biblical teaching.

His Arminian views were affront enough to his ministerial colleagues in Boston. But within a few years, he gave the scions of orthodoxy even more reason to shudder when he drifted toward Arian views as well. Arianism, condemned as a heresy since the fourth century, denied the Trinity and the divinity of Christ. Mayhew's embrace of this theological position would pave the way for later Unitarians, who held similar views. He was relatively secure in a pulpit that superintended the spiritual needs of merchants and those who themselves tended to the interests of trade and were happy to receive a spiritual diet other than that dispensed to the inhabitants of Boston's older environs. Mayhew, who admitted that his "natural temper [was] perhaps too warm," was thus able to endure the disapproval of more orthodox Bostonians and insisted that their adherence to outmoded creeds was itself a scandal against Christianity. Creeds were, he declared, "imperious and tyrannical: and contrary to the spirit and doctrines of the gospel." It mattered not that they boasted a venerable lineage. "[A] falsehood of a thousand years standing, remains as much a falsehood as ever, although it may have been consecrated by the church and transmitted to posterity in a creed."

As if theological controversy alone were not enough to satisfy Mayhew's appetite for disputation, he also plunged into political quarrels that would ripen into the American Revolution a generation later. In his sermon *A Discourse Concerning Unlimited Submission and Non-Resistance to the Higher Powers,* Jonathan Mayhew argued that righteous living did not require acquiescence to tyranny. "[W]hen Iniquity comes to be thus established by a Law; it cannot be any iniquity to transgress that law by which it is established. On the contrary, it is a sin not to transgress it." Mayhew died before a rising tide of patriotic fervor joined his voice in opposing British tyranny over the colonies, but his protests were a prelude to the many that would follow.

Mayhew married Elizabeth Clarke in 1756, but loss was a steady companion of their marital union. Though they had three children together, only one—a daughter—survived infancy. Mayhew himself died in Boston on July 9, 1766, after suffering a cerebral hemorrhage, three months before his 46th birthday.

Jonathan Mayhew championed a partnership between reason and religion that carried him beyond the bounds of Congregational orthodoxy.

Combining liberal theology with liberal politics, he would probably have been at home in 19th-century New England. There, a Unitarianism kindred to his spiritual views flourished, as well as a nation that had formed itself out of war against British tyranny.

Further Reading

Akers, Charles W. *Call unto Liberty: A Life of Jonathan Mayhew, 1720–1766.* Cambridge, Mass.: Harvard University Press, 1964.

Bradford, Alden. *Memoir of the Life and Writings of Jonathan Mayhew.* Boston: C. C. Little, 1838.

Corrigan, John. *The Hidden Balance: Religion and the Social Theories of Charles Chauncy and Jonathan Mayhew.* Cambridge: Cambridge University Press, 1987.

Mayhew, Jonathan. *Christian Sobriety.* Boston: Richard and Samuel Draper, 1763.

———. *A Defense of the Observations on the Charter and Conduct of the Society for the Propagation of the Gospel in Foreign Parts.* Boston: R. & S. Draper, 1763.

———. *A Discourse Concerning Unlimited Submission and Non-Resistance to the Higher Powers.* Boston: D. Fowle, 1750. Available online. URL:http://www.lexrex.com/informed/otherdocuments/sermons/mayhew.htm. Downloaded on April 27, 2002.

———. *Observations on the Charter and Conduct of the Society for the Propagation of the Gospel in Foreign Parts.* Boston: Richard and Samuel Draper, 1763.

McCabe, Charles Cardwell
(1836–1906) *Methodist Episcopal bishop*

A chaplain in the Union army and later a bishop in the Methodist Episcopal Church, Charles Cardwell McCabe combined the talents of an evangelist and a fund-raiser. A gregarious temper and solid speaking skills made him an important advocate for the Methodist Episcopal Church in the closing decades of the 19th century. McCabe was born on October 11, 1836, in Athens, Ohio, the son of Robert McCabe and Sarah Robinson McCabe. He experienced a religious conversion when he was eight years old—or, by some accounts, at a revival meeting when he was 14. Thereafter he decided to prepare himself to become a Methodist minister. In

1854, he enrolled in Ohio Wesleyan University at Delaware, Ohio, where an uncle was a professor. While a student at Ohio Wesleyan, he wore himself out with extracurricular revival preaching. Finally, he contracted typhoid fever after tending to his uncle, who nearly died of the same illness, and had to withdraw from the university in 1858. The school subsequently granted him a B.A. degree in 1860 in spite of this early departure.

After leaving Ohio Wesleyan, McCabe taught school for a time and then worked as a high school principal in Ironton, Ohio. In 1860, he married Rebecca Peters, with whom he had one child. That same year he was ordained a deacon in the Methodist Episcopal Church.

When the Civil War began, McCabe plunged into the work of raising volunteers for the Union army, helping to assemble the 122d Regiment of the Ohio Volunteer Infantry. By September 1862, McCabe had been ordained an elder in the Methodist Episcopal Church. A month later, he became a chaplain for the 122d Regiment. In June of the following year, he was captured after the battle of Winchester, while tending to the wounded left behind after his regiment escaped. He was consigned to Libby Prison in Richmond, Virginia, where he remained until mid-October 1863. In later years he frequently entertained audiences with tales from this experience, in his lecture "The Bright Side of Life in Libby Prison."

Even before McCabe had joined the 122d Regiment as chaplain, he had discovered in *Atlantic Monthly* a poem by Julia Ward Howe, "Battle Hymn of the Republic." After hearing the poem later sung to the tune of "John Brown's Body," McCabe, who possessed a fine baritone voice, began to sing the "Battle Hymn" regularly. After he was released from prison and took a job raising funds for the U.S. Christian Commission, he had the opportunity to sing the song at a commission meeting held at the Hall of the House of Representatives in February 1864, at which President Abraham Lincoln was in attendance. McCabe described the occasion in a letter to his wife:

> I made a brief address and wound up as requested, by singing the "Battle Hymn," Col. Powell singing bass. When we came to the

chorus the audience rose. O, how they sang! I happened to strike exactly the right key and the band helped us. I kept time for them with my hand and the mighty audience sang in exact time. Some shouted out loud at the last verse, and above all the uproar Mr. Lincoln's voice was heard: "Sing it again!"

The next year, after Lincoln lay slain by an assassin's bullet, McCabe sang the song again for some of the memorial services conducted for the president. He is often credited with having popularized "The Battle Hymn of the Republic."

After the Civil War, McCabe briefly pastored Spencer Chapel in Portsmouth, Ohio, from 1865 to 1868. He joined the Church Extension Society in 1868, first as a financial agent and subsequently as assistant corresponding secretary. In 1884, he was appointed corresponding secretary for the Missionary Society, a position he held until 1896, when he was elected a bishop of the Methodist Episcopal Church. Six years later, McCabe added to this ecclesiastical appointment service as the chancellor of American University in Washington, D.C. He continued in both posts until 1906, when he fell ill while helping the Methodist Episcopal Church in Torrington, Connecticut, raise funds to pay off a mortgage. McCabe died in New York City on December 9, 1906.

Charles Cardwell McCabe possessed a talent crucial to institutional expansion—that of fund-raising—and he lent this talent to the cause of Methodism for more than three decades. In his early adulthood he disclosed to his journal, "I seem doomed to raise money." But McCabe was an evangelist as well as a fund-raiser, an indefatigable herald of the Christian gospel whose labors helped expand the reach of American Methodism in the last half of the 19th century.

Further Reading

Allen, Robert Willis. "Chaplain Charles Cardwell McCabe, 122nd Ohio V: The Man Who Made Howe's 'Battle Hymn' Famous." Available online. URL: http://johnbrownsbody.net/CCMcCabe.htm. Downloaded on November 15, 2001.

Bristol, Frank Milton. *The Life of Chaplain McCabe: Bishop of the Methodist Episcopal Church.* New York: F. H. Revell, 1908.

Crook, Isaac. "Reminiscences of Bishop McCabe." *Methodist Review* 90 (March 1908): 210–22.

Stuart, Charles M. "Charles Cardwell McCabe." *Methodist Review* 90 (January 1908): 8–19.

McCosh, James

(1811–1894) *educator, philosopher*

The 11th president of what became Princeton University, Scottish-born James McCosh towered over the life of his institution for 20 years. An evangelical friendly to scientific investigation, he imbued his presidency with a distinctive character, which sought to encourage religious devotion even as it championed a course of study appropriate to the modern world. He was born on April 1, 1811, in Patna, Scotland, the son of Andrew McCosh and Jean Carson McCosh, prosperous farmers. After education in a local parish school, he received an undergraduate degree from Glasgow University in 1829 and theological training from the University of Edinburgh, from which he graduated with a master of arts in divinity degree in 1834. That year he was licensed as a minister of the Church of Scotland, and the following year he became the pastor of the Abbey Chapel in Arbroath, where he labored for five years. In 1839, he accepted a position at the West Church in Brechin. Four years later, though, McCosh joined other evangelical ministers in withdrawing from the established Church of Scotland and creating the Free Church of Scotland. In Brechin, McCosh met and in 1845 married Isabella Guthrie, with whom he had five children.

While a parish minister, McCosh pursued philosophical studies that he had begun as a student, fixing himself securely within the stream of Scottish realism, or Scottish Common Sense philosophy, as it is sometimes known. During his later years at Brechin, he published his first book, *The Method of Divine Government* (1850), which attempted to support theistic beliefs with the tool of philosophic realism. The book quickly made McCosh's name prominent on both sides of the Atlantic and earned him an appointment in 1852 at Queen's College in Belfast, Ireland, as professor of metaphysics and logic. The following decade, he

made a visit to America in 1866 and favorably impressed the Presbyterians he met there. Consequently, when the presidency of the College of New Jersey (subsequently Princeton University), a Presbyterian institution, became vacant in 1868, McCosh was named the college's 11th president.

At Princeton, McCosh labored industriously for two decades to transform the college. He sought to reverse the pattern of faculty inbreeding that dominated affairs before his arrival and to expand the college's institutional and financial resources. He worried some conservative evangelicals by his enthusiastic embrace of Darwinism, though his own evangelical temper made him an advocate of campus revivals. In contrast with Harvard University's president, Charles W. Eliot, with whom he had a celebrated debate in 1885, McCosh distrusted the new open elective system Eliot had established at Harvard. Students need to be told what to study, McCosh insisted. The future would eventually produce a compromise between the stark alternatives the two men advocated.

McCosh retired as president in 1888, though he continued to live in a house built for him on the college grounds. The address he gave on the occasion of his retirement captures something of the spirit that he displayed in Princeton.

> It is not without feeling that I take the step which I now take. It recalls that other eventful step in my life when I gave up my living, one of the most enviable in the Church of Scotland, when the liberties of Christ's people were interfered with. . . . I may feel a momentary pang in leaving the fine mansion, which a friend gave to the college and to me—it is as when Adam was driven out of Eden. I am reminded keenly that my days of active work are over. But I take the step firmly and decidedly. The shadows are lengthening, the day is declining. My age, seven years above the threescore and ten, compels it, Providence points to it, conscience enjoins it, the good of the college demands it. . . . I leave the college in a healthy state, intellectually, morally, and religiously, thanks be to God and man. I leave it with the prayer, that the blessing of Heaven and the good-will of men may rest upon it, and with the prospect of its having greater usefulness in the future than even that which it has had in the past.

McCosh died on November 16, 1894, at Princeton, New Jersey.

From his early career as an evangelical Scottish minister, James McCosh had philosophical interests that eventually turned him to the life of an academic and, still later, transplanted him to America, where he became the president of one of the nation's premier educational institutions. The preacher who had shown himself to be a first-rate scholar proved that he could also be an outstanding college administrator. In later years, he was happy to boast about his accomplishments: "It's me collidge," he liked to declare with a thick Scottish brogue. "I made it."

Further Reading

Hoeveler, J. David. *James McCosh and the Scottish Intellectual Tradition: From Glasgow to Princeton*. Princeton, N.J.: Princeton University Press, 1981.

McCosh, James. *First and Fundamental Truths: Being a Treatise on Metaphysics*. New York: C. Scribner's Sons, 1889.

———. *Gospel Sermons*. New York: R. Carter & Brothers, 1888.

———. *The Method of the Divine Government, Physical and Moral*. New York: R. Carter, 1852.

———. *The Religious Aspect of Evolution*. New York: G. P. Putnam's Sons, 1888.

Patton, William Donald. "James McCosh: the Making of a Reputation. A Study of the Life and Work of the Rev. Dr. James McCosh in Ireland, from His Appointment as Professor of Logic and Metaphysics in Queen's College, Belfast, 1851, to His Appointment as President of Princeton College, New Jersey, and Professor of Philosophy in 1868." Ph. D. dissertation, Queen's University of Belfast, 1993.

McGarvey, John William

(1829–1911) *Disciples of Christ minister, educator*

From his position as professor and later president of the College of the Bible in Lexington, Kentucky, John William McGarvey oversaw training of ministers for the Disciples of Christ tradition for nearly half a century. He lived to see his denomination splinter into three main lines, each of which was happy to claim him as a significant spiritual influence. McGarvey was born on March 1, 1829, near Hopkinsville, Kentucky, the son of John McGarvey and Sarah Ann Thomson McGarvey. After the death of his father when he was four years old and his mother's subsequent remarriage, McGarvey moved with his family to Tremont, Illinois, in 1839. There he attended a private school run by James K. Kellogg.

In the spring of 1847, McGarvey entered Bethany College in Bethany, Virginia (later West Virginia). There he encountered the college's leading professor, ALEXANDER CAMPBELL, the founder of the restorationist movement that became the Disciples of Christ denomination. Campbell championed a theological vision that sought to recover a primitive, authentic Christian faith, which had been lost beneath the weight of competing creeds and sectarian loyalties. In 1848, while a student at Bethany, McGarvey experienced a religious conversion and was baptized in a creek near the college church he attended.

Although at the time of his graduation from Bethany in the summer of 1850, McGarvey was determined to become a minister, he did not feel equipped to undertake this vocation at once. Rather than accept the offer of a traveling evangelist to accompany him as an apprentice, McGarvey moved to Fayette, Missouri, where his family had relocated. In Fayette he opened a boys' school and studied the Bible independently for two years. At the end of this period he was ordained in the fall of 1852 and, at the beginning of the following year, was installed as the pastor of a Disciples of Christ church in Dover, Missouri. In the spring of 1853 he married Atwayanna Francis Hix (known as "Ottie"), with whom he had eight children. After nine years in Dover, McGarvey moved to Lexington, Kentucky, where he became the pastor of the Main Street Christian Church.

In 1865, however, McGarvey's career turned down a new avenue when he was appointed a Bible professor at Kentucky University's College of the Bible in Lexington. Unlike Bethany College, which had provided little in the way of specific preparation for the ministerial vocation, the College of the Bible placed special emphasis on training ministers for the Disciples of Christ. Within a dozen years after the university had been reorganized as a new institution in 1865, the College of the Bible separated from the university and became an independent institution. McGarvey, though, remained at the College of the Bible through this transition and ultimately served the institution until 1911, first as a professor and then, from 1895 to 1911, as president. He died on October 6, 1911, in Lexington, Kentucky.

Toward the end of McGarvey's long tenure as a Bible professor, the denomination founded by Alexander Campbell divided along precise doctrinal fault lines. McGarvey himself joined the contest among Disciples on one issue in particular—the use of higher criticism in the study of the Bible. Along with more conservative Disciples, he warred against this higher criticism and the theological liberalism it engendered. Also, with more conservative Disciples, he opposed the use of instrumental music in worship. Unlike them, however, he did not resist the formation of cooperative societies devoted to the cause of missions. By the early 20th century, Disciples had divided themselves along the lines created by their differences on these issues. Conservatives, who came to be known as the Churches of Christ, resisted theological liberalism and instrumental worship. Independent Disciples, known commonly as Christian Churches, opposed missionary associations as an unscriptural innovation. Finally, Disciples of Christ churches followed the drift of other mainstream Protestant denominations toward theological liberalism, even as they championed a variety of cooperative associations. Each of these traditions had reason to count McGarvey as an ally on at least some of the issues that divided them from other Disciples.

Further Reading

Boring, M. Eugene. "The Disciples and Higher Criticism: The Crucial Third Generation." In *A Case Study of Mainstream Protestantism.* Edited by D. Newell Williams. Grand Rapids, Mich.: W. B. Eerdmans, 1991.

Harrison, Richard. "Disciples Theological Formation: From a College of the Bible to a Theological Seminary." In *A Case Study of Mainstream Protestantism:*
The Disciples' Relation to American Culture, 1880–1989. Edited by D. Newell Williams. Grand Rapids, Mich.: W. B. Eerdmans, 1991.

McGarvey, J.W. *Autobiography.* Lexington, Ky.: College of the Bible, 1960.

———. *The Authorship of the Book of Deuteronomy, with Its Bearings on the Higher Criticism of the Pentateuch.* Cincinnati, Ohio: Standard Publishing, 1902.

Morro, William Charles. *"Brother McGarvey": The Life of President J. W. McGarvey of the College of the Bible, Lexington, Ky.* St. Louis: Bethany Press, 1940.

Stevenson, Dwight. *Lexington Theological Seminary: 1865–1965—The College of the Bible Century.* St. Louis: Bethany Press, 1965.

Trimble, John C. "The Rhetorical Theory and Practice of John W. McGarvey." Ph.D. dissertation, Northwestern University, 1966.

McGlynn, Edward

(1837–1900) *Catholic priest, social reformer*

Briefly exiled not only from the Catholic priesthood but from the church itself, Edward McGlynn became a center of controversy in the late 19th century. His reformist zeal collided with the authority of his more conservative archbishop, MICHAEL AUGUSTINE CORRIGAN, and earned him a temporary excommunication from the Catholic Church. He was born on September 27, 1837, in New York City, the son of Irish immigrant parents, Peter McGlynn and Sarah McGlynn. After attending public school, he was dispatched to Rome, where he studied at the Urban College of the Propaganda Fide from 1850 to 1859. He briefly served as vice rector of the North American College after it opened in 1859, before being ordained the following year and returning to the United States.

At home again in New York, McGlynn served in several parishes during his first years as a priest, including St. Joseph's Church in Greenwich Village, where the reform-minded Thomas Ferrell was pastor. McGlynn eventually became involved in a group of progressive priests, led by Ferrell, called the Academia, who began meeting in 1866 to discuss theological and social issues of the day. Before this, though, McGlynn spent the three years from 1862 to 1865 as chaplain of a military hospital in Central Park, absorbing firsthand experiences of poverty and loss, which partially inspired the reformist zeal that characterized much of his later pastoral ministry.

In the late summer of 1865, McGlynn was assigned as assistant pastor at St. Stephen's Church on the Lower East Side of New York. When St. Stephen's senior pastor, Jeremiah Cummings, died at the beginning of 1866, McGlynn assumed his position and spent the next 21 years ministering in this parish, tending to the spiritual needs of mostly poor and working-class parishioners. He might have remained a dedicated—and largely unknown—Catholic priest except for the circumstances that caused the orbit of his life to intersect that of Henry George.

George was a social reformer famous for advocating the abolition of all taxes except a single tax on real estate. After McGlynn read Henry George's *Progress and Poverty* (1880), which diagnosed the sources of poverty and proposed the single tax as a remedy, McGlynn became an ardent supporter of the single-tax proposal. His increasingly prominent political activity displeased his spiritual superiors, though, and he was instructed in 1883 to refrain from further activity. Nevertheless, when Henry George became a candidate for mayor of New York in 1886, McGlynn ignored these instructions and campaigned actively on George's behalf.

The New York archbishop, Michael Corrigan, responded to George's defiance by suspending him as pastor of St. Stephen's late in 1886, and in December, McGlynn was summoned to Rome to respond to charges concerning the matter over which he had been suspended. Pleading ill health and other personal circumstances, McGlynn insisted that he was unable to go to Rome. Subsequently in early May 1887, he was ordered to appear in Rome within 40 days or be automatically excommunicated. McGlynn, again, declined to venture to Rome and was, in due course, excommunicated in July 1887.

Apparently unchastened by this turn of events, McGlynn continued an active round of campaigning and lecture events. For example, he supported Henry George's candidacy for New York secretary of

state on the United Labor Party ticket in 1887. But even as he pursued this course, allies of McGlynn within the church pressed his cause before the Vatican. Eventually the Vatican charged the papal legate, Archbishop Francesco Satolli, with the task of reconciling McGlynn. Toward the end of 1892, Satolli received from McGlynn a statement of his ideas and determined that they were in accord with Catholic teaching. He subsequently absolved McGlynn of his excommunication in December 1892. In the summer of 1893 McGlynn traveled to Rome, where he had an audience with the pope. On his return to the United States, he received an assignment to serve as pastor of St. Mary's Church in Newburgh, New York. A few years later he spoke at the funeral of Henry George, declaring in the course of his remarks that "[t]here was a man sent from God, and his name was Henry George." McGlynn himself died a little more than two years later, on January 7, 1900, in Newburgh, New York.

In the final decades of the 19th century a growing number of American religious leaders were convinced of the need to respond to the social problems created in the wake of the Industrial Revolution. For Protestants, commitment to issues of social justice expressed itself chiefly through the Social Gospel movement, which labored to apply the teachings of Christ to the social ills of the day. Edward McGlynn represented the Catholic counterpart to the Protestant social gospel. He, and a growing number of progressive Catholics, became convinced that neither private nor institutional charities were a sufficient remedy for the disparities in wealth that had become increasingly prominent by the latter half of the 19th century. Poverty, McGlynn believed, had its roots in systemic injustices, and these required concrete political action to correct. In the century that followed his death, an increasing number of Catholic thinkers would agree with his analysis.

Further Reading

Bell, Stephen. *Rebel, Priest, and Prophet: A Biography of Dr. Edward McGlynn.* New York: The Devin-Adair Co., 1937; Westport, Conn.: Hyperion Press, 1975.
Malone, Sylvester L., ed. *Dr. Edward McGlynn.* New York: Dr. McGlynn Monument Association, 1918; New York: Arno Press, 1978.

Scibilia, Dominic Pasquale. "Edward McGlynn, Thomas McGrady, and Peter C. Yorke: Prophets of American Social Catholicism." Ph.D. dissertation, Marquette University, 1990.

Shanaberger, Manuel Scott. "The Reverend Dr. Edward McGlynn: An Early Advocate of the Social Gospel in the American Catholic Church, an Intellectual History." Ph.D. dissertation, University of Virginia, 1993.

McKay, David Oman

(1873–1970) president of the Church of Jesus Christ of Latter-day Saints

The ninth president of the Mormon Church, David Oman McKay, presided over the church during a period of significant growth. His spiritual superintendence emphasized the strengthening of its educational institutions and its missionary outreach. McKay was born on September 8, 1873, in Huntsville, Utah, the son of David McKay and Jennette Evans McKay. When McKay was eight years old, his father left his family for two years to serve as a Mormon missionary in Scotland. McKay obtained his early education from public schools and then at the Weber Stake Academy in Ogden, Utah, a Mormon school. After two years at the academy, McKay returned to his hometown to serve a year as principal of the community school. After this brief interlude in his education, McKay enrolled in the University of Utah, from which he graduated first in his class in 1897.

After two years of service as a missionary in Scotland, McKay returned to the United States in 1899 and began work at the Weber Stake Academy, first as a teacher and then, beginning in 1902, as principal. Within four years, though, after three members of the Mormon Church's Quorum of the Twelve Apostles died in quick succession, McKay was ordained an apostle in the church. He remained at Weber Academy until 1908, when his administrative responsibilities with the church made it impossible to continue with his duties as principal. Thereafter, however, McKay continued to concentrate his energies as a church leader on educational issues. He served on the boards of a succession of institutions:

Weber Academy from 1908 to 1922, the University of Utah from 1921 to 1922, and Utah State Agricultural College (later Utah State University) from 1940 to 1941. He assumed oversight of the Mormon Church's Sunday School program as superintendent from 1918 to 1934, and in 1919 he was appointed as the church's first commissioner of education.

To his keen interest in the Mormon Church's educational affairs, McKay added an expansive missionary zeal. In 1920 he became the most traveled Mormon leader of his time after conducting a 13-month worldwide tour of Mormon missions. Soon after completing this tour, he returned to Europe as president of the European mission. By 1924, McKay was back in the United States and reported enthusiastically to the assembled general conference the following year:

> I testify to you that God lives, that he is near to his servants, and will hear and answer them when they come to him. I know that my Redeemer lives. I know it! I know that he has spoken to man in this age. I know that his church is established among men. God help us all to be true to it and help the world to see it as it is.

In 1934, McKay joined the Mormon Church's highest ecclesiastical body, the First Presidency, when the Mormon president, Heber J. Grant, chose him to be one of his two counselors. While in this office, McKay suffered embarrassment when his niece, the historian Fawn McKay Brodie, published a controversial biography of JOSEPH SMITH, JR., the founder of the Mormon Church. The book, *No Man Knows My History* (1945), suggested that Smith had manufactured the revelations that he had professed to have received and that formed the basis for the religious claims of the church. It so alienated Brodie from the church that she requested and received excommunication. This controversy, however, did not diminish McKay's own standing with the church. Six years after the publication of Fawn Brodie's book, after the death of the Mormon president, George Albert Smith, McKay became the ninth president of the Church of Jesus Christ of Latter-day Saints.

In McKay's 19-year tenure as president, the Mormon Church's membership increased dramatically, from 1.1 million to 2.8 million. In part, this growth reflected a significant change in Mormon missionary activity. McKay ended the church's policy of encouraging non-American converts to Mormonism to immigrate to the United States and, beginning in the mid-1950s, oversaw the opening of Mormon temples in other countries. McKay died in Salt Lake City, Utah, on January 18, 1970.

David O. McKay's enthusiasm for Mormon missions while he was a member of the Quorum of the Twelve Apostles predicted the course of his presidency. His movement to build Mormon temples overseas announced a new period in Mormon history in which the United States no longer represented a kind of Mecca for Mormon believers. McKay's leadership thus helped to transform Mormonism from an American to a world religion.

Further Reading

Armstrong, Richard N. *The Rhetoric of David O. McKay: Mormon Prophet.* New York: P. Lang, 1993.

Brodie, Fawn. *No Man Knows My History: The Life of Joseph Smith the Mormon Prophet.* 2d ed. New York: Knopf, 1971.

Gibbons, Francis M. *David O. McKay: Apostle to the World, Prophet of God.* Salt Lake City, Utah: Deseret, 1986.

McKay, David Lawrence. *My Father, David O. McKay.* Edited by Lavina Fielding Anderson. Salt Lake City, Utah: Deseret, 1989.

McKay, David Oman. *Cherished Experiences, from the Writings of President David O. McKay.* Compiled by Clare Middlemiss. Rev. ed. Salt Lake City, Utah: Deseret, 1976.

———. *Gospel Ideals: Selections from the Discourses of David O. McKay.* Salt Lake City, Utah: Bookcraft, 1998.

———. *What E'er Thou Art Act Well Thy Part: The Missionary Diaries of David O. McKay.* Edited by Stan Larson and Patricia Larson. Salt Lake City, Utah: Blue Ribbon Books, 1999.

McKay, Llewelyn R. *Home Memories of President David O. McKay.* Salt Lake City, Utah: Deseret, 1956.

Morrell, Jeanette. *Highlights in the Life of President David O. McKay.* Salt Lake City, Utah: Deseret, 1966.

McKendree, William
(1757–1835) *Methodist Episcopal bishop*

The first American-born bishop of the Methodist Episcopal Church, William McKendree has sometimes been referred to as the father of western Methodism. In addition to laboring in the newly created Western Conference of the Methodist Episcopal Church, he inaugurated administrative changes in the church that had a lasting effect on its life. McKendree was born on July 6, 1757, in King William County, Virginia, the son of John and Mary McKendree. He was raised in the Anglican Church, which prevailed in the southern colonies, but in around 1776 he first associated himself with the Methodists. During the Revolutionary War he served in the Continental army and was present at the surrender of Cornwallis at Yorktown. He experienced a religious conversion in 1787, which he described in the following terms:

> The great deep of my heart was broken up; its desperately wicked nature was disclosed and the awfully ruinous consequences clearly appeared. My repentance was sincere. I was desirous of salvation, and became willing to be saved upon any terms; and after a sore and sorrowful travail of three days . . . I ventured my all on Christ. In a moment my soul was delivered of a burden too heavy to be borne, and joy instantly succeeded sorrow.

Nine months after his conversion, McKendree became an itinerant Methodist preacher. He was admitted on trial in 1788 as a preacher in the Virginia Conference and assigned to the Mecklenburg Circuit. Over the following several years he preached in a number of Virginia circuits. Bishop FRANCIS ASBURY ordained him first a deacon in the summer of 1790 and then an elder on Christmas Day the following year.

McKendree's career in the Methodist Episcopal Church almost ended abruptly in 1792, when he briefly joined the ecclesiastical rebellion of his presiding elder, James O'Kelly. That year, O'Kelly attempted to subvert the authority of Bishop Asbury by proposing a resolution at the General Conference held in Baltimore, the first such conference since the organization of the Methodist Episcopal Church in 1784. O'Kelly proposed to limit the authority of the bishops—then Asbury and THOMAS COKE, who spent much of his time in England—by giving "any preacher who may think himself injured by the appointment of the bishop the liberty to appeal to the Conference." When this resolution failed to pass, O'Kelly promptly withdrew from the Methodist Episcopal Church and established the Republican Methodist Church. McKendree briefly staged a miniature rebellion of his own by declining to accept an itinerant circuit for the coming year. Nevertheless, Bishop Asbury sought out the young minister, invited McKendree to travel with him for a time, and effected his reconciliation with the Methodist Episcopal Church.

After several more years of itinerant preaching in Virginia, McKendree was ordained a presiding elder in 1796. Five years later he took charge of the Kentucky District of the newly formed Western Conference, where he devoted his copious energy, speaking ability, and administrative gifts to founding new Methodist churches and circuits. His labors during this period won him acknowledgment as the "father of western Methodism."

At the General Conference in 1808, McKendree was elected the third bishop of the church. Early in his tenure as bishop, McKendree introduced an important administrative change. Bishop Asbury had previously made preaching assignments for the ministers of the church without consulting others. McKendree began the practice of seeking the advice of his presiding elders on matters of appointments, declining to make these decisions solely by himself.

McKendree never married. He labored as bishop of the Methodist Episcopal Church past the death of Francis Asbury in 1816, though his own health began to decline after 1820. On his donation of nearly 500 acres to Lebanon Seminary in Lebanon, Illinois, in 1830, the institution was re-

named McKendree College in his honor. He died five years later, on March 5, 1835, in Summer County, Tennessee, at his brother's home.

William McKendree worked for the cause of Methodism across nearly half a century. He became the church's first native-born bishop, even though he almost left the church early in his ministerial career. Prodigious efforts, though, coupled with great speaking and administrative gifts, eventually made him one of the most influential leaders of early American Methodism.

Further Reading

Bangs, Nathan. *A History of the Methodist Episcopal Church.* 4 vols. New York: T. Mason and G. Lane, 1838–40.

Fry, Benjamin St. James. *The Life of Rev. William M'Kendree.* Edited by Daniel P. Kidder. New York: Carlton & Phillips, 1852.

Paine, Robert. *Life and Times of William M'Kendree, Bishop of the Methodist Episcopal Church.* Nashville: Publishing House of the Methodist Episcopal Church, South, 1880.

Wigger, John H. *Taking Heaven by Storm: Methodism and the Rise of Popular Christianity in America.* New York: Oxford University Press, 1998.

McPherson, Aimee Semple
(Aimee Elizabeth Kennedy)
(1890–1944) *Pentecostal preacher*

A Pentecostal evangelist and founder of the Church of the Foursquare Gospel, Aimee Semple McPherson was one of the most controversial and flamboyant preachers of the 20th century. Preaching an optimistic and entertaining gospel, she attracted large audiences, though controversy clouded the last two decades of her ministry. She was born Aimee Elizabeth Kennedy on October 9, 1890, in Ontario, Canada, the daughter of James Morgan Kennedy and Mildred ("Minnie") Pearce. Her father was a Methodist farmer and her mother an active member of the Salvation Army. While in high school, Aimee Kennedy was a skeptic for a time but eventually experienced conversion to Pentecostalism after hearing the preaching of Irish

Pentecostal preacher Aimee Semple McPherson founded the Church of the Foursquare Gospel. *(Library of Congress, Prints and Photographs Division LC-USZ62-92329)*

evangelist Robert James Semple, whom she married in 1908, at the age of 17.

After a brief preaching ministry in the United States, Aimee Semple and her husband became missionaries to China in 1910. Shortly after their arrival, however, both contracted malaria and Robert Semple died of complications of the illness on August 17, 1910. A month after his death, Aimee gave birth to their daughter, Roberta Star Semple, in Hong Kong. She returned to the United States and settled for a time in New York City, where her mother had moved to work in a Salvation Army mission. Soon, though, Aimee Semple struck out on her own. In the course of her travel she met and married Harold ("Mack") McPherson, a Chicago accountant, in 1912. The new couple moved to Rhode Island, where she

gave birth to Rolf Kennedy McPherson in 1913, but, in the wake of prolonged illness, McPherson soon became convinced that God had called her to the work of evangelism. She left her husband in 1915 to begin an itinerant preaching career. Harold joined her for a time but ultimately tired of traveling; the couple separated permanently in 1918, then divorced in 1921.

In the later part of 1918, McPherson believed it was time to find a more permanent center of ministry, and she moved with her children to California, where, the following year, she began to preach at Victoria Hall in downtown Los Angeles. She combined ministry at this location with continued preaching tours that drew increasingly large audiences in tents, auditoriums, and coliseums. By 1921, she had raised enough money to begin construction on the Angelus Temple, at the edge of Echo Park in Los Angeles, and the 5,300-seat auditorium was opened at the first of the year in 1923. There, she attracted large crowds with her dynamic preaching, theatrical presentations, and reputation for having the gift of healing. Four years after the Angelus Temple opened, McPherson established the Church of the Foursquare Gospel, which, by the closing years of the 20th century, would be a separate branch of Pentecostalism with more than 2 million members and more than 20,000 local congregations.

In the spring of 1926, McPherson became the center of a lurid controversy after she disappeared while swimming at a beach in Venice, California. When she reappeared at the end of June that year, claiming to have been kidnapped and to have escaped, rumors circulated that she had disappeared to have an affair with an employee at the Angelus Temple. A local district attorney charged her with obstructing justice and falsifying police reports but eventually dropped the charges. McPherson made a "Vindication Tour" in 1927, but controversy seemed to have become a permanent fixture of her evangelistic ministry. In 1931 she married David Hutton, a singer at the Angelus Temple, but this marriage disappointed many of her followers, who believed that remarriage while one's spouse was still alive violated scriptural teaching. The marriage dissolved in divorce by the beginning of 1934 and was followed by a series of legal battles that estranged McPherson from her daughter and her mother. Eventually she turned operation of the Foursquare Church over to her son in 1944, though she continued her preaching ministry. She died on September 27, 1944, in Oakland, California, of an overdose of sleeping pills, which was ruled accidental by a medical examiner.

Aimee Semple McPherson believed she lived in the last days, when miraculous signs such as speaking in tongues and healing presaged the coming of Christ. In a sermon preached five years before her death at Angelus Temple, she captured the sense of expectancy and urgency that characterized her phenomenal success as a charismatic preacher. "Jesus is coming soon," she assured her audience. "Jesus is so exquisitely glorious! Salva-tion is so real and so to be desired. It must be had. The whole success or failure of these last few days depends on you, and God help me, upon me." Revivalism has had many preachers of fire and brimstone who pummeled their audiences with the prospect of eternal damnation. McPherson, instead, captivated thousands with a message of hope and redemption, delivered with an appreciation for the value of spectacle and entertainment that proved an enduring spiritual combination during the 20th century.

Further Reading

Austin, Alvyn. *Aimee Semple McPherson.* Don Mills, Ont.: Fitzhenry and Whiteside, 1980.

Bahr, Robert. *Least of All Saints: The Story of Aimee Semple McPherson.* Englewood Cliffs, N.J.: Prentice-Hall, 1979.

Blumhofer, Edith Waldvogel. *Aimee Semple McPherson: Everybody's Sister.* Grand Rapids, Mich.: W. B. Eerdmans, 1993.

Epstein, Daniel Mark. *Sister Aimee. The Life of Aimee Semple McPherson.* New York: Harcourt Brace Jovanovich, 1993.

Mavity, Nancy Barr. *Sister Aimee.* Garden City, N.Y.: Doubleday, Doran, 1931.

McPherson, Aimee Semple. *In the Service of the King; The Story of My Life.* New York: Boni & Liveright, 1927; Waco, Tex.: Word Books, 1973.

———. *This Is That: Personal Experiences, Sermons and Writings of Aimee Semple McPherson.* Los Angeles: Echo Park Evangelistic Association, Inc., 1923; New York: Garland, 1985.

Mendes, Henry Pereira
(1852–1937) *Orthodox rabbi*

H. Pereira Mendes, as he was known, served as rabbi of the oldest Jewish congregation in America for more than 40 years. He added to his pastoral and preaching responsibilities an active engagement in the Jewish cultural and social life of New York City. Henry Pereira Mendes was born on April 13, 1852, in Birmingham, England, the son of Abraham Pereira Mendes and Eliza de Sola Mendes. Mendes sprang from a long line of Sephardic rabbis, including both his father and his maternal grandfather, David Aaron de Sola. He studied at Northwick College in London, a religious school established by his father, from when he was 12 years old, and he later attended University College of the University of London from 1870 to 1872. Subsequently, he served for a few years as a rabbi in Manchester, England.

Mendes found a lasting station in 1877, when he accepted the invitation to become the rabbi of Congregation Shearith Israel in New York City, the city's Spanish and Portuguese synagogue and the country's oldest Jewish congregation, established in the mid-17th century. He served in this position actively for the next 43 years and assumed emeritus status on his retirement in 1920. Thirteen years after he arrived in the United States, Mendes married Rosalie Rebecca Piza, with whom he had two sons.

Mendes prominently defended Orthodox Judaism from the 19th-century encroachments of the Reform Judaism movement, laboring energetically to defend traditional Jewish beliefs and practices from those who would submerge them through assimilation to American culture. Together with Rabbi SABATO MORAIS of the Mikveh Israel congregation in Philadelphia, Pennsylvania, he helped found the Jewish Theological Seminary in New York City in 1887. He and Morais intended this institution to serve as an Orthodox counterpart to the Hebrew Union College in Cincinnati, Ohio, which had been established by Rabbi ISSAC MAYER WISE and other leaders of Reform Judaism in 1875. Morais undertook the first presidency of the seminary, but after his death in 1897, Mendes occupied this post from 1897 to 1902. Mendes, though, ultimately severed his relationship with the seminary after it was captured as an arm of Conservative Judaism. During this period, Mendes also advanced the cause of Orthodox Judaism by helping to found the Union of Orthodox Jewish Congregations of America in 1898 and serving as the organization's president during its first decade and a half.

Mendes seized every opportunity to expand the organizational and cultural resources of American Jews, helping to found, for example, the Horeb Home and School for Jewish Deaf-Mutes, which later became the Lexington School for the Deaf, and the Montefiore Hospital. He also played a key role in promoting the cause of Zionism. He did not do so, though, simply as a means of securing a Jewish homeland. He emphasized the "spiritual side of Zionism," a vision he described in the following terms:

> I consider that the spiritual side of Zionism doesn't mean only the possession of a legalized home in the land of our fathers. It means that, and much more. Our possession is already legalized by Him who gave it to us forever and who gives all lands to whom He pleases.

To his many activities on behalf of Orthodox Judaism and Zionism, Mendes added as well a prolific writing career. He wrote a stream of poems and articles for the *American Hebrew* and worked with other Jews to publish *The Jewish Encyclopedia* and a new English translation of the Hebrew Bible. He also published books of his own, including *Derech Hayim: The Way of Life,* which he finished three years before his death. Mendes died on October 20, 1937, in Mount Vernon, New York.

H. Pereira Mendes arrived in the United States at a time when Orthodox Judaism found itself on the defensive against reformist impulses that urged American Jews to embrace their country and its culture more emphatically, even at the cost of sacrificing traditional Jewish beliefs and practices. More affluent Jewish congregations, especially, found the appeals of Reform Judaism powerful and frequently turned away from Orthodox Judaism. Mendes, though, became a powerful ally for beleaguered Orthodoxy. As a rabbi trained in England and leader of a Jewish congregation with roots in colonial America, he offered a persuasive counterargument to Reform Jews who characterized Orthodoxy as too steeped in Old World traditions and not sufficiently in touch with American life. He helped demonstrate that traditional Judaism need not surrender either its beliefs or its practices to find a prominent place in the religious life of the nation.

Further Reading

Fierstien, Robert E. "From Foundation to Reorganization: The Jewish Theological Seminary of America,

1886–1902." Ph.D. dissertation, Jewish Theological Seminary of America, 1986.

Markovitz, Eugene. "Henry Pereira Mendes: Builder of Traditional Judaism in America." Ph.D. dissertation, Yeshiva University, 1961.

Mendes, Henry Pereira. *The Jewish Religion Ethically Presented.* 5th ed. New York: Bloch, 1921.

———. *Looking Ahead: Twentieth Century Happenings.* London: F. T. Neely, 1899.

Nadell, Pamela Susan. *Conservative Judaism in America: A Biographical Dictionary and Sourcebook.* New York: Greenwood Press, 1988.

Pool, David deSilva. *H. Pereira Mendes: A Biography.* New York: n.p., 1938.

Sachar, Howard M. *A History of the Jews in America.* New York: Knopf, 1992.

Merton, Thomas
(Brother Louis)
(1915–1968) *Trappist monk, writer*

Although Thomas Merton adopted the contemplative spiritual vocation of a Trappist monk, he became one of the most popular Catholic writers of the 20th century. The autobiographical account of his conversion to Catholicism, *The Seven Storey Mountain,* is regarded as a classic narrative of spiritual life. Merton was born on January 31, 1915, in Prades, France, the son of Owen Merton, a New Zealander, and Ruth Jenkins Merton, an American. Merton's family moved to the United States the year after he was born, and his mother died of cancer in 1921. The remainder of his childhood and youth witnessed a series of geographical dislocations as he moved with his father—an artist—first to Bermuda, then to New York, then to France, and finally to England, where Thomas enrolled in the Oakham School in 1923. Three years later, Merton's father died of a brain tumor.

In 1933, Merton matriculated at Clare College, Cambridge, but his unruly behavior apparently caused his guardian to remove him from Cambridge the following year. Subsequently, Merton returned to the United States, where he enrolled in Columbia University, from which he graduated with a B.A. in English in 1935. He fol-

lowed this degree with work toward an M.A., which he ultimately received in 1841. During his graduate years, Merton became attracted to Catholicism under the influence of two of his professors, Mark Van Doren and Daniel Walsh. He was baptized into the Catholic Church and, in November 1938, received his first communion, an event whose significance he later described in *The Seven Storey Mountain:*

> For now I had entered into the everlasting movement of that gravitation which is the very life and spirit of God: God's own gravitation towards the depths of His own infinite nature, His goodness without end. And God, that center Who is everywhere, and whose circumference is nowhere, finding me, through incorporation with Christ, incorporated into this immense and tremendous gravitational movement which is love, which is the Holy Spirit, love me.
>
> And He called out to me from His own immense depths.

Soon after his conversion, Merton began exploring the possibility of becoming a priest. Although he first considered joining the Franciscans and taught for this order at St. Bonaventure's College (later St. Bonaventure University), the Franciscans ultimately declined to receive him into their order. In the wake of the emotional turmoil occasioned by this rejection, Merton turned instead to the Trappist order, of which he had formed a favorable impression after attending a retreat at Our Lady of Gethsemane, a Trappist abbey in Kentucky. He became a postulate of the order in December 1941 and, two months later, a novice in the order formally known as the Cistercians of the Strict Observance. He made final vows in the order in 1947 and was ordained a Trappist priest two years later.

At the urging of his superiors in the order, Merton, known as Brother Louis among the Trappists, turned to writing a few years later, publishing *Thirty Poems* in 1944 and *The Seven Storey Mountain* in 1948. The latter, an account of his spiritual pilgrimage, eventually became a best-seller, establishing Merton as an important Catholic writer. He wrote prolifically after this; some of his works appeared only after he died. Toward the last decade of his life, he became interested in the mystical traditions of Eastern religions and eventually arranged permission from his order to travel to India and Thailand. While in Bangkok, he died of a heart attack on December 10, 1968, apparently caused by an electric shock received from a fan with faulty wiring.

Of Thomas Merton's first Christmas in a Trappist monastery, he wrote in an early draft of *The Seven Storey Mountain*, "Christ always seeks the straw of the most desolate cribs to make his Bethlehem." Merton's retreat from the barrenness of materialism to the spiritually contemplative life became an inspiration to many believers in the last half of the 20th century. Mystical traditions of both the West and the East experienced a rebirth during this period, and Merton served as an exemplar of the spiritual possibilities available in contemplative communities. His first Christmas in a monastery found him stretched out on a stone floor, prostrate in worship of the Christ of Bethlehem. For the many who desired to find a faith that was not married to late 20th-century materialism, Merton's contemplative experience became an important spiritual beacon.

Further Reading

Forest, James H. *Living with Wisdom: A Life of Thomas Merton.* Maryknoll, N.Y.: Orbis Books, 1991.

Furlong, Monica. *Merton: A Biography.* New York: Harper & Row, 1980.

Griffin, John Howard. *Follow the Ecstasy: The Hermitage Years of Thomas Merton.* Edited by Robert Bonazzi. Maryknoll, N.Y.: Orbis Books, 1993.

Merton, Thomas. *The Seven Storey Mountain.* New York: Harcourt, Brace, 1948.

———. *Thomas Merton, Spiritual Master: The Essential Writings.* Edited by Lawrence S. Cunningham. New York: Paulist Press, 1992.

Nouwen, Henri J. M. *Thomas Merton, Contemplative Critic.* San Francisco: Harper & Row, 1981.

Padovano, Anthony T. *The Human Journey: Thomas Merton, Symbol of a Century.* Garden City, N.Y.: Doubleday, 1982.

Pennington, M. Basil. *Thomas Merton, Brother Monk: The Quest for True Freedom.* San Francisco: Harper & Row, 1987.

Shannon, William Henry. *Silent Lamp: The Thomas Merton Story.* New York: Crossroad, 1992.

Wilkes, Paul, ed. *Merton, by Those Who Knew Him Best.* San Francisco: Harper & Row, 1984.

Woodcock, George. *Thomas Merton, Monk and Poet: A Critical Study.* New York: Farrar, Straus, Giroux, 1978.

Michel, Virgil George
(George Francis Michel)
(1890–1938) *Catholic monk*

Virgil George Michel founded the American liturgical movement. He also played a prominent role in the development of Catholic social thought during the early decades of the 20th century. He was born George Francis Michel on June 24, 1890, in Saint Paul, Minnesota, the son of Fred Michel and Mary Griebler Michel. Growing up in a Catholic family, Michel attended elementary school at Assumption School in Saint Paul and high school at St. John's Preparatory School in Collegeville, Minnesota. In 1909, he entered the novitiate of St. John's Abbey. He took monastic vows as a Benedictine monk in 1913 and assumed the name *Virgil*. He pursed college education at St. John's University, where he earned a B.A., a Ph.B., and an M.A. in 1909, 1912, and 1913, respectively. He followed these degrees with study at the Catholic University of America, where he earned an S.T.B. in 1917 and a Ph.D. in English in 1918. During this last year, he was ordained a priest.

From 1918 to 1924, Michel served at St. John's in a variety of administrative and teaching positions. At the end of this period, his abbot sent him to Rome to study scholastic philosophy. Once arrived in Rome, however, Michel found his interest drawn to the subject of liturgical reform within the church, and he met and was deeply influenced by another Benedictine monk, Lambert Beauduin of the Belgian monastery of Mont-César. Beauduin encouraged Michel's study of liturgy as an expression of the Mystical Body of Christ, a liturgical idea that emphasized the corporate nature of Catholic spirituality rather than purely individual piety. As a consequence of Beauduin's influence, Michel visited a variety of religious communities in

Europe to familiarize himself with the main currents of liturgical renewal at work there.

On his return to St. John's in 1925, Michel cast himself into the labor of transplanting the liturgical ideas he had seen cultivated in Europe to American soil. Two publishing ventures undertaken in 1926 served as the central focus of his work: the Liturgical Press, which he used at first to publish translations of European works concerning liturgy, and *Orate Fratres* (renamed *Worship* in 1951), a journal devoted to the study and discussion of liturgical issues. In addition to these efforts, Michel collaborated with the Dominican Sisters of Grand Rapids, Michigan, to publish the Christ-Life series, a series of textbooks for use in elementary and secondary parochial schools. With the Grand Rapids Dominicans, he undertook a similar project for college students, *The Christian Religion Series for College*.

A whirlwind of activity in the five years after his return from Europe eventually took its toll on Michel's health. He had to be hospitalized for a time and afterward was assigned less strenuous responsibilities as a missionary to Native Americans in northern Minnesota. He returned to St. John's in 1933, however, and resumed oversight of the Liturgical Press and *Orate Fratres*. In the following years, Michel devoted significant attention to the connection between liturgy and issues of social justice. As the nation struggled through the Great Depression, he became convinced that a proper focus on lay participation in liturgical elements of the church such as the mass offered the promise of creating a sense of religious community. This renewed sense of community, in turn, might be marshaled to address issues of social justice. Five years after his return to St. John's, however, Michel's health again collapsed under the weight of his many activities. He contracted pneumonia and died on November 26, 1938, in Collegeville, Minnesota.

In the brief years of his mature work as a Benedictine monk, Virgil Michel left an indelible mark on the liturgical life of the Catholic Church in the United States. He is generally acknowledged as the founder of the liturgical movement, which sought to make the Catholic liturgy not simply the spiritual possession of priests and religious workers but the corporate expression of worship within the mystical Body of Christ. Through the articles he wrote for *Orate Fratres*, the books he published through the Liturgical Press, and an energetic, if brief, career as a preacher and a teacher, Virgil Michel helped steer the course of liturgical development in the United States long after his life had ended. He also labored to show the connection between Catholic spirituality and social thought, a connection increasingly prominent among 20th-century Catholics in the decades after Michel's untimely death.

Further Reading

Franklin, R. W. *Virgil Michel: American Catholic.* Collegeville, Minn.: Liturgical Press, 1988.

Marx, Paul. *Virgil Michel and the Liturgical Movement.* Collegeville, Minn.: Liturgical Press, 1957.

Michel, Virgil George. *Christian Social Reconstruction: Some Fundamentals of the Quadragesimo Anno.* Milwaukee: Bruce, 1937.

———. *Liberal Education: Essays on the Philosophy of Higher Education.* Edited by Robert L. Spaeth. Collegeville, Minn.: Office of Academic Affairs, Saint John's University, 1981.

———. *The Liturgy of the Church, According to the Roman Rite.* New York: Macmillan, 1937.

Wilson, Stephen Bradley. "Liturgical Life: Elements of a Contemporary Account of the Christian Moral Life Based on a Macintyrean Read of Virgil Michel's Thought." Ph.D. dissertation., University of Notre Dame, 2000.

Miller, William

(1782–1849) *founder of the Adventist movement*

For a brief period during the 19th century, William Miller gained national notoriety when he named a precise date for the return of Christ to earth. When this event failed to come to pass, Miller was quickly forgotten, though the millennial expectations that fueled his initial popularity survived into the 21st century. He was born on February 15, 1782, in Pittsfield, Massachusetts, the son of William Miller and Paulina Phelps Miller, and he grew up in Low Hampton, New York.

Miller married Lucy Smith in 1803, and the couple settled in Poultney, Vermont, and eventually had 10 children together. Though he had grown up in a pious family, which included a grandfather and an uncle who were Baptist ministers, Miller became a skeptic in his young adult years. He worked for a time as a constable and a sheriff before joining the Vermont militia and then the army, through which he saw action during the War of 1812.

After the war, Miller experienced a religious conversion at a camp meeting and began to study the Bible seriously. The fruit of these studies was a growing conviction that Jesus would return to earth to establish his millennial kingdom around 1843. He derived this date from the Old Testament book of Daniel, chapter 8, which prophesied an interval of 2,300 days before the inauguration of the Messiah's millennial kingdom. Dating this prophesy at 457 B.C., and construing the days referred to as years, Miller concluded that Christ's return was imminent. Although Miller soon began sharing this belief in local revival speeches, he might have remained relatively unknown but for his association with Joshua W. Himes, a Boston minister who became convinced of the truth of Miller's views and helped to promote them. By 1836, he had helped Miller publish a tract setting forth the basis for his astonishing prediction: *Evidences from Scripture and History of the Second Coming of Christ about the Year A.D. 1843, and of His Personal Reign of 1000 Years.* Six years later, Himes purchased an enormous tent that Miller used to lecture ever increasing crowds on the subject of Christ's return.

When the year 1843 finally arrived, Miller's disciples pressed him for a more precise announcement concerning the date of Christ's appearance, and Miller responded by suggesting that it would occur sometime between March 21, 1843, and March 21, 1844. When the later date passed, however, Miller revised his original calculations and concluded that Jesus would return to earth on October 22, 1844. The failure of this prediction yielded what came to be known as "the great disappointment," and the abrupt decline of Miller's influence. It did not, however, spell the end of Adventism as a movement. Some of those who had been influenced by his teaching, such as Ellen

Gould Harmon Smith—the founder of Seventh Day Adventism—continued to believe that October 22, 1844, had inaugurated Christ's millennial kingdom, though not openly and visibly, on earth. This offshoot of Adventism survived into the 21st century, long after Miller himself had been forgotten. Miller died in Low Hampton several years after the great disappointment, on December 20, 1849.

Enthusiasm for the imminent return of Christ and speculation concerning the signs of his appearance featured prominently in the history of American religion during the 19th and 20th centuries. Miller's brief popularity owed much to enduring interest in the subject of the end times, an interest that continues to thrive in many Christian denominations, especially those with a populist and conservative cast. But Miller became famous not simply because he shared a common anticipation of the inauguration of Christ's millennial kingdom but because he was willing to name the date for the inauguration. Time eventually proved his prediction wrong, but it could not erase the keen millennial interest that survived the discrediting of this one overly confident seer.

Further Reading

Bliss, Sylvester. *Memoirs of William Miller, Generally Known as a Lecturer on the Prophecies, and the Second Coming of Christ.* Boston: J. V. Himes, 1853; New York: AMS Press, 1971.

Dick, Everett Newfon. *William Miller and the Advent Crisis, 1831–1844.* Edited by Gary Land. Berrien Springs, Mich.: Andrews University Press, 1994.

Doan, Ruth Alden. *The Miller Heresy, Millennialism, and American Culture.* Philadelphia: Temple University Press, 1987.

Gale, Robert. *The Urgent Voice: The Story of William Miller.* Washington, D.C.: Review and Herald Publishing Association, 1975.

Gordon, Paul A. *Herald of the Midnight Cry.* Edited by Glen Robinson. Boise, Idaho: Pacific Press Publishing Association, 1990.

Miller, William. *Evidence from Scripture and History of the Second Coming of Christ.* Troy, N.Y.: E. Gates, 1838.

Numbers, Ronald L., and Jonathan M. Butler, eds. *The Disappointed: Millerism and Millenarianism in the*

Nineteenth Century. Bloomington: Indiana University Press, 1987.

White, James. *Sketches of the Christian Life and Public Labors of William Miller, Gathered from His Memoir by the Late Sylvester Bliss, and from Other Sources.* Battle Creek, Mich.: Steam Press of the Seventh-Day Adventist Publishing Association, 1875; New York: AMS Press, 1972.

Mitchell, Jonathan

(1624–1668) *Puritan minister*

A leading intellectual of New England's second generation, Jonathan Mitchell occupied the prestigious pulpit of the Congregational Church at Cambridge. For nearly 20 years he preached to the students and faculty of Harvard, as well as to the other inhabitants of that town, and played a crucial role in the synod that produced the Half-Way Covenant. He was born in 1624 in Yorkshire, England, to Matthew Mitchell and Susan Butterfield Mitchell. His parents migrated to New England in 1635 along with the famous Puritan preacher RICHARD MATHER. They settled eventually in Connecticut, where Jonathan received his preparatory education from Abraham Pierson. He matriculated in 1642 at Harvard College and achieved such academic success there that he became a teaching fellow at the college in 1649 after his graduation.

The church at Cambridge had been established in 1636, and its first pastor, Thomas Shepard, was one of New England's most influential preachers. When Shepard died in 1649, the church invited Mitchell to assume his place. Mitchell accepted this offer in 1650 and that same year also married Shepard's widow, Margaret Boradel Shepard, with whom he had six children. This spiritual post placed Jonathan Mitchell at the center of Harvard's religious life.

Soon after he became minister of the Cambridge Church, Mitchell had to confront one of the most notorious defections from the Puritan fold of the 17th century. In the mid- to late 1630s, religious dissenters such as ROGER WILLIAMS and ANNE MARBURY HUTCHINSON had disturbed the fondly constructed thoroughfares of New England's experiment in holy commonwealth. But neither had held an important place of leadership within the affairs of the colony. In 1654, though, HENRY DUNSTER, the president of Harvard and a member of Mitchell's own congregation, demonstrated that heterodoxy might issue even from prominent places. Dunster became convinced that the baptism of infants—a prominent practice among the New England Puritans of the 17th century—was contrary to scriptural teaching. By thus aligning himself with the so-called Anabaptists—those who believed that baptism should be reserved for adults who had experienced conversion—Dunster scandalized his Puritan contemporaries, in whose minds Anabaptists were "incendiaries of commonwealths" because they attacked what Puritans believed to be a crucial religious and social covenant between parents and their children and God. Mitchell and other New England ministers endeavored in vain to sway Dunster from his opinions. Ultimately, Dunster resigned as Harvard's president in 1654 and relocated to Plymouth Colony.

The following decade, Mitchell found himself again at the center of spiritual controversy when the Synod of 1662 met to consider another issue relating to infant baptism. The synod addressed the controversial question of whether churches should baptize the children of parents who had themselves been baptized as infants but had never had an adult conversion experience and thus had never become full church members. The synod adopted the Half-Way Covenant, which provided that these children could themselves be baptized though they, like their parents, would not be admitted to full church membership unless they were later able to demonstrate that they had experienced conversion. Mitchell played a crucial role in the adoption of this covenant. "To leave the Children of non-scandalous Orthodox Christians Unbaptized," he preached in a sermon the year before his death, "will (I doubt not) be one day found a thing displeasing unto Jesus Christ." Mitchell published the synod's official results and also defended the Half-Way Covenant in his work *A Defense of the Answer and Arguments of the Synod Met at Boston in the Year 1662* (1664). Jonathan Mitchell died four years later in Cambridge on July 9, 1668.

The man who graduated from Harvard with such distinction toward the end of the 1640s lived less than 20 years after this event. But during his brief adult life he earned a reputation as one of New England's brightest spiritual stars. He wrote an influential appeal to Massachusetts's General Court, seeking financial support of Harvard, *Modell for the Maintaining of Students and Fellows of Choise Abilities at the College in Cambridge* (1664). New England suffered from his untimely death, much as it had from the untimely death of Thomas Shepard, his predecessor at the Cambridge church. An epitaph preserved in the Puritan historian COTTON MATHER's *Magnalia Christi Americana* captures the sting of this loss, as experienced by Mitchell's contemporaries:

Here lies the darling of his time,
Mitchell expirëd in his prime;
Was four years short of forty-seven,
Was found full ripe and plucked for heaven.

Massachusetts did not forget Mitchell but preserved his memory as a young man who helped to guide New England Puritanism through its perilous second generation.

Further Reading

Mather, Cotton. *Magnalia Christi Americana.* London, 1702; New York: Arno Press, 1972.

Mitchell, Jonathan. *A Discourse of the Glory to Which God Hath Called Believers by Jesus Christ.* 2d ed. Boston: B. Green, 1721.

———. *Nehemiah on the Wall in Troublesome Times.* Cambridge, Mass.: S.G. & M.J., 1671.

Sibley, John Langdon. *Biographical Sketches of Those Who Attended Harvard College.* Boston: Massachusetts Historical Society, 1873.

Moody, Dwight Lyman
(1837–1899) *revivalist*

Dwight Lyman Moody was a layman who became the greatest revival preacher of the last decades of the 19th century. He pioneered techniques of mass urban evangelism that would be carried forward into the next century through preachers such as BILLY SUNDAY and BILLY GRAHAM, and he established several educational institutions, most prominently among them, the Moody Bible Institute in Chicago. Moody was born on February 5, 1837, in Northfield, Massachusetts, the son of Edwin Moody and Betsey Holton Moody. His father was a bricklayer, and Moody grew up in rural western Massachusetts, where he received only the equivalent of a fifth-grade education.

In 1854, Moody moved to Boston and became a shoe salesman in his uncle's store, began attending a Congregationalist church, and had a conversion experience. In 1856, he relocated to Chicago, where he continued to work as a shoe salesman but also cast himself energetically into religious ministry. Two years after his arrival in Chicago, he took charge of a mission Sunday school in the

Dwight L. Moody introduced revivalism to the major urban centers of late 19th-century America. *(Library of Congress, Prints and Photographs Division LC-USZ62-122752)*

city's slums, and in 1858 he gave up his employment in the shoe store to devote himself full-time to Christian work.

During the Civil War, Moody worked for the United States Christian Commission, which ministered to Union soldiers. In 1862 he married Emma C. Revell, and their union produced three children. After the war, he returned to Chicago and became president of the Chicago Young Men's Christian Association (YMCA) in 1866, but he soon began to supplement his work for the YMCA with preaching engagements in Illinois churches. At a national YMCA meeting in 1870, Moody formed an association with the singer IRA DAVID SANKEY that would contribute immeasurably to the success of his later revival career. The turning point in their association occurred in 1873, when the two men traveled to Great Britain for what would become two years of revival campaigns across England and Scotland.

News of the success of their revivals in Great Britain preceded Moody and Sankey when they returned to the United States in 1875 and launched a decade of revival campaigns in the urban centers of the northern and midwestern United States. Unlike many revivalists who both preceded and followed him, Moody delivered sermons that emphasized the love of God and the potential for salvation within each person's grasp rather than the torments of hell. Combined with Sankey's talents as a singer and composer of popular revival hymns, Moody's preaching soon made him the most prominent evangelist in the country. Though a Congregationalist, he delivered sermons calculated to call his hearers to conversion rather than to expound the doctrines of any particular denomination. "I look upon this world as a wrecked vessel," he was happy to say. "God has given me a lifeboat and said to me, 'Moody, save all you can.'" But in spite of the general ecumenical tenor of his preaching, Moody's own theology placed him among the ranks of Christian conservatives and made him a forerunner of the fundamentalists who would follow in the 20th century.

Dwight L. Moody's early experiences as a Sunday School teacher in the Chicago slums had convinced him of the value of Christian education, and from the late 1870s he took steps to establish institutions that would have a more continuous spiritual impact on the lives of young men and women. In 1879, he founded the Northfield Seminary for Girls in his hometown of Northfield, Massachusetts, and the Mount Hermon School for boys two years later. As his vigorous evangelistic schedule began to slow somewhat, he turned his attention to providing a venue for Christian students and adults to have their faith deepened and did so by establishing the Northfield Conferences in 1880. These conferences drew influential evangelical ministers together in Northfield during the summers and attracted a wide variety of believers in search of spiritual renewal and edification. In 1886, the Student Volunteer movement, an organization devoted to encouraging foreign missions, grew out of that year's conference at Northfield.

Although Moody had originally contemplated that his schools for boys and girls would assist in the preparation of a new generation of Christian workers, he eventually believed that a different kind of institution, more focused on fulfilling this purpose, was required. Accordingly, in 1887, Moody established a Bible training school named the Chicago Evangelization Society, whose first building was erected two years later. Eventually named the Moody Bible Institute after its founder's death, the school was intended to provide a measure of Bible study and a strong dose of hands-on experience for young men who desired to become Christian ministers. This institute would become a leading center of evangelical education in the United States.

Toward the end of his life, Moody spent more of his time in Northfield but maintained a rigorous revival schedule. In the end, heart problems exacerbated by excessive weight were his downfall. In November of 1899, while he was conducting revival services in Kansas City, his health failed him and he had to make one last return to Northfield. As his family gathered around him, it soon became apparent that he was dying. At the end of his life, on December 22, 1899, he exclaimed, "Earth is receding and Heaven is calling," and then breathed his last.

America's most prominent revivalists have frequently managed to step beyond their particular denominational boundaries and address a wider audience. Dwight L. Moody was such an evangelist. Though his personal theology tracked a course that was solidly conservative, he could name as friends some of the liberal religious thinkers of his day. And his preaching avoided the theological controversies that had divided Protestant America into separate camps in favor of a simple call for sinners to receive salvation and for Christians to undertake service in the name of Christ.

Further Reading

Curtis, Richard Kenneth. *They Called Him Mister Moody.* Garden City, N.Y.: Doubleday, 1962.

Dorsett, Lyle W. *A Passion for Souls: The Life of D. L. Moody.* Chicago: Moody Press, 1997.

Findlay, James F. *Dwight L. Moody: American Evangelist, 1837–1899.* Chicago: University of Chicago Press, 1969.

Harvey, Bonnie C. *D.L. Moody: The American Evangelist.* Uhrichsville, Ohio: Barbour, 1997.

Moody, Dwight Layman. *The Best of D. L. Moody: Sixteen Sermons by the Great Evangelist.* Edited by Wilbur M. Smith. Chicago: Moody Press, 1971.

———. *Commending the Faith: The Preaching of D. L. Moody.* Edited by Garth Rosell. Peabody, Mass.: Hendrickson Publishers, 1999.

———. *D. L. Moody Collection: The Highlights of His Writings, Sermons, Anecdotes, and Life Story.* Edited by James S. Bell, Jr. Chicago: Moody Press, 1997.

———. *Dwight L. Moody: The Best from All His Works.* Edited by Stephen Rost. Nashville: T. Nelson Publishers, 1989.

Moody, Paul Dwight. *My Father: An Intimate Portrait of Dwight Moody.* Boston: Little, Brown, 1938.

Moody, William R. *D. L. Moody.* New York: Macmillan, 1930; New York: Garland, 1988.

Pollock, John Charles. *Moody.* Chicago: Moody Press, 1983.

Moon, Lottie
(Charlotte Diggs Moon)
(1840–1912) *Baptist missionary*

A Baptist missionary to China, Lottie Moon struggled against traditional stereotypes about women's roles to become one of the most famous mission-

Lottie Moon devoted her life to Baptist missionary activity in China. *(Southern Baptist Historical Library and Archives)*

aries in Southern Baptist history. During the last quarter of the 19th century and the early years of the 20th, she endured significant hardship and danger to take the Christian message to China. Charlotte Diggs Moon was born on December 12, 1840, at a family plantation named Viewmont in Albemarle County, Virginia, the daughter of Edward Harris Moon and Anna Maria Barclay Moon. She studied at Virginia Female Seminary (later Hollins College) in Botetourt Springs and then at Albemarle Female Institute in Charlottesville, Virginia. During her years at Albemarle, she experienced in 1859 a religious conversion after hearing the preaching of Baptist minister and future seminary professor JOHN ALBERT BROADUS.

One of her teachers at Albemarle was a young man named Crawford H. Toy, who later taught for a time at the Southern Baptist Theological Seminary in Louisville, Kentucky, until his sympathies for emerging theories of biblical criticism caused his dismissal from this post in 1879. He subsequently joined the faculty of Harvard College, as a professor of Hebrew and Semitic languages. Toy and Moon appear to have had a romantic attachment, and it seemed for a time after his move to Harvard that Lottie Moon would join him in Cambridge as his wife. But for reasons not fully understood, perhaps because of the divergence between Toy and Moon's theological views, this never happened.

In the years after her graduation from Albemarle, Lottie Moon taught school, first in Danville, Kentucky, from 1866 to 1873, and then in Cartersville, Georgia, in 1873. In this final year, she was appointed a missionary to China by the Foreign Missions Board of the Southern Baptists. When she arrived in China late in 1873, she worked initially with her sister, Edmonia Harris Moon, overseeing a school for boys in Tengchow. But her sister's health failed within a few years, and she and Lottie Moon returned to the United States in 1876. The following year, Lottie Moon set out for China without her sister. After seven more years of labor at a school for girls she established in Tengchow, during which she seems to have first considered and then abandoned thought of marrying Crawford H. Toy, she relocated to P'ingtu in the interior of Shantung Province. She chafed at traditional views that would have limited her work to that thought appropriate for a woman. In an article written for *Woman's Work in China*, she expressed her dissatisfaction with these views: "Can we wonder at the mortal weariness and disgust, the sense of wasted powers and the conviction that her life is a failure, that comes over a woman when, instead of the ever-broadening activities she had planned, she finds herself tied down to the petty work of teaching a few girls." Over the following years, she demonstrated the capacity of women to serve as equal partners in missionary activity.

Apart from a furlough to the United States in 1903 to 1904, Moon remained in China for the rest of her life. From 1910, plague and famine assailed Shantung Province, and Moon suffered along with the Chinese people. By the end of 1912, she had taken to depriving herself of food so she might relieve the hunger of those around her. She grew so weak and so despondent about the lack of financial support for her missionary work that her life was threatened. Missionary associates tried to salvage her health by transporting her back to the United States, but while on board a ship in a Japanese harbor en route to the United States, she died on December 24, 1912.

Lottie Moon served on the mission field of China for almost four decades. During those years she supplemented her evangelistic efforts among the Chinese with constant efforts to persuade other Southern Baptists to join her in China or at least to support mission work there. Though these appeals had little success while she was alive, in the years that followed her death, Southern Baptists recognized her as a kind of patron saint of foreign missions by naming their annual fund-raising drive for foreign missions after her.

Further Reading

Allen, Catherine B. *The New Lottie Moon Story.* 2d ed. Birmingham, Ala.: Woman's Missionary Union, 1997.

Estep, William Roscoe. *Whole Gospel—Whole World: The Foreign Mission Board of the Southern Baptist Convention, 1845–1995.* Nashville: Broadman & Holman, 1994.

Hyatt, Irwin T. *Our Ordered Lives Confess: Three Nineteenth-Century American Missionaries in East Shantung.* Cambridge, Mass.: Harvard University Press, 1976.

Lawrence, Una Roberts. *Lottie Moon.* Nashville: Sunday School Board of the Southern Baptist Convention, 1927.

Monsell, Helen Albee. *Her Own Way: The Story of Lottie Moon.* Nashville: Broadman Press, 1958.

Rankin, Jerry. *A Journey of Faith and Sacrifice: Retracing the Steps of Lottie Moon.* Birmingham, Ala.: New Hope, 1996.

Moon, Sun Myung
(1920–) *founder of the Unification Church*

Korean-born Sun Myung Moon founded one of the best-known new religious movements of the 20th century, the Unification Church. Though the movement remains most prominent in Korea and Japan, it migrated to the United States in the 1960s and Moon himself spent a significant amount of time in America during the final decades of the 20th century. He was born on January 6, 1920, in P'yeongan Pukto, Korea. When he was a child his parents converted to Presbyterianism. As a teenager, Moon believed that Jesus had appeared to him and commissioned him to complete the work that Jesus had been unable to finish. At the age of 19, Moon began to study electrical engineering, first in Seoul and then at Waseda University in Japan.

By 1945 he had returned to Korea and begun preaching the doctrines that would subsequently be published as *The Divine Principle* (1973). Not well received by other Christian ministers in South Korea, Moon relocated to Soviet-occupied North Korea. Soon after his arrival, he was arrested, tortured, and left for dead to be retrieved by his disciples. Though he recovered from this first ordeal, Moon was arrested again in February 1948 for "advocating chaos in society" and sentenced to five years of hard labor at the Tong Mee Special Labour Concentration Camp in Hungnam, famous for its deadly abuse of prisoners. After the beginning of the Korean War in the summer of 1950, United Nations forces liberated the Tong Nee prisoners, including Moon, in October of that year. He then settled in Pusan early in 1951. By 1953 he had relocated to Seoul, and there, on May 1, 1954, he founded the Holy Spirit Association for the Unification of World Christianity, commonly referred to as the Unification Church.

On March 16, 1960, Moon married Ha Ja Han. Over the next decade, missionaries from the Unification Church took Moon's teachings to other parts of the world, including the United States. Young Oom Kim was perhaps the most important of these early missionaries to the United States, working first in Eugene, Oregon, and later

in San Francisco, California. Other missionaries subsequently arrived, though their evangelistic efforts threatened to splinter into separate groups until Moon himself visited the United States in the early 1970s and reorganized the growing affairs of the Unification Church there. *The Divine Principle,* written by Unification Church leader Hyo Won Eu and chiefly representing the revelations received by Moon, was published in English translation in 1973.

According to Moon's teaching, the present world is engulfed in sin because Satan sexually seduced Eve and tainted the human bloodline with his pernicious influence. Jesus came as Messiah and accomplished the spiritual redemption of the world but was not able to accomplish its physical redemption by finding and marrying a perfect wife and producing sinless children. This task remained for a Second Messiah, or "Lord of the Second Advent." During its first decades of existence, the Unification Church sometimes hinted that Moon himself was this Second Messiah, and Moon formally acknowledged that he was Messiah in 1992. Through his marriage to Ha Ja Han, Moon and his wife became the "True Parents." The Unification Church teaches that their marriage creates the possibility that church members can be grafted into the "heavenly family" inaugurated by Moon and his wife and can participate in the Kingdom of Heaven.

In its American incarnation, especially, the Unification Church has generated a significant amount of controversy. Claims that the church brainwashes new members abound, as well as complaints that it uses a variety of "front" organizations to accomplish its purposes without readily revealing the connection between these organizations and the church. Moon himself was convicted of tax evasion in the early 1980s and spent 18 months in prison in the United States. The Unification Church also attracted widespread media attention through its mass marriages. At a "Blessing Ceremony" conducted in Seoul in 1999, for example, Moon presided over a wedding ceremony for more than 40,000 couples. By the beginning of the 21st century, Moon was in his 80s and had designated his wife, some

20 years younger, as his successor within the Unification Church.

The members of the Unification Church, derisively called "Moonies," have made more substantial proselytizing gains in Korea and Japan than in the United States. Nevertheless, the religious group continues to have a controversial presence in America. In the last three decades of the 20th century, Moon did much to court the acceptance of American leaders, especially of the conservative persuasion. The Unification Church, for example, owns *The Washington Times*, an influential conservative newspaper. But at the beginning of the 21st century, it remained to be seen whether the church would flourish after the death of its aging founder.

Further Reading

Boettcher, Robert B. *Gifts of Deceit: Sun Myung Moon, Tongsun Park, and the Korean Scandal.* New York: Holt, Rinehart & Winston, 1980.

Chryssides, George D. *The Advent of Sun Myung Moon: The Origins, Beliefs, and Practices of the Unification Church.* New York: St. Martin's Press, 1991.

Dean, Roger Allen. *Moonies: A Psychological Analysis of the Unification Church.* New York: Garland, 1992.

Horowitz, Irving Louis. *Science, Sin, and Scholarship: The Politics of Reverend Moon and the Unification Church.* Cambridge, Mass.: MIT Press, 1978.

Moon, Sun Myung. *Home Church: The Words of Reverend Sun Myung Moon.* New York: Holy Spirit Association for the Unification of World Christianity, 1983.

Sontag, Frederick. *Sun Myung Moon and the Unification Church.* Nashville: Abingdon Press, 1977.

Morais, Sabato
(1823–1897) *rabbi*

Sabato Morais was the rabbi of the Mikveh Israel congregation in Philadelphia, Pennsylvania, for nearly half a century. During this period he was a vigorous defender of Orthodox Judaism and the founder of the Jewish Theological Seminary in New York City. He was born on April 13, 1823, in Livorno, Italy, the son of Samuel Morais and Buonina Wolf. He grew up in the Sephardic Jewish tradi-

tion, descended from Jews who had lived in Spain and Portugal prior to their expulsion in the last decade of the 15th century, and he received a rabbinical education in Livorno that led to his ordination as a rabbi in 1845. Subsequently, Morais moved to London, where, from 1846, he served as the head of a Jewish school for orphans for five years. In 1851, Morais moved to Philadelphia, where he was elected to the post of "hazan and lecturer," the reader and minister, at the Mikveh Israel congregation in Philadelphia, a Sephardic congregation that was one of the oldest Jewish congregations in the United States. In a century when rabbis seldom held their positions with particular congregations for long periods, Morais was a prominent exception. He served the Mikveh Israel congregation from 1851 until he died 46 years later. He married Clara Esther Weil in 1855, and they had seven children together.

Morais's career as a rabbi was characterized by a readiness to speak out about controversial subjects, a devotion to traditional Jewish beliefs and practices, and a lively social conscience. He was an outspoken proponent of abolitionism in the years leading up to the Civil War and an equally vigorous supporter of President Abraham Lincoln and the Union cause. Some of the members of Morais's congregation were "copperheads"—that is, northern supporters of southern secession. When Morais gave a Thanksgiving sermon in 1864 championing the cause of the North in the Civil War, his congregation subjected him to a three-month-long ban on speaking about political matters. Though he endured this particular restriction, he routinely used his Sabbath sermons to pronounce upon controversial subjects.

Morais's long efforts to defend Orthodox Jewish principles and practices placed him at the center of what was called the "Historical school" of Judaism at the time. Like many other religious leaders before and after him, Morais envisioned a prominent place for education in preserving the beliefs and practices of his religious tradition. To this end, he undertook teaching responsibilities as a professor of biblical literature at Maimonides College from 1867 until the college closed in 1873. Thereafter, Morais cooperated for a time with ISAAC MAYER WISE, a leader of Reform Judaism, in helping to found the Hebrew Union College in Cincinnati in 1875. But a college banquet that included nonkosher shellfish and Wise's failure to exhibit any sympathy for Orthodox scruples regarding this issue convinced Morais that close cooperation between the Historical school and Reform Judaism was not possible. In the following decade, Morais helped found the Jewish Theological Seminary in New York in 1886 as a conservative alternative to Hebrew Union College. He served as president and professor of the Bible at the seminary from 1887 until his death. Building upon the foundation that Morais laid, the institution became a center of Conservative Judaism's intellectual and spiritual life.

Sabato Morais added an active social engagement to his career as an educator and a leader of the Mikveh Israel congregation. He plunged into a variety of benevolent causes. When immigrants from southern and eastern Europe began to arrive in Philadelphia in the last quarter of the 19th century, Morais assumed a prominent role in seeing them settled. He also helped negotiate a peaceful conclusion to the Great Cloakmaker's Strike of 1890. Sabato Morais died on November 11, 1897, in Philadelphia.

Religious conservatism in its various manifestations has sometimes clothed itself in a preoccupation with the past at the expense of the present. Sabato Morais's long career as a rabbi, an educator, and a social reformer demonstrated that a marriage between traditional faith and a lively engagement with the present world was possible. He labored across five decades to preserve Orthodox Jewish beliefs and practices from the encroachments of modernity, and he matched these labors with equally vigorous attempts to respond to the contemporary social issues and needs of his day.

Further Reading

Davis, Moshe. The Emergence of Conservative Judaism: The Historical School in Nineteenth Century America. Westport, Conn.: Greenwood Press, 1977.

Fierstien, Robert E. A Different Spirit: The Jewish Theological Seminary of America, 1886–1902. New York: The Seminary, 1990.

Morais, Henry S. Sabato Morais: A Memoir. New York: Press of P. Cowen, 1898.

Nussenbaum, Max Samuel. "Champion of Orthodox Judaism: A Biography of the Reverend Sabato Morais, LL.D." D.H.L. dissertation, Yeshiva University, 1964.

Morse, Jedidiah
(1761–1826) *Congregationalist minister, geographer*

Jedidiah Morse was a Congregationalist minister whose widely published books on geographical subjects led him to be called "the father of American geography." In the spiritual geography of the late 18th and early 19th centuries, Morse was located squarely on the side of orthodox Congregationalism against the rising Unitarian tide. He was born on August 23, 1761, in Woodstock, Connecticut, to Jedidiah Morse and Sarah Child Morse. The elder Morse occupied a number of political posts in Connecticut and served as a deacon in the local Congregational church. The younger Morse suffered a variety of illnesses in his childhood, which inclined him to bookishness. In 1779, he entered Yale College, winning an exemption from the draft during the Revolutionary War because of his poor health. Two years later, he joined the church in New Haven; he wrote to his father at the time that he hoped he had "an Interest in the Merits of a Crucified Saviour, & that I have had a desire to forsake all & follow him."

After his graduation from Yale in 1783, Morse taught at a New Haven school for girls and also studied with JONATHAN EDWARDS, JR., a pastor in North Haven, and Yale's theology professor, Samuel Wales, to prepare himself for a clerical ministry. During this period, Morse's interest in geography yielded *Geography Made Easy*, published in 1784 and the first of many books on this subject. The next year, he was licensed to preach and invited to occupy the pulpit of the church in Norwich, but he soon decided that he lacked the maturity to settle at once into a permanent pastorate, choosing instead to return to Yale as a tutor. He arranged another temporary preaching assignment at a friend's church in Midway, Georgia, and planned to use the journey there as a basis for collecting more information to revise his geography book. En route to Georgia, he had the opportunity of meeting some of the most eminent men of his day, including Benjamin Franklin and George Washington. By the spring of 1787, he had returned north, where he worked on his geography and in 1788 undertook another preaching assignment at the Collegiate Presbyterian Church in New York City. The following year, he published *American Biography;* married Elizabeth Ann Breese, with whom he had 11 children; and accepted the pastorate of the First Congregational Church of Charlestown, Massachusetts, where he remained until 1819.

For the next three decades, Morse tried to tend to his responsibilities as a pastor while also publishing a steady stream of geographical books, although his talent at geography was clearly superior to his talent as either a preacher or a theologian. In spite of lackluster success in both of these latter categories, Morse threw himself energetically into the central theological contest of his day, which involved the debate between the conservative and liberal wings of Congregationalism. By the beginning of the 19th century, liberal Congregationalists had drifted toward Unitarianism. Morse vehemently opposed this theological migration and enlisted himself in the battle to preserve traditional Calvinistic doctrines such as the Trinity, the divinity of Jesus, and the depravity of humankind. To thwart the progress of liberalism among Congregational churches, in 1805 he founded and began to edit the magazine *The Panoplist.* This literary effort arose partially out of a heated campaign by conservative Congregationalists to block the appointment of a Unitarian to a chair of theology at Harvard College. Though Morse and his allies lost this battle, they were able to coordinate other steps to oppose Unitarianism, including founding Andover Theological Seminary in 1808, the New England Tract Society in 1814, and the American Bible Society in 1816.

Over the years, Morse's congregation grew to resent his various extracurricular activities, especially his continued work on books of geography and their frequent revisions. Ordinary pastoral responsibilities, such as visiting parishioners and even preparing weekly sermons, suffered from inattention. Eventually, his Charlestown church forced him to resign, effective at the beginning of 1820. Thereafter, he undertook work for the Department of Indian Affairs by surveying the condition of Native American tribes in the Northeast. He died on June 9, 1826, in New Haven, Connecticut.

Jedidiah Morse typified the breed of evangelical Protestants possessed by a boundless intellectual curiosity. He communicated this curiosity to his children, and one of his sons, Samuel Finley Breese Morse, would become the inventor of the telegraph. Whereas later evangelicals would sometimes find themselves at odds with science, Morse viewed scientific discovery as the natural ally of faith. In a speech delivered in 1821 to the American Bible Society, he embraced the advances yet to be made in scientific knowledge.

> It will be prodigy on prodigy, wonder following wonder, greater as they go, till wonders become the order of the day, wonders on wonders, the steady and established method of Providence. Besides, they will anticipate us, not we them. New resources will be opened. New truth will be learned—new only to us, though old itself as its Eternal Author!

His confidence in the progress of science, though, did not seem to him inconsistent with theological orthodoxy. Morse, along with other evangelicals, waged war against liberalism in its various forms—especially Unitarianism—and his success at this warfare would help to make Protestant evangelicalism an enduring feature of American religious life.

Further Reading

Morse, James King. *Jedidiah Morse: A Champion of New England Orthodoxy.* New York: Columbia University Press, 1939.

Moss, Richard J. *The Life of Jedidiah Morse: A Station of Peculiar Exposure.* Knoxville: University of Tennessee Press, 1995.

Phillips, Joseph W. *Jedidiah Morse and New England Congregationalism.* New Brunswick, N.J.: Rutgers University Press, 1983.

Sprague, William Buell. *The Life of Jedidiah Morse.* New York: A. D. F. Randolph, 1874.

Mott, John Raleigh
(1865–1955) *ecumenical leader*

One of the 20th century's preeminent ecumenical statesmen, John Raleigh Mott labored tirelessly for the cause of world missions across nearly 70 years. In recognition of his influence as a missionary and ecumenical activist, he shared the Nobel Peace Prize in 1946. Mott was born on January 25, 1865, in Livingston Manor, New York, the son of John Stitt Mott and Elmira Dodge Mott, who were Methodist farmers. He studied at Upper Iowa University from 1881 to 1885 and then at Cornell University, where he earned a Ph.D. in history in 1888. Two years later he married Leila Ada White, with whom he had four children.

In 1886, while at Cornell, Mott met C.T. Studd, the famous English athlete turned missionary, who inspired Mott to consider becoming a missionary himself. Later that year, Mott attended one of the summer student conferences organized by DWIGHT LYMAN MOODY in Northfield, Massachusetts, and he joined other students who dedicated themselves to the cause of missions. Although Mott never served as a missionary himself, he became the foremost evangelist for the cause of missions in the first half of the 20th century. On leaving Cornell, he accepted a position as a traveling secretary for the national Young Men's Christian Association (YMCA) College Committee. By 1901, he had become general secretary for the YMCA's foreign department, a post that gave him oversight of YMCA organizations around the world. Mott remained active in YMCA affairs until near the end of his life, but he simultaneously plunged into organizational work of other missionary agencies.

The Student Volunteer Movement for Foreign Missions (SVM) grew out of one of Dwight L. Moody's summer conferences, and once it was formally organized in 1888, Mott became the secretary to its executive committee. He held this position for more than 30 years, assisting in the work of persuading young men and women to give their lives to the cause of missions. His work for the YMCA and the SVM increasingly took on an ecumenical cast, as Mott attempted to coordinate the energies of different Protestant groups. He helped to establish the Foreign Missions Conference of North America, an alliance of various Protestant mission boards, in 1893. By 1910, he had expanded his horizons to seek international cooperative efforts as well, and he helped to plan and preside over the world missionary conference held in Edinburgh, Scotland. In a speech before the conference, he summarized the measure of the challenge to evangelism.

> It is a startling and solemnizing fact that even as late as the twentieth century, the Great Command of Jesus Christ to carry the Gospel to all mankind is still so largely unfulfilled. . . . The church is confronted today, as in no preceding generation, with a literally worldwide opportunity to make Christ known.

By the time of the Edinburgh conference, Mott had become internationally recognized as a champion of missions. His stature in the international community was so prominent that President Woodrow Wilson even sought to make him an ambassador to China, an appointment that Mott declined.

In the 1920s, Mott resigned his various posts with the YMCA and the SVM to apply his energies more directly to the International Missionary Council, which had grown out of the Edinburgh conference. He served as chairman of the council from 1928 to 1946. This labor gave him contact with religious leaders who sought to form ecumenical bonds more substantial than mere cooperative missionary efforts. He thus played a prominent role in the planning that finally produced the World Council of Churches (WCC), which held its inaugural meeting in Amsterdam in 1948. He had served as one of five provisional presidents of the organization prior to this meeting; subsequently, he was made honorary president of the WCC. This honor was added to one that he had received in 1946, when he shared the Nobel Peace Prize with Emily Greene Balch, an American economist. Mott died in Orlando, Florida, on January 31, 1955.

Scarcely any individual made a more profound contribution to the organization of world missions in the first half of the 20th century than John R. Mott. While the world careened through two global wars, he steered the course of missionary activity down paths that would recruit thousands to the cause of world evangelism. In the years leading up to World War II, he added to his mission work an abiding commitment to seeing the church recover a measure of the unity of which denominationalism had deprived it. It was therefore fitting that the Nobel Prize honor him as one of the 20th century's architects of peace.

Further Reading

Barnes, Michael Craig. "John R. Mott: A Conversionist in a Pluralist World." Ph.D. dissertation, University of Chicago, 1992.

Fisher, Galen Merriam. *John R. Mott: Architect of Co-Operation and Unity*. New York: Association Press, 1952.

Hopkins, Charles Howard. *John R. Mott, 1865–1955: A Biography*. Grand Rapids, Mich.: Eerdmans, 1979.

Mackie, Robert C. *Layman Extraordinary: John R. Mott, 1865–1955*. New York: Association Press, 1965.

Mathews, Basil Joseph. *John R. Mott, World Citizen*. New York: Harper & Brothers, 1934.

Mott, John Raleigh. *Addresses and Papers of John R. Mott.* 6 vols. New York: Association Press, 1946–47.

———. *Confronting Young Men with the Living Christ.* New York: Association Press, 1923.

———. *The Decisive Hour of Christian Missions.* New York: Student Volunteer Movement for Foreign Missions, 1910.

———. *The Evangelization of the World in this Generation.* New York: Student Volunteer Movement for Foreign Missions, 1900; New York: Arno Press, 1972.

———. *Liberating the Lay Forces of Christianity.* New York: Macmillan, 1932.

Muhammad, Elijah
(Robert Poole)
(1897–1975) *Nation of Islam leader*

Though Elijah Muhammad did not found the Nation of Islam, he made it a nationally prominent black religious movement. At its height in the 1960s, the Nation of Islam boasted some 500,000 members. Muhammad was born Robert Poole on October 10, 1897, in Sandersville, Georgia, the son of William Poole and Mariah Hall Poole. Soon after Poole's birth, his family moved to Cordelle, Georgia, where he attended public school until he dropped out in the fourth grade to help support his family by working. Poole married Clara Evans in 1919; with her he had eight children.

Early the following decade, Poole relocated with his family to Detroit, Michigan, where he found work in an automobile factory. There, in 1931, he met Wallace Fard, an itinerant salesman who in 1930 had begun preaching a form of Islam in the homes of his customers. By July 1930, Fard had founded the Lost-Found Nation of Islam in a rented hall. Soon after Fard and Poole met, Poole became Fard's chief deputy and changed his name to *Elijah Muhammad*. Fard taught a racial mythology that maintained that blacks were the original humans but that a mad scientist named Yacub had created whites, referred to as devils. In Fard's cosmology, whites would rule Earth for six millennia, but blacks would ultimately rule the world after an apocalypse.

After the disappearance of Fard in June 1934, the Nation of Islam splintered into several groups. Fearful of violence against him, Muhammad resettled in Chicago, Illinois, in 1936; there he made the recently established Temple of Islam No. 2 the national headquarters of the Nation of Islam. He announced that Fard had been the incarnation of Allah and that he was Allah's messenger. Under his direction, the Nation of Islam began to celebrate February 26, Fard's birthday, as Savior's Day.

Muhammad was imprisoned from 1942 to 1946 for violating the Selective Service Act by refusing to be drafted during World War II. But in the two decades that followed, the Nation of Islam grew rapidly. Muhammad emphasized the necessity of financial independence for Nation of Islam members, insisting that welfare be shunned and that members attempt to start their own businesses. After his own imprisonment, Muhammad corresponded with a young prison inmate named Malcolm Little. Converted to the Nation of Islam while in prison, Malcolm Little changed his name to MALCOLM X after his parole in 1952,—choosing the X to replace what he considered his slave name—and he quickly became prominent with the Nation of Islam. Two years after his release from prison, Muhammad appointed Malcolm X to lead Temple No. 7 in Harlem, New York, and in 1962, he designated Malcolm X his national representative.

Soon afterward, though, Muhammad and Malcolm X became estranged as a result of Muhammad's fear that his protégé had aspirations to take over the Nation of Islam and of Malcolm X's knowledge of rumors of Muhammad's affairs with women in the Nation of Islam. Tension between the two men reached a climax after the assassination of President John F. Kennedy. Muhammad had instructed Malcolm X and other Black Muslim leaders to refrain from commenting about the assassination, but Malcolm X announced publicly that the slain president "never

foresaw that the chickens would come home to roost so soon." Muhammad responded to Malcolm X's statement by suspending him for three months, beginning in December 1963. Several months later, Malcolm X left the Nation of Islam to form his own organization, Muslim Mosque, Inc. In February 1965, Malcolm X was assassinated by members of the Nation of Islam.

After the death of Malcolm X, Muhammad appointed LOUIS ABDUL FARRAKHAN to take over as minister of the Harlem temple and as his national representative. In his final years, Muhammad spent an increasing amount of time at his home in Phoenix, Arizona, where he sought relief from respiratory ailments. He died on February 25, 1975, in Chicago, Illinois.

With little formal education, Elijah Muhammad became the leader of one of the 20th century's more prominent new religious movements.

Elijah Muhammad transformed the Nation of Islam into a prominent African-American religious movement in the United States. *(Library of Congress, Prints and Photographs Division LC-USZ62-116389)*

His theology of racial pride and self-sufficiency resonated within the African-American community and formed a counterpoint to the Christian influence underpinning the civil rights activism of other black leaders such as MARTIN LUTHER KING, JR. The antiwhite rhetoric he had inherited from Wallace Fard, which had been grafted onto Islamic beliefs, provoked continuing controversy. Nevertheless, it fueled dissatisfaction with the systemic subordination of African Americans in the United States and thus fertilized the social ground that produced the Civil Rights movement.

Further Reading

Clegg, Claude Andrew. *An Original Man: The Life and Times of Elijah Muhammad.* New York: St. Martin's Press, 1997.

Evanzz, Karl. *The Messenger: The Rise and Fall of Elijah Muhammad.* New York: Pantheon Books, 1999.

Lincoln, C. Eric. *The Black Muslims in America.* Boston: Beacon Press, 1961.

Muhammad, Elijah. *The Fall of America.* Chicago: Muhammad's Temple of Islam No. 2, 1973.

———. *Message to the Blackman in America.* Chicago: Muhammad Mosque of Islam No. 2, 1965.; Newport News, Va.: United Brothers Communications Systems, 1992.

———. *The Theology of Time.* Hampton, Va.: U.B. & U.S. Communications Systems, 1992.

Rashad, Adib. *Elijah Muhammad and the Ideological Foundation of the Nation of Islam.* Hampton, Va.: U.B. & U.S. Communications Systems, 1994.

Muhlenberg, Henry Melchior
(1711–1787) *Lutheran minister*

Henry Melchior Muhlenberg arrived in America nearly 40 years after the first Lutheran congregation was organized near Philadelphia, Pennsylvania. But he helped to meld the scattered Lutheran churches into a coordinated body of congregations, thus earning the common designation as the father of American Lutheranism. He was born on September 6, 1711, in Einbeck, in the province of Hanover, the son of Nicolaus Muhlenberg and Anna Maria Kleinschmidt. His father's death when Henry was 12 years old interrupted his early

education, and Muhlenberg did not enter the University of Göttingen until he was 23 years old. He graduated in 1737 and then taught at a school for orphans in Halle, a center of German pietism. After being ordained and serving as pastor of a congregation in Grosshennersdorf, Muhlenberg left Germany in 1742, at the age of 30, to become pastor of three Lutheran congregations in Pennsylvania. These congregations had written to Hermann Francke, a Lutheran leader of the pietist movement at the University of Halle, seeking a pastor. Francke persuaded Muhlenberg to undertake this charge.

In Pennsylvania, Muhlenberg had to contend initially with attempts by Count NIKOLAUS LUDWIG VON ZINZENDORF, who had arrived in America in 1741, to organize the various German-speaking churches into a synod. Zinzendorf, a pietist like Muhlenberg, had been influential in establishing the Moravian Church in Saxony. By immigrating to America, he hoped to expand the church's influence there by uniting German congregations into the Church of God in the Spirit. Partially because of the opposition of Muhlenberg, Zinzendorf's plan ultimately failed, and Muhlenberg was able to prevent the absorption of his Lutheran congregations into Zinzendorf's more radical pietism.

In 1745, Muhlenberg married Anna Maria Weiser, and their union produced 11 children. Three of Muhlenberg's sons became even better known than their father: John Peter Gabriel Muhlenberg was a brigadier general in the Continental army during the Revolutionary War; Frederick Augustus Conrad Muhlenberg served as the Continental Congress's first Speaker of the House of Representatives; and Henry Gotthilf Heinrich Ernst Muhlenberg became a Lutheran pastor and a famous botanist. Muhlenberg himself became a U.S. citizen in 1754.

Over the next years, Muhlenberg served not only as a pastor for the Lutheran congregation in Philadelphia, which became the center of his ministry, but as a general leader among the Lutheran churches rapidly planted across North America. Over the course of his 45-year ministry in North America, he tended to scattered Lutheran congregations from Nova Scotia to Georgia, mediating disputes, planting new churches, and helping to train leaders. He was instrumental in the creation of the first Lutheran Ministerium, or synod, in 1748 and served as its first president. In later years, he helped develop principles of ecclesiastical governance for the American Lutheran churches.

When the Revolutionary War began in North America, Muhlenberg tried to remain neutral, insisting that Lutheran pastors had more than enough responsibilities without meddling in political matters. He saw "no Christian principle at stake, nothing humane about the war." He saw one son serve under George Washington in the Continental army but applied himself instead to Lutheran affairs. He died on October 7, 1787, in Trappe, Pennsylvania. The Latin epitaph on his tomb states simply, "Who and what he was, future ages will know without a stone."

For his long and faithful labor among the German-speaking Lutherans of North America, Henry Melchior Muhlenberg became known as the patriarch of American Lutheranism. Originally sent to America to tend three congregations, he made the entire eastern seaboard his parish. Through nearly half a century of prodigious labor, Muhlenberg created the foundation for an enduring Lutheran presence in the New World.

Further Reading

Frick, William K. *Henry Melchior Muhlenberg: "Patriarch of the Lutheran Church in America."* Philadelphia: Lutheran Publication Society, 1902.

Kleiner, John W., ed. *Henry Melchior Muhlenberg—The Roots of 250 Years of Organized Lutheranism in North America: Essays in Memory of Helmut T. Lehmann.* Lewiston, N.Y.: Edwin Mellen Press, 1998.

Muhlenberg, Henry Melchior. *The Correspondence of Heinrich Melchior Mühlenberg.* Edited and translated by John W. Kleiner and Helmut T. Lehmann. Camden, Maine: Picton Press, 1993.

———. *The Notebook of a Colonial Clergyman, Condensed from the Journals of Henry Melchior Muhlenberg.* Translated and edited by Theodore G. Tappert and John W. Doberstein. Philadelphia: Muhlenberg Press, 1959; Minneapolis: Fortress Press, 1998.

Riforgiato, Leonard R. *Missionary of Moderation: Henry Melchior Muhlenberg and the Lutheran Church in En-glish America.* Lewisburg, Pa,: Bucknell University Press, 1980.

Seebach, Margaret R. *An Eagle of the Wilderness: The Story of Henry Melchior Muhlenberg.* Philadelphia: United Lutheran, 1924.

Stoever, M. L. *Memoir of the Life and Times of Henry Melchior Muhlenberg.* Philadelphia: Lindsay & Blakiston, 1856.

Strohmidel, Karl Otto. "Henry Melchior Muhlenberg's European Heritage." *Lutheran Quarterly* 6 (1992): 5–34.

Mullins, Edgar Young
(1860–1928) *Baptist minister, educator*

A leading Baptist at the turn of the 20th century, Edgar Young Mullins presided over the Southern Baptist Theological Seminary in Louisville, Kentucky, for almost three decades. During this period his intelligence and moderate temperament made him a leading voice for early 20th-century Baptists. He was born on the eve of the Civil War, on January 5, 1860, in Franklin County, Mississippi, the son of a Baptist minister, Seth Granberry Mullins, and Cornelia Blair Tillman Mullins. When he was eight years old, his family moved to Corsicana, Texas. In his teenaged years, he worked at odd jobs, including telegraph operator, to help pay for his older siblings' college education. In 1876, though, he was able to enroll in Texas Agricultural and Mechanical College (later Texas A & M University), and he graduated three years later. He initially planned to become a lawyer, but after experiencing a religious conversion at a revival in Dallas in 1880, he reconsidered his vocational plans. Mullins began studies to prepare himself for the ministry in 1881 at the Southern Baptist Theological Seminary in Louisville, Kentucky, and graduated in 1885.

Mullins hoped initially to become a missionary to Brazil, but poor health discouraged him from this course. Instead, soon after his graduation from the seminary, he accepted a position as minister of a Baptist church in Harrodsburg, Kentucky, and in 1886, he married Isla May Hawley, with whom he had two children. By 1888 he and his family had relocated to Baltimore, Maryland,

Edgar Young Mullins served as president and theology professor at the Southern Baptist Theological Seminary in Louisville, Kentucky, during the early decades of the 20th century. *(Southern Baptist Historical Library and Archives)*

where he served as the pastor of the Lee Street Baptist Church for seven years and had the chance to study for a time at Johns Hopkins University. At the end of this period he assumed the post of assistant secretary of the Foreign Mission Board of the Southern Baptist Convention and moved to Richmond, Virginia. Feeling ill equipped for the responsibilities of this position, Mullins readily accepted the offer presented to him in 1895 to be pastor of a Baptist church in Newton Center, Massachusetts. But this pastorate proved to be only a temporary station preceding the start of his main life's work. In 1899 Mullins accepted the appointment as president and professor of theology of the Southern Baptist Theological Seminary in Louisville, Kentucky.

Mullins arrived at the seminary at a time when theological controversy had forced the res-

ignation of the seminary's previous president, William Heth Whitsitt. But Mullins proved more able at navigating the currents of denominational politics. He doubled the seminary's endowment as well as its faculty, and he directed the school's relocation in 1926 to a better site in Louisville. Mullins found room among his responsibilities as seminary professor to write prolifically and earned a reputation as the leading Southern Baptist theologian of the first quarter of the 20th century. His signature doctrinal emphasis was on "soul competency," which he considered the traditional Baptist emphasis on the soul's capacity for an encounter with God unmediated by priests or creeds.

In his position at the helm of the seminary, Mullins also played a leading role in Baptist affairs. He served as president of the Southern Baptist Convention from 1921 to 1924 and helped establish the Baptist World Alliance, of which he was president from 1923 to 1928. He also chaired the Southern Baptist committee that proposed *The Baptist Faith and Message*, the influential statement of faith for Southern Baptists. Mullins died on November 23, 1928, in Louisville, Kentucky.

Edgar Young Mullins was the leading spokesman for Southern Baptists in the early decades of the 20th century. He successfully administered the affairs of his denomination's most prominent seminary, and he wielded his influence as seminary president and professor to affect the lives of countless ministerial students and the churches they would ultimately serve. Active in denominational affairs, he made one of his most enduring contributions to the history of the Southern Baptists in the preparation of *The Baptist Faith and Message*. This statement of faith, designed to be a canopy broad enough to shelter a wide variety of Baptist views, served as a basis for cooperative efforts in a denomination known for its fractiousness.

Further Reading

Carrell, William D. M. "Edgar Young Mullins and the Competency of the Soul in Religion." Ph.D. dissertation, Baylor University, 1993.

Ellis, William E. *"A Man of Books and a Man of the People": E. Y. Mullins and the Crisis of Moderate South-*

ern Baptist Leadership. Macon, Ga.: Mercer University Press, 1985.

Maddux, Clark. "Edgar Young Mullins and Evangelical Developments in the Southern Baptist Convention." *Baptist History and Heritage* 33 (1998): 62–73.

Moore, David Edwin. "Ecclesiological Implications of Religious Experience in the Theologies of Edgar Young Mullins and Henry Wheeler Robinson." Ph.D. dissertation, Southwestern Baptist Theological Seminary, 1999.

Mullins, Edgar Young. *The Axioms of Religion: A New Interpretation of the Baptist Faith*. Philadelphia: American Baptist Publication Society, 1908.

———. *The Christian Religion in Its Doctrinal Expression*. Philadelphia: Roger Williams Press, 1917.

Mullins, Isla May Hawley. *Edgar Young Mullins: An Intimate Biography*. Nashville: Sunday School Board of the Southern Baptist Convention, 1929.

Murray, John Courtney

(1904–1967) *Catholic priest, theologian*

America's leading Catholic theologian of the 20th century, John Courtney Murray helped to establish the principle of religious freedom as a tenet of modern Catholic teaching. Though Murray was initially censored for holding heterodox views concerning church-state issues, his thinking ultimately dominated official Catholic understanding of the issue, beginning with Vatican II. He was born on September 12, 1904, in New York City, the son of Michael John Murray and Margaret Courtney Murray. After attending St. Francis Xavier High School in New York City, Murray entered the Society of Jesus (better known as the Jesuits) in 1920. He subsequently received a B.A. and an M.A. from Boston College in 1926 and 1927, respectively. After teaching for a few years in the Philippines, Murray resumed theological studies at Woodstock College, Maryland, and then at the Gregorian University in Rome, from which he received a doctorate in sacred theology (S.T.D) in 1926, having been previously ordained a Catholic priest in 1933. On his graduation from the Gregorian University, Murray assumed an academic post at Woodstock College that he held until his death three decades later. In 1941 he became editor of

Theological Studies, a Jesuit journal. He held this position for the remainder of his life.

Early in his academic career, John Courtney Murray turned his attention to issues involving the relationship between church and society. Initially, he insisted that the only coherent basis for social action lay in a correct apprehension and application of traditional Christian doctrines such as the Trinity, the incarnation, and the atonement. Eventually, though, he believed that cooperative action for the common good was possible among adherents of a wider spectrum of religious beliefs. Cooperation, in fact, was not only possible; it was necessary to withstand the destructive influence of those Murray described as "barbarians" in his book *We Hold These Truths* (1960).

> The barbarian need not appear in bearskins with a club in hand. He may wear a Brooks Brothers suit and carry a ball-point pen with which to write his advertising copy. In fact, even beneath the academic gown there may lurk a child of the wilderness, untutored in the high tradition of civility, who goes busily and happily about his work, a domesticated and law-abiding man, engaged in the construction of a philosophy to put an end to all philosophy, and thus put an end to the possibility of a vital consensus and to civility itself.

Convinced that civil cooperation among different traditions of religious belief—and unbelief—was both possible and necessary, Murray reconsidered Catholic teachings on the appropriate relationship between church and state in modern society. In the mid-20th century, official Catholic teaching insisted that the ideal church-state relationship was one in which the Catholic Church was the official religion of the state and in which other varieties of belief and unbelief were suppressed. Religious toleration might be appropriate under some limited circumstances but only as a necessary exception to the general rule of Catholic primacy. Murray, however, became convinced that this teaching was not applicable in modern democratic societies such as the United States.

By the 1950s, Murray's church-state views had begun to create conflict with some Catholic authorities. In particular, Murray found himself at odds with Cardinal Augustus Ottaviani, the secretary of the Vatican Holy Office, whose opposition to Murray's views eventually resulted in Murray's being censored by Jesuit authorities in Rome when he produced further articles on the subject of church-state relations. The Vatican, however, could not suppress Murray's growing reputation in the United States as a leading Catholic intellectual. After the publication of *We Hold These Truths: Catholic Reflections on the American Proposition* (1960), his influential collection of essays, Murray even appeared on the cover of *Time* magazine.

When the first session of Vatican II began in October 1962, Murray was not present. Subsequently, however, Cardinal FRANCIS JOSEPH SPELLMAN had Murray appointed as an expert on church-state affairs for the U.S. delegation. Eventually, Murray played a significant role in drafting the council's statement of religious liberty, formally titled *Dignitatis humanae personae* (1965). Vatican II's pronouncement on this issue vindicated Murray's church-state views, but the theologian did not live long after the event. He died of a heart attack in New York on August 16, 1967.

John Courtney Murray is generally thought to be the leading Catholic theologian yet produced in the United States. He grappled with the issue of how believers were to engage with the society in which they found themselves and viewed religious toleration as a key feature of this engagement. He championed the idea of religious liberty even when it conflicted with prevalent Catholic teaching, although he ultimately saw his views embraced by the Catholic Church after Vatican II.

Further Reading

Ferguson, Thomas P. *Catholic and American: The Political Theology of John Courtney Murray.* Kansas City, Mo.: Sheed & Ward, 1993.

Hughson, D. Thomas. *The Believer as Citizen: John Courtney Murray in a New Context.* New York: Paulist Press, 1993.

Love, Thomas T. *John Courtney Murray: Contemporary Church State Theory.* Garden City, N.Y.: Doubleday, 1965.

Murray, John Courtney. *Bridging the Sacred and the Secular: Selected Writings of John Courtney Murray.* Edited by J. Leon Hooper. Washington, D.C.: Georgetown University Press, 1994.

———. *We Hold These Truths: Catholic Reflections on the American Proposition.* New York: Sheed & Ward, 1960.

Pelotte, Donald E. *John Courtney Murray: Theologian in Conflict.* New York: Paulist Press, 1976.

N

Nevin, John Williamson
(1803–1886) *theologian, educator*

During the heyday of 19th-century Protestant revivalism, John Williamson Nevin became a staunch critic of evangelical Protestantism. As a central proponent of what came to be known as "Mercersburg theology," he championed an ecclesiastical vision that gave central place to the historic Christian community and its liturgy rather than to spontaneous acts of individual piety. He was born on February 20, 1803, near Shippensburg, Pennsylvania, the son of John Nevin and Martha McCracken Nevin. Nevin's parents were Presbyterians, and he received his early education from a Presbyterian school and then from his father before entering Union College in Schenectady, New York, from which he received a B.A. in 1821. While at Union, Nevin had a revivalistic conversion experience. After graduation, he returned home to work on his father's farm for a time before enrolling in Princeton Theological Seminary. He graduated from Princeton in 1826 and was invited to remain there as an instructor for the next two years.

From 1828 to 1840, Nevin served on the faculty of the Western Theological Seminary in Allegheny City, Pennsylvania. During this period, he married Martha Jenkins in 1835 with whom he had eight children. At Western Theological, he was influenced by the writings of Johann August Neander, and through this encounter Nevin eventually turned away from Presbyterian ecclesiology. In keeping with this theological migration, he left Western Theological Seminary in 1840 and joined the faculty of the German Reformed seminary in Mercersburg, Pennsylvania. The following year, he accepted the presidency of Marshall College, also located in Mercersburg. Over the next decade, Nevin wrote a number of books, beginning with *The Anxious Bench* (1843), which developed key elements of what came to be known as Mercersburg theology. Nevin's views represented a sharp departure from the individualist conversion theologies of evangelists such as CHARLES GRANDISON FINNEY, which emphasized the unmediated encounter between the individual and God in salvation. Though nominally Protestant, Nevin's theology emphasized traditional Catholic concern for the historic church and its sacraments. In *The Mystical Presence* (1846), for example, he urged that

> [t]he life of the single Christian can be real and healthful only as it is born from the general life of the church, and carried by it onward to the end. We are Christians singly, by partaking (having *part*) in the general life revelation, which is already at hand organically in the church, the living and life-giving body of Jesus Christ.

Nevin found a theological ally for a time in PHILIP SCHAFF, a Swiss scholar who joined the Mercersburg faculty in 1844 and who shared with Nevin views that might be described as "evangelical Catholicism," emphasizing in Protestant fashion the centrality of the gospel but holding the tradition of the historic Catholic Church in high regard as well. The Catholic sympathies of the two men soon placed them at odds with their denomination. During the 1840s, Schaff was tried for heresy twice—unsuccessfully. Nevin, for his part, toyed with converting to Catholicism but settled on retiring from the Mercersburg seminary—and from his presidency of Marshall College—for reasons of health in 1853. Franklin and Marshall College in Lancaster, Pennsylvania, lured him back to academia, first as a lecturer in 1861 and then as president from 1866 to 1876, when he retired permanently. He died on June 6, 1886, in Lancaster.

John Williamson Nevin lived at a time not propitious for those—such as he—with ecumenical impulses. The century in which he lived would be drawing to a close before other American religious thinkers would return to the themes he and Philip Schaff developed at Mercersburg. In his time, Nevin had to content himself with appeals for the preservation and acknowledgment of the historic traditions and sacraments of the church that fell on uninterested ears. The currents of revivalism swept passed his jeremiads unimpeded, reinforcing an individualist strand of Protestantism that ignored, he thought, the historic and communitarian life of the church.

Further Reading

Appel, Theodore. *The Life and Work of John Williamson Nevin.* Philadelphia: Reformed Church Publication House, 1889; New York: Arno Press, 1969.

DiPuccio, William. *The Interior Sense of Scripture: The Sacred Hermeneutics of John W. Nevin.* Macon, Ga.: Mercer University Press, 1998.

Hamstra, Sam, Jr., and Arie J. Griffioen, eds. *Reformed Confessionalism in Nineteenth-Century America: Essays on the Thought of John Williamson Nevin.* Lanham, Md.: Scarecrow Press, 1995.

Hewitt, Glenn Alden. *Regeneration and Morality: A Study of Charles Finney, Charles Hodge, John W. Nevin, and Horace Bushnell.* Brooklyn, N.Y.: Carlson, 1991.

Nevin, John Williamson. *Antichrist: Or, the Spirit of Sect and Schism.* New York: J. S. Taylor, 1848.

———. *Catholic and Reformed: Selected Theological Writings of John Williamson Nevin.* Edited by Charles Yrigoyen, Jr. and George H. Bricker. Pittsburgh: Pickwick Press, 1978.

———. *My Own Life: The Earlier Years.* Lancaster, Pa.: n.p., 1964.

———. *The Mystical Presence, and Other Writings on the Eucharist.* Edited by Bard Thompson and George H. Bricker. Philadelphia: United Church Press, 1966.

Nichols, James Hastings. *Romanticism in American Theology: Nevin and Schaff at Mercersburg.* Chicago: University of Chicago Press, 1961.

Wentz, Richard E. *John Williamson Nevin: American Theologian.* New York: Oxford University Press, 1997.

Niebuhr, Helmut Richard
(1894–1962) *theologian, educator*

H. Richard Niebuhr, as he was known, never quite escaped the shadow of his more famous brother, the theologian REINHOLD NIEBUHR. Nevertheless, many observers named him the "theologians' theologian," and he had a profound impact on 20th-century American theology and must be reckoned among the century's most enduring religious voices. Helmut Richard Niebuhr was born on September 3, 1894, in Wright City, Missouri, the son of Gustav Niebuhr and Lydia Hosto Niebuhr. His father was a minister in the German Evangelical Synod of North America, a Protestant denomination originally founded by German immigrants from the Lutheran and Reformed traditions. Both H. Richard Niebuhr and his brother, Reinhold, followed their father's vocation by studying at Elmhurst College, in Elmhurst, Illinois, a small denominational school, and subsequently at Eden Seminary, then located in Wellstone, Missouri, from which H. Richard Niebuhr graduated in 1915.

After seminary, Niebuhr was ordained and began a brief tenure as a minister of the Walnut Park Evangelical Church in Saint Louis in 1916. While in Saint Louis, he received a master's degree from Washington University. By 1919, however, Eden Theological Seminary had invited Niebuhr to join its faculty, and he returned to Webster Groves to take the first step of what would be a luminous career as an academic and a theologian. A year later, he married Florence Marie Mittendorf, with whom he had two children.

In 1922, the desire to further his education led Niebuhr to enroll in the Yale Divinity School, from which he received a bachelor of divinity degree the following year, soon to be accompanied in 1924 by a Ph.D. from Yale University, where he wrote his dissertation on Ernst Troelsch, the liberal German theologian whose influence would mark much of Niebuhr's subsequent work. After leaving Yale, he became president of his undergraduate alma mater, Elmhurst College, from 1924 to 1927, before returning to Eden Theological Seminary for four years. There he taught theology and wrote one of his most important books, *The Social Sources of Denominationalism* (1929), which traced denominational divisions among churches in the United States to a variety of cultural factors, including class, race, and regionalism.

After studying briefly in Germany, Niebuhr joined the faculty of the Yale Divinity School; he rose through the faculty ranks the remainder of his academic career to become first a professor and then in 1954 the Sterling Professor of Theology and Christian Ethics. At Yale, he became one of the most important American theologians of the 20th century, though his elder brother Reinhold, on the faculty of Union Theological Seminary, had the brighter reputation. H. Richard, like Reinhold, was deeply influenced by neoorthodox thinkers such as Karl Barth, who chastised theological liberals for making faith a subjective matter rather than a response to divine revelation. Revelation, he suggested in *The Meaning of Revelation* (1941), is

> the moment in our history through which we know ourselves to be known from beginning to end, in which we are apprehended by the knower; it means the self-disclosing of that eternal knower. . . . Revelation means that we find ourselves to be valued rather than valuing and that all our values are transvaluated by the activity of a universal valuer. . . . When we speak of revelation we mean that moment when we are given a new faith, to cleave to and to betray, and a new standard, to follow and deny.

Embracing what he termed "radical monotheism," Niebuhr denied the existence of any absolute ex-

cept God, even religious claims about God: these were inevitably incomplete. Niebuhr died on July 5, 1962, in Greenfield, Massachusetts.

In the decades after his death, H. Richard Niebuhr's reputation as a theologian has not suffered decline. Though overshadowed by his more widely respected brother during his life, H. Richard's had an impact that has seemed to some observers more enduring than that of Reinhold, whose theological career frequently focused on the leading events and issues of the day. H. Richard Niebuhr, on the other hand, has often been recognized as having grappled with more lasting issues about the relationship between faith and culture, and between the finite and the Absolute.

Further Reading

Diefenthaler, Jon. *H. Richard Niebuhr: A Lifetime of Reflections on the Church and the World.* Macon, Ga.: Mercer University Press, 1986.

Fadner, Donald Edward. *The Responsible God: A Study of the Christian Philosophy of H. Richard Niebuhr.* Missoula, Mont.: Published by Scholars Press for the American Academy of Religion, 1975.

Fowler, James W. *To See the Kingdom: The Theological Vision of H. Richard Niebuhr.* Nashville: Abingdon Press, 1974; Lanham, Md.: University Press of America, 1985.

Godsey, John D. *The Promise of H. Richard Niebuhr.* Philadelphia: Lippincott, 1970.

Hoedemaker, L.A. *The Theology of H. Richard Niebuhr.* Philadelphia: Pilgrim Press, 1970.

Irish, Jerry A. *The Religious Thought of H. Richard Niebuhr.* Atlanta: J. Knox Press, 1983.

Kliever, Lonnie D. *H. Richard Niebuhr.* Waco, Tex.: Word Books, 1977; Peabody, Mass.: Hendrickson Publishers, 1991.

Niebuhr, H. Richard. *Christ and Culture.* New York: Harper, 1951.

———. *The Meaning of Revelation.* New York: Macmillan, 1941.

———. *The Responsible Self: An Essay in Christian Moral Philosophy.* New York: Harper & Row, 1963.

———. *The Social Sources of Denominationalism.* New York: H. Holt, 1929.

Thiemann, Ronald F. *The Legacy of H. Richard Niebuhr.* Minneapolis: Fortress, 1991.

Niebuhr, Reinhold
(Karl Paul Reinhold Niebuhr)
(1892–1971) *theologian, educator*

Together with the transplanted German scholar PAUL JOHANNES TILLICH, Reinhold Niebuhr is generally regarded as one of the two most prominent American theologians of the 20th century. He self-consciously endeavored to escape the narrow technical bounds that sometimes limit the influence of academics, and he became one of the foremost public intellectuals of the century. Karl Paul Reinhold Niebuhr was born on June 21, 1892, the son of Gustav Niebuhr and Lydia Hosto Niebuhr. Gustav Niebuhr was a minister in the German Evangelical Synod of North America, and both Reinhold and his brother, HELMUT RICHARD NIEBUHR, followed their father in preparing for the ministry, first at Elmhurst College, in Elmhurst, Illinois, a small denominational school, and subsequently at Eden Theological Seminary, then located in Wellstone, Missouri. Niebuhr graduated from the seminary in 1913, with a bachelor of divinity degree, and then proceeded on to Yale Divinity School, where he received an additional B.D. in 1914 and an M.A. in 1915.

After leaving Yale, Niebuhr became the minister of the Bethel Evangelical Church in Detroit, Michigan, where he remained from 1915 to 1928. During this period, his gifts as speaker made him an increasingly popular voice among liberal Christians, with whom he had aligned himself since his seminary days. He also contributed regularly to the liberal Protestant periodical *Christian Century*. Over his years as minister at Bethel, especially as a result of opposition to the industrial practices of Henry Ford, Niebuhr became increasingly supportive of the labor movement and increasingly critical of those (chiefly liberal Christians) who trusted in the power of reason and love to secure a just society. The achievement of justice required the exercise of power, not an overly confident optimism in the benevolent potential of human nature.

After 13 years as a minister, Niebuhr joined the faculty of Union Theological Seminary in 1928 as an associate professor of ethics. He also joined the Socialist Party and, over the next few years, twice ran for political office—for the state senate

in 1930 and for the U.S. Congress in 1932—on the Socialist ticket. Both efforts failed resoundingly. During the same period, Niebuhr married Ursula Keppel-Compton in 1931, and the couple subsequently had two children. More successful than Niebuhr's political aspirations were his early efforts as a scholar. His 1932 book, *Moral Man and Immoral Society*, developed the argument that the moral aspirations fit for individuals were not necessarily appropriate to govern the conduct of nations. "Religion is always a citadel of hope, which is built on the edge of despair," he insisted, but hope alone could not secure justice. Niebuhr was no Thomas More, dreaming of utopia from his academic perch: his expectations concerning human possibilities were more modest.

> [C]ollective man, operating on the historic and mundane scene, must content himself with a more modest goal. His concern for some centuries to come is not the creation of an ideal society in which there will be uncoerced and perfect peace and justice, but a society in which there will be enough justice, and in which coercion will be sufficiently non-violent to prevent his common enterprise from issuing into complete disaster.

In the years that followed, Niebuhr's stature as an American intellectual steadily ascended, both within his own country and internationally. He gradually migrated away from socialism and finally resigned from the Socialist Party in 1940, although he did not surrender the political and social realism that had drawn him to the party. A year later he established a periodical called *Christianity and Crisis*, which he edited over the next two decades. He also published a string of influential books, such as the two-volume *The Nature and Destiny of Man* (1941–43) and *The Children of Light and the Children of Darkness* (1944). "Man's capacity for justice makes democracy possible, but man's inclination to injustice makes democracy necessary," he wrote in the latter, again applying his own religious realism to the threat posed to collective society by fascist regimes such as Nazi Germany.

In 1952, Niebuhr suffered the first of several strokes that partially incapacitated him and tethered him more closely to Union Theological Seminary. He continued to teach for the remainder of the decade, but he eventually retired in 1960, shortly after being admitted in 1959 to the highly selective and enormously prestigious American Academy of Arts and Sciences. Five years later, President Lyndon Johnson awarded Niebuhr the Medal of Freedom. Niebuhr died in Stockbridge, Massachusetts, on June 1, 1971.

Academic theologians often toil in relative isolation from the larger currents of public thought. Reinhold Niebuhr was a prominent exception. Though lacking a sterling educational background, he became one of the 20th century's premier public sages, turning his thoughts to the great issues of the day and communicating them to a wide assortment of listeners and readers. Though moored to the beliefs and convictions of liberal Protestantism, Niebuhr nevertheless challenged theological liberals to consider more seriously the realities of present human circumstances. Moreover, in at least one respect he had a wider audience even than intellectuals, for he composed the prayer that has become famous in 12-step programs such as Alcoholics Anonymous: "God, grant me serenity to accept the things I cannot change, courage to change the things I can, and wisdom to know the difference."

Further Reading

Ausmus, Harry J. *The Pragmatic God: On the Nihilism of Reinhold Niebuhr.* New York: P. Lang, 1990.

Bingham, June. *Courage to Change: An Introduction to the Life and Thought of Reinhold Niebuhr.* New York: Scribner, 1961; Lanham Md.: University Press of America, 1993.

Brown, Charles C. *Niebuhr and His Age: Reinhold Niebuhr's Prophetic Role in the Twentieth Century.* Philadelphia: Trinity Press International, 1992.

Carnell, Edward John. *The Theology of Reinhold Niebuhr.* Grand Rapids, Mich.: Eerdmans, 1951.

Davies, D. R. *Reinhold Niebuhr: Prophet from America.* New York: Macmillan, 1948; Freeport, N.Y.: Books for Libraries Press, 1970.

Durkin, Kenneth. *Reinhold Niebuhr.* Harrisburg, Pa.: Morehouse, 1990.

Fackre, Gabriel J. *The Promise of Reinhold Niebuhr.* Philadelphia: Lippincott, 1970; Lanham, Md.: University Press of America, 1994.

Fox, Richard Wightman. *Reinhold Niebuhr: A Biography.* New York: Pantheon Books, 1985; Ithaca, N.Y. Cornell University Press, 1996.

Gilkey, Langdon Brown. *On Neibuhr: A Theological Study.* Chicago: University of Chicago Press, 2001.

Merkley, Paul. *Reinhold Niebuhr: A Political Account.* Montreal: McGill-Queen's University Press, 1975.

Niebuhr, Reinhold. *The Children of Light and the Children of Darkness.* New York: C. Scribner's Sons, 1944.

———. *Christian Realism and Political Problems.* New York: Scribner, 1953.

———. *Leaves from the Notebook of a Tamed Cynic.* Chicago: Willett, Clark & Colby, 1929.

———. *Moral Man and Immoral Society: A Study in Ethics and Politics.* New York: C. Scribner's Sons, 1932.

———. *Remembering Reinhold Neibuhr: Letters of Reinhold and Ursula M. Niebuhr.* Edited by Ursula M. Niebuhr. San Francisco: HarperSanFrancisco, 1991.

Patterson, Bob E. *Reinhold Niebuhr.* Waco, Tex.: Word Books, 1977; Peabody, Mass.: Hendrickson Publishers, 1991.

Scott, Nathan A. Jr., ed. *The Legacy of Reinhold Niebuhr.* Chicago: University of Chicago Press, 1975.

Stone, Ronald H. *Professor Reinhold Niebuhr: A Mentor to the Twentieth Century.* Louisville, Ky.: Westminster/John Knox Press, 1992.

Norris, J. Frank
(John Franklyn Norris)
(1877–1952) *Baptist minister*

J. Frank Norris presided over fundamentalist Baptist pulpits during the first half of the 20th century. He courted controversy and used his substantial skills as an orator to rail against a variety of social ills such as gambling and political corruption, even as he assailed theological liberals and Catholics. He was born John Franklyn Norris on September 18, 1877, in Dadeville Alabama, the son of James Warren Norris and Mary Davis Warren. When Norris was 11 years old, he and his family moved to Hubbard, Texas, where they were sharecroppers. Two years later, Norris was converted in a revival meeting. By the time he left home for college, he had determined to pursue a vocation as a minister. While a student at Baylor University, he married

Lillian Gaddy, with whom he had four children. He earned a B.A. from Baylor in 1903 and then attended Southern Baptist Theological Seminary in Louisville, Kentucky, from which he graduated first in his class with a Th.M. in 1905.

After seminary, Norris served from 1905 to 1908 as pastor of the McKinney Avenue Baptist Church in Dallas, Texas, where his preaching and leadership expanded the church's membership 10-fold. During the same period he worked for the *Baptist Standard,* the leading newspaper for Southern Baptists in Texas, in which he used his influence as an editor to campaign against racetrack gambling. He also spearheaded the drive to relocate the Southwestern Baptist Theological Seminary from the campus of Baylor University in Waco to Forth Worth. Norris himself moved to Fort Worth in 1909 to become the pastor of the First Baptist Church there, and he occupied this pulpit for the next 44 years. In 1912, he had his first significant brush with the law, when he was charged—and ultimately acquitted—of arson after his church was destroyed by fire. He seized this opportunity to build bigger facilities for the church.

Norris's penchant for controversy drew increasingly large audiences as the years progressed, but it also earned him the opposition of many other Texas Baptists, as well as politicians and businessmen who felt the sting of his pulpit tirades. His intemperate criticism of denomination leaders fractured his relationship with the Baptist General Convention of Texas to the degree that in 1923 the convention refused to accept delegates from Norris's church, and the following year it expelled Norris and his congregation from the convention. In 1926, his criticisms of Fort Worth's mayor, H.C. Meachem, for allegedly funneling public funds to Catholic institutions ultimately led to an altercation in Norris's office in which he shot and killed a friend of the mayor. Though tried for murder, Norris won his second criminal acquittal, this time on the ground of self-defense. The fiery preacher's anti-Catholicism took center stage again in 1928, when he campaigned vigorously against the Catholic presidential candidate Alfred E. Smith and is credited with having helped Herbert Hoover win the election.

Not content with the influence he wielded from his Fort Worth pulpit, Norris seized both the written word and the infant medium of radio broadcasting to extend the reach of his fundamentalist message. Over the years, he published a succession of newspapers: *Fence Rail* from 1917 to 1921, *The Searchlight* from 1921 to 1927, and *The Fundamentalist* from 1927 to 1952. In the 1920s, he also established one of the first religious radio ministries. Even one pulpit eventually proved too narrow to contain his energy. From 1934 to 1948, he added another congregation—the Temple Baptist Church in Detroit, Michigan—to his pastoral responsibilities at the First Baptist Church in Fort Worth. He shuttled back and forth by rail and plane to preach on alternate Sundays at these two congregations, whose combined membership—which Norris claimed was 25,000—made it the largest pastorate in the world.

After his falling out with the Baptist General Convention of Texas, Norris founded his own church association in 1933, first called the Premillennial Baptist Missionary Fellowship and later renamed the Fundamental Baptist Missionary Fellowship. Shortly before his death, this organization splintered in 1950 between the World Baptist Fellowship, over which Norris exercised leadership, and the Baptist Bible Fellowship. Norris died on August 20, 1952, in Keystone, Florida.

J. Frank Norris preached a blend of theology that emphasized the inerrancy of the Bible and the imminent premillennial return of Christ, even as it castigated Darwinism, theological modernism, and Roman Catholicism. He combined these theological emphases with a vigorous social critique, warring from pulpit and newspaper against liquor, gambling, organized labor, and, especially after World War II, communism. His opponents demonized him, both for his archconservative theological and social views and for his intemperate language and sensationalist tactics. Nevertheless, supporters and allies revered J. Frank Norris as one of 20th-century fundamentalism's most articulate and influential prophets.

Further Reading

Hankins, Barry. *God's Rascal: J. Frank Norris and the Beginnings of Southern Fundamentalism.* Lexington: University Press of Kentucky, 1996.

Inside History of First Baptist Church, Fort Worth, and Temple Baptist Church, Detroit: Life Story of Dr. J. Frank Norris. New York: Garland, 1988.

The Story of the Fort Worth Norris-Wallace Debate: A Documentary Record of the Facts Concerning the Norris-Wallace Debate, Held in Fort Worth, Texas, November, 1934. Nashville: F.E. Wallace, Jr., Publications, 1968.

Tatum, E. Ray. *Conquest or Failure? Biography of J. Frank Norris.* Dallas: Baptist Historical Foundation, 1966.

Noyes, John Humphrey

(1811–1886) *utopian leader*

John Humphrey Noyes founded one of the 19th century's most famous utopian societies, the Oneida community. Convinced that spiritual perfection was possible, he led his followers to adopt controversial social practices, such as "complex marriage," as a means of achieving the perfection he believed was within human grasp. Noyes was born on September 3, 1811, in Brattleboro, Vermont, the son of John Noyes and Polly Hayes Noyes. Raised in the family of an agnostic father and a religiously devout mother, Noyes had a revivalist conversion experience shortly after graduation from Dartmouth College in 1830. Though he had been preparing to practice law, he abandoned further thought of this vocation and studied first at Andover Theological Seminary and then at Yale Divinity School.

By 1834 Noyes had become convinced that Christ had returned to earth in A.D. 70 and had opened the door to the possibility of human perfection on Earth. He married Harriet A. Holton in 1838, but by this time he had rejected traditional notions of monogamy. In their place, he had begun to teach a small group of disciples that the marriage relationship should not be confined to a single man and woman but should be as unrestrained as eating and drinking. The complex marriage he proposed in place of traditional domestic relationships encouraged taking multiple sexual partners within the community that had now established itself around him in Putney, Vermont. As he explained in a private letter, later published without his permission in the radical newspaper *The Battle Ax and Weapons of War* in August 1837:

> [W]hen the will of God is done on earth, as it is in heaven, *there will be no marriage.* . . . Exclusiveness, jealousy, quarrelling, have no place there, for the same reason as that which forbids the guests at a thanksgiving dinner to claim each his separate dish, and quarrel with the rest for his rights. In a holy community, there is no more reason why sexual intercourse should be restrained by law, than why eating and drinking should be—and there is as little occasion for shame in the one case as in the other.

By the mid-1840s Noyes's community consisted of about 37 members, who shared three houses, ran a store and two farms, and worshiped together in a small chapel. Eventually, however, public hostility to the sexual practices of his community among Noyes's Vermont neighbors resulted in his being charged with adultery in 1847. This charge prompted the community to relocate to Oneida, New York, where Noyes and his followers continued to live communally until 1879. Noyes led the Oneida community to add two interrelated refinements to the idea of complex marriage: First, he instituted the requirement of male continence, which required that males who engaged in sexual intercourse refrain from climax, thus constituting a limited form of birth control. Second, he caused the community to adopt the practice of what he called "stirpiculture," which involved allowing only couples designated by Noyes to produce children.

In the mid-1870s, Noyes attempted to name his son, Dr. Theodore Noyes, an agnostic, to take over leadership of the Oneida community, a move opposed by many in the community. By the end of the decade, Noyes's sporadic leadership and continued external criticism of the community's sexual practices finally caused its members to abandon their communal relationship and, in 1881, reorganize their property holdings as a joint stock company. Noyes himself migrated to Niagara Falls, Canada, where he died on October 20, 1886.

The 19th century witnessed a strong current of perfectionist aspirations, flowing chiefly through John Wesley's Methodism. But occasionally the desire to find perfection in this life, rather than in one to come, found its way down more unusual and isolated tributaries. The Oneida community of John Humphrey Noyes was one such expression of perfectionist impulse, and the social forms of life embraced by this community strayed far from the conventions of the day, especially those relating to sexual intercourse. Claiming to repudiate the possessiveness and jealousies of worldly life, Noyes led his followers for a time to attempt an experiment that would be renewed in various forms of "free love" associations during the 20th century.

Further Reading

Carden, Maren Lockwood. *Oneida: Utopian Community to Modern Corporation.* Baltimore: Johns Hopkins University Press, 1971.

Free Love in Utopia: John Humphrey Noyes and the Origin of the Oneida Community. Compiled by George Wallingford Noyes; edited by Lawrence Foster. Urbana: University of Illinois Press, 2001.

Klaw, Spencer. *Without Sin: The Life and Death of the Oneida Community.* New York: Allen Lane, 1993.

Noyes, Pierrepont. *My Father's House: An Oneida Boyhood.* New York: Farrar & Rinehart, 1937.

Parker, Robert Allerton. *A Yankee Saint: John Humphrey Noyes and the Oneida Community.* New York: G.P. Putnam's Sons, 1935.

Thomas, Robert David. *The Man Who Would Be Perfect: John Humphrey Noyes and the Utopian Impulse.* Philadelphia: University of Pennsylvania Press, 1977.

Occom, Samson
(Samson Occum)
(1723–1792) *Presbyterian minister*

A Native American convert to Christianity, Samson Occom became an ordained Presbyterian minister and evangelist to Indian tribes in New England. He also played an important role in raising support for the school established by Eleazar Wheelock, which would eventually become Dartmouth College. Occom was born in 1723 near New London, Connecticut, a member of the dwindling Mohegan tribe and son of Joshua and Sarah Occom. He had some contact with Christian missionaries during his childhood, and through the preaching of James Davenport, he eventually became a Christian convert during the Great Awakening. "I was born a Heathen," he later wrote, "and Brought up in Heathenism, till I was between 16 & 17 years of age." At that time, he said,

> I had, as I trust, a Discovery of the way of Salvation through Jesus Christ, and was enabled to put my trust in him alone for Life & Salvation. From this Time the Distress and Burden of my mind was removed, and I found Serenity and Pleasure of Soul, in Serving God.

In 1743, Occom entered the school run by Eleazar Wheelock in Lebanon, Connecticut. He progressed rapidly for four years but ultimately had to abandon his studies because of eye troubles occasioned by his scholarly efforts. In 1749, Occom was able to secure a position as a teacher for the Montauk Indians of Long Island, New York, where he labored for 12 years. He married Mary Fowler, a Montauk, in 1751, and this union produced 10 children. Among the Montauk, Occom soon combined teaching responsibilities with those of a minister, as he began to conduct weekly religious services. During this period, the Long Island Presbytery ordained him as a minister in August 1759.

During the 1760s Occom traveled widely, conducting evangelistic missions to the Oneida of New York and to other New England Indian communities. Most significantly, in 1765 he traveled to Great Britain with Nathaniel Whitaker, a Norwich pastor, to raise funds on behalf of a school for Native Americans (called the Indian Charity School) that Eleazar Wheelock had established in 1754. Occom's educational accomplishments under Wheelock's tutelage partially inspired the founding of the Indian Charity School, and his aid in raising support for the school secured its future prospects. He preached widely in England and Scotland from 1765 to 1768 and helped raise more than £11,000 for the school. After Occom returned to North America, these funds enabled Wheelock to relocate the school to New Hampshire and to rename the institution Dartmouth College.

Though warmly received in Great Britain, Occom found his reception in New England significantly less cordial. Many colonial authorities were already cool to Occom because he had sided with the Mohegan in a dispute involving Connecticut lands. Occom's relationship with Wheelock suffered when he began to suspect that Wheelock intended Dartmouth College, and the money that Occom had raised, to educate whites rather than Native Americans. Without steady employment and with a substantial family to care for, Occom endured a steady stream of financial worries even as he continued to minister to the Native Americans in his area. Rumors of Occom's occasional drunkenness further soured his relationship with Wheelock and others. The whispers against him prompted Occom to observe, "Christians are some times worse than the Savage Indians."

In 1771, Occom received an unusual request that would increase his reputation in New England. Moses Paul, a Native American who was convicted of murdering a man and sentenced to die, asked Occom to preach his execution sermon. The sight of one Native American's ascending the pulpit to preach on the occasion of another's execution could not fail to be gripping. "By the melancholy providence of God," Occom began,

> and at the earnest desire and invitation of the poor condemned criminal, I am here before this great concourse of people at this time, to give the last discourse to the poor miserable object who is to be executed this day before your eyes, for the due reward of his folly and madness and enormous wickedness.

The sermon created such a sensation that it was published and went through a number of editions. In the same decade, Occam published a collection of hymns and appears to have been the author of at least some of them.

During the 1770s, Occom developed plans to create a Christian–Native American community in New York but was not able to accomplish this dream until 1789, when he moved with his family to Brothertown (Eeayam Quittoowau Connant). He died in Stockbridge, New York, three years later, on July 14, 1792.

Samson Occom was colonial America's most famous Native American convert to Protestant Christianity. Intelligent and independent, he nevertheless suffered from his reliance on white patrons to meet the financial needs of his large family. That he could not always depend on the generosity and support of the society that had been instrumental in his conversion lent an aspect of disillusionment to an otherwise notable life.

Further Reading

Blodgett, Harold. *Samson Occom.* Hanover, N.H.: Dartmouth College Publications, 1935.

Love, William DeLoss. *Samson Occom and the Christian Indians of New England.* Boston: Pilgrim Press, 1899.

McCarthy, Keely E. "'Reducing Them to Civilitie': Religious Conversions and Cultural Transformations in Protestant Missionary Narratives, 1690–1790." Ph.D. dissertation, University of Maryland, College Park, 2000.

Moore, Cynthia Marie. "'Rent and Ragged Relation(s)': Puritans, Indians, and the Management of Congregations in New England, 1647–1776." Ph.D. dissertation, State University of New York at Stonybrook, 1999.

Occom, Samson. *A Sermon, Preached at the Execution of Moses Paul, an Indian.* New Haven, Conn.: Thomas and Samuel Green, 1772.

Peyer, Bernd C. "Samson Occom: Mohegan Missionary and Writer of the Eighteenth Century." *American Indian Quarterly* 6 (1982): 208–17.

Olcott, Henry Steel
(1832–1907) *Theosophical Society founder*

After brief careers as a farmer, a journalist, a Union officer, and a lawyer, Henry Steel Olcott helped found a new religious movement, the Theosophical Society, in his middle years. He also became instrumental in the revitalization of Hinduism and especially Buddhism in India. He was born on August 2, 1832, in Orange, New Jersey, the son of pious Presbyterians, Henry Wyckoff Olcott and Emily Steel Olcott. When Olcott was 16, his father's business failed, and Olcott subsequently went to work on his uncle's farm. He brought an avid intellectual curiosity to this work, which led him to found an agricultural school in New Jersey when he was in his early 20s, and in 1858 he published a book about sugarcane. After the school failed in 1859, Olcott became an assistant agricultural editor of the *New York Tribune* from 1858 to

1860. At the end of this period, he married Mary Eplee Morgan, and their union would eventually produce four children. With the outbreak of the Civil War, Olcott joined the Union army. He was eventually assigned the task of investigating fraud associated with army procurement and was promoted to the rank of colonel.

After the war, Olcott returned to journalism but found time to study law and pass the New York bar examination. He practiced law from 1868 to 1878. He and his wife were divorced in 1870, and, soon thereafter, he began to investigate spiritualism phenomena, an interest he had held since he was a teenager. In 1874 he traveled to a farm in Chittenden, Vermont, that was reputed to be the site of psychic phenomena. His research into the phenomena resulted in his 1875 publication of *People from the Other World*, but an even more important consequence of his visit to Chittenden was his encounter there with HELENA PETROVNA BLAVATSKY, a Russian aristocrat who had immigrated to the United States a few years previously. In 1875, the year after they met at the Vermont farm, Olcott and Blavatsky founded the Theosophical Society, with Olcott as its president. This religious movement sought to harness elements of Western occultism with certain features of Eastern religious thought. Soon after the creation of the Theosophical Society, Blavatsky made a first attempt to explain its key ideas in *Isis Unveiled* (1877).

The year after the publication of this book, Blavatsky and Olcott set sail together for India. Once there, they established a magazine called *Theosophist* in 1879; lectured widely on Theosophy; and established local chapters of the movement. In 1882, they were able to purchase an estate at Adyar, which became the world headquarters of the Theosophical Society. In addition to their work as apologists for Theosophy, Olcott and Blavatsky also took a keen interest in local Hindu and Buddhist practice and thought, and through respectful support of these Eastern religious traditions they helped inaugurate their late-19th-century renaissance, which itself played a prominent role in the movement toward Indian independence in the following century. Both Olcott and Blavatsky became Buddhists in 1880,

Henry S. Olcott was a cofounder (with Helena Blavatsky) of the Theosophical Society. *(Library of Congress, Prints and Photographs Division LC-USZ62-105248)*

though they maintained their devotion to Theosophy. Olcott, especially, became an ardent defender and popular expositor of Buddhist teachings. In a move reminiscent of his childhood Presbyterianism, he prepared and published his *Buddhist Catechism* in 1885.

The close association between Olcott and Blavatsky ended in the mid-1880s, after the Society for Psychical Research in England sent an investigator to India to investigate certain psychic phenomena attributed to Blavatsky. The investigator eventually published a report accusing her of fraud, and this finding, coupled with her declining health, prompted Blavatsky to leave India and eventually settle in London. Olcott remained in India at the Theosophical Society headquarters as the society's president, but he had to contend in subsequent years with a variety of internal conflicts within the Theosophy movement, including disagreements with Blavatsky and with the American branch of the society, led by William Q. Judge. He died on February 17, 1907, in Adyar.

The 20th century would see Eastern religious thought imported to the United States on a wide scale. Henry Steel Olcott must be accorded a prominent place in the history of this religious commerce. The main thrust of his influence, though, was not in introducing Eastern religious traditions to the United States but in seeking out these traditions himself and attempting to reinvigorate them in their indigenous habitats. Along the way, he helped to found what would become one of the 20th century's most influential new religious movements.

Further Reading

Murphet, Howard. *Hammer on the Mountain: Life of Henry Steel Olcott (1832–1907)*. Wheaton, Ill.: Theosophical Publishing House, 1972.

Olcott, Henry Steel. *Old Diary Leaves: The True Story of the Theosophical Society*. New York: G. P. Putnam's Sons, 1895.

———. *People from the Other World*. Hartford, Conn.: American, 1875.

Prothero, Stephen R. *The White Buddhist: The Asian Odyssey of Henry Steel Olcott*. Bloomington: Indiana University Press, 1996.

Oxnam, Garfield Bromley

(1891–1963) *Methodist bishop, ecumenical leader*

Garfield Bromley Oxnam served the Methodist Church from 1916 until his retirement in 1960. One of the most influential Methodist leaders of the 20th century, Oxnam also rose to prominence in national and international ecumenical organizations. He was born on August 14, 1891, in Sonora, California, the son of Thomas Henry Oxnam and Mary Ann Jobe Oxnam, known to family and friends as "Mamie." The parents of Bromley Oxnam, as he was known, were devout Methodists, and at the age of 17, while attending a revival meeting, Oxnam determined to become a Methodist minister. He commented on the event in his journal: "Christianity has changed me, now I have sweet peace, a joy in it, all is just right, Christ has made life worth while to me." Although he had dropped out of high school to help support his family, Oxnam was able to attend the

University of Southern California, from which he received a B.A. in 1913. Subsequently, he attended Boston University School of Theology and graduated in 1915. The previous year he had married Ruth Fisher, with whom he had three children. After leaving Boston, Oxnam briefly pursued graduate studies at Harvard University and the Massachusetts Institute of Technology.

Ordained a deacon in the Methodist Episcopal Church in 1916, Oxnam was first assigned to a rural church in Poplar, California. In October 1917, Oxnam's bishop appointed him to the Newman Methodist Episcopal Church in East Los Angeles, a struggling urban congregation in a multiethnic neighborhood. Within a few years, Oxnam arranged to sell the Newman church and to purchase new property, where he founded the Church of All Nations in 1921. An ardent supporter of the social gospel movement, Oxnam opened the church to labor union meetings and quickly earned the attention of the Los Angeles office of the Federal Bureau of Investigation (FBI), which began a file on his activities. Eventually, the Church of All Nations functioned less as a church and more as a community center.

In 1927, Oxnam returned to Boston to accept a position on the faculty of the Boston University School of Theology. By the following year, he had assumed the presidency of De Pauw University in Greencastle, Indiana, a Methodist institution. As he grappled with the impact of the Great Depression on the university, Oxnam earned a reputation as an authoritarian. His penchant for firing professors without consideration of their tenured status and without input from other university constituencies ultimately earned the university censure by the American Association of University Professors.

After eight years at DePauw, in 1936, Oxnam was elected a bishop of the Methodist Episcopal Church, the youngest bishop in the history of the church. Three years later he participated in the merger of the Methodist Episcopal Church, South, and the Methodist Protestant Church with his own denomination. In the years after his election as bishop, he served in bishoprics in Omaha (1936–39), Boston (1939–44), New York (1944–52), and Washington, D.C. (1952–60). In the decade after he became a bishop, Oxnam also rose to prominence in a succession of ecumenical organizations. He served as president of the Federal Council of Churches from 1944 to 1946. Oxnam played a central role in the transformation of this body into the National Council of Churches in 1950, and he served as its inaugural president. He also labored actively in the creation of the World Council of Churches in 1948 and was one of its six inaugural presidents, the only American initially to hold this executive position.

With a distaste for theology and a preference for social activism, Oxnam could be found in some of the progressive social movements of his day. He helped found Protestants and Other Americans United for the Separation of Church and State in 1948 and was the group's first president. He also orchestrated the Methodist Crusade for a New World Order, which supported the creation of the United Nations. His long years as a friend of organized labor and an ally of the social gospel movement made it inevitable that the cold war would cause some people to cast a baleful eye in his direction. Oxnam began the last decade of his life with a voluntary appearance before the House Un-American Activities Committee, to respond to allegations that he was a communist. Afflicted by Parkinson's disease toward the end of his life, Oxnam had to retire in 1960; he died on March 12, 1963, in White Plains, New York.

G. Bromley Oxnam was the model of liberal Protestantism's ecumenical and socially progressive temper in the first half of the 20th century. If he was not also a leading light of liberal theology, it was because theological inquiry and conflict bored him. He fastened his attention, instead, on the social contributions that Christianity might make to the world, and he proved adept at steering the institutional structures fashioned by mainstream Protestants to make these contributions.

Further Reading

Miller, Robert Moats. *Bishop G. Bromley Oxnam: Paladin of Liberal Protestantism.* Nashville: Abington Press, 1990.

Miller, Wayne Lowell. "A Critical Analysis of the Speaking Career of Bishop G. Bromley Oxnam." Ph.D. dissertation, University of Southern California, 1961.

Oxnam, Garfield Bromley. *I Protest.* New York: Harper, 1954.

———. *A Testament of Faith.* Boston: Little, Brown, 1958.

P

Palmer, Phoebe Worrall
(1807–1874) *Methodist lay preacher*

An early leader within the Holiness movement, Phoebe Worrall Palmer became convinced that perfection was attainable in this life. Through revival preaching, writing, and practical humanitarian efforts, Palmer labored to convey this spiritual vision to others and in the process became one of the 19th century's most prominent lay ministers. She was born on December 18, 1807, in New York City, the daughter of Henry Worrall and Dorothea Wade Worrall. Her father had been converted to Methodism before immigrating to the United States in 1785, and as she grew older, Phoebe embraced the faith that he taught his family. In 1827 she married Walter Clarke Palmer, a New York physician, and the couple had six children, only three of whom survived childhood.

On July 26, 1837, Palmer experienced a spiritual awakening after she had become convinced that she had lost three of her children because she loved them more than she loved God. Believing that she had experienced what Methodists called "entire sanctification" on this date, Palmer became an ardent apostle for the possibility that Christians could attain perfection at once. This view contrasted with the belief held by most Methodists and other Protestants that spiritual sanctification or perfection entailed a lengthy process, often thought to be completed only after death. Palmer, in contrast, insisted that perfection was immediately accessible to believers through an experience she identified from the New Testament as the "baptism of the Holy Sprit." Her view of Christian perfection was centered in what has been named *altar theology*, the idea that Christians could, in a single moment of dedication, present themselves to God as on an altar and receive entire sanctification.

After her 1837 experience, Palmer traveled widely as a revival preacher, first in the United States, and later in Canada and Great Britain. She also conducted a weekly meeting, the Tuesday Meeting for the Promotion of Holiness, which played an important role in the growth of the Holiness movement, for some 40 years. In 1845, with the publication of her first book, *The Way of Holiness*, Palmer began to use the written word as a vehicle for spreading the Holiness message. In addition to authoring numerous books, she also edited *Guide to Holiness*, a magazine that had some 30,000 readers at the peak of its popularity, from 1862 to 1874.

Palmer's Holiness teaching did not contemplate only a life of pious insularity. By 1847 she had become an officer in the Ladies' Home Missionary Society of the Methodist Episcopal Church. In this position she prompted the organization to establish the Five Points Mission in New York City, which offered rent-free apartments, baths, and a chapel to the poor, as well as a variety of other rescue missions. She died in New York City on November 2, 1874.

"It is my solemn conviction, before God," Phoebe Worrell Palmer once wrote to a friend, "that women have a work to do, beyond what they are now doing." Though her ideas about the roles of women are far removed from those of modern feminists, Palmer defended a role for women that was decisively greater than that which 19th-century American society routinely allocated to them. Charles Edward White, a modern biographer, characterized her accomplishments as follows: "[S]he addressed thousands in an age when some thought it unseemly for a woman to speak . . . she wrote theological works when some thought it impossible for a woman to reason, and . . . she established a mission in the slums when some thought it unsafe for a woman to venture too far from the home." But Phoebe Palmer was more than an exemplar of the possible contributions that women might make to American religion and society. She also had a formative influence on the Holiness movement, which itself is the main current from which spring modern-day tributaries such as the Nazarenes, the Pentecostal and Assembly of God Churches, the Salvation Army, and the charismatic movement.

Further Reading

Hogan, Lucy Anne Lind. "The Overthrow of the Monopoly of the Pulpit: A Longitudinal Case Study of the Cultural Conversation Advocating the Preaching and Ordination of Women in American Methodism 1859–1924." Ph.D. dissertation, University of Maryland College Park, 1995.

Palmer, Phoebe. *The Devotional Writings of Phoebe Palmer.* New York: Garland, 1985.

———. *Incidental Illustrations of the Economy of Salvation, Its Doctrines and Duties.* Boston: H.V. Degen, 1855.

———. *Phoebe Palmer: Selected Writings.* Edited by Thomas C. Oden. New York: Paulist Press, 1988.

———. *The Way of Holiness, with Notes by the Way; Being a Narrative of Religious Experience Resulting from a Determination to Be a Bible Christian.* New York: G. Lane & C. B. Tippett, 1845.

Raser, Harold E. *Phoebe Palmer, Her Life and Thought.* Lewiston, N.Y.: Edwin Mellen Press, 1987.

Wheatley, Richard. *The Life and Letters of Mrs. Phoebe Palmer.* New York: Garland, 1984.

White, Charles Edward. *The Beauty of Holiness: Phoebe Palmer as Theologian, Revivalist, Feminist, and Humanitarian.* Grand Rapids, Mich.: F. Asbury Press, 1986.

Parker, Quanah
(Kwahnah)
(ca. 1852–1911) *Native American religious leader*

A leader of the Comanche after the tribe was consigned to reservation life, Quanah Parker served as a principal representative of the Comanche in their relations with the U.S. government. He also supported the rise of sacramental peyote use among Native Americans. Quanah Parker (whose first name means "fragrant") was born around 1852 to Peta Nocona, a Comanche warrior, and Cynthia Ann Parker. His mother was a white woman who had been captured by the Comanche when she was nine years old and had become acculturated to Native American life. She spent 25 years with the Comanche before being discovered and forced to return to her white family. During the Red River War of 1874–75, Quanah Parker led Comanche raids against buffalo hunters in the Texas panhandle. He was eventually wounded and forced to surrender at Fort Sill, Oklahoma.

In the following years, after Parker and his people were consigned to a reservation in Oklahoma, he grew in influence, partially as a result of notoriety associated with his being the son of a white woman but also of his own ability and determination. He served as an intermediary between Native Americans and ranchers eager to use reservation grasslands and eventually became the principal leader of his people. Over the course of the years, his personal wealth became substantial and included a 10-room home referred to as the "Star House."

Though Parker absorbed some elements of white civilization, he also continued to practice certain Native American customs, including polygamy. He had eight wives and 25 children. Parker also participated in the sacramental use of peyote, and he became an important influence in the rise of peyoteism among Native Americans and in the popularization of religious beliefs and ceremonies that combined elements of traditional tribal religion with some of those borrowed from Christianity. Peyote, a small, spineless variety of cactus that grows in the Rio Grande Valley, the top of which is harvested and dries in the form of a button, is believed by adherents of peyote religion to possess healing and teaching properties. A hallucinogen, it is consumed during religious meetings that include singing, drumming, and praying. Quanah Parker's name is today associated with one of two principal ceremonies of peyote religion: the Half-Moon, also called the Quanah Parker Way, and the Big Moon. The two variants differ in the form of altar on which a

Quanah Parker, a Native American religious leader, represented the Comanche tribe in its relations with the U.S. government. *(Library of Congress, Prints and Photographs Division LC-USZ62-98166)*

larger peyote button, referred to as the Chief Peyote, sits during the peyote ceremony. In the Quanah Parker Way, this altar is crescent-shaped; in the Big Moon, the altar is larger and horseshoe-shaped. Near the end of Parker's life, Native American followers of peyote religion institutionalized their sacramental use of peyote in the Native American Church.

Because of his prominence among his people, Quanah Parker served for a time as a tribal judge. He was a chief Native American negotiator meeting with the federal government in the sessions that ultimately produced the 1900 Jerome Agreement, which guaranteed that each reservation inhabitant receive 160 acres. Ironically, this agreement diminished his own property holdings. So influential was Parker among the Native Americans on the Oklahoma reservations that President Theodore Roosevelt invited him to participate in the president's inaugural parade in 1905. He died in Oklahoma, at Star House, on February 23, 1911.

Quanah Parker was a principal Native American political and religious leader during the last half of the 19th century. Consistent with the last name he assumed from his mother to join with his own Indian name, Parker successfully navigated the intersection between Native American culture and the dominant white culture that forced the Native Americans onto the reservations of Oklahoma. He contributed to the flourishing of a religious tradition that continues to claim substantial Native American adherents.

Further Reading

Dees, Mary Reaves. *Quanah Parker's Strange Encounters: A Biography.* DeSoto, Tex.: Marmor Publishing, 1997.

Hagan, William T. *Quanah Parker, Comanche Chief.* Norman: University of Oklahoma Press, 1993.

Jackson, Clyde L., and Grace Jackson. *Quanah Parker, Last Chief of the Comanches: A Study in Southwestern Frontier History.* New York: Exposition Press, 1963.

Neeley, Bill. *The Last Comanche Chief: The Life and Times of Quanah Parker.* New York: J. Wiley, 1995.

Wilson, Claire. *Quanah Parker: Comanche Chief.* New York: Chelsea House, 1992.

Parker, Theodore

(1810–1860) *Unitarian minister, abolitionist, social reformer*

Theodore Parker outstripped most Unitarians of his day in his zeal to hurry beyond orthodox formulations of Christian doctrine to what he perceived to be the enduring essence of Christianity. The same independent temper inspired him to insist on the abolition of slavery at a time when the nation was not prepared to do so. Parker was born on August 24, 1810, in Lexington, Massachusetts, the son of John Parker and Hannah Stearns Parker. Though he was sufficiently intellectually gifted to be accepted as a student at Harvard College, Parker was prevented by financial circumstances from attending college. Instead, while teaching school, Parker studied the Harvard curriculum and eventually passed the examinations required of graduates. He did not receive an undergraduate degree, but Harvard Divinity School was happy to accept him as a student and he graduated in 1836. The following year he was ordained and became the minister of the Unitarian church in West Roxbury, Massachusetts. The same year he married Lydia Dodge Cabot; the marriage produced no children.

Most Unitarians of the first half of the 19th century viewed themselves as still lodged securely within the household of Christendom, even though they had abandoned belief in the Trinity. Parker, though, was prepared to jettison far more of traditional Christian orthodoxy, and he soon found himself at odds with other Unitarians. In 1841, he seized the opportunity of preaching at the ordination of a new minister in Boston to deliver his own homily on Christian truth, "The Transient and Permanent in Christianity." He shocked many of his listeners by his willingness to classify much of Christian doctrine in the "transient" category.

> Many tenets, that pass current in our theology, seem to be the refuse of idol temples; the offscourings of Jewish and heathen cities, rather than the sands of virgin gold, which the stream of Christianity has worn off from the rock of ages, and brought in its bosom for us. . . . The stream of Christianity, as men receive it, has caught a stain from every soil it has filtered through, so that now it is not the pure water from the well of Life, which is offered to our lips, but streams troubled and polluted by man with mire and dirt.

Parker's suggestion that the pollutions of Christianity included preoccupation with the nature of Christ and with the authority of the Scriptures shocked even the Unitarians of his day. They disassociated themselves from him, in the main, and prompted Parker and those more receptive to his views to establish the Twenty-Eighth Congregational Society, which served as his pulpit for the remainder of his life, in 1846.

A lively social conscience accompanied Theodore Parker's spiritual radicalism, exhibiting itself especially on the subject of slavery. He railed against the traffic in souls from pulpit and lecture podium, arguing, as he wrote in a letter to a southern slaveholder, that slave owners were "doing a great wrong to themselves, to their slaves, and to mankind." He buttressed his words with deeds, moreover, and cast himself into organizations such as Boston's Committee of Vigilance, which sought to help escaped slaves elude recapture. To his diatribes against slavery, Parker also added theological and social critiques on a wide range of issues, including women's rights, public corruption, poverty, and U.S. government treatment of Native Americans. His views influenced some listeners but aggravated even more, making him one of his generation's most popular and most reviled speakers. Eventually, however, recurring sickness prompted by overexertion began to plague him. While on a European trip seeking rest and recovery, he died on May 10, 1860, in Florence, Italy.

In his day, Theodore Parker was virtually exiled from the fellowship of other Unitarians who could not follow the radical theological paths he sought to blaze. Toward the beginning of the 20th century, however, the spiritual descendants of these early Unitarians found cause to embrace Parker as one of their patron saints. The American Unitarian Association, happy to banish Parker from spiritual fraternity in the 1840s, published a centenary edition of his works in 1907. The lonely pilgrimage Parker had undertaken away from

Christian orthodoxy in the mid-19th century no longer seemed so radical. Moreover, his zeal as a social reformer became a model for 20th-century Unitarians who sought to confront the needs of their society.

Further Reading

Albrecht, Robert C. *Theodore Parker.* New York: Twayne Publishers, 1971.

Chadwick, John White. *Theodore Parker, Preacher and Reformer.* Boston: Houghton, Mifflin, 1900; St. Clair Shores, Mich.: Scholarly Press, 1971.

Chesebrough, David B. *Theodore Parker: Orator of Superior Ideas.* Westport, Conn.: Greenwood Press, 1999.

Commager, Henry Steele. *Theodore Parker.* Boston: Little, Brown, 1936; Boston: Beacon Press, 1960.

Frothingham, Octavius Brooks. *Theodore Parker: A Biography.* Boston: J. R. Osgood, 1874.

Parker, Theodore. *An Anthology.* Edited by Henry Steele Commager. Boston: Beacon Press, 1960.

———. *Theodore Parker: American Transcendentalist: A Critical Essay and a Collection of His Writings.* Edited by Robert E. Collins. Metuchen, N.J.: Scarecrow Press, 1973.

Weiss, John. *Life and Correspondence of Theodore Parker: Minister of the Twenty-eighth Congregational Society, Boston.* 2 vols. New York: D. Appleton, 1864; New York: Da Capo Press, 1970.

Peale, Norman Vincent

(1898–1993) *Methodist minister, author*

The author of one of the 20th century's most popular religious books, *The Power of Positive Thinking* (1952), Norman Vincent Peale became famous for his message of hope and optimism. He emphasized the possibility of spiritual and personal power to listeners and readers, choosing to focus on practical issues of life rather than abstract theological questions. In doing so, he found an enormous audience across more than 60 years of ministry as a Christian preacher and writer. He was born on May 31, 1898, in Bowersville, Ohio, to Charles Clifford Peale, a Methodist preacher, and Anna DeLaney Peele. Peale received a B.A. from Ohio Wesleyan, a Methodist college, in 1920. After a brief attempt to pursue a career in journalism, Peale decided to prepare for the Methodist ministry and enrolled at Boston University in 1921; he graduated three years later with an M.A. and an S.T.B.

Peale's first ministerial assignment was St. Mark's Methodist Church in Brooklyn, New York, which he began in the summer of 1924. St. Mark's was a small congregation that met in a run-down building. Within three years, though, Peale had engineered its relocation to a new building and renamed the church, whose membership had climbed from 40 to around 900, as the Kings Highway Methodist Church. When assigned to the University Church in Syracuse, New York, in 1927, Peale accomplished a similar result, seeing the church's membership swell and its ministry among college students expand.

In 1932, Peale accepted the pastorate of the Marble Collegiate Church, a Dutch Reformed congregation in New York City. As had his previous pastorates, his new church had fallen on hard times: its facilities south of Midtown Manhattan had deteriorated and its membership had declined. Even Peale's energy and abilities did not immediately engineer an improvement in the church's condition. During a vacation in his second year there, however, Peale found himself spiritually rekindled, and he returned to his church full of new hope and energy. That year, the Federal Council of Churches (subsequently the National Council of Churches) invited him to start a radio program, which he called *The Art of Living* and which would become a central aspect of his ministry for the next 40 years. To his pastoral and radio ministry, Peale added a career as an author. In 1937, he published *The Art of Living,* the first of more than 20 books.

Before Peale's father became a Methodist minister, he had pursued a career as a physician for a time, and this heritage may have influenced Peale's own interest in medicine and psychiatry in the 1940s. He became convinced that many of his parishioners lacked both faith and mental health, and he began to explore avenues for seeking some alliance between his own pastoral ministry and the

Norman Vincent Peale's best-selling book *The Power of Positive Thinking* popularized the "gospel of success" during the middle years of the 20th century. *(Library of Congress, Prints and Photographs Division, LC-USZ62-126496)*

services of mental health experts. He eventually collaborated with the psychiatrist Smiley Blanton to establish a "religion-psychiatric clinic" at his church, an enterprise later renamed the Blanton-Peale Institute of Religion and Health.

In 1952, Norman Vincent Peale, already an established author, crossed over into best-seller territory with the publication of *The Power of Positive Thinking*. Although Peale's working title for the book had been *The Power of Faith*, his publisher persuaded him—correctly, as it turned out—that Peale might find a wider audience if he changed the title. Combining anecdote, aphorism, and practical principles, Peale's book en-

couraged his readers with a gospel of optimistic possibility intended to overcome self-doubt and assure personal success.

The success of Peale's *Positive Thinking* and of other books that followed in its wake made him one of the most popular preachers and Christian writers of the 20th century. But in spite of this success, Peale was a magnet for criticism, from both theological conservatives and liberals. Conservatives assailed his self-help theology; liberals blanched at the intellectual shallowness of his books and sermons. Liberals found even more offense as Peale cast his increasingly considerable reputation behind social conservative causes, not the least of which was his public political support for and friendship with Richard Nixon.

Peale weathered the criticism, though, and continued his prodigious preaching, speaking, and writing career. He transformed *Guideposts*—a magazine he founded in the 1940s—into a periodical with millions of readers. He also became the president of the Reformed Church in America in 1969, even while he continued to preach at the Marble Collegiate Church until his retirement in 1984 at the age of 86. He died in Pawling, New York, on Christmas Eve 1993.

Norman Vincent Peale's infectious optimism found a receptive audience in the years after World War II, when America's economy and world station seemed limitlessly ascendant. His critics assailed the endlessly self-congratulatory element of his message: conservatives, because they believed it obscured the reality of sin and the necessity of grace; liberals, because it ignored systemic social problems in favor of a native and intellectually impoverished individualism. But those who admired him and those who believed themselves helped by his message tended to overwhelm the voice of critics and make Norman Vincent Peale one of the 20th century's most popular Christian representatives.

Further Reading

Broadhurst, Allan R. *He Speaks the Word of God: A Study of the Sermons of Norman Vincent Peale*. Englewood Cliffs, N.J.: Prentice-Hall, 1963.

George, Carol V. R. *God's Salesman: Norman Vincent Peale and the Power of Positive Thinking*. New York: Oxford University Press, 1993.

Gordon, Arthur. *One Man's Way: The Story and Message of Norman Vincent Peale, a Biography*. Englewood Cliffs, N.J.: Prentice-Hall, 1972.

———. *The Power of Positive Thinking*. New York: Prentice-Hall, 1952.

Peale, Norman Vincent. *This Incredible Century*. Wheaton, Ill.: Tyndale House Pub., 1991.

———. *The True Joy of Positive Living: An Autobiography*. New York: Morrow, 1984.

Westphal, Clarence. *Norman Vincent Peale, Christian Crusader: A Biography*. Minneapolis: Denison, 1964.

Penn, William

(1644–1718) *Quaker leader, founder of Pennsylvania*

Born the son of a wealthy military hero, William Penn became a Quaker while a young man. Thereafter, he used the benefits of his social and economic rank to support the cause of Quakerism. In particular, he founded the colony of Pennsylvania partially as a haven for Quakers from religious persecution. He was born on October 14, 1644, in London, England, the son of Sir William Penn and Margaret Jasper Vanderschuren Penn. His father, an admiral, was able to have William educated at the Chigwell Free Grammar School in Essex and then at Christ Church College, Oxford. Unfortunately for the father's aspirations for his son, Oxford expelled William Penn in 1662 for complaining about compulsory chapel attendance at services of the Church of England. Hoping to cure Penn of his flirtation with Protestant dissent, his father dispatched him to the European continent for a time; there Penn studied at L' Académie Protestante de Saumur. When Penn returned to England, he studied law at Lincoln's Inn and then undertook to assist in his father's various affairs. But he earned his father's lasting displeasure in 1667 by becoming a Quaker while on a business expedition for his father in Ireland.

William Penn had leadership abilities that his father had hoped to turn down paths of business and politics, but he employed them instead to advance the cause of Quakerism. As an outspoken defender of the Quakers both in speeches and in books, Penn spent time in jail on more than one occasion. His arrest in 1670 for inciting a riot resulted in a jury verdict of not guilty despite the court's demand that the jurors find Penn and his codefendant guilty. This case established an important precedent about the power of jurors to reach verdicts amendable to their own judgment rather than the instructions of judges. Penn responded to his arrests by becoming an ardent champion of religious liberty, using both his rhetorical abilities and his family connections to defend other Quakers from persecution. He poignantly described the hardships wrought by persecution for cause of conscience. "For not to be able to give us faith, or save our consciences harmless, and yet to persecute us for refusing conformity, is intolerable hard measure," he complained in *The Great Case for Liberty of Conscience* (1670). Must believers, he asked, "be persecuted here if they do not go against their consciences, and punished hereafter if they do?" But Penn also denied that civil rulers had any authority to superintend the religious beliefs of their subjects. "[I]mposition, restraint, and persecution, for matters relating to conscience," he insisted, "directly invade the Divine prerogative, and divest the Almighty of a due, proper to none besides himself."

After the death of his father in 1670, Penn possessed significant wealth; in 1672, he married Gulielma Maria Springett, with whom he had three children who survived infancy. Throughout the 1670s, Penn traveled widely in England and abroad, advancing the Quaker message. He still maintained cordial relations with important people in England, though, not the least of whom was Charles II. In 1681, Charles repaid a debt he had owed to Penn's father by awarding William Penn a charter for the colony of Pennsylvania.

Penn seized this opportunity to attempt the creation of a "holy experiment" in civil government, one that would erect a godly commonwealth where Quakers, and other believers as well, could live untroubled by religious persecution. The colony's governing document, the Frame of Government, produced in 1682, specifically guaranteed religious liberty to all those who believed in God, though it limited the right to hold office to Christians. Penn went to America for two years in his role as proprietor of the colony to oversee its early development. But his financial affairs, already precarious before he received the Pennsylvania charter, were not improved by the king's grant. Quickly overwhelmed by debt, Penn found himself on the losing end of a lawsuit by creditors and spent some nine months in a debtor's prison. He was also caught up in a boundary dispute with the proprietors of the Maryland colony.

By 1684, Penn had returned to England, and though in 1699 he visited his colony again for two years, he acted mostly as a long-distance proprietor for the remainder of his life. He suffered political setbacks, including being temporarily stripped of authority over the colony in 1692. His first wife died in 1694, and two years later he married Hannah Callowhill, with whom he had seven children. Penn suffered a stroke in 1712 and died six years later, on July 30, 1718, in Ruscombe, Berkshire, England.

William Penn's stature as the founder of Pennsylvania is almost mythical in its grandeur: the son of privilege who devoted himself to the cause of a new religious sect and founded an American colony to create a safe harbor for Quakers and other religious dissenters. Although he spent only a few years in America, he played a significant role in early American history, especially in the struggle to secure

The Quaker leader William Penn founded the colony of Pennsylvania. *(Library of Congress, Prints and Photographs Division, LC-USZ62-106735)*

religious liberty. But financial difficulties cast a shadow across his own dream of launching a "holy experiment" in the New World. These surely did not take him by surprise, for in spite of his prominent social position, his conversion to Quakerism had exposed him to suffering in general and to the sting of religious persecution in particular. While imprisoned for his beliefs in 1669, Penn had written lines in the pamphlet *No Cross, No Crown,* that would form a fitting epitaph: "No pain, no palm; no thorns, no throne; no gall, no glory; no cross, no crown."

Further Reading

Dobrée, Bonamy. *William Penn, Quaker and Pioneer.* Boston: Houghton Mifflin, 1932; Folcroft, Pa.: Folcroft Library Editions, 1978.

Dunn, Mary M. *William Penn: Politics and Conscience.* Princeton, N.J.: Princeton University Press, 1967.

Endy, Melvin B., Jr. *William Penn and Early Quakerism.* Princeton, N.J.: Princeton University Press, 1973.

Fantel, Hans. *William Penn: Apostle of Dissent.* New York: Morrow, 1974.

Geiter, Mary K. *William Penn.* New York: Longman, 2000.

Hull, William Isaac. *William Penn: A Topical Biography.* London: Oxford University Press, 1937; Freeport, N.Y.: Books for Libraries Press, 1971.

Morris, Kenneth R. "Theological Sources of William Penn's Concept of Religious Toleration." *Journal of Church and State* 35 (1993): 83–111.

Peare, Catherine Owens. *William Penn: A Biography.* Philadelphia: Lippincott, 1957.

Penn, William. *The Papers of William Penn.* Edited by Mary Maples Dunn and Richard S. Dunn. Philadelphia: University of Pennsylvania Press, 1981–87.

Pennington, James William Charles
(James Pembroke)
(1807–1870) *Congregationalist and Presbyterian minister, abolitionist*

James W. C. Pennington escaped from slavery as a young man and became a respected African-American minister. He served in a number of Congregationalist and Presbyterian churches and lent his considerable talents to the abolitionist movement. He was born in 1807 on a plantation in Queen Ann's County, Maryland, the son of Nelly and Brazil, slaves owned by James Tilghman. At birth, he was given the name James Pembroke, though he later adopted James William Charles Pennington as his name.

During his childhood and teenage years, Pennington was trained first as a stonemason and later as a blacksmith, but his escape from slavery in 1827 gave him the opportunity to find the education denied him as a slave. After his escape he took refuge at first one and then another Quaker farm in Pennsylvania, where he learned to read and write. By 1829 he had made his way to Brooklyn, New York, where he worked during the day while he attended evening classes and continued studying on his own. During this period he was converted to Christianity, an event he subsequently described in his autobiography, *The Fugitive Blacksmith:*

> Day after day for about two weeks, I found myself more deeply convicted of personal guilt before God. . . . Burning with a recollection of the wrongs man had done me— mourning for the injuries my brethren were still enduring, and deeply convicted of the guilt of my own sin against God . . . one evening in the third week of the struggle, while alone in my chamber, and after solemn reflection for several hours, I concluded that I could never be happy or useful in that state of mind, and resolved that I would try to become reconciled to God.

In 1833 Pennington became a teacher at a school for African Americans in New Town, Long Island. But his continued thirst for education sent him two years later to the Yale Divinity School, which refused to admit him as a student but allowed him to attend lectures. By 1837 he had been licensed to preach and had begun a long career as a minister, mainly in Presbyterian and Congregationalist churches.

In the 1840s, while he served as minister of a Congregational church in Hartford, Connecticut, Pennington played an influential role in the *Amistad* affair, which involved Africans of the Mendi tribe who had revolted on board the slave ship *Amistad* and who had ultimately been captured by an American navy cutter. Pennington supported the cause of the Mendi while their case made its way through U.S. courts, and he helped to see them returned to their home in Africa. During this period, he helped found the Union Missionary Society to advance the antislavery cause and African missions, and he served as an early president of the society. In 1846, he suffered the death of his first wife, Harriet; two years later he married Almira Ray. Late in that decade, he traveled abroad and was awarded an honorary doctorate in 1849 by the University of Heidelberg.

The following decade saw the height of Pennington's influence. He managed to procure his freedom from his former slave master in 1851 while abroad in Europe. He subsequently returned to New York City, where he had been the minister of the Shiloh Presbyterian Church since 1847, and was soon elected moderator of the Third Presbytery and president of the National Negro Convention in 1853. In the wake of these prestigious appointments, Pennington led a successful drive against segregated transportation in New York City. But soon thereafter, he succumbed to alcoholism, which blunted the influence of his remaining years. He lost his position at the Shiloh church and was forced to accept less prominent pastorates. By 1858, he had returned to the Colored Presbyterian Church at New Town, where his ministerial career had begun.

At the conclusion of the Civil War, Pennington was convinced of the necessity of spiritual labor in the South among the newly freed slaves, and he ministered for a time in Natchez, Mississippi, in the African Methodist Episcopal denomination. He returned north in 1868 and accepted the pastorate of the Fourth Congregational Church in Portland, Maine, until 1870, when he traveled to Florida in hopes of improving his health. He found energy to help establish an African-American Presbyterian Church in Jacksonville that year, but it would be his last spiritual post. He died in Jacksonville in 1870 on October 20 or 22.

James W. C. Pennington, the fugitive blacksmith, as he called himself, helped to forge the tradition of evangelical abolitionism. Choosing to be ruled by God rather than by slave masters, he devoted himself to a career as a Christian minister

and as an implacable foe of slavery. His persistent thirst for education made him one of the nation's most prominent African-American ministers in the years leading up to the Civil War and a steady, if not so influential figure in African-American Christianity in the decade that followed it.

Further Reading

Pennington, James W. C. *The Fugitive Blacksmith: Or, Events in the History of James W. C. Pennington*. 3d ed. London: C. Gilpin, 1850; Westport, Conn.: Negro Universities Press, 1971.

———. *A Text Book of the Origin and History, &c. Of the Colored People*. Hartford, Conn.: L. Skinner, 1841; Detroit: Negro History Press, 1969.

Thomas, Herman Edward. *James W.C. Pennington: African American Churchman and Abolitionist*. New York: Garland, 1995.

Washington, Joseph R. *The First Fugitive Foreign and Domestic Doctor of Divinity: Rational Race Rules of Religion and Realism, Revered and Reversed or Revised by the Reverend Doctor James William Charles Pennington*. Lewiston, N.Y.: Edwin Mellen Press, 1990.

White, David O. "The Fugitive Blacksmith of Hartford: James W. C. Pennington." *Connecticut Historical Society Bulletin* 49 (Winter 1984), 4–29.

Pierson, Arthur Tappan

(1837–1911) *Presbyterian minister, missionary advocate*

Beginning his ministerial career as a Presbyterian, Arthur Tappan Pierson became a prominent evangelical leader during the last years of the 19th century. He typified those individuals whose theological commitments would characterize fundamentalism in the early decades of the 20th century. Pierson was born on March 6, 1837, in New York City, the son of Stephen Haines Pierson and Sally Ann Wheeler Pierson. Pierson entered the Mount Washington Collegiate Institute in New York when he was 11 years old. At 13 he left home for boarding school at the Collegiate Institute at Tarrytown-on-the-Hudson. While there he experienced a religious conversion at a revival meeting, and two years later became a member of the Thirteenth Street Presbyterian Church in New York City, where his father was an elder. After a year at Tarrytown, Pierson transferred to the Ossining School at Sing Sing, New York, where he completed his preparatory education. He subsequently attended Hamilton College, from which he graduated in 1857, and Union Theological Seminary, which awarded him a bachelor of divinity degree in 1860. In 1860 he was also ordained a Presbyterian minister, and he married Sarah Frances Benedict, with whom he had seven children.

After serving as minister of the First Congregational Church in Binghamton, New York, from 1860 to 1863, and the Presbyterian church of Waterford, New York, from 1863 to 1869, Pierson became the pastor of the Fort Street Presbyterian Church in Detroit, Michigan, in 1862; he remained there until 1882. During his Detroit years, Pierson became dissatisfied with the prospect of a comfortable ministry to middle-class parishioners and became earnest about reaching a broader spectrum of the city's inhabitants with the Christian gospel. After the destruction of his church building by fire in 1878, he began to hold services in a local opera house, hoping to attract wider audiences.

In 1882, Pierson moved to the Second Presbyterian Church in Indianapolis, Indiana, and the following year, to Philadelphia, Pennsylvania. There he became the minister of the Bethany Church, formed from the Sunday School originally established by evangelical lay minister, department store owner, and later U.S. postmaster John Wanamaker. During his years in Philadelphia, Pierson became involved in the evangelical conferences organized by the revivalist DWIGHT LYMAN MOODY in Northfield, Massachusetts. In the summer of 1886, Moody held a conference for college students at Mount Hermon. Although the scheduled conference had no specific missionary emphasis, when ROBERT PARMALEE WILDER and other students besieged Moody with the request to hold sessions concerning missions, Moody invited Pierson to speak on the subject. Pierson's sermon, "God's Providence in Modern Missions," helped spark a commitment from 100 students to pledge themselves to the work of foreign missions. The "Mount Hermon Hundred" went on to form the nucleus of the Student Volunteer movement

established two years later, which took as its motto an aspiration often attributed to Pierson: "the evangelization of the world in this generation." In the years that followed, Pierson himself became a leading advocate of missions, and beginning in 1888 he served as editor of the *Missionary Review of the World* for 20 years.

Pierson attended the World Missionary Conference in London in 1888 as well, and the following year, he resigned from Bethany Church to begin a full-time speaking and writing career. During a tour of Great Britain in 1891, the Baptist preacher Charles Hadden Spurgeon invited Pierson to preach at his church, the Metropolitan Temple in London. Five years later, Pierson became convinced of the Baptist view that baptism was an ordinance appropriate to adult believers rather than infants, and he was rebaptized. This event prompted the severance of his ministerial connection with Presbyterianism. In 1897, Pierson became involved in the Keswick movement, which emphasized the role of the Holy Spirit in personal sanctification, and he acted as a forerunner of the charismatic movement in the 20th century. He died on June 3, 1911, in Brooklyn, New York.

Arthur Tappan Pierson shared many of the theological commitments of the early 20th-century evangelicals who increasingly found themselves at odds with liberal Protestantism. He held premillennialist views, expecting that Christ might return to earth at any time, views that made him a prominent advocate of missions. In contrast with more mainstream Protestants, who were beginning to warm to higher critical views about the Bible, Pierson joined other conservatives in insisting on the inerrancy of Scripture. He authored, for example, some of the articles in *The Fundamentals* (1910–15), the influential series of books published to defend orthodox Christian doctrines. Finally, Pierson embraced the Keswick movement, which was a powerful influence for personal Christian devotion in the closing years of the 19th century and the early decades of the 20th. In all, he represented the emergence of a nondenominational evangelical Christianity that played a prominent role in 20th-century American religion.

Further Reading

Pierson, Arthur Tappan. *The Divine Art of Preaching*. New York: Baker & Taylor, 1892.

———. *Evangelistic Work in Principle and Practice*. New York: Baker & Taylor, 1887.

———. *In Christ Jesus*. New York: Funk & Wagnalls, 1898.

Pierson, Delavan Leonard. *Arthur T. Pierson: A Spiritual Warrior, Mighty in the Scriptures; a Leader in the Modern Missionary Crusade*. New York: F. H. Revel, 1912; New York: Garland, 1988.

Robert, Dana L. "'The Crisis of Missions': Premillennial Mission Theory and the Origins of Independent Evangelical Missions." In *Earthern Vessels: American Evangelicals and Foreign Missions, 1880–1980*. Edited by Joel A. Carpenter and Wilbert R. Shenk. Grand Rapids, Mich.: W. B. Eerdmans, 1990.

———. "The Legacy of Arthur Tappan Pierson." *International Bulletin of Missionary Research* 8 (July 1984): 120–25.

Pike, James Albert

(1913–1969) *Episcopal bishop*

During the last half of the 20th century, theological conservatives tended to find themselves more often the subject of media attention than did liberals. One prominent exception to this pattern was Bishop James Albert Pike, a controversial Episcopalian who stretched the bounds of orthodoxy enough to be charged with heresy and then embarked on a brief, but sensational, career as an investigator of psychic phenomena. James Pike was born on February 14, 1913, in Oklahoma City, Oklahoma, the son of James Pike and Pearl Agatha Wimsatt Pike. When Pike was two years old, his father died, and his mother later moved to Hollywood, California, where she raised her son in the Roman Catholic faith. After high school, Pike enrolled in the University of Santa Clara, a Jesuit institution, expecting to become a priest. But during his college years, he grew disaffected with the Catholic Church and with religion generally, abandoned thought of a ministerial career in favor of a legal one, and transferred to the University of California, Los Angeles, (UCLA), where he graduated in 1934 with an A.B. in political science and law.

Two years later he received an LL.B. degree from UCLA, and then in 1938, a J.S.D. from Yale University. He married Jane Alvies in the late 1930s; the couple had divorced by 1940.

From 1938 to 1942, Pike practiced law in Washington, D.C., as an attorney for the Securities and Exchange Commission. During these years, he also taught part-time, first at the School of Law of the Catholic University of America, and then at George Washington University Law School. In 1942, he married one of his students from George Washington, Esther Yanovsky, with whom he had four children. That same year, Pike was commissioned as a lieutenant in the navy; he served initially in navy intelligence and later as a lawyer for the U.S. Maritime Commission and the War Shipping Administration. During these years, Pike began to study in preparation for a ministry as an Episcopal priest. In 1944, he became a curate at St. John's Church in Washington and a chaplain at George Washington University. In 1945, Pike began two years of study at the Virginia Theological Seminary. He was ordained an Episcopal priest in 1946.

By 1947, Pike had become rector of Christ Church in Poughkeepsie, New York, and the Episcopal chaplain at the town's Vassar College. From 1949 to 1952, he served as chaplain at Columbia University and as head of the university's department of religion. While in New York, Pike studied at Union Theological Seminary and obtained a B.D. in 1951. In 1952, Pike became dean of the Cathedral of St. John the Divine, the largest Episcopal church in the United States, where he served for the next six years. He achieved national prominence during this period, in part through hosting a television program devoted to the discussion of contemporary issues from a religious perspective and in part through the publication of an article about him, "The Joyful Dean," in a 1958 issue of *Reader's Digest*.

In 1958, Pike was elected Episcopal bishop of California. In this position, he regularly preached on controversial social subjects, such as the perils of McCarthyism and the immorality of segregation. He also shocked theological conservatives in 1960, when he announced in a *Christian Century* article that he no longer believed in the Trinity, the virgin birth, or salvation through Jesus alone.

This announcement prompted official charges of heresy against him. The same decade added personal crisis and loss to Pike's already controversial character, when he joined Alcoholics Anonymous in 1964 to deal with chronic alcoholism and when, two years later, his son committed suicide. In 1967, Pike's wife divorced him.

The death of Bishop Pike's son prompted one further coda to Pike's public career, when he began to investigate spiritualism and published in 1968 a book of his findings, *The Other Side: An Account of My Experiences with Psychic Phenomena.* That year he resigned as bishop of California and became a staff member of the Center for the Study of Democratic Institutions. Charged again with heresy, he was censured by the House of Bishops in 1968. That same year he married Diane Kennedy, a former student who had helped him write *The Other Side.* The following year, while on an expedition in Israel, the couple became lost in the Judaean desert and Pike died sometime between September 3 and 7, 1969, while his wife was seeking to find her way out of the desert and obtain help.

Bishop James A. Pike's much publicized departures from orthodox Christianity made him a controversial figure during the 1960s and a symbol of that turbulent decade's social upheavals. His heresies were, in the main, milder than many others witnessed in the 20th century. Nevertheless, his prominent position in the Episcopal Church hierarchy magnified them.

Further Reading

Holzer, Hans. *The Psychic World of Bishop Pike.* New York: Crown Publishers, 1970.
Laughlin, Paul A. "James A. Pike." In *Twentieth-Century Shapers of American Popular Religion.* Edited by Charles H. Lippy. New York: Greenwood Press, 1989.
Morris, Frederick M. *Bishop Pike: Ham, Heretic, or Hero.* Grand Rapids, Mich.: Eerdmans, 1967.
Pike, Diane Kennedy. *Search: The Personal Story of a Wilderness Journey.* Garden City, N.Y.: Doubleday, 1969.
Pike, James A. *If This Be Heresy.* New York: Harper & Row, 1967.
Pike, James A. with Diane Kennedy. *The Other Side: An Account of My Experiences with Psychic Phenomena.* New York: Doubleday, 1968.

Spraggett, Allen. *The Bishop Pike Story.* New York: New American Library, 1970.
Stringfellow, William, and Anthony Towne. *The Bishop Pike Affair: Scandals of Conscience and Heresy, Relevance and Solemnity in the Contemporary Church.* New York: Harper & Row, 1967.

Pilmore, Joseph
(1739–1825) *Methodist minister, Episcopal priest*

Joseph Pilmore advanced the cause of two denominations in America: Methodism and later Anglicanism. Disagreement with Methodism's founder, John Wesley, eventually caused Pilmore to seek ordination in the Anglican Church in America, in which he served for nearly four decades. He was born on October 31, 1739, in Tadmouth, Yorkshire, England, of parents whose names are unknown, who were devout members of the Church of England. He was converted through the preaching of John Wesley when he was 16 years old and thereafter attended Wesley's Kingwood School, located near Bristol. In the late summer of 1765, Pilmore was admitted on a trial basis as a Methodist preacher and undertook the East Cornwall circuit in August 1766. After a year spent tending the Methodist societies in East Cornwall, Pilmore was assigned to a circuit in South Wales, where he labored for two years. But John Wesley planted the seeds of a different ministry for Pilmore in August 1768, when he proposed to the Methodist Conference meeting in Bristol that missionaries be dispatched to America. The conference took no action on this proposal in 1768, but at its meeting the following year, Joseph Pilmore and Richard Boardman volunteered to undertake a preaching mission to the American colonies. Pilmore subsequently explained in his journal the course of thinking that led him to accept Wesley's challenge:

> I was frequently under great exercise of mind respecting the dear Americans, and found a willingness to sacrifice everything for their sakes. I was happy enough as to my situation and connexions [sic], . . . yet I could not be satisfied to continue in Europe. A sense of

duty so affected my mind, and my heart was drawn out with such longing desires for the advancement of the Redeemer's kingdom that I was made perfectly willing to forsake my kindred and native land, with all that was the most near and dear to me on earth, that I might spread abrode [sic] the honours of his glorious Name.

Pilmore and Boardman left England on August 21, 1769, and arrived in New Jersey on October 21, the first official representatives of Methodism in America.

The two men decided at first to divide their efforts, one taking responsibility for the Methodist societies in Philadelphia and the other for those in New York, and to alternate their stations every four months. Pilmore began work in Philadelphia, which became his favorite American city. He dedicated a partially finished structure there, which was purchased from Dutch Presbyterians and became St. George's Methodist Church. After the arrival of FRANCIS ASBURY and Richard Wright, new ministers from England sent by John Wesley in the fall of 1771, Pilmore made a preaching tour through the southern colonies. He returned to Philadelphia in June 1773, in time to meet Thomas Rankin, Wesley's newly designated superintendent for American Methodism, and to participate in the first conference of American Methodist preachers, held at St. George's church in Philadelphia in July 1773. Perhaps because this conference produced some criticism of the laxity of discipline in the American Methodist societies—an implicit criticism of Pilmore and Boardman—the two men departed the colonies for England at the first of the year in 1774.

Of the decade that followed, little is known of Joseph Pilmore's life. From August 1774, he appears to have held no ministerial appointment for the two years. After that period, he served circuits in England, Ireland, and Scotland until 1784. That year John Wesley drew up his Deed of Declaration, a document in which he named 100 permanent members of the General Conference and that constituted the formal organization of Methodism. Pilmore's name did not appear in the list. Instead, history next notes his ordination in Connecticut first as a deacon and then as a priest of the Protestant Episcopal Church in November 1785. The

reasons for his departure from Methodism are unclear, but they perhaps included tensions in his dealings with other American Methodist leaders—particularly Francis Asbury—and his dissatisfaction with the separation of Methodists from the Church of England, which was formalized in Wesley's Deed of Declaration.

In his early years as a priest in the Episcopal Church, Pilmore served parishes in and around Philadelphia until 1794, when he became the rector of Christ Church in New York City. A decade later he returned to Philadelphia as rector of St. Paul's Church. In 1790, he married Mary Benezet Wood, a widow with whom he had one child before her death in 1808. Pilmore may have married again, but this is not certain. He retired from St. Paul's Church in 1821, and he died four years later in Philadelphia, on July 24, 1825.

Though he became an early convert to Methodism, Joseph Pilmore never abandoned his love for the Anglican Church. When John Wesley turned Methodism down a separate ecclesiastical path from the Church of England, Pilmore departed Methodist company and reinvigorated his attachment to Anglicanism. In the course of this spiritual turning, the American colonies enjoyed the labors of Joseph Pilmore first as a Methodist missionary and later as an Episcopal priest.

Further Reading

"Mr. Wesley's Preachers: Joseph Pilmore," The John Rylands Library. Available online. URL:http://rylibweb.man.ac.uk/data1/dg/methodist/pil.html. Downloaded on November 24, 2001.

Pilmore, Joseph. *The Journal of Joseph Pilmore, Methodist Itinerant, for the Years August 1, 1769, to January 2, 1774.* Edited by Frederick E. Maser and Howard T. Maag. Philadelphia: Printed by Message Publishing Company for the Historical Society of the Philadelphia Annual Conference of the United Methodist Church, 1969.

Powell, Adam Clayton, Sr.
(1865–1953) *Baptist minister*

Born two weeks after the end of the Civil War, Adam Clayton Powell, Sr., eventually became the most prominent African-American minister of his day. He presided over Abyssinian Baptist Church in Harlem, New York, for almost three decades and transformed it into the largest black church in America as well as a social and political center for Harlem. He was born on May 5, 1865, in Martin's Mill, Virginia, the son of a German planter, known to him only as "Powell," and a mother named Sally, who was recently freed from slavery. His father died during the Civil War, and Powell subsequently moved with his mother to West Virginia. During his childhood, he managed to obtain three years of schooling.

Powell left West Virginia in 1884 and moved to Rendville, Ohio, where he worked in a coal mine. The year after he arrived in Ohio, Powell experienced a religious conversion during a revival, though he did not at first pursue a ministerial career. Instead he hoped to become a lawyer and a politician, and he studied for a time at Rendville Academy. He moved to Washington, D.C., in 1887 and applied for admission to Howard University Law School, but he was rejected. Subsequently, however, he undertook to prepare himself for the Christian ministry by studying at the Wayland Seminary in Washington (later Virginia Union University), from which he graduated in 1892. While in seminary, Powell married Mattie Fletcher Shaffer, with whom he had two children, one of whom, Adam Clayton Powell, Jr., also became a minister and later was the first African American elected to the U.S. Congress from New York.

After seminary, Powell served as minister at a succession of small churches before becoming the pastor of Immanuel Baptist Church in New Haven, Connecticut, in 1893. While there, he studied at Yale Divinity School. After 15 years in New Haven, however, Powell was invited in 1908 to become the pastor of the Abyssinian Baptist Church in New York City, the ministerial post where he would become famous. Founded in 1808, Abyssinian was one of the oldest black churches in America. When Powell assumed the leadership of the church, its membership numbered 1,600 and the church shouldered a substantial debt. Over the years that followed, Powell's dynamic preaching and spiritual superintendence of the congregation

swelled its membership to some 13,000 by the 1930s, making it the largest black congregation in America and one of the largest congregations of any religious body in the country.

A pivotal moment for the church occurred in the early 1920s, when Powell persuaded its membership to relocate from West 40th Street to Harlem. After purchasing several lots on 138th Street, Powell and his congregation built new facilities, dedicated in 1923, to house the church's growing membership and its growing ministries. The Gothic and Tudor structure, which boasted imported stained glass windows and an Italian marble pulpit, became a center of African-American social and cultural life during the 1920s and 1930s. During these years, Abyssinian Baptist Church hosted a broad range of social services for the African-American community, including a home for the aged and extensive adult education programs.

From his pulpit in Harlem, Adam Clayton Powell became one of the most prominent African-American leaders of his generation. He helped found the Urban League in 1910 and served on the board of directors and as vice president of the National Association for the Advancement of Colored People (NAACP), though both his theology and his politics were generally conservative. He retired as pastor of the Abyssinian church in 1937 but was able to see his son, Adam Clayton Powell, Jr., succeed him as pastor. His first wife died in 1945, and the next year he married Inez Means Cottrell. Powell died on June 12, 1953, in New York City.

During the 20th century, African-American ministers frequently served as prominent leaders within the black community. With the same rhetorical power they marshaled in the service of gospel preaching, they also devoted to broader social and cultural issues such as civil rights. MARTIN LUTHER KING, JR., and JESSE JACKSON were prominent examples of this pattern later in the 20th century, but they followed pathways already well worn by their predecessors, none perhaps more famous than Adam Clayton Powell, Sr. For nearly 30 years he labored to plant the gospel firmly in Harlem and to lead his congregation in the service of both the spiritual and the temporal needs of the African-American community there.

Further Reading

Clingan, Ralph Garlin. *Against Cheap Grace in a World Come of Age: An Intellectual Biography of Clayton Powell, 1865–1953.* New York: Peter Lang, 2002.

Gore, Bob. *We've Come This Far: The Abyssinian Baptist Church, a Photographic Journal.* New York: Stewart, Tabori & Chang, 2001.

Powell, A. Clayton. *Against the Tide: An Autobiography.* New York: R. Richard Smith, 1938; New York: Arno Press, 1980.

Hickey, Neil, and Ed Edwin. *Adam Clayton Powell and the Politics of Race.* New York: Fleet, 1965.

Woolridge, Pearlena Lewis. "An Historical Study of Leadership: Adam Clayton Powell, Senior, at the Abyssinian Church." M.A. thesis, Howard University, 1972.

Pratt, Parley Parker

(1807–1857) *Mormon leader, author*

The foremost Mormon apologist of the mid-19th century, Parley Parker Pratt used his skills as a writer to defend the Mormon Church from the frequent attacks on it in its earliest years. He also seized the printed word as an evangelistic tool to win converts for the Church of Jesus Christ of Latter-day Saints. Pratt was born on April 12, 1807, in Burlington, New York, the son of Jared Pratt and Charity Dickinson Pratt, who were farmers. When he was 19 years old, Pratt struck out alone for Ohio and became a farmer there. The following year, in 1827, he married Thankful Halsey, with whom he had one son. Soon afterwards he experienced a religious conversion through the preaching of SIDNEY RIGDON, a minister associated with ALEXANDER CAMPBELL and the restorationist movement that would later become the Disciples of Christ denomination. After Pratt read the *Book of Mormon* on its publication in 1830, however, he converted to Mormonism. That same year JOSEPH SMITH, JR., the founder of the Mormon Church, dispatched Pratt and several other Mormon missionaries to the western frontier to preach to Native Americans there. While on this mission, Pratt and his associates visited Sidney Rigdon in Ohio. As Pratt had been converted under Rigdon's preaching, now Rigdon

and many members of his church in Mentor, Ohio, became Mormons.

Over the following years Pratt played an influential role in the early affairs of the Mormon Church. He was named to the Quorum of the Twelve Apostle's for the church in 1835, joining 11 other men who assisted Joseph Smith in the leadership of church affairs. Pratt shared in the early travails of the Mormons, including the clashes with Missouri citizens, which eventually led Missouri's governor to order the Mormons to leave the state or suffer extinction. After the Mormons settled in Nauvoo, Illinois, Pratt joined BRIGHAM YOUNG and other Mormon missionaries in a successful evangelistic mission to England in 1839–41.

While he was in England, Pratt in 1840 founded and began editing a newspaper, the *LDS Millennial Star*; this was neither the first nor the last occasion when he took up the pen to advance the cause of Mormonism. As early as 1837 he had published an evangelistic tract, *Voice of Warning,* and in 1839 he authored *History of the Late Persecution,* an account of the Mormons' trials in Missouri. On the eve of the church's formal announcement of the practice of plural marriages in 1852—a practice in which Pratt and other Mormon leaders had secretly engaged for more than a decade—Pratt defended Mormon polygamy in print in *"Mormonism!" "Plurality of Wives!" An Especial Chapter, for the Especial Edification of Certain Inquisitive News Editors.* In addition to these and other apologetic works on behalf of the Church of Jesus Christ of Latter-day Saints, Pratt wrote several volumes of poems, some of which became hymns for the Mormon Church.

Pratt accomplished these literary endeavors even as he took an active part in the pioneering work that eventually settled the Mormons in the Great Salt Lake Basin after the death of Joseph Smith. During the 1850s, he served in the territorial legislature of Utah while Brigham Young was territorial governor, and later he served as president of the Mormon mission in California. That same decade he also wrote perhaps his most important work, a treatise on Mormon theology, *Key to the Science of Theology* (1855).

Before Joseph Smith died at the hands of an Illinois mob, he had instituted the practice of plural marriage. Along with other Mormon leaders, Pratt embraced this practice. After the death of his first wife, Pratt married Mary Ann Frost, with whom he had four children. In 1843, he married the first of 10 additional women and fathered 25 children by them. His marriage to Mary Ann Frost ended in divorce in 1853, but the remainder of his wives survived him. His last plural wife, Eleanor J. McComb, had been married to a man named Hector McLean before her marriage to Pratt. McLean blamed Pratt for stealing his wife, and, while Pratt was on a missionary trip to the southern states, McLean attacked and killed him in Alma, Arkansas, on May 13, 1857.

Parley Parker Pratt was one of the earliest converts to Mormonism, and he played a prominent role in the main events of the church's life. As a pioneer leader alone, he would have won an important place in Mormon history. But his talent as a writer, both in defending and in propagating Mormon doctrines, made him a central figure in the Church of Jesus Christ of Latter-day Saints during its first half century.

Further Reading

Pratt, Parley P. *Autobiography of Parley P. Pratt*. Edited by Scot Facer Proctor and Maurine Jensen Proctor. Salt Lake City, Utah: Deseret, 2000.

———. *The Essential Parley P. Pratt*. Salt Lake City, Utah: Signature Books, 1990.

Pratt, Steven. "Eleanor McLean and the Murder of Parley P. Pratt." *Brigham Young University Studies* 15 (Winter 1975): 225–56.

Scott, Reva Lucile. *A Biography of Parley P. Pratt, the Archer of Paradise*. Caldwell, Idaho: The Caxton Printers, 1937.

Smart, William B., and Donna T. Smart, eds. *Over the Rim: The Parley P. Pratt Exploring Expedition to Southern Utah, 1849–50*. Logan: Utah State University Press, 1999.

Priestley, Joseph

(1733–1804) *theologian, scientist, educator*

Remembered today primarily as the scientist who discovered oxygen, Joseph Priestley considered

himself a Christian minister. He served a number of dissenting congregations—that is, non-Anglican churches—in England but by the time he immigrated to the United States in 1794, his sympathies for the French Revolution and his unorthodox theology generally denied him access to pulpits in America. He was born in Yorkshire, England, the son of Jonas Priestley and Mary Swift Priestley. After his mother's death in 1739, Priestley was adopted in 1742 by one of his father's sisters. In 1751 he enrolled in an academy for dissenting ministerial students run by Caleb Ashworth in Daventry. While there, he migrated away from belief in the Trinity to the Arian view that Jesus was a created being. In 1755, Priestley began to serve dissenting congregations, in Needham Market, Suffolk, and at Nantwich in Cheshire. In the latter post, Priestley opened a private academy, and his interest in education would consume a significant portion of his energies over the years that followed.

Priestley left Nantwich in fall 1761 to undertake a position as a tutor at Warrington Academy. The following year he married Mary Wilkinson, with whom he had four children. At Warrington, he was able to pursue scientific investigations of his own, and his growing reputation as an investigator led to his appointment as a fellow of the Royal Society in the summer of 1766. This interlude as a teacher and a scientist did not permanently interrupt Priestley's career as a minister, though. He took charge of a dissenting congregation in Mill-Hill Chapel, Leeds, in 1767. While there, he pursued studies that produced *An Essay on the First Principles of Government* (1768) and his three-volume work on religion, *The Institutes of Natural and Revealed Religion* (1772–74).

The opportunity in 1772 to become the private librarian and family tutor for Sir William Petty, second early of Shelburne, gave Priestley freedom to press forward with scientific experiments. One product of these was his discovery of oxygen in 1774. After eight years in this position, however, Priestley left the service of Petty and soon afterward became the minister of a dissenting congregation in Birmingham, though he continued an active career as a writer. Priestley's public support for the French Revolution, however, eventually made him unwelcome in Birmingham. After riots during the summer of 1791, he moved to Hackney, where he became the minister of the Gravel Pit Meeting.

Following Britain's declaration of war against France in early 1793, Priestley's sympathy for the French Revolution made it impossible for him to remain safely in England. Accordingly, he chose to follow his two sons, who had immigrated to America in the late summer of 1793. He set sail with his wife for the United States in the spring of 1794 and settled eventually in Northumberland, Pennsylvania. Though welcomed generously by many distinguished Americans on his arrival in the United States, Priestley spent the next years leading a quiet life in the main, pursuing his own research, writing, and occasionally preaching to such Unitarian audiences as he could attract.

Priestley's political sympathies ran toward the Democrat-Republicans and against the Federalists. When the Federalists assumed control of both the presidency and the Congress after the inauguration of President John Adams in 1797, Priestley could not resist criticizing the new administration publicly. In 1798, Congress passed the Alien and Sedition Acts, which gave the president power to deport foreign nationals who criticized the U.S. government, and at least some observers urged that the act be leveled against Priestley. Adams declined to expose Priestley to this indignity, however. Priestley, for his part, lived to see his friend Thomas Jefferson elected president. He died at his home in Northumberland on February 6, 1804.

Joseph Priestley, a respected scientist, scholar, and minister on both sides of the Atlantic, lived the last 10 years of his life in the United States. His devotion to "rational religion," especially in the form of Unitarianism, won him the high regard of some Americans. Nevertheless, both because he resided briefly in America and because orthodox Christianity still dominated the religious life of the young nation, Priestley never enjoyed popular success as a preacher in the United States. He spent his last years chiefly pursuing the scientific investigations and literary projects that had dominated the course of his life.

Further Reading

Clark, John Ruskin. *Joseph Priestley, a Comet in the System: Biography.* San Diego, Calif.: Torch Publications, 1990.

Crowther, J. G. *Scientists of the Industrial Revolution: Joseph Black, James Watt, Joseph Priestley and Henry Cavendish.* London: Cresset Press, 1962.

Gibbs, F. W. *Priestley: Revolutions of the Eighteenth Century.* Garden City, N.Y.: Doubleday, 1967.

Graham, Jenny. *Revolutionary in Exile: The Emigration of Joseph Priestley to America, 1794–1804.* Philadelphia: American Philosophical Society, 1995.

Holt, Anne. *A Life of Joseph Priestley.* London: Oxford University Press, 1931; Westport, Conn.: Greenwood, 1970.

Priestley, Joseph. *Autobiography of Joseph Priestley.* Bath: Adams & Dart, 1970.

———. *Joseph Priestley, Selections from His Writings.* Edited by Ira V. Brown. University Park: Pennsylvania State University Press, 1962.

———. *Political Writings.* Edited by Peter N. Miller. Cambridge, England: Cambridge University Press, 1993.

Schofield, Robert E. *The Enlightenment of Joseph Priestley: A Study of His Life and Work from 1733 to 1773.* University Park: Pennsylvania State University Press, 1997.

Schwartz, A. Truman, and John G. McEvoy, ed. *Motion Toward Perfection: The Achievement of Joseph Priestley.* Boston: Skinner House Books, 1990.

Thorpe, Thomas Edward. *Joseph Priestley.* New York: AMS Press, 1976.

Randolph, Paschal Beverly
(1825–1875) *occultist*

A leading spiritualist of the 19th century, Paschal Beverly Randolph introduced the Rosicrucian Fraternity (Fraternitas Rosæ Crusis) to the United States. He also devoted himself to the study and teaching of sexual magic, or "Affectional Alchemy." Randolph was born on October 8, 1825, in New York City, the son of William Randolph and Flora Beverly. His father was a wealthy plantation owner from Virginia. His mother apparently was a slave from Madagascar who died of smallpox when he was a child, though Randolph spent his life denying that his mother was black. Randolph ran away from home when he was around 15, and he worked as a sailor until an injury when he was about 20 forced him to support himself at a variety of jobs. He became interested in the occult during this period.

In 1850 he married a woman named Mary Jane—whose maiden name is unknown—with whom he had three children. That same year, while on a trip to Europe, Randolph was admitted to the Fraternitas Rosæ Crusis. In 1858, on a return visit to Europe, Randolph was appointed grand master of the Fraternitas for the Western world and was inducted as a knight of the L'Ordre du Lis. On his arrival again in the United States, he launched a speaking and writing career aimed at establishing the Fraternitas securely in American soil.

After the Civil War, President Abraham Lincoln, who shared a friendship with Randolph for some years, requested that he undertake a mission to educate blacks in Louisiana. After Lincoln's assassination, Randolph rode the train carrying the slain president's body back to Illinois for a time, but, disgruntled whites who opposed the idea of a black man's occupying the train with them eventually put Randolph off.

The chief occupations Randolph pursued during the 1860s and 1870s were the practice of medicine and the development of his ideas relating to sexual magic. According to Randolph, at the moment of sexual climax the powers of the cosmos were accessible and made possible the realization of goals such as spiritual enlightenment, physical health, or financial success. He combined his medical practice with counseling for couples that included instruction in Affectional Alchemy. Some critics accused Randolph of promoting free love, and he was briefly imprisoned in 1872 for encouraging immorality before his acquittal.

Toward the end of his life, he married Kate Corson, with whom he had one child, Osiris Budh. It is not known, however, either when his first marriage ended or when the second began. He moved to Toledo, Ohio, at some point shortly before his death. After discovering that his wife was having an affair, he was found dead of an apparently self-inflicted gunshot wound to his head. The coroner ruled the death a suicide on July 29, 1875, in Toledo.

A prominent 19th-century occult leader in the United States, Paschal Beverly Randolph is primarily responsible for the early growth of Rosicrucianism in America. His preoccupation with the relationship between sex and magic represented a common occult theme. Partially through his influence, both Rosicrucianism and sexual alchemy would continue to find devotees into the 21st century.

Further Reading

Clymer, R. Swinburne. *The Rose Cross Order: A Short Sketch of the History of the Rose Cross Order in America, Together with a Sketch of the Life of Dr. P. B. Randolph, the Founder of the Order.* Allentown, Pa.: Philosophical, 1916.

Deveney, John P. *Paschal Beverly Randolph: A Nineteenth-Century Black American Spiritualist, Rosicrucian, and Sex Magician.* Albany: State University of New York Press, 1997.

Randolph, Paschal Beverly. *After Death: The Immortality of Man; the World of Spirits, Its Location, Extent, Appearance; the Route Thither; Inhabitants; Customs, Societies; Also Sex and Its Uses There, Etc., Etc.; with Much Matter Pertinent to the Question of Human Immortality.* Rev. ed. Quakertown, Pa.: Philosophical, 1970.

———. *The Immortality of Love: Unveiling the Secret Arcanum of Affectional Alchemy.* Edited by Paul P. Ricchio. Quakertown, Pa.: Beverly Hall, 1978.

———. *Ravalette: The Rosicrucian's Story.* Quakertown, Pa.: Philosophical Publishing Company, 1939.

Ransom, Reverdy Cassius

(1861–1959) *bishop of the African Methodist Episcopal Church, civil rights leader*

A founding member of the National Association for the Advancement of Colored People (NAACP) and an ardent champion of the social gospel, Reverdy Cassius Ransom waged a long campaign against racial inequality. He died on the eve of the Civil Rights movement, not living to see the victories for which he had been a crucial advance agent. Ransom was born on January 4, 1861, in Flushing, Ohio, the son of Harriet Johnson and a father whose identity is unknown. His mother subsequently married George Ransom in 1865, and Reverdy assumed his stepfather's surname. Shortly before he entered college, he married Leanna Watkins in 1881, and the couple had one child before their divorce in 1886.

Ransom began his college education at Wilberforce University in Green County, Ohio, in 1881. The following year, however, he transferred to Oberlin College, where he was awarded a small scholarship and worked at odd jobs to support himself. After he organized a protest of a college regulation that segregated black women at a separate table in the women's dining room, he lost his scholarship and returned the next year to Wilberforce, from which he graduated in 1886. That same year he was ordained a deacon in the African Methodist Episcopal (A.M.E.) Church and married Emma Sarah Conner, with whom he had one child.

For the first 14 years after his graduation, Ransom was pastor of a number of A.M.E. churches: in Altoona, Ollisdaysburg, and Allegheny City, Pennsylvania, from 1886 to 1890; in Springfield and Cleveland, Ohio, from 1890 to 1896; and in Chicago, Illinois, where he was minister of the Bethel A.M.E. Church from 1896 to 1900. Ransom's pastoral experience with the plight of urban blacks made him an advocate of the Social Gospel movement, which flourished among liberal Protestants during the last decades of the 19th century and the first of the 20th. It emphasized the social dimensions of Christian salvation, insisting that the New Testament gospel was applicable not simply to the salvation of individuals but to the regeneration of social relations and institutions. The Social Gospel movement thus provided a theological justification for Christian participation in the various progressive programs of the day. Following the impetus of this movement, in 1900 Ransom organized a new Chicago congregation called the Institutional Church and Social Settlement. This venture attempted not only to minister to the spiritual needs of the African-American community in Chicago, but to provide educational and recreational resources, as well as to meet the material needs of members. It met significant opposition from other A.M.E. ministers, who protested Ransom's elevation of temporal concerns over spiritual ones.

Ransom left Chicago in 1904 and, after briefly occupying the pulpit of an A.M.E. church in New Bedford, Massachusetts, served as minister of the

Charles Street A.M.E. Church in Boston. While there he joined the Niagara Movement, which W. E. B. Du Bois had helped form, thus siding publicly with Du Bois against the more conservative and accommodationist racial policies of Booker T. Washington. He delivered the address "The Spirit of John Brown" at the Niagara Movement's annual meeting in 1906. In the following year he became pastor of the Bethel A.M.E. Church in New York and participated in the founding of the NAACP. From 1912 to 1924, he was the editor of *The A.M.E. Church Review*. The following years saw him in 1913 beginning a Manhattan mission church called the Church of Simon of Cyrene and waging an unsuccessful write-in campaign for a seat in Congress in 1918.

In 1924, Reverdy C. Ransom was ordained a bishop in the A.M.E. Church. Though he was 63 years old at the time, his energy was still far from spent. After the death of his second wife, he married Georgia Myrtle Teal Hayes in 1943. He served as president of the board of trustees for Wilberforce University from 1932 to 1948, and he became the first African American to hold the position of commissioner of the Board of Pardon and Paroles for the state of Ohio, a role he filled from 1936 to 1940. He died at Wilberforce on April 22, 1959.

Reverdy C. Ransom believed that American Christianity had to confront the scar of race. In an editorial published in *The A.M.E. Review* in October 1914, "The Thin Veneer of Christianity on European Civilization," Ransom wrote: "The practical application of Christianity meets a real test every time it is confronted by an American Negro. The Negro is a standing challenge to the earnestness of its faith." A keen sense of the ways that American society, in general, and American Christians, in particular, had betrayed the gospel by their treatment of African Americans made him one of the 20th century's prophets of racial equality.

Further Reading

Morris, Calvin S. *Reverdy C. Ransom: Black Advocate of the Social Gospel.* Lanham, Md.: University Press of America, 1990.

Ransom, Reverdy C. *Making the Gospel Plain: The Writings of Bishop Reverdy C. Ransom.* Edited by An-thony B. Pinn. Harrisburg, Pa.: Trinity Press International, 1999.

———. *The Negro: The Hope or the Despair of Christianity.* Boston: Ruth Hill, 1935.

———. *The Pilgrimage of Harriet Ransom's Son.* Nashville: Sunday School Union, 1949.

Wills, David. "Reverdy C. Ransom, The Making of an A.M.E. Bishop." In *Black Apostles: Afro-American Clergy Confront the Twentieth Century.* Edited by Randall K. Burkett and Richard Newman. Boston: G. K. Hall, 1978.

Rapp, George
(Johann Georg Rapp)
(1757–1847) *utopian leader*

George Rapp, a German pietist who immigrated to the United States with his followers, founded one of the most prosperous utopian communities of the 19th century. While he and the other members of the Harmony Society waited for Christ's imminent return, they cast themselves into the work of establishing a thriving community. Rapp was born Johann Georg Rapp on November 1, 1757, in Iptingen, Würtemberg, Germany, the son of Hans Adam Rapp and Rosina Berger Rapp. From the time he was a young man, Rapp chafed against the spiritual formality and sterility he perceived in the Lutheran Church in Germany. Consequently, Rapp, who was a weaver by trade, found himself drawn to pietistic fellowships, which emphasized the primacy of personal holiness and devotion to God over mere assent to creedal formulations. In 1783, he married Christine Benzinger, with whom he had two children. By the last decade of the 18th century, Rapp had declared himself a prophet of God and had begun to attract followers, who numbered as many as 10,000 by the early 1800s.

After being harried by German authorities for their nonconformist beliefs, Rapp and his followers eventually decided to immigrate to the United States, where by 1805 they had established the town of Harmony near Pittsburgh, Pennsylvania. There, the newly arrived religious community formed themselves into the Harmony Society, a collective social and economic enterprise in which members shared their possessions and worked together to support themselves by farming and other occupations. Rapp and the other Harmonists were convinced that Christ would return to Earth soon and establish his millennial kingdom. They also doubted that the proper measure of spiritual devotion might be attained without some sacrifice of worldly pleasures. As a consequence, the Harmony Society eventually practiced celibacy.

The Harmonists were industrious while they awaited the appearance of Christ and soon established a thriving community. Dissatisfaction with the location Rapp had originally settled on, though, prompted them to relocate to southwestern Indiana in 1814 and 1815. In the new Harmony settlement, Rapp and his followers again established a productive community. By 1817, additional German immigrants had joined them in Indiana, raising the number of Harmonists to around 900. Their neighbors, however, disapproved of the German community, which persisted in the practice of celibacy and did not hurry to embrace American culture. The Harmonists, as a result, after 10 years in Indiana, relocated again. This time they returned to Pennsylvania to a site near their original town and established a new community they named *Economy.* The Harmonists sold their property in Indiana to Robert Owen, who wished to establish his own commune there and renamed the town *New Harmony.*

In its final incarnation, the Harmonists' collective enterprise was again successful. The community profited not only from the spiritual leadership of George Rapp, but from the business and organizational acumen of his adopted son, Frederick Rapp. In the early 1830s, a significant number of Harmonists split off from the main body of the community to follow Bernhard Müller. These ultimately established their own community nearby, the New Philadelphia Congregation. Rapp, however, continued to lead his remaining followers until he died on August 7, 1847, in Economy, Pennsylvania.

Nineteenth-century America witnessed the brief flourishing of several utopian Christian communities. The most prominent among these were JOHN HUMPHREY NOYES's Oneida community in New York, Mother ANN LEE's Shakers in New England, and George Rapp's Harmonists in Pennsylvania and, for a time, Indiana. Of these, the Harmonists were the most economically successful. Though pietistic devotion and millennial hopes undergirded the spiritual life of Rapp and his followers, their industry made them prosper materially. Nevertheless, the community's practice of celibacy and the centrality of Rapp as a leader resulted in its sharp decline after his death. Even so, however, its stability and its success have made it a source of continued study by those who would emulate its communal life.

Further Reading
Arndt, Karl John Richard, ed. *Economy on the Ohio, 1826–1834: The Harmony Society During the Period of Its Greatest Power and Influence and its Messianic Crisis.* Worcester, Mass.: Harmony Society Press, 1984.
———. *George Rapp's Harmony Society, 1785–1847.* Philadelphia: University of Pennsylvania Press, 1965.
———, ed. *George Rapp's Separatists, 1700–1803: The German Prelude to Rapp's American Harmony Society: A Documentary History.* Worcester, Mass.: Harmony Society Press, 1980.
———, ed. *George Rapp's Years of Glory: Economy on the Ohio, 1834–1847.* New York: P. Lang, 1987.
Bole, John A. *The Harmony Society: A Chapter in German American Culture History.* Philadelphia: Americana Germanica Press, 1905.
Kring, Hilda Adam. *The Harmonists: A Folk-Cultural Approach.* Metuchen, N.J.: Scarecrow Press, 1973.
Rapp, George. *Thoughts on the Destiny of Man.* New Harmony, Ind.: The Harmonie Society, 1824.
Reichmann, Eberhard, La Vern J. Rippley, and Jörg Nagler, eds. *Emigration and Settlement Patterns of German Communities in North America.* Indianapolis: Max Kade German-American Center, Indiana University-Purdue University at Indianapolis, 1995.

Rauschenbusch, Walter
(1861–1918) *Baptist theologian, educator, social reformer*

A leading voice in the Social Gospel movement, Walter Rauschenbusch labored to apply the message of the New Testament gospel to the problems of modern industrial society. His attempt to recruit the Christian Church to the work of alleviating the social sources of poverty had a significant impact on liberal Protestantism at the beginning of the 20th century. Rauschenbusch was born on October 4, 1861, in Rochester, New York, the son of Augustus Rauschenbusch and Caroline Rhomp Rauschenbusch. His father was a New Testament professor at Rochester Seminary who had originally emigrated from Germany to the United States. He saw to it that his son received an education at the school in Gütersloh, Westphalia. On returning to the United States, Rauschenbusch earned a B.A. from the University of Rochester in 1884 and subsequently graduated from Rochester Seminary in 1886.

The year he completed seminary, Walter Rauschenbusch became the pastor of the Second German Baptist Church in New York, located in Hell's Kitchen, an impoverished area of the city's West Side. The plight of immigrants and other poor workers galvanized Rauschenbusch's conscience and directed the course of his theological imagination toward social reform. During his years in Hell's Kitchen, Rauschenbusch helped organize in 1892 the Brotherhood of the Kingdom, a nondenominational group devoted to practical social service. The following year he married Pauline Rother, with whom he had five children.

In 1897, Rauschenbusch joined the faculty of Rochester Seminary, first as a New Testament professor and later as a professor of church history. He did not, however, surrender his social conscience. In years that followed Rauschenbusch joined other liberal Protestant thinkers, such as SOLOMON WASHINGTON GLADDEN and JOSIAH STRONG, in insisting that Christians could not remain indifferent to the social problems carried in the wake of industrialism. With the publication of his *Christianity and the Social Crisis* (1907), he became a leading voice in what came to be known as the Social Gospel movement. As a scholar, a preacher, and a popular lecturer, Rauschenbusch called attention to the complicity of religious believers in business and social patterns that visited misery and hardship on the weakest members of society. He wrote in *Christianizing the Social Order* (1913):

For the last ten years our nation has been under conviction of sin. We had long been living a double life, but without realizing it. Our business methods and the principles of our religion and our democracy have always been at strife, but not until our sin had matured and brought forth wholesale death did we understand our own obliquity.

Convinced that righteousness and justice might be secured in the workaday world, Rauschenbusch urged Christians to live out the ethics of Jesus, especially with respect to his special concern for the poor.

Rauschenbusch's concern for a vigorous Christian social ethic was largely embraced by the Federal Council of Churches, founded in 1908, though the onset of World War I in the following decade somewhat dimmed his optimistic view of human nature and human potential. Nevertheless, Rauschenbusch's ideas became part of the general current of progressivism that resurfaced in the years after the war, especially during the New Deal era. Rauschenbusch died in Rochester, New York, on July 25, 1918.

The Social Gospel movement flourished in America during the last two decades of the 19th century and the first two of the 20th. Walter Rauschenbusch's early experiences as a minister in Hell's Kitchen made him at first an ally of and then a key voice within this movement. The church, he urged, had a peculiar responsibility to attack the sources of poverty and injustice. "Once more the fate of a nation is rocking in the balance," he announced in *Christianizing the Social Order*. "Let the Church of Christ fling in, not the sword, but the cross, not against the weak, but for them."

Further Reading
Beckley, Harlan. *Passion for Justice: Retrieving the Legacies of Walter Rauschenbusch, John A. Ryan, and Reinhold Niebuhr.* Louisville, Ky.: Westminster/John Knox Press, 1992.

Jaehn, Klaus Juergen. *Rauschenbusch: The Formative Years.* Valley Forge, Pa.: Judson Press, 1976.

Minus, Paul M. *Walter Rauschenbusch: American Reformer.* New York: Macmillan, 1988.

Peitz, Darlene Ann. *Solidarity as Hermeneutic: A Revisionist Reading of the Theology of Walter Rauschenbusch.* New York: P. Lang, 1992.

Ramsay, William M. *Four Modern Prophets: Walter Rauschenbusch, Martin Luther King, Jr., Gustavo Gutiérrez, Rosemary Radford Ruether.* Atlanta Ga.: John Knox Press, 1986.

Rauschenbusch, Walter. *Christianity and the Social Crisis.* New York: Macmillan, 1907; Louisville, Ky.: Westminster/John Knox Press, 1991.

———. *Dare We Be Christians?* Boston: Pilgrim Press, 1914; Cleveland: Pilgrim Press, 1993.

———. *For God and the People: Prayers of the Social Awakening.* Boston: Pilgrim Press, 1910; Folcroft, Pa.: Folcroft Library Editions, 1977.

———. *The Social Principles of Jesus.* New York: Association Press, 1916; Philadelphia: R. West, 1978.

———. *A Theology for the Social Gospel.* New York: Macmillan, 1917; Louisville, Ky.: Westminster John Knox Press, 1997.

———. *Walter Rauschenbusch: Selected Writings.* Edited by Winthrop S. Hudson. New York: Paulist Press, 1984.

Sharpe, Dores Robinson. *Walter Rauschenbusch.* New York: Macmillan, 1942.

Smucker, Donovan E. *The Origins of Walter Rauschenbusch's Social Ethics.* Montreal: McGill-Queen's University Press, 1994.

Rice, John Holt

(1777–1831) *Presbyterian minister, educator*

A prominent Virginia Presbyterian of the early 19th century, John Holt Rice achieved renown as a preacher and a religious editor and writer. His most enduring accomplishment was the founding of the Union Theological Seminary in Virginia. He was born on November 28, 1777, near New London, Virginia, the son of Benjamin Rice and Catharine Holt Rice. After studying with a variety of private tutors, Rice attended Liberty Hall Academy (later Washington and Lee University) under the direction of William Graham and subsequently an academy run by George Baxter in New London, Virginia. Around 1794 he left Baxter's academy and began his own teaching career by becoming a private tutor to a family in Malvern Hill.

In 1796 Rice exchanged this post for a position as tutor at Hampden-Sidney College. In all but one year, beginning in the fall of 1799, when he worked as a private tutor for a succession of families, Rice remained at Hampden-Sidney for eight years. During this period he briefly considered a career as a physician but determined, instead, to become a Presbyterian minister. Returning to Hampden-Sidney in 1800 after a year's absence, he continued his work as a tutor while he pursued theological studies under the direction of ARCHIBALD ALEXANDER, president of Hampden-Sidney and later the first professor at Princeton Theological Seminary. He married Ann Smith Morton in the summer of 1802; the couple had no children. After completing his theological studies, Rice was licensed to preach by the Hanover Presbytery in the fall of 1803 and the following year ordained a minister of a congregation in Cub Creek. Soon afterward he resigned his tutoring position at Hampden-Sidney.

Rice supplemented his pastoral responsibilities at Cub Creek—and his income—by starting a school in his home, a practice common among Presbyterian ministers in Virginia at the time. He also wrote for the *Virginia Religious Magazine.* During this period Rice helped to raise money for the Theological Library and School at Hampden-Sidney College, a project that formed the genesis in the early 1820s of the Union Theological Seminary, over which Rice would subsequently preside.

In the spring of 1812, a new congregation of Presbyterians in Richmond, Virginia—later organized as the First Presbyterian Church—summoned Rice as its minister. Arrangements for the construction of a church building consumed much of his early years in Richmond, but within a few years he had begun publishing a paper, *Christian Monitor,* from 1815 to 1817, until Rice replaced it in 1818 with a monthly paper, titled the *Virginia Evangelical and Literary Magazine,* which he edited for 10 years. After his relocation to Richmond, Rice also became increasingly prominent among Virginia Presbyterians. He attended the 1816 General Assembly on behalf of the Hanover Presbytery and three years later was elected moderator of the General Assembly itself.

In fall 1822, Rice was offered the presidency of the College of New Jersey (later Princeton University), but he turned down this opportunity in favor of remaining in the South. Shortly after Rice had been elected president of the College of New Jersey, Hampden-Sidney College moved to transfer its theology department to the oversight of the Hanover Presbytery. The presbytery accepted this transfer and, reconstituting the department as Union Theological Seminary, proposed to make Rice a professor of the seminary and its chief administrator. Rice accepted this position in 1824, and, until his death at the beginning of the next decade, he labored to put the institution on a sound footing. He died on September 3, 1831, in Hampden-Sydney, Virginia.

John Holt Rice was a son of the South who refused to leave his native region even to accept the prestigious position of president of Presbyterianism's most important institution, the College of New Jersey. Instead, he chose to climax a long career as a minister and a writer by turning his hand to the creation of a new theological institution in the South. In this he proved successful and, in doing so, provided southern Presbyterians with an institution that, though never seriously rivaling the prestige of Princeton University, would educate a long succession of Presbyterian ministers across future years.

Further Reading

Balmer, Randall, and John R. Fitzmier. *The Presbyterians.* Westport, Conn.: Greenwood Press, 1993.

Hood, Fred J. *Reformed America: The Middle and Southern States, 1783–1837.* University: University of Alabama Press, 1980.

Maxwell, William. *A Memoir of the Rev. John H. Rice, D.D. First Professor of Christian Theology in Union Theological Seminary, Virginia.* Philadelphia: J. Whethan, 1835.

Price, Philip B. *The Life of the Reverend John Holt Rice, D.D.* Richmond: Library of Union Theological Seminary in Virginia, 1963.

Thompson, Ernest Trice. *Presbyterians in the South.* 3 vols. Richmond, Va.: John Knox Press, 1963–73.

Weeks, Louis B., III. "John Holt Rice and the American Colonization Society." *Journal of Presbyterian History* 46 (March 1968): 26–41.

Rigdon, Sidney
(1793–1876) *Mormon leader*

Sidney Rigdon followed a spiritual migration, first a Baptist, later an early Disciples of Christ minister, and finally a member of the Church of Jesus Christ of Latter-day Saints, also known as the Mormons or Latter-day Saints (LDS). His missionary zeal on behalf of LDS made him second only to JOSEPH SMITH JR., in influence among the first generation of Mormons. Rigdon was born on February 19, 1793, on a farm near St. Clair Township, Pennsylvania, the son of William and Nancy Rigdon. He received a limited education in a log schoolhouse but voraciously read the Bible and books concerning history, even as he worked on the family farm. He experienced a religious conversion in 1817 and became a member of a United Baptist church. Soon afterward, his mother, left a widow after the death of Rigdon's father in 1810, sold the family farm, and Rigdon began studying with a minister during the winter of 1818–19. He was subsequently licensed to preach and, in spring 1819, associated himself with Adamson Bentley, a Baptist minister in Warren, Ohio. The following year he married Phebe Brooks, with whom he appears to have had 12 children.

By 1821 Rigdon had been ordained the minister of the First Baptist Church of Pittsburgh, Pennsylvania. That same year he met ALEXANDER CAMPBELL, the founder of the Disciples of Christ, who communicated to Rigdon his zeal for the restoration of primitive Christianity. Rigdon's developing restorationist principles eventually alienated him from his congregation, and in 1824, he left the First Baptist Church and worked as a tanner to support himself, while he preached intermittently. By 1826, he had moved to Bainbridge, Ohio, where he founded congregations first at Mantua and then at Mentor. The latter became the seat of his preaching activities in the final years of the 1820s. During this period, Rigdon's understanding of primitive New Testament principles began to diverge from that of Alexander Campbell. In particular, Rigdon was attracted to the communal patterns of living practiced by the New Testament church described in the early chapters of the book of Acts, an attraction Campbell did not share. In 1830 differences between the men came to a head, and Rigdon separated himself and his congregation in Mentor from the Campbellite movement.

That same year, PARLEY PARKER PRATT, a young man who had been converted under Rigdon's preaching and who had subsequently become a member of the Church of Jesus Christ of Latter-day Saints, visited Rigdon and showed him the *Book of Mormon.* Rigdon was initially skeptical of the claims of Joseph Smith, Jr., the founder of the Mormon Church, but after studying the book, he became convinced that its revelation contained the key to the recovery of the apostolic church. That year he embraced Mormonism and led his congregation to do so as well. In 1831, Rigdon met Joseph Smith and persuaded him to relocate Mormon headquarters from New York to Kirtland, Ohio, where Rigdon's preaching had been influential. There, Rigdon promptly became an important leader within the new movement, and word of his conversion to Mormonism attracted additional converts to the faith. Within a few years, however, the Mormons' opponents began to claim that the *Book of Mormon* had been plagiarized from an unpublished novel written by Solomon Spaulding and given to Joseph Smith by Sidney Rigdon.

Over the following years, Rigdon's preaching ability naturally cast him into a role as a principal spokesman for the Mormons as he suffered the travails of the church. Internal dissension, external allegations of financial improprieties, and the threat of mob violence persuaded Smith and Rigdon to leave Ohio for Far West, Missouri, in early 1838. Controversy followed them there as well. Rigdon preached an inflammatory sermon on July 4 of that year, encouraging resistance among Mormons to the opposition that had tracked them to Far West. By the fall of 1838, Missouri's governor, Lilburn Boggs, declared that Mormons had to be driven from the state or else "exterminated." Rigdon himself was arrested and charged with treason, murder, and other criminal offenses, but the judge in his criminal case dismissed the charges after listening to Rigdon's persuasive argument in his own behalf.

By early 1839, Rigdon had joined Smith and other Mormons in Illinois, where they built the town of Nauvoo, which was 60 miles north of Quincy on the Mississippi River. Five years later,

Joseph Smith decided to run for president of the United States, and he chose Rigdon as his running mate, though by this time Rigdon no longer had his previous influence among the Mormons. This campaign came to naught after Smith, while in jail for allegedly ordering the destruction of a newspaper in Nauvoo that had published articles critical of the Mormons, was killed by a mob. Rigdon lost out to BRIGHAM YOUNG in the power struggle within the Mormon church that followed Smith's death. He relocated to Pittsburgh, where he published the *Later Day Saint's Messenger and Advocate,* which criticized Joseph Smith but continued to recognize the *Book of Mormon* as an inspired book. He briefly presided over a congregation called the Church of Christ, organized in 1845 in Franklin County, Pennsylvania, until it dissolved and he moved to Friendship, New York, where he died on July 14, 1876.

Sidney Rigdon's restless quest for an authentic church led him from the Baptists, to the Disciples of Christ, and finally, to the Church of Jesus Christ of Latter-day Saints. His gifted preaching won converts within each of these traditions and made him, for a time, potential heir apparent to Joseph Smith. But by the time of Smith's death, Rigdon had already lost much of his influence among the Mormons and could not endure subordination to a new leader. He left the main current of Mormonism and died in obscurity.

Further Reading

Chase, Daryl. "Sidney Rigdon—Early Mormon." M.A. thesis, University of Chicago, 1931.

Knowles, Lloyd Alan. "The Appeal and Course of Christian Restorationism on the Early Nineteenth Century American Frontier: With a Focus on Sidney Rigdon as a Case Study." Ph.D. dissertation, Michigan State University, 2000.

McKiernan, F. Mark. *The Voice of One Crying in the Wilderness: Sidney Rigdon, Religious Reformer 1793–1876.* Lawrence, Kans.: Coronado Press, 1971.

Van Wagoner, Richard S. *Sidney Rigdon: A Portrait of Religious Excess.* Salt Lake City, Utah: Signature Books, 1994.

White, Joseph W. "The Influence of Sidney Rigdon upon the Theology of Mormonism." M.A. thesis, University of Southern California, 1947.

Roberts, Benjamin Titus
(1823–1893) *founder, general superintendent of the Free Methodist Church*

Expelled from the Methodist Episcopal Church in 1858, Benjamin Titus Roberts helped organized the Free Methodist Church soon afterward. His energetic leadership as the church's first general superintendent contributed significantly to the new denomination's early growth. Roberts was born on July 25, 1823, in Cattaraugus County, New York, the son of Titus Roberts and Sally Ellis Roberts. With such rudimentary education as he was able to obtain, Roberts was teaching school by the time he was 16 years old. He later took up the study of law, but the religious conversion he experienced in 1844 convinced him to become a minister. To prepare for this vocation he studied briefly at Genesee Wesleyan Seminary in Lima, New York, and then at Wesleyan University in Middletown, Connecticut, from which he graduated in 1848. The following year he married Ellen Lois Stowe, with whom he had seven children.

Roberts had been licensed to preach in the spring of 1847 while he was still in college. The month after his graduation he joined the Genesee Conference of the Methodist Episcopal Church as minister. Over the next decade, Roberts tended a series of New York congregations. As early as 1853, he published an article in the *Northern Advocate,* a Methodist paper, in which he challenged the spiritual condition of the Methodist Episcopal churches in the Genesee Conference. During the same period he began to voice opposition to the common practice of renting or selling pews in Methodist churches, insisting that attempts to carry the Christian message to the unconverted required free pews.

Roberts and his spiritual allies who advocated a return to old-time Methodism were derisively branded "Nazarites" by other members of the Genesee Conference, a reference derived from the Old Testament and referring to a class of holy men separated from the rest of the people by the vigorousness of their spiritual discipline. In a letter to the conference bishop, T. A. Morris, in the fall of 1856, Roberts characterized the divide

among ministers within the conference: "What we call religion they call fanaticism; what they denominate Christianity, we consider formalism." Roberts sharpened this distinction in a controversial article, "New School Methodism," which he published in the *Northern Independent* in 1857. The "Old School Methodists," with whom he aligned himself,

> rely for the spread of the gospel upon the agency of the Holy Ghost, and the purity of the Church. The New School Methodists appear to depend upon the patronage of the worldly, the favor of the proud and the aspiring; and the various artifices of worldly policy.

Roberts's rhetoric earned him a condemnation from the Genesee Conference in 1857 and expulsion the following year, an action affirmed by the General Conference of the Methodist Episcopal Church when it considered the issue in May 1860.

In August of the same year, a number of laypersons and ministers who aligned themselves with Roberts's critique of the Methodist Episcopal Church met in Pekin, New York, and organized the Free Methodist Church. They elected Benjamin Roberts the first general superintendent or bishop of the church, an office he held for more than three decades. Soon after the formation of the church, Roberts sought to provide the new denomination a place for the education of ministers by establishing the Chili Seminary (later named the A. M. Chesbrough Seminary and still later Roberts Wesleyan College) in North Chili, New York, in 1866. He also published the religious newspaper *The Earnest Christian* from 1860 until his death, as well as editing *The Free Methodist* from 1886 to 1890. He died in Cattaraugus, New York, on February 27, 1893.

Benjamin Titus Roberts became a minister toward the end of Methodism's first century in America. He found the Methodist Episcopal Church of his day to be lethargic and worldly and asserted that it had forgotten the evangelical zeal of its youth. Not content to endure his jeremiads, the church expelled him, forcing Roberts and his spiritual allies to frame a new denominational organization. In great part as a result

Roberts's energetic labors on behalf of the Free Methodist Church, it grew rapidly and survives into the 21st century.

Further Reading

Blews, Richard R. *Master Workmen: Biographies of the Late Bishops of the Free Methodist Church During Her First Century, 1860–1960.* Winona Lake, Ind.: Light and Life Press, 1960.

Demaray, Donald E. *The People Called Free Methodist: Snapshots.* Winona Lake, Ind.: Light and Life Press, 1985.

Hogue, Wilson T. *History of the Free Methodist Church of North America.* Chicago: The Free Methodist Publishing House, 1915.

McPeak, Rick Hughes. "Earnest Christianity: The Practical Theology of Benjamin Titus Roberts." Ph.D. dissertation, Saint Louis University, 2001.

Roberts, Benjamin Titus. *Fishers of Men.* Rochester, N.Y.: G. L. Roberts, 1878.

———. *Pungent Truths: Being Extracts from the Writings of the Rev. Benjamin Titus Roberts.* Edited by William B. Rose. Chicago: The Free Methodist Publishing House, 1912.

———. *Why Another Sect.* New York: Garland, 1984.

Roberts, Benson Howard. *Benjamin Titus Roberts, Late General Superintendent of the Free Methodist Church: A Biography.* North Chile, N.Y.: n.p., 1900.

Zahniser, Clarence Howard. *Earnest Christian: Life and Works of Benjamin Titus Roberts.* Winona Lake, Ind.: Free Methodist Publishing House, 1957.

Robertson, Pat
(Marion Gordon Robertson)
(1930–) *television personality*

Through the Christian Broadcasting Network (CBN), the television network he founded, Pat Robertson became the most prominent conservative religious voice on television during the final decades of the 20th century. He eventually used this prominence as a basis for attempting to obtain the Republican presidential nomination in 1988 and to found the Christian Coalition, a conservative Christian political organization. He was born Marion Gordon Robertson on March 22, 1930, in Lexington, Virginia, the son of A. Willis Robert-

son and Gladys Churchill Robertson. Robertson's father was a politician who served 34 years in Congress, both in the U.S. House of Representatives and in the Senate, a circumstance that undoubtedly influenced Robertson's own later political ambitions. He graduated from a military prep school in Chattanooga, Tennessee, and then entered Washington and Lee University in 1946 and received a B.A. in 1950. During college he joined the Marine Corps Reserve and served in Korea for two years after graduation. On returning to the United States, Robertson earned a J.D. from Yale University Law School in 1955. While in law school he married Adelia ("Dede") Elmer, and this union produced four children. His legal career met unexpected frustration, however, when he failed to pass the New York bar examination and had to settle for a job as a management trainee and financial analyst with W. R. Grace & Company in New York City.

Dissatisfied with his prospects as a businessman, Robertson experienced a religious conversion and subsequently felt called to the vocation of minister. He enrolled in New York Theological Seminary in 1956, and three years later he obtained a master of divinity degree. During his seminary years, he served as an associate pastor at the First Reformed Church in Mount Vernon, New York. That church's senior minister was prominent in the charismatic movement, which emphasized the present-day reality of gifts of the Spirit such as healing, prophesy, and speaking in tongues, an emphasis that Robertson himself would share in future years.

After graduation from the seminary, Robertson moved with his family to Virginia, where he raised the money to purchase a bankrupt ultra-high-frequency (UHF) television station in Portsmouth; he founded the Christian Broadcasting Network in 1960 and aired its first programming on October 1, 1961. CBN became the first Christian television network. That same year, Robertson was ordained a Southern Baptist minister, an ordination he would eventually relinquish in 1987 prior to his bid to obtain the Republican presidential nomination. To raise funds to cover CBN's expenses, Robertson asked 700 individuals to become "faith partners" in

1963, by pledging to give $10 each month. Three years later, he premiered what would become the cornerstone of CBN's programming, the *700 Club*, a Christian version of the television talk show, which rapidly catapulted Robertson to national prominence. By the mid-1970s he was able to use revenues from CBN to purchase land in Virginia Beach that would become CBN University (later Regent University) in 1978. The former Yale law student saw his university add its own law school in 1986.

In the 1980s, Pat Robertson with other conservative Christians shifted his attention to a political context that seemed ever more alien to his values. In *America's Dates with Destiny* (1986), he complained that contemporary America had betrayed the Christian values that had originally supported its founding and engineered its flourishing. Two years later, he made an attempt to capture the Republican Party's nomination for president. Though Robertson outperformed many expectations for his candidacy in the early primaries, George Herbert Walker Bush eventually won the nomination, and Robertson was left to funnel his remaining political influence into the formation of the Christian Coalition in 1989. This organization's purpose was, according to Robertson, "to mobilize Christians—one precinct at a time, one community at a time—until once again we are the head and not the tail, and at the top rather than the bottom of our political system." The organization remained an influential political force during the 1990s, though, by the beginning of the 21st century, its influence had begun to wane.

The 20th century knew more than a few religious leaders who recognized the potential of radio and television to broadcast their religious message. These were, in the main, ministers of churches who combined broadcasts with their pastoral ministries. Robertson, however, plunged directly into the medium of television, knowing no congregation other than the audiences he attracted. Moreover, he adapted the secular talk show model to his religious message, allowing him to communicate without precisely preaching and to address a broader range of topics than many other television evangelists. This range, in turn, created a platform

from which Robertson has been influential in coaxing his electronic church into political activism on behalf of conservative Christian causes.

Further Reading

Boston, Rob. *The Most Dangerous Man in America? Pat Robertson and the Rise of the Christian Coalition.* Amherst, N.Y.: Prometheus Books, 1996.

Donovan, John B. *Pat Robertson: The Authorized Biography.* New York: Macmillan, 1988.

Foege, Alec. *The Empire God Built: Inside Pat Robertson's Media Machine.* New York: John Wiley & Sons, 1996.

Harrell, David Edwin. *Pat Robertson: A Personal, Religious, and Political Portrait.* San Francisco: Harper & Row, 1987.

Hertzke, Allen D. *Echoes of Discontent: Jesse Jackson, Pat Robertson, and the Resurgence of Populism.* Washington, D.C.: CQ Press, 1993.

Ide, Arthur Frederick. *Evangelical Terrorism: Censorship, Falwell, Robertson, and the Seamy Side of Christian Fundamentalism.* Irving, Tex.: Scholars Books, 1986.

Morken, Hubert. *Pat Robertson: Where He Stands.* Old Tappan, N.J.: F.H. Revell, 1988.

Robertson, Pat, with Jamie Buckingham. *The Autobiography of Pat Robertson: Shout It from the Housetops!* Rev. ed. South Plainfield, N.J.: Bridge, 1995.

———. *The Plan.* Nashville: T. Nelson, 1989.

———, with Bob Slosser. *The Secret Kingdom.* Nashville: T. Nelson, 1982.

Straub, Gerard Thomas. *Salvation for Sale: An Insider's View of Pat Robertson's Ministry.* Buffalo, N.Y.: Prometheus Books, 1986.

Russell, Charles Taze

(1852–1916) *founder of the Watch Tower Bible and Tract Society*

Charles Taze Russell established one of the most enduring and controversial adventist groups of the late 19th century. The religious organization he founded, called the Watch Tower Bible and Tract Society, eventually was known as the Jehovah's Witnesses. Russell was born on February 16, 1852, in Allegheny, Pennsylvania, the son of Joseph Lytle Russell and Ann Eliza Birney Russell. Although his parents were Presbyterians, Russell in his spiritual migration traveled through Congregationalism for a time, then skepticism, and finally adventism. By the early 1870s he had become the pastor for a small Bible study group, and within a few years he was publishing a magazine, with Nelson H. Barbour, that insisted that Jesus had spiritually returned to earth—or, more precisely, to the "upper air"—in 1874, an event he termed the "Millennial Dawn," and that Christ's millennial kingdom would begin in 1914. Although Barbour had provided the scriptural calculations to produce these dates, he and Russell parted ways in 1879, and Russell started a new publication, initially titled *Zion's Watch Tower and Herald of Christ's Presence.*

Russell's study of the Bible led him not only to these millennial projections but to other beliefs that strayed from the path of mainstream Christian orthodoxy. Among these were his insistence that Jesus was not God, but a created spirit, and his denial of the existence of hell and belief that the fate of nonbelievers was to be painlessly annihilated rather than eternally tormented. In addition to these beliefs, Russell articulated complicated views entailing the number of believers who would be included in the true church (144,000) and the possibility of a second opportunity to accept the truth for those who failed to do so in their present life.

In 1879 Russell married Maria Frances Ackley, with whom he had no children and from whom he was later divorced. In the following decade, he founded the Watch Tower Bible and Tract Society in 1884. This organization became known as the Jehovah's Witnesses in 1931, after the death of Russell. In the meantime, however, Russell concentrated on producing a series of Bible studies, eventually titled *Studies in Scripture* and published by the Watch Tower and Tract Society from 1906 to 1917. Three years after the appearance of the first volume in this series, Russell relocated the headquarters of the Watch Tower from Pittsburgh, Pennsylvania, to Brooklyn, New York.

While editing his periodical, *Zion's Watch Tower,* and publishing the volumes of *Studies in Scripture,* Russell also lectured widely in the United States, Canada, and Europe, and he attracted a significant following. As he continued

to insist that Christ's kingdom would finally appear in 1914, Russell's followers adopted as their marching banner the slogan "Millions will never die." Russell died on October 31, 1916, while riding on a train passing through Pampa, Texas, in the course of a lecture tour. He was succeeded within the Watch Tower and Tract Society by JOSEPH FRANKLIN RUTHERFORD, and in 1931 the organization came to the known as the Jehovah's Witnesses.

The Watch Tower Bible and Tract society sprang from the fertile soil of 19th-century millennial expectations, already well tilled by religious leaders such as WILLIAM MILLER and ELLEN GOULD HARMON WHITE. The society shared the confidence of other adventist groups that Christ's appearance was imminent and as they did, had to respond to the failure of the Almighty to act according to the timetable they established. In the case of Russell, who had named 1914 as the date the millennial kingdom would be established, the onset of World War I provided ample demonstration that the essence of his apocalyptic vision was accurate. Russell's retreat from Trinitarian Christianity—especially his denial of Christ's divinity—set him apart from other adventists. This theological difference, coupled with the aggressive evangelizing methods the group adopted under Russell's successor, Joseph Franklin Rutherford, helped to make the society Russell established one of the more controversial adventist faiths of the 20th century.

Further Reading
Curry, Melvin D. *Jehovah's Witnesses: The Millenarian World of the Watch Tower.* New York: Garland, 1992.

Holden, Andrew. *Jehovah's Witnesses: Portrait of a Contemporary Religious Movement.* London: Routledge, 2002.

Horowitz, David. *Pastor Charles Taze Russell: An Early American Christian Zionist.* New York: Philosophical Library, 1986.

Penton, M. James. *Apocalypse Delayed: The Story of Jehovah's Witnesses.* 2d ed. Toronto: University of Toronto Press, 1997.

Russell, C. T. *Studies in the Scriptures.* 7 vols. Allegheny, Pa.: Watch Tower Bible & Tract Society, 1906–17.

Rutherford, Joseph Franklin
(1869–1942) *Jehovah's Witnesses leader*

On the death of CHARLES TAZE RUSSELL, the founder of the Watch Tower Bible and Tract Society, Joseph Franklin Rutherford took control of the affairs of the society. In 1931, he renamed the organization the Jehovah's Witnesses, and under his leadership, the group launched an aggressive evangelization campaign that made it one of the most controversial religious groups of the 20th century. Rutherford was born on November 8, 1869, in Morgan County, Missouri, the son of James Calvin Rutherford and Lenore Strickland Rutherford. His parents were farmers who were members of a local Baptist church. The circumstances of Rutherford's childhood and education are unclear, but he received his license to practice law in Missouri in 1892 after preparing—as did many other would-be lawyers in the 19th century—by apprenticing himself with an established lawyer, in Rutherford's case, Judge E. L. Edwards. In addition to his apprenticeship with Edwards, Rutherford served as a court reporter prior to becoming a lawyer. He practiced law at first in Booneville, Missouri, and served from time to time as a specially appointed judge, a fact that would later prompt Jehovah's Witnesses to refer to his as "Judge" Rutherford. At some point he apparently married a woman named Mary, but his wife's maiden name and the details of their marriage, including its date, have not survived. Rutherford and his wife appear to have had one child. They eventually became estranged.

Soon after beginning his law practice, Rutherford met some missionaries of the Watch Tower Bible and Tract Society, who in 1894 sold him copies of several volumes in what would eventually be Charles Taze Russell's seven-volume Bible commentary, *Studies in Scripture*. It was not until more than a decade later, however, that Rutherford became formally associated with Russell's society through baptism in 1906. Within a few years, he had relocated to New York, where he became a lawyer for the Watch Tower Bible and Tract Society. By 1916, Rutherford had gained seats on the board of directors of the key organizations through which the society operated.

After the death of Charles Russell in the fall of 1916, Rutherford was able to seize control of the various Watch Tower organizations. By the following year, he had been elected president of these organizations, and he promptly engineered the dismissal of board members opposed to his leadership. These actions generated heated controversy among Watch Tower members and led significant numbers of them to form splinter organizations, but Rutherford managed to tame the main body of the Watch Tower Bible and Tract Society to his new spiritual superintendence.

Rutherford opposed U.S. involvement in World War I and counseled members of the Watch Tower Bible and Tract Society—sometimes called International Bible Students—to resist the draft. In 1918, U.S. authorities arrested Rutherford and other Watch Tower leaders on charges of violating the Espionage Act of 1917, which prohibited obstruction of the draft. Rutherford and his companions were found guilty at trial and sentenced, in the case of Rutherford and six others, to 20-year prison terms; a remaining defendant received a 10-year prison sentence. Rutherford and the others served nine months in prison until they were finally released on bail. In May 1919, a federal court of appeals reversed their convictions on the basis of improper conduct by the original trial judge, and the government declined to try them again.

After the war, Rutherford led the Watch Tower society in launching an aggressive campaign to carry its message to unbelievers. The society began to distribute house to house a new publication targeted to this audience, *Golden Age* (which eventually became *Awake!*). Its members also used phonograph records of sermons by Rutherford—often excoriating other religious traditions, especially Catholicism—as a means of evangelizing. Over the years that followed, these strategies would increasingly land society members in conflicts with localities, who frequently used laws against disturbing the peace, leafleting, and unwanted solicitation to harry missionaries of the Watch Tower Bible and Tract Society. Eventually, the U.S. Supreme Court heard a number of cases arising out of activities of the society; the Court often used these cases to establish more expansive freedoms of religion and speech.

In 1920 Rutherford published the booklet "Millions Now Living Will Never Die," which predicted that the end of the world—"the completion of all things"—would occur in 1925, and that the Old Testament saints and heroes of faith would be resurrected. Even after the passage of this date, Rutherford so anticipated the imminent appearance of these resurrected saints that he purchased a mansion near San Diego, California, called Beth Sarim, where he expected them to reside. Rutherford's prediction helped to swell the ranks of the Watch Tower society for a time, though many adherents withdrew from the society after 1925 passed uneventfully. Nevertheless, he remained at the helm of a rapidly growing society of followers, whom he named Jehovah's Witnesses in 1931. Rutherford died at Beth Sarim on January 8, 1942.

By the end of the 20th century, Jehovah's Witnesses had more than 5 million members in some 230 countries. Although Joseph Rutherford neither founded the organization nor established the core details of its spiritual vision, he shepherded the Witnesses through a period of precipitous growth. His strategy of aggressively evangelizing the United States—and the world—with the Witnesses' message chiefly accounted for its steady growth in the 20th century and its regular collisions with localities resistant to this message.

Further Reading

Curry, Melvin D. Jehovah's Witnesses: The Millenarian World of the Watch Tower. New York: Garland, 1992.

Holden, Andrew. Jehovah's Witnesses: Portrait of a Contemporary Religious Movement. London: Routledge, 2002.

Penton, M. James. Apocalypse Delayed: The Story of Jehovah's Witnesses. 2d ed. Toronto: University of Toronto Press, 1997.

Rutherford, J. F. Jehovah's Witnesses. I. The Early Writings of J.F. Rutherford. Edited by Jerry Bergman. New York: Garland 1990.

Ryan, John Augustine

(1869–1945) *Catholic priest, theologian, social reformer*

The leading Catholic voice for social reform in the first half of the 20th century, John Augustine Ryan refused to recognize a faith that had no application to the needs of society. He attempted to infuse economics with ethics and thus to craft an ethical basis for securing social justice. He was born on May 25, 1869, in Vermillion, Minnesota, the son of William Ryan and Maria Elizabeth Luby Ryan. His parents were Catholic farmers, and by the time he was a young man Ryan had determined to become a Catholic priest. He studied at Saint Thomas Seminary in Minneapolis and was ordained a priest in 1898. Subsequently, he earned an S.T.D. from the Catholic University of America in 1906.

Ryan published his doctoral dissertation as *A Living Wage: Its Ethical and Economic Aspects* in 1906, and the title of this work expressed the essence of his social thought. He protested against the modern separation between ethical and economic inquiries, blaming the Protestant Reformation for severing these two subjects from one another. He urged in place of this dichotomy a reinvigorization of concern for the common good rather than for the maximization of wealth by discrete individuals.

While he worked on his dissertation, Ryan taught moral theology and economics at St. Paul's Seminary, and he remained there for 13 years. In 1915 he joined the faculty of Catholic University in Washington, D.C., first as a professor of political science and, from 1916, as a professor of theology. By the end of the decade he had been appointed dean of the School of Sacred Sciences. He remained at Catholic University until 1939.

From early in his tenure at Catholic University, Ryan supplemented his teaching responsibilities with efforts to engineer social reform. In 1917, he began several years as editor of *Catholic Charities Review*, though he opposed the view that social ills such as poverty could be remedied solely through private or institutional charity. Charity, he believed, was no substitute for justice. Justice, in turn, required progressive legal reform, and Ryan allied himself with public interest groups such as the National Consumers' League to lobby for reforms such as a minimum wage and progressive taxation. He also outlined a systematic program for social reform adopted and published by the National Catholic Welfare Conference in 1920, "The

Bishops' Program of Social Reconstruction." In 1919, he became director of the Social Action Department of the National Catholic Welfare Conference, a position he held until shortly before his death in 1945.

Ryan sowed the seeds for future controversy in 1922, when he published with M. F. X. Millar the book *The State and the Church*. In spite of his progressive views on the subject of social justice, Ryan adhered to more traditional Catholic views concerning church-state relations. He argued with Millar that separation of religious institutions and government represented a merely pragmatic surrender to modern reality. The ideal, though, would be a close alliance between state and church, meaning the Catholic Church. Later that decade, during the presidential election of 1928, Ryan's position furnished ammunition for those who opposed Democratic candidate Al Smith, the first Catholic presidential candidate.

In the 1930s, Ryan became a natural ally of President Franklin D. Roosevelt's New Deal policies. He squared off publicly against the controversial, but immensely popular, radio priest Father CHARLES EDWARD COUGHLIN, a vitriolic critic of Roosevelt and the New Deal. Ryan's support of Roosevelt earned him Father Coughlin's label of "Right Reverend New Dealer." With whatever enmity this brand may have been accompanied, it nevertheless captured Ryan's political sensibilities. At the beginning of Roosevelt's second term in office, the harmony between his views and those of the president earned Ryan the opportunity to become the first Catholic to deliver a benediction at a presidential inauguration. It also won him appointment to the Industrial Appeals Board of the National Recovery Administration in the summer of 1934.

Ryan retired from Catholic University in 1939, on his 70th birthday. He died on September 16, 1945 in Saint Paul, Minnesota.

The early decades of the 20th century witnessed a flourishing of Catholic social thought, and John Augustine Ryan was a principal theoretician and architect of the Catholic movement for social reform. As early as his seminary days, he pondered the implications of Catholic teaching concerning social justice, especially as expressed in Pope Leo XIII's encyclical *Rerum Novarum*. In his most significant work, *Distributive Justice: The Right and Wrong of Our Present Distribution of Wealth* (1916), he insisted that workers had a right to a "living wage," that is, one sufficient to secure those economic necessities required to maintain human dignity. Any lower wage was not only socially harmful but immoral. This insistence undergirded his social thought and prompted him to encourage active Catholic involvement in the political process to secure social justice.

Further Reading

Beckley, Harlan. *Passion for Justice: Retrieving the Legacies of Walter Rauschenbusch, John A. Ryan, and Reinhold Niebuhr.* Louisville, Ky.: Westminster/John Knox Press, 1992.

Broderick, Francis L. *Right Reverend New Dealer: John A. Ryan.* New York: Macmillan, 1963.

Gearty, Patrick William. *The Economic Thought of Monsignor John A. Ryan.* Washington, D.C.: Catholic University of America Press, 1953.

Ryan, John Augustine. *The Catholic Church and the Citizen.* New York: Macmillan, 1928.

———. *Declining Liberty and Other Papers.* New York: Macmillan, 1927; Freeport, N.Y.: Books for Libraries Press, 1968.

———. *Economic Justice: Selections from Distributive Justice and a Living Wage.* Edited by Harlan R. Beckley. Louisville, Ky.: Westminster/John Knox Press, 1996.

———. *Social Doctrine in Action: A Personal History.* New York: Harper & Brothers, 1941.

S

Sankey, Ira David
(1840–1908) *revival singer, hymn composer*

Allied with the famous revivalist DWIGHT LYMAN MOODY, Ira Sankey helped to shape evangelical Christian music in the last decades of the 19th century. As a revival singer and a composer of hymn music, he popularized the gospel hymn and planted his musical vision in hymnbooks where his melodies can still be found nearly a century after his death. Ira David Sankey was born on August 28, 1840, in Edinburg, Pennsylvania, the son of David Sankey and Mary Leeper Sankey. His parents were devout Methodists who taught him to sing hymns at an early age. Sankey himself was converted during a revival in 1856, and when his family moved to New Castle, Pennsylvania, so his father could become president of a local bank, Sankey joined the New Castle Methodist Church. Within a few years of his family's arrival in New Castle, he was superintendent of the church's Sunday School program and director of its choir.

After the outbreak of the Civil War, Sankey joined the Union army and served from 1861 to 1863. Following his discharge, he returned to Pennsylvania, found a job as a tax collector, and in 1863 married Fanny V. Edwards, with whom he had two children. As a result of his talent as a singer, Sankey soon was appearing regularly at revivals and churches in Pennsylvania, where he might have remained but for the circumstances that led to his meeting Dwight L. Moody, the most famous revivalist in the second half of the 19th century.

In 1867, when a branch of the Young Men's Christian Association (YMCA) opened in New Castle, Sankey enthusiastically joined in its work; eventually he became president of the New Castle YMCA. Because of his local prominence in the YMCA, he was selected as a delegate to an international meeting of the organization held in Indianapolis in 1870. There, according to Sankey's autobiography, Moody heard Sankey sing at a prayer meeting and immediately confronted him afterward, asking, "Where are you from? Are you married? What is your business?" When Sankey answered that he had a wife, two children, and a job working for the government, Moody announced abruptly, "You will have to give that up. You must; I have been looking for you the last eight years." Sankey eventually agreed, and the two men worked together for most of the next three decades, until Moody's death in 1899 ended their partnership.

After a revival campaign in Great Britain from 1873 to 1875, both Moody and Sankey returned to the United States to become the most prominent revivalists of their generation. Sankey became a prolific composer of hymn music, seldom writing his own lyrics but setting those of others such as FANNY CROSBY to popular tunes and rhythms. Perhaps his best-known melody is the gospel ballad "The Ninety and Nine," which he set to music and sang regularly in revivals and church services. His musical influence stretched far beyond the memory of those who heard him sing, however, since he compiled and published a series of songbooks

Ira D. Sankey's gospel music contributed to the success of Dwight L. Moody's evangelistic campaigns. *(Library of Congress, Prints and Photographs Division, LC-USZ62-108534)*

Revivalism swept across the urban centers of the United States during the last half of the 19th century and flowed deeply into the religious life of the 20th. It reverberated to the voices of preachers such as Dwight L. Moody, and in the new century, AIMEE SEMPLE MCPHERSON, BILLY SUNDAY, and BILLY GRAHAM. The current of revivalism also moved to the melody and rhythms of gospel hymns, which gave musical life to the content of evangelical preaching. Though other songwriters such as Fanny Crosby played a more prominent role in the creation of the lyrics to these hymns, Ira D. Sankey supplied much of the music that animated these lyrics. His influence stretched far into the 20th century and, in fact, beyond. New musical idioms gained prominence in some Protestant churches as the 20th century wore on. Nevertheless, gospel hymns, including many that Sankey helped write and popularize, continued to hold an important place in many southern evangelical churches especially, even into the 21st century.

Further Reading

Everett, Betty Steele. *Ira Sankey: First Gospel Singer.* Fort Washington, Pa.: Christian Literature Crusade, 1999.

Goodspeed, Edgar Johnson. *A Full History of the Wonderful Career of Moody and Sankey in Great Britain and America.* New York: H.S. Goodspeed, 1876; New York, AMS Press, 1973.

The Ira D. Sankey Centenary: Proceedings of the Centenary Celebration of the Birth of Ira D. Sankey, Together with Some Hitherto Unpublished Sankey Correspondence. New Castle, Pa.: Lawrence County Historical Society, 1941.

Ludwig, Charles. *Sankey Still Sings.* Anderson, Ind.: The Warner Press, 1947.

Rhodes, Richard S., ed. *Dwight Lyman Moody's Life Work and Gospel Sermons as Delivered by the Great Evangelist in His Revival Work in Great Britain and America, Together with a Biography of His Co-laborer, Ira David Sankey.* Chicago: Rhodes & McClure, 1900.

Robertson, Darrel M. *The Chicago Revival, 1876: Society and Revivalism in a Nineteenth-century City.* Metuchen, N.J.: Scarecrow Press, 1989.

Sankey, Ira David. *My Life and the Story of the Gospel Hymns and of Sacred Songs and Solos.* Philadelphia: Sunday School Times, 1907; New York, AMS Press, 1974.

containing many of his own hymns as well as others in the gospel hymn tradition.

Sankey worked with Moody until the latter died in 1899, though ill health during the 1890s caused Sankey to limit his traveling schedule somewhat. When Moody died, Sankey summoned a creative energy he only rarely possessed to write in the funeral both the lyrics and the music for the hymn "Out of the Shadow-Lands." Sankey himself lived on for nearly another decade, though glaucoma robbed him of sight after 1903 and severely curtailed the activities of his remaining years. He died in Brooklyn, New York, on August 14, 1908.

Schaff, Philip
(1819–1893) *theologian, educator*

The dean of church history studies in late 19th-century America, Philip Schaff devoted a long and eminent career as a scholar to the study of the historical development of the church. Together with JOHN WILLIAMSON NEVIN, Schaff was a key proponent of what came to be known as the Mercersburg theology, which attempted to harness appreciation for the Reformation with reverence for the historic Catholic Church. He was born on January 1, 1819, in Chur, Switzerland, the son of Philip Schaf or Schaaf and Anna Louis Schindler, a couple who were not married. He later changed his name to *Schaff*. The early death of his father and the exile of his mother from Chur caused by the illegitimate birth of her son, left him an orphan at an early age. A minister in Chur eventually recognized his academic promise and sent Schaff to a pietist school at Kornthal, Württemberg, where he experienced a religious conversion and was confirmed in a Lutheran church. From this school, Schaff transferred to the Stuttgart Gymnasium, where he studied for two years before enrolling in the University of Tübingen in 1837. After two years at Tübingen, he continued studies in Halle and Berlin before beginning his academic career as a university professor in Berlin, where he worked from 1842 to 1844.

Europe, however, was not to be the seat of Schaff's scholarly career. After being ordained in the spring of 1844, he set out for America to join the faculty of the German Reformed seminary at Mercersburg, Pennsylvania. There he found a spiritual ally in his fellow faculty member John Williamson Nevin. Together, these two men articulated a vision of the church that came to be known as the Mercersburg theology. Schaff's inaugural address at Mercersburg, "The Principle of Protestantism," created the framework for much of his further thought by emphasizing both the value and the necessity of the Protestant Reformation and its organic unity with the medieval Catholic Church. The hospitableness between the Mercersburg theology and Roman Catholicism did not escape the notice of the German Reformed denomination. Within a few years of his arrival in Pennsylvania, Schaff had twice been tried for heresy—unsuccess-fully in each case. A more cordial event during this period was his 1845 marriage to Mary Elizabeth Schley, with whom he had eight children.

Mercersburg remained the center of Schaff's scholarly activities until the mid-1860s, when he, while on a leave of absence in New York City, tendered his resignation to the seminary. He lectured for several years at seminaries in the New York area, and he joined the faculty of Union Theological Seminary in New York City in 1870. At the same time he became a member of the Presbyterian Church (U.S.A.), the denomination with which the seminary was then associated.

In the years that followed Schaff completed a number of significant scholarly projects, the most important of which were his three-volume work *The Creeds of Christendom* (1877) and another multivolume project, his *History of the Christian Church* (1882–92). Schaff's energy, however, could not be contained solely in scholarly writing projects: he also worked on behalf of organizations such as the New York Sabbath Committee; the Evangelical Alliance, an organization with an ecumenical temper matching his own; and the American Committee of Bible Revision, responsible for the publication in 1885 of a new version of the King James Bible. Toward the end of his long career at Union Theological Seminary, Schaff founded the American Society of Church History in 1888, and he served as its president for the remainder of his life. He also guided the society in its preparation of a multivolume treatise on American church history published from 1893 to 1897. Schaff died on October 20, 1893, in New York City.

The monumental products of Philip Schaff's a scholarship still line library shelves, weighty in their learning and expansive in their breadth. In his day, though, Schaff made his home not only among the noiseless stacks of books from which he pried open the past, but in the lively affairs of late 19th-century Christendom. To all his labors he gave a capacious appreciation for the church and its history, eager to portray it as he believed it to be: an organic unity stretching across nearly two millennia. Shortly before his death, he addressed the World's Parliament of Religions in Chicago in his lecture "The Reunion of Christendom," a fitting coda for his life's work.

Further Reading

Nichols, James Hastings. *Romanticism in American Theology: Nevin and Schaff at Mercersburg*. Chicago: University of Chicago Press, 1961.

Penzel, Klaus. *The Private Life of Philip Schaff: Another Centennial Appraisal for the Friends of the Burke Library of Union Theological Seminary in the City of New York*. New York: Union Theological Seminary, 1995.

Pranger, Gary K. *Philip Schaff (1819–1893): Portrait of an Immigrant Theologian*. New York: P. Lang, 1997.

Schaff, David Schley. *The Life of Philip Schaff, in Part Autobiographical*. New York: C. Scribner's Sons, 1897.

Schaff, Philip. *Philip Schaff, Historian and Ambassador of the Universal Church: Selected Writings*. Edited and with introductions by Klaus Penzel. Macon, Ga.: Mercer University Press, 1991.

Shriver, George H. *Philip Schaff: Christian Scholar and Ecumenical Prophet*. Macon, Ga.: Mercer University Press, 1987.

Schmucker, Samuel Simon

(1799–1873) *Lutheran minister, educator, theologian*

Samuel Simon Schmucker helped shape American Lutheranism during the first half of the 19th century. He played an important role in the creation of the Lutheran General Synod, a national governing body, and Gettysburg Seminary in Pennsylvania. Schmucker was born on February 28, 1799, in Hagerstown, Maryland, the son of John George Schmucker and Elizabeth Gross Schmucker. His father was a Lutheran minister; Samuel Schmucker prepared for the ministry by studying first at the University of Pennsylvania from 1814 to 1816 and then at Princeton Theological Seminary, from which he graduated in 1820. He was ordained as a Lutheran minister in 1821 and served for the next five years as minister for several congregations in Virginia. During his early years as a minister, he married Elenora Geige in 1821, with whom he had one child, and then two years after her death in 1823, Mary Catherine Steenbergen, with whom he had 12 children.

Schmucker's most enduring contributions to Lutheranism in America would be as an educator and theologian rather than as a minister, however. In 1826 he helped found the Gettysburg Theological Seminary in Pennsylvania and served on its faculty for nearly 40 years, until his retirement in 1864. The following decade he participated in organizing Pennsylvania College (now Gettysburg College) and serving as its president from 1832 to 1834. In 1834, he published *Elements of Popular Theology*, the first Lutheran systematic theology written in English and published in the United States. Schmucker also played an important leadership role in the Lutheran General Synod, formed in 1820, for which he served as president from 1828 until 1845.

Schmucker possessed the spiritual impulses of pietism, with its focus on personal devotion and sanctity rather than creedal conformity. The revivals that periodically punctuated 19th-century religious life left an abiding mark on him. Schmucker preferred to concentrate on individual spiritual renewal rather than on the fine points of doctrine, and this evangelical temper, which caused him to seek spiritual allies across confessional lines, made him an early forebear of the ecumenical movement that would begin to flourish toward the turn of the 20th century. In 1838, he published an early ecumenical manifesto, *Appeal to the American Churches*.

By the middle of the 19th century, however, Schmucker's evangelical piety had lost favor among most Lutherans, who increasingly championed creedal orthodoxy. In the interest of ecumenical unity and evangelistic efforts, Schmucker saw no need for Lutherans to insist on rigid adherence to every element of the Augsburg Confession of 1530, the spiritual yardstick of traditional Lutheranism. By the midpoint of the 19th century, however, American Lutherans, whose numbers had been augmented by German and Scandinavian immigrants, were less inclined than Schmucker to retreat from any portions of the Augsburg Confession. In 1864 disputes among the faculty of the Gettysburg Theological Seminary over these issues resulted in the creation of a new Lutheran seminary in Philadelphia.

Schmucker's second wife, Mary Catherine, died in 1848, and he married Esther M. Wagner the following year. He eventually retired from his faculty position at the Gettysburg Theological Seminary in 1864 but not before the seminary grounds had been overrun by Confederate soldiers during the battle of Gettysburg in the Civil War. While occupying the grounds, the soldiers apparently took pains to seek out and destroy Schmucker's writings because of the antislavery sentiments they regularly expressed. He died on July 26, 1873, in Gettysburg, Pennsylvania.

Revivalism in America has frequently made friends out of spiritual strangers and encouraged believers to leap over doctrinal boundaries to join hands with those who share their zeal for spiritual renewal. Samuel Schmucker sought to invigorate early 19th-century Lutheranism with this ecumenical spirit, even at the risk of sacrificing particular canons of Lutheran orthodoxy. Although he played an important role in founding and shepherding early Lutheran institutions in America, he nevertheless could not ultimately communicate to most other Lutherans the essence of his evangelical piety.

Further Reading

Anstadt, Peter. *Life and Times of Rev. S.S. Schmucker.* York, Pa.: P. Anstadt, 1896.

Crews, Warren Earl. "Three Men, One Vision: Samuel Schmucker, John Nevin, William Muhlenberg and a Church Evangelical and Catholic." Ph.D. dissertation, Saint Louis University, 1995.

Ferm, Vergilius Anselm. *The Crisis in American Lutheran Theology: A Study of the Issue Between American Lutheranism and Old Lutheranism.* New York: Century, 1927.

Kuenning, Paul P. *The Rise and Fall of American Lutheran Pietism: The Rejection of an Activist Heritage.* Macon, Ga.: Mercer University Press, 1988.

Noll, Mark. "The Lutheran Difference." *First Things* 20 (February 1992): 31–40.

Schmucker, Luke. *The Schmucker Family and the Lutheran Church in America.* N.p., 1937.

Schmucker, Samuel Simon. *Appeal to the American Churches, with a Plan for Catholic Union.* New York: Gould & Newman, 1838; Philadelphia: Fortress Press, 1965.

———. *Elements of Popular Theology.* Andover Mass.: Gould & Newman, 1834.

Wentz, Abdel Ross. *Pioneer in Christian Unity: Samuel Simon Schmucker.* Philadelphia: Fortress Press, 1967.

Schneerson, Menachem Mendel
(1902–1994) *rebbe of Lubavitcher Hasidim*

Menachem Mendel Schneerson was the leading force among ultra-Orthodox American Jews during the second half of the 20th century. He helped to reinvigorate Orthodox traditions and practices during this period. Schneerson was born on April 18, 1902, in Nikolayev, Ukraine, the son of Levi Yitzchak Schneerson and Chana Yanovsky Schneerson. His father was a rabbi in the Lubavitcher Hasidim, a branch of Hasidim known as Chabad; his great-grandfather had been the third *rebbe,* or spiritual head, of the Chabad; his cousin, Yosef Yitzchak Schneerson, was the sixth rebbe. By the time of Menachem Schneerson's bar mitzvah, he had been recognized as a religious prodigy, and he received his ordination as a rabbi at the age of 17. In 1928 he married Chaya Mushka Schneerson, the daughter of his cousin, Rebbe Schneerson. Five years later the couple moved to Berlink, where Schneerson, in a move viewed as unusual by some Hasidic Jews, studied at secular universities: math and science at the University of Berlin and engineering at the Sorbonne.

In 1941, Schneerson immigrated with his family to the United States, where he joined his father-in-law, Rebbe Schneerson, who had settled in the Crown Heights area of Brooklyn. There, for the next nine years, Schneerson supervised the educational programs of the Chabad until he was named the seventh Lubavitch rebbe, after the death of his father-in-law in 1950. Unlike many American Jews who had surrendered Orthodox beliefs and traditions as the price of admission to mainstream American culture, the Lubavitch Hasidim steadfastly resisted cultural assimilation. Moreover, under the leadership of Rebbe Schneerson, the Chabad launched an aggressive campaign to renew spiritual devotion among nonobservant Jews. Schneerson saw to the establishment of Chabad Houses near college campuses as an outreach to Jewish students, as well as the distribution of literature and the organization of public services. Through these and other evangelistic enterprises, the rebbe rejected the insularity that sometimes characterizes small religious sects in favor of an active spiritual colonization of the secular world. His efforts were quite successful: By the last decade of the 20th century the Chabad claimed some 200,000 members across the world, as well as the support of many nonobservant Jews not prepared to undertake the Hasidic life-style but appreciative of the Lubavitchers' spiritual mission.

During the early 1990s, speculation flourished among some Lubavitchers that Rebbe Schneerson might be the Messiah. He and his wife were childless, and Schneerson had not designated a successor, circumstances that helped to fuel messianic expectations. But these were significantly frustrated in 1992 after the rebbe suffered a stroke, which severely incapacitated him for a time. With his gradual recovery, though, expectations again increased among some of the Chabad that he would soon reveal himself as the Messiah. When Schneerson died on June 12, 1994, in New York City, however, and was not resurrected, as some of his followers had hoped, the messianic hopes centered on him were decisively frustrated.

During the 19th and 20th centuries, Reform Judaism became the dominant religious tradition of Jews in America. Transplanted from Germany in the 19th century, this tradition—eagerly embraced by Jews seeking to find their place within American culture—revised traditional Jewish practices to make them more amenable to modern American society. By the mid-20th century, Jewish Orthodoxy was in decline. Rebbe Menachem Mendel Schneerson, though, became the leader of a prominent Jewish counterculture, Orthodox to its core and not embarrassed to be identified as such. Through Schneerson's campaign to entice nonobservant Jews back to traditional beliefs and practices, the Chabad became a highly visible alternative to the more acculturated forms of Judaism that continue to dominate the lives of most American Jews. Although expectations that Schneerson might be the Messiah waned after his death, the Chabad continues to perpetuate the rebbe's wisdom and teaching through its literature.

Further Reading

Deutsch, Shaul Shimon. *Larger than Life: The Life and Times of the Lubavitcher Rebbe Rabbi Menachem Mendel Schneerson.* 2 vols. New York: Chasidic Historical Productions, 1995–97.

Ehrlich, Avrum M. *Leadership in the Habad Movement: A Critical Evaluation of Habad Leadership, History, and Succession.* Northvale, N.J.: J. Aronson, 2000.
Hoffman, Edward. *Despite All Odds: The Story of Lubavitch.* New York: Simon & Schuster, 1991.
Levin, Faitel. *Heaven on Earth: Reflections on the Theology of the Lubavitcher Rebbe.* Brooklyn, N.Y.: Kehot Publication Society, 2000.
Schneerson, Menachem Mendel. *Toward a Meaningful Life: The Wisdom of the Rebbe.* Edited by Simon Jacobson. New York: William Morrow, 1995.

Scofield, Cyrus Ingerson

(1843–1921) *Congregationalist-Presbyterian minister, author of* Scofield Reference Bible

C. I. Scofield produced one of fundamentalist Christianity's most significant works, the *Scofield Reference Bible,* published in 1909. Through notes appended to the biblical text, Scofield did more than any other individual to popularize a view of end times known as dispensational premillennialism. Cyrus Ingerson Scofield was born near Clinton, Michigan, the son of Elias Scofield and Abigail Goodrich Scofield. He served in the Confederate army for a year in 1861, but otherwise the circumstances of his early life are obscure. By 1866, he was working in a law office in Saint Louis, Missouri, and that year he married Leontene Cerré, with whom he had two children. At the end of the decade, he relocated to Atchison, Kansas, where he was admitted to practice law in 1869. In short order, he was twice elected to the Kansas legislature in 1871 and 1872 and then appointed U.S. attorney for Kansas in 1873.

In the years immediately afterward, Scofield suffered a precipitous personal decline into dishonesty and criminal conduct, speculated to have been caused by alcoholism. By 1877 he appears to have been separated from his wife, and he returned two years later to Saint Louis without his wife and children. That year, however, he had a conversion experience that reoriented the course of his life. He joined the Pilgrim Congregational Church and became involved in the Saint Louis chapter of the Young Men's Christian Association. In 1880 he was licensed to preach as a Congregational minister and became the minister of the Hyde Park Congregational Church, which he had helped to establish. Two years later, he moved to Dallas, Texas, where he was briefly pastor of a small mission church and then became the minister for the First Congregational Church in Dallas in 1883, where he remained for the next 12 years. The same year Scofield, divorced by his first wife, married Hettie Hall von Wartz, with whom he had one child.

In 1895, the revivalist DWIGHT LYMAN MOODY persuaded Scofield to leave Dallas and become the minister of Moody's home church in Massachusetts, the Trinitarian Congregationalist Church of East Northfield. There, Scofield also became president of the Northfield Bible Training School. Since his conversion in 1879, Scofield had been immersed in the currents of a particular theological tributary known as premillennial dispensationalism. This view of human history identified separate eras—or dispensations—in which God dealt with humans according to a specific pattern. The view Scofield held was premillennialist in that he believed Christ would return to earth before beginning a literal 1,000-year reign that would precede the end times. Scofield had previously published a defense of this view, *Rightly Dividing the Word of Truth,* in 1888. In Northfield, he conceived the more ambitious project of creating an edition of the King James Bible with his own interpretive notes, designed to guide readers through the intricacies of Scofield's version of premillennial dispensationalism. The *Scofield Reference Bible* was published by Oxford University Press in 1909.

While working to prepare his Bible edition, Scofield returned to Dallas, but during this period he migrated away from Congregationalism and into the Presbyterian Church (U.S.A.), which was, at the time, more hospitable to his theological views. He eventually relocated to New York, where he opened a correspondence school for Bible students. Still later, in 1914, he established a similar school in Philadelphia, Pennsylvania. Scofield died in Douglaston, Long Island, on July 24, 1921.

Premillennial dispensationalism found its roots in literal readings of the Bible that created a dominant strain of 20th-century Protestant fundamentalism. Within the strata of religious experi-

ence characterized by this theological vision, no work exercised a more significant and enduring influence than the *Scofield Reference Bible.* Conceived and produced by a man with an obscure and even disreputable past, the *Scofield Reference Bible* nevertheless became fundamentalism's best-selling reference tool. Its opponents railed against the presumption that would lead a man to add his words to pages that bore the written word of God. But the many readers of the *Scofield Reference Bible* found it an indispensable guide to the Bible and to the end times in which they believed themselves immersed.

Further Reading

Canfield, Joseph M. *The Incredible Scofield and His Book.* Vallecito, Calif.: Ross House, 1988.
Gaebelein, Frank E. *The Story of the Scofield Reference Bible, 1909–1959.* New York: Oxford University Press, 1959.
The Holy Bible: Containing the Old and New Testaments. Edited by C. I. Scofield. Lake Wylie, S.C.: Christian Heritage, 1995.
Sandeen, Ernest R. *The Roots of Fundamentalism: British and American Millenarianism 1800–1930.* Chicago: University of Chicago Press, 1970.
Trumbull, Charles G. *The Life Story of C.I. Scofield.* New York: Oxford University Press, 1920.
Weston, Charles G., and Emma Moore Weston. *Analyzing Scofield: The Life and Errors of C. I. Scofield.* Croton-on-Hudson, N.Y.: Morgan Brown, 1997.

Scott, Orange
(1800–1847) *Methodist minister, abolitionist*

Conflicts over his vehement opposition to slavery and to ecclesiastical authority ultimately drove Orange Scott out of the Methodist Episcopal Church. He subsequently participated in the formation of a new Methodist denomination, the Wesleyan Methodist Connexion. Scott was born on February 13, 1800, in Brookfield, Vermont, the son of Samuel Scott and Lucy Whitney Scott. During Scott's childhood, his father had to move the family repeatedly in search of work, and Scott himself obtained less than two years of formal education. In August 1820, Scott began to read the Bible and resolved, as he later described in his autobiography, "to seek God till I found him precious to my soul." The following month, he attended a series of revival meetings held in Barre, Vermont, where he was working at the time, and he experienced a religious conversion: "I was," he later described, "enabled to surrender all to God, take Christ without reserve, trust him with all my ransomed powers, and find peace in believing, and joy in the Holy Ghost!" Within a few months of this experience, Scott committed himself to the work of preaching.

He was admitted provisionally to the New England Annual Conference of the Methodist Episcopal Church as an itinerant minister in 1822 and permanently in 1824. He spent his early years tending to Methodist circuits in Vermont, Massachusetts, and New Hampshire. Scott married Amy Fletcher in 1926; with her he had five children before her death from tuberculosis in 1835. Also in 1926, he was ordained an elder.

In 1830 Scott received his ordination as a presiding elder—the ecclesiastical office in the Methodist Episcopal Church that is second in authority only to that of bishop—and was given responsibility over the Springfield District in Massachusetts. In addition to the work of preaching in revivals and district churches during this period, Scott began to wrestle with the issue of slavery. By 1834 he was an avowed abolitionist and began writing articles against slavery in *Zion's Herald*, a newspaper published for the New England Conference of the Methodist Episcopal Church. The following year, after the death of his first wife, Scott married Eliza Dearborn, with whom he had two children. That year he was also reappointed a presiding elder and assigned to the Providence District in Rhode Island.

The New England Conference, in support of his abolitionist views, made him a delegate to the 1836 Methodist Episcopal General Conference in Cincinnati, Ohio, where he vigorously pressed the abolitionist position. In response to the conflict over slavery at this conference, the bishops of the Methodist Episcopal Church released a statement suggesting that the only appropriate course was to refrain from further discussion of the subject. Scott, however, would not be muzzled. As a consequence, the presiding bishop for the next New England Conference refused to reappoint him a presiding elder. After spending a year ministering in Lowell, Massachusetts, Scott went to work for the American Anti-Slavery Society, establishing chapters of the organization across New England and earning the displeasure of his superiors within the Methodist Episcopal Church. He finally withdrew from the church in the fall of 1841.

Scott spent the following years pressing the cause of abolitionism and complaining about the kinds of abuses of ecclesiastical power that had driven him from the church. From early 1843 until his death, he published *The True Wesleyan*, a weekly newspaper that gave him a forum to express his views. That same year, Scott joined with others to lay the framework for the creation of a new Methodist denomination, which was formalized as the Wesleyan Methodist Connexion at a conference held in Utica, New York, the next year. When elected president of the conference, Scott declined the post; however, he agreed to serve as the book agent for the new denomination. He died soon afterward, on July 31, 1847, from illness prompted by overwork and excessive travel.

The national debate over slavery that eventually spilled onto the battlefields of the Civil War produced collateral battles among and often within various American religious traditions. The Methodist Episcopal Church was a case in point. Conflict over slavery led to Orange Scott's exodus from the church and to his help in the formation of a new Wesleyan denomination, the Wesleyan Methodist Connexion. It would subsequently produce even greater fractures, as Southern Methodists left the Methodist Episcopal Church in 1844 to form their own Methodist Episcopal Church, South.

Further Reading

"Library Reference Guide: Methodism, A Brief History," Boston University School of Theology. Available online. URL: http://www.bu.edu/sth/library/methodismhistory.html#WMC. Updated on October 18, 2001.

Matthews, Donald G. "Orange Scott the Methodist Evangelist as Revolutionary." In *The Antislavery Vanguard: New Essays on the Abolitionists*. Edited by Martin B. Duberman. Princeton, N.J.: Princeton University Press, 1965.

Scott, Orange. *The Grounds of Secession from the M.E. Church.* New York: Arno Press, 1969.

———. *The Life of Rev. Orange Scott: Compiled from His Personal Narrative, Correspondence, and Other Authentic Sources of Information.* Edited by Lucius C. Matlack. New York: C. Prindle and L.C. Matlack, 1847–48; Freeport, N.Y.: Books for Libraries Press, 1971.

Scott, Walter
(1796–1861) *Disciples of Christ minister, author, educator*

Walter Scott helped to steer the early course of the Disciples of Christ. A friend and spiritual ally of ALEXANDER CAMPBELL, he shared Campbell's unyielding concern for restoring the primitive patterns of New Testament Christianity. He was born on October 31, 1796, in Moffatt, County Dumfriesshire, Scotland, the son of John Scott and Mary Innes Scott, Scottish Presbyterians. In the second decade of the 19th century, Scott attended the University of Edinburgh; the actual dates of his attendance and whether he graduated remain unclear. In 1818, however, one of Scott's uncles suggested that his parents send him to America, and they accordingly dispatched Scott across the Atlantic.

Scott arrived in the summer of 1818 in New York, where, with his uncle's assistance, he found work teaching English, Greek, and Latin at the Union Academy of Jamaica, Long Island. The following year he relocated to Pittsburgh, Pennsylvania, where he met George Forrester, who ran an academy where Scott began teaching and also led a small congregation of believers interested in restoring the primitive beliefs and patterns of the church. After Forrester's accidental death by drowning in 1820, Scott assumed the leadership both of Forrester's academy and of his congregation.

In the early 1820s, Scott met Alexander Campbell, and the two men quickly discovered their common zeal for a restoration of primitive Christianity. After Campbell began publication in 1823 of a religious periodical—named the *Christian Baptist* at Scott's suggestion–Scott contributed articles to the early issues. The same year he married Sara Whitsett, with whom he had five children.

Scott moved with his family to Steubenville, Ohio, in 1826; there he ran an academy for a year. But Campbell's suggestion that Scott attend the annual meeting of the Mahoning Baptist Association that year proved to be a turning point in his life. In 1827, the association, now familiar with the young Scottish minister, elected him to serve as its full-time evangelist. For the next three years, Scott traveled widely on behalf of the association, preaching what he believed to be a restored gospel message, trimmed of reliance on creeds and fastened only to the Bible. In time, however, Campbell and other reform-minded members of the Mahoning Baptist Association believed that the idea of an association among churches had no scriptural warrant. Accordingly, the association voted in 1830 to abolish itself. From that time, Campbell, Scott, and their spiritual allies came to be known simply as "Disciples." Two years later, they allied themselves with a similar reformist group led by BARTON WARREN STONE.

In the following years, Scott lived first in Philadelphia, then in Cincinnati, and still later in Carthage, Ohio, while he toured the surrounding areas on evangelistic preaching missions. He published a periodical of his own, the *Christian Evangelist,* for all but three years from 1832 to 1844. He also turned to writing books of his own, publishing over the course of his life *A Discourse on the Holy Spirit* (1831), *The Gospel Restored* (1836), *To Themelion: The Union of Christians* (1852), *The Death of Christ* (1853), and *The Messiahship* (1859). Beginning in late 1836, he served briefly as the president of a Disciples institution, Bacon College, in Georgetown, Kentucky. During most of the period from 1827 to 1844, he centered his itinerant preaching and editorial activities in Carthage.

In 1844 he returned to Pittsburgh, where he started a new periodical, *The Protestant Unionist,* which he edited until 1847, and where he served as minister of two churches even as he continued sporadic revival preaching. In 1849, his first wife died; after her death he moved to May's Lick, Kentucky, where he became the minister of a church. In 1850 he married Nannie B. Allen, one of his church members, with whom he had a daughter. Two years later, he moved his new family to Covington, Kentucky, where he started a female academy, but after his second wife's death in 1854, he returned to May's Lick. He married Elza Sandridge in 1855. He died on April 23, 1861, in May's Lick.

Walter Scott tends to be overshadowed in the history of the Disciples of Christ by his more prominent friend, Alexander Campbell. But he brought indefatigable zeal to the work of spreading what he and Campbell called the "ancient gospel." If Campbell was the Luther of this 19th-century reformation, as Disciples were accustomed to think of it, then Scott was happy to think of himself as Melanchthon. A gifted speaker and talented writer, he did much to advance the cause of the early Disciples of Christ.

Further Reading

Baxter, William. *Life of Elder Walter Scott: With Sketches of His Fellow Laborers.* Cincinnati: Bosworth, Chase & Hall, 1874.

Gerrard, William A. *A Biographical Study of Walter Scott, American Frontier Evangelist.* Joplin, Mo.: College Press, 1992.

Neth, John Watson. *Walter Scott Speaks: A Handbook of Doctrine.* Milligan College, Tenn.: Emmanuel School of Religion, 1967.

Scott, Walter. *The Autobiography of Walter Scott: 1796–1861.* Edited by Roscoe M. Pierson. Lexington, Ky.: Bosworth Memorial Library, The College of the Bible, 1952.

Stevenson, Dwight Eshelman. *Walter Scott: Voice of the Golden Oracle, a Biography.* St. Louis: Christian Board of Publication, 1946.

Toulouse, Mark G., ed. *Walter Scott: A Nineteenth-Century Evangelical.* St. Louis: Mo.: Chalice Press, 1999.

Seabury, Samuel
(1729–1796) *Episcopal bishop*

Samuel Seabury was an Episcopal clergyman and a British Loyalist during the Revolutionary War period. Nevertheless, he became a leading force in the attempt to secure a bishop for the Episcopal Church after the war, and ultimately he was ordained its first American bishop in 1784. He was born on November 30, 1729, in Groton, Connecticut, to Samuel Seabury and Abigail Mumford Seabury. His father was a Congregationalist minister who became an Episcopal convert around the time of Samuel's birth and soon afterward was ordained an Episcopal priest and served as a colonial missionary for the English Society for the Propagation of the Gospel (SPG). The younger Samuel Seabury attended Yale College and graduated in 1748. He obtained an M.A. from Yale in 1751.

Because he was too young to be ordained a priest on his graduation from Yale, young Samuel served initially as a catechist under his father. Like many 18th-century clergy, Samuel Seabury hoped to combine careers as a clergyman and a physician, and to this end he studied both theology and medicine with his father while waiting to become old enough for ordination as a priest. In 1752, he traveled to Great Britain to study medicine at the University of Edinburgh, and the following year, he was ordained. He returned to America in 1754 and served as a missionary for the SPG at Christ Church in New Brunswick, New Jersey. In 1757, he became the rector of a church in New York City, and, a decade later, he assumed the position of rector of St. Peter's Church in Westchester, New York. During this later ministry, Seabury became involved in the movement by Episcopal clergy in New York to seek permission from the Church of England to install an American Episcopal bishop.

Like other priests of the Church of England, Seabury had taken an ordination vow that included a pledge of allegiance to the British throne, a pledge that he did not abandon when a revolutionary temper began to possess the American colonies. To support the Loyalist cause, Seabury penned several influential tracks that opposed the movement for independence under the name "A. W. Farmer." "[I]f I must be enslaved," he declared in one of these, "let it be by a KING at least, and not by a parcel of upstart lawless Committee-men. If I must be devoured, let me be devoured by the jaws of a lion, and not *gnawed* to death by rats and vermin!" So vigorous was Seabury's loyalism that he eventually had to take refuge behind British lines on Long Island.

After the Revolutionary War, the cause of obtaining an American Episcopal bishop seemed all the more pressing to Seabury and other Episcopal clergy. They first attempted to choose Jeremiah Leaming to seek this position, but he declined for reasons of age and health. Seabury's Episcopal colleagues then selected him to seek ordination from the Church of England as a bishop. When Seabury arrived in England in 1783, however, Anglican Church authorities declined to ordain him, chiefly because they did not feel free to waive the traditional ordination requirement of pledging fealty to the English Crown and because Seabury was no longer in a position to pledge such loyalty. Seabury turned instead to the bishops in Scotland, called the nonjuring bishops because they had refused to take the oath of allegiance to William and Mary after they had already sworn allegiance to King James II. On November 1784, Seabury was consecrated bishop of Connecticut. He returned to Connecticut the following year and served as America's first Episcopal bishop until he died on February 25, 1796, in New London, Connecticut.

The Revolutionary War presented obvious difficulties for American members of the Church of England, especially for clergy who had sworn allegiance to the English Crown as part of their ordination. The Episcopal Church in America survived its severance from England through accommodation to new political circumstances. Samuel Seabury's career as the first Episcopal bishop illustrates both the difficulties experienced by Episcopal ministers in the colonies and their resourcefulness in finding a path to sustain the life of their church in the newly created United States.

Further Reading

Beardsley, Eben Edwards. *Life and Correspondence of the Right Reverend Samuel Seabury, D.D., First Bishop of Connecticut, and of the Episcopal Church in the United States of America.* Boston: Houghton Mifflin, 1881.

Cameron, Kenneth Walter, ed. *Samuel Seabury, 1729–1796: His Election, Consecration, and Reception—The Documentary History.* Hartford, Conn.: Transcendental Books, 1978.

———, ed. *Samuel Seabury among His Contemporaries.* Hartford, Conn.: Transcendental Books, 1980.

Ferguson, Randall Lee. "The Anti-Revolutionary Rhetoric of Thomas Chandler, Myles Copper, Charles Inglis, and Samuel Seabury: An Analysis of Metaphor." Ph.D. dissertation, University of Minnesota, 1998.

Rowthorn, Anne W. *Samuel Seabury: A Bicentennial Biography.* New York: Seabury Press, 1983.

Steiner, Bruce E. *Samuel Seabury, 1729–1796: A Study in the High Church Tradition.* Athens: Ohio University Press, 1971.

Sheen, Fulton John
(Peter Fulton Sheen)
(1895–1979) Catholic priest, educator, radio and television personality

One of the 20th century's most prominent Catholic evangelists, Archbishop Fulton J. Sheen combined a rigorous intellect, schooled in philosophical study, with the gifts of a public speaker. He popularized Catholic teaching in the new electronic media of the century, first on radio and later television. He was born Peter Fulton Sheen on May 8, 1895, in El Paso, Illinois, the son of Newton Morris Sheen and Delia Fulton Sheen. In later years, he adopted Fulton as his first name and John, his confirmation name, as a middle name. He graduated from high school at the Spalding Institute in Peoria, Illinois, in 1913, and then received a B.A. and an M.A. from St. Viator's College and Seminary in Bourbonnais, Illinois. He was ordained a Catholic priest in 1919 and spent the next six years pursuing additional studies: He was awarded a Ph.D. from the University of Louvain in 1923 and studied afterward at the Sorbonne and the Collegio Angelico in Rome, where he received an S.T.D. in 1924.

At home again in the United States, Sheen followed a brief period of service in St. Patrick's parish in Peoria with an academic career, joining the faculty of the Catholic University of America in 1926. He remained there for the next 24 years, teaching philosophy and theology and producing a staggering number of books and articles. In 1925, he published the first of 60 books, *God and Intelligence in Modern Philosophy: A Critical Study in the Light of the Philosophy of Saint Thomas,* in which he declared that "[t]he wisdom of the ages and the epitome of our experience is given in the simple truth understood by the simple and forgotten by many a philosopher, that we are not 'God-makers but God-made.'" Sheen followed this initial work with dozens of others. Especially during the middle years of the 20th century, he became well known for books challenging communism and modern theories of psychology that undermined traditional teachings of the church. He viewed communism as both a threat to the Western world and a judgment on the West's spiritual vacuity. "[U]nless there is a moral revival in our Western world," he wrote in *Communism and the Conscience of the West* (1948), "*especially* a rebirth of family life, Communism may be the instrument for the liquidation of a bourgeois civilization that has forgotten God." In *Peace of Soul* (1949), he indicted modern psychology for offering false remedies for 20th-century anxiety, which, he said,

Fulton John Sheen used radio and television to popularize the Catholic faith in the 20th century. *(Library of Congress, Prints and Photographs Division, LC-USZ62-91049)*

cannot be cured by a surrender to passions and instincts; the basic cause of our anxiety is a restlessness within time, which comes because we are made for eternity. If there were anywhere on earth a resting place other than God, we may be very sure that the human soul in its long history would have found it before this.

Though Sheen's prolific pen might have led to renown as a writer, in fact, it was his speaking career that catapulted him to prominence. In 1930, he launched a series of radio broadcasts, the *Catholic Hour*, that attracted national recognition. Over the next 20 years, his preaching and radio appearances made him the nation's foremost Catholic apologist, and he was influential in the conversions of multitudes, including prominent figures such as Clare Boothe Luce and Henry Ford II. In the 1950s, Sheen migrated to television; from 1951 to 1957, he hosted the enormously popular program *Life Is Worth Living*, which eventually claimed an audience of more than 20 million and aired on 123 television stations. He followed this broadcast success with *The Bishop Sheen Program*, which aired from 1961 to 1968.

In 1950, Sheen left the faculty of Catholic University and became the national director for the Society for the Propagation of the Faith, for which he worked tirelessly on behalf of the cause of Catholic missions. The following year, he was consecrated titular bishop of Caesariana and made auxiliary bishop of the Archdiocese of New York, where he served under Cardinal FRANCIS JOSEPH SPELLMAN. He held both offices until 1966. In 1966, after a dispute with Cardinal Spellman, Sheen was reassigned as bishop of the Diocese of Rochester, New York. As a Catholic administrator, Sheen proved to be less adept than as a Catholic apologist, and his attempts to implement changes in his diocese after Vatican II became the subject of substantial controversy. He resigned in 1969 and was named titular archbishop of Newport, Wales. He retired in Manhattan, where he died on December 9, 1979 at the age of 84.

During the middle years of the 20th century, there was no more well-known Catholic priest in the United States than Fulton J. Sheen. He gave to his long service of the Catholic Church copious gifts of communication, through both the written and the spoken word. He also adapted quickly to radio and television technology and was without peer as a 20th-century Catholic apologist.

Further Reading

Conniff, James C.G. *The Bishop Sheen Story.* Greenwich, Conn.: Fawcett, 1953.

Lynch, Christopher Owen. *Selling Catholicism: Bishop Sheen and the Power of Television.* Lexington: University Press of Kentucky, 1998.

Murphy, Myles P. *The Life and Times of Archbishop Fulton J. Sheen.* New York: Alba House, 2000.

Noonan, D. P. *The Passion of Fulton Sheen.* New York: Dodd, Mead, 1972.

Sheen, Fulton J. *God Love You.* Garden City, N.Y.: Garden City Books, 1955.

———. *Peace of Soul.* New York: Whittlesey, 1949.

———. *The Quotable Fulton Sheen: A Topical Compilation of the Wit, Wisdom, and Satire of Archbishop Fulton J. Sheen.* Edited by George J. Martin, Richard P. Rabatin, and John L. Swan. New York: Doubleday, 1989.

———. *Treasure in Clay: The Autobiography of Fulton J. Sheen.* Garden City, N.Y.: Doubleday, 1980; San Francisco: Ignatius Press, 1993.

Shabazz, Malik el-   See MALCOLM X.

Sheldon, Charles Monroe
(1857–1946) *Congregationalist minister, author*

A Congregationalist pastor and passionate social reformer, Charles Monroe Sheldon penned *In His Steps,* one of the 20th century's most popular inspirational classics. The novel depicts the social consequences when a group of Christians attempt to imagine how Jesus would respond to the various social issues of their day. Charles Sheldon was born on February 26, 1857, in Wellsville, New York, the son of Stewart Sheldon and Sarah Ward Sheldon. His father was a Congregationalist pastor who served in pulpits in New York, Missouri, Rhode Island, and Michigan before becoming a superintendent of home missions in the Dakota Territory.

There the family took up residence on a 160-acre farm. They attended the First Congregationalist Church of Yankton, where Charles's uncle was a pastor and where, in his late teens, Charles experienced conversion. In 1877, he enrolled in Phillips Academy in Andover, Massachusetts, working part-time as a janitor to make ends meet. After two years, he matriculated at Brown University in Providence, Rhode Island. He received a B.A. in 1883 and a B.D. from Andover Theological Seminary in 1886; in that year he was also ordained a Congregationalist minister. After a brief tenure as pastor of a church in Waterbury, Vermont, in 1888, Sheldon accepted a call to the Central Congregational Church in Topeka, Kansas, where he would remain for the rest of his pastoral ministry. Three years later he married Mary Abby Merriam, with whom he had one child, a son named Merriam.

The year after Sheldon arrived in Topeka, his church moved to a new building, and he seized the occasion to announce what would become his guiding principles. He would preach, he declared:

> a Christ for the common people. A Christ who belongs to the rich and poor, the ignorant and learned, the old and young, the good and the bad. A Christ who knows no sect or age, whose religion does not consist alone in cushioned seats, and comfortable surroundings, or culture, or fine singing or respectable orders of Sunday services, but a Christ who bids us all recognize the Brotherhood of the race, who bids us throw open this room to all.

To preach a Christ "for the common people," Sheldon insisted on discovering the needs of the common people, and to this end he devoted weeks to living among various social groups, including African Americans in nearby Tennesseetown, a black ghetto near Sheldon's church. The experiences of these weeks became the subjects of articles and stories he published, but, more significantly, they also became the impetus for social reform work. Responding to his concerns for the education of children, Sheldon's church established a kindergarten and a small library for the black community in Tennesseetown. Sheldon also organized professionals to provide a variety of social services to Tennesseetown.

Charles Sheldon associated himself with the Social Gospel movement, which began to flourish about the time he arrived in Topeka and emphasized the necessity of Christian commitment to social reform. He wrote regularly for the movement's chief periodical, *The Kingdom.* He also cast himself into one after another social reform project, believing that the gospel required no less.

In 1897, Sheldon published *In His Steps,* which described a fictional town where a midwestern pastor challenged his congregation to live their lives in answer to a simple question, "What would Jesus do?" One by one, the congregation attempted this spiritual exercise, to find that it had vast social consequences. Sheldon wrote the book in installments that he read to his congregation on Sunday evenings, a practice begun in 1891 and continuing until he left the church in 1919. The book, when published, sold millions of copies, many of them in unauthorized editions made possible by a flaw in Sheldon's copyright.

In 1919, illness forced Sheldon to resign as pastor of the Central Congregational Church. He became editor in chief of the *Christian Herald* for five years and then continued as a contributing editor from 1926 until 1946. Before death finally forced him to lay aside his pen, he had written more than 50 books and hundreds of articles. He died on February 24, 1946, in Topeka, at the age of 88.

More than a century after Charles Sheldon wrote *In His Steps,* his book remains perennially in print. Though Sheldon possessed no intellectual brilliance, he was a master of providing popular dress for abstract theological principles and of applying those principles to meet social needs of his day. His simple book continues to resonate among readers who find in the Christian gospel not simply a statement of theological truth but a mandate for action within their own social and cultural contexts.

Further Reading

Boyer, Paul. "*In His Steps:* A Re-Appraisal." *American Quarterly* 23 (Spring 1971): 60–78.
Ferrée, John P. *A Social Gospel for Millions: The Religious Bestsellers of Charles Sheldon, Charles Gordon, and Harold Bell Wright.* Bowling Green, Ohio: Bowling Green University Popular Press, 1988.
Miller, Timothy. *Following in His Steps: A Biography of Charles M. Sheldon.* Knoxville: University of Tennessee Press, 1987.
Sheldon, Charles Monroe. *In His Steps.* Philadelphia: H. Altemus, 1899; Nashville: Thomas Nelson Publishers, 1999.

Silver, Abba Hillel
(Abraham Silver)
(1893–1963) *Reform rabbi, Zionist leader*

One of the 20th century's most prominent American Zionists, Abba Hillel Silver labored energetically for the creation of a Jewish state in Palestine. He was equally dedicated to the preservation of Jewish religious faith in the face of attempts by secular Jews to dismiss its importance. He was born Abraham Silver on January 28, 1893, in Newstadt-Schirwindt, Lithuania, the son of Moses Silver and Dina Seaman Silver. His father was a rabbi—the son and grandson of rabbis, as well—who immigrated to the United States in 1898. By 1902, the rest of the family, including Abe Silver, had joined Moses Silver in America.

Abe Silver attended public school in the morning and yeshiva in the afternoon. When he was 11 years old, he helped organize the Dr. Herzl Zion Club, named after the founder of the modern Zionist movement, Theodore Herzl, who had died two years before the club was organized. After Silver's bar mitzvah in 1906, he became the club's president. A year later he represented the club at the 10th Annual Convention of the Federation of American Zionists, addressing the convention although he was only 14 years old. After graduation from high school in 1911, Silver pursued a joint course of studies at the University of Cincinnati and the nearby Hebrew Union College, the chief educational institution of Reform Judaism. Though Silver's theological inclinations were largely in harmony with the Reform views of Hebrew Union College, his Zionist loyalties were distinctly out of place. The Pittsburgh Platform of 1885, Reform Judaism's statement of theological principles, had declared the anti-Zionist view that still animated Reform Judaism in the early 20th century: "We consider ourselves no longer a nation but a religious community and therefore expect neither a return to Palestine nor a sacrificial worship under the administration of the sons of Aaron nor the restoration of any of the laws concerning the Jewish state." Silver refused to surrender his Zionism, but he nevertheless prospered at Hebrew Union College and graduated first in his class in 1915. That same year he undertook his first rabbinate at Congregation Leshem Shomayim in Wheeling, West Virginia. Two years later he assumed leadership of the more prominent Reform congregation Tifereth Israel in Cleveland, Ohio. He remained associated with this congregation for the remainder of his life, although involvement in the Zionism movement increasingly consumed his energies over the following years. In 1923 he married Virginia Horkheimer, with whom he had two sons.

In subsequent years, as the threat of nazism loomed and war eventually engulfed the world, Silver began to represent a militant form of Zionism. The Holocaust, especially, radicalized him and made him impatient with the more diplomatic efforts of moderates, such as STEPHEN S. WISE, to establish a Jewish state in Palestine. Wise was prepared to be patient with President Franklin D. Roosevelt's focus on domestic economic concerns during the 1930s and with the war effort in the 1940s, rather than on the interests of Zionists. Silver, on the other hand, relentlessly prodded American and British officials first to permit more substantial Jewish immigration to Palestine and later to recognize an independent Jewish state there. By late summer 1943, Silver had been named cochair with Wise of the American Zionist Emergency Council. In the years that followed, Silver used his influence to press aggressively the cause of Zionism. The culmination of his and other Zionists' efforts was the recognition of Israel as an independent state by the administration of President Harry Truman in 1948.

Soon after this recognition, Silver retreated from active political engagement. He contented himself chiefly with leadership of his Cleveland congregation. More aggressive strains of secularism among the Jewish community attracted his attention after World War II. In an address before the 40th Biennial of the Union of American Hebrew Congregations in Boston during mid-November 1948, he asserted the primacy of religion:

> To the thoughtful Jews it is becoming increasingly clear that there are no substitutes in Jewish life for religion. Neither philanthropy nor culture nor nationalism is adequate for the stress and challenge of our lives. All these interests can and must find their rightful place within the general pattern of Judaism. But the pattern must be of Judaism, the Judaism of the priest, the prophet, the saint, the mystic and the rabbi; the Judaism which speaks of God, and the worship of God, and the commandments of God, and the quest for God.

Silver died on November 28, 1963, in Cleveland, Ohio.

Abba Hillel Silver, one of the leading orators of the 20th century, helped to give Jewish Americans a greater voice within the American political process. His relentless advocacy of Zionism assisted not only in the creation of an independent Jewish state, but in the enhancement of the public space occupied by Jews in America. He also helped to harness the energies of Reform Judaism to the cause of 20th-century Zionism, in an alliance that proved to be crucial for the eventual birth of Israel in 1948.

Further Reading

Abba Hillel Silver and American Zionism. Edited by Mark A. Raider, Jonathan D. Sarna, and Ronald W. Zweig. London: Frank Cass, 1997.

Raphael, Marc Lee. *Abba Hillel Silver: A Profile in American Judaism.* New York: Holmes & Meier, 1989.

Silver, Abba Hillel. *Moses and the Original Torah.* New York: Macmillan, 1961.

———. *Religion in a Changing World.* New York: R. R. Smith, 1930.

———. *Therefore Choose Life; Selected Sermons, Addresses, and Writings of Abba Hillel Silver.* Edited by Herbert Weiner. Cleveland: World, 1967.

———. *Vision and Victory: A Collection of Addresses, 1942–1948.* New York: Zionist Organization of America, 1949.

———. *Where Judaism Differed: An Inquiry into the Distinctiveness of Judaism.* New York: Macmillan, 1956.

Smith, Hannah Whitall

(1832–1911) *Holiness preacher, author*

Hannah Whitall Smith wrote one of the classics of Christian devotional literature, *The Christian's Secret of a Happy Life* (1875). Together with her husband, Robert Pearsall Smith, she lectured widely in both the United States and Great Britain as part of the Higher Life movement. She was born on February 7, 1832, in Philadelphia, Pennsylvania, the daughter of John Mickle Whitall and Mary Tatum Whitall. Her parents were prosperous and prominent Quakers, who saw that their daughter received an education at a Quaker school in Philadelphia. In the summer of 1851, the 19-year-old Hannah Whitall married Robert Pearsall Smith, with whom she had seven children, four of whom survived to adulthood. One of her daughters, Alys Pearsall Smith, eventually became the first wife of the famous British philosopher Bertrand Russell.

Both Smith and her husband were Quakers, but both had conversion experiences during a revival meeting in 1858. In the late 1860s, both also had the experience of "entire sanctification" or "second blessing" characteristic of Holiness groups. The following decade, Robert and Hannah Smith became popular lay evangelists at Holiness conferences and meetings on both sides of the Atlantic. In Great Britain and the European continent from 1873 to 1875, the couple became prominent at gatherings devoted to seeking a "higher life." These events culminated in the Brighton Conference for the Promotion of Holiness in the spring of 1875, predecessor of the subsequent Keswick movement, whose first meeting occurred in the summer of 1875. This movement shared the emphasis on personal sanctification of the Holiness groups but spilled beyond the traditional Wesleyan congregations that made up the Holiness groups into a variety of other Christian denominations.

In 1875 Hannah Whitall Smith produced one of the most important devotional works of the Higher Life movement, *The Christian's Secret of a Happy Life,* in which she explained the possibilities for Christian sanctification.

The maturity of Christian experience cannot be reached in a moment, but is the result of the work of God's Holy Spirit, who, by His energizing and transforming power, causes us to grow up into Christ in all things. . . . But the sanctification the Scriptures urge as a present experience upon all believers does not consist in maturity of growth, but in purity of heart, and this may be as complete in the babe in Christ as in the veteran believer. . . . All that we claim then in this life of sanctification is, that by a step of faith we put ourselves into the hands of the Lord, for Him to work in us all the good pleasure of His will; and that by a continuous exercise of faith we keep ourselves there. This is our part in the matter. And when we do it, and while we do it, we are, in the Scripture sense, truly pleasing to God, although it may require years of training and discipline to mature us into a vessel that shall be in all respects to His honor, and fitted to every good work.

Although Robert and Hannah Smith were the most prominent speakers at the Brighton Conference, soon afterward they returned to the United States under a cloud for alleged doctrinal and moral indiscretions by Robert. This scandal aborted their continued active participation in the Higher Life movement. Hannah Whitall Smith, though, redirected her energies to the temperance movement and became active in both American and British expressions of this social reform movement. The Smiths moved to England in 1887. Hannah Smith died on May 1, 1911, at Iffly Place, near Oxford.

The Holiness movement had its impetus from 19th-century Methodist groups who rediscovered John Wesley's idea of Christian perfectionism. But longing for more tangible holiness in the personal lives of believers eventually spilled over into other denominations, and the broader spiritual impulse as expressed during the late 19th century became known as the Higher Life movement. Hannah Whitall Smith and her husband, Robert Smith, were, for a brief period of years leading up to 1875, two of the most important lay leaders within this movement. Although their active ministry within the Higher Life movement declined abruptly after 1875, Hannah Whitall Smith's devotional classic, *The Christian's Secret of a Happy Life,* proved to be an enduring monument to the influence of Christian perfectionism as well a spiritual guide to subsequent Christians seeking a more holy life.

Further Reading

Allen, Kerri. "Representation and Self-representation: Hannah Whitall Smith as Family Woman and Religious Guide." *Women's History Review* 7 (1998): 227–39.

Dieter, Melvin Easterday. *The Holiness Revival of the Nineteenth Century.* 2d ed. Lanham, Md.: Scarecrow Press, 1996.

Henry, Marie. *The Secret Life of Hannah Whitall Smith.* Grand Rapids, Mich.: Chosen Books, 1984.

Meneghel-McDonald, Meg Ann. "Becoming a 'Heretic': Hannah Whitall Smith, Quakerism, and the Nineteenth-Century Holiness Movement." Ph.D. dissertation, Indiana University, 2000.

Smith, Hannah Whitall. *The Christian's Secret of a Happy Life.* Chicago: F. H. Revell, 1883; Nashville: T. Nelson Publishers, 1999.

———. *The Christian's Secret of a Holy Life: The Unpublished Personal Writings of Hannah Whitall Smith.* Edited by Melvin E. Dieter. Grand Rapids, Mich.: Zondervan, 1994.

———. *Philadelphia Quaker: The Letters of Hannah Whitall Smith.* Edited by Logan Pearsall Smith. New York: Harcourt, Brace, 1950.

———. *The Unselfishness of God and How I Discovered It: A Spiritual Autobiography.* New York: Fleming H. Revell, 1903; New York: Garland, 1985.

Strachey, Barbara. *Remarkable Relations: The Story of the Pearsall Smith Family.* London: Gollancz, 1980.

Joseph Smith, Jr., founded the Church of Jesus Christ of Latter-day Saints. *(Library of Congress, Prints and Photographs Division LC-USZ62-90309)*

Smith, Joseph, Jr.

(1805–1844) *founder of the Church of Jesus Christ of Latter-day Saints*

By the time of his death at the age of 38, Joseph Smith, Jr., had founded a growing religious movement that still thrives more than a century and a half later. The Church of Jesus Christ of Latter-day Saints, commonly referred to as the Mormon Church, recognizes Smith as its architect and prophet. Smith was born in Sharon, Vermont, the son of Joseph Smith, Sr., and Lucy Mack Smith, poor farmers. After repeated relocations, his family settled near Palmyra, New York, in 1816. By Smith's account, when he was 14 years old he asked God to tell him which church to join. As a consequence of this prayer, two beings appeared to him, calling themselves the Father and the Son, and informed him that he should not join any church, because they were all infected with error.

Several years later, in the fall of 1823, Smith claimed to have a new vision, this time of an angel named Moroni. The angel told Smith where to find golden plates buried in a nearby hill. These were inscribed with an ancient language and accompanied by two stones, the Urim and the Thummim, which would assist in the translation of the plates. Four years later, Smith retrieved the plates and began the work of translating them. By this time he had married Emma Hale, with whom he had nine children, the last of whom was born several months after Smith's death. The couple also adopted two children. In work of translation Smith dictated the contents of the plates alternately to his wife, to a local farmer named Martin

Harris, and to a schoolteacher named Oliver Cowdery. None of these scribes was permitted to see the plates, although in 1829 some of Smith's followers claimed that they were visited by the angel Moroni and shown them. In 1830, Smith published the translation he had produced as the *Book of Mormon,* which recounted the history of an ancient America where Christ had appeared after his crucifixion. That same year he organized the Church of Jesus Christ, later renamed the Church of Jesus Christ of Latter-day Saints.

Smith claimed to receive a continued stream of revelations, the most important of which were published in *Doctrine and Covenants* in 1835. One of these early revelations prompted Smith to dispatch a band of missionaries to the western frontier. There, they won a number of converts, including the former Campbellite minister SIDNEY RIGDON, who traveled to New York in 1831 and persuaded Smith to relocate the infant church's headquarters to Kirtland, Ohio, where Rigdon had an influential following.

Smith agreed to this proposal and moved to Kirtland, though for a time he hoped to build a new Jerusalem near Independence, in Jackson County, Missouri. In 1833, however, Jackson County residents expelled the Mormons who had settled there, and Smith redirected his focus to Kirtland. There, in 1836, he completed construction of a temple for the church. Soon afterward, however, a bank that he had founded in Kirtland failed and prompted Smith and his followers to leave the area in the face of widespread criticism and potential mob violence.

Joseph Smith and other Mormons settled next in Far West, Missouri. This destination proved to be no haven, however. Violence erupted between Mormons and their opponents in mid-1838. By the fall, Missouri's governor, Lilburn Boggs, ordered the Mormons to leave the state or suffer extermination. Smith and other Mormon leaders were arrested for treason, murder, and other crimes, and they were jailed for five months until they were finally allowed to leave the state.

By the end of 1839, Smith had established a new community, named Nauvoo, located 60 miles north of Quincy, Illinois, on the Mississippi River. There, in 1841, Smith added to the controversy

that would ultimately surround the Mormon Church by announcing the doctrine of plural marriage to his inner circle of followers and encouraging them to join him in the practice of polygamy. The success of Mormon missionaries in winning converts for the church inspired Smith to declare his candidacy for president of the United States in 1844, with Sidney Rigdon as his vice-presidential running mate.

Smith's campaign for president suffered its first turbulence when a local group, who had splintered from the Mormon Church and started their own congregation, published the newspaper *Nauvoo Expositor.* The paper catalogued the errors of the Mormon Church and promptly earned the unfavorable attention of Nauvoo's mayor, Joseph Smith, who declared the paper a public nuisance and ordered it shut down. For this action, Smith was arrested and confined to a jail in Carthage, Illinois. While in jail, however, he and his brother Hyrum were attacked and killed by a mob on June 27, 1844.

Joseph Smith founded one of the most controversial new religious movements of the 19th century. In spite of—or perhaps at least partially because of—the opposition that it engendered, the Church of Jesus Christ of Latter-day Saints expanded rapidly once relocated west. Violence accompanied its early years, finally creating of Joseph Smith a martyr for the faith that has continued to flourish into the 21st century.

Further Reading

Brodie, Fawn. *No Man Knows My History: The Life of Joseph Smith, the Mormon Prophet.* 2d ed. New York: Knopf, 1971.
Bushman, Richard L. *Joseph Smith and the Beginnings of Mormonism.* Urbana: University of Illinois Press, 1984.
Hill, Donna. *Joseph Smith: The First Mormon.* Garden City, N.Y.: Doubleday, 1977.
Persuitte, David. *Joseph Smith and the Origins of the Book of Mormon.* Jefferson, N.C.: McFarland, 1985.
Smith, Joseph. *The Papers of Joseph Smith.* Edited by Dean C. Jessee. 2 vols. Salt Lake City, Utah: Deseret Book Company, 1989–92.
———. *The Personal Writings of Joseph Smith.* Edited by Dean C. Jessee. Salt Lake City, Utah: Deseret Book, 1984.

Smith, Joseph, III
(1832–1914) *president of the Reorganized Church of Jesus Christ of Latter Day Saints*

Joseph Smith III presided over the Reorganized Church of Jesus Christ of Latter Day Saints (formally renamed *Community of Christ* in the spring of 2001) for more than a half century. This prominent splinter movement from the main body of the Mormon Church—which his father had founded—rejected the more controversial aspects of early Mormonism, especially the practice of polygamy. Smith was born on November 6, 1832, in Kirkland, Ohio, the son of JOSEPH SMITH, JR., and Emma Hale Smith. His father was the founder of the Church of Jesus Christ of Latter-day Saints, commonly referred to as the Mormon Church. Joseph Smith III followed the early migrations of his father, who sought repeatedly to find a location where the Mormons might establish their religious community. Smith lived for a time with his parents in Far West, Missouri, until armed conflict between Mormons and other state residents prompted the governor of Missouri to order the Mormons to leave the state or face extinction. After this expulsion in 1839, the Mormons made their way to a location that they named Nauvoo, along the Mississippi River in Illinois. It was there that Joseph Smith, Jr., was arrested for inciting the destruction of a local newspaper and, while jailed in the county seat, Carthage, Illinois, was killed by a mob on June 27, 1844.

After the death of Joseph Smith, Jr., the Mormons wrestled with the issue of who would succeed him. Some Mormons believed that their founder had determined that his son, Joseph Smith III, 12 years old at the time of his father's death, should assume his father's place of leadership. The larger proportion of Mormons, however, accepted BRIGHAM YOUNG as the new president of the Church of Jesus Christ of Latter-day Saints and eventually followed him in a migration to Utah. When in 1852 Brigham Young publicly endorsed the practice of polygamy—which he and other Mormon leaders had practiced secretly for a decade—those disaffected with Young's leadership had even more pressing justification to establish a "reorganized" Mormon Church. Joseph Smith III at first refused to assume the leadership of this splinter faction within Mormonism. Nevertheless, when the Reorganized Church of Jesus Christ of Latter Day Saints (RLDS) was formally organized on April 6, 1860, at Amboy, Illinois, Smith agreed to become its president. He occupied this position until his death, more than 50 years later. In 1856, several years before he assumed this position, Smith had married Emmeline Griswold, with whom he had five children. After his first wife's death in 1869, he married Bertha Madison the same year, and the couple had nine children. Bertha Madison Smith died in 1896 in a carriage accident, and Smith married Ada Rachel Clark, with whom he had three sons.

Under Smith's leadership, the RLDS proceeded down theological paths less estranged from traditional Christian teachings than those traveled by the Mormon Church. Geography may have affected the church's doctrinal development in this regard. The main body of Mormons, led by Brigham Young to the geographically isolated Utah Territory, had gained a space to develop a distinctive spiritual vision, sharply at odds with the more traditional expression of American religion. The Utah Mormons discovered, of course, that they were not as isolated as they might have hoped, and in the second half of the 19th century they clashed with the federal government. The RLDS, however, never had the protective benefits of isolation, since the reorganized Mormon Church lived its infancy and adolescence in the American heartland. In any event, the RLDS steadfastly rejected such Mormon practices as polygamy, baptisms of the dead, and other temple ceremonies.

Joseph Smith III labored to wrest the Church of Jesus Christ of Latter-day Saints away from the spiritual byways down which Brigham Young was directing it. He sent missionaries to Utah to distribute countless tracts and other printed materials that sought to disclose the church's deviation from the plan of its founder, Joseph Smith, Jr. Nevertheless, these efforts proved almost completely unsuccessful. Smith had to content himself with oversight of the slow and steady growth of his own new denomination, since he never enjoyed any significant defections from the Mormon Church. He died on December 10, 1914, in Independence, Missouri, where he made his home.

Joseph Smith III was not yet a teenager when his father died at the hands of an Illinois mob. The violent death of its founder left the Mormon Church in perilous circumstances, which made it unlikely that its leadership would pass to a 12-year-old boy either directly or through some form of ecclesiastical guardianship. In fact, Brigham Young won control of the Mormon Church and transplanted it to the Utah Territory. Although Joseph Smith III attempted to assume the mantle of his father when he came of age, time and circumstances had already carried the Mormon Church down trails that Brigham Young had blazed. Smith had to content himself with the spiritual superintendence of a small fraction of his father's original followers. The Reorganized Church of Jesus Christ of Latter Day Saints, which he had helped organize and shepherd through its first half century, survived into the 21st century.

Further Reading

Launius, Roger D. *Father Figure: Joseph Smith III and the Creation of the Reorganized Church.* Independence, Mo.: Herald, 1990.

———. *Joseph Smith III: Pragmatic Prophet.* Urbana: University of Illinois Press, 1988.

Smith, Joseph, III. *Joseph Smith III and the Restoration.* Edited by Mary Audentia Smith Anderson. Independence, Mo.: Herald House, 1952.

———. *The Memoirs of Joseph Smith III (1832–1914): The Second Prophet of the Church.* Edited by Mary Audentia Smith Anderson. Independence, Mo.: Price, 2001.

Smohalla
(Wak-wei, Kuk-kia)
(ca. 1815–1895) *Native American prophet, founder of the Dreamer Religion*

Credited with revitalizing the Washani Religion and developing it into the Dreamer Religion, Smohalla was a prophet among the Pacific Northwest Indians. He began his career as a shaman and later established himself as a prophet. He was born Wak-wei or Kuk-kia, meaning "arising from the dust of the Earth Mother," between 1815 and 1820, around the area of current-day Walla Walla, Washington. He was a Shahaptian speaker of the Wanapam tribe. After he became a shaman, he was known by a variety of new names, the most commonly used of which was Smohalla, meaning either "dreamer" or "preacher." Smohalla's years as a medicine man suffered significant disappointment when he failed to prevent the illness-related death of his adolescent daughter. This and similar episodes may have prompted him to redirect his attention to the idea of a resurrection, which became central to his later thought.

A crucial turning point in Smohalla's career as a shaman occurred in the late 1850s, as a result of a fight with Chief Moses of the Sinkiuse tribe in which he was left for dead. According to the traditional account, Smohalla managed to escape to Mexico and eventually returned to Washington via Utah, where he had contact with Mormons. Although the story of Smohalla's battle with Moses and his subsequent southern journey may be apocryphal, Smohalla emerged from this period proclaiming a revitalized Washani Religion (Washani means "dancers"), which became known as the Dreamer Religion. He settled with his followers at P'na Village in the Columbia River valley, in present-day Yakima County, Washington.

Smohalla preached that in a future millennial period, Native Americans would be resurrected and restored to their land, which had been cleansed by God of whites. In the interim, he insisted that Native Americans refrain from unnatural practices such as farming. Captain J. W. MacMurray, who visited Smohalla in the summer of 1884, recorded the prophet's answer to suggestions that he and his people undertake such practices.

> You ask me to plough the ground! Shall I take a knife and tear my mother's bosom? Then when I die she will not take me to her bosom to rest.
>
> You ask me to dig for stone! Shall I dig under her skin for her bones! Then when I die I can not enter her body to be born again.
>
> You ask me to cut grass and make hay and sell it, and be rich like white men, but how dare I cut off my mother's hair?

The ceremonial rites of the Dreamer Religion practiced by Smohalla included the Waashat Dance, as well as the use of bells, which Smohalla claimed would be rung at the world's end and would be heard only by those who were pure. Though the federal government's agents worked hard to consign Smohalla and his followers to a reservation, the Wanapam prophet managed to frustrate these efforts and to pursue his revitalized Washani religious vision until the end of his long life. Smohalla died in 1895 on a visit to the Yakima Reservation in Washington.

Even before Smohalla's death, many of his followers had abandoned the prophet's religious vision and had relocated to reservations. More would do so in the years after his death. But for a time in the second half of the 19th century, Smohalla's prophetic ministry among the Wanapam inspired a temporary resistance to the encroachment of white civilization. Through the ritual of the Waashat Dance, the prophecy of a coming millennial age, and an emphasis on a "natural" pattern of life, Smohalla offered his followers a religious and cultural vision that briefly frustrated the inevitable march of white settlement in the Pacific Northwest and the attempt to confine Native Americans to reservations.

Further Reading

Huggins, Eli. "Smohalla, the Prophet of Priest Rapids." *Overland Monthly* 5 (February, 1891): 208–15.

Hunn, Eugene S. *Nch'i-wána, "The Big River": Mid-Columbia Indians and Their Land.* Seattle: University of Washington Press, 1990.

Relander, Click. *Drummers and Dreamers: The Story of Smohala the Prophet and His Nephew Puck Hyah Toot, the Last Prophet of the Nearly Extinct River People, the Last Wanapums.* Caldwell, Idaho: Caxton Printers, 1956.

Ruby, Robert H., and John A. Brown. *Dreamer-Prophets of the Columbia Plateau: Smohalla and Skolaskin.* Norman: University of Oklahoma Press, 1989.

Walker, Paul Robert. "Smohalla." In *Spiritual Leaders.* New York: Facts On File, 1994.

Spalding, Martin John
(1810–1872) *Catholic archbishop*

A leading Catholic prelate of 19th-century America, Martin John Spalding combined enormous in-

tellectual and administrative gifts to become a dominant force within the Catholic Church in the United States. He added to this leadership a prominent role in Vatican I, the ecumenical counsel most notable for its declaration of the doctrine of papal infallibility. Spalding was born on May 23, 1810, in Washington County (later renamed Marion County), Kentucky, the son of Richard Spalding and Henrietta Hamilton Spalding. He was educated at St. Mary's College in his home county. Afterward he prepared for the Catholic priesthood by studying at St. Joseph's Seminary in Bardstown, Kentucky. After his graduation from St. Joseph with a bachelor of divinity degree in 1830, Spalding traveled to Rome, where he received an S.T.D. from the Urban College of Propaganda and was ordained a priest in 1834.

Spalding spent the early years of his ministry as a parish priest in Bardstown and in Lexington, Kentucky, and as president from 1838 to 1840 of St. Joseph's College in Bardstown. By 1844, he had been appointed vicar general of the Louisville diocese. Four years later he became coadjutor bishop of Louisville and, after the death of Benedict Joseph Flaget at the beginning of 1850, the second bishop of Louisville. In this ecclesiastical position, Spalding demonstrated the energy and administrative talent, as well as the scholarly ability, that characterized his remaining years. A stream of books poured from his pen from the mid-1840s through 1860, including works such as *General Evidences of Catholicity* (1847) and his two-volume *History of the Protestant Reformation* (1860), which proved him to be one of the foremost Catholic apologists of his generation, second only to ORESTES AUGUSTUS BROWNSON. In the late 1850s he made a European tour to attract religious workers to staff the steadily increasing institutional resources of his diocese and, along the way, was influential in establishing the American College of Louvain in Belgium.

In 1864, Spalding became the seventh archbishop of Baltimore. At the Second Plenary Council of Baltimore held two years later, he had the opportunity to demonstrate the leadership abilities that had taken him to the Baltimore archdiocese. Previous archbishops had tended to address various ecclesiastical concerns in a patchwork fashion, but

Spalding supervised the adoption of more than 500 decrees that amounted to a comprehensive guide for a wide range of issues. He was not successful in achieving all his goals, such as the adoption of a uniform catechism, but many of these would find expression in the Third Plenary Council of 1884, held 14 years after Spalding's death. He did succeed in protecting the fragile beginnings of the American labor movement, which would promote the interests of many immigrant Catholics, by seeing that labor organizations were exempted from the general condemnation levied against secret societies in the Plenary Council of 1866.

Toward the end of his life, Archbishop Spalding demonstrated that his influence as a Catholic prelate extended beyond the borders of his own country. At the First Vatican Council, which met in Rome from December 1869 until September 1870, Spalding played a significant role in the deliberations that eventually yielded the declaration concerning papal infallibility. Although Spalding initially supported an implicit rather than an explicit statement of papal infallibility, achieved through the condemnation of views that denied this infallibility, he eventually sided with those who pressed for, and ultimately obtained, an explicit recognition of infallibility. This labor proved to be one of his last. Illness began to plague him soon after his return to the United States. He suffered from attacks of gastritis and eventually contracted bronchitis, of which he died in Baltimore on February 7, 1872.

Martin John Spalding served the Catholic Church in America at a time when its numbers were being swelled by an influx of European immigrants. Though Spalding's Catholic heritage stretched much further back in American history, he emphatically sided with the needs and concerns of mid-19th-century Catholic immigrants to the United States. He sought to defend Catholics from the attacks of the Know-Nothing Party, which waged a campaign of fear against Catholic immigrants, even as he sought to expand the institutional resources of the Louisville diocese and later the Baltimore archdiocese to respond to the needs of these immigrants. But his more enduring historical place arises from his skill in directing the larger course of American Catholic affairs. His energetic

leadership earned him recognition as the unofficial primate of the American Catholic Church during the 1860s and early 1870s.

Further Reading

"Archbishop Martin Spalding." From Richard H. Clarke's Three-volume *History of the Church in the United States* (1888). Available online. URL: http://www.archbalt.org/history/spalding.htm. Downloaded on October 24, 2001.

Micek, Adam Andrew. *The Apologetics of Martin John Spalding.* Washington D.C.: Catholic University of America Press, 1951.

Spalding, M. J. *Miscellanea: Comprising Reviews, Lectures, and Essays, on Historical, Theological, and Miscellaneous Subjects.* Louisville, Ky.: Webb, Gill & Levering, 1855.

———. *Sketches of the Early Catholic Missions of Kentucky: From Their Commencement in 1787 to the Jubilee of 1826–7.* New York: Arno Press, 1972.

Spalding, Thomas W. *Martin John Spalding: American Churchman.* Washington, D.C.: Catholic University of America Press, 1973.

———. *The Premier See: A History of the Archdiocese of Baltimore, 1789–1989.* Baltimore: Johns Hopkins University Press, 1989.

Spellman, Francis Joseph
(1889–1967) *Catholic cardinal*

One of the most prominent American Catholics of the 20th century, Francis Joseph Spellman enjoyed access to a president and friendship with a pope. His contacts within the Roman curia and the relationships he cultivated with American leaders allowed him to play an important part in securing broader acceptance for Catholics in American society. Spellman was born on May 4, 1889, in Whitman, Massachusetts, the son of William Spellman and Ellen Conway Spellman. After attending public schools in Whitman, Spellman earned his undergraduate degree from New York's Fordham College in 1911. Thereafter, in preparation for a vocation as a priest, he traveled to Rome, where he studied at the North American College. He graduated with a doctorate in theology in 1916 and was ordained a priest the same year. Spellman's time in Rome played a decisive role in his future career, for it allowed him to make contacts with men who would subsequently be in positions to aid his advancement within the American Catholic hierarchy. The most important of these was Francesco Borgonini-Duca, one of his seminary professors.

When Spellman returned to the United States, he found himself almost immediately at odds with Boston's archbishop, Cardinal William Henry O'Connell. For the next decade, O'Connell exiled the young priest to a series of insignificant posts, including work on the staff of the diocesan newspaper and as archivist for the diocese. In 1925, however, Spellman returned to Rome, where he was appointed director of the Knights of Columbus playgrounds in Rome and assigned a position with the Vatican secretary of state. There he became friends with Eugenio Pacelli, appointed secretary of state in 1930. In 1931, after Pope Pius XI condemned fascism in *Non Abiamo Bisogno*, Pacelli gave Spellman the document to smuggle to Paris, where it was published.

Spellman returned to the United States in 1932 as auxiliary bishop of Boston, but once again, he had to endure Archbishop O'Connell's displeasure, expressed in the form of disagreeable assignments. Not the least of these was O'Connell's decision to consign Spellman to the financially troubled Newton Center parish. Spellman, for his part, used his seven years as auxiliary bishop to cultivate a relationship with Joseph P. Kennedy and, through him, ultimately had contact with President Franklin D. Roosevelt. Spellman also had the opportunity to escort Cardinal Eugenio Pacelli on a tour of the United States in 1936, thus reinvigorating his ties with the man who would, three years later, become Pope Pius XII. In April 1939, soon after Pacelli became pontiff, he appointed Spellman archbishop of New York, the largest diocese in the United States.

Archbishop Francis Spellman promptly turned his attention to the task of establishing diplomatic relations between the United States and the Vatican. As World War II began in Europe, President Roosevelt appointed Myron C. Taylor as his representative to Pope Pius XII. Furthermore, adding to Spellman's prominence as an American prelate,

Roosevelt designated him vicar for the U.S. armed forces in December 1939. By the end of World War II, Spellman's international stature as archbishop of New York and military vicar prompted Pius XII to offer him a position as Vatican secretary of state. When Spellman declined this post, the pope appointed him a cardinal in 1946.

After the war, Cardinal Spellman's influence declined somewhat. Other Catholic prelates in the United States saw to it that Spellman's influence was generally confined to the East Coast. In addition, President Roosevelt's death in 1945 deprived Spellman of his most important political relationship. President Harry Truman proved a less attentive ear for Spellman than his successor, and Spellman's long cherished ambition of formalizing diplomatic relations between Vatican City and the United States seemed ever more distant. Not even Spellman's carefully cultivated political contacts could deliver this prize, as he discovered when President John F. Kennedy, son of Spellman's old friend Joseph Kennedy, announced that the United States would not pursue formal diplomatic ties with the Vatican.

In the years after World War II, Spellman demonstrated his conservative leanings by his anti-Communist zeal, including his implicit support of the Wisconsin senator Joseph McCarthy and his later support of American involvement in the Vietnam War. But he made himself a difficult target for ideological labels in other ways. After the death of Pius XII and the election of John XXIII as pope, Archbishop Egidio Vagnozzi became the new pontiff's apostolic delegate to the United States. When Vagnozzi complained about Catholic biblical scholars who were using the tools of higher criticism in their work, Spellman rushed to the defense of the American scholars. He also supported Catholic theologian JOHN COURTNEY MURRAY, whose defense of religious liberty and religious disestablishment had originally caused him to be excluded from participation in the Second Vatican Council. Spellman died in New York City several years after Vatican II, on December 2, 1967.

Though enormously influential within the American Catholic Church, Cardinal Francis Spellman was chiefly important as a result of his dealings with political leaders such as President

Roosevelt rather than the ordinary affairs of the church. He was the most prominent Catholic prelate in America during the middle years of the 20th century, and he helped to forge a climate in which Catholics became increasingly at home in the United States. At the turn of the 20th century, the americanist controversy called into question Catholic support of American values and institutions as against the traditional practices of the church. Spellman helped to settle the underlying issue of this dispute by demonstrating the possibility of being thoroughly Roman, as he was, while being thoroughly American. When John F. Kennedy became the first Roman Catholic elected president of the United States in 1960, he inherited a cultural reality made possible, in part, by the influence of Cardinal Francis Spellman.

Further Reading

Cooney, John. *The American Pope: The Life and Times of Francis Cardinal Spellman.* New York: Times Books, 1984.

Gannon, Robert Ignatius. *The Cardinal Spellman Story.* Garden City, N.Y.: Doubleday, 1962.

Spellman, Francis Cardinal. *The Foundling.* New York: C. Scribner, 1951.

———. "An Incentive to Prayer." Available online. URL: http://www.ewtn/.com/library/PRAYER/INCENTIVE.TXT. Downloaded on April 29, 2002.

———. *Prayers and Poems by Francis Cardinal Spellman.* New York: C. Scribner's Sons, 1946.

———. *What America Means to Me, and Other Poems and Prayers.* New York: Scribner, 1953.

Steibel, Warren. *Cardinal Spellman, the Man.* New York: Appleton-Century, 1966.

Steinberg, Milton
(1903–1950) *rabbi, author*

Before his untimely death at the age of 46, Milton Steinberg had earned a reputation as one of his generation's most gifted writers and speakers. More than a half century after his death, both his printed sermons and his other writings continue to provide insight into the Jewish faith. Steinberg was born on November 26, 1903, in Rochester, New York, the son of Samuel Steinberg and Fannie Sternberg Steinberg. In 1919, he moved with his family to New York City. He graduated from DeWitt Clinton High School as valedictorian in 1921 and promptly enrolled in the City College of New York, from which he received a B.A. in 1924. Four years later he graduated from the Jewish Theological Seminary in New York City and was ordained a rabbi.

After seminary, Steinberg accepted a position as rabbi at Beth-El Zedeck in Indianapolis, Indiana, in 1928. In the year after his arrival, he married Edith Alpert, whom he had dated since 1925, and they had two children. At Beth-El Zedeck, he labored for five years, concentrating especially on developing Jewish education programs. "You can throw away every note you've ever taken at the Seminary," he wrote to his childhood friend Ira Eisenstein during this period; "you won't need them. There isn't a man in a radius of 50 miles who knows the difference between the *Midrash* and the *Talmud*."

In 1933, Steinberg returned to New York, where he accepted a position as rabbi of Manhattan's prestigious Park Avenue Synagogue. He remained there for the rest of his life. While in seminary, Steinberg had studied with MORDECAI MENAHEM KAPLAN, the founder of the branch of American Judaism known as Reconstructionism, whose interest in envisioning Judaism without reference to a belief in God Steinberg did not share. Conversant with the major theological currents of his day, including those within Christianity, Steinberg ultimately rejected the project of Reconstructionism as theologically impoverished. He remained firmly anchored within the tradition of Conservative Judaism, which sought to find a middle way between Orthodox and Reform Judaism by preserving traditional Jewish beliefs while being open to potential innovation with respect to particular Jewish laws and practices.

Steinberg won recognition as a gifted preacher, and his writing also received praise. By 1934 he had published his first book, *The Making of the Modern Jew*, and several more followed in the next decade and a half, including one novel, *As a Driven Leaf* (1939). This book is a fictional account of the renegade Talmudic sage Elisha ben Abuyah, who struggled to harmonize Jewish faith and Greek culture.

Steinberg's *Basic Judaism* (1947) was—and is—a highly regarded primer on Jewish life and thought.

One of his more popular sermons, "To Hold with Open Arms," which was preached in 1944, used Steinberg's own experience of a heart attack to reflect on the preciousness of life and surrender to God's will:

> Given God, everything becomes more precious, more to be loved and clung to, more embraceable; and yet at the same time easier to give up. For these belong to the universe and the God who stands behind it. . . . I let go of them the more easily because I know that as parts of the divine economy they will not be lost. When they slip from my hands they will pass to hands better, stronger, and wiser than mine. For only when He is given, can we hold life at once infinitely precious and yet as a thing lightly to be surrendered.

The heart attack that prompted this sermon was not Steinberg's last. After recurring heart problems, Steinberg suffered a final heart attack, which caused his death on March 20, 1950, in New York City.

Rabbi Milton Steinberg lacked the technical training and scholarship that would have led to recognition as a theologian. Nevertheless, he applied himself diligently to the study of modern religious thought. The fruit of this study, and of his gifts of written and spoken expression, made Steinberg a popular and respected commentator on the Jewish faith. Historians frequently ponder what further impact he might have made had death not seized him so early in life. In spite of his early death, however, Steinberg briefly occupied one of the most important Jewish pulpits of his day, and he won high praise for the spirit and the gifts that he exhibited there.

Further Reading

Goldman, Alex J. *Giants of Faith: Great American Rabbis.* New York: Citadel Press, 1965.

Noveck, Simon. *Milton Steinberg: Portrait of a Rabbi.* New York: Ktav Publishing House, 1978.

Steinberg, Milton. *Anatomy of Faith.* Edited by Arthur A. Cohen. New York: Harcourt, Brace, 1960.

———. *As a Driven Leaf.* Indianapolis, Ind.: Bobbs-Merrill, 1939.

———. *Basic Judaism.* New York: Harcourt, Brace, 1947; Northvale, N.J.: J. Aronson, 1987.

———. *A Believing Jew: The Selected Writings of Milton Steinberg.* New York: Harcourt, Brace, 1951; Freeport, N.Y.: Books for Libraries Press, 1971.

———. "The Creed of an American Zionist." Available online. URL: http://www.theatlantic/com/unbound/bookauth/zionism/steinberg.htm. Downloaded on April 29, 2002.

———. *The Making of the Modern Jew: From the Second Temple to the State of Israel.* Rev. ed. New York: Behrman House, 1948; Lanham, Md.: University Press of America, 1987.

Stetson, Augusta Emma Simmons
(1842–1928) *Christian Science leader*

Augusta Emma Simmons Stetson rose quickly to prominence in the Christian Science Church and founded the First Church of Christ, Science, in New York City. Ultimately, however, unorthodox teachings and perceptions that her influence might supplant that of Christian Science founder, MARY BAKER EDDY, led to Stetson's excommunication from the church. Augusta Emma Simmons was born on October 12, 1842, in Waldoboro, Maine, the daughter of Peabody Simmons and Salome Sprague Simmons, devout Methodists. She grew up in Damariscotta, Maine, where she graduated from high school before attending Lincoln Academy in New Castle, Maine.

Augusta Simmons married Frederick J. Stetson in 1864; the couple had no children. Frederick Stetson was a Civil War veteran and a shipbuilder who worked for a London company. His work took the couple to England, as well as India and Burma, over the following years, but physical infirmity eventually forced his retirement. Stetson and her husband subsequently returned to the United States and settled in Boston. There, she decided to pursue a career in public speaking and enrolled in the Blish School of Oratory in 1882.

In 1884, Stetson happened to attend a lecture by Mary Baker Eddy, who had founded the Church of Christ, Scientist, five years previously. Stetson quickly embraced Eddy's teaching, and Eddy as quickly recognized Stetson's promise as a leader

Augusta E. Stetson played a prominent role in Christian Science before she was dismissed from the church for her heterodox ideas. *(Library of Congress, Prints and Photographs Division LC-USZ62-111854)*

and a teacher. During the fall of 1884, Stetson completed a three-week course at Eddy's Massachusetts Metaphysical College in Boston, and she promptly undertook a healing mission to Skowhegan, Maine. Eddy, though, wished Stetson to work with her and summoned her back to Boston, where she made Stetson one of the five preachers at the home church of Christian Science, which met in Chickering Hall.

By 1886, however, Eddy had dispatched Stetson to New York City to take charge of the Christian Science societies located there. Stetson and other Christian Scientists in the city formally organized the First Church of Christ, Scientist, New York City, in 1888. Two years later, she was ordained the church's first minister, an officer later

renamed *reader*. In 1891 Stetson established the New York City Christian Science Institute as a means of training Christian Science practitioners. Through both the First Church and this institute, she was successful in attracting new Christian Science adherents in New York, attached not only to Eddy's doctrines but to Stetson's own personality. The growth of the First Church forced it to relocate regularly, until Stetson was able to oversee construction of an ornate granite edifice at 96th Street and Central Park West at a cost of more than $1 million by the time of its dedication in 1903. To this impressive structure, larger even than the mother church in Boston, Stetson's congregation added a $100,000 residence next door for Stetson in the following year.

As Stetson's influence in New York magnified, Eddy and her closest supporters became increasingly suspicious of Stetson's possible ambitions. As early as 1895, Eddy had formalized the structure of the Church of Christ, Science, to prohibit preaching by individual ministers in favor of a focus on "readings" of the Bible and Eddy's own *Science and Health with Key to the Scriptures*. In 1902, Eddy changed the organizational structure of the Church of Christ, Scientist, to limit readers (as ministers were now called) to terms of only three years. This change removed Stetson from her position as reader of the New York church—but not from her post as principal of the institute she had established or from the opulent residence in which she made her home. In the final year of that decade, the Christian Science board of directors began an investigation of Stetson's views. After the board found evidence of such heterodoxies as a belief that sexual relations were inherently evil and of attempts by Stetson to use mental suggestion against various enemies, her license as a Christian Science practitioner was revoked in September 1909.

Stetson refused to recriminate Mary Baker Eddy for her exile. She remained active as a speaker and an author over the years that followed, choosing to construe her excommunication as the fault of the Christian Science board of directors rather than of Eddy herself. She died on October 12, 1928, in Rochester, New York.

A central figure in the early life of the Church of Christ, Science, Augusta Emma Simmons Stetson exercised an influence second only to that of Mary Baker Eddy herself. A gifted speaker and organization builder, she planted Christian Science teaching firmly in the urban soil of America's most prominent city. Though her banishment from the church might have inspired her to organize a competing Christian Science movement, her personal loyalty to Mary Baker Eddy forestalled this avenue. She contented herself during her final years with publishing sermons, letters, and memoirs to demonstrate this loyalty, even though she no longer enjoyed a place of responsibility within the Church of Christ, Scientist.

Further Reading

Cunningham, Sarah Gardner. "A New Order: Augusta Emma Simmons Stetson and the Origins of Christian Science in New York City, 1886–1910." Ph.D. dissertation, Union Theological Seminary, 1994.

Eddy, Mary Baker. *Letters of Mary Baker Eddy to Augusta E. Stetson, C.S.D., 1889–1909.* Cuyahoga Falls, Ohio: Emma Publishing Society, 1990.

Stetson, Augusta E. *Poems: Written on the Journey from Sense to Soul.* 4th ed. Cuyahoga Falls, Ohio: Emma Publishing Society, 1992.

———. *Reminiscences, Sermons, and Correspondence: Proving Adherence to the Principle of Christian Science as Taught by Mary Baker Eddy.* Cuyahoga Falls, Ohio: Emma Publishing Society, 1989.

———. *Sermons Which Spiritually Interpret the Scriptures and Other Writings on Christian Science: A History of Pioneer Steps.* Cuyahoga Falls, Ohio: Emma Publishing Society, 1992.

Swihart, Altman K. *Since Mrs. Eddy.* New York: H. Holt, 1931.

Stiles, Ezra

(1727–1795) *Congregational minister, educator*

Ezra Stiles was a prominent Congregational clergyman who became the president of Yale College and helped to produce its early prominence. He was born on November 29, 1727, in North Haven, Connecticut, to Isaac Stiles and Kezia Taylor Stiles. His father was a Congregationalist minister and his mother, the daughter of Edward Taylor, one of New England's preeminent early poets. Kezia Stiles died four days after giving birth to Ezra.

Ezra Stiles attended Yale College, graduated in 1746, and then received a master's degree in 1749 after additional theological studies. The college then invited him to remain as a tutor, and he served in this capacity from 1749 until 1755, during which period he was licensed to preach, wrestled with skepticism, drifted away from Calvinism—especially its emphasis on human depravity—and flirted with a career in law. Anglicans tried to tempt him into a ministerial position with one of their churches. Eventually, though, Stiles left Yale to become the pastor of the Second Congregational Church in Newport, Rhode Island, where he remained for nearly 20 years. On February 10, 1757, he married Elizabeth Hubbard, and the couple subsequently had eight children.

In Newport, Stiles's theological views turned toward a more evangelical, orthodox Calvinism than the faith with which he had begun his pastoral ministry. His pastoral responsibilities were not so demanding that Stiles was unable to pursue studies on a variety of subjects. Though he published little concerning his scholarly investigations, over the years his reputation as a serious thinker increased dramatically. After his wife, Elizabeth, died in May 1775, he married Mary Checkley, the widow of an acquaintance, in 1782.

In the spring of 1776, after British ships took up a forbidding presence in Newport Harbor, many of the town's residents fled, including Stiles and his children. He preached temporarily in Dighton, Massachusetts, and in 1777 he was invited to become minister of the First Congregational Church in Portsmouth, New Hampshire. By early summer, he had moved his family there; however, he did not remain in this pulpit for long. In September of the same year, he received word that Yale had elected him its new president, and by the following June, Stiles had moved to New Haven to begin his life's final career. He marked the event by freeing a slave he had owned for some years.

At the time that Stiles assumed the presidency of Yale, the college's financial affairs were in wreckage and its reputation in tatters. In the years that followed, Stiles wedded his own reputation to Yale's, and the college profited from this marriage. He finally convinced the Connecticut legislature to provide a secure financial basis of support for the college, and he modernized and improved the instruction offered there so that students flocked to it.

Throughout his adult life, Stiles believed that ministers should avoid overt engagement in political matters, but he was devoted to the cause of democracy and liberty. During the Revolutionary War, he defended his abstention from political matters in a letter:

> I am a Friend to American Liberty; of the final prevalence of which I have not the least doubt, though by what means and in what ways God only knows. . . . I am a Spectator indeed of Events, but intermeddle not with Politics. We [ministers] have another Department, being called to an Office and Work, which may be successfully pursued (for it has been pursued) under every species of *Civil Tyranny* or *Liberty*. We cannot become the Dupes of Politicians without Alliances, Concessions and Connexions dangerous to evangelical Truth and spiritual Liberty.

In later years, this reticence to engage in political matters did not prevent Stiles from enthusiastically supporting the French Revolution, even when it turned down the path of tyrannicide with the execution of Louis XVI in 1793. In religious affairs, a similar devotion to liberty imbued Stiles with a reluctance to see government cast its weight behind any particular religious orthodoxy. In his personal relations with the members of other religious groups, Stiles displayed an ecumenical temper.

Stiles remained intellectually active until the end of his life, although his health declined in later years. He died in New Haven on May 12, 1795.

Ezra Stiles possessed an insatiable appetite for learning that made him one of the most educated men of his day. He lacked creative brilliance and therefore failed to ally his name to any great development in the history of American ideas generally, or of theology in particular. But the capaciousness of his learning and his reputation combined to make him one of the first great American college presidents.

Further Reading

Bergman, Marvin Lavon. "Public Religion in Revolutionary America: Ezra Stiles, Devereux Jarratt, and John Witherspoon." Ph.D. dissertation, University of Chicago, 1990.

Morgan, Edmund S. *The Gentle Puritan: A Life of Ezra Stiles.* New Haven, Conn.: Yale University Press, 1962.

Stiles, Ezra. *Extracts from the Itineraries and Other Miscellanies of Ezra Stiles.* Edited by Franklin Bowditch Dexter. New Haven, Conn: Yale University Press, 1916.

———. *Letters & Papers of Ezra Stiles, President of Yale College, 1778–1795.* Edited by Isabel M. Calder. New Haven, Conn.: Yale University Library, 1933.

———. *The Literary Diary of Ezra Stiles.* Edited by Franklin Bowditch Dexter. New York: C. Scribner's Sons, 1901.

Stoddard, Solomon
(1643–1729) *Puritan minister*

Solomon Stoddard became famous in his Puritan generation for liberalizing the requirements for church membership and participation in the sacrament of the Lord's Supper. His grandson, JONATHAN EDWARDS, would become one of the most famous preachers in American history. Solomon Stoddard was born in Boston on September 27, 1643, to Anthony Stoddard, a successful merchant, and Mary Downing Stoddard, niece of Massachusetts governor John Winthrop and sister-in-law of Governor Simon Bradstreet. Solomon received his preparatory education in Elijah Corlet's school in Cambridge and then matriculated at Harvard College, where he received an undergraduate degree in 1662 and a master's degree three years later. He was invited to become a tutor at the college in 1666 and to occupy a position as Harvard's first librarian. Soon, though, he departed for Barbados, where he served as chaplain for two years before returning to Massachusetts in 1669. That year, he was invited to become minister of the church at Northampton, after the death of its pastor, Eleazer Mather. Stoddard cemented his relationship with this congregation by marrying the former minister's widow,

Esther Warham Mather, on March 8, 1670. Together the couple had nine children, added to the three from Esther's previous marriage.

Solomon Stoddard began his ministerial career less than a decade after a synod convened in Boston had adopted the Half-Way Covenant. Prior to this synod, the accepted practice in the Massachusetts churches was to require an applicant for church membership to give a public account of a conversion experience. The children of church members were baptized, but by the second half of the 17th century it became apparent that many of these children, now grown to adulthood and having children of their own, never became church members because they never made the necessary public account of their conversion experience. The Half-Way Covenant established an arrangement that permitted the baptism of children whose parents had themselves been baptized but had not become full members of churches. It stipulated, however, that these children, though baptized, would not be admitted to full church membership, including participation in the ordinance of the Lord's Supper, until they had given testimony to a conversion experience of their own.

Solomon Stoddard, installed as the minister of the Northampton church, soon deviated from the terms of the Half-Way Covenant by admitting as members in his church both those who had experienced conversion and those who had simply been baptized as infants. Eventually, he added to this innovation the further step of permitting church members who had not given evidence of a conversion experience to participate in the Lord's Supper. These ecclesiastical innovations mirrored the pattern of Stoddard's personal religious life. Though baptized as an infant, Stoddard did not become a member of a church during his teenage and college years, because he had not had a conversion experience. In fact, this experience does not appear to have occurred until after he began preaching at the Northampton church. By one account, it was during a service in which he presided over the administration of the Lord's Supper that Stoddard experienced conversion. In later years, he would refer to the ordinance of communion as a "converting ordinance." He would accordingly permit individuals to partake of this ordinance if they led

a morally upright life and professed belief in the essential tenets of the church, even if they had not had a conversion experience.

"Stoddardism," as Stoddard's positions on church membership and participation in the ordinance of communion were called, proved enormously influential in western Massachusetts and Connecticut, partially because Stoddard's son and several sons-in-law who became New England ministers reflected his theological influence. Significant revivals that his church experienced during the years of his ministry also enhanced Stoddard's influence. Though liberal in his understanding of church membership, Solomon Stoddard was a staunchly evangelical preacher. His preaching, in fact, served as a precursor for the Great Awakening that occurred in New England from 1720 through 1740. In 1727, Stoddard's grandson, Jonathan Edwards, became his ministerial associate and heir apparent at the Northampton church. Edwards would continue his grandfather's evangelical ministry but would ultimately attempt to reinvigorate restrictions on church membership and be dismissed by the congregation.

Solomon Stoddard led the migration of many New England churches toward less exclusive standards of membership. Since church membership in 17th-century New England was often a prerequisite to important citizenship rights, Stoddard's ecclesiastical practices helped democratize New England politics. He also continued to call for the radical conversion of his hearers in the face of spiritual laxity, and he thus became an important predecessor of the Great Awakening that began its spread across New England in the last decade of Stoddard's life.

Further Reading

Coffman, Ralph J. *Solomon Stoddard*. Boston: Twayne Publishers, 1978.

Husband, Paul Edward. "Church Membership in Northampton: Solomon Stoddard versus Jonathan Edwards." Ph.D. dissertation, Westminster Theological Seminary, 1990.

Miller, Perry. "Solomon Stoddard, 1643–1729." *Harvard Theological Review* 34 (1941): 277–320.

Schafer, Thomas A. "Solomon Stoddard and the Theology of the Revival." In *A Miscellany of American*

Christianity: Essays in Honor of H. Shelton Smith. Edited by Stuart C. Henry. Durham, N.C.: Duke University Press, 1963.

Stone, Barton Warren
(1772–1844) *evangelical Christian preacher, leader in Christian restorationist movement*

Barton Warren Stone played a significant role in the 19th-century Christian restorationist movement, in which a variety of believers sought to recover a primitive and more authentic Christian faith. Stone and his followers eventually aligned themselves with the Disciples of Christ, an association of restorationist churches led by ALEXANDER CAMPBELL. He was born on December 24, 1772, near Port Tobacco, Maryland, the son of John Stone and Mary Warren Stone. After his father died when Stone was very young, his mother moved the family to Pittsylvania County, Virginia. Stone intended at first to become a lawyer and enrolled in the Guilford Academy in North Carolina to prepare for this vocation. While there, however, he was influenced by the preaching of the Presbyterian revivalist James Gready and eventually experienced a religious conversion, which he described in his autobiography:

> Jesus came to seek and save the lost. . . . I yielded and sunk at his feet a willing subject. I loved him—I adored him—I praised him aloud in the silent night,—in the echoing grove around. I confessed to the Lord my sin and folly in disbelieving his word so long— and in following so long the devices of men. I now saw that a poor sinner was as much authorized to believe in Jesus at first, as at last—that *now* was the accepted time, the day of salvation.

This experience redirected Stone's vocational plans. He became a Presbyterian minister rather than a lawyer and was ordained by the Orange Presbytery of North Carolina in 1796. He eventually settled near Paris, Kentucky, where he served as minister for congregations at Cane Ridge and Concord. By the time of his ordination in the Transylvania Presbytery, however, his devotion to

Presbyterian doctrine had already suffered decline. At his ordination in 1798 he was asked, "Do you receive and adopt the Confession of Faith, as containing the system of doctrine taught in the Bible?" Stone replied, "I do, as far as I see it consistent with the word of God." The Transylvania Presbytery accepted Stone in spite of his equivocation, and he cemented another union three years later by marrying Elizabeth Campbell, with whom he had five children.

In August 1801, Stone sought to spread the revivalism of his former spiritual mentor, James McGready, to the Kentucky frontier by joining with other ministers to hold revival services in Cane Ridge. Thousands of people flocked to the Cane Ridge Revival, but in its aftermath, Stone and several other Presbyterian ministers found themselves increasingly at odds with the Transylvania Presbytery, until they were finally expelled from it in 1803. The following year, Stone and the other ministers formed their own association, still nominally Presbyterian, and named it the Springfield Presbytery. Nevertheless, within a year they dissolved this union and published "The Last Will and Testament of the Springfield Presbytery," whose declarations included the following:

> We *Will*, that the people henceforth take the Bible as the only sure guide to heaven, and as many as are offended with other books, which stand in competition with it, may cast them into the fire if they choose; for it is better to enter into life having one book, than having many to be cast into hell.

Having thus terminated their bonds with Presbyterianism, Stone and his spiritual allies elected to call themselves, simply, Christians.

After the death of his first wife in 1810, Stone married his wife's cousin, Celia Wilson Bowen, with whom he had six children. Over the following years, the ministers who had originally formed the Springfield Presbytery gradually turned down other spiritual paths, but under the influence of Barton Stone, the "Christian" movement continued to flourish. In 1826, Stone founded the *Christian Messenger*, a periodical devoted to the cause of Christian unity and to the abolition of denominations. That same decade, Stone met Alexander

Barton Stone was an early leader in the Christian Restorationist movement, which ultimately became the Disciples of Christ, and is pictured here to the right with other Disciples leaders. *(Library of Congress, Prints and Photographs Division)*

Campbell, the leader of a like-minded restorationist movement known as the Disciples of Christ, and in the early 1830s Stone led his group of believers to join the Disciples of Christ. He suffered a stroke in 1841 and died three years later, on November 9, 1844, in Hannibal, Missouri.

The splintering of Protestant Christianity into an ever increasing multiplicity of sects and denominations has troubled more than a few Christians. In the 19th century, especially, believers such as Barton Warren Stone sought to leap past the doctrinal and ecclesiastical fractures that divided Christians and, by returning to primitive Christian principles and practices, to forge a foundation for Christian unity. Stone's Christian movement became an important tributary of 19th-century Christian restorationism, and, when joined with the Disciples of Christ, helped to form an enduring branch of Protestant Christianity.

Further Reading

Cane Ridge in Context: Perspectives on Barton W. Stone and the Revival. Edited by Anthony L. Dunnavant. Nashville: Disciples of Christ Historical Society, 1992.

Conkin, Paul Keith. *Cane Ridge: America's Pentecost.* Madison.: University of Wisconsin Press, 1990.

Garrett, Leroy. *The Stone-Campbell Movement: An Anecdotal History of Three Churches.* Joplin, Mo.: College Press, 1981.

Stone, Barton W. *The Biography of Eld. Barton Warren Stone.* Cincinnati: Published for the author by J. A. & U. P. James, 1847; New York: Arno Press, 1972.

Voices from Cane Ridge. Edited by Rhodes Thompson. St. Louis, Mo.: Bethany Press, 1954.

Williams, D. Newell. *Barton Stone: A Spiritual Biography.* St. Louis, Mo.: Chalice Press, 2000.

Strong, Augustus Hopkins
(1836–1921) *Baptist theologian, educator*

Augustus Hopkins Strong's *Systematic Theology* (1876) was still in print more than 75 years after his death, though this theologian is generally unknown. In his own era, however, Strong was one of conservative Protestantism's most prominent voices. He was born on August 3, 1836, in Rochester, New York, the son of Alvah Strong and Catherine Hopkins Strong. His father was a wealthy journalist, and Strong ever afterward was comfortable in the company of affluence. He completed his undergraduate education at Yale College in 1857, and after a year of European travel, he enrolled in Rochester Theological Seminary, in Rochester, New York, a citadel of Northern Baptist education, from which he graduated in 1859. Thereafter, he studied in Berlin before being ordained a Baptist minister and beginning an 11-year ministry as a pastor in 1861. That same year he married Harriet Savage, with whom he enjoyed a union of more than half a century and had six children.

After an initial ministry as pastor of the First Baptist Church of Haverhill, Massachusetts, which lasted from 1861 to 1865, the 29-year-old Strong was invited to become pastor of the First Baptist Church in Cleveland, Ohio, a large and prominent congregation. His learned sermons from that prestigious pulpit soon garnered offers to become a professor at Crozer Seminary in Pennsylvania and the president of Brown University in Rhode Island, which he refused. Nevertheless, when Ezekial Robinson, former professor of theology at Rochester Theological Seminary, accepted the presidency of Brown in 1872, Strong agreed to assume the professorial chair that Brown had left, as well as the presidency of the seminary. He thus returned to his alma mater and held both posts for the next four decades.

Strong's most enduring work as a theologian was his *Systematic Theology*, published four years after his arrival at the helm of Rochester Theological Seminary, a work of immense erudition, which he carried through eight editions and which found a home in conservative seminaries especially well into the 20th century. His theology generally accepted all the essentials of traditional orthodoxy, except insofar as it was friendly toward HORACE BUSHNELL's view of the atonement as the demonstration of God's love for humankind rather than as a substitution to satisfy the demands of God's wrath or justice. But Strong's career as a theological thinker intersected strong currents of modernity, and, unlike more conservative Protestants, he refused to reject these absolutely. Thus, he came to accept Darwin's theory of evolution and to respect the results of higher critical study of the Bible.

On the eve of the 20th century, Strong published the study *Christ in Creation and Ethical Monism* (1899), in which he attempted to grapple with what he saw as an emerging philosophical monism that had demonstrated its influence across a wide spectrum of disciplines. The choice, as he saw it, was not to swim against the stream of these philosophical tendencies, but to turn it down channels that would enrich belief rather than reinforce unbelief.

> This universal tendency toward monism, is it a wave of unbelief set agoing by an evil intelligence in order to overwhelm and swamp the religion of Christ? Or is it a mighty movement of the Spirit of God, giving to thoughtful men, all unconsciously to themselves, a deeper understanding of truth and preparing the way for the reconciliation of diverse creeds and parties by disclosing their hidden ground of unity? . . . Monism is, without much doubt, the philosophy of the future, and the only question would seem to be whether it shall be an ethical and Christian, or a non-ethical and anti-Christian monism. If we refuse to recognize this new movement of thought and to capture it for Christ, we may find that materialism and pantheism perversely launch their craft upon the tide and compel it to further their progress. Let us tentatively accept the monistic principle and give to it a Christian interpretation. . . . Let us see in this forward march of thought a sign that Christ and his kingdom are conquering and to conquer.

Strong lived to see the destructive beginnings of the controversy between Protestant liberals and fundamentalists. Toward the end of his life, he declared himself hesitantly against at least some of the manifestations of liberalism, though his own views would have never allowed him to be completely at home in the camp of fundamentalists. He retired from Rochester Theological Seminary in 1912 and died on November 29, 1921, in Rochester, New York.

Augustus Hopkins Strong played a dominant role in the life of northern Baptists at the turn of the 20th century. In addition to exerting influence as president and theology professor at Rochester Theological Seminary, he served as president of the American Baptist Foreign Mission Society from 1892 to 1895 and of the General Convention of Baptists of North America from 1905 to 1910. He was, in many ways, relatively progressive in his thinking, at least compared with those who would recruit his name to their banner in the fundamentalist-liberal conflicts that would follow his death. Nevertheless, his most enduring contribution was his *Systematic Theology,* a classic statement of conservative Protestant faith.

Further Reading

Henry, Carl F. H. Henry. *Personal Idealism and Strong's Theology.* Wheaton Ill.: Van Kampen Press, 1951.

Strong, Augustus Hopkins. *Autobiography of Augustus Hopkins Strong.* Edited by Crerar Douglas. Valley Forge, Pa.: Judson Press, 1981.

———. *Christ in Creation and Ethical Monism.* Philadelphia: Roger Williams Press, 1899. Available online. URL:http://www.ucalgary.ca/~nurelweb/papers/other/monism-1.html. Downloaded on April 29, 2002.

———. *Systematic Theology: A Compendium and Commonplace-book Designed for the Use of Theological Students.* 3 vols. Philadelphia: Griffith & Rowland Press, 1907–09.

Wacker, Grant. *Augustus H. Strong and the Dilemma of Historical Consciousness.* Macon, Ga.: Mercer University Press, 1985.

Strong, Josiah

(1847–1916) *Congregationalist minister, social reformer*

Josiah Strong was a principal architect of the Social Gospel movement. In the final decades of the 19th century, Strong and other liberal Protestants became convinced that churches had a responsibility to work toward the cure of the social ills of modern society. He labored for more than 30 years to challenge and organize Christian communities to accept this responsibility and, in the process, became a prominent voice for both Christian engagement in social reform activities and ecumenical unity with which to pursue these activities. Strong was born on January 19, 1847, in Naperville, Illinois, the son of Josiah Strong and Elizabeth Webster Strong. He grew up in Hudson, Ohio, where he attended

Western Reserve College and obtained a B.A. in 1867. Strong subsequently studied at Lane Theological Seminary in Cincinnati, Ohio, and was ordained a Congregationalist minister in September 1871. His first pastoral assignment, which he began the same month, accompanied by his wife, Alice Bisbee, whom he had married in late August 1871, was in a church in Cheyenne, Wyoming.

Over the next decade and a half, Strong spent two years in Cheyenne, after which he served as an instructor and chaplain at Western Reserve College from 1873 to 1876; as a minister in Sandusky, Ohio, from 1876 to 1881; as regional secretary of the Congregational Home Missionary Society from 1881 to 1884; and as a minister in Cincinnati from 1884 to 1886. Toward the end of this period, Strong published his first book, *Our Country: Its Possible Future and Its Present Crisis* (1885), which helped to chart the course of his future life. This work, which cataloged a variety of social problems and proposed solutions for them, represented an early manifesto in what would become the Social Gospel movement. In the book, Strong urged Christians to address the ills of American society, suggesting that the United States, as a chief representative of the "Anglo-Saxon" race, was poised to play a key role in the world's history.

Widely and favorably received, Strong's first book earned him appointment as the general secretary of the Evangelical Alliance in 1886. He used this position to advance the cause of Christian engagement in the work of social reform. The alliance, however, eventually proved more conservative in its reformist zeal than Strong preferred, and in 1898 he founded the American League for Social Service (renamed the American Institute for Social Service in 1902), an organization that would be more responsive to his progressive vision. Strong presided over this organization for the remainder of his life.

Eager to see the church as a whole committed to the work of social reform in the name of Christ, Josiah Strong was an early supporter of the ecumenical movement. He felt that a united church offered the best hope for social engagement, and he was consequently a natural ally of ecumenism. He took an active role in the Federal Council of Churches, including, not surprisingly, its Commission on the Church and Social Service.

Strong authored a steady stream of books over the following years. However, his confidence about the providential role to be played by the Anglo-Saxon race earned him criticism by later historians. Some observers have accused him of racism and imperialism on the basis of passages such as the following from *The New Era* (1893):

> In seems to me that God with infinite wisdom and skill, is here training the Anglo-Saxon race for an hour to come in the World's future. . . . [T]his race of unequaled energy, with all the majesty of numbers and the might of wealth behind it—the representative, let us hope, of the largest liberty, the purest Christianity, the highest civilization—having developed peculiarly aggressive traits calculated to impress its institutions on mankind, will spread itself over the earth.

In spite of these criticisms, in his own day Strong was widely regarded as a progressive voice for social reform. He died in New York City, on April 28, 1916.

By the beginning of the 20th century, evangelical Protestantism had a long history of active engagement in social reforms, including the antislavery and temperance movements. The Social Gospel movement, primarily in the liberal wing of Protestantism, represented a similar reformist impulse, though one trained on new social ills occasioned by the industrialization of late-19th-century America. Josiah Strong played an important role in this religious movement, which inspired in its turn ecumenical ventures to harness the collective energies of mainline churches to the task of applying the gospel of Christ to the pressing social needs of the day.

Further Reading

Deichmann, Wendy Jane. "Josiah Strong: Practical Theologian and Social Crusader for a Global Kingdom." Ph.D. dissertation, Drew University, 1991.

Muller, Dorothea R. "Josiah Strong and the Challenge of the City." Ph.D. dissertation, New York University, 1955.

Root, Edward T. "Josiah Strong: A Modern Prophet of the Social Gospel." *New Church Review* (June 1922): 47–54.

Strong, Josiah. *Expansion under New World Conditions.*
New York: Baker and Taylor, 1900; New York: Garland, 1971.

———. *My Religion in Everyday Life.* New York: Baker & Taylor, 1910.

———. *The New Era.* New York: Baker & Taylor, 1893.

———. *Our Country: Its Possible Future and Its Present Crisis.* New York: Baker & Taylor for the American Home Mission Society, 1885; Cambridge, Mass.: Belknap Press of Harvard University Press, 1963.

———. *The Twentieth Century City.* New York: Baker and Taylor, 1898; New York: Arno Press, 1970.

Sunday, Billy
(William Ashley Sunday, Jr.)
(1862–1935) *revivalist*

The most prominent American revivalist during the years leading up to World War I, Billy Sunday traded a professional baseball career for an itinerant preaching ministry. He extended the urban revivalism movement of 19th-century Protestant evangelists such as CHARLES GRANDISON FINNEY and DWIGHT LYMAN MOODY into the 20th century. He was born William Ashley Sunday on November 19, 1862, on a farm in Story County, Iowa, the son of William Ashley Sunday, Sr., and Mary Jane Corey Sunday. His father, a private in the Union army during the Civil War, died of pneumonia a few months later. His mother, eventually unable to support Billy Sunday and his brother financially, had to send them to the Soldiers' Orphan Home in Glenwood, Iowa, in 1872. Both brothers struck out on their own in 1876, working as farm hands. They split up eventually when Billy moved, in 1877, to Nevada, Iowa, where he attended school and worked at a number of odd jobs. He also played for a local baseball team before moving in 1880 to Marshalltown, Iowa, where he worked for a furniture store and the volunteer fire department, while playing with the Marshalltown baseball team.

In 1883, Sunday tried out for and won a place on the Chicago White Stockings, with whom he played five seasons before the Pittsburgh Alleghenies bought his contract in 1888. Midway through the 1890 season, the Alleghenies traded him to the Philadelphia Phillies. During his years as a pro-

Billy Sunday's evangelistic campaigns in early 20th-century America foreshadowed the success of later evangelists such as Billy Graham. *(Library of Congress, Prints and Photographs Division LC-USZ62-108493)*

fessional baseball player, Billy Sunday excelled as a base runner and a fielder, but other events in his life rerouted its course at the height of his athletic success. Around 1885 he was converted to Christianity at the Pacific Garden Mission in Chicago; he then joined the Jefferson Park Presbyterian Church and began working with the Chicago Young Men's Christian Association (YMCA) during the off-season. Sunday's decision to become a Presbyterian appears to have owed much to his desire to pursue a romantic relationship with Helen A. Thompson, the daughter of a wealthy Presbyterian businessman. "If she had been a Catholic I would have been a Catholic," he later admitted. The two were married in 1888, and their union produced four children.

With the encouragement of his wife, Billy Sunday gave up professional ball in 1891 to work full-time as assistant secretary of the Chicago YMCA.

Two years later, Sunday, who had taught Bible classes and occasionally preached for the YMCA, decided to travel with JOHN WILBUR CHAPMAN, an itinerant evangelist. Sunday served mainly as Chapman's advance agent, helping to coordinate preparations for Chapman's revival services. At the end of 1895, however, Chapman gave up his itinerant ministry in favor of a settled pulpit in Philadelphia, Pennsylvania. Chapman suggested that the ministers of Garner, Iowa, invite Billy Sunday to preach a weeklong series of revival services, and these, held during January 1896, launched Sunday's career as a revivalist in his own right.

Over the next 20 years, Sunday's homespun preaching style, laced with slang and copious baseball analogies, won him renown as the "baseball evangelist." At the beginning of his ministry, Sunday's revivals took him to a variety of small towns, mostly in the Midwest. By the end, he had carried his gospel message into Chicago and New York, the great urban centers of his day. Though he was ordained a Presbyterian minister by the Chicago Presbytery in 1903, he avoided denominational labels in his zeal to call men and women to Christ. In 1905, he began to hold revivals in temporary wooden structures that were built to order for his services and whose aisles were covered with sawdust. The services invariably concluded with an altar call, when Sunday coaxed his hearers to leave their seats and go forward to make or renew their profession of faith in Christ. Those who experienced conversion were "hitting the sawdust trail," in Sunday's parlance.

Billy Sunday's reputation reached its apex in the years immediately preceding World War I, but it declined after 1918. He ran for the Republican presidential nomination in 1920 but failed to win it. After the war, he increasingly supported conservative causes such as Prohibition and the campaigns of Republican candidates, offending some observers, and took in substantial income from his revivals, alienating many others, including journalists. He continued the work of a traveling evangelist, but the crowds began to diminish in size and the towns that invited him to hold services tended to become smaller. He suffered a heart attack in 1933, but he kept preaching until another felled him and he died on November 6, 1935, in Chicago.

Sunday preached to more people than any man before him: estimates place the number at more than 100 million across a 40-year ministry. He stood in a long line of American revivalists stretching back to the years preceding the Great Awakening: he was the 20th-century successor of GEORGE WHITEFIELD, JONATHAN EDWARDS, Charles Finney, and Dwight L. Moody. The essential continuity of his own life, from orphan and rural beginnings during the Civil War to the increasing urbanization of the 1900s, became a pattern for his religious influence. He was able to meld elements of traditional Christian faith with the commercialism and industrialism of 20th-century America, delivering a gospel at home in rural tent revivals as well as in the heart of the nation's great cities.

Further Reading

Brown, Elijah P. The Real Billy Sunday: The Life and Work of Rev. William Ashley Sunday, D.D., the Baseball Evangelist. New York: Fleming H. Revell, 1914.

Bruns, Roger. Preacher: Billy Sunday and Big-time American Evangelism. New York: W. W. Norton, 1992.

Dorsett, Lyle W. Billy Sunday and the Redemption of Urban America. Grand Rapids, Mich.: W. B. Eerdmans, 1991.

Ellis, William T. Billy Sunday: The Man and His Message. Philadelphia: John C. Winston, 1936.

Knickerbocker, Wendy. Sunday at the Ballpark: Billy Sunday's Professional Baseball Career, 1883–1890. Lanham, Md.: Scarecrow Press, 2000.

McLoughlin, William Gerald. Billy Sunday Was His Real Name. Chicago: University of Chicago Press, 1955.

Sunday, Billy. Billy Sunday Speaks. Edited by Karen Gullen. New York: Chelsea House Publishers, 1970.

———. Great Love Stories of the Bible and Their Lessons for Today. New York: G. P. Putnam's Sons, 1917.

Thomas, Lee. The Billy Sunday Story: The Life and Times of William Ashley Sunday, an Authorized Biography. Grand Rapids, Mich.: Zondervan, 1961.

Suzuki, Daisetz Teitarō
(1870-1966) Buddhist teacher and writer

Daisetz Teitarō Suzuki was a central figure in the concourse between Eastern and Western religions that occurred during the 20th century. More than any other single individual, he helped to popularize Zen Buddhism in the United States. He was born Teitarō Suzuki on October 18, 1870, in present-day Kanazawa, Japan, the son of Ryojun Suzuki and Masu Suzuki. His father, grandfather, and great-grandfather were all physicians. Family financial difficulties that followed the early death of Suzuki's father ultimately forced him to withdraw from high school before graduation. Beginning in 1891, though, he studied at Waseda University and Tokyo Imperial University. Soon afterward he began to study informally at Engakuji, a Zen Buddhist temple in Kamakura, first with Kōsen Imagia and then, after Imagia's death in 1892, with Sōen Shaku.

Suzuki's first significant contact with the West came when he translated into English a speech made by Sōen at the World's Parliament of Religions, which met in Chicago, Illinois, in 1893. Shortly before Suzuki traveled to the United States himself in 1897, he achieved *satori,* or enlightenment, and received from Sōen the name Daisetsu, frequently spelled Daisetz in English, which means "Great Simplicity." In the United States, Suzuki helped Paul Caros, the editor of the magazine *Open Court,* translate the *Tao te ching* into English and he eventually published his own English introduction to eastern religious thought in 1907, *Outlines of Mahayana Buddhism.*

By 1909, Suzuki had returned to Japan, where he taught first as a lecturer at Gakushūin University and Tokyo Imperial University and later as a professor at Gakushūin University. Two years later he married Beatrice Lane. The couple worked together closely to popularize Zen Buddhism to the English-speaking world. In 1919 they moved to Kyoto, where Suzuki served first as lecturer and then professor at Ōtani University and where, beginning in 1921, they published *The Eastern Buddhist,* a further attempt to convey Buddhist teaching to an English-speaking audience. Suzuki also authored a number of books in English concerning Buddhism.

After the death of his wife in 1939, Suzuki retired to Kamakura, where he remained during World War II. Following the war, however, he ended his seclusion, teaching first at the University of Hawaii, and then, in 1951, at Columbia University, in New York City. There he had a profound influence on figures such as the pyschoanalyst Erich Fromm, composer John Cage, and poet Allen Ginsberg. Two years after arriving in New York, Suzuki took up residence with the family of one of his students who became his secretary, Mihoko Okamura. He retired from Columbia in the summer of 1957. Thereafter he helped to establish the Cambridge Buddhist Society in Cambridge, Massachusetts, and lectured widely until his death on July 12, 1966, in Tokyo.

In the period after World War II, especially, America discovered the religions of the East. This concourse in understanding had predecessor's such as the Theosophy Society, with its blend of Eastern religion and Western occultism, established by Henry Steel Olcott and Helena Petrovna Blavatsky in the 1870s. But in the 20th century, the East no longer had to rely on Western interpreters but instead found voices of its own through which to speak. Daisetz Teitarō Suzuki was one of the most influential of these voices. He transported the teachings of Buddhism to the United States and helped prompt a growing appreciation for and fascination with Eastern religious thought in the West.

Further Reading

A Zen Life: D.T. Suzuki Remembered. Edited by Masao Abe. New York: Weatherhill, 1986.

Suzuki, Daisetz Teitaro. *The Essentials of Zen Buddhism, Selected from the Writings of Daisetz T. Suzuki.* Edited by Bernard Phillips. New York: Dutton, 1962.

———. *An Introduction to Zen Buddhism.* Edited by Christmas Humphreys. London: Rider, 1983; New York: Grove Weidenfield, 1991.

———. *Living by Zen: A Synthesis of the Historical and Practical Aspects of Zen Buddhism.* London: Rider, 1991.

Switzer, A. Irwin. *D. T. Suzuki: A Biography.* Edited and enlarged by John Snelling. London: The Buddhist Society, 1985.

Szold, Henrietta
(1860–1945) *Zionist leader, founder of Hadassah*

Henrietta Szold forged a prominent place for Jewish women in the Zionist movement, which sought to create an independent state for Jews in Palestine, their historic homeland. History remembers her as the founder of Hadassah, a Zionist women's organization, and as a tireless architect of health and education programs in Palestine. She was born on December 21, 1860, in Baltimore, Maryland, the daughter of Benjamin Szold and Sophie Schaar Szold. Her father was a rabbi, and early in her life she displayed both interest in and aptitude for rabbinical studies that might have led her to become a rabbi had she been a man. As it was, however, she found work as a teacher at a private girls' school after she graduated from high school in 1877. In the late 1880s, Szold began to offer night classes for Russian immigrants.

Szold had written articles for Jewish periodicals since her teenage years and had aided her father in his scholarship, and these experiences prepared her to accept a position in Philadelphia as literary secretary of the Jewish Publication Society of America in 1893. There, her responsibilities included translating Heinrich Graetz's multivolume *History of the Jews*. After three years, however, she returned to Baltimore to care for her ailing father. In Baltimore, she began the first of her public associations with the Zionist movement by joining the Zionist Association of Baltimore in 1897. Two years later she became a member of the executive council of the Federation of American Zionists. Szold's father died in the summer of 1902, and she subsequently moved with her mother to New York City, where she became the first female student at the Jewish Theological Seminary. Of even more consequence for the future course of her life, she joined the Hadassah Study Circle, a small women's club devoted to the cause of Zionism.

In 1909, Szold's commitment to Zionism took a significant step forward after she made a trip to Palestine, where she was dismayed by health conditions and the prevailing poverty. The next year, she became the unpaid secretary of the Federation of American Zionists. Even more significantly, in 1912 her study group became the heart of a new Zionists women's organization, of which Szold was elected president: the Daughters of Zion, later renamed Hadassah, for the group that had been its genesis. Henrietta Szold served as president of Hadassah from 1912 to 1926, then as honorary

president from 1926 until her death in 1945. Under her guidance, Hadassah played a prominent role in sponsoring medical and educational services in Palestine; Szold herself spent a large portion of the following decades there overseeing various humanitarian projects. After her resignation from her position as active president of Hadassah in 1926, Szold was elected to a seat on the Palestine Zionist executive committee and given oversight of health and education matters.

In the 1930s, after the rise of nazism in Germany threatened the safety of Jews there, Szold plunged herself into efforts to rescue Jewish young people from Germany, and later from occupied Europe, and to transplant them to Palestine. Called the Jugendaliyah, the "coming out of the youth," this project occupied much of Szold's attention from 1933 until her death. She never had children of her own, but she became a surrogate mother to many displaced young people, and she saw that they were trained and incorporated within the Jewish settlements in Palestine. She died on February 13, 1945, in Jerusalem, a few months before Germany surrendered.

By the last decade of the 20th century, Hadassah, the organization that Henrietta Szold founded, had more than 300,000 members and was the largest Jewish organization in the United States. Unlike many American Zionists, who supported the cause of a Jewish homeland in Palestine from their homes in the United States, Szold lived for the better part of 20 years out of a suitcase in hotels in Jerusalem, laboring to create the framework for the Zionist vision whose ultimate fulfillment in the creation of the state of Israel in 1948 she did not live to see. Her indefatigable humanitarian efforts, both in supervising medical and educational programs in Palestine and in orchestrating the rescue of more than 20,000 Jewish young people from the Holocaust, made her one of the 20th century's most revered Jewish leaders.

Further Reading

Dash, Joan. *Summoned to Jerusalem: The Life of Henrietta Szold*. New York: Harper & Row, 1979.

Fineman, Irving. *Woman of Valor: The Life of Henrietta Szold, 1860–1945*. New York: Simon & Schuster, 1961.

Gidal, Tim. *Henrietta Szold: A Documentation in Photos and Text.* Jerusalem: Gefen Publishing House, 1997.

Krantz, Hazel. *Daughter of My People: Henrietta Szold and Hadassah.* New York: Dutton, 1987.

Levinger, Elma Ehrlich. *Fighting Angel: The Story of Henrietta Szold.* New York: Behrman House, 1946.

Lowenthal, Marvin. *Henrietta Szold: Life and Letters.* Westport, Conn.: Greenwood Press, 1975.

Szold, Henrietta. *Lost Love, the Untold Story of Henrietta Szold: Unpublished Diary and Letters.* Edited by Baila Round Shargel. Philadelphia: Jewish Publication Society, 1997.

Zeitlin, Rose. *Henrietta Szold: Record of a Life.* New York: Dial Press, 1952.

T

Taylor, Nathaniel William

(1786–1858) *Congregationalist minister, theologian, educator*

Nathaniel William Taylor helped to shape what became known as the New Haven theology, a reaction against the influence of JONATHAN EDWARDS. As a professor at Yale Divinity School, Taylor championed a less deterministic vision of Calvinism, which played a prominent role during the later decades of the 19th century. He was born on June 23, 1786, in New Milford, Connecticut, the son of Nathaniel Taylor and Anne Northrop Taylor. His grandfather had been a minister of the Congregationalist church in New Milford and a trustee of Yale College. Taylor himself attended Yale, where he fell under the influence of TIMOTHY DWIGHT, president and professor at the college, and graduated in 1807. Three years later he married Rebecca Maria Hine, with whom he had six children. He was licensed to preach the same year. In the spring of 1812, he was ordained as the pastor of the First Church of New Haven, Connecticut.

As a preacher—and later, as a divinity school professor—Taylor championed a version of Calvinism that departed sharply from the prominent influence of Jonathan Edwards. Taylor welcomed the revivalism of the Second Great Awakening and attempted to articulate a theology more hospitable to revivalism and more immune to the steady encroachments of Unitarianism. Edwards had emphasized a theological determinism in which the inherent sinfulness of humans incapacitated them to choose to receive God's salvation. In contrast, Taylor downplayed the idea of inherent sinfulness and found a place for human freedom to accept salvation. Though he accepted the doctrine of original sin, he nevertheless insisted that "sin is in the sinning," and he maintained that men and women had "power to the contrary." Men and women were sinful because they chose to sin, not merely because they were descendants of Adam, the first sinner, as Edwards had contended. Taylor's revision of Calvinistic theology admirably served the cause of revivalism. Revival was no longer the inexplicable product of God's sovereign ways, but the rational consequence of revival preaching that called on listeners to turn away from sin and exercise their "power to the contrary." In general, Taylor's theology paved the way for Arminianism, a system of Christian belief that would become prominent throughout the remainder of the 19th century. It also laid the foundation for the many reform movements that traveled in the wake of revivalism and would finally produce the Social Gospel movement of the late 19th and early 20th centuries.

After a decade as a minister, Taylor was appointed the first professor at the newly established theology department of Yale College, which would become Yale Divinity School. In this position, he was able to exercise a powerful influence on the development of Congregationalist theology, and he used this influence to continue his assault of Edwardian determinism. In an important address, "Concio ad Clerum," which he delivered at the college commencement on September 10, 1828, Taylor reiterated his view that sin had to be traced not to an inevitable disposition to sin but to "man's own act consisting in a free choice of some object rather than God as his chief good."

Taylor remained at Yale for more than a quarter of a century, influencing a generation of New England preachers. He died on March 10, 1858, in New Haven.

Nathaniel Taylor's modified Calvinism suited the democratic temper of Jacksonian America. Old School Calvinism had chained human potential to the weight of inherent human depravity, and, as Americans spilled west across the frontier, this theological weight was ill suited to the general optimism of the times. Taylor crafted a theology infused with a more hopeful view of human potential, a theology with a larger place for free will and consequently a more prominent role for human endeavors of all kinds. The New Haven theology energized revivalism by teaching that humans could choose to receive God's gracious gift of salvation; it inspired men and women to undertake social reform by promising that humans could choose the right path. These new spiritual certainties eventually dominated the 19th century, and their dominance must be traced in part to the preaching and teaching of Nathaniel Taylor.

Further Reading

Hirrel, Leo P. *Children of Wrath: New School Calvinism and Antebellum Reform.* Lexington: University Press of Kentucky, 1998.

Mead, Sidney Earl. *Nathaniel William Taylor, 1786–1858: A Connecticut Liberal.* Chicago: University of Chicago Press, 1942.

Taylor, Nathaniel William. *Essays, Lectures, etc. upon Select Topics in Revealed Theology.* New York: Clark, Austin & Smith, 1859; New York: Garland, 1987.

———. *Lectures on the Moral Government of God.* 2 vols. New York: Clark, Austin & Smith, 1859; New York: Garland, 1987.

———. *Practical Sermons.* New York: Garland, 1987.

Wayland, John Terrill. *The Theological Department in Yale College, 1822–1858.* New York: Garland, 1987.

Tekakwitha, Kateri
(Kateri Tegakwitha, Kateri Tegakouita, Catherine Tekakwitha)
(1656–1680) *Catholic lay leader, candidate for Catholic sainthood*

A Native American convert to Catholicism, Kateri Tekakwitha (sometimes rendered Tegakwitha or Tegakouita) lived a short life, made prominent by her devotion to the Christian faith and by the sufferings she experienced because of it. She was known as "the Lily of the Mohawks" for the vow of chastity she took and the gentle and pious character of her life, and she became the first Native American proposed for sainthood. Tekakwitha was born in 1656 in a Mohawk village near present-day Auriesville, New York, the daughter of a Mohawk chief and an Algonquin mother who had been converted to Christianity. When she was four years old, a smallpox epidemic in her village killed both her parents and left her face scarred and her eyes weakened. Tekakwitha was thereafter raised by her uncle.

In 1667, the French forced the Mohawk to allow Jesuits into the village where Tekakwitha lived, and her uncle, the village chief, required her to attend to their needs. This encounter with the Jesuits, when Tekakwitha was 11 years old, left a lasting impression on the young girl, even though her uncle continued to be fiercely opposed to Christianity. Seven years later, Father James de Lamberville visited Tekakwitha's village. He instructed her in the Catholic faith and baptized her Catherine Tekakwitha on Easter Sunday 1676.

Initially remaining in her village, Tekakwitha suffered the animosity of the other Mohawks. When she refused to work in the fields on Sunday, the village denied her food and pelted her with stones. She became the brunt of insults and rebukes, scornfully designated "the Christian." Eventually, she escaped from her village and made a 200-mile trek to the French mission of St. Francis Xavier at Sault St. Louis on the St. Lawrence River, near Montreal, Canada. The mission, called Kahnawake by the Indians, sheltered a vital community of Native American Christians.

At Kahnawake, Tekakwitha took a vow of chastity and undertook a pattern of spiritual devotion characterized by its extreme austerity. She fasted twice a week, walked barefoot in snow and ice, and slept over the course of three nights on a bed of thorns. These physical mortifications apparently took their toll, and Kateri Tekakwitha died on April 17, 1680, at Kahnawake, when she was 24 years old. Almost immediately, Native American and French pilgrims began to seek the site of he grave, and over the years, miracles were attributed to her intervention.

In the late 19th century, efforts began to have Tekakwitha declared a saint. She became a candidate for canonization in 1884. The Catholic Church declared her venerable in 1943, and in 1980 she was beatified by Pope John Paul II. Her feast day is July 14, and she is considered among Catholics to be the patron of the environment and ecology.

Encounters between Native American and white cultures in North America during the 17th century often proceeded violently, and Kateri Tekakwitha's conversion to Christianity exposed her to one form of this violence. Exposed to loss at an early age through the death of her parents and the disfiguring effects of disease on her own body, Tekakwitha through her conversion became an outsider and the object of abuse in her Mohawk village. Though she eventually found a spiritual home at the mission in Canada, she nevertheless voluntarily embraced new forms of suffering in her devotion to her adopted faith.

Further Reading

Buehrle, Marie Cecilia. *Kateri of the Mohawks.* Milwaukee, Wis.: Bruce, 1954.

Koppedrayer, K. I. "The Making of the First Iroquois Virgin: Early Jesuit Biographies of Kateri Tekakwitha." *Ethnohistory* 40 (1993): 277–306.

Sargent, Daniel. *Catherine Tekakwitha.* New York: Longmans, Green, 1936.

Walworth, Ellen H. *The Life and Times of Kateri Tekakwitha.* Buffalo, N.Y.: P. Paul & Brother, 1891.

Tennent, Gilbert

(1705–1764) *Presbyterian minister*

Gilbert Tennent, an important revivalist during the Great Awakening, has tended to be eclipsed by GEORGE WHITEFIELD, the Awakening's premier preacher, and by JONATHAN EDWARDS, its theologian. But his participation both in Presbyterian divisions brought about by the Great Awakening and in attempts to heal those divisions in later years made him one of Presbyterianism's most significant figures during the middle years of the 18th century. He was born on February 5, 1705, in Vinnecash, Ireland, to WILLIAM TENNENT and Katherine Kennedy Tennent. Gilbert's father was a minister of the Church of Ireland who began to oppose many of the church's beliefs and practices in the second decade of the 18th century. Dissatisfied with spiritual prospects in Ireland, William Tennent migrated with his family to Philadelphia, Pennsylvania, in 1718, and promptly allied himself with the Presbyterian synod there. The father became a crucial teacher and spiritual mentor for the son. In 1723, Gilbert had a conversion experience, and though for a time he had contemplated a career in medicine, his conversion inspired him to prepare to preach. On the basis of his long tutelage under his father, he was able to obtain an M.A. from Yale College in 1725, though he had no undergraduate degree.

On graduation from Yale, Tennent was licensed by the Philadelphia Presbytery to preach in 1725, and the following year he was ordained as the pastor of a church in New Brunswick. There he became friends with THEODORUS JACOBUS FRELINGHUYSEN, the minister of a nearby Dutch Reformed congregation. Under Frelinghuysen's influence, Tennent began to see the progress of conversion as consisting of three distinct stages: law work, in which a sinner became aware of his sinfulness and need of God's grace; spiritual rebirth; and a life given to the practice of piety. At first, Tennent despaired that his efforts to see hearers converted were producing no fruit. He would later describe this early experience.

> I was then exceedingly grieved that I had done so little for God, and was very desirous to live one *half Year* more if it was his Will, that I might stand upon the Stage of the World as it were, and plead more faithfully for his Cause, and take more earnest Pains for the *Conversion of Souls.*

Eventually, though, Tennent developed a revivalistic preaching style that anticipated the evangelistic preaching of George Whitefield and helped initiate the Great Awakening in the 1740s. Tennent, in fact, met Whitefield and accompanied him on his first preaching tour through the middle colonies in 1739. Like Whitefield, Gilbert Tennent earned criticism for his unsettling jeremiads against ministers he believed to be unconverted. But this criticism deterred neither Tennent nor Whitefield from regular attacks on preachers who lacked their zeal for the conversion of souls. In 1740, Tennent published the sermon *The Danger of an Unconverted Ministry*. Just as they spared no criticism of unregenerate clergy, Tennent's sermons bristled with sharp descriptions of the perilous situation of those who had not yet experienced conversion. "Preaching the terrors," he believed, was a necessary prerequisite to sermons describing the grace of God.

In 1740 Tennent suffered the death of his first wife, whose name and background are unknown. He married Cornelia Bancker de Pyster Clarkson, a widow who brought several children to their union, in 1742. After her death in 1753, Tennent married Sarah Spoffard, with whom he had three children.

During the 1740s, Presbyterians split over ideas generated by the Great Awakening, as evangelical Presbyterians such as Tennent formed a new synod in New York, distinct from the Philadelphia synod, in which an antirevivalistic spirit prevailed. Tennent also migrated from his church in New Brunswick to Philadelphia, where he eventually became the pastor of the Second Presbyterian Church. Gilbert Tennent's father had established the "Log College," an influential academy for Presbyterian ministers, and Gilbert demonstrated a devotion to education similar to that of his father. In 1746, he became a trustee of the College of New Jersey (later Princeton University). In the following decade, he traveled with SAMUEL DAVIES, a Virginia minister and later president of the college, to raise funds for its support in Great Britain.

In his later years Tennant became a force for reconciliation among Presbyterians who had been divided in the course of the Great Awakening. The New York and Philadelphia synods merged in 1758, and Tennent became the first moderator to preside over the unified body. He died in Philadelphia on July 23, 1764.

Although George Whitefield's preaching sparked the Great Awakening, the decade-long progress of that American spiritual movement owed much to the local labors of men such as Gilbert Tennent. Tennent provided fuel for the fires that Whitefield ignited and strove to create and sustain institutions such as the College of New Jersey to convey their evangelical faith to the next generation.

Further Reading

Brink, Frederick W. *The Contribution of Gilbert Tennent to American Christianity and the American Nation.* Philadelphia: Temple University Press, 1942.

———. "Gilbert Tennent, Dynamic Preacher." *Journal of the Presbyterian Historical Society* 32 (March 1954): 91–107.

Coalter, Milton. J., Jr. *Gilbert Tennent, Son of Thunder: A Case Study of Continental Pietism's Impact on the First Great Awakening in the Middle Colonies.* New York: Greenwood Press, 1986.

Sermons of the Log College. Edited by Archibald Alexander. Ligonier, Penn.: Soli Deo Gloria Publications, 1993.

Tennent, Gilbert. *The Danger of an Unconverted Ministry.* Philadelphia: Benjamin Franklin, 1740.

Tennent, William
(1673–1746) *Presbyterian minister*

The father of Presbyterian education in North America, William Tennent contributed an Old World respect for learning to the infant Presbyterianism of the New World. The school he established, dubbed the "Log College" by its detractors, became a model for future Presbyterian institutions of learning, including the College of New Jersey (later Princeton University). Tennent was born in Scotland in 1673, the son of John Tennent and Sarah Hume Tennent. Although details of his early life are unknown, he graduated with an M.A. from Edinburgh University in 1695 and thereafter served as a chaplain in the household of Anne, duchess of Hamilton. He seems to have been licensed to preach by the presbytery in Scotland before he migrated to Ireland, where he was admitted to the Ulster Synod of the Presbyterians in 1701. In 1702, he married Katherine Kennedy, with whom he had five children, including a son, GILBERT TENNENT, who became an influential Presbyterian minister in North America's middle colonies.

In 1704, Tennent abandoned Presbyterianism to become a deacon and then a presbyter in the Church of Ireland. Over the next 14 years, however, he became disenchanted with that church. He never had a parish of his own and eventually contemplated a return to Presbyterianism, which he accomplished by migrating with his family to North America in 1718 and promptly seeking admittance to the Presbyterian Synod in Philadelphia. His stated reasons for leaving the Church of Ireland included his opposition to "the Churches conniving at the Practice of Arminian Doctrine inconsistent with the eternal Purpose of God, and an Encouragement to Vice." "Besides," he informed the Philadelphia Presbyterians, "I could not be satisfied with their Ceremonial way of worship. These . . . have so affected my Conscience, yet I could no longer abide in a Church where the same are practiced."

Admitted as a Presbyterian minister after some debate, William Tennent ministered briefly to a congregation in East Chester, New York, before moving with his family to Bedford, New York. In Bedford, he earned sufficient respect from other ministerial colleagues in the area to be considered for the position of minister at the Yale College church. When this opportunity did not materialize, Tennent found his situation insufficient to support his family. In 1726, he moved them to Bucks County, Pennsylvania, where he preached to a Dutch congregation in Bensalem and to a Scottish congregation that had settled near the mouth of the Neshaminy River. Later he added to these ministries preaching at Deep Run.

Tennent's purchase of 100 acres in Warminster Township in 1735 would constitute a crucial transition in his life. There he established an academy, in what the famous revivalist GEORGE WHITEFIELD would describe as a "log-house, about twenty feet long, and nearly as many broad," which Tennent's opponents would mock as the Log College. However inauspicious its physical setting, Tennent's academy infused Presbyterianism in the middle colonies with a strong dose of respect for an edu-

cated ministry. Almost all of his students went on to become Presbyterian ministers, and his school became the model for other Presbyterian colleges that would follow, not the least of which was the College of New Jersey founded in 1746. Tennent died on May 6, 1746, in Neshaminy, Pennsylvania.

William Tennent is remembered more as an educator than as a preacher. But the education he provided to future Presbyterian ministers from 1735 on was infused with religious faith even as it sought to emulate the educational standards of great European institutions such as Edinburgh University. By Tennent's influence, evangelical Presbyterianism of the 18th century allied itself with higher education and thus attained a more significant influence on American culture than it might otherwise have had.

Further Reading

Alexander, Archibald. *The Log College: Biographical Sketches of William Tennent and His Students, Together with an Account of the Revivals under Their Ministries.* Philadelphia: Presbyterian Board of Education, 1851; London: Banner of Truth Trust, 1968.

Ingram, George H. "Biographies of the Alumni of the Log College, II: William Tennent, Sr., the Founder." *Journal of Presbyterian History* 14 (March 1930): 1–27.

Pears, Thomas Clinton, Jr. *Documentary History of William Tennent and the Log College.* Philadelphia: Presbyterian Historical Society, 1940.

Sermons of the Log College. Edited by Archibald Alexander. Ligonier, Penn.: Soli Deo Gloria Publications, 1993.

Tennent, Mary A. *Light in Darkness: The Story of William Tennent, Sr. and the Log College.* Greensboro, N.C.: Greensboro, 1971.

Tenskwatawa
(Lalawethika, the Shawnee Prophet)
(1775–1836) *Native American religious leader*

A Native American religious leader known as the Shawnee Prophet, Tenskwatawa briefly led a revitalization of traditional Indian religion in the early years of the 19th century. After he had prophesied that his followers would be immune to the weapons of U.S. soldiers at the battle of Tippecanoe, the failure of this prophecy stripped him of most authority among his people. He was born Lalawethika ("the Noisemaker") in 1775, at Old Piqua, a Shawnee village in Ohio. His father, Puckeshinwa, was a Shawnee war chief who died prior to Lalawethika's birth. His mother, Methoataske, was a Creek Indian. Methoataske left Ohio after her husband's death, and left her children—including the famous Shawnee leader Tecumseh—in the care of one of her daughters. As he grew up, Lalawethika lacked the physical prowess of his brother, Tecumseh, and, in an accident with bow and arrow, lost an eye. He consequently found himself overshadowed by his brother. Moreover, adding to his alienation among the Shawnee, he became an alcoholic.

After 1795, Lalawethika came of age, married, and had several children. But he had difficulty supporting his family, because he was a poor hunter and because he had problems with alcohol. Lalawethika eventually became friends with a Shawnee medicine man, Penagashe, who taught him some of his skills. After Penagashe died in 1804, Lalawethika attempted to replace him as shaman, but his skill as a medicine man proved as uneven as his skill at hunting, and his fellow Shawnee did not accept him.

In 1805, however, Lalawethika claimed to have experienced the first of a series of visions, which would establish him as a religious leader among his people. In his first vision, he visited the spirit world and saw paradise, where the Shawnee lived a life of abundance and happiness. But sinful Shawnee were turned back from the door to this paradise and consigned to an enormous lodge where they suffered torment. On awakening from this vision, Lalawethika swore never to drink alcohol again, abandoned the name given him at birth, and chose instead to be called Tenskwatawa, which means "Open door."

In the months that followed, Tenskwatawa elaborated the substance of additional visions to a growing number of followers. The people of the world, he said, sprang from two sources. The Creator of Life had made the Shawnee and other Native Americans; the Great Serpent, a force of primordial evil, had created whites. The Creator of Life insisted that the Shawnee distance themselves from whites and their ways. Tenskwatawa's message offered a convincing explanation to many Native Americans of the turmoil they experienced as a result of the unrelenting advance of white civilization. In the summer of 1806, the Shawnee Prophet, as he was now called, was able to obtain advance warning of an impending eclipse and used his knowledge to impress the skeptical among his people by his prediction of a "black sun."

In 1808, Tenskwatawa and Tecumseh relocated to a village named Prophetstown in the Indiana Territory, near the juncture of the Tippecanoe and Wabash Rivers. There Tecumseh tried to leverage his brother's religious authority to unite Native American tribes into a common alliance against further territorial threats from white settlers. Alarmed at this development, William Henry Harrison, the governor of the Indiana Territory, led a military

Tenskwatawa, known as the Shawnee Prophet, led in a revitalization of Native American religion during the early years of the 19th century. *(Library of Congress, Prints and Photographs Division, LC-USZ62-23787)*

force against the Native Americans at Prophetstown in the fall of 1811. Although Tenskwatawa assured his followers that they would be immune to the weapons of the white soldiers, Harrison and his force destroyed Prophetstown and killed many Native Americans. After this defeat, Tenskwatawa's influence suffered precipitous decline.

Together with Tecumseh, Tenskwatawa sided with the British during the War of 1812. But after Tecumseh's death in 1813 at the Battle of Thames, Tenskwatawa fled to Canada, where he remained in exile for more than a decade, attempting unsuccessfully to regain the spiritual authority that he had once had. He returned to the United States in 1825, however, and federal authorities persuaded him to help them relocate Shawnee in Ohio to a new reservation west of the Mississippi. Eventually, Tenskwatawa and other Shawnee settled at a reservation in Kansas along the Kansas River. He died there in November 1836.

Religious awakenings often travel in the wake of social upheaval, as those unmoored from a stable past seek to make sense of a turbulent present. Tenskwatawa's religious influence among the Shawnee and other Native Americans illustrates this common pattern. One consequence of the collision between Native American and white cultures was that this pattern would repeat itself in the future, as Native Americans sought to understand a world that seemed increasingly inhospitable to their traditional patterns of life.

Further Reading

Cave, A. A. "The Failure of the Shawnee Prophets Witch-hunt." *Ethnohistory* 42 (1995): 445–75.

Drake, Benjamin. *Life of Tecumseh and of His Brother the Prophet, with a Historical Sketch of the Shawanee Indians.* New York: Arno Press, 1969.

Edmunds, R. David. *The Shawnee Prophet.* Lincoln: University of Nebraska Press, 1983.

Eggleston, Edward, and Lillie Eggleston Seelye. *Tecumseh and the Shawnee Prophet.* New York: Dodd, Mead, 1878.

Jacobs, Lyn Richard. "Native American Prophetic Movements of the Eighteenth and Nineteenth Centuries." Ph.D. dissertation, Syracuse University, 1995.

Tillich, Paul Johannes
(1886–1965) *theologian*

One of the most prominent American theologians of the 20th century, German-born Paul Tillich was exiled from his country during the 1940s and became a U.S. citizen. His theology, firmly anchored to the philosophy of existentialism, sought to bridge the widening gap between traditional Christian doctrines and 20th-century secularism. He was born Paul Johannes Tillich on August 20, 1886, in Starzeddel, East Prussia (a province of the German Empire), to Johannes Tillich and Wilhelmina Mathilde Düselen Tillich. His father was a Lutheran pastor, but in the course of his university years, studying at Berlin, Tübingen, and Halle, Tillich migrated from his father's conservative faith. He obtained a Ph.D. from the University of Breslau in 1911 and his licentiate in theology from the University of Halle the following year.

In 1912, Tillich was ordained a minister in the Evangelical Lutheran Church and became the pastor of a church in Berlin. He married Margareth ("Grethi") Wever in 1914 and, within the week, volunteered to serve as an army chaplain, a post he held until 1919. Tillich's marriage to Margareth produced one child, who died in infancy. The couple divorced in 1921, and, after adopting a bohemian life-style for several years, in 1924 Tillich married Hannah Werner Gottschow, with whom he had two children.

After World War I, Tillich found a home in academia and taught at universities in Berlin, Marburg, Dresden, Leipzig, and finally Frankfurt over the following years. Disillusioned by the war, Tillich embraced socialism and attempted to meld its political philosophy with his own theological reflections. He published widely and soon became an important figure within the German intellectual community. When the Nazi Party rose to power in 1933, however, Tillich, who publicly defended Jewish students, found himself suspended from his professorship at the University of Frankfurt. At this point, the American theologian REINHOLD NIEBUHR secured Tillich an academic appointment at Union Theological Seminary in New York City. In 1937 the seminary tenured Tillich and made him an endowed professor, and three years later, the German-born theologian became a U.S. citizen.

After World War II, Tillich's reputation continued to increase, especially as he found in the language of existentialism a vocabulary for his own theological reflections. Two world wars had driven many intellectuals to despair of finding meaning in existence and to feel a sense of helplessness in the face of chaos, and Tillich deemed the task of theology one of responding to questions posed by the cultural context in which it finds itself. This "method of correlation," as he referred to it, "explains the contents of the Christian Faith through existential questions and theological answers in mutual interdependence."

To the angst of 20th-century society, Tillich offered a renewed focus on a God who was not the supernatural other standing above and outside a chaotic world, but rather the ground of all being, "being-itself." This God was not to be found in creeds or catechisms or churches with their various pontifications and pronouncements. Tillich referred to the necessity of rejecting all pretensions of spiritual certainty as the "Protestant principle." This principle was, he said, "the guardian against the attempts of the finite and conditioned to usurp the place of the unconditional in thinking and acting. It is the prophetic judgment against religious pride, ecclesiastical arrogance, and secular self-sufficiency and their destructive consequences." The God on whom he sought to focus attention was the "God beyond God," the God who grounded all other being but also transcended it and transcended as well every human attempt to name the unnameable deity. The "New Being" in Jesus as the Christ represented the possibility of human reconciliation with the ground of being, since Jesus experienced the conditions of existence and nevertheless overcame existential estrangement. In light of this possibility, one need not succumb to existential paralysis in the face of chaos and nothingness. Nor does the reality of doubt destroy the possibility of faith. In an enigmatic final sentence to his most popular book, *The Courage to Be*, Tillich declared that "[t]he courage to be is rooted in the God who appears when God has disappeared in the anxiety of doubt."

Paul Tillich remained at Union Theological Seminary until 1955, when he joined the faculty at Harvard University. He accepted his final university appointment in 1962, by becoming the Nu-veen Professor of Theology at the University of Chicago Divinity School. He died on October 22, 1965, in Chicago.

Tillich, as much as any other American theologian of the 20th century, attempted to stand at the crossroads between Christian faith and modern anxiety. Often obscure, he nevertheless became deeply influential to other religious thinkers who tried to occupy a similar ground. Orthodox Christians often complained that in his attempt to answer the questions of modern secular society, Tillich had strayed outside the fold of Christianity altogether. But his defenders answered that Tillich had simply staked out a theological territory at the boundary between faith and unbelief, arguing that this was the only vantage from which authentic theology could proceed.

Further Reading

Adams, James Luther. *Paul Tillich's Philosophy of Culture, Science, and Religion.* New York: Harper & Row, 1965.

Pauck, Wilhelm & Marion Pauck. *Paul Tillich: His Life and Thought.* New York: Harper & Row, 1976.

Tait, Leslie Gordon. *The Promise of Tillich.* Philadelphia: Lippincott, 1971.

Thomas, J. Heywood. *Paul Tillich.* Richmond: John Knox Press, 1966.

Tillich, Hannah. *From Time to Time.* New York: Stein & Day, 1973.

Tillich, Paul. *The Courage to Be.* New Haven, Conn.: Yale University Press, 1952.

———. *Dynamics of Faith.* New York: Harpers, 1956.

———. *My Search for Absolutes.* New York: Simon & Schuster, 1967.

———. *On the Boundary: An Autobiographical Sketch.* New York: Scribner, 1966.

———. *Systematic Theology.* 3 vols. Chicago: University of Chicago Press, 1951–63.

Visick, Vernon Mansell. "Paul Tillich and the University." Ph.D. dissertation, University of Chicago, 2000.

Torrey, Reuben Archer

(1856–1928) *Congregationalist minister, revivalist, educator*

Reuben Archer Torrey linked late 19th-century revivalism with the fundamentalist movement of the next century. Though not as gifted a revival preacher as DWIGHT LYMAN MOODY, his mentor, Torrey had abilities as an educator and a popular writer that played a crucial role in sustaining and enriching the essential theological commitments of evangelical Protestantism in the early 20th century. Torrey was born on the eve of the Civil War, on January 28, 1856, in Hoboken, New Jersey, the son of Reuben Slayton Torrey and Elizabeth Archer Swift Torrey. Torrey's father was a banker and a wealthy manufacturer, and neither the Civil War nor its aftermath disturbed the son's privileged childhood. He attended Yale University, where he received a B.A. in 1875, and then Yale Divinity School, where he received a bachelor of divinity degree in 1878. The following year Torrey married Clara Belle Smith, with whom he had five children.

After several years as pastor of a Congregationalist church in Garrettsville, Ohio, Torrey spent a year studying theology at Leipzig and Erlangen in Germany. Exposed there to higher criticism of the Bible, Torrey returned to the United States convinced of the danger of liberal theological tendencies and committed to the inerrancy of the Bible. He settled in Minneapolis, Minnesota, first as the minister of the Open Door Congregational Church from 1883 to 1886, then as superintendent of the Minneapolis City Missionary Society from 1886 to 1889. While in Minneapolis, Torrey attracted the attention of revivalist Dwight L. Moody, who invited him to take charge of the Chicago Bible Institute, which Moody had founded in 1887 and whose first building was constructed in the year that Torrey became its superintendent. The institute, intended to train urban evangelists, became a crucial force in the perpetuation of Moody's evangelical Protestant vision, through both the students who passed through its doors and the allied institutions whose creation it inspired.

Torrey captained the Chicago Bible Institute (renamed the Moody Bible Institute after Moody's death in 1899) from 1889 through 1908. During this period, he also served as pastor of the Chicago Avenue Church from 1894 through 1906. From these influential posts, Torrey quickly assumed the mantle as Moody's anointed successor. In fact, two years after Moody's death, Torrey took a sabbatical

from his responsibilities in Chicago in order to conduct a four-year worldwide revival campaign reminiscent of Moody's own career as an urban revivalist. This new direction of his energies eventually caused Torrey to resign as pastor of the Chicago Avenue Church in 1906 and as president of the Moody Bible Institute two years later.

Torrey joined his new incarnation as a revival preacher with a steady career as a Christian author and eventually published more than 40 books. By the second decade of the 20th century, however, he had settled in California, where, in 1912, he became the dean of the Bible Institute of Los Angeles. Three years later he added to this undertaking service as the pastor of the nondenominational Church of the Open Door in Los Angeles. He held both positions until his retirement in 1924.

By the early 20th century, the theological differences that had simmered between liberals and conservatives for decades finally flared into open conflict. Leading evangelical conservatives sought to draw a sharp demarcation between themselves and the currents of liberalism by publishing *The Fundamentals* (1910–15), a 12-volume series of articles by leading conservatives. The articles defended tenets of Protestant orthodoxy such as the virgin birth of Christ and the reality of hell, and—against the theories of higher biblical criticism that had taken root among Protestant liberals—they explicitly affirmed the Bible's inerrancy. Torrey placed himself at the center of this theological movement, named *fundamentalism,* for the books that gave it expression, by editing the last two volumes of *The Fundamentals.* After his retirement in 1924, Torrey moved to North Carolina. He died on October 26, 1928, in Asheville, North Carolina.

As the successor of the 19th century's premier revivalist, Reuben Archer Torrey helped to shepherd evangelical Protestantism into the century that followed. He did so through gifts that complemented and supplemented those of his mentor, Dwight L. Moody. He possessed a sufficient measure of Moody's revivalistic temper to provide continuity for the spiritual movement that Moody's revival preaching had sparked. But he also excelled Moody in some respects: he was more comfortable with reasoned appeals than with emotional ones, more the teacher than the preacher. These gifts made him an able advocate of conservative Christianity in the 20th century.

Further Reading

Brereton, Virginia Lieson. *Training God's Army: The American Bible School, 1880–1940*. Bloomington: Indiana University Press, 1990.

Davis, George Thompson Brown. *Torrey and Alexander: The Story of a World-Wide Revival, a Record and Study of the Work and Personality of the Evangelists R. A. Torrey, D.D., and Charles M. Alexander*. New York: Fleming H. Revell, 1905.

Harkness, Robert. *Reuben Archer Torrey: The Man, His Message*. Chicago: The Bible Institute Colportage Association, 1929.

Marsden, George M. *Fundamentalism and American Culture: The Shaping of Twentieth Century Evangelicalism, 1870–1925*. New York: Oxford University Press, 1980.

Martin, Roger. *R. A. Torrey: Apostle of Certainty*. Murfreesboro, Tenn.: Sword of the Lord Publishers, 1976.

Torrey, Reuben Archer. *Conservative Call to Arms*. Edited by Joel A. Carpenter. New York: Garland, 1988.

———. *Revival Addresses*. Chicago: Fleming H. Revel, 1903; Cambridge, England: J. Clarke, 1974.

Turner, Henry McNeal

(1834–1915) *bishop of the African Methodist Episcopal Church*

A forerunner of the modern Civil Rights movement, Henry McNeal Turner served 35 years as a bishop of the African Methodist Episcopal (A.M.E.) Church. As a leader of the premier African-American institution of the late 19th and early 20th centuries, Turner was one of the most important black leaders of his day. He was born on February 1, 1834, in Newberry, South Carolina, the son of Hardy Turner and Sarah Greer Turner, who were free blacks. Turner was converted at a camp meeting when he was a teenager and subsequently determined to become a Methodist minister.

By 1853, at the age of 19, Turner was licensed as an itinerant minister by the Methodist Episcopal Church, South. In 1856, he married Eliza Ann Peacher, with whom he had 14 children. In 1858, he joined the A.M.E. Church, and for the next

five years, he served as a minister for churches in Baltimore and Washington, D.C. After President Abraham Lincoln issued the Emancipation Proclamation in 1863, Turner helped to organize a regiment of black soldiers, the First U.S. Colored Troops, and then served as the regiment's chaplain, the first African American commissioned as a chaplain in the United States Army. At the conclusion of the Civil War, he settled in Georgia, where he worked briefly for the Freedman's Bureau and then turned to missions work for the A.M.E. Church. Largely confined to the North and Midwest before this time, the church grew rapidly over the following years, in large part because of Turner's evangelistic efforts. Perhaps more than any single individual, Turner helped to make it a national institution by spearheading its growth in the former states of the Confederacy.

During the late 1860s, Turner added a political career to his religious one, working to organize the Republican Party in Georgia and winning election to the Georgia legislature in 1868. After he and 23 other black legislators were illegally deprived of their seats the following year, he served briefly as postmaster in Macon, before a scandal that involved alleged consorting with a prostitute and passing of false bank notes forced him to resign. He was able to reclaim his legislative seat by congressional order in 1870 but lost it in his first reelection bid the same year. He subsequently was pastor of an A.M.E. church in Savannah until 1876, when he was appointed manager of the A.M.E. Church's publishing house and moved to Philadelphia, Pennsylvania, to take charge of its affairs. In 1880, he returned to Georgia and settled in Atlanta, after he was elected a bishop of the A.M.E. Church.

Over the following years, Turner continued to press the expansion of the A.M.E. Church in the South, even as he remained a vocal critic of race relations in the United States. He challenged the racial presuppositions of dominant American Christianity, controversially claiming in 1895 that "God is a Negro" and urging blacks to produce a new translation of the Bible that would remove the racist undertones he saw planted there by whites. He wrote in a column for *The Voice of Missions* in August 1899:

The white man's digest of Christianity or Bible doctrines are not suited to the wants, manhood growth, and progress of the Negro. Indeed he has colored the Bible in his translation to suit the white man, and made it, in many respects, objectionable to the Negro. And until a company of learned black men shall rise up and retranslate the Bible, it will not be wholly acceptable and in keeping with the higher conceptions of the black man.

Dismayed by the treatment of African Americans, Turner eventually became a fervent advocate of colonization schemes that would send blacks to Africa, where they might form a political community of their own and spread the message of Christianity to that continent's inhabitants. He also accepted a position as honorary vice president of the American Colonization Society in 1876, though this appointment produced friction with many in the African-American community who suspected the organization of racist designs. Turner founded and edited two newspapers to communicate his ideas on the subject, *The Voice of Missions,* published from 1893 to 1900, and *The Voice of the People,* from 1901 to 1904. He died of a stroke while conducting A.M.E. business in Windsor, Canada, on May 8, 1915.

Henry McNeal Turner was a relatively young man when the Thirteenth Amendment to the U.S. Constitution abolished slavery and the Fourteenth guaranteed the equal protection of law to all American citizens. He briefly tasted the promise of these amendments in the late 1860s, when he won election to the state legislature of Georgia and served briefly as a postmaster. But the course of his years after the Civil War was mainly characterized by disappointment, as southern whites found ways to frustrate the promise of the Constitution's Reconstruction Amendments. The disillusionments of these years made Turner an advocate of African colonization schemes, but they did not prevent him from playing a leading role in the growth of the A.M.E. Church in the South. His part in the strengthening of African-American churches would bear important fruit in the second half of the 20th century, when these institutions provided crucial support for the Civil Rights movement.

Further Reading

Angell, Stephen Ward. *Bishop Henry McNeal Turner and African-American Religion in the South.* Knoxville: University of Tennessee Press, 1992.

Ponton, Mungo Melanchthon. *Life and Times of Henry M. Turner: The Antecedent and Preliminary History of the Life and Times of Bishop H. M. Turner, His Boyhood, Education and Public Career, and His Relation to His Associates, Colleagues and Contemporaries.* Atlanta: A. B. Caldwell, 1917; New York: Negro Universities Press, 1970.

Turner, Henry McNeal. *The Genius and Theory of Methodist Polity; Or, the Machinery of Methodism, Practically Illustrated Through a Series of Questions and Answers.* Philadelphia: Publication Department, A.M.E. Church, 1885; Northbrook, Ill.: Metro Books, 1972.

———. *Respect Black: The Writings and Speeches of Henry McNeal Turner.* Edited by Edwin S. Redkey. New York: Arno Press, 1971.

Tyler, Bennet

(1783–1858) *Congregationalist minister, educator*

Bennet Tyler composed the last significant chapter in the history of what is known as the New Divinity theology. This collection of theological emphases, inherited from JONATHAN EDWARDS, sought to harmonize Calvinist doctrines such as predestination with the spiritual psychology of revivalism. Tyler was born on July 10, 1783, in Middlebury, Connecticut, the son of James Tyler and Anne Hungerford Tyler. While a student at Yale College, he experienced a religious conversion during a revival that occurred at the college in the summer of 1802. After graduation from Yale in 1804, he taught school briefly before studying privately for the ministry with the Congregational minister Asahel Hooker of Goshen, Connecticut. He was licensed to preach in 1806. The following year Tyler was invited to become the minister of a small Congregational church in South Britain, Connecticut. The same year he married Esther Stone, with whom he had nine children. He was ordained the pastor of the South Britain church in the summer of 1808.

The content of Tyler's preaching placed him securely within the ranks of the New Divinity. This school of theology traced its lineage to Jonathan Edwards, the famous Calvinist theologian and friend of the Great Awakening, and to two of Edwards's students, Samuel Hopkins and Joseph Bellamy. The core of the New Divinity was its emphasis on the sovereignty of God, the accountability of men and women for their sinfulness, and the call for sinners to immediate conversion. Edwards—and Tyler, after him—argued that human beings are naturally free to choose to obey God, even if they are morally incapable of doing so apart from God's grace, and that they are therefore accountable for their sin. Conversely, this natural ability to choose the right course made it possible for revivalists to call on men and women to be converted at once, without relying on the lengthy process of "preparation for grace" central to older forms of Calvinism.

Tyler's preaching sparked revivals in his own church before he was appointed president of Dartmouth College in 1822 and left his ministerial post to become an educator. He proved not particularly effective as a college administrator, and so in 1828 he returned to the ministry by accepting the call to become the pastor of Second Church in Portland, Maine. There, over the next several years, he engaged in a vigorous polemic against the teachings of NATHANIEL WILLIAM TAYLOR, a theology professor at Yale College. Taylor, like Tyler, was interested in developing a theology hospitable to revivalism but traveled down a sharply different path that would come to be known as New Haven theology. Unlike Tyler, Nathaniel Taylor rejected the idea that sin had incapacitated men and women to choose salvation. He insisted, instead, that human beings always had "power to the contrary." Tyler believed that Taylor had overemphasized the freedom of the human will and railed against Taylor's views in a series of books and journal articles. The theological war waged by the two men came to be known as the "Taylor-Tyler Controversy."

Tyler eventually joined other opponents of the New Haven theology to establish in 1834 the Theological Institute of Connecticut in East Windsor, Connecticut, where Jonathan Edwards had been born. He hoped this institute would counter the influence of Yale, and he became its president and professor of theology in 1834. He held these positions until 1857, when he retired. Tyler died in East Windsor on May 14, 1858.

The history of American Protestantism subsequently resolved the Taylor-Tyler Controversy in favor of Nathaniel Taylor and the New Haven theology. Its Arminian-flavored emphasis on free will became dominant over the course of the century that followed, giving a distinctly non-Edwardsian flavor to the great 19th-century revivals led by men such as CHARLES GRANDISON FINNEY and DWIGHT LYMAN MOODY. Bennet Tyler lived near the end of the New Divinity as a theological current. Its attempt to fasten revivalism to an essentially Calvinistic theology had spent its energy by the time of Tyler's death. He therefore had the historical fate of those who witness the passing of an idea rather than those—such as Jonathan Edwards—who participate in its creation: relative historical obscurity.

Further Reading

Foster, Frank Hugh. *A Genetic History of the New England Theology.* Chicago: University of Chicago Press, 1907; New York: Russell & Russell, 1963.

Guelzo, Allen C. *Edwards on the Will: A Century of American Theological Debate.* Middletown, Conn.: Wesleyan University Press, 1989.

Tyler, Bennet. *Lectures on Theology.* Edited by Nahum Gale. Boston: J. E. Tilton, 1859.

———. *Letters on the Origin and Progress of the New Haven Theology.* New York: R. Carter and E. Collier, 1837.

———. *New England Revivals.* Boston: Massachusetts Sabbath School Society, 1846.

Verot, Jean Pierre Augustin Marcellin
(1805–1876) *Catholic bishop*

Transplanted from France to the United States in 1830, Jean Pierre Augustin Marcellin Verot eventually migrated south to Florida. There he supported the southern cause during the years leading up to and during the Civil War, and afterward he labored to tend the spiritual terrain left in the war's aftermath. Verot was born on May 23, 1805, in Le Puy, France, the son of Jean Pierre Augustin Vérot and Magdeleine Marcet Vérot. From 1821 to 1830, he studied at the Issy Seminary in France under the direction of the Society of St. Sulpice (known as the Sulpicians). In 1828, he was ordained a Sulpician priest, and after his completion of seminary he was sent to St. Mary's College in Baltimore, Maryland, to teach.

Verot remained at St. Mary's College, teaching mathematics and science, for the next 22 years, until the institution closed in 1852. Subsequently, he served as a parish priest in Ellicott's Mills, Maryland, and surrounding parishes until he was appointed vicar apostolic of Florida in late 1857. By the summer of 1858, he had arrived in Saint Augustine, Florida, where he found extensive needs but few resources to meet them. Undaunted, he journeyed to France, where he recruited additional priests and religious workers to assist him. On July 22, 1861, his responsibilities were enlarged when he was named the third bishop of Savannah, with continued spiritual oversight of the Florida vicariate as well.

During the Civil War, Verot achieved some notoriety by speaking out in favor of secession and the property rights of slave owners, even as he condemned the slave trade and the treatment of slaves by their owners. A sermon he delivered at the beginning of the year of 1861 was later published as a tract and circulated widely in the North, earning Verot the nickname of "Rebel Bishop." In spite of his sympathy for the cause of the South, Verot attempted to attend to the spiritual needs of federal prisoners at Andersonville, Georgia, during the Civil War. After the war, he confronted the needs of his spiritual jurisdiction by attempting to reconstitute race relations even as he sought to heal the wounds that had been inflicted on that jurisdiction. By 1867, he had established a Catholic school for the children of freed slaves in Saint Augustine, relying on the help of the Sisters of St. Joseph from Le Puy, his hometown in France. He also engineered a significant educational innovation by securing tax support for two parochial schools in Savannah, Georgia, an arrangement—referred to as the Savannah Plan—that lasted until 1916.

Verot attended the First Vatican Council in Rome from 1869 to 1870, and he quickly established himself as one of the most vocal American prelates. Though he had lent his spiritual support to slavery in previous years, now he urged the council to recognize the equal humanity of blacks. He also argued vocally against any recognition of the pope's infallibility, and when the council moved to a declaration of this point, he absented himself rather than cast a negative vote. In the spring of 1870, the Florida vicariate was reconstituted as the diocese of Saint Augustine and Verot named its first bishop. He presided over the newly created diocese for the next six years. He died in Saint Augustine on June 10, 1876.

The South's Rebel Bishop assumed his spiritual oversight of Florida on the eve of the Civil War and, five months after Georgia seceded from the Union, undertook similar responsibility for its territory as well, serving as Savannah's third bishop. For lending his spiritual authority to defend the cause of the South, Jean Pierre Augustin Marcellin Verot might have earned a more damning judgment from history, but for his postwar attempts to improve the condition of the newly freed slaves. Soon after the close of the Civil War, the Rebel Bishop attended Vatican I, where he stood up in the august assembly of Catholic prelates to declare the humanity of those whose slavery he had previously condoned. He remains a colorful and controversial figure in American religious history, though his action at Vatican I to some extent has tempered what otherwise might have been a less cordial historical judgment.

Further Reading

Gannon, Michael. *Rebel Bishop: Augustin Verot, Florida's Civil War Prelate.* Milwaukee, Wis.: Bruce, 1964; Gainesville: University Press of Florida, 1997.

McNally, Michael J. *Catholic Parish Life on Florida's West Coast, 1860–1968.* [S.I.]: Catholic Media Ministries, 1996.

———. *Catholicism in South Florida, 1868–1968.* Gainesville: University Presses of Florida, 1982.

Wight, W. E. "Bishop Verot and the Civil War." *Catholic Historical Review* 47 (July 1961): 153–63.

W

Walther, Carl Ferdinand Wilhelm
(1811–1887) *Lutheran minister, educator*

Carl Ferdinand Wilhelm Walther migrated to the United States in the mid-19th century and—over the course of the next 40 years—became a principal leader of the Lutheran Missouri Synod. As a minister, a seminary professor, and the chief architect of his denomination, Walther championed a conservative Lutheranism that still commands significant adherents at the beginning of the 21st century. He was born on October 25, 1811, in Langenchursdorf, Saxony, the son of Gottlob Heinrich Walther and Johanna Wilhelmina Zschenderlein Walther. Three generations of Walthers who preceded Carl had been Lutheran ministers, and Carl Walther and his older brother, Otto Hermann Walther, also followed this vocational path. After graduation from a preparatory school in September 1829, Carl Walther joined his older brother at the University of Leipzig a month later. After graduation in spring 1833, Walther was ordained a Lutheran minister and became the pastor of the Lutheran Church in Bräunsdorf.

During his university years, Walther found a spiritual mentor in Martin Stephan, a Lutheran minister in Dresden. Their association continued after Walther became a minister and eventually prompted him to join Stephan, who led Walther and some 800 other conservative Lutherans from Saxony into migrating to the United States. They arrived in New Orleans in January 1839 and made their way to Saint Louis, Missouri. Soon after their arrival, however, Martin Stephan was accused of financial and sexual misconduct and expelled from the group of immigrants. Two years later, members of the immigrant community debated the question of whether they might legitimately consider themselves a spiritual congregation after their departure from Germany and the banishment of their leader. In April 1841, at a series of meetings referred to as the Altenburg Debate, Walther argued that the immigrants were a legitimate church. The following month, he became the minister of Trinity Lutheran Church in St. Louis, of which his brother had been pastor before he died. In September 1841, Walther married Emilie Buenger, with whom he had six children.

Within a few years of assuming the leadership of the Trinity church, Walther undertook a wider ministry to German Lutherans in the St. Louis area. He began publishing *Der Lutheraner* in September 1844, and in the first issue explained the spiritual needs he was attempting to meet. Lutherans who had settled in the West, he complained, "live so scattered from each other; they are stripped and bare of all means, and in many places are unable to organize a congregation and call a minister to serve them." In this perilous spiritual condition, they were "tempted to abandon their father's faith . . . or seek fulfillment of their spiritual needs in other, already existing congregations."

> Therefore, in these parts of their new father-land, our precious brothers-in-the-faith are in need of encouragement to remain true to

their faith; they need to be warned of the dangers of apostasy which is threatening here; they need the tools necessary to defend themselves against those who deny that what they have learned in their youth from the Catechism is the true faith; they need the assurance that the church to which they profess to belong has not disappeared; and that therefore they do not have cause to seek refuge at other congregations.

In the wake of this publishing venture, in 1847, Walther took the lead in organizing the Lutheran immigrants into the German Evangelical Lutheran Synod of Missouri, Ohio, and Other States, later known simply as the Missouri Synod of the Lutheran Church. He served as the synod's president from 1847 to 1850 and from 1864 to 1878. Two years after the synod's formation, Walther was chosen to serve as a professor of theology at the synod's seminary in Saint Louis, Concordia, and, in 1854, he became the seminary's president.

Until his death in 1887, Walther labored with great industry to defend the orthodox Lutheran congregations planted in Missouri and surrounding states from their many spiritual antagonists. From 1855 to his death, he edited the theological journal *Lehre und Wehre* (doctrine and defense), which he founded to provide a forum for the expression of Lutheran orthodoxy. By January 1887, the 50th anniversary of Walther's ordination, he was very ill. He died in Saint Louis on May 7, 1887.

Unlike his mentor, Martin Stephan, Walther distrusted autocratic ministerial leadership and led the Missouri Synod to emphasize instead a greater measure of lay participation in ecclesiastical affairs by vesting the synod's authority in the collected Lutheran congregations rather than in the ministers. But Walther's commanding presence cast a broad shadow across the early affairs of the synod. As a polemical defender of Lutheran orthodoxy, as an energetic seminary president and professor, and as a dedicated pastor, Walther dominated the early life of the Missouri Synod.

Further Reading

Klug, Eugene F. A. *Church and Ministry: The Role of Church, Pastor, and People from Luther to Walther.* St. Louis, Mo.: Concordia, 1993.

Polack, William Gustave. *The Story of C. F. W. Walther.* St. Louis, Mo.: Concordia, 1935.

Reckzin, Dale Markham. "Three Doctors of the American Lutheran Church: Charles Porterfield Krauth, Carl Ferdinand Wilhelm Walther, Gustav Adolph Theodor Felix Hoenecke," Western Lutheran Seminary. Available online. URL: http://www.wls.wels.net/library/Essays/Authors/R/ReckzinDoctors/ReckzinDoctors.html. Downloaded on December 5, 2001.

Spitz, Lewis William. *The Life of Dr. C. F. W. Walther.* St. Louis, Mo.: Concordia, 1961.

Steffens, Diedrich Henry. *Doctor Carl Ferdinand Wilhelm Walther.* Philadelphia: Lutheran Publication Society, 1917.

Suelflow, August Robert. *Servant of the Word: The Life and Ministry of C. F. W. Walther.* St. Louis, Mo.: Concordia, 2000.

Walther, C. F. W. *Correspondence of C. F. W. Walther.* Translated and edited by Roy A. Suelflow. St. Louis, Mo.: R.A. Suelflow, 1980.

———. *Essays for the Church.* 2 vols. St. Louis, Mo.: Concordia, 1992.

Warfield, Benjamin Breckinridge
(1851–1921) *Presbyterian theologian*

A leading Christian theologian at the turn of the 20th century, Benjamin Breckinridge Warfield applied his immense learning to the exposition of orthodox Christian doctrine. The open conflict between Christian liberals and fundamentalists did not erupt until shortly after his death, but Warfield was in many ways the father of modern fundamentalism. He was born on November 5, 1851, on his family's estate, "Grasmere," located near Lexington, Kentucky, the son of William Warfield and Mary Cabell Breckinridge Warfield. After attending private schools for his elementary and secondary education, Warfield enrolled in the College of New Jersey (later Princeton University), from which he graduated first in his class in 1871. He traveled subsequently to Europe, where he studied first at Edinburgh and then at Heidelberg. Though he had become a member of the Second Presbyterian Church in Lexington when he was 16 years old, Warfield did not seem poised to become a minister. While he was at Heidelberg, however, he announced his intention to pursue this vocation. He subsequently returned to the United States and enrolled in Princeton Theological Seminary, from which he graduated in 1876. The same year he married Annie Pearce Kinkead.

After seminary Warfield set off for Europe again to study at Leipzig, Germany. While there, his wife suffered a trauma that made her a semiinvalid the rest of her life. The couple never had children, and Warfield seldom ventured far from his wife for the remainder of their life together. This personal circumstance, added to Warfield's scholarly temperament, meant that his theological influence, which became substantial in later years, was communicated through his pen rather than through public speeches and appearances.

After the Warfields returned from Europe, he served briefly as assistant pastor of the First Presbyterian Church of Baltimore, beginning in the summer of 1877. But his talents and training had fitted him better to be an academic, and he accepted an appointment in 1878 as a New Testament instructor at Western Theological Seminary in Pennsylvania. The following year he was ordained a minister of the Presbyterian Church (U.S.A.). After nearly a decade of scholarly work that won Warfield increasing recognition, Princeton Theological Seminary invited him to occupy the chair of didactic and polemic theology left vacant by the death of Archibald Alexander Hodge. Hodge had inherited this position from his father, CHARLES HODGE, one of Presbyterianism's most eminent theologians of the 19th century and with whom Warfield had studied while a student in seminary. Warfield accepted Princeton's offer and, from 1887, made that seminary the seat of his scholarly activities for the next 34 years.

A torrent of books and articles flowed from the pen of Benjamin B. Warfield over the following years. Added to these were his labors as editor of a series of Presbyterian periodicals, *Presbyterian Review, Presbyterian and Reformed Review,* and *Princeton Theological Review.* In his various scholarly roles, Warfield became one of the 20th century's most distinguished theologians. But in a century when many theologies abandoned fundamentals of traditional orthodoxy in favor of systems more at home with modernity, Warfield was the champion

of orthodoxy, particularly of the Presbyterian orthodoxies expressed in the Westminster Confession, the summary of Presbyterian doctrine adopted in the 1640s by English Presbyterians. At a time when higher criticism of the Bible had called into question its authority and reliability, Warfield defended biblical infallibility. "We believe this doctrine," he insisted in his article "The Inspiration of the Bible" in the 1894 edition of *Bibliotheca Sacra,* "primarily because it is the doctrine which Christ and his apostles believed, and which they have taught us. It may sometimes seem difficult to take our stand frankly by the side of Christ and his apostles. It will always be found safe." The weight of his influence dominated the General Assembly of the Presbyterian Church (U.S.A.) for the years surrounding the beginning of the 20th century. Though in the generation after Warfield this mainline denomination veered toward a different course; for the time, at least, his defense of orthodoxy prevailed against the more liberal views of scholars such as CHARLES AUGUSTUS BRIGGS of the Union Theological Seminary, who was suspended from the Presbyterian ministry for contesting the inerrancy of the Bible. Warfield died on February 16, 1921, at Princeton, New Jersey.

Soon after Warfield's death, the Presbyterian Church (U.S.A.) followed the course of other mainline Protestant denominations in retreating from central tenets of traditional Christian orthodoxy. For a time, however, the weight of Warfield's influence and erudition helped forestall this development. During his life, the fracture between liberalism and fundamentalism loomed on the horizon but had not yet added new divisions to the Protestant tradition. Warfield could not prevent this fracture, but he helped to hold it largely at bay during his lifetime. Even after that schism, Warfield's scholarship continued to influence conservative Christian thinking into the 21st century.

Further Reading

Gilbreath, S. Burkhart. *Professor Benjamin Breckinridge Warfield, D.D., L.L.D., LITT.D.: Princeton Poise and Power, Princeton, New Jersey.* Shippensburg, Pa.: Beidel Printing House, 1996.
Hoffecker, W. Andrew. "Benjamin B. Warfield." In *The Princeton Theology: Reformed Theology in America.*

Edited by David F. Wells. Grand Rapids, Mich.: Baker Book House, 1989.

Mark A. Noll, ed. *The Princeton Theology, 1812–1921: Scripture, Science, and Theological Method from Archibald Alexander to Benjamin Breckinridge Warfield.* Grand Rapids, Mich.: Baker Academic, 2001.

Warfield, Benjamin Breckinridge. *Evolution, Scripture, and Science: Selected Writings.* Edited by Mark A. Noll & David N. Livingstone. Grand Rapids, Mich.: Baker Books, 2000.

———. *The Inspiration and Authority of the Bible.* Philadelphia: Presbyterian & Reformed Publishing Company, 1948.

———. *Selected Shorter Writings of Benjamin B. Warfield.* Edited by John E. Meeter. Nutley, N.J.: Presbyterian & Reformed Publishing Company, 1970–73.

Webb, Muhammad Alexander Russell
(1846–1916) *convert to Islam*

Alexander Russell Webb, known after his conversion to Islam as Muhammad Alexander Russell Webb, is frequently cited as the first white convert to Islam in America. He became well known at the turn of the 20th century as a fervent missionary for the Islamic faith. He was born on November 9, 1846, in Hudson, New York, the son of Alexander Nelson Webb, a newspaper owner and editor, and Caroline Elizabeth Lefferts Webb. His parents were Presbyterians. Webb appears to have studied at and perhaps received an undergraduate degree from Claverack College in Claverack, New York. By around the age of 20, he had rejected Christianity.

After college, Webb worked for a time as a journalist, first purchasing a small newspaper, *The Missouri Republican* of Unionville, Missouri, and subsequently working as an editor first for the *Missouri Gazette* of Saint Joseph, Missouri, and then for *The Missouri Republican* of Saint Louis. In 1887, President Glover Cleveland appointed Webb consul general for Manila, in the Philippines. The same year he appears to have married a widow whose name is not known with whom he had three children in addition to the child she brought to their marriage. While in Manila, Webb, who had been studying oriental religions for some time,

converted to Islam. He later described his migration from Christianity to Islam in an essay published in *Islam, Our Choice*.

> I have been requested to tell you why I, an American, born in a country which is nominally Christian, and reared under the drippings, or more properly perhaps the drivelling, of an orthodox Presbyterian pulpit, came to adopt the faith of Islam as my guide in life. . . . I adopted this religion because I found, after protracted study, that it was the best and only system adapted to the spiritual needs of humanity. . . . When I reached the age of 20, and became practically my own master, I was so tired of the restraint and dullness of the Church, that I wandered away from it and never returned to it. . . . About eleven years ago I became interested in the study of Oriental religions. I saw Mill and Locke, Kant, Hegel, Fichte, Huxley, and many other more or less learned writers discoursing with a great show of wisdom concerning protoplasm and monads, and yet not one of them could tell me what the soul was or what became of it after death. . . . I have spoken so much of myself in order to show you that my adoption of Islam was not the result of misguided sentiment, blind credulity, or sudden emotional impulse, but it was born of earnest, honest, persistent, unprejudiced study and investigation and an intense desire to know the truth.

In 1892, Webb surrendered his position as consul general and commenced a lecture tour to India, followed by a return to the United States in 1893. That year he settled in New York and launched the Oriental Publishing Company, which he used as a vehicle for distributing tracts on the subject of Islam. He also published *Moslem World,* a periodical devoted to the propagation of Islam. He achieved a measure of prominence the same year by attending the World's Parliament of Religion in Chicago, where he was a vocal advocate for the Muslim faith. Toward the end of the 19th century, Webb settled in Rutherford, New Jersey, where he spent the remainder of his life. He died on October 1, 1916, in Rutherford.

After abandoning Christianity as a young man, Muhammad Alexander Russell Webb eventually turned to Islam. He was, for a brief period in the closing years of the 19th century and the early years of the 20th, a vigorous missionary on behalf of his newfound faith in the United States. He founded no enduring religious movement, but his embrace of Islam would form a pattern followed by other Americans in the century that followed his conversion.

Further Reading

"Alexander Russell Webb." Available online. URL: http://www.muslim.org/islam/webb1.htm. Downloaded on May 1, 2002.

Islam, Our Choice. Edited by Ebrahim Ahmed Bawany. 5th abridged ed. Karachi: Begum Aisha Bawany Waqf, 1970.

Webb, Mohammed Alexander Russell. *Islam in America: A Brief Statement of Mohammedanism and an Outline of the American Islamic Propaganda.* New York: The Oriental Publishing Co., 1893.

White, Alma Bridwell
(Mollie Alma Bridwell)
(1862–1946) *Pentecostal evangelist*

Alma Bridwell White founded what became known as the Pillar of Fire denomination. She was ordained a bishop of the denomination she established, the first woman to hold such a position in the history of the Christian Church. White was born Mollie Alma Bridwell on June 16, 1862, in Lewis County, Kentucky, the daughter of William Bridwell and Mary Ann Harrison Bridwell. Her parents were farmers and Methodists. A church member by the time she was 12, White had a conversion experience when she was 16 years old and thereafter believed that God had called her to be a preacher. For a time, however, she pursued a career as a teacher. After studying first at the Female Seminary in Vanceburg, Kentucky, and then at the Millersburg Female College in Millersburg, Kentucky, she taught school for a year in Millersburg. Subsequently, she moved to Bannack, Montana, where she taught from 1882 to 1886. During this period she met Kent White, a Methodist ministerial student whom she married in 1887, and with whom she had two sons. Both of her sons would

become ministers in the denomination their mother would later found.

After their marriage, Alma and her husband moved to Lamar, Colorado, where Kent White became the minister of a small Methodist church. Alma took an active part in the affairs of her husband's church—active enough, in fact, that some members of the church thought her role unsuitable for a woman. In 1893, White experienced a spiritual renewal known among Holiness groups as the "second blessing" or "entire sanctification." Awakened again to the conviction that God wished her to preach, White undertook a career as an itinerant Holiness evangelist. By 1896, her success as a preacher had led her to establish the Pentecostal Home Mission in Denver, Colorado. Her husband, Kent, joined her in the mission's activities, and, in 1901, they and others formally organized the Pentecostal Union Church. A year later, Alma White was ordained a minister of the church. Alma and her husband produced a religious newspaper, the *Pentecostal Mission Herald*, later renamed the *Pillar of Fire*, and the latter eventually became the name of the association of congregations that sprang up under White's leadership.

By 1908, White had relocated the center of her fledgling denomination to a farm in New Jersey she named "Zarephath." There, she and her followers shared a spiritual vision consistent with that embraced by other Holiness groups, maintaining their confidence in the possibility of entire perfection in this life. The following year Kent White became a Pentecostal. His subsequent attempts to lead the Pillar of Fire movement to embrace glossolalia or "speaking in tongues" collided, however, with Alma White's resolute opposition to Pentecostalism. Though Alma White's religious services had some elements in common with Pentecostal churches, such as the practice of spiritual healing, she opposed in general the use of spiritual gifts such as the gift of speaking in tongues. Alma White prevailed in the ensuing power struggle with Kent over control of the Pillar of Fire churches and was, in fact, ordained bishop of the denomination in 1918, an ecclesiastical office no woman had ever held in a Christian denomination.

In the 1920s, Alma White's anti-Catholicism led her to endorse the Ku Klux Klan (KKK), and to speak regularly at Klan meetings in New York and New Jersey. At the same time, however, she became an increasingly prominent advocate of women's rights. Her denomination thus had the distinction of being the only religious group that openly endorsed the KKK and both supported the Equal Rights Amendment to the U.S. Constitution. Alma White died on June 26, 1946.

The denomination that Alma Bridwell White started remains a rather minor tributary within the broader current of American Holiness groups. White herself, though, was a charismatic figure whose historical influence extends beyond the boundaries of the Pillar of Fire congregations that still trace their lineage to her. Her distinction as the first woman ordained as a bishop in the history of the Christian Church accounts for part of her historical significance. But the curious intersections of her religious vision and contemporary social issues, demonstrated by her associations with both the KKK and the women's rights movement, have also made her an enduring enigma in the history of American religion.

Further Reading

Stanley, Susie Cunningham. *Feminist Pillar of Fire: The Life of Alma White.* Cleveland: Pilgrim Press, 1993.

White, Alma. *Everlasting Life.* Zarephath, N.J.: Pillar of Fire, 1944.

———. *Looking Back from Beulah.* New York: Garland, 1987.

———. *Short Sermons.* Zarephath, N.J.: Pillar of Fire, 1932.

———. *The Story of My Life and Pillar of Fire.* 5 vols. Zarephath, N.J.: Pillar of Fire, 1935–43.

White, Arthur K. *Some White Family History.* Denver: Pillar of Fire, 1948.

White, Ellen Gould Harmon
(1827–1915) *founder of Seventh-Day Adventist Church*

Together with her husband, James White, Ellen Gould Harmon White founded one of the most influential of the many adventist groups in 19th-century America, the Seventh-Day Adventists. Adventists in general focused their spiritual atten- tions on the anticipated imminent return of Christ to earth, and Ellen White helped to fasten the practice of Saturday or Sabbatarian worship to one important strand of adventism. She was born Ellen Gould Harmon on November 26, 1827, near Gorham, Maine, the daughter of Robert Harmon and Eunice Gould Harmon. The most significant event of her childhood occurred when she was struck in the head by a rock thrown by a classmate when she was about nine years old. The injury she suffered contributed to a lifetime of pain and physical ailments and effectively disabled her from obtaining further formal education.

Ellen Harmon's parents were devoted Methodists, and she experienced a religious conversion while at a Methodist camp meeting in 1840 and was subsequently baptized. Soon afterward, she was influenced by the adventist WILLIAM MILLER, who preached that Christ would shortly return to earth. Miller and his followers eventually set their hopes on the appearance of Christ on October 22, 1844. Many Millerites, as they were called, turned away from adventism after the October date passed without event, experiencing what became known as "the great disappointment," but Harmon remained convinced that the return of the Messiah was imminent. That same year, she fell into a trance and experienced the first of what would be innumerable visions that confirmed her faith. She also became a convinced Sabbatarian, believing that Saturday, the Jewish Sabbath, was the proper day of worship for Christians as well.

By the mid-1840s, Ellen Harmon began a traveling ministry and was soon accompanied in her travels by another Millerite, James S. White, whom she subsequently married in the summer of 1846 and with whom she had four sons. James White undertook the publication of his wife's visions and served as editor first of *Present Truth*, beginning in 1849, and later of *Review and Herald*, beginning the following year. After settling briefly in Rochester, New York, White and her family eventually made their home in Battle Creek, Michigan. Together the couple oversaw the designation of the churches associated with them as Seventh-Day Adventists in 1860 and the subsequent organization of the churches into a religious body in 1863.

During the 1860s, Ellen White communicated to her fellow adventists numerous visions and teachings on the subject of health, generally disparaging resort to physicians and to the drugs they prescribed. She, together with many other 19th-century hydropaths, championed the curative potential of water treatments, especially when combined with other natural remedies and with abstention from rich diets, tobacco, and alcohol. In 1866, White established her own sanitorium in Battle Creek, called the Western Health Reform Institute.

In the last two decades of the 19th century, after her husband's death in 1881, White traveled extensively outside the United States, spending a significant amount of time preaching in Europe, Australia, and New Zealand. Eventually she returned to America and settled near Saint Helena, California. She died there on July 16, 1915. By the time of her death, she had written thousands of articles and 40 books, including perhaps her most popular work, *Steps to Christ* (1892).

The Seventh-Day Adventists numbered more than 100,000 members at the time of Ellen Gould Harmon White's death in 1915, and, by the end of the century, the religious body for which she had been the principal midwife claimed a membership in excess of 11 million. Revered as a prophet of God by Seventh-Day Adventists, White cast a long shadow of influence across both the years of her life and the decades that followed it. Her books continue to be published, her visions studied, and her testimony to the imminent return of Christ embraced.

Further Reading

Douglass, Herbert E. *Messenger of the Lord: The Prophetic Ministry of Ellen G. White*. Nampa, Idaho: Pacific Press Publishing Association, 1998.

Graham, Roy E. *Ellen G. White: Co-Founder of the Seventh-Day Adventist Church*. New York: P. Lang, 1985.

Numbers, Ronald L. *Prophetess of Health: A Study of Ellen G. White*. New York: Harper & Row, 1976; Knoxville: University of Tennessee Press, 1992.

White, Arthur L. *Ellen G. White*. 6 vols. Washington, D.C.: Review and Herald Publishing Association, 1981–86.

———. *Ellen White: Woman of Vision*. Hagerstown, Md.: Review and Herald Publishing Association, 2000.

White, Ellen Gould Harmon. *The Complete Published Ellen G. White Writings* [computer file]. Version 3.0. Silver Spring, Md.: Ellen G. White Estate, 1999.

White, James. *Life Sketches: Ancestry, Early Life, Christian Experience, and Extensive Labors of Elder James White, and His Wife Mrs. Ellen G. White*. Battle Creek, Mich.: Press of the Seventh-Day Adventist Publishing Association, 1880.

Whitefield, George
(1714–1770) *revivalist*

One of the most famous Christian evangelists in the history of American religion, George Whitefield sparked a revival in North America during the first half of the 18th century. He held audiences on two continents spellbound by his extemporaneous preaching, finding a pulpit in fields as

George Whitefield's preaching helped to spark the Great Awakening. *(Library of Congress, Prints and Photographs Division, LC-USZ62-75073)*

often as in church buildings. He was born in Gloucester, England, on December 16, 1714, in an inn kept by his parents, Thomas and Elizabeth Edwards Whitefield. His father died when he was two, leaving his mother's financial circumstances straitened, but he was nevertheless able to enroll at Pembroke College in Oxford when he was 18 years old. There he met John and Charles Wesley and, after an extended period of soul searching, experienced conversion in the spring of 1735.

> One day, perceiving an uncommon Drought and a disagreeable Claminess in my Mouth, and using things to allay my Thirst, but in vain, it was suggested to me, that when *Jesus Christ* cried out, "I thirst," His sufferings were near at an End. Upon which I cast myself down on the Bed, crying out, I thirst! I thirst!—Soon after this, I found and felt in myself that I was delivered from the Burden that had so heavily oppressed me! The Spirit of Mourning was taken from me, and I knew what it was truly to rejoice in God my Saviour, and, for some Time, could not avoid singing Psalms wherever I was.

Whitefield obtained a B.A. from Oxford in 1736 and was ordained the same year as an Anglican minister. Two years later, the Wesleys suggested that Whitefield undertake a preaching mission to America in Georgia. Whereas another might have found it difficult to relinquish the crowds who had already began to attend his preaching, Whitefield became convinced that God had called him to Georgia. Once there, he determined to establish an orphanage and promptly returned to England to raise funds for this project. By November 1739, he had returned to the colonies, where thousands of people soon flocked to hear him preach and where, in the midst of extensive evangelistic tours, he found time to establish an orphanage, Bethesda. His revivalistic preaching would be influential in launching the Great Awakening, which spread across British North America during the 1740s.

Over the next 30 years, George Whitefield traveled regularly between England and North America, preaching to large audiences on both sides of the Atlantic Ocean. Enthusiastically received by many, Whitefield also drew criticism from many established pulpits, whose ministers railed at his emotionally laden sermons. In the main, his theological beliefs tracked those of traditional Calvinism, focusing on God's gracious provision of salvation to sinful men and women. He was eager, though, to call on all of his hearers to receive salvation without fretting whether they might be among the elect. But the degree to which Whitefield sought to ignite a passionate response from his hearers differed from the practices of many Anglican and Congregational pulpits, which focused more on the mind than on the heart. Opposition from established churches often left their pulpits closed to Whitefield, but he proved as able to preach in a field as in a finely constructed church. After his first experience preaching in a field, he described his impression: "Blessed be God, *I have now broke the Ice; I believe I never was more acceptable to my Master than when I was standing to teach those Hearers in the open Fields.*" If anything, he attracted larger crowds in the open air than he could have hoped to have ministered to in the church buildings of his day.

Whitefield married Elizabeth Burnell James in 1741. The couple had only one child, who died in infancy. Whitefield maintained an abiding commitment to the Georgia orphanage he established and remained attentive to the needs of poor children throughout his life. He preached until the very end of his life: He died in Newburyport, Massachusetts, on September 30, 1770, less than 24 hours after he had delivered what would be his last sermon.

George Whitefield's revival preaching drew thousands of people to a renewed spiritual life. Never at home with abstract questions of theology, he focused on a simple appeal to sinners to receive the grace of God made available through Christ, an appeal that leaped across boundaries that had traditionally divided Christians into separate denominational traditions. But Whitefield's preaching created its own divisions: between those who saw him as a herald of "New Light" and those "Old Lights" who resented his criticism of established churches and their ministers.

Further Reading

Clarkson, George E. *George Whitefield and Welsh Calvinistic Methodism.* Lewiston, N.Y.: Edwin Mellen Press, 1996.

Dallimore, Arnold A. *George Whitefield: The Life and Times of the Great Evangelist of the Eighteenth-century Revival.* London: Banner of Truth Trust, 1970.

Gillies, John. *Memoirs and Sermons of Rev. George Whitefield.* Rev. ed. Philadelphia: Leary & Getz, 1854.

Henry, Stuart C. *George Whitefield: Wayfaring Witness.* New York: Abingdon Press, 1957.

Lambert, Frank. *"Pedlar in Divinity": George Whitefield and the Transatlantic Revivals, 1737–1770.* Princeton, N.J.: Princeton University Press, 1994.

Ninde, Edward Summerfield. *George Whitefield: Prophet-Preacher.* New York: Abingdon Press, 1924.

Pollock, John. *George Whitefield and the Great Awakening.* Garden City, N.Y.: Doubleday, 1972.

Stout, Harry S. *The Divine Dramatist: George Whitefield and the Rise of Modern Evangelicalism.* Grand Rapids, Mich.: Eerdmans, 1991.

Whitefield, George. *Journals, 1737–1741.* Gainesville, Fla.: Scholars' Facsimiles & Reprints, 1969.

Whitman, Marcus

(1802–1847) *physician, medical missionary*

Marcus Whitman, together with his wife, Narcissa, labored for a little more than a decade to evangelize Native Americans in the Oregon Territory. Their ministry as medical missionaries met an abrupt end, however, when they were massacred, along with other white settlers, by the Cayuse Indians. Whitman was born on September 4, 1802, in Federal Hollow (later Rushville), New York, the son of Beza Whitman and Alice Green Whitman. His father died when he was a child and his mother dispatched him soon afterward to Massachusetts, where he was raised by his uncle and grandfather. While a teenager, Whitman studied at a school taught by a Congregationalist minister in Plainsfield, Massachusetts. When he was 17 years old, he experienced a religious conversion, which he described in a subsequent letter: "I was awakened to a sense of my sin and danger and brought by Divine grace to rely on the Lord Jesus for pardon and salvation."

The year after his conversion, Whitman returned to Rushville intent on becoming a minister. Discouraged by his family from pursuing this course, however, he worked instead for his stepfather's shoe shop for a few years and then turned to the study of medicine by apprenticing himself to a Rushville physician. In 1825, he enrolled in the College of Physicians and Surgeons of the Western District of New York, located in Fairfield. After 16 weeks of study, he was licensed to practice medicine, and he spent the next two and a half years pursuing this vocation in Niagara, Canada. By 1831 he had returned to Fairfield to complete his medical studies and earn an M.D., and after this, he practiced medicine for a few years in Wheeler, New York, where he became an elder of the Wheeler Presbyterian Church.

Marcus Whitman had never completely surrendered his teenage aspiration to become a minister. In 1834 he began to explore the possibility of becoming a medical missionary for the American Board of Commissioners for Foreign Missions (ABCFM), an organization that sponsored Presbyterian and Congregationalist missionary activities. In February 1836, he married Narcissa Prentiss, with whom he had one child, and the two joined an expedition to Oregon. Later that year, Whitman chose Waiilatpu on the Walla Walla River for the site of an ABCFM-sponsored mission. Over the next several years, he and his wife helped to create a thriving missionary community, where they dispensed medical care, lessons about farming, and spiritual instruction to the Cayuse Indians.

Their missionary labors were not wholly successful. None of the Cayuse was converted to Christianity, even those who could be persuaded to attend Sunday preaching services. Furthermore, divisions and other conflicts erupted among the white settlers who had joined the Whitmans at Waiilatpu. These proved sufficiently serious that the ABCFM took action to remove the couple from the mission and relented only after Whitman returned east in 1842 to defend the progress of his work. After his return to Waiilatpu, however, Whitman found his time increasingly consumed with tending to the needs of the steady flow of white settlers arriving in the Oregon territory. The Cayuse, apparently angered by the encroachment of these settlers and alarmed at the diseases the settlers brought with them to the area, massacred 13 members of the Waiilatpu settlement, including Marcus and Narcissa Whitman, on November 29, 1847.

As a sad coda to the deaths of Marcus and Narcissa Whitman, in 1850 five Cayuse were turned over to territorial officials and hanged for their role in the Waiilatpu massacre. One of Whitman's associates erected a seminary on the site of the mission, later relocated to Walla Walla and named Whitman College. Whitman himself was honored with a statue erected in the National Statuary Hall in Washington, D.C.

Further Reading

Drury, Clifford Merrill. *Marcus and Narcissa Whitman, and the Opening of Old Oregon*. Glendale, Calif.: A. H. Clark, 1973.

Hulbert, Archer Butler, and Dorothy Printup Hulbert, eds. *Marcus Whitman, Crusader*. Colorado Springs: The Stewart Commission of Colorado College, 1936–41.

Jeffrey, Julie Roy. *Converting the West: A Biography of Narcissa Whitman*. Norman: University of Oklahoma Press, 1991.

———. "Empty Harvest at Waiilatpu." *Columbia: The Magazine of Northwest History* 6 (1992): 22–32.

Jones, Nard. *The Great Command: The Story of Marcus and Narcissa Whitman and the Oregon Country Pioneers*. Boston: Little, Brown, 1959.

Mowry, William A. *Marcus Whitman and the Early Days of Oregon*. New York: Silver, Burdett, 1901.

Sprague, Roderick. "Plateau Shamanism and Marcus Whitman." *Idaho Yesterdays* 31 (1987): 55–56.

Webster, Johnathan H. "The Oregon Mission and the ABCFM." *Idaho Yesterdays* 31 (1987): 24–34.

Whitman, Marcus. *More about the Whitmans: Four Hitherto Unpublished Letters of Marcus and Narcissa Whitman*. Edited by Clifford M. Drury. Tacoma: Washington State Historical Society, 1979.

Wilder, Robert Parmalee

(1863–1938) *missions advocate*

Robert Parmalee Wilder devoted a lifetime of energy to the cause of Christian missions. Raised in the home of missionary parents, he never veered from the steadfast purpose of seeing the work of evangelism supported and expanded. He was born on August 2, 1863, in Kolhapur, India, the son of Royal Gould Wilder and Eliza Jane Smith Wilder.

Wilder's parents were missionaries in India, where Robert Wilder spent his earliest years, before his family returned to the United States in 1875 and settled in Princeton, New Jersey. When he was 10 years old, Wilder had a dream in which he was falling into a dark pit and saw a star. "As long as my eyes were fastened on the star," he later described, "I was lifted higher and higher but when I looked around me to ascertain what lifted me, down I went. Finally, my eyes were fastened continuously on the star until it drew me out of the pit." The meaning of the dream was clear to Wilder: "The star was Jesus who lifted me out of the pit of self and sin." Together with his 12-year-old sister, Wilder committed himself to serve God. After the two informed their father of this decision, he gave them each a Sunday School class to teach and admitted them to church membership.

Wilder studied at Princeton Preparatory School and Williston Seminary in Easthampton, Massachusetts. He matriculated at Princeton College in 1881. The missionary zeal that Wilder gained from his parents did not slumber during his college years at Princeton, where he was a member of the First Presbyterian Church. He attended the Inter-Seminary Alliance summer conference at Hartford, Connecticut, in 1883. When he returned to college that fall, he and the two other Princeton students who had been delegates to the conference established the Princeton Foreign Missionary Society. Illness forced Wilder to leave college briefly in 1885, but he graduated the next year and, the following summer, attended the student conference organized by DWIGHT LYMAN MOODY at Mount Hermon, Massachusetts. Wilder persuaded Moody to devote a portion of the conference to a discussion of missions, which resulted in 100 students' pledging themselves to become foreign missionaries. This "Mount Hermon Hundred" became the nucleus of the Student Volunteer Movement (SVM) for Foreign Missions, established in 1888, whose motto was "The evangelization of the world in this generation." Wilder was instrumental in the creation of this organization by traveling across the country in 1886 and 1887 to secure additional pledges from students to become missionaries.

Wilder attended Union Theological Seminary in New York City from 1887 until 1891, when he graduated. That year he traveled to India as a missionary and decided to stop in Great Britain to encourage the cause of student missionary volunteers there. As a result of his efforts in this regard, the Student Volunteer Missionary Union of Great Britain and Ireland was formed in spring 1892. In the fall of that year, he married Helen Olsoon, whom he had met on a walking tour in Norway the previous year, and with whom he had four children. The Wilders labored as missionaries in India until the spring of 1897.

Over the following four decades, Wilder worked with a variety of missions organizations. After spending two years in the United States working with the SVM and the Young Men's Christian Association (YMCA), Wilder returned to India as the national secretary of that country's YMCA from 1899 to 1902. After a period in Norway recovering his health, he became secretary of the British Student Christian Movement from 1905 to 1916. Back in the States soon after World War I began, Wilder worked again for the YMCA until 1919, when he became general secretary of the Student Volunteer Movement, a position he held for the next eight years. His final active service was as executive secretary of the Christian Council for Western Asia and Northern Africa (later the Near East Christian Council) from 1927 to 1933. Though officially retired after 1933, Wilder continued to travel widely in support of missions. He died in Oslo, Norway, on March 27, 1938.

Robert Parmalee Wilder's infectious enthusiasm for missions helped to launch the Student Volunteer Movement, one of the most prominent missionary endeavors of the early 20th century, in both the United States and Europe. Most effective during its first three decades, the movement inspired thousands of students to dedicate themselves to mission work. After 1920, however, increasing friction between the liberal and conservative wings of Protestantism began to blunt the effectiveness of cooperative missionary movements such as the SVM. Liberal Protestants, especially, retreated from the movement's evangelistic focus in favor of social reform efforts and interfaith dialogue with non-Christians. Wilder, though, never abandoned his belief that the message of Christianity was good news, to be communicated to every corner of the globe.

Further Reading

Braisted, Ruth Evelyn Wilder. *In this Generation: The Story of Robert P. Wilder*. New York: Published for the Student Volunteer Movement by Friendship Press, 1941.

Kelleher, Matthew Hugh. "Robert Wilder and the American Foreign Missionary Movement." Ph.D. dissertation, St. Louis University, 1974.

Parker, Michael. *The Kingdom of Character: The Student Volunteer Movement for Foreign Missions (1886–1926)*. Lanham, Md.: University Press of America, 1998.

Wilder, Robert Parmalee. *Christ and the Student World*. London: Simpkin Marshall, 1935.

———. *The Great Commission: The Missionary Response of the Student Volunteer Movements in North America and Europe*. London: Oliphants, 1937.

Williams, Roger
(ca. 1603–1683) *colonial leader*

Expelled from the Massachusetts Bay Colony in 1635, Roger Williams was one of the founders and early political leaders of the Providence colony, which eventually became Rhode Island. History remembers him most, however, as one of America's earliest advocates of religious liberty and of separation of government and religious affairs. He was born in the first few years of the 17th century in London, England, the son of James Williams and Alice Pemberton Williams. During his teenaged years he joined the ranks of the Puritans, who believed that the Church of England had not sufficiently cleansed itself of impure Catholic beliefs and practices. During the same period, Roger Williams received the benevolent attention of Sir Edward Coke, one of England's premier jurists. Through Coke's sponsorship, Williams received a preparatory education from the Charterhouse School, beginning in 1621, and the subsequent opportunity to study at Cambridge's Pembroke Hall, where he received an undergraduate degree at the beginning of 1627.

Though qualified to hold a post as an Anglican minister, Williams held Puritan views that placed him at odds with the Church of England. Accordingly, he accepted a position as the chaplain for the estate of Sir William Masham in Essex.

There he met and married Mary Barnard, a maid in Masham's household, on December 15, 1629. Williams and his wife soon followed the course of many other English Puritans by migrating to the New World. The two arrived on February 5, 1631, in Boston, where Williams was promptly invited to become minister of the church there. But Williams declined this opportunity, explaining later that he dared not "officiate to an unseparated people." The Boston church, he complained, had not sufficiently repudiated its ties with the Church of England. Although the Massachusetts Puritans shared in principle Williams's opposition to the Anglican religious establishment, they owed their colonial patent to King Charles I and were anxious not to offend Charles's Anglican sensibilities. Williams eventually relocated to Salem, where he became pastor of the church in 1634. From the Salem pulpit, Williams began to advocate positions increasingly objectionable to the authorities of the Massachusetts Bay Colony. He was eventually tried before the Massachusetts General Court and banished from the colony in the fall of 1635 for his heterodox views. These views included his insistence that Charles I had no authority to grant patents in the New World without purchasing land from Native Americans and that the affairs of Massachusetts government were impermissibly entangled with religion. When Massachusetts authorities attempted to ship Williams back to England, he fled instead to Narragansett Bay in the winter of 1635–36. There, joined by a few other families, Williams obtained land from the Narragansett Indians and established the colony of Providence.

In the following years, Williams played a prominent role in the affairs of the Providence Colony, even as he continued a spiritual pilgrimage that eventually placed him outside the fraternity of organized religion. He helped establish the first Baptist church in America in 1639, but he soon became convinced that no true church existed any longer in the world. Churches require properly ordained ministers, he believed, and none existed since the Emperor Constantine had polluted the church in the fourth century by declaring Christianity the official Roman religion. By this act, Williams insisted, the chain of apostolic succession—extending from Jesus to the original apostles

and then to their successors—had been disrupted. Thereafter, the ordination of proper ministers became impossible, as did the establishment of new Christian communities. He believed that Christians had been left to wander an Earth that was barren of true churches.

In the decade after Williams founded the Providence Colony, he took up his pen to chastise the Massachusetts Bay Colony for its unholy alliance of church and state. In books such as *The Bloody Tenet of Persecution*, Williams waged rhetorical war against the use of law to coerce religious uniformity. "Forced worship," he charged, "stinks in God's nostrils." The Puritans of Massachusetts Bay wielded legal sanctions such as whippings and banishments, confident that they could distinguish the true believer from the false. Williams, however, doubted the capacity of their spiritual discernment. On hearing in 1651 that the colony had punished three Baptists who had held a religious service in Massachusetts, he wrote to the colony's governor and complained.

> Sir, I must be humbly bold to say, that 'tis impossible for any man or men to maintain their Christ by the sword, and to worship a true Christ! to fight against all consciences opposites to theirs, and not to fight against God in some of them, and to hunt after the precious life of the true Lord Jesus Christ.

As a leader in the Providence Colony, Roger Williams undertook a mission to England in the 1640s to obtain a patent for the colony from Parliament. Though he successfully completed this mission with the grant of a patent in 1644, continued turmoil concerning the colony's political footing led him to return to England again the following decade. During the 1640s and 1650s, Williams also served several years as the colony's highest official, all the while continuing to pen a steady progression of books, including one on Native American language and others in defense of religious liberty. When not occupied with the colony's business, Williams applied his copious energies to the operation of a successful trading post.

In the later years of his life, Roger Williams contended with the variety of spiritual radicalisms drawn to Providence's more religiously tolerant climate, chief among them the Quakers. He was happy to elaborate what he believed to be the doctrinal errors of the Quakers, even as he championed their right to enjoy religious freedom. But he also contended with Quakers and others who claimed exemption from taxes and military service on conscientious grounds, arguing that religious liberty did not entitle citizens to exemptions from such crucial social obligations. Active to the end of his life, Williams eventually died in the winter or early spring of 1683.

In the early 19th century, Thomas Jefferson would popularize the idea of a "wall of separation" between church and state. But Roger Williams had envisioned such a separation nearly two centuries before, when he agitated relentlessly for a sharp demarcation between the church and the world or—as he phrased it—between the garden and the wilderness. His commitment to the cause of religious liberty and religious disestablishment was not the product of indifference to religion but instead of faith that he believed would be polluted by alliances with political authority.

Further Reading

Brockunier, Samuel Hugh. *The Irrepressible Democrat: Roger Williams*. New York: Ronald Press, 1940.

Covey, Cyclone. *The Gentle Radical: A Biography of Roger Williams*. New York: Macmillan, 1966.

Easton, Emily. *Roger Williams: Prophet and Pioneer*. Boston: Houghton Mifflin, 1930.

Ernst, James. *The Political Thought of Roger Williams*. Seattle: University of Washington Press, 1929.

———. *Roger Williams: New England Firebrand*. New York: Macmillan, 1932.

Garrett, John. *Roger Williams: Witness Beyond Christendom, 1603–1683*. New York: Macmillan, 1970.

Gaustad, Edwin S. *Liberty of Conscience: Roger Williams in America*. Grand Rapids, Mich.: Eerdmans, 1991.

Gilpin, W. Clark. *The Millenarian Piety of Roger Williams*. Chicago: University of Chicago Press, 1979.

Hall, Timothy L. *Separating Church and State: Roger Williams and Religious Liberty*. Urbana: University of Illinois Press, 1998.

Miller, Perry. *Roger Williams: His Contribution to the American Tradition*. Indianapolis: Bobbs-Merrill, 1953.

Morgan, Edmund. *Roger Williams: The Church and the State*. New York: W. W. Norton, 1967.

Spurgin, Hugh. *Roger Williams and the Puritan Radicalism in the English Separatist Tradition*. Lewiston, N.Y.: Edwin Mellen Press, 1989.

Williams, Roger. *Complete Writings of Roger Williams*. 7 vols. New York: Russell & Russell, 1963.

———. *The Correspondence of Roger Williams*. Edited by Glen W. Lafantasie. 2 vols. Providence, R.I.: Brown University Press, 1988.

Winslow, Ola Elizabeth. *Master Roger Williams*. New York: Macmillan, 1957.

Wise, Isaac Mayer
(1819–1900) *Reform rabbi*

Isaac Meyer Wise, the father of Reform Judaism in the United States, contributed indefatigable energy and copious organizational skills to the work of unifying American Judaism. In substantial measure because of his labors, Reform Judaism became the dominant religious tradition among American Jews during the 19th century. Wise was born on March 29, 1819, in Steingrub, Bohemia (today Kammeny Dvur, Bohemia), the son of Leo Weis and Regina Weis. He studied at yeshivas in Bohemia and Austria before in 1843 becoming a rabbi in Radnitz, a town in Bohemia. The following year he married Theresa Block, with whom he had four sons and four daughters. He did not remain long in Radnitz, however, but made his way to the United States with his family in 1846.

After a few months, Wise and his family settled in Albany, New York, where he became the rabbi of Congregation Beth-El. Wise discovered almost at once the fragmented and disorganized character of American Judaism, and he began a half-century-long crusade to give order to what he perceived as religious chaos. One source of conflict among American Jews was that between Orthodox and Reform Judaism, the latter begun in Germany during the early 19th century. Wise's alignment with Reform Judaism set him on an inevitable collision course with Orthodox Judaism and partially frustrated his attempts to promote Jewish unification. In 1850, after his congregation attempted to dismiss him for his Reformist zeal and Wise refused to recognize the dismissal, physical conflict erupted at the synagogue during New Year services and Wise found himself arrested for inciting a mob. In the aftermath of this fracture within his congregation, Wise and his supporters established the Anshe Emeth congregation.

Four years after the split within the Albany congregation, Isaac Meyer Wise accepted an offer to become the rabbi of Congregation B'nai Yeshrun in Cincinnati, Ohio. He occupied this post for the remainder of his life and made Cincinnati the center of his efforts to unite American Jews under the Reform banner. The year that he arrived at B'nai Yeshrun he began publication of a weekly English newspaper, *The Israelite,* and a German paper, *Die Deborah.* Both publishing ventures served as platforms for Wise to advance the cause of unification among Jewish congregations in America. He also sought to create liturgical unity and reform in the diverse practices of Jewish synagogues by publishing a reformed prayer book, *Minhag America,* in 1857.

In subsequent years Wise sought to establish further institutional structures to support Jewish unity. He helped found the Union of American Hebrew Congregations in 1873 and, in 1875, the Hebrew Union College in Cincinnati. He served as president of the college for the remainder of his life and, with the creation of the Central Conference of American Rabbis in 1883, assumed a lifetime presidency of this organization as well. Although he seems to have hoped that this triumvirate of institutions might find a basis of support broader than Reform Judaism, the fractures between Reform and Orthodox congregations were too deep for even Wise's organizational gifts to heal. A decade after the creation of the Hebrew Union College, Orthodox Jews, led by SABATO MORAIS and HENRY PEREIRA MENDES, established the Jewish Theological Seminary in New York to perpetuate their distinct spiritual vision.

Wise's first marriage lasted for 30 years, until the death of his wife in 1874. Two years later he married Selma Bondi, with whom he had four children. Wise died on March 26, 1900, in Cincinnati.

By the time of his death at the verge of the 20th century, Isaac Meyer Wise had become the most prominent Jewish religious leader in America. He labored prodigiously and incessantly to find a common voice for American Judaism and to erect institutional structures that would sustain Jewish religious life in America. His own sympathies for Reform Judaism partially defeated his unification efforts, as more Orthodox believers saw that the voice with which Wise attempted to speak for Jews in America had an overwhelmingly Reform accent. He succeeded, nevertheless, in unifying Reform Judaism in the United States, in creating an educational institution to train American rabbis, and in making the Reform tradition the dominant one among American Jews.

Further Reading

Knox, Israel. *Rabbi in America: The Story of Isaac M. Wise.* Boston: Little, Brown, 1957.
May, Max B. *Isaac Mayer Wise: The Founder of American Judaism, A Biography.* New York: G. P. Putnam's Sons, 1916.
Temkin, Sefton D. *Isaac Meyer Wise: Shaping American Judaism.* Oxford: Oxford University Press, 1992.
Wise, Isaac Mayer. *Reminiscences.* Translated and edited by David Philipson. Cincinnati: L. Wise, 1901; New York: Arno Press, 1973.
———. *Selected Writings of Isaac Mayer Wise.* Edited by David Philipson and Louis Grossmann. New York: Arno Press, 1969.
———. *The Western Journal of Isaac Mayer Wise, 1877.* Edited by William M. Kramer. Berkeley, Calif.: Western Jewish History Center, Magnes Museum, 1974.

Wise, Stephen Samuel
(1874–1949) *Reform rabbi, Zionist leader*

Unlike most Reform rabbis of his generation, Stephen S. Wise played an active role in the Zionist movement. He lived long enough to see both the Nazi atrocities committed against the Jews during World War II and the creation of an independent Jewish state in Palestine after the war. Wise was born on March 17, 1874, in Erlau, Hungary, near Budapest, the son of Aaron Weisz and Sabine de Fischer Farkashazy Weisz. His father immigrated to the United States in 1874, and Stephen followed with the rest of the Weisz family soon afterward. After private studies with his father, Stephen Wise prepared to continue six generations of family tradition by becoming a rabbi himself. He earned a B.A. from Columbia University in 1892 and began private rabbinical studies in the United States and Austria. In 1893, he was ordained a rabbi in Austria.

After his return to the United States, Wise accepted a position as assistant rabbi of Congregation B'nai Jeshurun in New York City. During this period he began work on a Ph.D. in Semitics from Columbia, a degree that he received in 1902. He also migrated from the tradition of Orthodox Judaism, in which he had been raised, toward Reform Judaism. But unlike most other Reform Jews, who downplayed the idea of the Jews as a people, Wise began a long association with the Zionist movement. He was a founding member of the Federation of American Zionists in 1898.

In 1900, Wise became rabbi at Beth Israel in Portland, Oregon, a Reform congregation. The same year, he married Louise Waterman, with whom he had two children. In Oregon, Wise created a pattern of engagement in progressive causes that would characterize the rest of his life. He returned to New York City after six years, and there in 1907 he formed the Free Synagogue, an independent Jewish congregation. For almost four decades he held services for this congregation in Carnegie Hall. As in Oregon, Wise saw his role as a religious leader as including active social involvement. He was a founding member of the National Association for the Advancement of Colored People (NAACP) in 1909 and of the American Civil Liberties Union (ACLU) in 1920. He also formed a close friendship with JOHN HAYNES HOLMES, the pastor of New York's Community Church, and the two men worked together to expose the corruption of Tammany Hall.

During World War I, Wise gradually acquired an international reputation through his labors on behalf of Zionism. In 1914, he began working with the future Supreme Court justice Louis Brandeis, who took charge of the American Zionist movement. Two years later, Wise was instrumental in the creation of the American Jewish Congress. These activities were not without their conflicts. In addition to rifts with other Reform Jews over

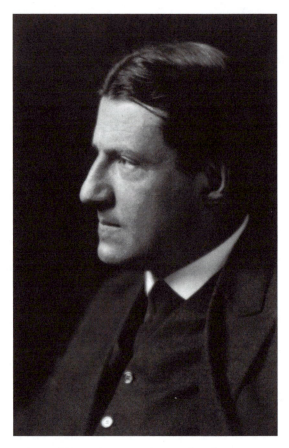

Reform rabbi Stephen Samuel Wise played a prominent role in the Zionist movement. *(Library of Congress, Prints and Photographs Division, LC-USZ62-75146)*

Zionism, Wise experienced tension over the relative status of American and European Zionist leaders. The domination of Chaim Weizmann, a European Zionist, of the American Zionist movement ultimately caused Brandeis, now an associate justice on the Supreme Court, and Wise to resign from the movement in 1921. The following year hostility among Reform Jews to the cause of Zionism, especially as exhibited at Reform's chief educational institution—Hebrew Union College in Cincinnati—prompted Wise to establish a competing educational institution in New York, the Jewish Institute of Religion.

In the years leading up to World War II, Wise had to contend with the growing threat of nazism.

He found himself sometimes alone in his harsh jeremiads about the dangers for democracy in Adolf Hitler's growing power. But he supported Franklin D. Roosevelt, even though the president's attention tended to be dominated by rescuing the country from the economic crisis of the Depression, and later waging war against the Axis powers, than by supporting the Zionist agenda. Wise has sometimes been criticized for not raising the alarm immediately after his discovery of Hitler's first efforts to implement his extermination policy against the Jews, the notorious "Final Solution," when he discovered it in the summer of 1942.

Wise's health declined sharply after the war. He lived, though, to see the fruition of his long years as a Zionist, the creation of an independent state for the Jews in Palestine in 1948. He died the following year, on April 19, 1949, in New York City.

Rabbi Stephen S. Wise occupied a popular pulpit in New York City for almost 40 years. His leadership of the American Zionist movement secured his prominent place in American religious history. He inherited from the Orthodox Judaism of his childhood an abiding respect for the idea of a Jewish people, and he labored tirelessly to secure a place for his people within their historic homeland of Palestine. He said of himself in an article published in *Time* magazine in 1938, "I am a Jew who is an American. I was a Jew before I was an American. I have been an American all my life, 64 years, but I've been a Jew for 4,000 years." Although the founding of the state of Israel in 1948 must be traced to the labors of many individuals, Wise must certainly be reckoned one of them.

Further Reading

"An Inventory to the Stephen S. Wise Collection." Available online. URL: http://www.huc.edu/aja/SWise.htm. Downloaded on April 29, 2002.

Shapiro, Robert Donald. *A Reform Rabbi in the Progressive Era: The Early Career of Stephen S. Wise.* New York: Garland, 1988.

Urofsky, Melvin I. *A Voice That Spoke for Justice: The Life and Times of Stephen S. Wise.* Albany: State University of New York Press, 1982.

Voss, Carl Hermann. *Rabbi and Minister: The Friendship of Stephen S. Wise and John Haynes Holmes.* Cleveland: World, Publishing, 1964.

Wise, Stephen Samuel. *Challenging Years: The Autobiography of Stephen Wise.* London: East and West Library, 1951.

———. *Stephen S. Wise: Servant of the People, Selected Letters.* Edited by Carl Hermann Voss. Philadelphia: Jewish Publication Society of America, 1969.

Witherspoon, John
(1723–1794) *Presbyterian minister, educator, Revolutionary War leader*

The only minister to sign the Declaration of Independence, John Witherspoon exerted enormous influence in the country that he made his own a little more than a decade before the Revolutionary War. As a preacher, a college president, and a patriot, he lent a vigorous mind to the support of the new nation. He was born on February 5, 1723, in Gifford, Scotland, the son of James Witherspoon and Anne Walker Witherspoon. He studied with his father, a minister of the Church of Scotland, and then, from the time he was 13 years old, at the University of Edinburgh, from which he received a master of arts degree in 1739. After another four years of theological study at the university, he was licensed to preach and subsequently ordained as minister of a church in Beith, Ayrshire, in early 1745. Three years later he married Elizabeth Montgomery, with whom he had 10 children.

The Church of Scotland divided itself between more orthodox or evangelical ministers, referred to, strangely enough, as the Popular party, and more liberal ones, called Moderates. Witherspoon identified himself with the Popularists and made a name for himself as the witty adversary of the more liberal party within the church. After a dozen years at Beith, he assumed the more prestigious pulpit of Laigh Kirk in Paisley. By 1766, his fame as a Scottish minister had crossed the Atlantic and won the attention of Presbyterians in America. That year, the College of New Jersey (later Princeton University) invited Witherspoon to assume its presidency. Although Witherspoon's wife initially opposed leaving Scotland, she eventually surrendered her reservations, and Witherspoon and his family finally arrived in late summer of 1768 in Princeton, where the Scottish minister assumed the helm of the College of New Jersey.

Witherspoon immediately took vigorous strides to raise financial support for the college and to increase its enrollment. To his administrative responsibilities, he added copious teaching duties, which he shared with one other professor (later in his administration, two) and several tutors. His personal contact with college students gave him a wide field of influence. He could boast among his students a president and a vice president of the United States, 21 senators, 39 congressmen, three Supreme Court justices, and 12 governors. Princeton sent nine of its graduates to the Constitutional Convention of 1787, at which a total of 55 delegates assembled. Five of these had been students of Witherspoon.

President Witherspoon had been in America less than a decade when he plunged enthusiastically into the rising current of sentiment in favor of independence from Britain. When future U.S. president John Adams met John Witherspoon in 1774, he promptly named him "an animated Son of Liberty." In the summer of 1776, New Jersey sent him as one of its delegates to the Continental Congress in Philadelphia, and he was the only minister to sign the Declaration of Independence. In the following years he served conspicuously in the Continental Congress until finally resigning in November 1782. Almost immediately, though, he undertook service in the New Jersey legislature from 1783 to 1789. His prominence in state politics earned him a place in the New Jersey ratifying convention in 1787 that made New Jersey the third state to ratify the U.S. Constitution.

In 1789, Witherspoon's wife, Elizabeth, died. That year he delivered the sermon at the newly organized General Assembly of the national Presbyterian Church. Two years later, he married a 24-year-old widow named Ann Dill, with whom he had two daughters. By 1792 he was totally blind, and on November 15, 1794, he died at his home, Tusculum, just north of Princeton.

John Witherspoon saw no contradiction between his ministerial and educational vocations and his service as a patriot. His religious devotion breathed the same air as his patriotic inclinations,

John Witherspoon, one of the signers of the Declaration of Independence, served as an early president of the College of New Jersey, which later became Princeton University. *(Library of Congress, Prints and Photographs Division, LC-USZ62-104656)*

and he did not hesitate to elaborate a connection between the two. In a speech delivered in Princeton in late spring of 1776, he argued:

> He is the best friend to American liberty, who is most sincere and active in promoting true and undefiled religion, and who sets himself with the greatest firmness to bear down profanity and immorality of every kind. Whoever is an avowed enemy of God, I scruple not to call him an enemy of his country.

The nation that John Witherspoon helped to construct would eventually have to ponder the relationship that ought to exist between government and religion. Witherspoon, though, illustrates how frequently faith and political activism have allied themselves in the American political tradition.

Further Reading

Collins, Varnum Lansing. *President Witherspoon.* 2 vols. Princeton, N.J.: Princeton University Press, 1925; New York: Arno Press, 1969.

Stohlman, Martha Lou Lemmon. *John Witherspoon: Parson, Politician, Patriot.* Philadelphia: Westminster Press, 1976.

Tait, L. Gordon. *The Piety of John Witherspoon: Pew, Pulpit, and Public Forum.* Louisville, Ky.: Geneva Press, 2001.

Witherspoon, John. *The Selected Writings of John Witherspoon.* Edited by Thomas Miller, Carbondale: Southern Illinois University Press, 1990.

Woods, David Walker, Jr. *John Witherspoon.* New York: F.H. Revell, 1906.

Woodruff, Wilford
(1807–1898) president of the Church of Jesus Christ of Latter-day Saints

As the fourth president of the Church of Jesus Christ of Latter-day Saints (the Mormon Church), Wilford Woodruff helped the church shed its identity as an embattled sect and find a place within the mainstream of American religious life. His most significant act as the church's leader was his official repudiation of the practice of polygamy. Woodruff was born on March 1, 1807, in Farmington, Connecticut, the son of Aphek Woodruff and Beulah Thompson Woodruff. He received a better than average education for the times by attending public schools and then Farmington Academy. He spent the next several years first working as an operator of flour mills and then tending a farm and a saw mill in Richland, New York, which he purchased with his brother, Azmon. During this period, Woodruff searched for an authentic church and was convinced that none of the denominations of his day provided it. In December 1833, however—three years after JOSEPH SMITH, JR., published the *Book of Mormon*—Woodruff was converted to Mormonism through the preaching of two Mormon missionaries who visited the area where he lived. The following year, he answered Joseph Smith's summons for Mormon volunteers to mount an expedition to Missouri. Smith proposed to recover property that Mormons who had settled in Jackson County had been forced to abandon when local residents drove them out of the county. The expedition, known as Zion's Camp, was unsuccessful, but Woodruff's participation in it helped to place him at the center of the

affairs of the new religious movement. Joseph Smith organized a Quorum of the Twelve Apostles in 1835 to assist in the leadership of the church, and after several years of missionary work, Woodruff was named to this council in 1839. Together with BRIGHAM YOUNG and other members of the council, Woodruff undertook a successful missionary journey to England in 1839–41. He returned to England on a second missionary venture in 1844.

After the death of Joseph Smith, Jr., in 1844, Woodruff joined the Mormon migration to Utah and arrived there among the advance party during the summer of 1847. The years that followed found him engaged in a variety of labors on behalf of the church. He also represented the interests of the church by serving in the Utah territorial legislature for 22 years. Perhaps his most important work during the middle years of his career as a Mormon leader was as a historian of Mormon affairs. He also tended the affairs of a large family, made so by his practice of plural marriage. In 1837 he married Phebe Whittemore Carter, with whom he had 4 children who survived infancy; he subsequently entered into plural marriages with eight other women, with whom he had 18 additional children who survived infancy. Four of these marriages ended in divorce.

After the death of Brigham Young in late August 1877, John Taylor was eventually selected to succeed him as president of the Mormon Church in the fall of 1880. At the same time, Woodruff became president of the Quorum of the Twelve Apostles, an office that made him the likely successor of Taylor. During the 1880s, the U.S. government launched a full-scale assault on the Mormon practice of polygamy. Two new federal laws, the Edmunds Act of 1882 and the Edmunds-Tucker Act of 1887, facilitated prosecution of polygamists, stripped them of the right to vote, and confiscated property of the Mormon Church. Especially during the middle of the decade, vigorous efforts by federal officials to enforce these laws forced Woodruff and other Mormon leaders into hiding. Woodruff, in particular, could not attend the funeral of his first wife, Phebe, in 1885 for fear of arrest.

Following the death of John Taylor in 1887, Woodruff eventually assumed the presidency of the

Mormon Church in 1889. Though he had originally believed that the federal campaign against the Mormons would usher in the end times, he eventually became convinced that Mormons would have to adjust themselves in significant ways to American society. He recorded in his diary entry for September 25, 1890, that he was

> under the necessity of acting for the Temporal Salvation of the Church. The United States Government has taken a Stand & passed Laws to destroy the Latter day Saints upon the Subjet [sic] of poligamy [sic] or Patriarchal order of Marriage. And after Praying to the Lord & feeling inspired by his spirit I have issued . . . [a] Proclamation which is sustained by my Councillors and the 12 Apostles.

The proclamation, called the "Manifesto," officially ended the practice of polygamy for Mormons. Woodruff died in San Francisco, while on a trip to California, on September 2, 1898.

Sometimes reckoned third in importance to Mormon history after Joseph Smith, Jr., and Brigham Young, Wilford Woodruff charted a course for the Mormon Church that would lead it into the mainstream of American religious and political life during the 20th century. By surrendering the church's commitment to plural marriage, he removed its chief source of offense. He also encouraged Mormons to take a less insular view of political activity, thus building a bridge for their full participation in American life in the century after his death.

Further Reading

Alexander, Thomas G. *Things in Heaven and Earth: The Life and Times of Wilford Woodruff, a Mormon Prophet.* Salt Lake City, Utah: Signature Books, 1991.

Cowley, Matthias Foss, ed. *Wilford Woodruff, Fourth President of the Church of Jesus Christ of Latter-day Saints: History of His Life and Labors.* Salt Lake City, Utah: The Deseret News, 1909; Salt Lake City, Utah: Bookcraft, 1964.

Gibbons, Francis M. *Wilford Woodruff: Wondrous Worker, Prophet of God.* Salt Lake City, Utah: Deseret, 1988.

Woodruff, Wilford. *Waiting for World's End: The Diaries of Wilford Woodruff.* Edited by Susan Staker. Salt Lake City, Utah: Signature Books, 1993.

Woodworth-Etter, Maria
(Maria Beulah Underwood)
(1844–1924) *Holiness and Pentecostal evangelist*

Maria Beulah Woodworth-Etter followed a spiritual migration that began in a Disciples of Christ church and ended in Pentecostalism. Along the way, she became the foremost female evangelist in America during the closing years of the 19th century and the first of the 20th. She was born on July 22, 1844, in New Lisbon (subsequently Lisbon), Ohio, the daughter of Samuel Underwood and Matilda Underwood. Her father, a farmer, apparently died of sunstroke in the summer of 1856. The following year, when she was 13, she experienced a religious conversion at a revival meeting in a Disciples of Christ church. During the Civil War, she met and soon married Philo Harrison Woodworth, a war veteran who had suffered a head injury in battle and was subsequently discharged.

Maria Woodworth's early years of marriage yielded a stream of disappointments and sorrows. She and her husband had little success at farming. Even more significantly, of the six children she bore, all but the first died in childhood. She experienced a spiritual renewal, however, at a revival service in a Quaker church in 1879 and this experience redirected her life's course. She began to preach in nearby churches and proved so effective that several denominations attempted to assign her to pulpits in the area. Woodworth joined a Disciples of Christ church during this period, but she refused to settle as a minister in any particular station, preaching itinerantly instead.

Woodworth's husband, Philo, initially tried to discourage her from traveling more widely, but he eventually agreed to accompany her on more far-reaching evangelistic tours throughout western Ohio and eastern Indiana. In 1884, she was licensed to preach by the 39th Indiana Eldership of the Churches of God; she remained associated with this denomination until 1904, when denominational authorities requested that she surrender her license. From 1885 to 1889, Woodworth preached throughout the Midwest, attracting crowds reportedly as large as 25,000 in one location. Along with the singing and shouting characteristic of Holiness meetings, Woodworth's revival services were marked by episodes of fainting among members of her audiences and by her own trancelike states, which sometimes caused her to stand motionless with her hands upraised for extended periods. She referred to these states as experiencing "the power," but they prompted critics to call her the "voodoo priestess."

In fall 1889, Woodworth took her revival campaign to Oakland, California. Her services in a tent there attracted significant attention, not a little of it unfavorable. Mobs threatened to disrupt the meetings, prompting local police to deputize some of the evangelist's followers to keep the peace during revival services. But the charismatic preacher gained even more attention when she predicted in early 1890 that an earthquake and a tidal wave would destroy Alameda, Oakland, and San Francisco on April 14 of that year. The failure of this prophecy and Woodworth's departure from California a few days before the predicted calamity dealt her preaching ministry a severe blow. The Oakland campaign also precipitated the separation of the Woodworths. In the proceedings that resulted in their divorce in 1891, she alleged that her husband had committed adultery several times.

Woodworth continued her itinerant career as an evangelist over the decades after the Oakland campaign. Her ministry continued to attract both praise and criticism. In meetings in Saint Louis in 1890, two doctors attempted—unsuccessfully—to have her committed as insane. A little more than a decade after her divorce from Philo Woodworth, she married Samuel Etter in 1902.

In about 1912, Woodworth-Etter became associated with the Pentecostal movement, which had taken root in the American religious soil the previous decade. Pentecostalism emphasized the postconversion experience of the "baptism by the Holy Spirit," as evidenced by its possessors by glossolalia, or speaking in tongues. Woodworth-Etter gained prominence in this movement through services she conducted in 1912 at a Pentecostal church in Dallas, Texas. Controversy continued to follow in the wake of her evangelistic career, though, perhaps most famously in Framingham, Massachusetts, where she was charged with obtaining money under false pretenses but acquitted—after a sensational four-day trial in 1913.

Toward the end of that decade, Woodworth-Etter established a church in Indianapolis where she preached when not traveling. She died in Indianapolis on September 16, 1924.

Maria Woodworth-Etter gained national prominence during an era when most Christian denominations frowned on women's becoming ministers. However, by her own account, God had charged her with the work of evangelism: "I heard the voice of Jesus calling me," she recorded in her book *Holy Ghost Sermons* (1918), "to go out in the highways and hedges and gather in the lost sheep." This summons initiated a preaching ministry that spanned more than four decades. First as a Holiness preacher and later as a Pentecostal evangelist, Woodworth-Etter established a pattern of ministry that had been presaged by the work of other women preachers such as PHOEBE WORRALL PALMER earlier in the 19th century and would be emulated in the 20th century by women such as AIMEE SEMPLE MCPHERSON and KATHRYN KUHLMAN.

Further Reading

Warner, Wayne E. "Maria Woodworth-Etter: A Powerful Voice in the Pentecostal Vanguard." Available online. URL: http://www.enrichmentjournal.ag.org/enrichmentjournal/199901/086_woodsworth_etter.cfm. Downloaded on November 24, 2001.

———. *The Woman Evangelist: The Life and Times of Charismatic Evangelist Maria B. Woodworth-Etter.* Metuchen, N.J.: Scarecrow Press, 1986.

Woodworth-Etter, Maria Beulah. *The Life, Work, and Experiences of Maria Beulah Woodworth.* St. Louis: by author, 1894.

———. *Marvels and Miracles.* Indianapolis: by author, 1922.

———. *The Original Maria Woodworth-Etter Devotional.* Edited by Larry Keefauver. Orlando, Fla.: Creation House, 1997.

———. *Signs and Wonders.* New Kensington, Pa.: Whitaker House, 1997.

Woolman, John
(1720–1772) *Quaker minister*

More than a century before the Civil War, President Abraham Lincoln's Emancipation Proclamation, and the ratification of the U.S. Constitution's Thirteenth Amendment, which abolished slavery, the Quaker John Woolman opposed slavery. In his life, he persuaded many Quakers to join him in this opposition, and after he died the Society of Friends decisively repudiated the commerce in human souls. His journal, published posthumously, became a classic account of American religious life. He was born on October 19, 1720, in Northampton, New Jersey, the son of Quaker parents, Samuel Woolman and Elizabeth Burr Woolman.

Until he was 21 years old, John Woolman worked on his family's farm. In 1741, he moved to Mount Holly, where he was employed in a local store. While working there, Woolman grew to believe that slavery was a great evil, being moved to this position after his employer at the time asked him to draw up a bill of sale for a female slave. Though he agreed to do so on this occasion, he subsequently declined further requests to participate—even in a minor capacity—in transactions involving slavery. During this decade, Woolman began to travel widely, especially in the South, and his travels gave him contact with many Quaker slaveholders. As he attempted to persuade these fellow Quakers to free their slaves, he became an even more decided opponent of slavery. In 1754, Woolman published *Some Considerations on the Keeping of Negroes Recommended to the Professors of Christianity of Every Denomination*, in which he argued at length against the institution of slavery: "[I]f we seriously consider that liberty is the right of innocent men; that the Almighty God is a refuge for the oppressed; that in reality we are indebted to them . . . to retain them in perpetual servitude, without present cause for it, will produce effects, in the event, more grievous than setting them free would do." In contrast with those who justified slavery by the supposed inherent inferiority of blacks, Woolman penned an eloquent hymn to human fraternity:

> There is a principle, which is pure, placed in the human mind, which in different places and ages hath had different names; it is, however, pure and proceeds from God.—It is deep, and inward, confined to no forms of religion, nor excluded from any, where the heart stands in perfect sincerity. In whomsoever this takes root, and grows, of what nation soever, they become brethren.

By 1758, Woolman's gentle persuasion resulted in the decision of the annual Philadelphia Quaker meeting to urge Quakers to free their slaves. Over the years, other annual meetings adopted the same position.

In his 20s, Woolman had already established a career as an itinerant Quaker minister, traveling mostly on foot. To support himself, he became a tailor in 1746, because this trade allowed him some measure of freedom to travel. In 1749, he married Sarah Ellis, with whom he had two children.

The years of Woolman's life were not marked by epochal transitions but by a patient witness to Quaker principles. A pacifist as well as an abolitionist, Woolman encouraged other Quakers to refuse support of wars. He also displayed a keen interest in the lives of Native Americans, especially their exploitation by rum merchants and those who would obtain their lands for a pittance. Toward the end of his life he decided to visit England, while there he contracted smallpox and died in York on October 7, 1772. Two years later, his journal was published.

Woolman was a prophet of abolitionism in the 18th century, but his prophetic character was not that of thunder and lightning. Instead, he rained on whoever would hear him a measured stream of arguments against the wrongs of his day, not the least of which was the traffic in slaves. His influence among Quakers was considerable during his life, and to this must be added the influence of his journal, which is a moving autobiography of American religious life.

Further Reading

Cady, Edwin H. *John Woolman: The Mind of the Quaker Saint.* New York: Washington Square Press, 1966.

Moulton, Phillips P. *The Living Witness of John Woolman.* Wallingford, Pa: Pendle Hill, 1973.

Peare, Catherine Owens. *John Woolman, Child of Light: The Story of John Woolman and the Friends.* New York: Vanguard, 1954.

Reynolds, Reginald. *The Wisdom of John Woolman.* London: G. Allen & Unwin, 1948.

Shore, W. Teignmouth. *John Woolman, His Life and Our Times: Being a Study in Applied Christianity.* London: Macmillan, 1913.

Sox, David. *John Woolman: Quintessential Quaker, 1720–1772.* Richmond, Ind.: Friends United Press, 1999.

Whitney, Janet Payne. *John Woolman, American Quaker.* Boston: Little, Brown, 1942.

Woolman, John. *The Journal and Major Essays of John Woolman.* New York: Oxford University Press, 1971.

Wovoka
(Jack Wilson)
(ca. 1856–1932) *Native American religious leader, prophet, founder of the Ghost Dance Religion*

A Northern Paiute (Numu) holy man, Wovoka (whose name means "cutter" or "wood cutter"), also known as Jack Wilson, became the founder of the Ghost Dance of 1890. This Native American religious movement emphasized the imminent restoration of the dead in a new Native American world. Wovoka was born around 1856 or 1858, probably near the Walker River in Mason Valley, Nevada. (Conflicting accounts suggest that it was either California or Nevada.) His father was Tavibo, a Northern Paiute shaman who followed Wodziwob, originator of the Ghost Dance of 1870. When Wovoka was a teenager his father died, and Wovoka became associated with the family of a white rancher named David Wilson. To non-Indians, he became known as Jack Wilson.

Over the following years, Wovoka worked for the Wilson family and also acquired a reputation as a medicine man among his people. In 1888–89, he claimed to have received a revelation that a messiah would shortly appear, that all of the Native American dead would soon return to life (along with the buffalo), and that the white settlers would disappear. He told his followers that they should participate in a regular series of ritual dances over four or five nights to bring about this remaking of the world, and these rituals were soon labeled the Ghost Dance. In the newly remade world, Wovoka prophesied, sickness would be eradicated and everyone would be young.

Many Native Americans perceived Wovoka himself to be the messiah, and the Ghost Dance spread rapidly after the first series of dances began in 1889. Wovoka claimed the ability to control the weather, and the Ghost Dance movement began to gain adherents in spring 1889, after Wovoka was believed to have drawn rain to drought-ridden western Nevada.

Wovoka seems to have counseled peace with whites. "Grandfather says," he is reported to have instructed his followers, "when your friends die you must not cry. You must not hurt anybody or do harm to anyone. You must not fight. Do right always. It will give you satisfaction in life." But some Native American tribes—the Lakota Sioux, in particular—found in the Ghost Dance a charter for militancy against whites. U.S. military authorities feared the Ghost Dance as a pretext for Native American rebellion; on December 29, 1890, federal troops massacred more than 200 Sioux men, women, and children at Wounded Knee on the Pine Ridge Indian Reservation in South Dakota. The massacre, accompanied by the failure of the Lakota representatives' assurances that Ghost Dance followers were protected by bulletproof ghost shirts, contributed to the rapid collapse of the Ghost Dance movement.

Wovoka remained influential for a time, though his prophesies regarding a new world did not immediately come to pass. He continued to counsel peace with the whites in teachings that combined elements of Native American religion with Christian concepts, such as reverence for Jesus.

> Do not tell the white people about this. Jesus is now upon the earth. He appears like a cloud. The dead are still alive again. I do not know when they will be here; maybe this fall or in the spring. When the time comes there will be no more sickness and everyone will be young again.

By 1895, Wovoka had severed his connections with such elements of the Ghost Dance as still survived. He worked at a ranch for a while and still later at a flour mill. By approximately 1905, Wovoka had begun teaching about the Ghost Dance again, and from 1910 to 1917 he influenced a revival of the movement.

Little is known about Wovoka's family life. He married a Northern Paiute woman named Mary (Tuuma) in the mid-1870s and he had four children, and in 1890, he took a second wife. Poverty afflicted his last years. His first wife, Mary, died in the summer of 1931, and a little more than a year later he died at his home in the Yerington Indian Colony townsite of Nevada on September 29, 1932.

Wovoka's life intersected the final subjugation of Native Americans by federal authorities. His religious teachings, especially as embraced by the Lakota Sioux, partially precipitated this subjugation. But the Ghost Dance survived even after Wounded Knee stripped it of its imminent messianic hope. It was a movement of peace and spiritual longing that managed to endure a tragic present.

Further Reading

Bailey, Paul Dayton. *Wovoka: The Indian Messiah.* Los Angeles: Westernlore Press, 1957.

Berube, David Michael. "The Lakotan Ghost Dance of 1890: A Historiocritical Performance Analysis." Ph.D. dissertation, New York University, 1990.

Hittman, Michael. *Wovoka and the Ghost Dance.* Edited by Don Lynch. Expanded ed. Lincoln: University of Nebraska Press, 1997.

Mooney, James. *The Ghost-Dance Religion and the Sioux Outbreak of 1890.* Washington: n.p., 1896; Lincoln: University of Nebraska Press, 1991.

X, Y

X, Malcolm   See MALCOLM X.

Young, Brigham
(1801–1877) *president of the Church of Jesus Christ of Latter-day Saints, territorial governor of Utah*

As the second president of the Church of Jesus Christ of Latter-day Saints (the Mormons), Brigham Young shepherded the infant religious movement through its second generation. He succeeded the founder of the Mormon Church, JOSEPH SMITH, JR., and his leadership and administrative abilities allowed the church to flourish during perilous times in its early life. Young was born on June 1, 1801, in Whitingham, Vermont, the son of John Young and Abigail Nabby Howe Young, who were farmers. He grew up on the New York frontier, where he received virtually no formal education, but his mother taught him to read the Bible and he learned the skills necessary to survive on the edge of the wilderness. His mother died of tuberculosis in 1815, and he soon left home to learn carpentry and related trades. He became a Methodist in 1824 and was baptized at 23 years of age. The same year he married Miriam Works, with whom he had two daughters before her death of tuberculosis eight years later.

By 1828, Young and his family had settled in Mendon, New York, where his father and several family members lived. There, two years later, Young encountered a Mormon missionary and learned about the *Book of Mormon.* He became a Mormon, baptized along with most of his family in April 1832. Young promptly devoted himself to preaching the Mormon faith. Soon after the death of his wife in September 1832, he set out for Kirtland, Ohio, where Joseph Smith, Jr., founder of the Mormons, had established his headquarters. After meeting Smith, Young returned to New York, where he took up the life of an itinerant Mormon evangelist. In February 1834, he married Mary Ann Angell and he returned with his family to Kirtland, where he rapidly earned Smith's trust. By 1835 he had been appointed one of the church's Quorum of the Apostles, the 12 men who helped Smith superintend Mormon affairs. Within three years he had become senior apostle. After the Mormon community migrated to Far West, Missouri, and was forced to flee almost immediately in the face of threatened violence, Young took charge of the exodus while Smith and other Mormon leaders languished for five months in jail. Once the Mormons had settled into Nauvoo, a new community in Illinois, Young traveled as a Mormon missionary to England, where he was successful in attracting many new converts to the faith. He returned to Nauvoo in the summer of 1841, and he promptly supported Smith by embracing the practice of plural marriage, a practice that remained secret for more than a decade. Eventually he took more than 50 women as wives and fathered 57 children through connubial relationships with 16 of his wives.

While in jail for criminal charges in 1844, Joseph Smith was killed by a mob and Brigham Young subsequently emerged from the ensuing internal power struggle as the new president of the Mormons. Convinced that the threat of violence against Mormons in Illinois necessitated relocation, Young orchestrated a mass migration of Mormons westward. When he arrived at the Great Salt Lake Valley in the summer of 1847, he declared the search for a new home over and organized additional waves of settlement in Utah over the years that followed. After Congress created the Utah Territory in 1850, he served until 1857 as territorial governor, though relations between the federal government and the Mormons were less than cordial, especially after the church publicly advocated its practice of polygamy in 1852. In 1857, President James Buchanan removed Young as governor and dispatched federal troops to Utah; the result was the short-lived and bloodless Utah War, which ended the following year.

Over the following two decades, Brigham Young superintended the religious and economic expansion of the Mormon Church. He oversaw the construction of the Utah portion of the transcontinental telegraph system and then linked church-owned telegraph stations to one another. He was similarly supportive of railroad construction in Utah, again seizing on railway lines as a means of creating transportation routes among Mormon settlements and interests in the territory. To these enterprises he added a host of other church-owned business ventures, not the least of which was his organization of Mormon communities into communal economic enterprises he named the United Order of Zion. He also oversaw the establishment in 1875 of Brigham Young Academy, later to become Brigham Young University. Young died in Salt Lake City on August 29, 1877.

Joseph Smith, Jr., was the charismatic prophet who gave birth to the Church of Jesus Christ of Latter-day Saints, but Brigham Young was the architect of the church's early life. He took control of the church after the violent end of its founder and guided it for more than three decades. He bears the credit for transplanting the Mormon Church to Utah, where it finally was able to obtain a measure of security from its opponents, and when this security was threatened during the Utah War, he guided the Mormons through the conflict without loss of life. He is second only to Joseph Smith, Jr., in importance to the history of the Mormon Church.

Further Reading

Arrington, Leonard J. *Brigham Young: American Moses.* New York: Knopf, 1985.

Bringhurst, Newell G. *Brigham Young and the Expanding American Frontier.* Edited by Oscar Handlin. Boston: Little, Brown, 1986.

Gibbons, Francis M. *Brigham Young, Modern Moses, Prophet of God.* Salt Lake City, Utah: Deseret, 1981.

Holzapfel, Richard Neitzel, and R. Q. Shupe. *Brigham Young: Images of a Mormon Prophet.* Salt Lake City, Utah: Religious Studies Center, Brigham Young University, 2000.

McCloud, Susan Evans. *Brigham Young: A Personal Portrait.* American Fork, Utah: Covenant Communications, 1996.

Stott, Clifford L. *Search for Sanctuary: Brigham Young and the White Mountain Expedition.* Salt Lake City: University of Utah Press, 1984.

Taves, Ernest H. *This Is the Place: Brigham Young and the New Zion.* Buffalo, N.Y.: Prometheus Books, 1991.

Walker, Ronald W. *Wayward Saints: The Godbeites and Brigham Young.* Urbana: University of Illinois Press, 1998.

Werner, Morris Robert. *Brigham Young.* New York: Harcourt, Brace, 1925; Westport, Conn.: Hyperion Press, 1975.

Z

Zeisberger, David

(1721–1808) *Moravian missionary*

A Moravian missionary to Native Americans during the 18th century, David Zeisberger devoted more than 60 years of his life to this work. Unlike some 17th- and 18th-century missionaries to the Indians, he endeavored to lead Native Americans to faith in Christ without uprooting their own cultural practices. He was born on April 11, 1721, in Zauchtenthal, Bohemia. His parents, David and Rosina Zeisberger, were members of a pietistic religious community called variously the Unitas Fractum or the Church of the Brotherhood, whose members were spiritual descendants of 15th-century reformer and martyr John Huss. Together with other members of the Unitas Fractum, Zeisberger's parents ultimately found a refuge on the estate of NIKOLAUS LUDWIG VON ZINZENDORF, a Lutheran pietist, in Saxony. There they established a village called Herrnhut, and in 1727, joined by Zinzendorf, they organized their religious community as the Church of the Brethren or the renewed Moravian Church.

Zeisberger's parents migrated to Georgia in 1736, and their son David followed them there the next year. A few years later the family moved to a Moravian community that had been established in Bethlehem, Pennsylvania. During Zinzendorf's 18-month stay in America, which began in 1741, he sought to encourage Moravian missions to the Native Americans, and, after his departure the following year, David Zeisberger determined to undertake this ministry. He began the study of the Iroquois language in a school operated by the Moravians in Bethlehem. In 1745, Zeisberger and another Moravian missionary made a venture into New York to visit a Mohawk tribe there. New York colonial authorities were hostile to the Moravians, however, and Zeisberger and his companion were ultimately arrested and spent almost two months in jail in New York City, suffering, as Zeisberger would later say, "for the Savior's sake," before being released and returning to Bethlehem.

This early experience did not deter Zeisberger from the course he had chosen. He spent much of the following years at a Moravian mission at the Native American village of Shamokin (now Sunbury, Pennsylvania) before traveling to Europe in 1750 to inform Count Zinzendorf of the progress of the Moravian missionary efforts. After his return to America the following year, Zeisberger devoted the next two decades to work among the Six Iroquois Nations. In the 1760s, he concentrated his efforts among the Delaware Indians in the Susquehanna valley and then, toward the end of that decade, migrated to the upper Ohio valley, where he continued to preach to the western Delawares. By 1772, he had established a mission at Schoenbrunn, where he built the first church west of the Ohio River.

The Revolutionary War disturbed the progress of Zeisberger's missionary activities. He found the time to marry Susan Lecron in the summer of 1781, and he continued his work in the Ohio country, even though the conflict between the colonies and

Great Britain had lured many Native Americans to ally themselves with the British. These alliances made Zeisberger's missionary efforts perilous. In fact, he was briefly captured by British forces in 1781. Although he was released and made his way back to Schoenbrunn in the spring of the following year, in his absence from the mission, American militiamen had massacred most of its Native American inhabitants on March 8, 1782. Zeisberger mourned when he heard about the awful event.

> This news sank deep into our hearts, so that these our brethren, who as martyrs, had all at once gone to the Saviour, were always day and night before our eyes and in our thoughts and we could not forget them, but this in some measure comforted us that they passed to the Saviour's arms and bosom in such resigned disposition of heart where they will forever rest, protected from the sins and all the wants of the world.

In the years that followed, Zeisberger chose to leave U.S. territory and live with Delaware (Lenni Lenape) Indians who had fled to British territory near Detroit. In 1792, he founded a mission in Ontario and named it Fairfield. Six years later, he returned to U.S. territory and established a mission near present-day New Philadelphia, Ohio. He died there on November 17, 1808.

Missionaries to Native Americans during the 17th and 18th centuries have sometimes been accused of making acculturation to Anglo-European values the price of admission to the kingdom of God. Zeisberger was, in the main, an exception to this pattern. For 20 years after the Schoenbrunn massacre, he accepted alienation from American society to remain with the Native American people whose spiritual care he had long tended.

Further Reading

Conrad, Maia Turner. "'Struck in Their Hearts': David Zeisberger's Moravian Mission to the Delaware Indians in Ohio, 1767–1808." Ph.D. dissertation, College of William and Mary, 1998.

De Schweinitz, Edmund Alexander. *The Life and Times of David Zeisberger, the Western Pioneer and Apostle of the Indians.* Philadelphia: J. B. Lippincott, 1870; New York, Johnson Reprint, 1971.

Olmstead, Earl P. *Blackcoats among the Delaware: David Zeisberger on the Ohio Froniter.* Kent, Ohio: Kent State University Press, 1991.

———. *David Zeisberger: A Life among the Indians.* Kent, Ohio: Kent State University Press, 1997.

Zeisberger, David. *Diary of David Zeisberger: A Moravian Missionary among the Indians of Ohio.* Translated and edited by Eugene F. Bliss. Cincinnati: R. Clarke for the Historical and Philosophical Society of Ohio, 1885; St. Clair Shores, Mich.: Scholarly Press, 1972.

———. *Schoenbrunn Story: Excerpts from the Diary of the Reverend David Zeisberger, 1772–1777, at Schoenbrunn in the Ohio Country.* Translated by August C. Mahr. Excerpted and introduced by Daniel R. Porter III. Columbus: Ohio Historical Society, 1972.

Zinzendorf, Nikolaus Ludwig von
(1700–1760) *Moravian missionary*

Born of noble Austrian lineage, Nikolaus Ludwig von Zinzendorf was an influential Lutheran pietist whose career briefly touched the New World with enduring consequences. He helped to unite a variety of German Protestant churches in North American and to carry out evangelistic missions to Native American tribes. He was born in Dresden, Saxony, on May 26, 1700, to George Ludwig, count von Zinzendorf, and Charlotte Justine von Gersdorf. His father died of tuberculosis when Zinzendorf was six weeks old, and after his mother's remarriage, he grew up in the castle of his maternal grandmother, the baroness von Gersdorf. There he formed a lifelong attachment to the principles and practices of pietism, a reform movement within German Lutheranism that emphasized personal spirituality and holiness rather than mere intellectual assent to creeds and participation in sacraments. As the heir of nobility, Zinzendorf received an education intended to fit him for statesmanship, first at the Paedagogium in Halle, where pietism flourished, and later at the University of Wittenberg, where he studied law from 1716 to 1719.

During his years at Wittenberg, Zinzendorf considered a ministerial career, but he was unwilling to oppose the wishes of his relatives, who viewed such a vocation as unfitting for a nobleman. When Zinzendorf was of age, however, he inherited assets that allowed him to purchase from his grandfather an estate, where he was able to pursue a different kind of religious calling. In 1722, he married Erdmuth Dorothea von Reuss, and their union produced 12 children, only 4 of whom survived childhood. That same year, religious refugees from Moravia obtained Zinzendorf's permission to settle on his estate, called Berthelsdorf. These religious believers belonged to a nearly extinct pietistic religious community called the Unitas Fractum, or the Church of the Brotherhood, descended from 15th-century followers of John Huss. On Zinzendorf's estate, they established a village called Herrnhut, with which Zinzendorf himself eventually became closely associated. In 1727, this religious community organized itself as the Church of the Brethren, or the renewed Moravian Church. Zinzendorf originally contemplated that the religious community established at Herrnhut would be a model for *ecclesiolae in ecclesia,* or "little churches within the church." But in succeeding years the Moravian Church formed an identity separate from the Lutheranism from which it had sprung.

Zinzendorf's involvement with the Moravians drew the displeasure of Saxon officials, and in 1736 he was exiled from Saxony. The following year, the Moravians bestowed the title of bishop on him and he traveled broadly as a representative of this religious community. He spent 18 months in North America, beginning in 1741; he centered his activities in Pennsylvania and attempted to unite the various German religious groups into synods. He also launched missionary efforts to various Native American tribes. He left the United States in 1742, after helping establish a significant Moravian community in Bethlehem, Pennsylvania.

Saxony relented its sentence of banishment of Zinzendorf in 1747 and allowed him to return to Hernhut, which he made a base of continued Moravian activities for the remainder of his life. Saxony officially recognized the Moravian Church in 1749, as did Parliament. Zinzendorf's wife Erd-

muth died in 1756, and he married Anna Nitschmann the following year. He died at Herrnhut on May 9, 1760.

A prolific hymn writer, Nikolaus Ludwig von Zinzendorf created lyrics that expressed the personal devotion to Christ that lay close to the heart of pietism. As a young man, he had experienced a particular closeness to Christ during a communion service, during which he later recalled, "I experienced an unusual stirring in my soul and promised my Saviour to be eternally true and to follow him." A few years later, he wrote a hymn describing the experience, whose first stanza declared:

> Happy, thrice happy hour of grace!
> I've seen, by faith, my Saviour's face:
> He did himself to me impart,
> And made a cov'nant with my heart.

In these lyrics, Zinzendorf reiterated the common pietistic concern with the believer's face-to-face encounter with Christ, a concern that he contributed to the history of American religious experience by his brief visit to North America and by the enduring influence of the Moravian Church.

Further Reading

Freeman, Arthur J. *An Ecumenical Theology of the Heart: The Theology of Court Nicholas Ludwig von Zinzendorf.* Bethlehem, Penn.: Moravian Church in America, 1998.

Lewis, Arthus J. *Zinzendorf, The Ecumenical Pioneer: A Study in the Moravian Contribution to Christian Mission and Unity.* Philadelphia: Westminster Press, 1962.

Stoudt, J. J. "Count Zinzendorf and the Pennsylvania Congregation of God and the Spirit." *Church History* 9 (1940): 366–438.

Weinlick, John R. *Count Zinzendorf: The Story of His Life and Leadership in the Renewed Moravian Church.* New York: Abington Press, 1956; Bethlehem, Pa.: The Moravian Church in America, 1984.

Zinzendorf, Nikolaus Ludwig von. *Nine Public Lectures on Important Subjects in Religion, Preached in Fetter Lane Chapel in London in the Year 1746.* Ed. and trans. by George W. Forell. Iowa City: University of Iowa Press, 1973.

Glossary

Advent Period during which Christians celebrate the birth of Jesus.

Adventists Christians whose central belief consists of anticipation of the imminent return of Christ.

agnosticism View that it is impossible to know the truth about the existence of God or other spiritual matters such as the immortality of the soul.

altar call Portion of some evangelical Protestant religious services when individuals are invited to go forward to the altar to profess or renew a faith in Christ.

Anabaptism Belief of some radical Protestant groups during the Reformation that baptism is not appropriate for infants and that adult believers who had been baptized as infants needed to be baptized again.

Anglicanism Beliefs and practices of the Church of England.

Antichrist Opponent of Christ during the end times.

anti-Semitism Hostility to Jews or Judaism.

apocalypse A revelation, typically of events concerning the end of times.

apologist A defender of a particular faith.

apostolic succession In the Christian tradition, the succession of ministers or spiritual authority from the original apostles of Jesus.

Arianism Theological beliefs considered heretical by orthodox Christians, originating with Arius, an Alexandrian priest of the fourth century A.D, who denied that Jesus was God but insisted that he had been created by God and was more than a human being.

Arminianism Named for Jacobus Arminius, a system of Christian belief that (in contrast with Calvinism) maintains that Christ died for everyone but that only those who believe in him will be saved; that individuals may resist grace; and that salvation, once received, may be lost.

asceticism Religious practices that deny physical pleasures or inflict pain or discomfort on the body.

atonement In Judaism and Christianity, the means by which sinful individuals are reconciled to God; in Jewish belief, atonement resulted originally from the use of sacrifices until the destruction of the temple in A.D. 70 ended the practice of sacrifice, and atonement was thereafter achieved through prayers, fasting, charity, and other religious observances; Christians locate atonement in the death of Jesus Christ on the cross but have proposed varying accounts of how Jesus' death secures human reconciliation with God.

Augsburg Confession Statement of faith adopted by Martin Luther and other Lutherans in 1530.

Azusa Street Revival Pentecostal revival experienced in 1906 in Los Angeles, California, led by the African-American preacher William Joseph Seymour.

baptism Mainly Christian rite of immersion or sprinkling with water as a sign of salvation or entrance into the community of faith.

Baptists Christian denomination of those who insist that the rite of baptism is appropriate for those to have professed faith in Christ and is therefore inappropriate for infants.

bar mitzvah/bat mitzvah The coming-of-age Jewish ceremony for boys—and, in Progressive Judaism, for girls—who are 13 years old.

biblical criticism The application of the methods of literary criticism to the Bible, including investigations into the origin and development of biblical texts.

Calvinism Theological movement within Protestant Christianity distinguished by its emphasis on the sovereignty of God and his election of those who will be saved.

canonization Process in the Catholic Church by which an individual, after death, is declared to be a saint.

canon law Body of rules and laws in the Catholic Church.

cardinal Ecclesiastical office in the Catholic Church inferior only to that of the pope.

catechism Statement of Christian doctrine in question-and-answer form.

cathedral A church that serves as the station of a bishop or as the central church of a diocese.

Catholic Church Understood by some Christians as the universal church, by others as the Roman Catholic Church in particular.

celibacy Abstention from sexual relations.

charismatic movement Christian renewal movement that began in the 20th century; emphasizes the contemporary presence of the Holy Spirit and the availability of "gifts of the Spirit" such as glossolalia, or speaking in tongues.

Christology Christian doctrine relating to the nature and significance of Christ.

Congregationalism Protestant religious tradition that emphasizes the importance and independence of local congregations.

cosmology A view or account of the nature of the universe, including its origin.

covenant In Jewish Scriptures, an agreement between God and the nation of Israel; used by Christians to refer to both the "new Covenant" ratified by the death of Christ and, in some traditions, agreements made by believers, as in establishment of a church.

Darwinism View propounded originally by Charles Darwin that various species evolved into their present forms over long periods.

deacon Ecclesiastical officer whose function is to assist a priest or minister.

deism Belief that the world was created by a deity who did not thereafter intervene in natural or human affairs.

dispensationalism Form of biblical interpretation associated with John Nelson Darby (1800–1882) and popularized through the Scofield Reference Bible that posits the existence of different periods of human history (or dispensations) in which God deals with the human race in distinct ways.

Dutch Reformed Church Reformed or Calvinistic movement within Protestant Christianity, originating in the Netherlands but transplanted to Europe, the American colonies, and South Africa.

ecclesiology Theological doctrines relating to the nature of the church.

ecumenism A movement within Christianity seeking to restore unity or cooperation among different Christian traditions and denominations.

encyclical Official letter from the pope, typically setting forth some doctrine or exhortation.

eschatology Theological doctrines relating to the end times.

Eucharist A central rite in Christian churches, based on Jesus' last supper with his disciples in which bread and wine represent his body and his blood; also referred to variously as communion, mass, and the Lord's Supper.

evangelicals Christians who emphasize a personal conversion experience.

fundamentalism Conservative Christian movement begun in the early 20th century that seeks to defend certain "fundamentals" of orthodox Christian faith such as belief in the virgin birth and the resurrection of Christ; by the end of the century used to refer generally to conservative Christians, especially those who believe in the inerrancy of the Bible.

Ghost Dance Native American religious movements that emphasize the imminent return of the dead to join the living in a new world.

glossolalia The experience recognized among Pentecostal and charismatic Christians of speaking in tongues—that is, in an unknown language.

Great Awakening Revival movement that flourished in the North American colonies during the 1740s.

Half-Way Covenant Doctrinal statement adopted by many Congregationalist churches in the 17th century that determined that the children of parents who had been baptized but had given no evidence of a conversion experience could be baptized but could not partake of the Lord's Supper without experiencing conversion.

Hanukkah Annual Jewish celebration in December that commemorates the rededication of the temple of Jerusalem after the defeat of the Syrians at the hands of Judas Maccabeus in 165 B.C.

Hasidism The practices and beliefs of ultraconservative Orthodox Jews

Higher Life movement Late-19th-century interdenominational movement that stressed the possibility of and necessity for sanctification in the present life.

Holiness groups Name given to churches and denominations that sprang from Methodism and emphasized the possibility of "entire sanctification" in the present life.

Holocaust The systematic attempt by Nazi Germany to destroy Jews during World War II.

Holy Spirit In orthodox Christian theology, the third person of the Trinity, along with God the Father and God the Son.

incarnation In Christian theology, the union of divinity and humanity in Jesus Christ, in whom, according to the Gospel of John, the "Word became flesh and dwelt among us."

jeremiad A type of sermon that calls attention to misfortune and calamity as a sign of God's displeasure with spiritual laxity.

kehillah Jewish community.

liturgical movement Movement that began in the 19th century to increase the involvement of laity in the liturgy.

liturgy The formal, corporate worship of God.

mass The sacrament of the Eucharist in the Roman Catholic Church, also known as communion or the Lord's Supper in other Christian traditions.

mesmerism The inducing of trance states, often as a means of healing or acquiring spiritual powers.

millenarianism Belief among some Christians in a thousand-year reign of the saints, immediately before or after the return of Christ to the world; also, more generally, religious beliefs that anticipate a sudden and radical transformation of the world.

missionary One who seeks to transmit religious beliefs to nonadherents.

monasticism Forms of religious life, especially common in Christianity and Buddhism, that emphasize the role of an ascetic life in spiritual progress, lived either alone or in a religious community.

monotheism Belief that there is only one God.

Moravian Brethren Evangelical Protestant group established in 1457 in Bohemia and later transplanted to Saxony and America; also known originally as Unitas Fratrum; characterized by strong missionary activity.

Mormons Members of the Church of Jesus Christ of Latter-day Saints (LDS) founded by Joseph Smith, Jr.

mosque Islamic house of worship and religious education.

Muslim An Islamic believer.

National Council of Churches Ecumenical association of Protestant, Eastern Orthodox, and National Catholic churches organized in the United States in 1950.

Native American Church Native American religious body with roots in the peyote religion of late 19th century; formally organized in 1918; characterized by sacramental use of peyote.

neoorthodoxy Reemphasis of Reformation doctrines of grace and faith in reaction to early-20th-century theological liberalism; prominent representatives include Karl Barth in Germany and Reinhold and H. Richard Niebuhr in the United States.

New Church Also known as the Church of the New Jerusalem or the Swedenborgian Church, named for its founder, Emanuel Swedenborg.

New Thought Name given to a family of spiritual movements that emphasize the presence of God (or the universal mind) in all individuals and posit the availability of "God-consciousness" to remedy the practical problems of life.

Nicene Creed Statement of Christian beliefs adopted by the Council of Nicaea (A.D. 325).

occult Named for a word meaning "hidden" and used to describe collection of religious beliefs and practices, such as magic and spiritualism, that have a religious dimension but are not associated formally with any religious group.

original sin Christian doctrine that maintains that as a result of humankind's initial disobedience to God, described in Genesis 3 and referred to as "the Fall," every subsequent individual has inherited a sinful nature.

Orthodox Judaism The branch of contemporary Judaism that insists on the authority of the Torah and remains most respectful of traditional Jewish beliefs and practices.

Oxford movement Reform movement within the Church of England during the 1830s and 1840s that stressed the importance of ritual and liturgy, as against theological liberalism within the church.

papal infallibility Doctrine of the Roman Catholic Church that declarations made by the pope in his official capacity ("ex cathedra") are guaranteed assistance by the Holy Spirit and are thus free of error.

Pentateuch The five books of Moses in the Hebrew Bible or the Old Testament.

Pentecostalism Christian movement dating from the early 20th century that emphasizes the power and presence of the Holy Spirit, thought to be manifested in part through spiritual gifts such as speaking in tongues (glossolalia) and healing.

People's Temple Religious movement established by Jim Jones, made famous by the mass suicide of its members in Guyana in November 1978.

pietism Movement within Protestant Christianity that emphasized good works and personal holiness as opposed to an emphasis on correct doctrine.

predestination Doctrine characteristic of Reformed Protestantism and certain other Christian groups that maintains that an individual's salvation or damnation is preordained by God.

Presbyterianism Form of church government associated with the Reformed churches, which consists of a hierarchy of local congregations, regional councils consisting of ministers and lay elders and referred to a presbyteries, and national councils referred to as General Assemblies.

Protestantism Religious traditions flowing from the Reformation in the 16th century, when Martin Luther, John Calvin, and others separated from the Roman Catholic church in protest of its doctrines and practices.

Puritans Name given to English Protestants who, in the late 16th and early 17th centuries, believed that the Church of England had not been sufficiently purified of vestiges of Catholicism.

Quakers Common name given to members of the Society of Friends, established by George Fox in the last half of the 17th century, who emphasized the importance of the Inner Light rather than established doctrines or forms of ecclesiastical discipline.

Qur'an (Koran) Sacred scripture of Islam, written by Muhammad in the seventh century A.D.

rabbi Title given to Jewish teachers and leaders after the fall of Jerusalem in A.D. 70.

rebbe The title given by Hasidic Jews to their spiritual leader.

Reconstructionist Judaism Twentieth-century movement within Judaism, established by Mordecai Kaplan, which seeks to revitalize Jewish culture, including Jewish religion, in accordance with contemporary needs.

rector In Anglican churches, a parish priest, or, in Roman Catholics churches, the priest in charge of a school or house.

Reformation The movement from which Protestantism sprang, in which Martin Luther, John Calvin, and others criticized the doctrines and practices of the Roman Catholic Church and eventually formed separate religious communities.

Reform Judaism Movement within Judaism that began in the 19th century and that sought to reinterpret Jewish theology and practice in ways that diminished the authority of the Torah and, at least initially, abandoned nationalistic aspirations.

reformed theology or churches Designation given to Christian theological views and churches that are Calvinistic in the sense of emphasizing God's sovereignty and the election of those who will be saved.

repentance In Christian theology, especially, a sincere regret for past actions and a turning toward God.

revivalism A focus on sudden, intense spiritual renewals such as characterized the Great Awakening in the 18th century.

Rosicrucianism Occult movement whose modern origins date from the early 17th century but traces its parentage to Christian Rosenkreutz (1378–1484), who allegedly founded the Order of the Rosy Cross and who claimed to possess occult knowledge.

sabbath The seventh day of the week, beginning traditionally before nightfall on Friday and lasting until Saturday evening, consecrated as a day of worship and rest; sometimes used to refer generally to the day of worship in most Christian communities (Sunday) or other religious traditions.

sacrament In Christian theology and practice, a rite or ceremony that recognizes or signifies inward grace; in Protestant churches sacraments include baptism and the Eucharist; the Roman Catholic and Orthodox Churches recognize seven sacraments.

saint Term used in the New Testament and in Protestant churches to refer to believers generally; in the Roman Catholic and Orthodox Churches, to an individual recognized as having a superior measure of holiness.

Salvation Army Religious organization founded by William Booth in 1865, devoted to evangelism and social service for the poor.

Satanism Religious movements, frequently associated with occult practices such as magic, that worship or glorify Satan or other antireligious symbols.

Scientology Twentieth-century religious movement founded by L. Ron Hubbard that seeks to free individuals of captivity to memories and experiences that deprive them of spiritual potential.

scriptures The sacred writings of a religious tradition.

Second Great Awakening Revival movement that flourished during the 1780s and 1790s.

see The area under the control of a bishop or an archbishop.

Sephardic Judaism Jews and Jewish practices descended from Jews expelled from Spain and Portugal in the 1490s.

Seventh-Day Adventist Millenarian Christian group with origins in the teachings of William Miller, who predicted that Christ would return to earth in the 1840s.

Shakers Popular name given to United Society of Believers in Christ's Second Appearing, founded in England and later transplanted to the United States, whose members believe that their leader, Ann Lee, was the incarnation of Christ.

Social Gospel Social reform movement that flourished among liberal Protestants at the end of the 19th and beginning of the 20th centuries, most prominently associated with the theologian Walter Rauschenbusch.

soteriology Doctrines concerning salvation.

spiritualism Religious beliefs holding that the spirits of individuals live on after death and may be communicated with through mediums.

Stoddardism Named for the Puritan preacher Solomon Stoddard, church practices during the late 17th and early 18th centuries that allowed membership and participation in communion without evidence of experience of conversion.

Swedenborgianism Views associated with the thought of the Swedish philosopher and mystic Emanuel Swedenborg (1688–1772), which included the idea that existence consists of the key principles of love and wisdom.

synagogue A Jewish meeting place for worship and religious education.

syncretism The merger of aspects of separate religious traditions.

Synod of Dort Conference of Calvinist ministers in 1618–19 that adopted the "Five Points of Calvinism," which emphasized that God had predestined those who would be saved, that Christ died only for them, and that grace could neither be resisted nor, once obtained, lost.

Talmud The authoritative collection of rabbinic traditions relating to Jewish life and law.

theism Belief in a transcendent, personal God.

theology The study (literally "science") of God.

Theosophy Religious movement founded by Helena Petrovna Blavatsky and Henry Steel Olcott that combined elements of Western occultism with Eastern religious thought.

Torah The Hebrew Scriptures generally, or, the Pentateuch—the five books of Moses.

Transcendentalism Philosophical movement associated most closely with Ralph Waldo Emerson that emphasized the role of intuition rather than sensory perception in discovery of truth, including religious truth.

Trinitarianism The orthodox Christian belief that God exists in three persons: the Father, the Son, and the Holy Spirit.

Unification Church Religious movement founded by the Korean-born Sun Myung Moon.

universalism The belief that all men and women will eventually receive salvation and eternal life.

Unitarianism Religious movement that rejected orthodox Christianity's Trinitarian concept of God.

Vatican Councils Two councils of the Roman Catholic church: the first met in 1869–70, and the second in 1962–65.

vicar Title given to priests in certain Christian denominations.

virgin birth The Christian belief that Jesus Christ had no earthly father but was conceived by Mary through the Holy Spirit.

Westminster Confession The confession of faith adopted by English Presbyterians in the 1640s and thereafter influential among churches in the Reformed tradition, including those in America.

World Council of Churches International ecumenical organization founded in 1948 and represented by mainstream Christian denominations.

yeshiva Jewish religious school.

Zionism Movement to restore Eretz Israel (the land of Israel) to the Jewish people.

BIBLIOGRAPHY AND RECOMMENDED SOURCES

Aberle, David. *The Peyote Religion Among the Navaho*. Chicago: Aldine, 1966.

Ahlstrom, Sydney E. *A Religious History of the American People*. New Haven, Conn.: Yale University Press, 1972.

Albanese, Catherine L. *America Religion and Religions*. 2d ed. Belmont, Calif.: Wadsworth, 1992.

———. *Nature Religion in America: From the Algonquin Indians to the New Age*. Chicago: University of Chicago Press, 1990.

Alexander, Hartley Burr. *The World's Rim: Great Mysteries of the North American Indians*. Lincoln: University of Nebraska Press, 1953.

Ammerman, Nancy Tatom. *Baptist Battles: Social Change and Religious Conflict in the Southern Baptist Convention*. New Brunswick, N.J.: Rutgers University Press, 1990.

Anderson, Edward. *Peyote: The Divine Cactus*. Tucson: University of Arizona Press, 1980.

Anderson, Victor. *Pragmatic Theology: Negotiating the Intersections of an American Philosophy of Religion and Public Theology*. Albany: State University of New York Press, 1998.

Antler, Joyce. *The Journey Home: Jewish Women and the American Century*. New York: Free Press, 1997.

Baker, Frank. *From Wesley to Asbury: Studies in Early American Methodism*. Durham, N.C.: Duke University Press, 1976.

Baum, Charlotte, Paula Hyman, and Sonya Michel. *The Jewish Woman in America*. New York: Dial Press, 1976.

Bellah, Robert N., and Fredrick E. Greenspahn. *Uncivil Religion: Interreligious Hostility in America*. New York: Crossroads, 1987.

Bengston, Gloria E. *Lutheran Women in Ordained Ministry, 1970–1995: Reflections and Perspectives*. Minneapolis, Minn.: Augsburg, 1995.

Beversluis, Joel D., ed. *A Sourcebook for the Community of Religions*. Chicago: Council for a Parliament of the World's Religions, 1993.

Bierhorst, John. *The Sacred Path: Spells, Prayers, and Power Songs of the American Indians*. New York: William Morrow, 1983.

Billington, Ray Allen. *The Protestant Crusade, 1800–1860: A Study of the Origins of American Nativism*. New York: Macmillan 1938.

Bonomi, Patricia U. *Under the Cape of Heaven: Religion, Society, and Politics in Colonial America*. New York: Oxford University Press, 1986.

Bowden, Henry Warner. *Native Americans and Christian Missions: Studies in Cultural Conflict*. Chicago: University of Chicago Press, 1981.

Braden, Charles Samuel. *These Also Believe: A Study of Modern American Cults and Minority Religious Movements*. New York: Macmillan, 1949.

Braude, Ann. *Radical Spirits: Spiritualism and Women's Rights in Nineteenth-Century America*. 2d ed. Bloomington: Indiana University Press, 2001.

Broches, Samuel. *Jews in New England*. 2 vols. New York: Bloch, 1942.

Butler, Jon. *Awash in a Sea of Faith: Christianizing the American People*. Cambridge, Mass.: Harvard University Press, 1990.

Carmody, Denise L. *The Republic of Many Mansions: Foundations of American Religion*. New York: Paragon House, 1990.

Carmody, Denise L., and John T. Carmody, *Exploring American Religion.* Mountain View, Calif.: Mayfield, 1990.

Choquette, Diane. *New Religious Movements in the United States and Canada: A Critical Assessment and Annotated Bibliography.* Westport, Conn.: Greenwood Press, 1985.

Cimino, Richard, and Don Lattin, *Shopping for Faith: American Religion in the New Millennium.* San Francisco: Jossey-Bass, 1998.

Contemporary American Religion. Edited by Wade Clark Roof. 2 vols. New York: Macmillan Reference USA, 2000.

Conway, Jill K., Linda Kealey, and Janet E. Schulte. *The Female Experience in Eighteenth- and Nineteenth-century America: a Guide to the History of American Women.* New York: Garland, 1982.

Cox, Harvey. *Fire From Heaven: The Rise of Pentecostal Spirituality and the Reshaping of Religion in the Twenty-first Century.* Reading, Mass.: Addison-Wesley, 1995.

Cross, F. L., ed. *The Oxford Dictionary of the Christian Church.* 2d rev. ed. London: Oxford University Press, 1984.

Dinnerstein, Leonard. *Anti-Semitism in America.* Oxford: Oxford University Press, 1994.

Dolan, Jay P. *The American Catholic Experience: A History from Colonial Times to the Present.* Garden City, N.Y.: Doubleday, 1985.

Donin, Hayim Halevy. *To Be a Jew: A Guide to Jewish Observance in Contemporary Life.* New York: HarperCollins, 1972.

Dooling, D.M., and Paul Jordan-Smith. *I Become Part of It: Sacred Dimensions in Native American Life.* New York: Parabola Books, 1989.

Eck, Diana L. *Encountering God: A Spiritual Journey from Bozeman to Bonaras.* Boston: Beacon Press, 1993.

Eerdmans' Handbook to Christianity in America. Grand Rapids, Mich.: Eerdmans, 1983.

Eliade, Mircea, Victor Turner, et al., eds. *The Encyclopedia of Religion.* New York: Macmillan, 1987.

Ellis, J. T., ed. *Documents of American Catholic History.* Milwaukee: Bruce, 1956.

Ellwood, Robert S., Jr. *Alternative Altars.* Chicago: University of Chicago Press, 1979.

Encyclopedia of Religion in the South. Edited by Samuel S. Hill. Macon, Ga.: Mercer, 1984.

Erdoes, Richard, and Alfonso Ortiz, eds. *American Indian Myths and Legends.* Westminster, Md.: Pantheon Books, 1984.

Fauset, Arthur. *Black Gods of the Metropolis.* New York: University of Pennsylvania Press, 1970.

Fein, Leonard. *Where Are We? The Inner Life of America's Jews.* New York: Harper & Row, 1988.

Feingold, Henry L., gen. ed. *The Jewish People in America.* 5 vols. Baltimore: Johns Hopkins University Press, 1992.

Finkelstein, Louis. *American Spiritual Autobiographies: Fifteen Self-Portraits.* New York: Harper, 1948.

Floyd, Samuel A., Jr. *The Power of Black Music.* Oxford: Oxford University Press, 1995.

Forcinelli, Joseph. *The Democratization of Religion in America: A Commonwealth of Religious Freedom by Design.* Lewiston, N.Y.: Edwin Mellen Press, 1990.

Fu, Charles W., ed. *Religious Issues and Interreligious Dialogues: An Analysis and Sourcebook of Developments Since 1945.* New York: Greenwood Press, 1989.

Gallagher, Edward J. *Early Puritan Writers, a Reference Guide: William Bradford, John Cotton, Thomas Hooker, Edward Johnson, Richard Mather, Thomas Shepard.* Boston: G.K. Hall, 1976.

Garrett, Leroy. *The Stone-Campbell Movement: An Anecdotal History of Three Churches.* Joplin, Mo.: College Press, 1981.

Gaustad, Edwin S. *A Documentary History of Religion in America.* 2 vols. Grand Rapids, Mich.: Eerdmans, 1982.

———. *A Religious History of America.* 2d ed. San Francisco: Harper & Row, 1990.

Glazer, Nathan. *American Judaism.* 2d ed. Chicago: University of Chicago Press, 1972.

Gordon, Milton. *Assimilation in American Life: The Role of Race, Religion, and National Origins.* New York: Oxford University Press, 1964.

Gort, Jerald D., et al., eds. *On Sharing Religious Experience: Possibilities of Interfaith Mutuality.* Grand Rapids, Mich.: Eerdmans, 1992.

Guillermo, Artemio R. *Churches Aflame: Asian Americans and United Methodism.* Nashville: Abingdon Press, 1991.

Hackett, David G. *Religion and American Culture, A Reader.* New York: Routledge, 1995.

Haddad, Yvonne Yazbeck, ed. *The Muslims of America.* New York: Oxford University Press, 1993.

Halvorson, Peter L., and William M. Newman. *Atlas of Religious Change in America, 1952–1990.* Atlanta: Glenmary Research Center, 1994.

Handy, Robert. *A Christian America: Protestant Hopes and Historical Realities.* 2d ed. New York: New York University Press, 1984.

Herberg, Will. *Protestant—Catholic—Jew: An Essay in American Religious Sociology.* Rev. ed. Garden City, N.Y.: Anchor Books, 1960.

Hertzberg, Arthur. *The Jews in America, Four Centuries of an Uneasy Encounter: A History.* New York: Simon & Schuster, 1989.

Hewitt, Glenn Alden. *Regeneration and Morality: A Study of Charles Finney, Charles Hodge, John W. Nevin, and Horace Bushnell.* Brooklyn, N.Y.: Carlson, 1991.

Hill, Samuel S. *Encyclopedia of Religion in the South.* Macon, Ga.: Mercer, 1984.

Hillman, Eugene. *Many Paths: A Catholic Approach to Religious Pluralism.* New York: Orbis Books, 1989.

Hoffecker, W. Andrew. *Piety and the Princeton Theologians: Archibald Alexander, Charles Hodge, and Benjamin Warfield.* Grand Rapids, Mich.: Baker Book House, 1981.

Holmes, David L. *A Brief History of the Episcopal Church.* Valley Forge, Pa.: Trinity Press International, 1993.

Hudson, Winthrop S., and John Corrigan. *Religion in America.* 5th ed. New York: Prentice-Hall, 1992.

Hultkrantz, Ake. *Native Religions of North America.* San Francisco: Harper & Row, 1987.

Hutchison, William R., ed. *Between the Times: The Travail of the Protestant Establishment in America 1900–1960.* Cambridge, England: Cambridge University Press, 1989.

———. *The Modernist Impulse in American Protestantism.* Cambridge, Mass.: Harvard University Press, 1976.

Jewish Women in America: An Historical Encyclopedia. Edited by Paula E. Hyman and Deborah Dash Moore. 2 vols. New York: Routledge, 1997.

Johnson, Jeff G. *Black Christians: The Untold Lutheran Story.* St. Louis: Concordia, 1991.

Jones, Charles Edwin. *Black Holiness.* Metuchen, N.J.: Scarecrow Press, 1987.

Joselit, Jenna Weissman. *The Wonders of America: Reinventing Jewish Culture 1880–1950.* New York: Hill & Wang, 1994.

Knitter, Paul. *No Other Name? A Critical Survey of Christian Attitudes Toward the World Religions.* Maryknoll, N.Y.: Orbis Books, 1985.

Kosmin, Barry A., and Seymour P. Lachman. *One Nation Under God: Religion in Contemporary American Society.* New York: Harmony Books, 1993.

Koszegi, Michael A., and J. Gordon Melton. *Islam in North America: A Sourcebook.* New York: Garland, 1992.

Krieger, David J. *The New Universalism: Foundations for a Global Theology.* Maryknoll, N.Y.: Orbis Books, 1991.

Laderman, Gary, ed. *Religions of Atlanta: Religious Diversity in the Centennial Olympic City.* Atlanta: Scholars Press, 1996.

Lebeson, Anita Libman. *Recall to Life: The Jewish Woman in America.* South Brunswick, N.J.: Yoseloff, 1970.

Leone, Mark P. *Roots of Modern Mormonism.* Cambridge, Mass.: Harvard University Press, 1979.

Lincoln, C. Eric, ed. *The Black Experience in Religion.* Garden City, N.Y.: Anchor Press, 1974.

Lincoln, C. Eric, and Lawrence H. Mamiya. *The Black Church in the African-American Experience.* Durham, N.C.: Duke University Press, 1990.

Lindley, Susan Hill. *"You Have Stept Out of Your Place": A History of Women and Religion in America.* Louisville, Ky.: Westminster John Knox, 1996.

Lippy, Charles H., and Peter W. Williams, eds. *Encyclopedia of the American Religious Experience.* 3 vols. New York: Charles Scribner's Sons, 1988.

Lochhead, David. *The Dialogical Imperative: A Christian Reflection on Interfaith Encounter.* Maryknoll, N.Y.: Orbis Books, 1988.

Lossky, Nicholas, et al., eds. *Dictionary of the Ecumenical Movement.* Geneva: World Council of Churches, 1991.

Lubarsky, Sandra B. *Tolerance and Transformation: Jewish Approaches to Religious Pluralism.* West Orange, N.J.: Cincinnati Hebrew Union College Press, 1990.

Ludlow, Daniel H., ed. *Encyclopedia of Mormonism.* 5 vols. New York: Macmillan, 1992.

Mallon, Elias D. *Neighbors: Muslims in North America.* New York: Friendship Press, 1989.

Marcus, Jacob R. *The American Jewish Woman: A Documentary History.* New York: Ktav; Cincinnati: American Jewish Archives, 1981.

———. *Early American Jewry.* 2 vols. Philadelphia: Jewish Publication Society of America, 1951.

Marsden, George M. *Religion and American Culture.* San Diego: Harcourt, Brace, Jovanovich, 1990.

Martin, William. *With God on Our Side: The Rise of the Religious Right in America.* New York: Broadway Books, 1996.

Marty, Martin. *Modern American Religion.* 3 vols. Chicago: University of Chicago Press, 1970–96.

———. *Pilgrims in Their Own Land: Five Hundred Years of Religion in America.* New York: Viking Penguin, 1985.

Marty, Martin E., and R. Scott Appleby. *The Glory and the Power: The Fundamentalist Challenge to the Modern World.* Boston: Beacon Press, 1992.

Mathews, Donald G. *Religion in the Old South.* Chicago: University of Chicago Press, 1977.

Matlins, Stuart M. *How to Be a Perfect Stranger: A Guide to Etiquette in Other People's Religious Ceremonies.* 2 vols. Woodstock, Vt.: Jewish Lights Publishing, 1997.

Matsuoka, Fumitaka. *Out of Silence: Emerging Themes in Asian American Churches.* Cleveland: United Church Press, 1995.

Mbiti, John. *African Religions and Philosophy.* Portsmouth, N. H.: Heinemann, 1990.

McCloud, Aminah Beverly. *African American Islam.* New York: Routledge, 1995.

McLoughlin, William Gerald. *Modern Revivalism: Charles Grandison Finney to Billy Graham.* New York: Ronald Press, 1959.

Melton, J. Gordon. *Religious Bodies in the United States, a Directory.* New York: Garland, 1992.

Moen, Matthew J. *The Transformation of the Christian Right.* Tuscaloosa: University of Alabama Press, 1992.

Moore, R. Laurence. *Religious Outsiders and the Making of Americans.* New York: Oxford University Press, 1986.

Morris, Charles R. *American Catholic: The Saints and Sinners Who Built America's Most Powerful Church.* New York: Times Books, 1997.

Muck, Terry. *Those Other Religions in Your Neighborhood: Loving Your Neighbor When You Don't Know How.* Grand Rapids, Mich.: Zondervan, 1992.

Murphy, Larry G., J. Gordon Melton, and Gary L. Ward, eds. *Encyclopedia of African American Religions.* New York: Garland, 1993.

Noley, Homer. *First White Frost: Native Americans and United Methodism.* Nashville: Abingdon Press, 1991.

Noll, Mark A. *A History of Christianity in the United States and Canada.* Grand Rapids, Mich.: Eerdmans, 1992.

———. ed. *The Princeton Theology, 1812–1921: Scripture, Science, Theological Method from Archibald Alexander to Benjamin Breckinridge Warfield.* Grand Rapids, Mich.: Baker Book House, 1983.

———. ed. *Religion and American Politics: From the Colonial Period to the 1980s.* New York: Oxford University Press, 1990.

O'Neil, Maura. *Women Speaking, Women Listening: Women in Interreligious Dialogue.* Maryknoll, N.Y.: Orbis Books, 1990.

Oren, Dan A. *Joining the Club: A History of Jews and Yale.* New Haven, Conn.: Yale University Press, 1985.

Orsi, Robert Anthony. *The Madonna of 115th Street: Faith and Community in Italian Harlem, 1880–1950.* New York: Yale University Press, 1985.

Peden, Creighton. *The Chicago School: Voices in Liberal Religious Thought.* Bristol, Ind.: Wyndham Hall Press, 1987.

Perry, Michael J. *Love and Power: The Role of Morality and Religion in American Politics.* New York: Oxford University Press, 1991.

Powers, William K. *Oglala Religion.* Lincoln: University of Nebraska Press, 1975.

Queen, Edward L., Stephen R. Prothero, and Gardiner H. Shattuck, Jr. *The Encyclopedia of American Religious History.* 2 vols. New York: Facts On File, 1996.

Raboteau, Albert J. *Slave Religion: "The Invisible Institution" in the Antebellum South.* New York: Oxford University Press, 1978.

Race, Alan. *Christians and Religious Pluralism.* Maryknoll, N.Y.: Orbis Books, 1982.

Reagon, Bernice Johnson, ed. *We'll Understand It Better, By and By.* Washington, D.C.: Smithsonian Institution Press; New York: Harper & Row, 1988.

Reid, Daniel G., ed. *Dictionary of Christianity in America.* Downers Grove, Ill.: InterVarsity, 1990.

Richardson, E. Allen. *East Comes West.* New York: Pilgrim Press, 1985.

———. *Strangers in This Land: Pluralism and the Response to Diversity in the United States.* New York: Pilgrim Press, 1988.

Roeber, A. G. *Palatines, Liberty, and Property: German Lutherans in Colonial British America.* Baltimore: Johns Hopkins University Press, 1993.

Sarna, Jonathan D., ed. *The Jews of Boston.* Boston: American Jewish Historical Society, 1996.

Schultz, Jeffrey D., John G. West, and Iain S. MacLean. *Encyclopedia of Religion in American Politics.* Phoenix, Ariz.: Oryx Press, 1999.

Seltzer, Robert M., and Norman J. Cohen, eds. *The Americanization of the Jews.* New York: New York University Press, 1995.

Sernett, Milton C. *Afro-American Religious History: A Documentary Witness.* Durham, N.C.: Duke University Press, 1985.

Shipps, Jan. *Mormonism: The Story of a New Religious Tradition.* Urbana: University of Illinois Press, 1984.

Shulman, Albert M. *The Religious Heritage of America.* San Diego: A.S. Barnes, 1981.

Silberman, Charles E. *A Certain People: American Jews and Their Lives Today.* New York: Summit, 1985.

Skerrett, Ellen, Edward B. Kantowicz, and Steven V. Avella. *Catholicism Chicago Style.* Chicago: Loyola University Press, 1993.

Smith, W. C. *Religious Diversity.* New York: Crossroads, 1981.

Spalding, Thomas W. *The Premier See. A History of the Archdiocese of Baltimore, 1789–1989.* Baltimore: Johns Hopkins University Press, 1989.

Sullivan, Lawrence E., ed.. *Native American Religions: North America.* New York: Macmillan, 1989.

Sweet, W. W. *Makers of Christianity: From John Cotton to Lyman Abbott.* New York: Macmillan, 1921.

Thiemann, Ronald F. *Religion in Public Life: A Dilemma for Democracy.* Washington, D.C.: Georgetown University Press, 1996.

Thompson, Ernest Trice. *Presbyterians in the South.* 3 vols. Richmond, Va.: John Knox Press, 1963–73.

Thompson, Norma H., ed. *Religious Pluralism and Religious Education.* Birmingham, Ala.: Religious Education Press, 1988.

Twentieth-Century Shapers of American Popular Religion. Edited by Charles H. Lippy. New York: Greenwood Press, 1989.

Underhill, Ruth M. *Red Man's Religion.* Chicago: University of Chicago Press, 1965.

Vecsey, Christopher. *Imagine Ourselves Richly: Mythic Narratives of North American Indians.* New York: HarperCollins, 1991.

———, ed. *Religion in Native North America.* Moscow: University of Idaho Press, 1990.

Villafane, Eldin. *The Liberating Spirit: Toward an Hispanic American Pentecostal Social Ethic.* Grand Rapids, Mich.: Eerdmans, 1993.

Wacker, Grant. *Heaven Below: Early Pentecostals and American Culture.* Cambridge, Mass.: Harvard University Press, 2001.

Wagenknecht, Edward. *Daughters of the Covenant: Portraits of Six Jewish Women.* Amherst: University of Massachusetts Press, 1983.

Wald, Kenneth D. *Religion and Politics in the United States.* 3d ed. Washington, D.C.: CQ Press, 1997.

Walker, Wyatt Tee. *Somebody's Calling My Name: Black Sacred Music and Social Change.* Valley Forge, Pa.: Judson Press, 1979.

Wall, Steve. *Shadowcatchers: A Journey in Search of the Teachings of Native American Healers.* New York: HarperCollins, 1994.

Washington, James Melvin. *Conversations with God: Two Centuries of Prayers by African Americans.* New York: HarperCollins, 1994.

Weber, Paul J., and W. Landis, Jones. *U.S. Religious Interest Groups: Institutional Profiles.* Westport, Conn.: Greenwood Press, 1994.

Weinberg, Sydney Stahl. *The World of Our Mothers: The Lives of Jewish Immigrant Women.* Chapel Hill: University of North Carolina Press, 1988.

Wentz, Richard E. *The Culture of Religious Pluralism.* Boulder, Colo.: Westview Press, 1998.

————. *Religion in the New World: The Shaping of Religious Traditions in the United States.* Minneapolis: Fortress Press, 1990.

Werblowsky, R.J. Zwi, and Geoffrey Wigoder, eds. *The Encyclopedia of the Jewish Religion.* New York: Holt, Rinehart & Winston, 1966.

Wilcox, Clyde. *God's Warriors: The Christian Right in the Twentieth Century.* Baltimore: Johns Hopkins University Press, 1991.

Williams, Peter W. *America's Religions: Traditions and Cultures.* New York: MacMillan Press, 1990.

————. *Popular Religion in America: Symbolic Change and the Modernization Process in Historical Perspective.* Englewood Cliffs, N.J.: Prentice-Hall, 1980.

Williams, Raymond Brady. *Religions of Immigrants from India and Pakistan: New Threads in the American Tapestry.* Cambridge: Cambridge University Press, 1988.

Williamson, William B., ed. *An Encyclopedia of Religions in the United States: One Hundred Religious Groups Speak for Themselves.* New York: Crossroads, 1992.

Wilmore, Gayraud S. *Black Religion and Black Radicalism: An Interpretation of the Religious History of the Afro-American People.* 2d ed. Maryknoll, N.Y.: Orbis Books, 1983.

Wilson, John F, ed. *Church and State in America: A Bibliographical Guide.* New York: Greenwood Press, 1986.

Wilson, John F., and Donald L. Drakeman, eds. *Church and State in American History: The Burden of Religious Pluralism.* Boston: Beacon Press, 1987.

Wind, James P., and James W. Lewis, eds. *American Congregations.* 2 vols. Chicago: University of Chicago Press, 1994.

Woodson, Carter G. *The History of the Negro Church.* Washington, D.C.: Associated Publishers, 1992.

Wuthnow, Robert. *The Restructuring of American Religion: Society and Faith Since World War II.* Princeton, N.J.: Princeton University Press, 1988.

Ziolkowski, Eric J., ed. *A Museum of Faiths: Histories and Legacies of the 1893 World's Parliament of Religions.* Atlanta, Ga.: Scholar's Press, 1993.

ENTRIES BY RELIGIOUS AFFILIATION

ADVENTIST/MILLENIALIST
Koresh, David
Miller, William
Russell, Charles Taze
Rutherford, Joseph Franklin
White, Ellen Gould Harmon

BAPTIST
Backus, Isaac
Broadus, John Albert
Cary, Lott
Clarke, John
Conner, Walter Thomas
Conwell, Russell Herman
Dixon, Amzi Clarence
Dunster, Henry
Falwell, Jerry
Fosdick, Harry Emerson
Graham, Billy
Jackson, Jesse
Judson, Adoniram
King, Martin Luther, Jr.
Leland, John
Moon, Lottie
Mullins, Edgar Young
Norris, J. Frank
Powell, Adam Clayton, Sr.
Rauschenbusch, Walter
Rigdon, Sidney
Robertson, Pat
Strong, Augustus Hopkins
Williams, Roger

BUDDHIST
Suzuki, Daisetz Teitaro

CATHOLIC
Avery, Martha Gallison Moore
Bayley, James Roosevelt
Black Elk
Brownson, Orestes Augustus
Burke, John Joseph
Cabrini, Francesca Xavier
Carroll, John
Cheverus, Jean Louis Lefebvre de
Cody, John Patrick
Corrigan, Michael Augustine
Coughlin, Charles Edward
Cushing, Richard James
Damien, Father
Day, Dorothy
De Smet, Pierre-Jean
Drexel, Katharine
Duchesne, Rose Philippine
England, John
Feehan, Patrick Augustine
Flanagan, Edward Joseph
Gibbons, James
Hecker, Isaac Thomas
Hughes, John Joseph
Ireland, John
Kino, Eusebio Francisco
Lamy, Jean Baptiste
Maurin, Aristide Peter
McGlynn, Edward
Merton, Thomas

Michel, Virgil George
Murray, John Courtney
Ryan, John Augustine
Sheen, Fulton John
Spalding, Martin John
Spellman, Francis Joseph
Tekakwitha, Kateri
Verot, Jean Pierre Augustin
    Marcellin

CHRISTIAN SCIENCE
Eddy, Mary Baker
Stetson, Augusta Emma
    Simmons

CONGREGATIONALIST
Abbott, Lyman
Beecher, Henry Ward
Beecher, Lyman
Brainerd, David
Chauncy, Charles
Clark, Francis Edward
Cotton, John
Dwight, Timothy
Edwards, Jonathan
Edwards, Jonathan, Jr.
Eliot, John
Emmons, Nathanael
Gladden, Solomon Washington
Hooker, Thomas
Kirk, Edward Norris
Mather, Cotton
Mather, Increase

Mather, Richard
Mayhew, Jonathan
Mitchell, Jonathan
Morse, Jedidiah
Scofield, Cyrus Ingerson
Sheldon, Charles Monroe
Stiles, Ezra
Stoddard, Solomon
Strong, Josiah
Taylor, Nathaniel William
Tyler, Bennet

DISCIPLES OF CHRIST
Ainslie, Peter
Ames, Edward Scribner
Campbell, Alexander
Garrison, James Harvey
Lipscomb, David
McGarvey, John William
Scott, Walter
Stone, Barton Warren

EPISCOPAL
Breck, James Lloyd
Brooks, Phillips
Chase, Philander
Cheney, Charles Edward
Crummell, Alexander
DuBose, William Porcher
Huntington, William Reed
Johnson, Samuel
Pike, James Albert
Seabury, Samuel

FUNDAMENTALIST
Torrey, Reuben Archer

HARMONIALIST
Davis, Andrew Jackson

HOLINESS
Mahan, Asa
Palmer, Phoebe Worrall
Smith, Hannah Whitall

HUMANIST, ATHEIST, ETC.
Ingersoll, Robert Green

JUDAISM
Adler, Cyrus
Adler, Felix
Einhorn, David
Ford, Arnold Josiah
Ginzberg, Louis
Gratz, Rebecca
Heschel, Abraham Joshua
Kaplan, Mordecai Menahem
Leeser, Isaac
Magnes, Judah Leon
Mendes, Henry Pereira
Morais, Sabato
Schneerson, Menachem Mendel
Silver, Abba Hillel
Steinberg, Milton
Szold, Henrietta
Wise, Isaac Mayer
Wise, Stephen S.

LUTHERAN
Krauth, Charles Porterfield
Muhlenberg, Henry Melchior
Schmucker, Samuel Simon
Walther, Carl Ferdinand
    Wilhelm

METHODIST
Allen, Richard
Asbury, Francis
Bangs, Nathan
Bresee, Phineas Franklin
Cadman, Samuel Parkes
Candler, Warren Akin
Cartwright, Peter
Coke, Thomas
Coppin, Fanny Jackson
Crosby, Fanny
Garrettson, Freeborn
Haven, Gilbert
Haygood, Atticus Greene
Heck, Barbara Ruckle
Knudson, Albert Cornelius
Lee, Jesse
McCabe, Charles Cardwell
McKendree, William
Mott, John Raleigh

Oxnam, Garfield Bromley
Pilmore, Joseph
Ransom, Reverdy Cassius
Roberts, Benjamin Titus
Scott, Orange
Turner, Henry McNeal

MISCELLANEOUS
Fillmore, Charles Sherlock
Fuller, Charles Edward
Hutchinson, Anne Marbury
Kuhlman, Kathryn
Pierson, Arthur Tappan

MISSIONARY
Brainerd, David
Breck, James Lloyd
Judson, Adoniram
Moon, Lottie
Pierson, Arthur Tappan
Whitman, Marcus
Wilder, Robert Parmalee

MORAVIAN
Zeisberger, David
Zinzendorf, Nikolaus
    Ludwig von

MORMON
Kimball, Spencer Woolley
McKay, David Oman
Pratt, Parley Parker
Smith, Joseph, Jr.
Smith, Joseph, III
Woodruff, Wilford
Young, Brigham

MUSLIM
Drew, Timothy
Webb, Muhammad Alexander
    Russell

NATION OF ISLAM
Farrakhan, Louis Abdul
Malcolm X
Muhammad, Elijah

NATIVE AMERICAN
Black Elk

Dreamer Religion
Smohalla
Tenskwatawa

Ghost Dance Religion
Wovoka

Longhouse Religion
Handsome Lake

Native American Church
Parker, Quanah

NEW RELIGIONS/NEW AGE
De, Abhay Charan
Divine, Father
Fox, Emmet
Grace, Sweet Daddy
Hubbard, L. Ron
Jones, Jim
Moon, Sun Myung

OCCULTIST
Randolph, Paschal Beverly

PENTECOSTAL
Branham, William Marrion
McPherson, Aimee Semple
White, Alma Bridwell
Woodworth-Etter, Maria

PRESBYTERIAN/REFORMED
Alexander, Archibald
Blake, Eugene Carson
Boehm, John Philip
Briggs, Charles Augustus
Cavert, Samuel McCrea
Coffin, Henry Sloane
Davies, Samuel
Dickinson, Jonathan
Ewing, Finis

Frelinghuysen, Theodorus
  Jacobus
Garnet, Henry Highland
Hodge, Charles
Makemie, Francis
McCosh, James
Nevin, John Williamson
Occom, Samson
Peale, Norman Vincent
Pennington, James William
  Charles
Rice, John Holt
Schaff, Philip
Tennent, Gilbert
Tennent, William
Whitman, Marcus
Wilder, Robert Parmalee
Witherspoon, John

QUAKER
Dyer, Mary
Hicks, Elias
Jones, Rufus Matthew
Keith, George
Penn, William
Woolman, John

REVIVALIST
Chapman, John Wilbur
Finney, Charles Grandison
Jones, Bob
Jones, Sam
Moody, Dwight Lyman
Sankey, Ira David
Sunday, Billy
Whitefield, George

SATANIST
LaVey, Anton Szandor

SECTARIAN/UTOPIAN
Harris, Thomas Lake

SPIRITUALIST
Cayce, Edgar

THEOLOGIAN
Bushnell, Horace
Edwards, Jonathan
Hodge, Charles
Knudson, Albert Cornelius
Lewis, Edwin
Machen, John Gresham
Macintosh, Douglas Clyde
Mathews, Shailer
Mullins, Edgar Young
Niebuhr, Helmut Richard
Niebuhr, Reinhold
Priestley, Joseph
Strong, Augustus Hopkins
Tillich, Paul Johannes
Warfield, Benjamin
  Breckinridge

THEOSOPHIST
Blavatsky, Helena Petrovna
Olcott, Henry Steel

UNITARIAN/UNIVERSALIST
Ballou, Hosea
Bellows, Henry Whitney
Blackwell, Antoinette Louisa
  Brown
Channing, William Ellery
Clarke, James Freeman
Frothingham, Octavius Brooks
Hale, Edward Everett
Hedge, Frederic Henry
Holmes, John Haynes
King, Thomas Starr
Parker, Theodore

UTOPIANS
Beissel, Johann Conrad
Lee, Ann
Noyes, John Humphrey
Rapp, George

1550–1599
Cotton, John
Hooker, Thomas
Hutchinson, Anne Marbury
Mather, Richard

1600–1649
Clarke, John
Dyer, Mary
Dunster, Henry
Eliot, John
Keith, George
Kino, Eusebio Francisco
Mather, Increase
Mitchel, Jonathan
Penn, William
Stoddard, Solomon
Williams, Roger

1650–1699
Beissel, Johann Conrad
Boehm, John Philip
Dickinson, Jonathan
Frelinghuysen, Theodorus
    Jacobus
Johnson, Samuel
Makemie, Francis
Mather, Cotton
Tekakwitha, Kateri
Tennent, William

1700–1749
Asbury, Francis

Backus, Isaac
Brainerd, David
Carroll, John
Chauncy, Charles
Coke, Thomas
Davies, Samuel
Edwards, Jonathan
Edwards, Jonathan, Jr.
Emmons, Nathanael
Handsome Lake
Heck, Barbara Ruckle
Hicks, Elias
Lee, Ann
Mayhew, Jonathan
Muhlenberg, Henry Melchior
Occom, Samson
Pilmore, Joseph
Priestley, Joseph
Seabury, Samuel
Stiles, Ezra
Tennent, Gilbert
Whitefield, George
Witherspoon, John
Woolman, John
Zeisberger, David
Zinzendorf, Nikolaus
    Ludwig von

1750–1759
Dwight, Timothy
Garrettson, Freeborn
Lee, Jesse
Leland, John

McKendree, William
Rapp, George

1760–1769
Allen, Richard
Cheverus, Jean Louis
    Lefebvre de
Duchesne, Rose Philippine
Morse, Jedidiah

1770–1779
Alexander, Archibald
Ballou, Hosea
Bangs, Nathan
Beecher, Lyman
Chase, Philander
Ewing, Finis
Rice, John Holt
Stone, Barton Warren
Tenskwatawa

1780–1789
Campbell, Alexander
Cartwright, Peter
Cary, Lott
Channing, William Ellery
England, John
Gratz, Rebecca
Judson, Adoniram
Miller, William
Taylor, Nathaniel William
Tyler, Bennet

1790–1799
Finney, Charles Grandison
Hodge, Charles
Hughes, John Joseph
Mahan, Asa
Rigdon, Sidney
Schmucker, Samuel Simon
Scott, Walter

1800–1809
Brownson, Orestes Augustus
Bushnell, Horace
De Smet, Pierre Jean
Einhorn, David
Hedge, Frederic Henry
Kirk, Edward Norris
Leeser, Isaac
Nevin, John Williamson
Palmer, Phoebe Worrall
Pennington, James William
    Charles
Pratt, Parley Parker
Scott, Orange
Smith, Joseph, Jr.
Verot, Jean Pierre Augustin
    Marcellin
Whitman, Marcus
Woodruff, Wilford
Young, Brigham

1810–1819
Bayley, James Roosevelt
Beecher, Henry Ward
Bellows, Henry Whitney
Breck, James Lloyd
Clarke, James Freeman
Crummell, Alexander
Garnet, Henry Highland
Hecker, Isaac Thomas
Lamy, Jean Baptiste
McCosh, James
Noyes, John Humphrey
Parker, Theodore
Schaff, Philip
Smohalla
Spalding, Martin John

Walther, Carl Ferdinand
    Wilhelm
Wise, Isaac Mayer

1820–1829
Blackwell, Antoinette Louisa
    Brown
Broadus, John Albert
Crosby, Fanny
Davis, Andrew Jackson
Eddy, Mary Baker
Feehan, Patrick Augustine
Frothingham, Octavius Brooks
Hale, Edward Everett
Harris, Thomas Lake
Haven, Gilbert
King, Thomas Starr
Krauth, Charles Porterfield
McGarvey, John William
Morais, Sabato
Randolph, Paschal Beverly
Roberts, Benjamin Titus
White, Ellen Gould Harmon

1830–1839
Abbott, Lyman
Blavatsky, Helena Petrovna
Bresee, Phineas Franklin
Brooks, Phillips
Cheney, Charles Edward
Coppin, Fanny Jackson
Corrigan, Michael Augustine
DuBose, William Porcher
Gibbons, James
Gladden, Solomon Washington
Haygood, Atticus Greene
Huntington, William Reed
Ingersoll, Robert Green
Ireland, John
Lipscomb, David
McCabe, Charles Cardwell
McGlynn, Edward
Moody, Dwight Lyman
Olcott, Henry Steel
Pierson, Arthur Tappan
Smith, Hannah Whitall
Smith, Joseph, III

Strong, Augustus Hopkins
Turner, Henry McNeal

1840–1849
Briggs, Charles Augustus
Conwell, Russell Herman
Damien, Father
Garrison, James Harvey
Jones, Sam
Moon, Lottie
Sankey, Ira David
Scofield, Cyrus Ingerson
Stetson, Augusta Emma
    Simmons
Strong, Josiah
Woodworth-Etter, Maria

1850–1859
Adler, Felix
Avery, Martha Gallison Moore
Cabrini, Francesca Xavier
Candler, Warren Akin
Chapman, John Wilbur
Clark, Francis Edward
Dixon, Amzi Clarence
Drexel, Katharine
Fillmore, Charles Sherlock
Mendes, Henry Pereira
Parker, Quanah
Russell, Charles Taze
Sheldon, Charles Monroe
Torrey, Reuben Archer
Warfield, Benjamin
    Breckinridge
Wovoka

1860–1869
Adler, Cyrus
Ainslie, Peter
Black Elk
Cadman, Samuel Parkes
Jones, Rufus Matthew
Mathews, Shailer
Mott, John Raleigh
Mullins, Edgar Young
Powell, Adam Clayton, Sr.

Ransom, Reverdy Cassius
Rauschenbusch, Walter
Rutherford, Joseph Franklin
Ryan, John Augustine
Sunday, Billy
Szold, Henrietta
White, Alma Bridwell
Wilder, Robert Parmalee

1870–1879
Ames, Edward Scribner
Burke, John Joseph
Cayce, Edgar
Coffin, Henry Sloane
Conner, Walter Thomas
Divine, Father
Ford, Arnold Josiah
Fosdick, Harry Emerson
Ginzberg, Louis
Holmes, John Haynes
Knudson, Albert Cornelius
Macintosh, Douglas Clyde
Magnes, Judah Leon
Maurin, Aristide Peter
McKay, David Oman
Norris, J. Frank
Wise, Stephen S.

1880–1889
Cavert, Samuel McCrea

Flanagan, Edward Joseph
Fox, Emmet
Fuller, Charles Edward
Grace, Sweet Daddy
Jones, Bob
Kaplan, Mordecai Menahem
Lewis, Edwin
Machen, John Gresham
Spellman, Francis Joseph
Tillich, Paul Johannes

1890–1899
Coughlin, Charles Edward
Cushing, Richard James
Day, Dorothy
Kimball, Spencer Woolley
McPherson, Aimee Semple
Michel, Virgil George
Muhammad, Elijah
Niebuhr, Helmut Richard
Niebuhr, Reinhold
Oxnam, Garfield Bromley
Peale, Norman Vincent
Sheen, Fulton John
Silver, Abba Hillel

1900–1909
Blake, Eugene Carson
Branham, William Marrion
Cody, John Patrick

Heschel, Abraham Joshua
Murray, John Courtney
Schneerson, Menachem Mendel
Steinberg, Milton

1910–1919
Graham, Billy
Kuhlman, Kathryn
Merton, Thomas
Pike, James Albert

1920–1929
King, Martin Luther, Jr.
Malcolm X
Moon, Sun Myung

1930–1939
Falwell, Jerry
Farrakhan, Louis Abdul
Jones, Jim
LaVey, Anton Szandor
Robertson, Pat

1940–1949
Jackson, Jesse

1950–1959
Koresh, David

INDEX

Boldface locators indicate main entries. *Italic* locators indicate photographs. Locators followed by *g* indicate glossary.

A

Abbott, Lyman **1–2**, *2*
ABC (American Broadcasting Company) 140
ABCFM (American Board of Commissioners for Foreign Missions) 378
Abernathy, Ralph 184
abolitionism. *See also* slavery
    Henry Ward Beecher 21
    Lyman Beecher 23
    Phillips Brooks 41
    Peter Cartwright 56
    William Ellery Channing 61
    Charles Finney 131
    Octavius Brooks Frothingham 138
    Henry Highland Garnet 141–143
    Freeborn Garrettson 144
    Gilbert Haven 160–161
    Elias Hicks 169
    George Keith 197
    Edward Norris Kirk 204
    Asa Mahan 225–226
    Sabato Morais 260
    Theodore Parker 287
    James W. C. Pennington 292–293
    Samuel Schmucker 321
    Orange Scott 323, 324
    John Woolman 390
Abyssinian Baptist Church 298
ACLU. *See* American Civil Liberties Union
activism. *See* social activism/social reform
Act of Toleration 227
Adam Bede (Eliot) 164
Adams, John 301
Address to the Roman Catholics of the United States of America (Carroll) 54
Adler, Cyrus **2–4**
Adler, Felix **4–5**
administrative service 58
Advent 398*g*
Adventists 253, 313, 398*g*. *See also* Seventh Day Adventist Church
African Americans. *See also* civil rights
    Richard Allen **8–10**
    Warren Akin Candler 53
    Lott Cary **57–58**
    Fanny Jackson Coppin **79–80**

Alexander Crummell **87–88**
    Father Divine **100–102**
    Timothy Drew **103–104**
    Katharine Drexel 104, *105*
    Arnold J. Ford **133–134**
    Henry Highland Garnet **141–143**
    Sweet Daddy Grace **151–152**
    Atticus Greene Haygood 162
    Jesse Jackson **184–186**
    Spencer W. Kimball 198
    Asa Mahan 225, *226*
    James W. C. Pennington **292–293**
    Adam Clayton Powell, Sr. **297–298**
    Paschal Beverly Randolph **302–303**
    Reverdy C. Ransom **303–304**
    Charles Sheldon 329
    Henry McNeal Turner **365–366**
    Augustin Verot 368, *369*
African Methodist Episcopal (AME) Church
    Richard Allen **8–10**
    Fanny Jackson Coppin 80
    James W. C. Pennington 293
    Reverdy C. Ransom **303–304**
    Henry McNeal Turner **365–366**
agnosticism 398*g*
AIDS 127
Ainslie, Peter **5–6**
Alcoholics Anonymous 275, 296
alcoholism 322
Alexander, Archibald **6–8**, 170, 307
Algonquian New Testament 120
Ali, Noble Drew. *See* Drew, Timothy
Alien and Sedition Acts 301
Allen, Richard 8, **8–10**
"All the Way My Savior Leads Me" (Crosby) 86
altar call 398*g*
altar theology 284
Alter Your Life (Fox) 136
AME Church. *See* African Methodist Episcopal Church
American Anti-Slavery Society 324
American Biography (Morse) 262
American Board of Commissioners for Foreign Missions (ABCFM) 378
American Broadcasting Company (ABC) 140

American Civil Liberties Union (ACLU) 172, 384
American Colonization Society 9, 57, 366
American Friend 190
American Friends Service Committee 191
American Indians. *See* Native Americans
Americanist controversy
    Michael Augustine Corrigan 81–82
    Isaac Hecker 164, *165*
    John Ireland 183
    Francis Spellman 340
American Jewish Congress 384
American liturgical movement. *See* liturgical movement
American Revolution. *See* Revolutionary War
America's Dates with Destiny (Robertson) 312
Ames, Edward Scribner **10–11**
amillennialism 102
Amistad affair 292–293
Anabaptism 398*g*
Andrew, James O. 56
Andros, Sir Edmund 230
Anglican Church
    Samuel Davies 93
    John Eliot 119
    Freeborn Garrettson 144
    Samuel Johnson 186, 187
    George Keith 197
    John Leland 216
    Francis Makemie 226–227
    Richard Mather 234
    Joseph Pilmore 296, 297
    Roger Williams 380, 381
Anglicanism 398*g*
Anthony, Susan B. 28
Antichrist 398*g*
Antinomians 83
anti-Semitism 398*g*
    Charles E. Coughlin 84, 85
    Louis Farrakhan 126, 127
    Abraham Joshua Heschel 168
    Isaac Leeser 215
antislavery movement. *See* abolitionism
Anxious Bench, The (Nevin) 271
Apocalypse 206–207, 313, 315, 398*g*
apologist 398*g*
apostolic succession 381, 398*g*

Appeal to the American Churches
    (Schmucker) 320
Appeal to the Public for Religious Liberty
    (Backus) 16
*Applied Christianity: Moral Aspects of Social
    Questions* (Gladden) 150
Arianism 61, 237–238, 398g
Arminianism 237, 356, 367, 398g
Art of Living (radio program) 288
As a Driven Leaf (Steinberg) 340
Asbury, Francis *11,* **11–13**
    Richard Allen 9
    Peter Cartwright 55
    Thomas Coke 75, 76
    Freeborn Garrettson 143–144
    Jesse Lee 214
    William McKendree 245, 246
    Joseph Pilmore 297
asceticism 398g
ATF. *See* Federal Bureau of Alcohol,
    Tobacco, and Firearms
atheism 181–182, 211
Atlantis 60
atonement 17, 46, 398g
Auburn Affirmation 74
Augsburg Confession 320, 398g
*Autobiography of Peter Cartwright, the
    Backwoods Preacher* 56
Avery, Martha Gallison Moore **13–14**
Awake! (magazine) 314
Azusa Street Revival 101, 398g

B
Backus, Isaac **15–16**
Ballou, Hosea **16–18,** 201
Bangs, Nathan **18–19**
baptism 51, 345, 398g. *See also* Half-Way
    Covenant
    Isaac Backus 15
    Charles Edward Cheney 66
    John Clarke 71
    Henry Dunster 108
    Adoniram Judson 193
    Jonathan Mitchell 254
    Arthur T. Pierson 294
Baptist Faith and Message 268
Baptists/Baptist Church 398g–399g
    Isaac Backus **15–16**
    Johann Conrad Beissel **24–25**
    John A. Broadus **39–40**
    Lott Cary **57–58**
    John Clarke **71–72**
    W. T. Conner **76–77**
    Russell H. Conwell **77–79**
    Amzi Clarence Dixon **102–103**
    Jerry Falwell **125–126**
    Harry Emerson Fosdick **134–135**
    Billy Graham **152–154**
    Jesse Jackson **184–186**
    Adoniram Judson **192–194**
    Martin Luther King, Jr. **199–201**
    John Leland **216–217**
    Douglas Clyde Macintosh **222–223**
    Lottie Moon **257–258**
    Edgar Young Mullins **267–269**
    J. Frank Norris **275–277**
    Adam Clayton Powell, Sr. **297–299**
    Walter Rauschenbusch **305–307**
    Sidney Rigdon 308

Augustus H. Strong **348–349**
    Roger Williams 381
Barbour, Nelson H. 313
Barclay, Robert 196
bar mitzvah/bat mitzvah 399g
Barth, Karl 218, 273
baseball 351
Basic Judaism (Steinberg) 340
"Battle Hymn of the Republic" 239
Bayley, James Roosevelt **19–20**
beatification 49, 93
Beauduin, Lambert 251
Becker, Peter 24
Beecher, Henry Ward *1,* **20–22,** *21, 22*
Beecher, Lyman 20, **22–24,** *23*
"Beecher's Bibles" 21
Beissel, Johann Conrad **24–25**
Bellamy, Joseph 117, 121, 367
Bellows, Henry Whitney **25–26,** 70, 138
Bible. *See also* biblical criticism; higher
    criticism
    William Ellery Channing 61
    Adoniram Judson 193
    Philip Schaff 319
    C. I. Scofield 322, 323
    Henry McNeal Turner 365
biblical criticism 258, 399g. *See also* higher
    criticism
biblical infallibility 372
biblical scholars 38–39
Bibliotheca Sacra 372
Big Moon peyote religion 286
birth control 90
Bishop Sheen Program (television show) 328
Black Elk **26–27**
Black Elk Speaks 27
Black Muslims. *See* Nation of Islam
Black Nationalism 133–134
Blackwell, Antoinette Louisa Brown **27–29**
Blackwell, Elizabeth 28
Blaine, James G. 181
Blake, Eugene Carson **29–30**
Blavatsky, Helena Petrovna **30–32,** 281
Blind Girl and Other Poems (Crosby) 86
Bloody Tenet of Persecution (Williams) 381
*Bloudy Tenent, Washed, and Made White in the
    Bloud of the Lambe* (Cotton) 83
Boardman, Richard 296, 297
Bob Jones University 152, 188
Boehm, John Philip **32–33**
Boggs, Lilburn 309, 334
Book of Common Prayer 178
Book of Mormon 309, 334, 393
Borgonini-Duca, Francesco 339
"born again" Christians 125
Boston
    Phillips Brooks 41–42
    Charles Chauncy 65
    Jean Lefebvre de Cheverus 67, 68
    James Freeman Clarke 70, 71
    John Cotton 83
    Richard Cardinal Cushing 88–90
    Mary Dyer 110–111
    Mary Baker Eddy 114
    John Eliot 119–120
    Louis Farrakhan 126–127
    Edward Everett Hale 156–157
    Anne Hutchinson 179
    Thomas Starr King 201–202

Edward Norris Kirk 204
Cotton Mather 230
Jonathan Mayhew 237–238
Theodore Parker 287
Bowne, Borden Parker 205
Brainerd, David **33–34**
Branch Davidians 206–207
Brandeis, Louis 384
Branham, William Marrion *34,* **34–35**
Breck, James Lloyd **35–36**
Bresee, Phineas Franklin **36–38**
*Brief Sketch of the History of the Catholic
    Church on the Island of New York* (Bayley)
    19
Briggs, Charles Augustus **38–39,** 372
broadcasting. *See* radio broadcasting;
    television broadcasting
Broadus, John Albert **39–40,** *40,* 102, 257
Brodie, Fawn McKay 244
Brooks, Phillips **41–42**
Brotherhood of the Kingdom 306
Brothertown 280
Brownson, Orestes Augustus **42–44,** *43,*
    164
Brownson's Quarterly Review 42–43
Brunner, Emil 218
Bryan, William Jennings 134
Buber, Martin 224
Buchanan, James 394
Buddhism 31, 281, 352–353
Buddhist Catechism (Olcott) 281
Burke, John Joseph **44–45**
Burma 193
Bush, George H. W. 312
Bushnell, Horace **45–47,** 149, 348

C
Cabrini, Francesca Xavier **48–49,** *49*
Cadman, S. Parkes **49–50**
Calles, Plutarco Elías 44
Calvinism 399g
    Nathan Bangs 18
    Henry Ward Beecher 20
    Lyman Beecher 22, 23
    Orestes A. Brownson 42
    William Ellery Channing 61
    Charles Chauncy 65, 66
    Timothy Dwight 109
    Jonathan Edwards, Jr. 118
    Nathanael Emmons 121
    Thomas Lake Harris 159–160
    Charles Hodge 170
    Edward Norris Kirk 203
    Jedidiah Morse 262
    Ezra Stiles 343
    Nathaniel William Taylor 356, 357
    Bennet Tyler 366, 367
    George Whitefield 377
Cambridge Platform 234
Campbell, Alexander *51,* **51–52**
    John W. McGarvey 241
    Parley P. Pratt 299
    Sidney Rigdon 308
    Walter Scott 325, 326
    Barton W. Stone 346, 348
Campbell, Thomas 51
Candler, Warren Akin **52–54**
canonization 105, 358, 399g
canon law 399g

cardinal 399g
Carlyle, Thomas 166
Carroll, John 54–55, 68
Cartwright, Peter 55–57, 56
Cary, Lott 57–58
cathedral 399g
Catholic Charities Review (Ryan) 315
Catholic Church xv, 399g
    Martha Moore Avery 13–14
    James Bayley 19–20
    Lyman Beecher 23
    Black Elk 27
    Orestes A. Brownson 42–44
    John J. Burke 44–45
    Francesca Cabrini 48–49
    John Carroll 54–55
    Jean Lefebvre de Cheverus 67–69
    John Patrick Cody 72–73
    Michael Augustine Corrigan 80–82
    Charles Coughlin 84–86
    Richard Cushing 88–90
    Father Damien 91–93
    Dorothy Day 95–97
    Pierre-Jean De Smet 98–99
    Katharine Drexel 104–105
    Philippine Duchesne 106–107
    John England 122–123
    Patrick Augustine Feehan 128–129
    Edward J. Flanagan 131–133
    Emmet Fox 135
    James Gibbons 146–148
    Isaac T. Hecker 164–165
    John Hughes 176–177
    John Ireland 182–183
    Eusebio Francisco Kino 202–203
    Jean Baptiste Lamy 210–211
    Peter Maurin 236–237
    Edward McGlynn 242–244
    Thomas Merton 250–251
    Virgil Michel 251–252
    John Courtney Murray 269–270
    J. Frank Norris 276
    J. F. Rutherford 314
    John A. Ryan 315–316
    Philip Schaff 319
    Fulton J. Sheen 327–329
    Martin Spalding 337–338
    Francis Spellman 338–340
    Kateri Tekakwitha 357–358
    Augustin Verot 368–369
Catholic Herald (newspaper) 176
Catholic Hour (radio show) 328
Catholic University of America 183
Catholic Ward (magazine) 165
Catholic Worker, The (newspaper) 96, 237
Catholic Worker movement 95–97, 236–237
Catholic World 44
Cavert, Samuel McCrea 58–59
Cayce, Edgar 59–60
Cayuse Nation 378–379
celestial sexuality 159, 160
celibacy 305, 399g
Channing, William Ellery 60–62, 68
Chapman, John Wilbur 62–63, 352
charismatic movement xiv, 399g
    William Branham 34–35
    Kathryn Kuhlman 208–209
Charles I, king of England 83, 234, 381

Charles II, king of England 291
Chase, Philander 63–65, 64
Chauncy, Charles 65–66
Cheney, Charles Edward 66–67
Cheverus, Jean Louis Lefebvre de 67–69
Chicago-Lambeth Quadrilateral 178
Chicago school 10, 235
Chicago World's Fair (1892–1893) 62
children, welfare of 132
China 257, 258
Christian Broadcasting Network (CBN) 311–312
Christian Church. *See* Disciples of Christ
Christian Coalition 311, 312
Christian Endeavor Society 69–70
Christian-Evangelist, The 145–146
Christian Herald 330
Christianity and Liberalism (Machen) 221
Christianity and the Social Crisis (Rauschenbusch) 306
Christianizing the Social Order (Rauschenbusch) 306
Christian Manifesto, A (Lewis) 218
"Christian Quakers" 197
Christian Religion Series for College (Michel) 252
Christian Right 126
Christian Science
    Mary Baker Eddy 113–115
    Charles Fillmore 129
    Emmet Fox 136
    Augusta E. Stetson 341–343
Christian's Secret of a Happy Life (Smith) 332
Christian System, The (Campbell) 51–52
Christian Union Quarterly 6
Christ in Creation and Ethical Monism (Strong) 349
Christology 399g
church and state, separation of. *See* separation of church and state
Churches of Christ. *See* Disciples of Christ
church history 7
Church-Idea: An Essay Toward Unity (Huntington) 178
Church of All Nations 282
Church of Christ, Scientist. *See* Christian Science
Church of England. *See* Anglican Church
Church of Jesus Christ of Latter-day Saints (Mormons) xiv, 400g
    Pierre-Jean De Smet 98
    Spencer W. Kimball 198–199
    David O. McKay 244–245
    Parley P. Pratt 299–300
    Sidney Rigdon 308–309
    Joseph Smith, Jr. 333–334
    Joseph Smith III 335–336
    Wilford Woodruff 387–388
    Brigham Young 393–394
Church of Satan 211–212
Church of the Foursquare Gospel 246, 248
Church of the Nazarene 36–38
citizenship rights 345
civil liberties 172, 173
civil rights
    Eugene Carson Blake 30
    Harry Emerson Fosdick 135

    Gilbert Haven 160–161
    Atticus Haygood 161–163
    Abraham Joshua Heschel 167, 168
    John Haynes Holmes 172, 173
    Jesse Jackson 184–186
    Martin Luther King, Jr. 199–201
    Malcolm X 227–229
    Elijah Muhammad 266
    Adam Clayton Powell, Sr. 298
    Reverdy C. Ransom 303, 304
    Henry McNeal Turner 365, 366
    Augustin Verot 368, 369
Civil War, U.S.
    Henry Ward Beecher 21
    Henry Whitney Bellows 26
    John A. Broadus 39–40
    Phillips Brooks 41
    Russell H. Conwell 77–78
    William Porcher DuBose 106
    Patrick Augustine Feehan 128
    Henry Highland Garnet 141, 143
    James H. Garrison 145
    James Gibbons 146
    Edward Everett Hale 156
    Gilbert Haven 160, 161
    Atticus Haygood 162
    John Hughes 177
    Robert Ingersoll 181
    John Ireland 182
    Thomas Starr King 202
    Edward Norris Kirk 204
    Charles Cardwell McCabe 239
    Dwight Lyman Moody 256
    Sabato Morais 260
    Henry Steel Olcott 281
    Ira D. Sankey 317
    Samuel Schmucker 321
    Henry McNeal Turner 365
    Augustin Verot 368, 369
Clark, Francis Edward 69–70
Clark, Tom C. 132
Clarke, James Freeman 70–71
Clarke, John 71–72
Clement XIV, Pope 54
Cleveland, Grover 373
Clinton, George 212
Code of Handsome Lake 158
Cody, John Patrick 72–73
Coffin, Henry Sloane 74–75
Coke, Thomas 75–76, 144, 246
Coleridge, Samuel Taylor 166
College of the Bible 241–242
colonization 366
Columbia University 186
Columbus Hospital 48
Comanche Nation 285
Commentary on the Palestinian Talmud (Ginzberg) 149
Common Cause Society 14
communal farms 96, 237
communes 24–25, 304–305, 308
communion. *See* Lord's Supper
Communism and the Conscience of the West (Sheen) 328
communitarianism 212
Community of Christ xiv, 335. *See also* Mormons
"complex marriage" 277–278
Compromise of 1850 160

Congregationalism/Congregational Church
  xiv, 399g
  Lyman Abbott **1–2**
  Archibald Alexander 7
  Isaac Backus 15
  Henry Ward Beecher **20–22**
  Lyman Beecher **22–24**
  Antoinette Brown Blackwell 28
  Horace Bushnell **45–47**
  William Ellery Channing 61
  Charles Chauncy **65–66**
  Francis E. Clark **69–70**
  Jonathan Dickinson 99
  Timothy Dwight **109–110**
  Jonathan Edwards **115–117**
  Jonathan Edwards, Jr. **117–118**
  Nathanael Emmons **120–122**
  Charles Finney 130
  Washington Gladden **149–150**
  Thomas Hooker 173, 174
  Samuel Johnson 186
  Adoniram Judson 192–193
  Edward Norris Kirk **203–204**
  John Leland 217
  Asa Mahan **225–226**
  Increase Mather 233
  Richard Mather 233–235
  Jonathan Mayhew **237–238**
  Jonathan Mitchell 254
  Dwight Lyman Moody 255, 256
  Jedidiah Morse **261–263**
  C. I. Scofield **322–323**
  Samuel Seabury 326
  Charles Sheldon **329–330**
  Ezra Stiles **343–344**
  Josiah Strong **349–351**
  Nathaniel Taylor **356–357**
  Nathaniel William Taylor 356
  Reuben Archer Torrey **363–365**
  Bennet Tyler **366–367**
Congress, U. S. 122, 143, 298
Conner, Walter Thomas **76–77**
Conquest of Canan, The (Dwight) 109
conscientious objection 214, 223
conservatism (conservative theology)
  Archibald Alexander 7
  Lyman Beecher 23
  Eugene Carson Blake 30
  Charles A. Briggs 38
  William Ellery Channing 61
  Michael Augustine Corrigan 81
  Jonathan Edwards, Jr. 117
  Billy Graham 152–154
  Charles Hodge 170–171
  Bob Jones 188
  Sabato Morais 261
  Jedidiah Morse 262
  J. Frank Norris 276
  Pat Robertson 311–312
  Augustus H. Strong 348–349
  Reuben Archer Torrey 363–365
  C. F. W. Walther 370–371
Conservative Judaism
  Cyrus Adler 3
  Mordecai M. Kaplan 195–196
  Isaac Leeser 216
  Sabato Morais 261
  Milton Steinberg 340

conservative politics
  Jerry Falwell 125–126
  J. Frank Norris 276
  Norman Vincent Peale 289–290
  Billy Sunday 352
Conservative Reformation and Its Theology
  (Krauth) 208
Constantine, emperor of Rome 381
Constitution, U.S. 16, 122, 216. *See also*
  individual amendments
Constitutional Convention 216
Constitution for the Diocese of Charleston
  122, 123
Continental Congress 386
conversion experiences. *See also* Half-Way
  Covenant
  Isaac Backus 15
  Eugene Carson Blake 29
  Charles A. Briggs 38
  John A. Broadus 39
  Horace Bushnell 45
  S. Parkes Cadman 49–50
  Peter Cartwright 55
  W. T. Conner 76
  Fanny Crosby 86
  Finis Ewing 123
  Charles Finney 130
  Theodorus Jacobus Frelinghuysen
    137
  Charles E. Fuller 139–140
  Freeborn Garrettson 144
  Atticus Haygood 162
  Sam Jones 191
  William Miller 253
  Lottie Moon 257
  Phoebe Palmer 284
  Arthur T. Pierson 293
  Adam Clayton Powell, Sr. 298
  Parley P. Pratt 299
  C. I. Scofield 322
  Solomon Stoddard 345
  Ellen G. White 375
  George Whitefield 377
  Marcus Whitman 378
Conwell, Russell Herman **77–79,** 78
Cook, Thomas 12
Coppin, Fanny Jackson **79–80**
Cornbury, Lord 226, 227
Cornplanter 158
Corrigan, Michael Augustine **80–82,** 81
  Francesca Cabrini 48
  James Gibbons 147
  John Ireland 183
  Edward McGlynn 242, 243
corruption/scandal
  John Patrick Cody 73
  Sweet Daddy Grace 151
  Sun Myung Moon 259
  Elijah Muhammad 265
  J. Frank Norris 276
  Henry Steel Olcott 281
  C. F. W. Walther 370
cosmology 399g
Cotton, John **82–84,** 83
  Mary Dyer 111
  Anne Hutchinson 179
  Cotton Mather 230
  Increase Mather 232
Coughlin, Charles Edward **84–86,** 316

Courage to Be, The (Tillich) 363
covenant 399g
"Covenant of Grace" vs. "Covenant of
  Works" 83, 111, 179
Creed and Deed (Adler) 4
Creeds of Christendom (Schaff) 319
Cristero Rebellion 44
Crosby, Fanny **86–87,** 317, 318
Crowley, Jeremiah 128
Crummell, Alexander **87–88,** 141
cults 188–189
Cumberland Presbytery 123–124
Cummins, George David 67
Cushing, Richard James **88–90,** 89

D

Damien, Father **91–93,** 92
Dartmouth College 279, 280
Darwinism 21, 240, 348, 399g. *See also*
  evolutionary theory
Davies, Samuel **93–94,** 359
Davis, Andrew Jackson **94–95,** 159
Day, Dorothy **95–97,** 96, 236, 237
De, Abhay Charan **97–98**
deacon 399g
Declaration of Independence 385, 386
Deed of Declaration 297
deism 399g
Delaware Nation 33, 395, 396
Democratic-Republican Party 301
denominationalism 5, 6
depression of 1930s. *See* Great Depression
deprogramming 189
Der Lutheraner 370
De Smet, Pierre-Jean **98–99**
Dewey, John 10
Dial, the 166
*Dianetics: The Modern Science of Mental
  Health* (Hubbard) 175
Dickinson, Jonathan **99–100**
Dignitatis humanae personae 270
diplomacy 44
Disciples of Christ
  Peter Ainslie **5–6**
  Edward Scribner Ames **10–11**
  Alexander Campbell **51–52**
  James H. Garrison **145–146**
  Jim Jones 189
  David Lipscomb **218–220**
  John W. McGarvey **241–242**
  Parley P. Pratt 299
  Sidney Rigdon 308
  Walter Scott **325–326**
  Barton W. Stone 346, 348
  Maria Woodworth-Etter 388
*Discourse Concerning Unlimited Submission and
  Non-Resistance to the Higher Powers* 238
Discourses on Christian Nurture (Bushnell) 45
dispensationalism 322, 323, 399g
*Distributive Justice: The Right and Wrong of Our
  Present Distribution of Wealth* (Ryan) 316
Divine, Father **100–102,** 189
Divine Light, The 226
Divine Principle, The (Moon) 259
Dixon, Amzi Clarence **102–103**
Doctrine and Covenants 334
Douglass, Frederick 143
draft resistance 314. *See also* conscientious
  objection

Dreamer religion 336–337
Drew, Timothy **103–104**
Drexel, Katharine **104–105**
Dubois, John 176
Du Bois, W. E. B. 88, 304
DuBose, William Porcher **105–106**
Duchesne, Rose Philippine **106–107**
Dukakis, Michael 185
Dunkards 24
Dunster, Henry **107–109**, 254
Dutch Reformed Church 62, 137–138, 288, 399g
Dwight, Timothy 22, *109*, **109–110**, 117, 356
Dyer, Mary **110–112**

E
Eastburn, Manton 177
Eastern Buddhist, The (Suzuki) 353
Eastern religions 251, 281, 282, 352–353
ecclesiology 399g
Economy community 305
ecumenism 399g
  Peter Ainslie 5–6
  Samuel McCrea Cavert **58–59**
  John R. Mott **263–264**
  Josiah Strong 349, 350
Eddy, Mary Baker 78, **113–115**, *114*, 136, 341–343
Edmunds Act of 1882 387
education
  Cyrus Adler 2–3
  Lyman Beecher 23
  Charles A. Briggs 38
  John A. Broadus 39–40
  Warren Akin Candler 53
  Philander Chase 64
  Henry Sloane Coffin 74
  W. T. Conner 77
  Fanny Jackson Coppin 79–80
  Alexander Crummell 87–88
  William Porcher DuBose 106
  Henry Dunster 107–108
  Timothy Dwight 109–110
  Jonathan Edwards, Jr. 117–118
  Louis Ginzberg 148–149
  Atticus Haygood 161–163
  Frederic Henry Hedge 166
  Charles Hodge 170–171
  Bob Jones 188
  Charles Porterfield Krauth 208
  Isaac Leeser 214–216
  Edwin Lewis 217–218
  David Lipscomb 219
  Douglas Clyde Macintosh 222–223
  Judah L. Magnes 224
  Asa Mahan 225–226
  Shailer Mathews 235–236
  James McCosh 240–241
  John W. McGarvey 241–242
  Dwight Lyman Moody 256
  Edgar Young Mullins 267–268
  John W. Nevin 271–272
  H. Richard Niebuhr 272–273
  Reinhold Niebuhr 274–275
  Joseph Priestley 300
  Walter Rauschenbusch 306
  John Holt Rice 307–308

Philip Schaff 319
Samuel Schmucker 320–321
Walter Scott 325–326
Fulton J. Sheen 327–328
Ezra Stiles 343–344
Augustus H. Strong 348–349
D. T. Suzuki 352–353
Nathaniel William Taylor 356–357
Reuben Archer Torrey 364
Bennet Tyler 367
C. F. W. Walther 371
John Witherspoon 385–386
Edwards, Jonathan xvi, **115–117**
  David Brainerd 33, 34
  Charles Chauncy 65
  Timothy Dwight 109, 110
  Nathanael Emmons 121
  Theodorus Jacobus Frelinghuysen 137
  Charles Hodge 171
  Nathaniel William Taylor 356
  Bennet Tyler 367
Edwards, Jonathan, Jr. 109, **117–118**, 261
Einhorn, David **118–119**
Elementa Philsophica (Johnson/Franklin) 186
Elements of Popular Theology (Schmucker) 320
Eliade, Mircea xv
Eliot, Charles W. 240
Eliot, George 164
Eliot, John **119–120**
Emancipation Proclamation 365
Emerson, Ralph Waldo 70, 136, 166
Emmons, Nathanael **120–122**
Emory University 53, 162
encyclical 399g
end of the world. *See* Apocalypse
end times 253, 322. *See also* Apocalypse
England, John **122–123**
Ephrata commune 24–25
epidemics 128
Episcopal Church
  James Roosevelt Bayley 19
  James Lloyd Breck **35–36**
  Charles A. Briggs 39
  Phillips Brooks **41–42**
  Philander Chase **63–65**
  Charles Edward Cheney **66–67**
  Alexander Crummell **87–88**
  William Porcher DuBose **105–106**
  William Reed Huntington **177–178**
  Samuel Johnson **186–187**
  James A. Pike **295–296**
  Joseph Pilmore **296–297**
  Samuel Seabury **326–327**
Equal Rights Amendment 198, 375
eschatology 399g
Espionage Act of 1917 314
Essay on the First Principles of Government (Priestley) 300
"Essay on the Laboring Classes" (Brownson) 42
establishment clause. *See* separation of church and state
Ethical Culture movement 4–5
Ethiopia 133
Eucharist 399g
evangelical abolitionism 293
evangelical Calvinism 343
evangelical Catholicism 164, 165, 271–272
evangelicals 399g

evangelism. *See also* revivalism
  J. Wilbur Chapman 62–63
  Charles Edward Cheney 66
  Amzi Clarence Dixon 102–103
  Charles E. Fuller 140
  Billy Graham 152–154
  Rebecca Gratz 155
  Sam Jones 191–192
  James McCosh 240–241
  Aimee Semple McPherson 247–248
  Dwight Lyman Moody 255–256
  Samson Occom 279–280
  Arthur T. Pierson 293–294
  J. F. Rutherford 314
  Walter Scott 325
  Solomon Stoddard 345
  Barton W. Stone **346–348**
  Maria Woodworth-Etter 389
Evidences from Scripture and History of the Second Coming of Christ (Miller) 253
Evolution and Religion (Beecher) 20
evolutionary theory xvi. *See also* Darwinism
  Lyman Abbott 2
  Henry Ward Beecher 21
  William Porcher DuBose 106
  Washington Gladden 150
  Shailer Mathews 236
  Augustus H. Strong 348
Ewing, Finis **123–124**
excommunication
  Patrick Augustine Feehan 128
  Edward McGlynn 243
  David O. McKay 244
  Augusta E. Stetson 341, 342
existentialism 363

F
faith healing. *See* healing
Faith of Modernism, The (Mathews) 235–236
Faith of Our Fathers (Gibbons) 146–147
Falwell, Jerry **125–126**
Fard, Wallace 104, 127, 264, 266
Farrakhan, Louis Abdul **126–128**, 185, 265
FBI. *See* Federal Bureau of Investigation
Federal Bureau of Alcohol, Tobacco, and Firearms (ATF) 206, 207
Federal Bureau of Investigation (FBI) xiv, 206–207, 282
Federal Council of Churches 306
Federalist Party 301
Feehan, Patrick Augustine **128–129**
Female Hebrew Benevolent Society (FHBS) 155
feminism 14
Fifteenth Amendment 28
Fillmore, Charles Sherlock 100–101, **129–130**
Finney, Charles Grandison **130–131**
  Lyman Beecher 23
  Phineas F. Bresee 37
  Fanny Jackson Coppin 79
  Charles Hodge 171
  Edward Norris Kirk 204
  Asa Mahan 226
  John W. Nevin 271
First Great Awakening. *See* Great Awakening

First Vatican Council. *See* Vatican I
Flanagan, Edward Joseph **131–133,** *132*
Ford, Arnold Josiah **133–134**
Ford, Henry 274
Ford, Henry, II 328
Fordham University 177
Fosdick, Harry Emerson **134–135**
Fourteenth Amendment 366
Fox, Emmet **135–137**
Fox, George 197
Franciscans 250
Franklin, Benjamin 54, 186
fraud. *See* corruption/scandal
Free African Society 9
Free Church of Scotland 240
freedom of religion. *See* religious liberty
free love 277–278, 302
Free Methodist Church 310–311
Free Religious Association 70, 138–139
free thought movement 5
free will 367
Frelinghuysen, Theodorus Jacobus
     137–138, 358
French Revolution 300, 301, 344
frontier. *See* westward expansion
Frothingham, Octavius Brooks 71, **138–139**
Fugitive Blacksmith, The (Pennington) 292
Fugitive Slave Law 9
Fuller, Charles Edward **139–140**
Fuller, Margaret 166
Fuller, Melville Weston 67
fundamentalism xvi, 399g
     Amzi Clarence Dixon 102, 103
     Jerry Falwell **125–126**
     Harry Emerson Fosdick 134
     Charles E. Fuller **139–140,** 140
     James H. Garrison 145
     Bob Jones **187–188,** 188
     J. Gresham Machen 221–222
     Shailer Mathews 235–236
     J. Frank Norris 275–276
     Arthur T. Pierson 293–294
     Pat Robertson 311–312
     C. I. Scofield **322–323**
     Augustus H. Strong 349
     Reuben Archer Torrey 363–365
     Benjamin B. Warfield 371, 372
Fundamentalist, The (newspaper) 276
Fundamentals, The
     Amzi Clarence Dixon 102, 103
     Shailer Mathews 235
     Arthur T. Pierson 294
     Reuben Archer Torrey 364
fund-raising
     Richard Cardinal Cushing 89
     Charles Cardwell McCabe 239
     Samson Occom 279
     Gilbert Tennent 359

G
Gambier Theological Seminary 64
Garnet, Henry Highland **141–143,** *142*
Garrettson, Freeborn 9, **143–145**
Garrison, James Harvey **145–146**
Garvey, Marcus 133
Genesee Conference 310
geography 261, 262
George, Henry 81, 243
Georgetown University 55

German Reformed Church 32–33
Germany
     Johann Conrad Beissel 24
     John Philip Boehm 32
     David Einhorn 118
     George Rapp 304
     Henrietta Szold 354
     Benjamin B. Warfield 372
Gettysburg Theological Seminary 320
Ghost Dance 26, 391–392, 399g
Gibbons, Abby Hopper 28
Gibbons, James 146, **146–148,** *147,* 165
Ginzberg, Louis **148–149**
Gladden, Solomon Washington **149–150,**
     306
Glorious Revolution 230
glossolalia 374, 400g
God and Intelligence in Modern Philosophy
     (Sheen) 327
God in Christ (Bushnell) 45
God in Search of Man: A Philosophy of Judaism
     (Heschel) 168
"God's Girls" 209
Golden Age 314
Golden Hour of the Little Flower (radio show)
     84
Goldstein, David 13, 14
Gospel Advocate 219
Grace, Sweet Daddy **151–152**
Graham, Billy **152–154,** *153,* 188
Graham, William 6
Grant, Heber J. 244
Gratz, Rebecca *154,* **154–155,** 215
Gready, James 346
Great Awakening xvi, 400g. *See also* Second
     Great Awakening
     Archibald Alexander 7
     Isaac Backus 15, 16
     David Brainerd 33
     Charles Chauncy 65, 66
     Samuel Davies 93
     Jonathan Dickinson 100
     Jonathan Edwards 116
     Nathanael Emmons 121
     Theodorus Jacobus Frelinghuysen 137
     Elias Hicks 170
     Solomon Stoddard 345
     Gilbert Tennent 358, 359
     Bennet Tyler 367
     George Whitefield 377
Great Britain
     Francis Asbury 11, 12
     Thomas Coke 75, 76
     Dwight Lyman Moody 256
     Samson Occom 279
     William Penn 291
     Arthur T. Pierson 294
     George Whitefield 377
     Roger Williams 380–381
Great Case for Liberty of Conscience (Penn)
     291
Great Depression 84, 217, 218, 252
Great Harmonia (Davis) 95
Greely, Horace 28
Green, Claude 104
Greenfield Hill (Dwight) 110
Guideposts (magazine) 290
Gulliford, Helen 209
Guyana 189

H
Hadassah 354
Haiti 123
Hale, Edward Everett 13, **156–157,** *157*
Half-Moon peyote religion 286
Half-Way Covenant 400g
     Jonathan Edwards 116
     Jonathan Edwards, Jr. 117
     Increase Mather 232–233
     Richard Mather 234–235
     Jonathan Mitchell 254
     Solomon Stoddard 345
Hampton, John 227
Handsome Lake **157–159**
Hanukkah 400g
"Hare Krishna" (mantra) 97
Harmony Society 304–305
Harney, William S. 98
Harris, Thomas Lake **159–160**
Harrison, William Henry 361–362
Harvard University 108
Hasidism 400g
Haven, Gilbert **160–161**
Hawaii 91–93
Hayes, Rutherford B. 181
Haygood, Atticus Greene **161–163**
healing
     William Branham 34–35
     Edgar Cayce 60
     Kathryn Kuhlman 208, 209
     Aimee Semple McPherson 248
     Alma White 374
Hebrew Sunday School 155
Hebrew Union College
     Sabato Morais 261
     Abba Hillel Silver 330–331
     Isaac Mayer Wise 383
     Stephen S. Wise 384
Hebrew University in Jerusalem 149,
     224–225
Heck, Barbara Ruckle **163–164**
Hecker, Isaac Thomas **164–165**
Hedge, Frederic Henry **165–167**
heresy
     Lyman Beecher 23
     Charles A. Briggs 38–39
     Horace Bushnell 46
     Anne Hutchinson 179
     John W. Nevin 272
     James A. Pike 295, 296
     Philip Schaff 319
Herrmenz, Mordecai 133
Heschel, Abraham Joshua *167,* **167–169**
Hicks, Elias *169,* **169–170**
higher criticism
     Charles A. Briggs 38
     defined 38
     William Porcher DuBose 106
     James H. Garrison 145
     Washington Gladden 150
     Francis Spellman 339
     Augustus H. Strong 348
     Reuben Archer Torrey 364
     Benjamin B. Warfield 372
Higher Life movement 332, 400g
Himes, Joshua W. 253
Hinduism 31, 97–98, 281
History of the Christian Church (Schaff) 319
History of the Late Persecution (Pratt) 299

History of the Methodist Episcopal Church (Bangs) 18
Hitler, Adolf 85, 127, 385
Hodge, Charles 7, **170–172,** 372
Holiness movement 400g
    Phineas F. Bresee 37
    Asa Mahan 226
    Phoebe Palmer 284, 285
    Hannah Whitall Smith 332, **332–333**
    Alma White 374
    Maria Woodworth-Etter **388–389**
Holmes, John Haynes *172,* **172–173,** 384
Holocaust 400g
    Cyrus Adler 3
    Abraham Joshua Heschel 167, 168
    Abba Hillel Silver 331
    Henrietta Szold 354
    Stephen S. Wise 385
Holy Koran of the Moorish Holy Temple of Science 104
Holy Spirit 400g
Hooker, Thomas **173–174**
Hoover, Herbert 276
Hopkins, Emma Curtis 129
Hopkins, Samuel 117, 121, 367
Hour of Decision (radio show) 153
House of Representatives, U.S. 56, 214
House Un-American Activities Committee 283
Howe, Julia Ward 239
Hubbard, L. Ron **174–176**
Hughes, John Joseph 164, *176,* **176–177**
humanism 5
human rights 29, 199
Huntington, William Reed **177–178**
Huss, John 397
Hussein, Saddam 185, 186
Hutchinson, Anne Marbury xiv, **178–180**
    John Clarke 71
    John Cotton 83
    Mary Dyer 111
    Thomas Hooker 174
Hyde, Charles McEwen 92
hymns
    Johann Conrad Beissel 24
    Fanny Crosby **86–87**
    Samuel Davies 94
    Frederic Henry Hedge 165
    Parley P. Pratt 299
    Ira D. Sankey **317–318**

I

I Believe in Miracles (Kuhlman) 209
ICY. *See* Institute for Colored Youth
immersion 51. *See also* baptism; baptism, infant
immigrants
    Jean Lefebvre de Cheverus 68
    Sabato Morais 261
    Walter Rauschenbusch 306
    Martin Spalding 338
incarnation 400g
Independent Liberal Church 138, 139
India 97, 98, 379
Industrial Revolution/industrialization
    Washington Gladden 150
    Edward McGlynn 243
    Reinhold Niebuhr 274
    Walter Rauschenbusch 306
    Josiah Strong 350

infallibility. *See* biblical infallibility; papal infallibility
infant baptism. *See* baptism, infant
Ingersoll, Ebon Clark 181, 182
Ingersoll, Robert Green **181–182**
In His Steps (Sheldon) 330
Inner Light 169–170
Institute for Colored Youth (ICY) 79, 80
Institutes of Natural and Revealed Religion (Priestley) 300
institution builders xiv–xv
integration 161. *See also* civil rights; segregation
International Society for Krishna Consciousness (ISKON) 97–98
Introduction to Philosophy (Johnson) 186
Ireland 128, 131, 182, 358
Ireland, John 81–82, 147, **182–183**
Iroquois language 395
Iroquois religion 157–158
Isis Unveiled (Blavatsky) 31, 281
Islam 127, 373–374. *See also* Nation of Islam
Islam, Our Choice 373
Israel 224, 331. *See also* Jewish state; Palestine
Ivanhoe (Scott) 154

J

Jackson, Jesse 127, **184–186,** *185*
James, William xiii, xv, 10
James II, king of England 327
Jefferson, Thomas
    Cyrus Adler 3
    William Ellery Channing 61
    Nathanael Emmons 121
    Handsome Lake 158
    John Leland 216
    Joseph Priestley 301
    Roger Williams 382
"Jefferson Bible" 3
Jehovah's Witnesses 312–315
jeremiad 400g
Jerome Agreement 286
Jerusalem 354
Jesuits
    Black Elk 27
    John Carroll 54
    Pierre-Jean De Smet 98
    Eusebio Francisco Kino 202
    John Courtney Murray 269
Jesus Christ and the Human Quest (Lewis) 218
Jewish Encyclopedia, The 148, 249
Jewish law 118
Jewish nationalism 224
Jewish state 3, 118, 330, 331
Jewish Sunday schools 215
Jewish Theological Seminary 249
John Birch Society 90
John Paul II, Pope 93, 105, 358
Johnson, Lyndon 275
Johnson, Samuel **186–187**
John XXIII, Pope 89, 339
Jones, Bob **187–188**
Jones, Jim xiv, **188–190**
Jones, Rufus Matthew **190–191**
Jones, Sam **191–192**
Jonestown 207
Joseph, Brother 91
Jubilee College 64

Judaism
    Cyrus Adler **2–4**
    Felix Adler 4
    Conservative. *See* Conservative Judaism
    David Einhorn **118–119**
    Arnold J. Ford **133–134**
    Louis Ginzberg **148–149**
    Rebecca Gratz **154–155**
    Abraham Joshua Heschel **167–169**
    Mordecai M. Kaplan **195–196**
    Isaac Leeser **214–216**
    Judah L. Magnes **224–225**
    H. Pereira Mendes **248–250**
    Sabato Morais **260–261**
    Orthodox. *See* Orthodox Judaism
    Reconstructionist. *See* Reconstructionist Judaism
    Reform. *See* Reform Judaism
    Menachem Mendel Schneerson **321–322**
    Sephardic 260, 402g
    Abba Hillel Silver **330–331**
    Milton Steinberg **340–341**
    Henrietta Szold **353–355**
    Isaac M. Wise **382–383**
    Stephen S. Wise **383–385**
Judson, Adoniram **192–194,** *193*
juvenile delinquency 132

K

Kahnawake 357
Kansas-Nebraska Bill 21
Kaplan, Mordecai Menahem **195–196,** 340
Keane, John J. 147
kehillah 224, 400g
Keith, George **196–198**
Keller, Helen 41
Kennedy, John F.
    Richard Cardinal Cushing 88, 89
    Malcolm X 229
    Elijah Muhammad 265
    Francis Spellman 339, 340
Kennedy, Joseph P. 89, 339
Kennedy, Rose 89
Kenyon College 64
Keswick movement 294, 332
Key to the Science of Theology (Pratt) 299
Kimball, Spencer Woolley **198–199**
King, Martin Luther, Jr. 199, **199–201**
    Eugene Carson Blake 30
    Abraham Joshua Heschel 168
    Jesse Jackson 184
    Malcolm X 228, 229
    Elijah Muhammad 266
King, Thomas Starr *201,* **201–202**
King James Bible 319, 323
King Philip's War 120, 233
King's College 186
Kino, Eusebio Francisco **202–203**
Kirk, Edward Norris **203–204**
Kirkland, James 53
KKK. *See* Ku Klux Klan
Knights of Columbus 147
Know-Nothing Party 338
Knudson, Albert Cornelius **205–206**
Kohler, Kaufman 119
Koran (Qur'an) 401g
Korea 259
Koresh, David xiv, **206–207**

Kosovo war 185
Kozlowski, Anthony 128
Krauth, Charles Porterfield **207–208**
Krishna 97–98
Kuhlman, Kathryn **208–209**
Ku Klux Klan (KKK) 374–375

L

labor unions 73, 150, 274
Lakota Sioux 26, 27, 99, 391, 392
Lammers, Arthur 60
Lamy, Jean Baptiste **210–211**
Latter-day Saints. *See* Church of Jesus Christ
   of Latter-day Saints
Latter Day Saint's Messenger and Advocate 309
LaVey, Anton Szandor **211–212**
lay leaders 154–155, 163–164
lay preachers 13, 14, 284–285
Lee, Ann **212–213**
Lee, Jesse **213–214**
Leeser, Isaac **214–216,** *215*
Legends of the Jews (Ginzberg) 148
Lehure und Wehre 371
Leland, John **216–217**
Leo XIII, Pope
   Francesca Cabrini 48
   Michael Augustine Corrigan 82
   Katharine Drexel 104
   James Gibbons 147
   Isaac Hecker 165
   John Ireland 183
   John A. Ryan 316
"Leper Priest of Molokai" 91–93
Letter from a Birmingham Jail (King) 200
Letters to God and the Devil (Ames) 10
Lewis, Edwin **217–218**
liberalism (liberal theology) xvi
   Edward Scribner Ames 10–11
   Henry Ward Beecher 20–21
   Charles A. Briggs 38
   Horace Bushnell 46
   William Ellery Channing 61
   Charles Chauncy 65
   James Freeman Clarke 70
   Henry Sloane Coffin 74–75
   William Porcher DuBose 105, 106
   Harry Emerson Fosdick 134–135
   Elias Hicks 169–170
   John Ireland 182–183
   Rufus Jones 190
   Albert Cornelius Knudson 205
   Edwin Lewis 217–218
   J. Gresham Machen 221–222
   Douglas Clyde Macintosh 222, 223
   Shailer Mathews 235–236
   Jonathan Mayhew 237–238
   John W. McGarvey 242
   H. Richard Niebuhr 273
   Reinhold Niebuhr 274
   James A. Pike 295
   Reverdy C. Ransom 303–304
   John A. Ryan 315–316
   Solomon Stoddard 344
   Augustus H. Strong 348–349
   Josiah Strong 350
Liberia 57–58, 87–88, 161
Liberty Federation 126
Life Experience and Gospel Labors of the Rt.
   Rev. Richard Allen 8–9

Life Is Worth Living (television show) 328
Liliuokalani, Princess 91
Lincoln, Abraham
   Phillips Brooks 41
   Peter Cartwright 56
   John Hughes 177
   Edward Norris Kirk 204
   Charles Cardwell McCabe 239
   Sabato Morais 260
   Paschal Beverly Randolph 302
   Henry McNeal Turner 365
Lipscomb, David **218–220**
liturgical movement 251–252, 400g
liturgical reform 178, 251–252
liturgy 400g
"living wage" 315, 316
Living Wage: Its Ethical and Economic Aspects
   (Ryan) 315
"Log College" 359, 360
Longhouse Religion 157–159
Longingqua Oceani 183
Lord's Prayer 137
Lord's Supper 116, 137, 344, 345. *See also*
   Half-Way Covenant
Los Angeles
   Phineas F. Bresee 37
   Billy Graham 152
   Aimee Semple McPherson 247–248
   G. Bromley Oxnam 282
   Reuben Archer Torrey 364
"Lost-Found Nation of Islam" 104, 264
Louis XVI, king of France 344
Louis XVIII, king of France 68
Loyalists 326
Lubavitcher Hasidim 321–322
Luce, Clare Boothe 328
Luther, Martin 165
Lutheran and Missionary magazine 208
Lutheran Church
   Charles Porterfield Krauth **207–208**
   Henry Melchior Muhlenberg **266–267**
   George Rapp 304
   Samuel Schmucker **320–321**
   Paul Tillich 362
   C. F. W. Walther **370–371**
   Nikolaus Ludwig von Zinzendorf 396
Lutheranism, conservative 370–371
lynching 53

M

MacArthur, Douglas 132
Machen, John Gresham **221–222**
Macintosh, Douglas Clyde **222–223**
MacMurray, J. W. 336
Madison, James 216
Magnes, Judah Leon **224–225**
Mahan, Asa **225–226**
Makemie, Francis **226–227**
Making of the Modern Jew (Steinberg) 340
Malcolm X 127, **227–230,** *228,* 264–265
Man Is Not Alone: A Philosophy of Religion
   (Heschel) 168
Manual of the Mother Church 114
"Man Without a Country, The" (Hale) 156
March on Washington (1963) 30, 200, 228,
   229
Marty, Martin 104
Marx, Karl 13
mass 400g

Massachusetts Bay Colony xiv
   John Clarke 71–72
   John Cotton 82–84
   Henry Dunster 107–108
   Mary Dyer 111
   Thomas Hooker 173, 174
   Anne Hutchinson 178–180
   Cotton Mather 230
   Roger Williams 381
Mather, Cotton **230–232,** *231*
   Henry Dunster 108
   Francis Makemie 227
   Increase Mather 232, 233
   Richard Mather 234
   Jonathan Mitchell 255
Mather, Increase 230, *232,* **232–233,** 234
Mather, Richard 230, 232, **233–235**
Mathews, Shailer **235–236**
Maurin, Aristide Peter 96, **236–237**
Mayhew, Jonathan **237–238**
McCabe, Charles Cardwell **238–240**
McCarthy, Joseph 90, 339
McCosh, James **240–241**
McCullough, Walter 152
McGarvey, John William **241–242**
McGlynn, Edward 81, **242–244**
McKay, David Oman **244–245**
McKendree, William 55, **245–246**
McPherson, Aimee Semple **246–248,** *247*
Meacham, H. C. 276
Meaning of Revelation, The (Niebuhr) 273
medicine 378
Mendes, Henry Pereira **248–250,** 383
mental health 288–289
"Mercersburg theology" 271–272, 319
Merton, Thomas **250–251**
mesmerism 94, 400g
Messiah 259, 322
Methodist Church
   Richard Allen **8–10**
   Francis Asbury **11–13**
   Nathan Bangs **18–19**
   Phineas F. Bresee 36, 37
   S. Parkes Cadman **49–50**
   Warren Akin Candler **52–54**
   Peter Cartwright **55–57**
   Thomas Coke **75–76**
   Freeborn Garrettson **143–145**
   Gilbert Haven **160–161**
   Atticus Haygood **161–163**
   Barbara Heck **163–164**
   Jim Jones 188
   Sam Jones **191–192**
   Albert Cornelius Knudson **205–206**
   Jesse Lee **213–214,** 214
   Edwin Lewis **217–218**
   Charles Cardwell McCabe **238–240**
   William McKendree **245–246**
   John Humphrey Noyes 277
   Garfield Bromley Oxnam **282–283**
   Phoebe Palmer **284–285**
   Norman Vincent Peale **288–290**
   Joseph Pilmore **296–297**
   Benjamin Titus Roberts **310–311**
   Orange Scott **323–325**
   Hannah Whitall Smith 332
   Alma White 374
   Ellen G. White 375
Methodist Missionary Society 18

Method of Divine Government (McCosh) 240
Mexico 44, 203
Michel, Virgil George **251–252**
"Mighty Fortress Is Our God" 165
Millar, M. F. X. 316
millennialism/millenarianism 400g
    Amzi Clarence Dixon 102
    William Miller 253
    Charles Taze Russell 313
    C. I. Scofield 322, 323
    Smohalla 336
Miller, William **252–254,** 375
Millerites 375
Million Man March 127
Mills, B. Fay 62
Milosevic, Slobodan 185
Minhag America (Wise) 383
minimum wage 315
missionaries xiv, 400g
    James Lloyd Breck **35–36**
    Francesca Cabrini **48–49**
    Alexander Crummell 87
    Father Damien **91–93**
    Pierre-Jean De Smet **98–99**
    Katharine Drexel **104–105**
    Philippine Duchesne **106–107**
    Jonathan Edwards, Jr. 118
    John Eliot **119–120**
    Henry Highland Garnet 143
    Adoniram Judson **192–194**
    Eusebio Francisco Kino **202–203**
    Jean Baptiste Lamy **210–211**
    David O. McKay 244
    Lottie Moon **257–258**
    Sun Myung Moon 259
    John R. Mott 263–264
    Marcus Whitman **378–379**
    Robert Wilder **379–380**
    David Zeisberger **395–396**
    Nikolaus Ludwig von Zinzendorf **396–397**
Missouri
    Parley P. Pratt 299
    Sidney Rigdon 309
    Joseph Smith, Jr. 334
    Joseph Smith III 335
    Brigham Young 393
Missouri Synod 370
Mitchell, Hinckley G. 205
Mitchell, Jonathan **254–255**
modernity xvi
Modern Thought 129
Mohawk Nation 357, 395
monasticism 400g
Mondale, Walter 184
monism 349
monotheism 400g
Montauk Nation 279
Moody, Dwight Lyman 255, **255–257**
    J. Wilbur Chapman 62
    Henry Sloane Coffin 74
    Fanny Crosby 86
    Amzi Clarence Dixon 102, 103
    John R. Mott 263
    Arthur T. Pierson 294
    Ira D. Sankey 317, 318
    C. I. Scofield 323
    Reuben Archer Torrey 364
    Robert P. Wilder 379

Moody Bible Institute 255, 256
Moon, Lottie 257, **257–258**
Moon, Sun Myung **259–260**
"Moonies" 260
Moorish Temple 103–104
Moorish Zionist Temple, Inc. 133
Morais, Sabato 3, 249, **260–261,** 383
Moral Majority 124, 125
Moral Man and Immoral Society (Niebuhr) 274
Moravian Brethren 400g
Moravian Church 32, 266, 397
Moravians 395–397
Mormons. *See* Church of Jesus Christ of Latter-day Saints
Morris, Samuel 101
Morse, Jedidiah 61, 117, **261–263**
Moses, chief of the Sinkiuse 336
Moslem World 373
mosque 400g
Mott, John Raleigh **263–264**
Mount Hermon Hundred 294
Mount Hermon School 256
Muhammad, Elijah 127, 228–229, **264–266,** 265
Muhammad, W. Deen 127
Muhlenberg, Henry Melchior **266–267**
Muldoon, Peter 128
Müller, Bernhard 305
Mullins, Edgar Young **267–269,** 268
Murray, James 136
Murray, John Courtney **269–270,** 339
music, in worship 219, 242. *See also* hymns
Muslim 400g
Muslim Mosque, Inc. 229, 265
Mutual Broadcasting Network 140
MX missile program 198
Mystery Hid from Ages and Generations, Made Manifest by the Gospel-Revelation (Chauncy) 66
Mystical Presence, The (Nevin) 271

N

NAACP. *See* National Association for the Advancement of Colored People
Nation, The 139
National Association for the Advancement of Colored People (NAACP)
    Katharine Drexel 105
    Harry Emerson Fosdick 135
    John Haynes Holmes 172
    Adam Clayton Powell, Sr. 298
    Reverdy C. Ransom 303, 304
    Stephen S. Wise 384
National Catholic Welfare Conference 44
National Conference of Unitarian and Other Christian Churches 25, 26
National Council of Churches 400g
National Council of the Churches of Christ in the United States of America (NCC) 59
National Negro Convention 9
National Vespers Hour (radio program) 135
National Woman Suffrage Association 28
Nation of Islam
    Timothy Drew 103, 104
    Louis Abdul Farrakhan **126–128**
    Malcolm X **227–230**
    Elijah Muhammad **264–266**

Native American Christianity
    Samson Occom 279, 280
    Kateri Tekakwitha 357–358
    Wovoka 391
Native American Church 400g
Native American education 198
Native American missions
    David Brainerd 33, 34
    James Lloyd Breck 36
    Pierre-Jean De Smet 98–99
    Katharine Drexel 104, 105
    Philippine Duchesne 106, 107
    John Eliot 119, 120
    Virgil Michel 252
    Samson Occom 279–280
    Marcus Whitman 378
    David Zeisberger 395
    Nikolaus Ludwig von Zinzendorf 397
Native Americans. *See also* specific tribes/nations
    Black Elk **26–27**
    Handsome Lake **157–159**
    Jedidiah Morse 262
    Samson Occom 279–280
    Quanah Parker **285–286**
    Smohalla **336–337**
    Kateri Tekakwitha **357–358**
    Tenskwatawa **360–362**
    John Woolman 390
    Wovoka **391–392**
Nauvoo 334, 335
Nazarites 310
Nazism 362, 384–385. *See also* Holocaust
NCC (National Council of the Churches of Christ in the United States of America) 59
Neander, Johann August 271
Neihardt, John G. 26, 27
neoorthodoxy 217, 218, 400g
Nevin, John Williamson **271–272,** 319
New Age spirituality 59
New Church 400g
New Deal 306, 316
New Divinity xvi, 65, 120–121, 366, 367
New Era, The (Strong) 350
New Harmony community 305
New Haven theology
    Lyman Beecher 23
    Charles Hodge 171
    Nathaniel William Taylor 356–357
    Bennet Tyler 367
New Lebanon community 213
"New Lights" 65, 93, 377
New School Methodism 310
New School Presbyterianism 7
New Side Presbyterianism 100
"New South" 161
New Thought 129, 135–136, 401g
New Views of Christianity, Society, and the Church (Brownson) 42
New York Tribune 28
Niagara Movement 304
Nicene Creed 401g
Niebuhr, Helmut Richard **272–273**
Niebuhr, Reinhold 74, 272, **274–275,** 362
Nineteenth Amendment 28
"Ninety and Nine, The" 317
Nixon, Richard M. 153, 290
Nobel Peace Prize 191, 200, 263, 264

No Man Knows My History (Brodie) 244
Non Abiamo Bisogno 339
nonviolent protest 200
Norris, J. Frank **275–277**
Northfield Academy 256
Nostra Aetate 168
Nothern Paiute Nation 391
Noyes, John Humphrey **277–278**

O
Oberlin College
    Lyman Beecher 23
    Antoinette Brown Blackwell 28
    Fanny Jackson Coppin 79
    Charles Finney 131
    Asa Mahan 225–226
*Observations on the Slavery of Africans and
    Their Descendants* (Hicks) 169
*Occident and the American Jewish Advocate,
    The* (newspaper) 215
Occom, Samson **279–280**
occult 30, 31, 60, 353, 401*g*
O'Connell, Henry 339
O'Kelly, James 246
Olcott, Henry Steel 31, **280–282**, *281*
Old Fashioned Revival Hour (radio program)
    139, 140
"Old Lights" 65, 377
Old School Methodism 310
Old School Presbyterianism 7, 23, 171
Old Side Presbyterianism 100
Old-Time Gospel Hour (television show)
    125, 126
Oliphant, Laurence 159
"O Little Town of Bethlehem" (Brooks) 41
Oneida colony 207, 277
Oneida Nation 279
Operation PUSH (People United to Save
    Humanity) 184, 185
Orate Fratres (journal) 252
Organization of African Unity 229
original sin 121, 356, 401*g. See also*
    Calvinism
orphanages 155
Orthodox Judaism 401*g*
    Mordecai M. Kaplan 195
    H. Pereira Mendes **248–250**, *249*
    Sabato Morais 260–261
    Menachem Mendel Schneerson
        321–322
    Isaac Mayer Wise 382, 383
Orthodox Presbyterian Church 222
orthodoxy 372. *See also* fundamentalism
*Other Side, The: An Account of My Experiences
    with Psychic Phenomena* (Pike) 296
Ottaviani, Augustus 270
Our Brother in Black (Haygood) 162
*Our Country: Its Possible Future and Its
    Present Crisis* (Strong) 350
Outlines of Mahayana Buddhism (Suzuki) 353
Outlook, The 1, 2
"Out of the Shadow-Lands" 318
Oxford movement 401*g*
Oxnam, Garfield Bromley **282–283**
oxygen 300

P
Pacelli, Eugenio 339
Pacific Northwest Indians 336

pacifism
    Harry Emerson Fosdick 135
    John Haynes Holmes 172
    David Lipscomb 219
    Douglas Clyde Macintosh 223
    Judah L. Magnes 224
    John Woolman 390
Paine College 53
Palestine
    Judah L. Magnes 224
    Abba Hillel Silver 330, 331
    Henrietta Szold 354
    Stephen S. Wise 385
Palestinian Jews 3
Palmer, Phoebe Worrall **284–285**
papal infallibility 337, 338, 401*g*
Parker, Quanah **285–286**, 286
Parker, Theodore 70, 138, **287–288**
Parks, Rosa 199
Paul, Moses 280
Paulists 164–165
Paul VI, Pope 73, 168
Payne, John 87
Peace Mission movement 100–102
Peace of Soul (Sheen) 328
Peale, Norman Vincent 136, **288–290**, 289
Penn, William 197, **290–292**, *291*
Pennington, James William Charles **292–293**
Pennsylvania 291
Pentateuch 401*g*
Pentecostal Christianity
    Sweet Daddy Grace **151–152**
    Jim Jones 189
    Aimee Semple McPherson **246–248**
    Alma White **373–374**
    Maria Woodworth-Etter 389
Pentecostalism 401*g*
People from the Other World (Olcott) 281
People's Temple xiv, 189, 401*g*
perfectionistic theology
    Phineas F. Bresee 37
    Asa Mahan 226
    John Humphrey Noyes 277–278
    Phoebe Palmer 284
    Hannah Whitall Smith 332
personalism 205
Petty, Sir William 300
peyote 284–285
philanthropy 105
Philippines 373
Philosophy of Personalism, The (Bowne) 205
Pierson, Arthur Tappan **293–295**
pietism 24, 320, 401*g*
Pike, James Albert **295–296**
Pillar of Fire 374
Pilmore, Joseph **296–297**
Pima Indians 203
Pius IX, Pope 164, 210, 339
Pius XI, Pope 44, 49
Pius XII, Pope 49, 73, 339
Plan of Union 7, 118
Plymouth Colony 108
polygamy
    Quanah Parker 285
    Parley P. Pratt 299, 300
    Joseph Smith, Jr. 334
    Joseph Smith III 335
    Wilford Woodruff 387
    Brigham Young 393

Posey, Thomas 6
positive thinking 129, 136, 288–290
postmillennialism 102
Potawatomi Nation 98, 107
Powell, Adam Clayton, Jr. 298
Powell, Adam Clayton, Sr. **297–299**
Power of Positive Thinking (Peale) 136, 288,
    289
Pratt, Parley Parker **299–300**, 309
predestination 401*g*
premillennial dispensationalism 322, 323
premillennialism 102, 294, 322, 323
Presbyterianism/Presbyterian Church 401*g*
    Archibald Alexander **6–8**
    Lyman Beecher 23
    Eugene Blake **29–30**
    David Brainerd **33–34**
    Charles A. Briggs 38
    Orestes A. Brownson 42
    J. Wilbur Chapman **62–63**
    Henry Sloane Coffin **74–75**
    Samuel Davies **93–94**
    Jonathan Dickinson **99–100**
    Finis Ewing **123–124**
    Charles Finney 130
    Harry Emerson Fosdick 134
    Henry Highland Garnet **141–143**
    Charles Hodge **170–172**
    Edward Norris Kirk 203–204
    J. Gresham Machen **221–222**
    Francis Makemie **226–227**
    John W. Nevin 271
    Samson Occom **279–280**
    Arthur T. Pierson **293–295**
    John Holt Rice **307–308**
    C. I. Scofield 323
    Billy Sunday 352
    Gilbert Tennent **358–359**
    William Tennent **359–360**
    Benjamin B. Warfield **371–373**
    John Witherspoon **385–387**
presidential campaigns
    Lyman Abbott 2
    Charles E. Coughlin 85
    Richard Cardinal Cushing 89
    Jerry Falwell 126
    Louis Farrakhan 127
    Robert Ingersoll 181
    Jesse Jackson 184–185
    J. Frank Norris 276
    Sidney Rigdon 309
    Pat Robertson 311, 312
    John A. Ryan 316
    Joseph Smith, Jr. 334
Presidential Medal of Freedom 275
Priestley, Joseph **300–301**
Princeton Theological Seminary 7
Princeton University 94, 100, 240
Principles of Mosaic Religion, The (Einhorn)
    118
*Principles of Nature, Her Divine Revelations,
    and a Voice to Mankind* (Davis) 95
Progress and Poverty (George) 243
Progressive reform. See social reform
progressivism. *See also* social activism; social
    reform
    Lyman Abbott 2
    Michael Augustine Corrigan 81
    James Gibbons 147
    Walter Rauschenbusch 306

prophecy 389
Prophetstown 361–362
Protestantism xv, xvi, 401g. *See also* specific
   religions
"Protestant principle" 363
Protestant Reformation. *See* Reformation
Protestant Unionist, The 325
psychic phenomena 281, 295, 296
psychics 59–60
Puritans/Puritanism 401g
   Charles Chauncy 65
   John Cotton **82–84**
   Henry Dunster **107–109**
   Mary Dyer 111
   John Eliot **119–120**
   Thomas Hooker **173–174**
   Anne Hutchinson **178–180**
   Cotton Mather **230–232**
   Increase Mather **232–233**
   Richard Mather **233–235**
   Jonathan Mitchell **254–255**
   Solomon Stoddard **344–346**
   Roger Williams **380–382**

Q

Quakers 401g
   Mary Dyer **110–112**
   Elias Hicks **169–170**
   Rufus Jones **190–191**
   George Keith **196–198**
   William Penn **290–292**
   Hannah Whitall Smith **332–333**
   Roger Williams 382
   John Woolman **389–391**
Quimby, Phineas Parkhurst 113, 136
Quorum of the Twelve Apostles
   Spencer W. Kimball 198
   David O. McKay 244, 245
   Parley P. Pratt 299
   Wilford Woodruff 387
Qur'an (Koran) 401g

R

rabbi 401g
racism 304, 350
Radical, The 139
radio broadcasting
   S. Parkes Cadman 50
   Charles E. Coughlin 84–85
   Richard Cardinal Cushing 89
   Jerry Falwell 125
   Harry Emerson Fosdick 135
   Charles E. Fuller 139–140
   Billy Graham 153
   Norman Vincent Peale 288
   Fulton J. Sheen 328
Randolph, Paschal Beverly **302–303**
Rankin, Thomas 12, 297
Ransom, Reverdy Cassius **303–304**
Rapp, George **304–305**
Rauschenbusch, Walter 135, **305–307**
Ray, James Earl 200
Reagan, Ronald 126
rebbe 401g
Reconstruction Amendments 366
Reconstructionist Judaism 195–196, 340,
   401g
rector 401g
Redemptionist order 164

Red River War 285
reform. *See* social activism/social reform
Reformation 52, 315, 319, 401g
Reformed doctrine 170
Reformed Episcopal Church 66–67
reformed theology/churches 402g
Reformers. *See* Disciples of Christ
Reforming Synod 233
Reform Judaism 402g
   Felix Adler 4
   David Einhorn **118–119**
   Isaac Leeser 215
   H. Pereira Mendes 249
   Sabato Morais 260–261
   Menachem Mendel Schneerson 322
   Abba Hillel Silver **330–331**
   Isaac M. Wise **382–383**
   Stephen S. Wise **383–385**
Regent University 312
Religion (Ames) 10
religious conservatism. *See* conservatism
religious conversion. *See* conversion
   experiences
religious liberalism. *See* liberalism
religious liberty
   Isaac Backus 15–16
   John Leland 216–217
   John Courtney Murray 270
   William Penn 290–291
   Francis Spellman 339
*Reminiscences of School Life and Hints on
   Teaching* (Coppin) 79
Reno, Janet 206
Reorganized Church of Jesus Christ of
   Latter-Day Saints xiv
   Joseph Smith III **335–336**
repentance 402g
reprobation 124
Republican Methodist Church 246
Republican Party
   Robert Ingersoll 181
   Pat Robertson 311, 312
   Billy Sunday 352
   Henry McNeal Turner 365
Rerum Novarum 316
restorationist movement. *See also* Disciples
   of Christ
   John W. McGarvey 241
   Parley P. Pratt 299
   Sidney Rigdon 308
   Barton W. Stone 346
retribution 17
revelation 273
revivalism 402g. *See also* evangelism
   Archibald Alexander 7
   Lyman Beecher 22, 23
   David Brainerd 33
   William Branham 35
   Phineas F. Bresee 37
   J. Wilbur Chapman 62–63
   Charles Chauncy 65
   Fanny Crosby 86
   Jonathan Dickinson 100
   Jonathan Edwards 115, 116
   Finis Ewing 123, 124
   Charles Finney **130–131**
   Theodorus Jacobus Frelinghuysen 137
   Billy Graham **152–154**
   Bob Jones **187–188**

   Sam Jones 191–192, **191–192**
   Edward Norris Kirk 204
   Charles Porterfield Krauth 207, 208
   Asa Mahan 226
   Charles Cardwell McCabe 239
   Dwight Lyman Moody **255–257**
   Ira D. Sankey 317–318
   Barton W. Stone 346
   Billy Sunday **351–352**
   Nathaniel William Taylor 356, 357
   Reuben Archer Torrey **363–365**
   Bennet Tyler 366, 367
   George Whitefield **376–378**
Revolutionary War
   Francis Asbury 12
   Isaac Backus 16
   John Carroll 54
   Charles Chauncy 66
   Timothy Dwight 109
   Freeborn Garrettson 143, 144
   Handsome Lake 157
   Barbara Heck 163
   Ann Lee 212
   Jesse Lee 214
   Jonathan Mayhew 238
   William McKendree 245
   Henry Melchior Muhlenberg 267
   Samuel Seabury 326, 327
   Ezra Stiles 343, 344
   John Witherspoon 386
   David Zeisberger **395–396**
Rhode Island 380–382
Rice, John Holt **307–308**
Rigdon, Sidney 299, **308–309**, 334
Rightly Dividing the Word of Truth (Scofield)
   323
Rights of Conscience Unalienable (Leland) 217
Riverside Church 135
Roberts, Benjamin Titus **310–311**
Robertson, Pat **311–312**
Robinson, Ezekial 348
Rochester Theological Seminary 348–349
Rockefeller, John D. 134
Roden, George 206
Roden, Lois 206
Roman Catholicism. *See* Catholic Church
Roosevelt, Franklin D.
   Charles E. Coughlin 85
   John A. Ryan 316
   Abba Hillel Silver 331
   Francis Spellman 339–340
   Stephen S. Wise 385
Roosevelt, Theodore
   Lyman Abbott 2
   James Gibbons 147
   Edward Everett Hale 156
   Quanah Parker 286
Rosicrucian Fraternity 302–303
Rosicrucianism 302–303, 402g
Russell, Charles Taze **312–313**, 314
Rutherford, Joseph Franklin 313, **314–315**
Ryan, John Augustine **315–316**
Ryan, Leo 189
Ryman, Tom 192

S

sabbath 402g
Sabbath Prayer Book (Kaplan) 195
sacrament 402g

St. Joseph's Mission 98
St. Patrick's Cathedral 177
saints xv, 49, 104, 105, 358, 402g
Salem witch trials 230–231, 233
Salvation Army 402g
Sanitary Commission, U.S. 26
Sankey, Ira David 86, 256, **317–318,** *318*
Satanic Bible, The (LaVey) 211
Satanism 211–212, 402g
Satolli, Francesco 243
satori 353
Sayville community 101
scandal. *See* corruption/scandal
Schaff, Philip 271–272, **319–320**
Schechter, Solomon 148
Schlatter, Michael 32
Schmucker, Samuel Simon 207, 208,
    320–321
Schneerson, Menachem Mendel **321–322**
science 236, 300, 301
Science and Health: With Key to the Scriptures
    (Eddy) 113, 114, 342
science fiction 175
Scientology 174–176, 402g
Scofield, Cyrus Ingerson **322–323**
Scofield Reference Bible 322, 323
Scott, Orange **323–325**
Scott, Sir Walter 154
Scott, Walter **325–326**
Scottish realism 240
scriptures 402g
Seabury, Samuel **326–327**
Second Great Awakening 16, 356, 402g
Second Messiah 259
Second Vatican Council. *See* Vatican II
Secret Doctrine, The (Blavatsky) 31
see 402g
segregation 160, 161, 182, 188. *See also* civil
    rights
Seixas, Isaac B. 215
Selective Service Act 264
Semple, Robert James 247
Senate, U.S. 157, 214
Seneca Nation 33
separation of church and state
    Isaac Backus 15–16
    John England 122
    Jerry Falwell 126
    John Ireland 183
    John Leland 216–217
    John Courtney Murray 269–270
    G. Bromley Oxnam 283
    William Penn 291
    John A. Ryan 316
    Roger Williams 382
Sephardic Judaism 260, 402g
"serpent's seed" 35
Seton Hall College 19
700 Club (television show) 312
Seven Storey Mountain (Merton) 250, 251
Seventh-Day Adventist Church 253,
    375–376, 402g
Seventh Day Baptists 24–25
sexuality. *See* "complex marriage"; free love
sexuality, celestial 159, 160
sexual magic 302–303
Seymour, William 101
Shabbazz, Qubilah 127
Shakers 212–213, 402g

Shawnee Prophet. *See* Tenskwatawa
Sheen, Fulton John **327–329,** *328*
Sheldon, Charles Monroe **329–330**
Shepard, Thomas 254
Short Essay on Universalism (Ballou) 17
*Short History of the Methodists, in the United
    States of America* (Lee) 214
Silver, Abba Hillel **330–331**
single tax 243
"Sinners in the Hands of an Angry God"
    115–116
Sitting Bull 99
slavery. *See also* abolitionism
    Richard Allen 8–9
    Lyman Beecher 23
    Lott Cary 57
    William Ellery Channing 61
    Arnold J. Ford 133
    Henry Highland Garnet 141, 143
    Freeborn Garrettson 144
    Gilbert Haven 160–161
    John Ireland 182
    Theodore Parker 287
    James W. C. Pennington 292–293
    Orange Scott 323
    Ezra Stiles 343
    Augustin Verot 368, 369
    John Woolman 390
SLCC. *See* Southern Christian Leadership
    Conference
Smith, Alfred 276, 316
Smith, Ellen Gould Harmon. *See* White,
    Ellen Gould Harmon
Smith, George Albert 244
Smith, Gerald L. K. 85
Smith, Hannah Whitall **332–333**
Smith, Joseph, Jr. *333,* **333–334**
    David O. McKay 244
    Parley P. Pratt 299, 300
    Sidney Rigdon 309
    Wilford Woodruff 387
    Brigham Young 393, 394
Smith, Joseph, III **335–336**
Smith, Robert Pearsall 332
Smithsonian Institute 3
Smohalla **336–337**
social activism/social reform. *See also*
    Catholic Worker movement; civil rights;
    Social Gospel
    Martha Moore Avery 14
    Henry Ward Beecher 21
    Lyman Beecher 22
    Antoinette Brown Blackwell 28
    Eugene Carson Blake 29, 30
    Phillips Brooks 41
    Orestes A. Brownson 42
    John J. Burke 44–45
    Francesca Cabrini 48–49
    Michael Augustine Corrigan 81
    Dorothy Day 95–97
    Sweet Daddy Grace 151–152
    Rebecca Gratz 155
    Atticus Haygood 161–163
    John Haynes Holmes 172–173
    Jim Jones 189
    Asa Mahan 225–226
    Edward McGlynn 242, 243
    Sabato Morais 261
    Reinhold Niebuhr 274

    G. Bromley Oxnam 283
    Phoebe Palmer 284
    Theodore Parker 287
    Adam Clayton Powell, Sr. 298
    Walter Rauschenbusch 306
    John A. Ryan 315–316
    Charles Sheldon 329–330
    Josiah Strong 349, 350
    Nathaniel William Taylor 356, 357
Social Gospel 402g
    Harry Emerson Fosdick 135
    Washington Gladden 149–150
    G. Bromley Oxnam 282, 283
    Reverdy C. Ransom 303
    Walter Rauschenbusch 305–306
    Charles Sheldon 330
    Josiah Strong 349, 350
    Nathaniel William Taylor 356
socialism 13–14, 362
Socialism: The Nation of Fatherless Children
    (Avery) 14
Socialist Party 274
Social Justice (newspaper) 85
social reform. *See* social activism/social
    reform
Social Sources of Denominationalism
    (Niebuhr) 273
Society for Ethical Culture 4
Society for Psychical Research 281
Society of Jesus. *See* Jesuits
Society of Silent Help 129
Society of the Sacred Heart 107
*Some Considerations on the Keeping of Negroes
    Recommended to the Professors of Christianity
    of Every Denomination* (Woolman) 390
soteriology 402g
"soul competency" 268
Southern Baptist Theological Seminary 39,
    40, 267, 268
Southern Christian Leadership Conference
    (SLCC) 184, 200
Southwestern Baptist Theological Seminary
    76, 77
Spalding, Martin John 146, **337–338**
Spellman, Francis Joseph 270, 328, **338–340**
Spirit of the Pilgrims 23
spiritualism 402g
    Helena Petrovna Blavatsky 30, 31
    Edgar Cayce 59–60
    Andrew Jackson Davis **94–95**
    Thomas Lake Harris 159
    Paschal Beverly Randolph **302–303**
Springfield Presbytery 346
Spurgeon, Charles Haddon 102, 103, 294
Stanton, Elizabeth Cady 28
State and the Church, The (Ryan and Millar)
    316
Steinberg, Milton **340–341**
Stephan, Martin 370, 371
Steps to Christ (White) 376
Stetson, Augusta Emma Simmons
    341–343, *342*
Stevenson, Robert Louis 92
Stewart, Milton and Lyman 103
Stiles, Ezra **343–344**
Stoddard, Solomon 115, 116, 233, **344–346**
Stoddardism 402g
Stone, Barton Warren 51, **346–348,** *347*
Stone, Lucy 28

Strong, Augustus Hopkins **348–349**
Strong, Josiah 306, **349–351**
Studd, C. T. 263
Student Volunteer Movement (SVM) for Foreign Missions 263, 379, 380
Studies in Scripture (Russell) 313, 314
Sturgis, Stokely 8
success, gospel of 78–79, 288–290
suffrage, African-American 41
suffrage, women's 14, 28, 46
Summerland 95
Sunday, Billy 62, 187, 188, *351*, **351–352**
Sunday school 86, 155
Survey of the Summe of Church-Discipline (Hooker) 174
Suzuki, Daisetz Teitaro **352–353**
SVM. *See* Student Volunteer Movement for Foreign Missions
Swedenborg, Emanuel 94–95, 159
Swedenborgianism 159, 402*g*
synagogue 402*g*
syncretism 402*g*
Synod of 1662 254
Synod of Dort 403*g*
Systematic Theology (Hodge) 171
Systematic Theology (Strong) 348
Szold, Henrietta 148, **353–355**

T

Talmud 148–149, 403*g*
Tammany Hall 384
Tao te ching 353
taxation 175, 259, 315, 382
tax support for religion 15, 217
Taylor, John 387
Taylor, Myron C. 339
Taylor, Nathaniel William 171, **356–357,** 367
"Taylor-Tyler Controversy" 367
Tecumseh 361
Tekakwitha, Kateri **357–358**
television broadcasting
    Richard Cardinal Cushing 89
    Jerry Falwell 125, 126
    James A. Pike 295
    Pat Robertson **311–312**
    Fulton J. Sheen 328
temperance movement 22, 28
Temple University 78
Ten Great Religions (Clarke) 71
Tennent, Gilbert 137, **358–359**
Tennent, William 358, **359–360**
Tenskwatawa **360–362,** *361*
Ten Times One Is Ten (Hale) 156
Testem benevolentiae 82, 165, 183
Thakura, Bhaktisddhanta Sarasvati 97
theism 403*g*
theological conservatism. *See* conservatism
theological liberalism. *See* liberalism
theology/theologians 403*g*
    Archibald Alexander **6–8**
    Edward Scribner Ames **10–11**
    Horace Bushnell 46
    W. T. Conner **76–77**
    William Porcher DuBose **105–106**
    Jonathan Edwards **115–117**
    Nathanael Emmons **120–122**
    Washington Gladden 149–150
    Abraham Joshua Heschel **167–169**
    Charles Hodge **170–172**
    Rufus Jones **190–191**
    Sam Jones 192
    George Keith **196–198**
    Albert Cornelius Knudson **205–206**
    Charles Porterfield Krauth **207–208**
    Edwin Lewis **217–218**
    J. Gresham Machen **221–222**
    Shailer Mathews **235–236**
    John Courtney Murray **269–270**
    John W. Nevin **271–272**
    H. Richard Niebuhr **272–273**
    Reinhold Niebuhr **274–275**
    Joseph Priestley **300–301**
    Walter Rauschenbusch **305–307**
    John A. Ryan **315–316**
    Philip Schaff **319–320**
    Samuel Schmucker **320–321**
    Augustus H. Strong **348–349**
    Nathaniel William Taylor **356–357**
    Paul Tillich **362–363**
    Bennet Tyler 367
    Benjamin B. Warfield **371–373**
Theosophical Society 30, 31, 280, 281, 353
Theosophy 60, 403*g*
Thirteenth Amendment 143, 366
Tillich, Paul Johannes 74, **362–363**
Tippecanoe, Battle of 361
Torah 403*g*
Torrey, Reuben Archer **363–365**
Toy, Crawford H. 258
Trail of Life in College (Jones) 190
trances 60
Transcendentalism 403*g*
    James Freeman Clarke 70
    Emmet Fox 136
    Octavius Brooks Frothingham 138
    Frederic Henry Hedge 165, 166
Transcendentalism in New England (Frothingham) 139
Transylvania Presbytery 123, 346
Treatise on Atonement (Ballou) 17
Treatise on the Preparation and Delivery of Sermons (Broadus) 40
Treaty of 1868 99
Trinitarianism 403*g*
Troelsch, Ernst 273
True Weslyean, The (newspaper) 324
Truman, Harry S.
    Father Flanagan 132
    Billy Graham 153
    Abba Hillel Silver 331
    Francis Spellman 339
Turner, Henry McNeal **365–366**
Twain, Mark 114
12-step programs 275
Tyler, Bennet **366–367**

U

Underground Railroad 141
Unification Church 259–260, 403*g*
unions. *See* labor unions
Union Theological Seminary 307, 308
Unitarianism/Unitarian Church 403*g*. *See also* Universalism/Universalist Church
    Martha Moore Avery 13
    Hosea Ballou 16
    Lyman Beecher 23
    Henry Whitney Bellows **25–26**
    Louisa Brown Blackwell **27–29**
    Horace Bushnell 46
    William Ellery Channing **60–62**
    Charles Chauncy 66
    James Freeman Clarke **70–71**
    Octavius Brooks Frothingham **138–139**
    Edward Everett Hale **156–157**
    Frederic Henry Hedge **165–167**
    Elias Hicks 170
    John Haynes Holmes **172–173**
    Thomas Starr King **201–202**
    Jonathan Mayhew 237, 238
    Jedidiah Morse 262
    Theodore Parker **287–288**
    Joseph Priestley 301
    Nathaniel William Taylor 356
United House of Prayer for All People 151–152
United Nations 283
United Society of Believers in Christ's Second Coming. *See* Shakers
United States Catholic Miscellany 122
United States v. MacIntosh 223
Unity School of Christianity 129–130
Unity Village 129
Universalism/Universalist Church 403*g*. *See also* Unitarianism/Unitarian Church
    Hosea Ballou **16–18**
    Orestes A. Brownson 42
    Charles Chauncy 66
    Elias Hicks 170
    Thomas Starr King **201–202**
Universal Negro Improvement Association 133
Urban League 298
urban missions 48–49, 68, 284
Utah
    Pierre-Jean De Smet 98
    Spencer W. Kimball 198
    David O. McKay 244–245
    Parley P. Pratt 299
    Joseph Smith III 335
    Wilford Woodruff 387
    Brigham Young 394
Utah War 394
utopian leaders
    Thomas Lake Harris **159–160**
    John Humphrey Noyes **277–278**
    George Rapp **304–305**

V

Vagnozzi, Egidio 339
Validity of Religious Experience, The (Bowne) 205
Van Doren, Mark 250
Vane, Henry 179
Varieties of Religious Experience (James) xiii, xv
Vatican Councils 403*g*
Vatican I (First Vatican Council) 165, 337, 338, 368
Vatican II (Second Vatican Council)
    John Patrick Cody 73
    Abraham Joshua Heschel 168
    John Courtney Murray 269, 270
    Fulton J. Sheen 328
    Francis Spellman 339
Verot, Jean Pierre Augustin Marcellin **368–369**

Vexed Questions in Theology (Clarke) 70
vicar 403g
Vietnam War 167, 168, 339
virgin birth 403g
visions 333–334
Voice of Warning 299

W
Waco, Texas. *See* Koresh, David
Walsh, Daniel 250
Walther, Carl Ferdinand Wilhelm **370–371**
Waltrip, Burroughs A. 209
Ward, Samuel 82
Wardley, James and Jane 212
Warfield, Benjamin Breckinridge 171, **371–373**
War of 1812 18, 362
Washani religion 336
Washington, Booker T. 304
Washington, D.C. *See* March on Washington (1963)
Washington, George 267
Washington Times 260
Watch Tower Bible and Tract Society 312–315
Watergate 153
Way of Holiness, The (Palmer) 284
WCC. *See* World Council of Churches
wealth, gospel of 78–79
Webb, Muhammad Alexander Russell **373–374**
Weeks, Eugene 129
We Hold These Truths: Catholic Reflections on the American Proposition (Murray) 269, 270
Weiss, George Michael 32
Weizmann, Chaim 384
Wesley, Charles 377
Wesley, John
  Francis Asbury 11, 12
  Thomas Coke 75, 76
  John Humphrey Noyes 277
  Joseph Pilmore 296, 297
  Hannah Whitall Smith 332
  George Whitefield 377
Wesleyan Methodist Connexion 323, 324
Western Conference (Methodist Episcopal Church) 245, 246
Western Messenger (magazine) 70
Westminster Confession 403g
  Charles A. Briggs 38
  Jonathan Dickinson 99–100
  Finis Ewing 124
  Harry Emerson Fosdick 134
  Charles Hodge 171
  Benjamin B. Warfield 372
westward expansion
  Lyman Beecher 23
  James Lloyd Breck 35–36
  Peter Cartwright 55–56
  Philander Chase 63–64
  Nathaniel William Taylor 357

Wharton, Charles Henry 54
What Christianity Means to Me: A Spiritual Autobiography (Abbott) 1
Wheelock, Eleazar 279
Wheelwright, John 179
Whig Party 121
Whitaker, Nathaniel 279
White, Alma Bridwell **374–375**
White, Ellen Gould Harmon 253, **375–376**
White, James S. 375
Whitefield, George 376, **376–378**
  Jonathan Dickinson 100
  Jonathan Edwards 116
  Theodorus Jacobus Frelinghuysen 137
  Jonathan Mayhew 237
  Gilbert Tennent 358, 359
  William Tennent 360
Whitehouse, Henry John 66–67
Whither? A Theological Question for the Times (Briggs) 38
Whitman, Marcus **378–379**
Widney, Joseph Pomeroy 37
Wilder, Robert Parmalee 294, **379–380**
Williams, Roger 72, 83–84, 174, **380–382**
Wilson, Jack. *See* Wovoka
Wilson, John 179
Winthrop, John 83
Wise, Isaac Mayer 118, 249, 260–261, **382–383**
Wise, Stephen Samuel 331, **383–385**, 384
witchcraft 158. *See also* Salem witch trials
Witherspoon, John **385–387**, 388
women's rights 28, 46, 375
Wonders of the Invisible World (Mather) 231
Woodruff, Wilford **387–388**
Woodworth-Etter, Maria **388–389**
Woolman, John 169, **389–391**
World Council of Churches (WCC) 58, 263, 283, 403g
World's Parliament of Religions (1893) 319, 353, 373
World War I
  Lyman Abbott 2
  Cyrus Adler 3
  John J. Burke 44
  Samuel McCrea Cavert 58
  Harry Emerson Fosdick 134
  John Haynes Holmes 172
  Rufus Jones 191
  Edwin Lewis 217, 218
  J. Gresham Machen 221
  Douglas Clyde Macintosh 223
  Judah L. Magnes 224
  Walter Rauschenbusch 306
  Charles Taze Russell 313
  J. F. Rutherford 314
  Paul Tillich 362
  Robert P. Wilder 380
  Stephen S. Wise 384

World War II
  Charles E. Coughlin 85
  Harry Emerson Fosdick 135
  Abraham Joshua Heschel 167, 168
  L. Ron Hubbard 175
  Elijah Muhammad 264
  Francis Spellman 339
  Henrietta Szold 354
  Paul Tillich 362
  Stephen S. Wise 384–385
Wounded Knee massacre 26, 391
Wovoka **391–392**
Wright, Richard 297

X
Xavier College 105

Y
Yacub 264
Yale University
  Timothy Dwight 109, 110
  Samuel Johnson 186
  Douglas Clyde Macintosh 223
  H. Richard Niebuhr 273
  Ezra Stiles 343–344
  Nathaniel William Taylor 356–357
yeshiva 403g
YMCA. *See* Young Men's Christian Association
Young, Brigham **393–394**
  Parley P. Pratt 299
  Sidney Rigdon 309
  Joseph Smith III 335
  Wilford Woodruff 387
Young Men's Christian Association (YMCA)
  S. Parkes Cadman 50
  J. Gresham Machen 221
  Dwight Lyman Moody 256
  John R. Mott 263
  Ira D. Sankey 317
  C. I. Scofield 322
  Billy Sunday 351–352
  Robert P. Wilder 380
Yugoslavia 185

Z
Zarephath farm 374
Zeisberger, David **395–396**
Zen Buddhism 353
Zinzendorf, Nikolaus Ludwig von 32, 266, 395, **396–397**
Zionism 403g
  Judah L. Magnes 224
  H. Pereira Mendes 249
  Abba Hillel Silver **330–331**
  Henrietta Szold **353–355**
  Stephen S. Wise **383–385**
Zion's Herald (newspaper) 324